Research, Invention, and Innovation Congress (RI2C 2023)

Held Online

E3S Web of Conferences Volume 428 (2023)

Bangkok, Thailand and Online
24-25 August 2023

Editors:

Malinee Sriariyanun
Yu-Shen Cheng
Debraj Bhattacharyya
Ponnusami Venkatachalam
Marttin Paulraj Gundupalli

ISBN: 978-1-7138-8427-9

Printed from e-media with permission by:

Curran Associates, Inc.
57 Morehouse Lane
Red Hook, NY 12571

Some format issues inherent in the e-media version may also appear in this print version.

For additional information, please contact EDP Sciences – Web of Conferences at the address below.

EDP Sciences – Web of Conferences
17, Avenue du Hoggar
Parc d'Activité de Courtabœuf
BP 112
F-91944 Les Ulis Cedex A
France

Phone: +33 (0) 1 69 18 75 75
Fax: +33 (0) 1 69 28 84 91

contact-edps@webofconferences.org

Additional copies of this publication are available from:

Curran Associates, Inc.
57 Morehouse Lane
Red Hook, NY 12571 USA
Phone: 845-758-0400
Fax: 845-758-2633
Email: curran@proceedings.com
Web: www.proceedings.com

TABLE OF CONTENTS

Preface

The 4th Research, Invention, and Innovation Congress (Ri2C2023) is hosted by King Mongkut's University of Technology Bangkok (KMUTNB) in online platform conference. The event was arranged on 24-25 August 2023 with three main sessions; i) Materials and Mechanics (iMM), ii) Electricals and Electronics (iEE), and iii) Sustainable Sciences (iSS). This proceeding focused on iSS session that covered the research topics in the fields of energy technology, environment and sustainable development and related fields. In iSS-Ri2C2023, we received contributions from editorial board members, scientific committee, reviewers and presenters worldwide.

We organized the online conference for our participants to allow all attendees worldwide to meet without limitations of travelling and accommodation. A total of 28 papers with the research topics related to energy technology and environment and sustainable development were peer-reviewed by at least 2 reviewers, and one editor and accepted for presentation in iSS-Ri2C2023 session. Due to continuous supports from all participants, we have an increase in international authors with the proportion at 60.71%, which was increased from iSS-Ri2C2022 event (at 42.3%). Furthermore all papers presented in iSS-Ri2C2019, iSS-Ri2C2021, and iSS-Ri2C2022 are published in E3S Web of Conference and indexed in SCOPUS database. The organizer committee will continue to host this event again in 2024 to be the stage for having international knowledge exchange and sharing in research to drive the sustainable society for our world.

Malinee Sriariyanun, Ph.D

Managing Editor

iSS-Ri2C2023

https://doi.org/10.1051/e3sconf/202342800002

Opening Address

Welcome Message from Advisory Chair

Dear colleagues, professors, researchers, ladies and gentlemen.

On behalf of King Mongkut's University of Technology North Bangkok (KMUTNB), I would like to express my sincere gratitude and welcome you to the 4th Research, Invention, and Innovation Congress (RI2C 2023). I would like to thank you all who sincerely contributed to this event in order to make it a success. This wouldn't have been possible without the support of each and everyone present here. Before we kick start the conference, I would like to take this opportunity to make some general remarks and touch briefly on the history of the RI2C Conference.

RI2C is the initials of Research, Invention, and Innovation Congress, the international conference carried out regularly by King Mongkut's University of Technology North Bangkok. RI2C is held first time in 2019 at Arnoma Grand Hotel Bangkok and since there it has been continued in a virtual platform from 2021 to this year 2023. As KMUTNB is a university of invention and innovation, RI2C aims to provide a forum for the knowledge exchange regarding the development of multidisciplinary researches for the novel invention and innovation. Moreover, our conference offers an opportunity for all accepted full papers to be submitted to the proceedings indexed by Scopus. Previous RI2C events successfully published more than 450 papers in the proceedings indexed by Scopus, such as Key Engineering Materials, Materials Today: Proceedings, E3S web of conference, and IEEE Xplore.

In this year, it is my hope that the 4th Research, Invention, and Innovation Congress would be able to achieve its objective in providing an effective forum for academician, researchers, and practitioners to advancing knowledge, research, technology and innovation, under the theme of the conference "Innovation for Better Life". Last but not least, my deepest gratitude goes to the International Advisory Board, Organizing Committee, Scientific Committee, all honored Keynote speakers, International Peer-Review team, all sponsors, and volunteer who have directly and indirectly supported the success of this conference. The Science and Technology Research Institute has organized a vibrant scientific program and is working hard to present highly respected and internationally notorious speakers. Although we try our finest to be professional, on behalf of KMUTNB, please accept our sincere apologies should there be inconveniences that occur before, during, or after the event.

I wish you a very productive conference with exciting and encouraging discussions and exchange of knowledge so that together we can anticipate a future of groundbreaking knowledge, research, and technology for innovations. Enjoy your participation in the RI2C 2023 and memorable time here. We hope you return next year with even more colleagues for RI2C 2024, KMUTNB's 65th Anniversary.

Thank you. Have a wonderful conference days.

Prof.Dr.-Ing.habil. Suchart Siengchin

President of KMUTNB, Thailand

https://doi.org/10.1051/e3sconf/202342800003

List of Conference Chairs

1. **Advisory Chair**

   Suchart Siengchin, KMUTNB, Thailand

2. **Conference Chair**

   Somrerk Chandra-ambhorn, KMUTNB, Thailand

   Kampanart Theinnoi, KMUTNB, Thailand

3. **General Secretary**

   Wanlop Harnnarongchai, KMUTNB, Thailand

4. **International Advisory Board**

   Leonado Simon, University of Waterloo, Canada

   Daniel Hissel, University of Franche-Comté, France

   Edmund Haberstroh, RWTH Aachen University, Germany

   Christopher O'Brien, University of Nottingham, United Kingdom

   Vincent Aroulmoji, Mahendra Engineering Colleges, India

   Yasushi Umeda, The University of Tokyo, Japan

   Yang Zhigang, Tsinghua University, China

   Damien Guilbert, Université de Lorraine, France

   Pankaj Koinkar, Institute of Technology and Science, Japan

   Sanjay Mavinkere Rangappa, KMUTNB, Thailand

5. **Innovative Sustainable Science (iSS)-Ri2C2023 Editors**

   Managing Editor: Malinee Sriariyanun, KMUTNB, Thailand

   Editorial members:

   Yu-Shen Cheng, National Yunlin University of Science and Technology, Taiwan

   Debraj Bhattacharyya, IIT Hyderabad, India

   Ponnusami Venkatachalam, Sastra deemed university, India

   Marttin Paulraj Gundupalli, University of Alberta, Canada

https://doi.org/10.1051/e3sconf/202342800003

6. Innovative Sustainable Science (iSS)-Ri2C2023 Academic committee

Aim and Scope of iss-Ri2C2023

Website: https://ri2c-kmutnb.com/home.aspx
Session: Innovative Sustainable Science (iSS)
Venue: Online Conference at King Mongkut's University of Technology North Bangkok, Thailand
Conference date: 24-25 August 2023

Aim and Scope

Main topic coverages: Environmental and Energy Technology
The other topics related to Environmental and Energy Technology include, but not limit to

- Energy and renewable energy
- Waste management and waste valorization
- Environment science and pollution management
- Sustainable development and management
- Natural Resource Management and improvement

Editorial policies

Paper submission guidelines

The full manuscript must be written in English language. Full papers in the forms of research or review articles should be original and unpublished anywhere else. The contents of submitted manuscript must follow the areas covered by the iSS-Ri2C aim and scope. The key compositions of the full research papers include 1) Abstract, 2) Introduction, 3) Materials and methods, 4) Results and discussion, 5) Conclusion, 6) Acknowledgement, 7) References. Authors can submit the manuscript via submission form posted in conference website.

Evaluation and review process

All full papers will be subjected to double blind peer-reviews with at least 2 reviewers. The evaluation will be based on the relevancy to the conference scope, structure of the manuscript, logical and scientific merits, innovative, presentation, format and ethic of publications. The communication between the editorial office and reviewers is kept confidential. Reviewers should not disclose any information. All submitted manuscript were screened for plagiarism by using Turnitin software to follow ethic of publication. After review of the manuscript by at least two independent reviewers, the decision will be made by the editor, which can be categorized in three conditions as follows; Accept without changes, Revisions Required, and Reject. The results of reviewing process will be informed via email from the conference organizer.

Ethics in publishing

Iss2023's Publication Ethics is based on the guidelines and standards developed by the Committee on Publication Ethics (COPE : https://publicationethics.org/).

Plagiarism

Plagiarism and self-copying contents are absolutely prohibited in iss's proceeding. All submitted manuscript will be screened with plagiarism detection software. The screened manuscript by software and editor will be proceeded to reviewing process.

2023 Research, Invention, and Innovation Congress (RI2C2023)

(https://ri2c-kmutnb.com/home.aspx)

Session: Innovative Sustainable Science (iSS)

Venue: Online Conference at King Mongkut's University of Technology North Bangkok, Thailand

Conference date: 24-25 August 2023

Main topic coverages: Environmental and Energy Technology

The other topics related to Environmental and Energy Technology include, but not limit to

- Energy and renewable energy
- Waste management and waste valorization
- Environment science and pollution management
- Sustainable development and management
- Natural Resource Management and improvement

Session Chairs:

1. Atthasit Tawai, KMUTNB, Thailand
2. Marttin Paulraj Gundupalli, University of Alberta, Canada
3. Prapakorn Tantayotai, Srinakarindwirot University, Thailand
4. Diana Jose, KMUTNB, Thailand

Presentation schedule for iSS-Ri2C2023

iSS No.	RI2C No.	Title	Authors
25 August 2023. ISS Section 1, Room 1. Visual platform. Time 9.00-12.30 Session Chairs: Atthasit Tawai Co-chair: Marttin Paulraj Gundupalli			
01009	Iss10	Optimization of Organosolv Pretreatment with Acid Catalyst to Enhance Enzymatic Saccharification of Corn Husk	**Engkarat Buakeaw**, Diana Jose, Wawat Rodiahwati, Marttin Paulraj Gundupalli, Keerthi Katam, Prapakorn Tantatotai, Malinee Sriariyanun, and Kraipat Cheenkachorn
01010	Iss11	Process Optimization of Deep Eutectic Solvent Pretreatment of Coffee Husk Biomass	**Sukunya Areeya**, Marttin Paulraj Gundupalli, Babu Dharmalingam, Baranitharan Paramasivam, Prapakorn Tantayotai, Patchanee Yasurin, Elizabeth Jayex Panakkal*
01008	Iss17	Oxalic Acid Pretreatment on Enhancement of Enzymatic Saccharification from Napier Grass for Biofuel Production	**Danipa Panyarachun**, Elizabeth Jayex Panakkal, Atthasit Tawai, Wawat Rodiahwati, Baranitharan Paramasivam, Suvaluk Asavasanti, Kraipat Cheenkachorn*
-	Iss01	The Effects of Combustion Phasing Induced by Water Injection on NOx Performance of GDI Engine at MBT Ignition Timing	**Nattapon Boontek**, Kampanart Theinnoi, Sak Sittichompoo
01001	Iss04	Activity for Diesel Particulate Matter Oxidation of Silver Supported on Al_2O_3, TiO_2, ZnO, and CeO_2: The Effect of Oxygen Concentration	**Punya Promhuad**, Boonlue Sawatmongkhon*, Nuwong Chollacoop, Kampanart Theinnoi, Thawatchai Wongchang, Ekachai Juntasaro
01002	Iss07	The Influence of Direct Non-Thermal Plasma Treatment on Soot Characteristics under Low Exhaust Gas Temperature	**Teerapong Iamcheerangkoon**, Nuwong Chollacoop, Boonlue Sawatmongkhon, Thawatchai Wongchang, Kampanart Theinnoi*, Ekachai Juntasaro
01004	Iss08	Performance Analysis of Integral Process of Bio-Oil Production, Bio-Oil Upgrading, and Hydrogen Production from Sewage Sludge	**Lida Simasatitkul***, Apiwat Lakkhanasombut, Worawit Morin, Supachai Jedsadajerm, Suksun Amornraksa, Karittha Im-orb
01003	Iss30	Nano-particle Characteristic Emitted from Gasoline Direct Injection Engine Equipped with Non-Thermal Plasma Device	**Pichitpon Neamyou**, Kampanart Theinnoi*, Boonlue Sawatmongkhon, Sak Sittichompoo
02012	Iss18	Manganese Constituent in Stainless Steels Oxidized in Oxygen Containing Water Vapor at 800 °C: High Temperature Oxidation and Volatilization	Methanan Sangsuebsri, Suwijak Pokwitidkul, **Panya Wiman**, Youhei Tanaka, Thammaporn Thublaor*
02003	Iss02	Immobilization of Cellulase on Zinc Oxide Deposited on Zeolite Pellets for Enzymatic Saccharification of Cellulose	**Tokla EOM**, Jantiya Isanapong, Pisist Kumnorkaew, Krisanavej Songthanasak, Peerapong Pornwongthong*
01007	Iss32	Performance Evaluation of Solar Radiation for Food and Agriculture Dryer	**Sriwichai Susuk***, Weerayuth Promjan, Natsacha Inchoorun, Rewadee Meesat, Wannee Suttivattanavet, Kusol Iamsub, Soravit Jamjumroon

01005	Iss23	Spirulina Cultivation Using Biogas CO_2 as the Carbon Source: Preliminary Study on Biomass Growth and Productivity	**Raj Kumar Oruganti**, Madhu Kumar Kumara, Rakesh Tejavath, Malinee Sriariyanun, Debraj Bhattacharyya*
01006	Iss03	Design and Development of Performance Rating Apparatus for Cold Room Refrigeration Unit Using Cooling-Load Balance Method	**Arruck Tragangoon**, Khemapat Tontiwattanakul, Montri Ngamprukvanit, Chayanon Serttikul*
25 August 2023. ISS Section 2, Room 1. Visual platform. Time 13.00-17.30 Session Chairs: Prapakorn Tantayotai Co-chair: Diana Jose			
02001	Iss22	The Relationship Between Environmental Technology Patenting and Environmental Performance Index in Countries: What Does It Mean and How Can We Measure It	Tatyana Maximova*, **Dmitry Verzilin**, Min Zhang
02002	Iss25	Economic Assessment of Medium and Large-Scale Landfill Mining Business: Case Study Thailand	**Anupong Muttaraid**, Sirintornthep Towprayoon, Chart Chiemchaisri, Thapat Silalertruksa, Komsilp Wangyao*
02013	Iss26	Machine Learning Techniques for the Design and Optimization of Polymer Composites: A Review	**J. Maniraj**, Felix Sahayaraj Arockiasamy *, C. Ram Kumar, D. Ashok Kumar, I. Jenish, Indran Suyambulingam, Sanjay Mavinkere Rangappa, Suchart Siengchin
02014	Iss27	Sustainable Smart Polymer Composite Materials: A Comprehensive Review	**A.Felix Sahayaraj***, S. Dhamotharan, D. Sandeep, P. Ramachandran, I. Jenish, Divya Divakaran, Indran Suyambulingam, M. R. Sanjay, Suchart Siengchin
-	Iss31	Mechanical properties of pyrolysis carbon black in rubber compound application	**Teerapat Anupabphan***, Noppakun Kaewdam, Bancha Seataew, Torlab Nangnoi, Napan Narischat, Chonlakarn Wongkhorsub
02015	Iss28	Understanding the Environmental Distribution and Potential Health Risks of Pollutants from Deodorant Products: A Review	**Meenakshi Kakara**, Srideep Dasari, Marttin Paulraj Gundupalli, Tawiwan Kangsadan, Keerthi Katam*
02016	Iss21	Pharmaceuticals and Agro-Chemicals in Groundwater of Hyderabad, India	**Kalyani Subbalakshmi Golakoti**, Sneha Maloth, Madhu Kumar Kumara, Murali Krishna Sabavath, Sukanya Areeya, Debraj Bhattacharyya, Keerthi Katam*
02017	Iss29	A Comparison of Fiber Types in Community for Mist Collection	Thana Ananacha, **Onvalee Amornleetrakul***
02008	Iss05	Utilization of Nongkhai Black Jasmine Rice Bran Oils for Development of Functional Drink Emulsion	**Ketinun Kittipongpittaya***, Teerawan Suwan, Piyarach Kullamethee, Premsak Puangploy, Pattaranan Yimchom, Tanyaporn Intaratul
02007	Iss19	Cider Production from King Mandarin (Citrus nobilis Lour.) and Its Antioxidant Activity	**Hao Thien Vo**, Bich Ngoc Thi Bui, Chau Minh Luu, Thanh Ngoc Nguyen, Long Dang Hoang Bui, Nhi Yen Thi Tran, Phat Tan Dao, Phong Xuan Huynh*
02006	Iss20	Antidiabetic Activity and Molecular Docking Analysis of Milky Mushroom (Calocybe indica) Grown on the Renewable Substrate	**Anne Sahithi Somavarapu Thomas**, Vijaya Lakshmi Murugan Kavitha, Jayapriya Sekar, Mahalakshmi Velmurugan, Malinee Sriariyanun, and Vinodhini Shanmugam*
02005	Iss24	Levan Production in Shake Flask and Fermenter - Influence of Feeding	**Bhuvaneshwari Veerapandian**, Saravanan Ramiah Shanmugam,

		Strategy on Levan Yield and Molecular Weight Distribution	Srividhya Krishnan, Subramaniyasharma Sivaraman, Malinee Sriariyanun, Ponnusami Venkatachalam*
01011	Iss12	Conversion of lignocellulose residue obtained from biorefinery stream to electricity by microbial fuel cell	Keerthi Katam, Maythee Saisriyoot, Supacharee Roddecha, Peerapong Pornwongthong, **Malinee Sriariyanun***
02004	Iss13	Climate-Conscious Food Preserving Technologies for Food Waste Prevention	Yousif Alhammadi, **Doris Ying Ying Tang**, Kit Wayne Chew, Suksun Amornraksa, Pau Loke Show*
02011	Iss14	Ultrasound-Assisted Food Processing: A Mini Review of Mechanisms, Applications, and Challenges	Mahra Alshehhi, **Guowei Wu**, Tawiwan Kangsadan, Kit Wayne Chew*, Pau Loke Show*
02009	Iss15	The Future of Food Preservation: Active Packaging with Controlled Release Systems	Khadija Farousha, **Pei En Tham**, Kit Wayne Chew, Suksun Amornraksa, Pau Loke Show*
02010	Iss16	From Kimchi to Kefir: An Exploration of Probiotics, Benefits, and Future	**Malak AbuZaid**, Sook Sin Chan, Kit Wayne Chew, Atthasit Tawai, Pau Loke Show*

*Presenter names are highlighted in Bold.

The 4th Research, Invention, and Innovation Congress (RI^{2}C 2023)

Session of Opening Ceremony & Keynote Lecture

Thursday, 24 August 2023 (9:00 a.m. – 3:30 p.m.)

KMUTNB
65
President of KMUTNB, Thailand
Prof.Dr.-Ing.habil. Suchart Siengchin
Dear colleagues, professors, researchers,

KMUTNB
65
(KMUTNB, Thailand)
Prof.Dr. Somrerk Chandra-ambhorn
On behalf of the organizing committee

INNOVATION
FOR BETTER
LIFE
2023
Science and Technology
Research Institute
KMUTNB
Assoc.Prof.Dr. Eugene Kowch
University of Calgary, Canada

INNOVATION
FOR BETTER
LIFE
2023
Assoc.Prof.Dr. Eugene Kowch
Professional Practice & Research Experience
Canada, USA, Spain, Hawaii, France, Australia, Italy, Panama, Mexico
United Kingdom, Thailand, S. Korea, Japan, China, Australia
SENIOR
ENGINEER
PRESIDENT

2023
INNOVATION
FOR BETTER
LIFE

2023
INNOVATION
FOR BETTER
LIFE

INNOVATION
FOR BETTER
LIFE
Dr. Siwarutt Boonyarattanakalin
SMS Corporation Co., Ltd., Thailand

INNOVATION
FOR BETTER
LIFE
SMS
www.smscor.com
PRODUCTS &
SOLUTIONS
HOW CAN WE HELP YOU ?
FOOD
PAPER
ADHESIVE
BIOPLASTIC
CONSTRUCTION
HEALTH CARE
TEXTILE
Dr. Siwarutt Boonyarattanakalin

INNOVATION
FOR BETTER
LIFE

INNOVATION
FOR BETTER
LIFE
พระนครเหนือ
Prof.Dr. Piya Kovintavewat
Nakhon Pathom Rajabhat
University, Thailand

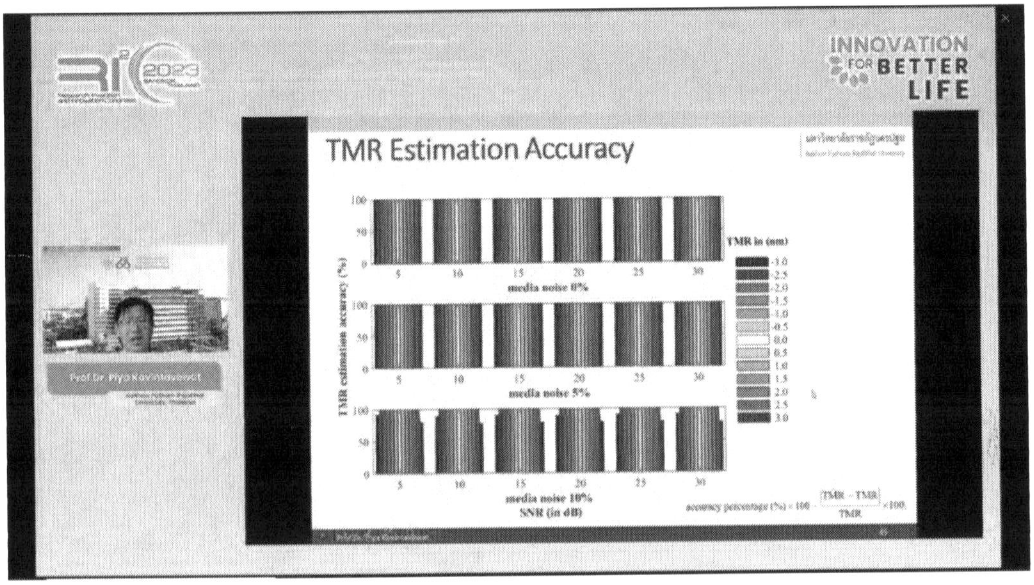
2023
INNOVATION FOR BETTER LIFE
TMR Estimation Accuracy
TMR estimation accuracy (%)
media noise 0%
media noise 5%
media noise 10%
SNR (in dB)
TMR in (nm)
-3.0
-2.5
-2.0
-1.5
-1.0
-0.5
0.0
0.5
1.0
1.5
2.0
2.5
3.0
Prof Dr. Piya Kovintavewat

2023
INNOVATION FOR BETTER LIFE
KMUTNB
พระนครเหนือ
Piya Kovintavewat
Titipong L

INNOVATION FOR BETTER LIFE
Prof.Dr. Gui Yun Tian
Newcastle University, UK

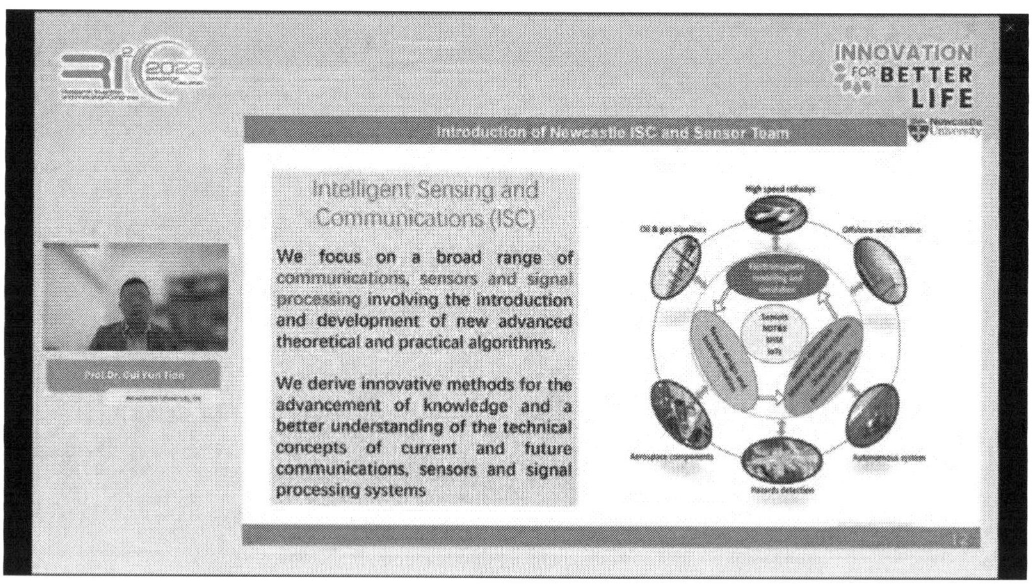
INNOVATION FOR BETTER LIFE
Introduction of Newcastle ISC and Sensor Team
Newcastle University
Intelligent Sensing and Communications (ISC)
We focus on a broad range of communications, sensors and signal processing involving the introduction and development of new advanced theoretical and practical algorithms.
We derive innovative methods for the advancement of knowledge and a better understanding of the technical concepts of current and future communications, sensors and signal processing systems
High speed railways
Oil & gas pipelines
Offshore wind turbine
Aerospace components
Autonomous system
Hazards detection
Prof.Dr. Gui Yun Tian
12

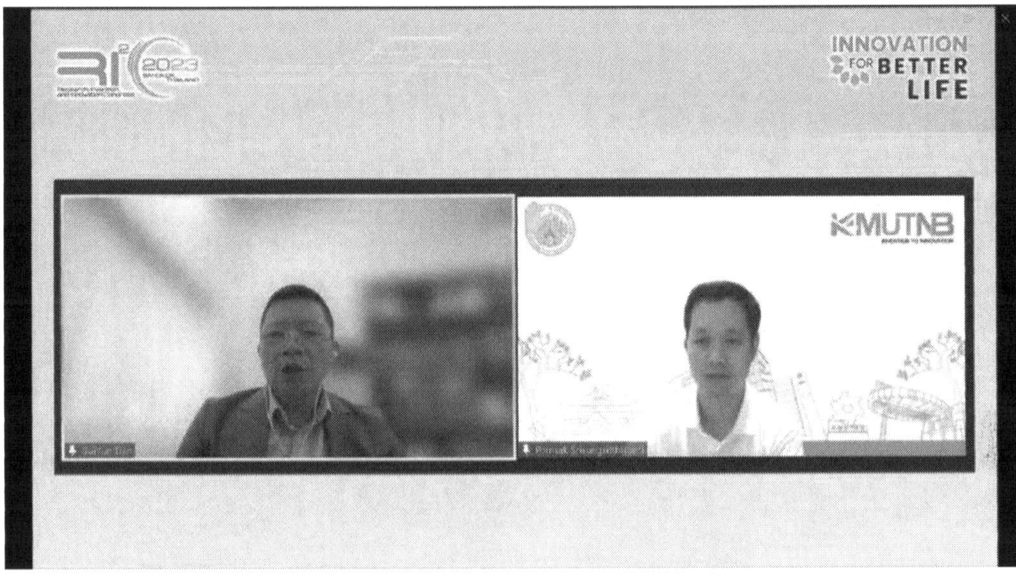
2023
INNOVATION
FOR BETTER
LIFE
KMUTNB

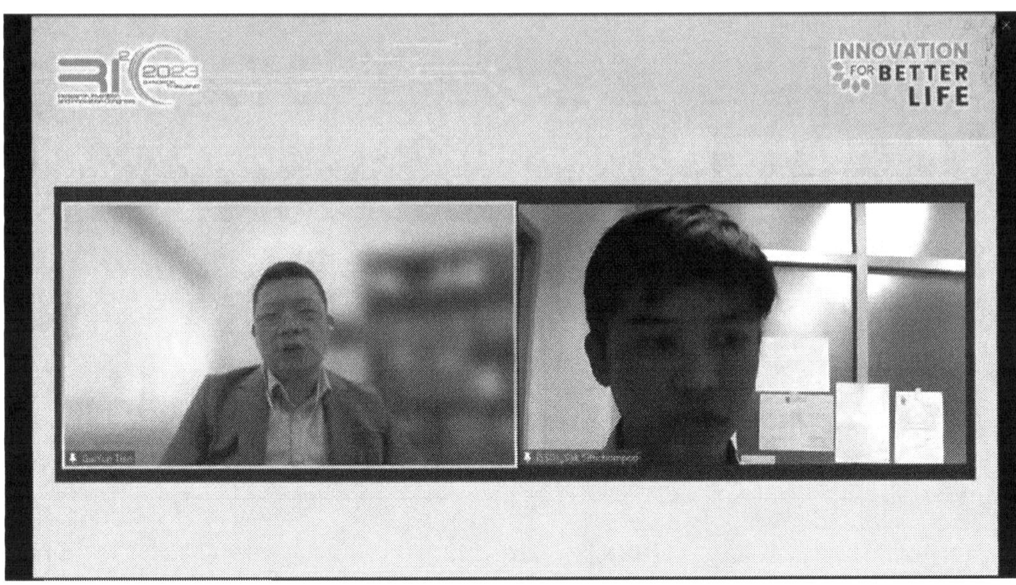
2023
INNOVATION
FOR BETTER
LIFE

Presentation Photo

25 August 2023. ISS Section 1, Room 1. Visual platform. Time 9.00-12.30
Session Chairs: Atthasit Tawai
Co-chair: Marttin Paulraj Gundupalli

- ISS_10 (01009)

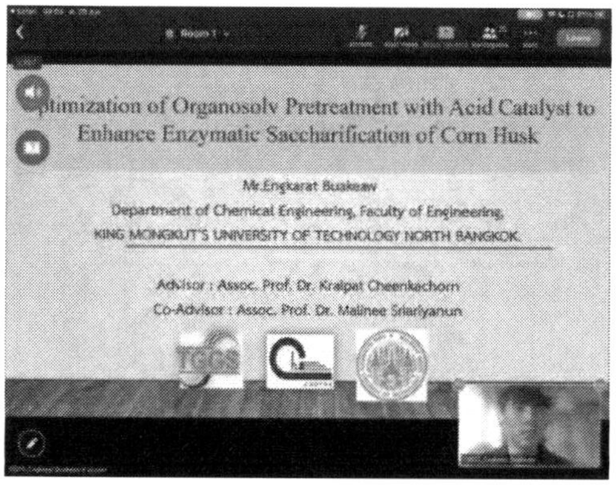

- ISS_11 (01010)

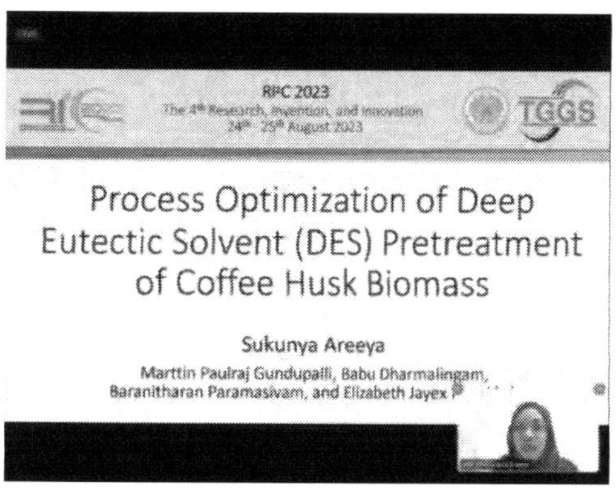

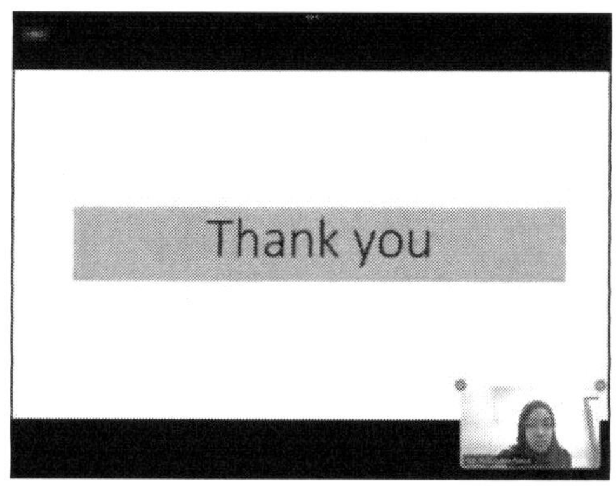

- ISS_17 (01008)

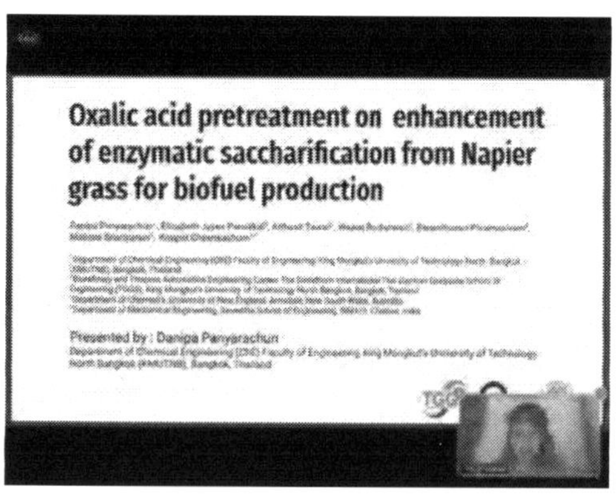

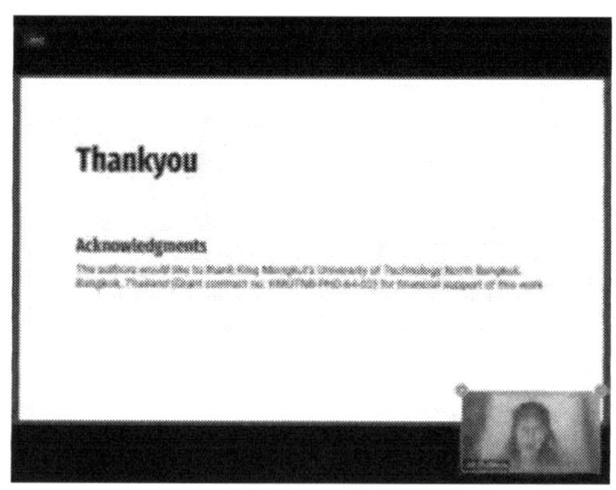

- ISS_01

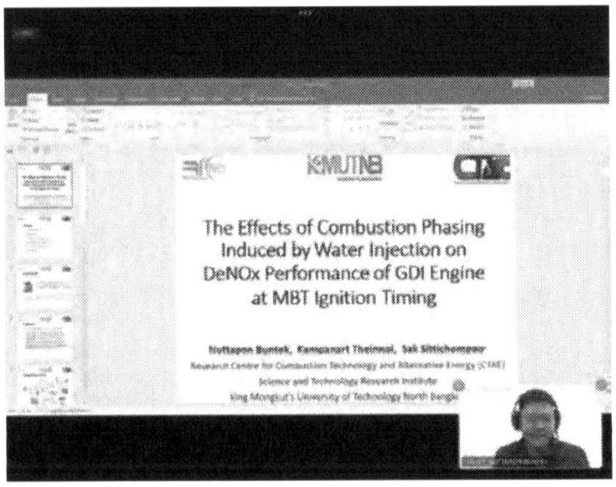

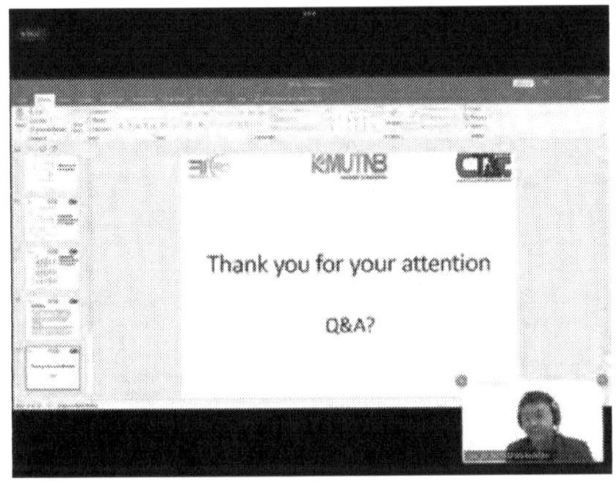

- ISS_04 (01001)

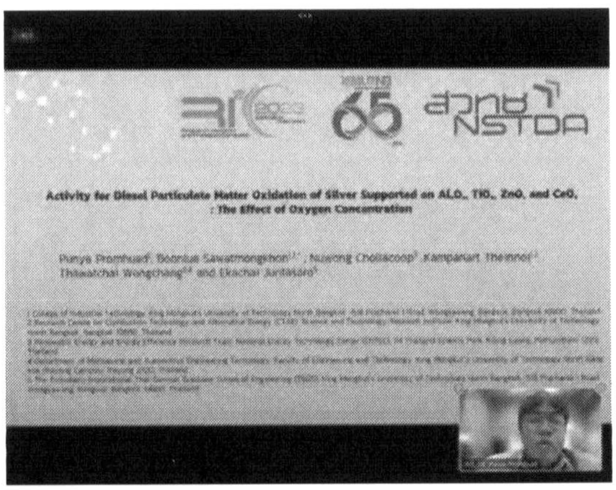

- ISS_07 (01002)

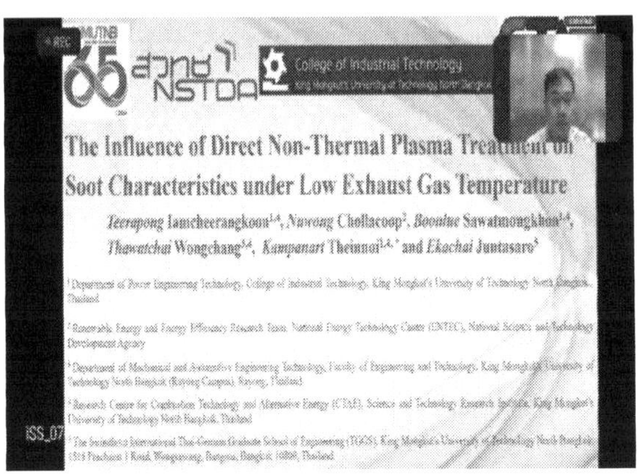

- ISS_08 (01004)

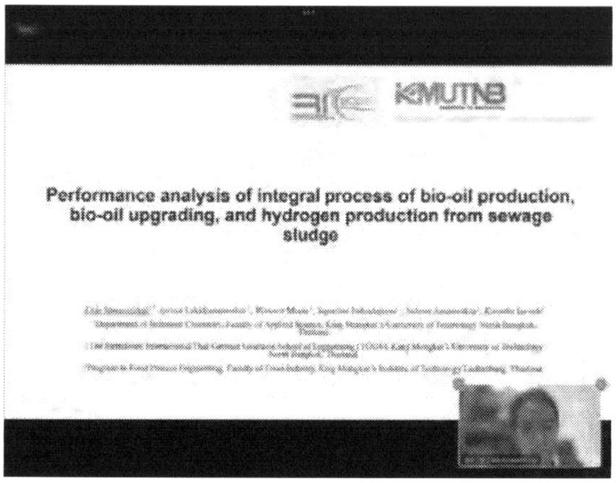

- ISS_30 (01003)

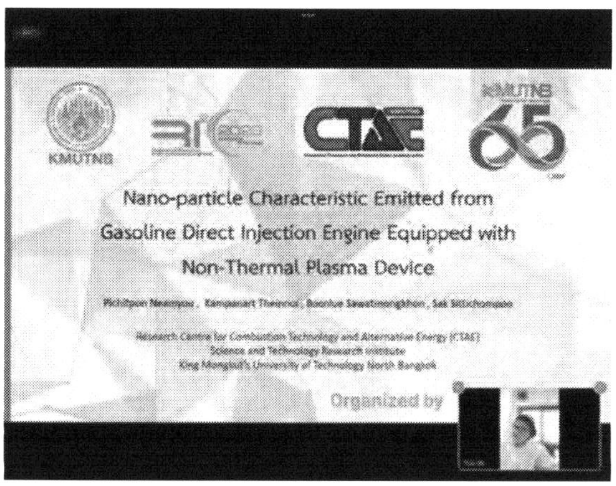

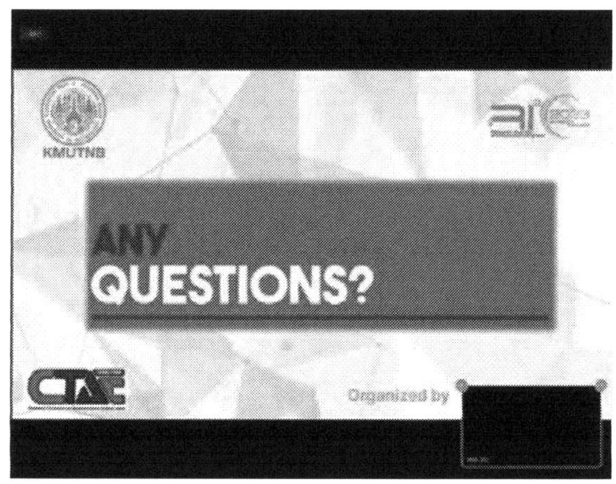

- ISS_18 (02012)

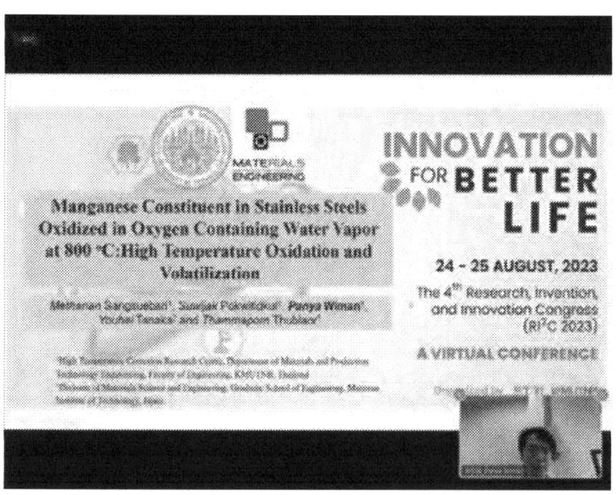

- ISS_02 (02003)

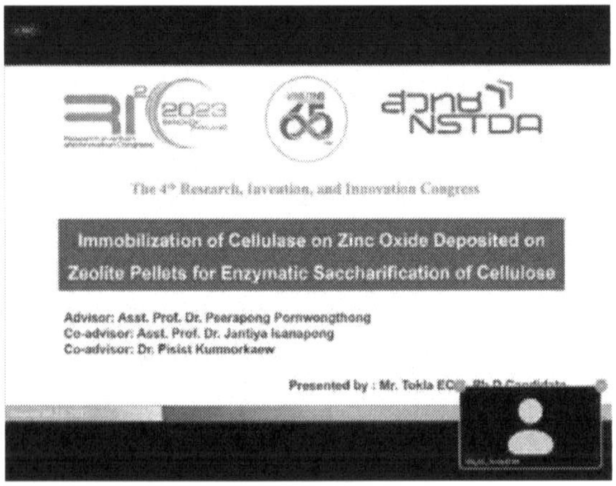

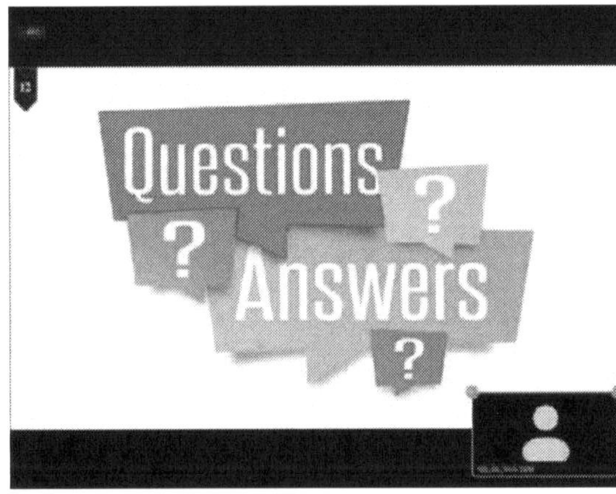

- ISS_32 (01007)

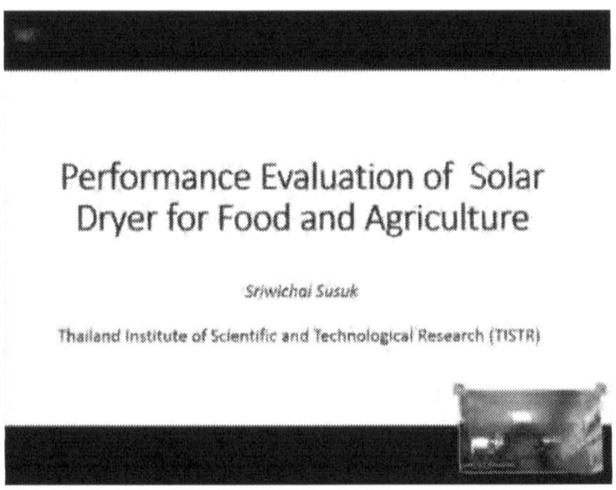

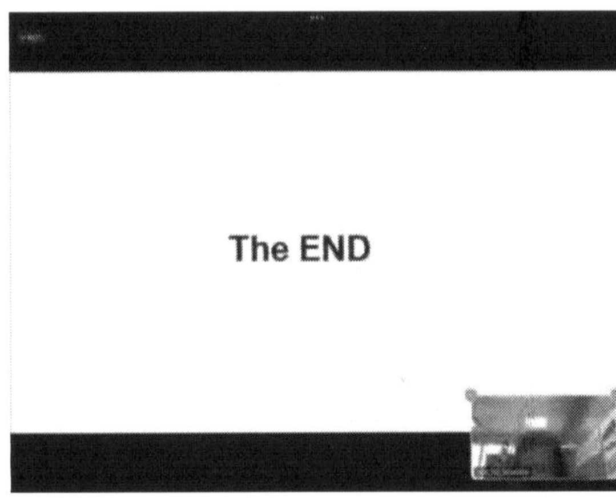

- ISS_23 (01005)

- ISS_03 (01006)

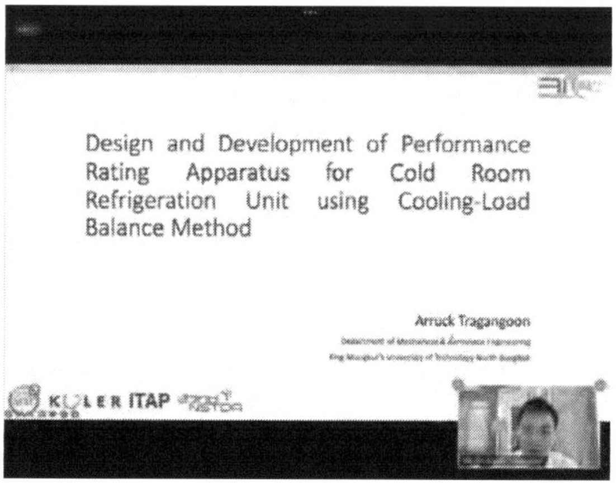

25 August 2023. ISS Section 2, Room 1. Visual platform. Time 13.00-17.30

Session Chairs: Prapakorn Tantayotai

Co-chair: Diana Jose

- ISS_22 (02001)

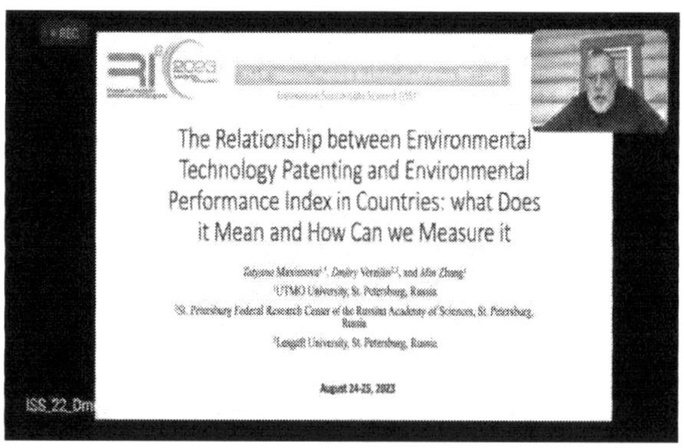

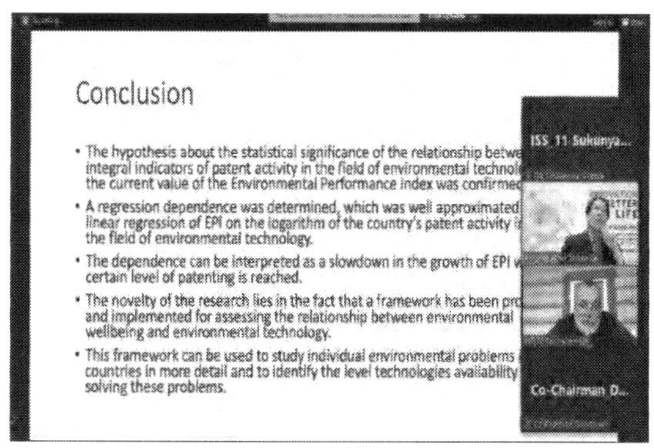

- ISS_25 (02002)

- ISS_26 (02013)

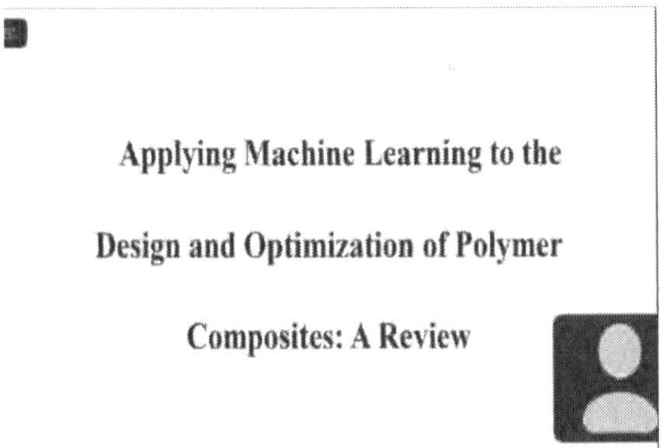

- ISS_27 (02014)

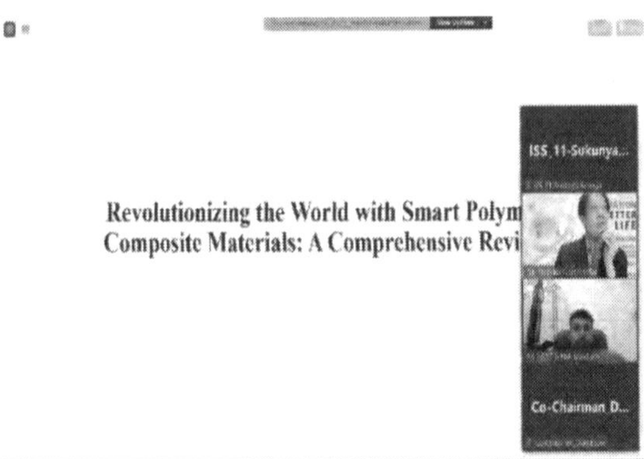

- ISS_31

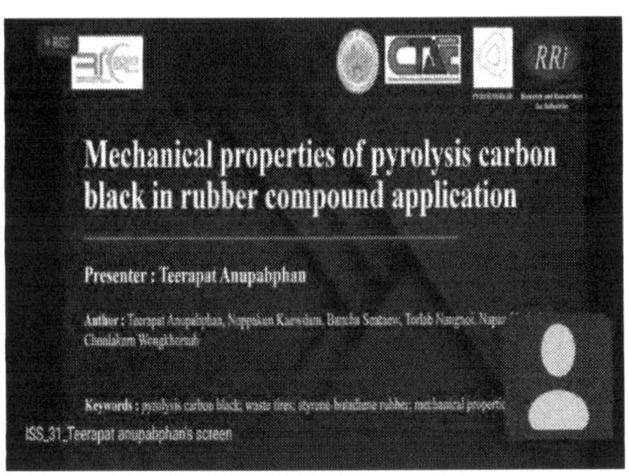

- ISS_28 (02015)

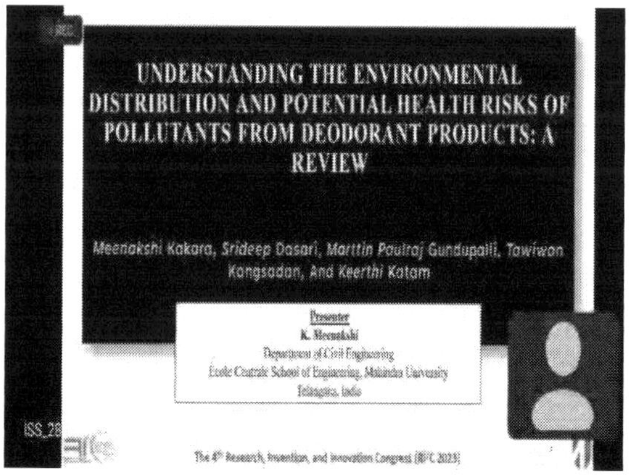

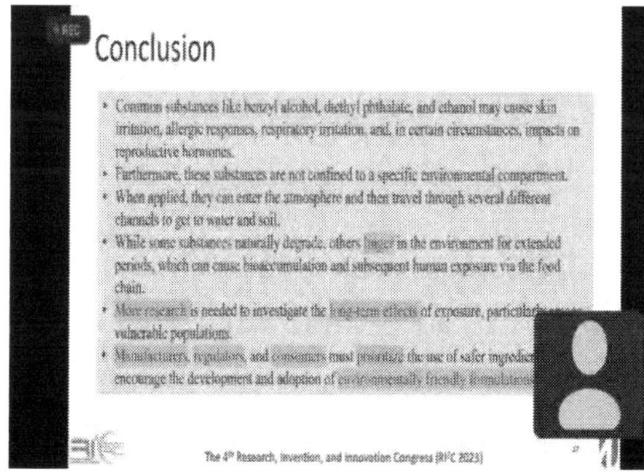

- ISS_21 (02016)

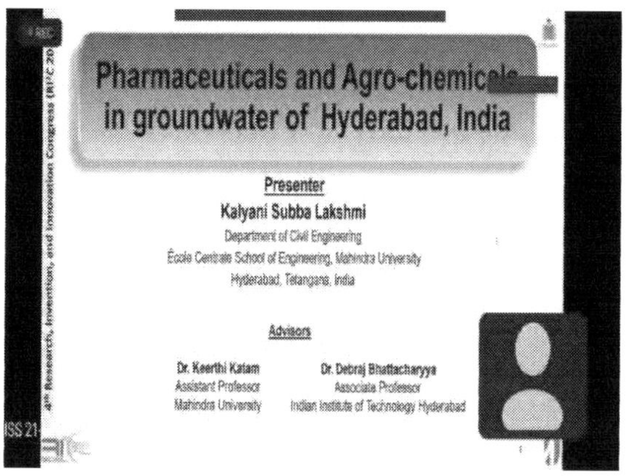

- ISS_29 (02017)

- ISS_05 (02008)

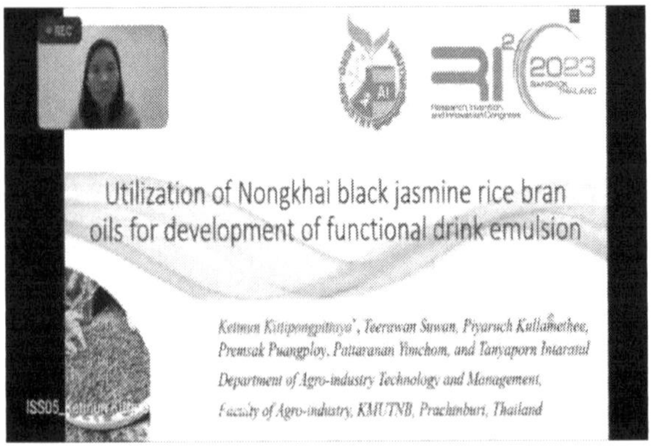

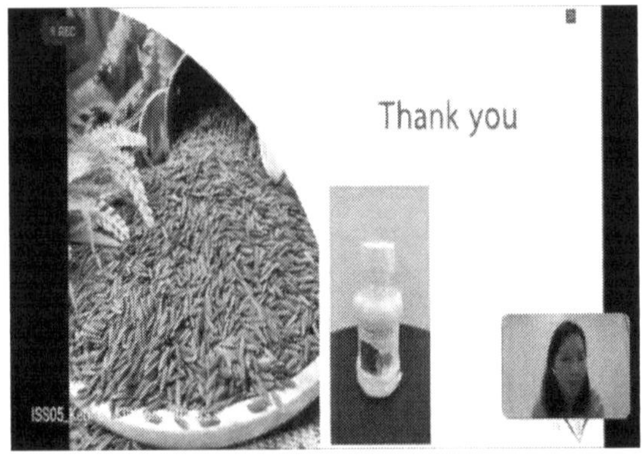

- ISS_19 (02007)

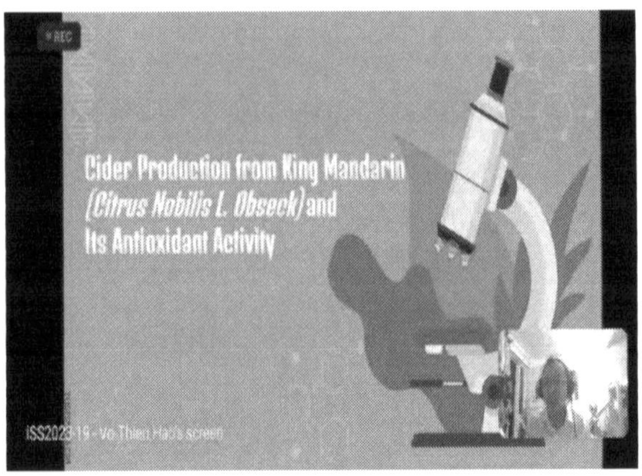

- ISS_20 (02006)

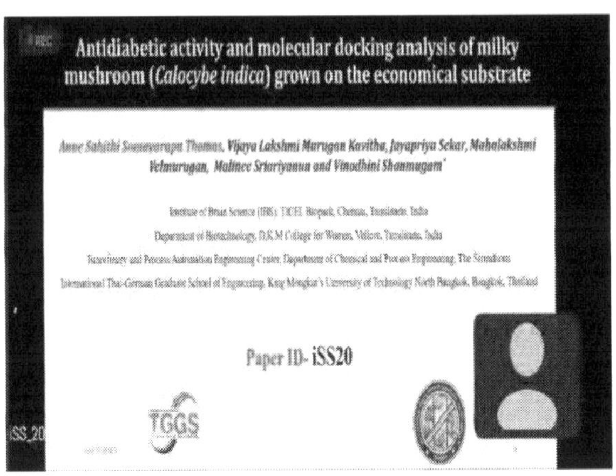

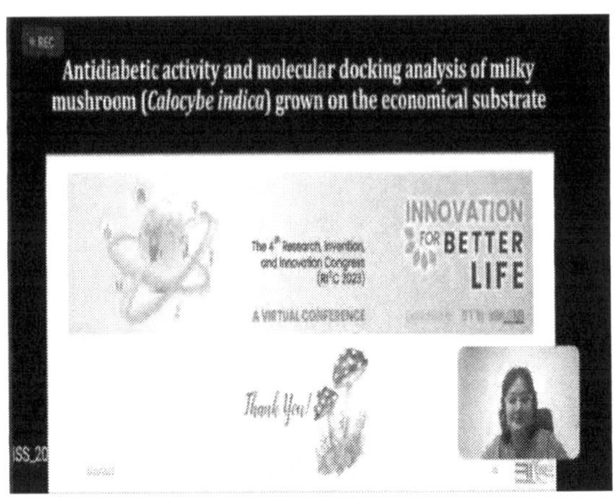

- ISS_24 (02005)

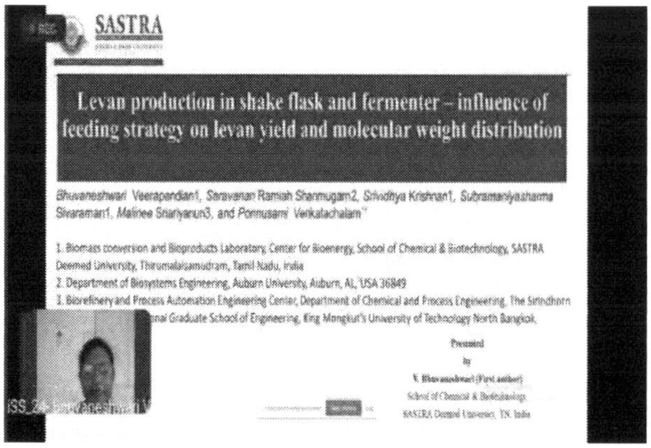

- ISS_12 (01011)

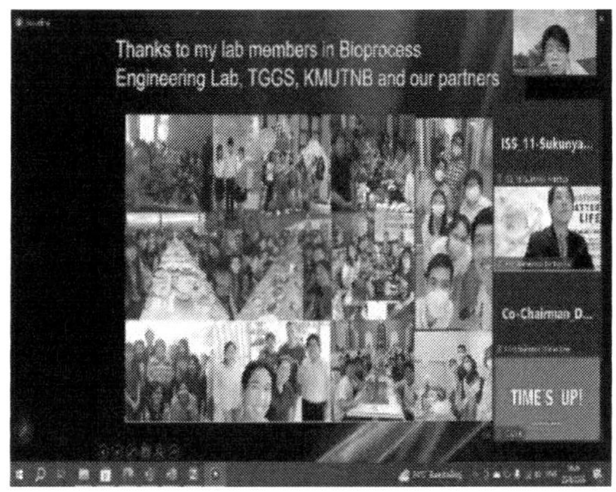

- ISS_13 (02004)

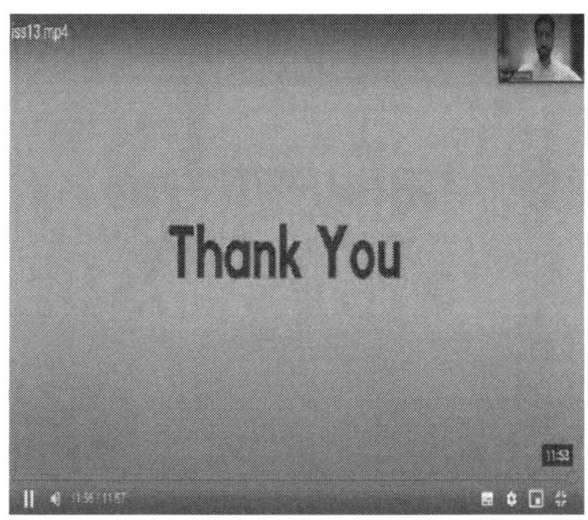

- ISS_14 (02011)

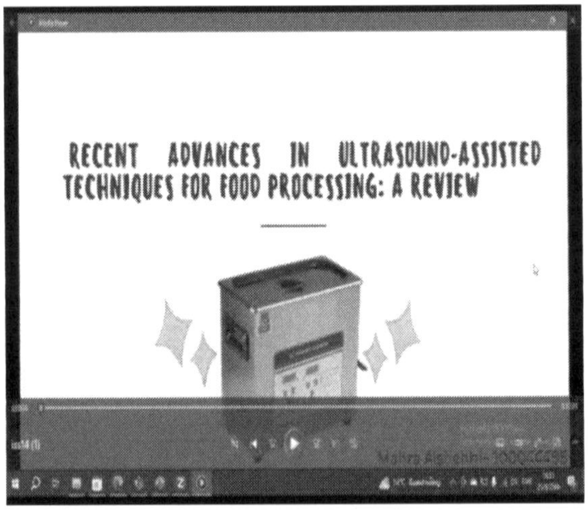

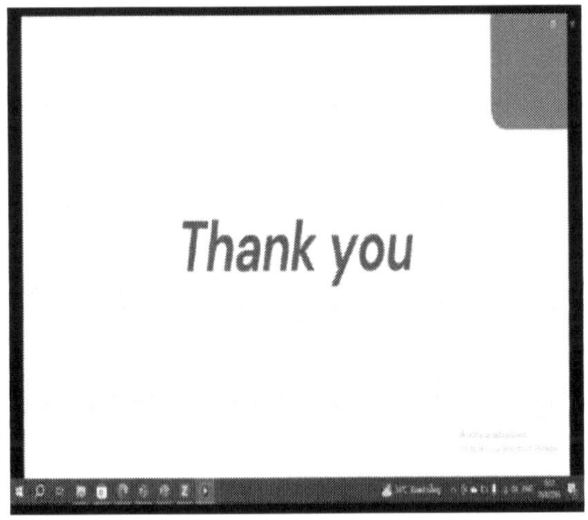

- ISS_15 (02009)

- ISS_16 (02010)

edp sciences

Web of Conferences

Statement of Peer review

In submitting conference proceedings to *Web of Conferences*, the editors of the proceedings certify to the Publisher that

1. They adhere to its **Policy on Publishing Integrity** in order to safeguard good scientific practice in publishing.
2. All articles have been subjected to peer review administered by the proceedings editors.
3. Reviews have been conducted by expert referees, who have been requested to provide unbiased and constructive comments aimed, whenever possible, at improving the work.
4. Proceedings editors have taken all reasonable steps to ensure the quality of the materials they publish and their decision to accept or reject a paper for publication has been based only on the merits of the work and the relevance to the journal.

Title, date and place of the conference

Title: 2023 Research, Invention, and Innovation Congress (RI2C2023)
Date: 24-25 August 2023
Place: Online conference at King Mongkut's University of Technology North Bangkok

Proceedings editor(s):

Malinee Sriariyanun, KMUTNB, Thailand
Yu-Shen Cheng, National Yunlin University of Science and Technology, Taiwan
Debraj Bhattacharyya, IIT Hyderabad, India
Ponnusami Venkatachalam, Sastra deemed university, India
Marttin Paulraj Gundupalli, University of Alberta, Canada

Date and editor's signature 1 Sep 2023

Activity for Diesel Particulate Matter Oxidation of Silver Supported on Al_2O_3, TiO_2, ZnO, and CeO_2: The Effect of Oxygen Concentration

Punya Promhuad[1], *Boonlue* Sawatmongkhon[1,2,*], *Nuwong* Chollacoop[3], *Kampanart* Theinnoi[1,2], *Thawatchai* Wongchang[2,4] and *Ekachai* Juntasaro[5]

[1] College of Industrial Technology, King Mongkut's University of Technology North Bangkok, 1518 Pracharat 1 Road, Wongsawang, Bangsue, Bangkok 10800, Thailand.
[2] Research Centre for Combustion Technology and Alternative Energy (CTAE), Science and Technology Research Institute, King Mongkut's University of Technology North Bangkok, Bangkok 10800, Thailand.
[3] Renewable Energy and Energy Efficiency Research Team, National Energy Technology Center (ENTEC), 114 Thailand Science Park, Klong Luang, Pathumthani 12120, Thailand.
[4] Department of Mechanical and Automotive Engineering Technology, Faculty of Engineering and Technology, King Mongkut's University of Technology North Bangkok (Rayong Campus), Rayong 21120, Thailand.
[5] The Sirindhorn International Thai-German Graduate School of Engineering (TGGS), King Mongkut's University of Technology North Bangkok, 1518 Pracharat 1 Road, Wongsawang, Bangsue, Bangkok 10800, Thailand.

Abstract. Particulate matter (PM) is a problem for human health the major producer of PM are diesel engines. The diesel particulate filters (DPFs) are used for the limitation of the PM. The DPF operation consists of two sequential functions: PM filtering and regeneration. One of the main contributing factors affecting the regeneration of DPF is the oxygen concentration in the exhaust gas. This study investigates the impact of different oxygen concentrations (99.99%, 10%, and 5%) on (PM) oxidation when using silver catalysts supported on CeO_2, ZnO, TiO_2, and Al_2O_3. The synthesized catalysts were characterized using XRD, SEM, SEMEDX, and H_2-TPR techniques, and the PM oxidation activity was evaluated using TGA. The results demonstrated that different oxygen concentrations had little effect on light VOCs oxidation compared to no catalyst or the same catalyst. However, heavy VOCs and soot combustion, which require a higher oxygen concentration, significantly reduce combustion performance when the oxygen concentration decreases.

Keyword. Al_2O_3, CeO_2, Oxygen concertation, PM oxidation, Silver catalyst, TiO_2, ZnO

1 Introduction

Air pollution is a significant environmental issue that adversely impacts human health [1], especially, the respiratory system, which could be damaged by the smaller size of particulate matter like inhalable PM_{10} (particulate matter with an aerodynamic diameter ≤ 10 µm,) and fine $PM_{2.5}$ [2]. Internal combustion engines, particularly diesel engines, are today a major producer of PM [3]. To mitigate this issue, the use of diesel particulate filters (DPFs) has emerged as a viable solution. The function of DPF comprises two main stages: filtration and regeneration [4]. During the filtration phase, particulate matter (PM) particles are trapped by the permeable structure of the diesel particulate filter (DPF), after which the accumulated PM is subjected to oxidation by oxygen at elevated temperatures, typically exceeding 600 °C, during the regeneration phase [5-7]. However, the temperature of exhaust gas produced by a diesel engine is normally less than 600 °C [8,9], so the exhaust gas cannot successfully be oxidized.

The application of catalyzed diesel particulate filter (cDPF) technology has been shown to reduce the temperature of regeneration [10]. Oxidation catalysts, typically composed of noble metals such as platinum (Pt), palladium (Pd), and silver (Ag), supported on metal oxide materials including ceria (CeO_2), alumina (Al_2O_3), and silica (SiO_2) [11-13]. Incorporating an oxidation catalyst can significantly lower the activation energy required for PM oxidation, thereby enabling combustion to occur at lower temperatures. Ag is well-known as a potential oxidation catalyst among the various noble metals [5]. Zhang and Jiang [5] studies revealed that Ag catalysts facilitate the synthesis of adsorbed active oxygen species such as peroxide (O_2^{-2}) and superoxide (O_2^-), also exhibit oxidative stability, which is crucial for Ag efficacy in promoting PM oxidation [11]. Moreover, Ag is a more affordable and cost-effective alternative for oxidation catalyst use than other noble metals [14].

* Corresponding author: boonlue.s@cit.kmutnb.ac.th

The support material has an important role in promoting PM combustion. Using alumina as a support material for oxidation catalysts, for example, Pt [15] and Ag [16], has been a good promoter for soot oxidation. Aneggi *et. al.*, [17] described the behavior of silver deposited on ceria in the oxidation of carbon soot particulate. The research was further expanded to include additional supports such as alumina and zirconia, which have been shown to be effective in numerous Ag oxidation processes. The addition of Ag to ZrO_2 or Al_2O_3 resulted in strong soot oxidation activity in both fresh and aged conditions. TiO_2 emerged as an additional oxide support material that demonstrated effectiveness in promoting particulate matter (PM) oxidation. This efficacy can be attributed to its notable surface area, optimal dispersion of the metal catalyst, and robust metal-support interaction (SMSI), thereby augmenting the catalytic activity. [18]. Ceria is one of the silver catalysts' most commonly used support materials due to its redox properties and oxygen storage capacity (OSC) [13]. The redox properties (the switching of Ce^{3+} to Ce^{4+}) promote high OSC performance [13], resulting in an increase in soot oxidation performance. The increase in oxygen vacancy due to a decrease in lattice oxygen also contributes to the soot oxidation activity [19]. The mechanisms of soot oxidation using CeO_2-based catalysts involve two consecutive steps [20,21]. First, the soot is combusted by lattice oxygen (OL), which affects the formation of oxygen vacancy (Ov) and reduces CeO_2 (Ce^{4+}) to CeO (Ce^{3+}). Then, the gas-phase oxygen adsorbs on the surface of CeO_2 and transforms into active oxygen [22].

The performance of PM oxidation was promoted by noble metals and supporters. Additionally, the oxygen concentration is the primary influence on effect the of PM oxidation performance. Zhao *et. al.*, [23] examined the combustion characteristics of soot and the impact of oxygen concentration and regeneration temperature on the continuous pulsation regeneration of a DPF. The study found that oxygen concentration is a highly effective indicator of regeneration efficiency, and that oxygen is the primary reactant in the soot regeneration reaction. In other words, the level of oxygen in the DPF directly affects the conditions necessary for successful soot combustion. The above research shows that oxygen concentration affects PM combustion when using Ag on different oxide supporters. It may be showing different promotions of PM combustion and its effect on PM oxidation performance. This paper aims to study the oxygen concentrations that impact PM oxidation performance when using silver catalysts on different oxide support (eg. CeO_2, ZnO, TiO_2, and Al_2O_3).

2 Experimental

2.1 Catalyst and Particulate matter preparation

This study's incipient wetness impregnation method employed the silver medal as a catalyst on four distinct supports. The synthesis process was initiated by dissolving silver nitrate (sourced from Thomas Baker Chemicals, India) in an appropriate quantity of distilled water, aiming to attain a silver loading of 16 wt% on the respective support materials. This study used 16wt% of Ag because of previous research conducted by our research group, which indicated that a 16 wt% Ag concentration on Al_2O_3 exhibited the best at promoting PM combustion [11]. The support materials employed in this study encompassed γ-alumina (sourced from Ajax Finechem, Australia) with a BET surface area measuring 142 m^2/g, titanium oxide (obtained from KEMAUS, Australia), and zinc oxide (procured from Quality Reagent Chemical, New Zealand). For ceria, a silver concentration of 5 wt% of the weight of CeO_2 was employed, as this concentration was determined to be conducive to promoting effective calcination. This study used 5wt% of Ag with CeO_2 as it is the best to promotes soot oxidation [13]. In this research, oxide supports were selected as representatives of different support material groups. For instance, Al_2O_3 was chosen as a representative of acidic support materials. TiO_2 (anatase structure) was selected as a representative of support materials classified as oxide semiconductors. ZnO was chosen as a representative of group II-VI semiconductor support materials. Lastly, CeO_2 was selected as a representative of reducible support materials. Subsequently, the precursor-laden supports were dried in an oven at 110 °C overnight and then calcined in static air at 600 °C for 2 h to obtain the final calcined samples.

The gaseous emissions generated by a diesel engine were employed as a direct reservoir for the retention of PM. The engine was operated under controlled conditions with varying speeds ranging from 1000 to 2000 rpm and loads ranging from 25% to 75% of the maximum load. To facilitate the experimental setup, a stainless-steel mesh with a mesh count of 500 per square inch was strategically placed inside the exhaust pipe, which possessed an inner diameter of 50 mm. The mesh was carefully rolled in a unidirectional manner for optimal positioning and effectiveness. The PM particles were trapped on the mesh and subsequently collected. The collected PM was then dried in a furnace at 110 °C for 8 h. For future studies, the dried PM was stored in an airtight container.

2.2 Material characterisation

The X-Ray Diffraction (XRD) patterns of the synthesized catalysts were examined using a Rigaku Miniflex 600 diffractometer (manufactured by Rigaku, Japan), with Cu-Kα radiation (λ = 1.5418 Å) employed as the X-ray source. The diffractograms were recorded within the angular range of 10° to 80° at a scanning rate of 2°/min. The average sizes of the crystallites were determined using Scherrer's equation. The catalysts underwent examination and characterization utilizing a ZEISS AURIGA field emission scanning electron microscope (FE-SEM) equipped with an Oxford Instruments energy-dispersive X-ray (EDX) spectrometer. This analytical setup allowed for the acquisition of microscopic images and the analysis of elemental compositions. The reducibility of the catalysts was investigated using H_2 temperature-programmed reduction (H_2-TPR) analysis. The measurements were performed using a ChemiSorb 2750 instrument (Micromeritics, United States) equipped with a thermal conductivity detector (TCD). Approximately 60 mg of the catalyst sample was loaded into a quartz reactor and subjected to a controlled temperature ramp. A gas mixture of 10 vol.% H_2 in He, flowing at a rate of 30 ml/min, was passed over the sample. The temperature was gradually increased from room temperature to 800 °C at a heating rate of 10 °C/min. The data were collected during the temperature ramp ranging from 80 °C to 700 °C.

2.3 Catalytic activity tests

The catalytic oxidation activity of PM was assessed using thermogravimetric analysis (TGA) with a PerkinElmer® Pyris 1 instrument. Prior to analysis, the PM samples were mixed with the catalyst at a predetermined weight ratio of 1/5. To ensure proper blending and close contact between the PM and catalyst, a stainless-steel mortar was employed for a 5-min duration. Next, an aliquot of approximately 10 mg from the prepared mixture was carefully transferred into a ceramic crucible. The temperature of the crucible was gradually raised from ambient temperature to 110 °C at a controlled heating rate of 10 °C/min, while maintaining a continuous flow of nitrogen gas. Subsequently, the purge gas was switched to oxygen (O_2) to facilitate the oxidation process, and the temperature was further increased to 700 °C, following the same heating rate of 5 °C/min. The purity of the oxygen was 99.99%, with concentrations of 10 vol.% O_2 in N_2 and 5 vol.% O_2 in N_2, flowing at a constant rate of 50 cm^3/min. The selection of oxygen concentration is necessary to align with the oxygen concentration within the exhaust gas of a diesel engine, which typically ranges from 5-17 vol% depending on the engine load [24,25]. However, in the exhaust gas of a diesel engine using biodiesel as fuel, the oxygen concentration is typically around 10 vol.% [26,27]. Based on these reasons, a concentration of 10 vol.% was chosen as the representative oxygen concentration derived from actual combustion in the engine. Additionally, a concentration of 5 vol% was selected as it represents the minimum concentration observed from combustion in a diesel engine, aiming to investigate the worst-case scenario of combustion. Lastly, the selection of a 99.99 vol.% concentration was made to examine the best performance of PM combustion. Continuous recording of sample weight was performed during the temperature ramp to monitor changes. PM oxidation activity was assessed based on several parameters. T_{20} corresponds to the temperature at which complete combustion of light volatile organic compounds (VOCs) occurs, defined as a 20% weight loss from the initial mass. T_{55} represents the temperature at which a 55% weight loss occurs from the initial mass, indicating the complete combustion of the heavy VOCs contained in the PM [11]. Finally, T_{90} is the temperature at which a 90% weight loss is observed and is used as an indicator of the performance of soot.

3 Result and discussion

A section of the results and discussion will show the result of the materials characterization, the PM oxidation activity and PM oxidation performance. The materials characterization shows the XRD result, SEM EDX image, and reducibility (H_2 -TPR). The TGA analyzer was used to define the PM oxidation activity and PM oxidation performance. The result and discussion of the PM oxidation activity show the activity when using different supporters and concentrations of oxygen. The silver used the different oxide supporters as follows: Al_2O_3, TiO_2, ZnO and CeO_2. The concentration of oxygen used was 99.99 %, 10 and 5 %vol of N_2.

3.1 The materials characterization

3.1.1 XRD

Figure 1 shows the XRD profiles of Ag on four supporters in this work. The 2Θ of metallic silver (JCPDS 04-0783) shows at 38.2°, 44.4°, 64.5°, 77.3°, and 81.4° indicate the (1 1 1), (2 0 0), (2 2 0), (3 1 1), and (2 2 2) [28,29]. The result in this work shows the same angle diffraction of Ag on all the oxide supporters except the case of Ag/CeO_2. As the Ag on the Ag/CeO_2 is 5 % by weight, it makes the small peak of silver for diffraction.

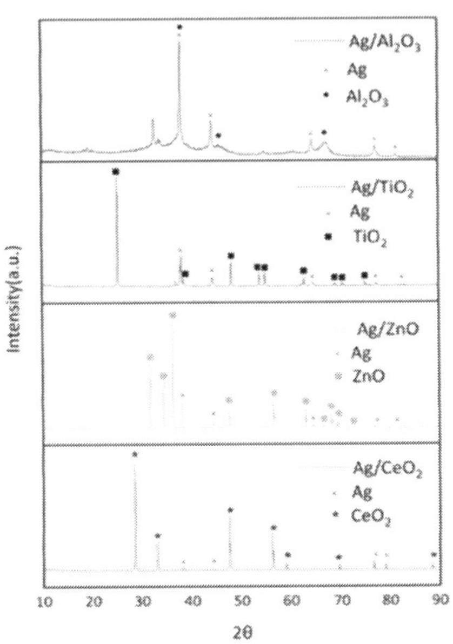

Fig. 1. The XRD profiles for Ag/Al_2O_3, Ag /TiO_2, Ag/ZnO and Ag/CeO_2.

The diffraction peak of Al_2O_3 (γ-Al_2O_3) was shown in the case of Ag/Al_2O_3, which is around 39.5°, 45.8°, and 67° [18]. Ag/TiO_2 shows the diffraction peaks of titanium the type anatase, which were angles at 25.64°, 38.26°, 48.40°, 63.00°, 69.26°, and 75.16° [26,27]. Corro *et. al.*, [30] used the XRD technique to identify the peaks of ZnO. The authors presented peaks at 32°, 34°, 36°, 47°, 56°, 63°, 66°, 68°, and 69o, which provided insights into the structural characteristics of ZnO as same in the case of Ag/ZnO of this work. Ag/CeO_2 showed the peaks of Ceria at 28.5° (1 1 1), 33.1° (2 0 0), 47.5° (2 2 0), 56.3° (3 1 1), 59.1° (2 2 2), 69.3° (4 0 0), 76.6° (3 3 1), 79.1 (4 2 0), and 88.5 (4 2 2). The mean Ag^0 crystallite size across each catalyst demonstrates that diverse supports have distinct impacts on the dispersion of the active metal and its interaction with the support material. The ascending sequence of average crystallite sizes of Ag^0 on different supports is as follows: Ag/Al_2O_3 (11 nm), Ag/TiO_2 (13 nm), Ag/ZnO (15 nm), and Ag/CeO_2 (41 nm).

3.1.2 SEM and SEM EDX

Figure 2 shows SEM and SEM EDX which present the element of catalyst and supporter. In the first group (i), the catalytic and supporter morphology is demonstrated with the following images: Ag/Al_2O_3 (a,i), Ag/TiO_2 (b,i), Ag/ZnO(c,i), and Ag/CeO_2 (d,i). The second group (ii) shows the composition of the support, which includes Al(a,ii), Ti (b.ii), Z(c,ii), and Ce(d,ii). Oxygen elements in all support materials are shown in group (iii) images. Finally, in group (iv) images, the dispersion of Ag on each support material is demonstrated, as follows: Ag/Al_2O_3 (a,iv), Ag/TiO_2 (b,iv), AgZnO (c,iv), and Ag/CeO_2 (d,iv). The SEM EDX images clearly show different Ag dispersions on different support materials. Moreover, it is evident that the Ag particles exhibit a greater size and increased agglomeration in the scenarios involving Ag/TiO_2 and Ag/ZnO catalysts, in comparison to the Ag/Al_2O_3 catalyst. The size of the catalyst particles may also influence the circumstances of interaction between the catalyst and the soot [31]. The small-sized catalyst particles have a large surface area, resulting in close or excellent contact conditions [11,35]. In the case of Ag/CeO_2 shows a low density of silver, which compare with another case because the perpetration of Ag is 5 wt% that it is lower than another support. The findings of the SEM EDX investigations agreed well with the XRD results.

3.1.3 H_2-TPR

Figure 3 shows the H_2 profile of Ag on several oxide supporters in each temperature range. The oxidation activity was promoted by active oxygen species from both the surface and lattice oxygen. The active oxygen species could respond with H_2. For example, the surface oxygen on Ag_2O responds with H_2 as follows: $Ag_2O+H_2 \rightarrow 2Ag^0+H_2O$ [3]. The consumption of H_2 was shown by a peak of the TCD signal in H_2-TPR. It is well known that the temperature was higher than 300 °C, Ag_2O completely changed to Ag^0 [33].

The TCD signal for Ag/CeO_2 exhibited two distinct peaks. The first peak, observed at 190 °C, indicated the consumption of H_2 by the surface oxygen of the material. The presence of Ag_2O was found to facilitate the reaction with H_2. Additionally, a surface reaction between H_2 and CeO_2 was observed, resulting in the formation of oxygen vacancies on the ceria surface. The second peak in the TCD signal is detected at a temperature of 700 °C, which exceeded the combustion range of particulate matter.

Ag/ZnO shows two distinct peaks in the TCD signal at temperatures of 212 °C and 600 °C, respectively. These peaks indicated the consumption of H_2 through active oxygen species from both surface and lattice oxygen. The surface oxygen was replenished by Ag_2O when the temperature was below 300 °C, while the lattice oxygen was released from ZnO. The reaction involved the reduction of Zn^0 to Zn^+, as expressed by the equation: $ZnO + H_2 \rightarrow Zn^0+H_2O$, which was catalyzed by metallic copper (Cu) [34]. The results obtained for Ag/ZnO are consistent with those reported by Zhao et al. [35], who observed only a single peak in the TCD signal at 600 °C.

Ag/TiO_2 shows the single peak in the TCD signal at a temperature of 176 °C, indicating the consumption of H_2 through active oxygen species originating from Ag_2O. As TiO_2 does not release lattice oxygen, the observed consumption of H_2 is attributed solely to the presence of active oxygen on Ag_2O. To enhance the active oxygen generation and delivery abilities, Kim et al. [40] employed ceria as a promoter for Ag/TiO_2 in soot oxidation. The authors also reported H_2-TPR results for Ag supported on anatase between 250 °C and 330 °C, which resemble the reducibility characteristics of Ag/TiO_2 observed in our study. Ag supported on alumina (Ag/Al_2O_3) exhibited a single peak in the TCD signal at around 100 °C, indicating the presence of active oxygen -originating from Ag_2O. The reaction temperature was lower than 300 °C, and no reduction peaks were observed in the profiles of pure Al_2O_3, which confirms that the source of active oxygen is indeed Ag_2O. Ousji et al. [41] also investigated Ag-based catalysts on different supports for formaldehyde oxidation and used the H_2-TPR technique to determine the reduction of metal oxides. Their results showed that in the case of Ag/Al_2O_3, the peak TCD around 100 °C was caused by the presence of large Ag_2O.

Additionally, our study found that there was no catalyst-driven oxygen release at temperatures exceeding 150 °C, as evidenced by the absence of TCD signal peaks. This finding is consistent with Aneggi et al. [18], who used TPR to assess the reducibility of Ag-based catalysts and found that Ag has no effect on TPR traces of ZrO_2 and Al_2O_3. H_2-TPR analysis also showed no observable reduction peaks for Ag_xO, which confirms the presence of zero-valent Ag at temperatures >110 °C. Based on these experimental findings, it can be concluded that Ag_2O is fully converted to Ag^0 once it releases oxygen to H_2.

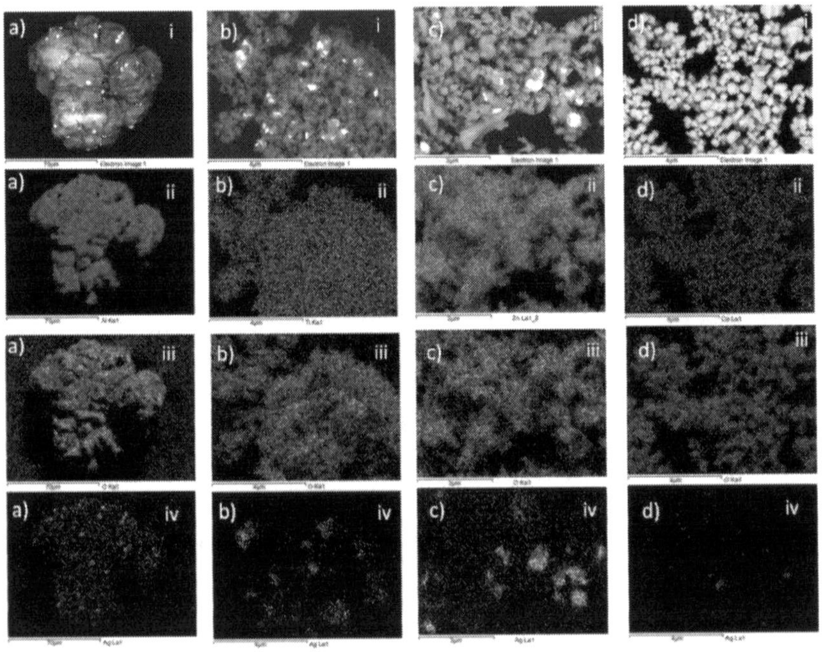

Fig. 2. SEM and SEM EDX images of a) Ag/Al_2O_3, b) Ag/ TiO_2, c) Ag/ZnO and Ag/ CeO_2. The number in fig 2 is a type of image as follows: SEM image (i), Type of the main element of supporter (ii) such as the image of Ag/ Al_2O_3 shows the Al, the element of oxygen (iii), and the element of silver (iv).

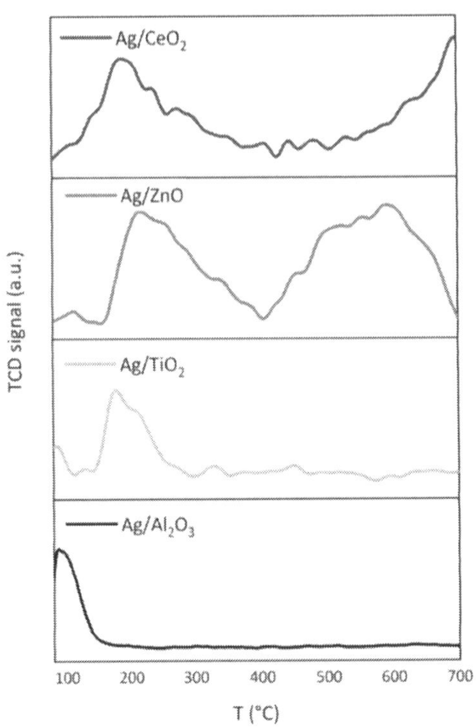

Fig. 3. H_2-TPR profiles of Ag/CeO_2, Ag/ZnO, Ag/TiO_2, and Ag/Al_2O_3 catalysts.

3.2 PM oxidation activity

3.2.1 Pure PM oxidation

Figure 4 shows the oxidation activity of pure PM and the percentage of weight loss, and the first derivative of weight loss (DTG) are shown in figure 4a and 4b, respectively. The combustion of PM is divided into three phases depending on its constituents: The initial combustion phase for light VOCs, the secondary combustion phase for heavy VOCs [11], and the final combustion phase for soot [32]. The phase of combustion is presented by DTG result.

Utilizing a 99.99% O_2 concentration, the DTG analysis exhibits three distinct peaks at 289 °C, 389 °C, and 517 °C, which correspond to the oxidation of light VOCs, heavy VOCs, and soot, respectively. In the case of a 10 vol% O_2 in N_2 concentration, two peaks of DTG are observed at 271 °C (light VOCs) and approximately 600 °C (heavy VOCs). Similarly, when a 5 vol% O_2 in N_2 concentration is employed, two peaks of DTG are observed at 266 °C (light VOCs) and approximately 600 °C (heavy VOCs). The TGA results indicated that the weight loss percentage of pure PM was affected by the oxygen concentration. Complete combustion of PM was achieved at 700 °C when 99.99% oxygen concentration was used, whereas at 10% oxygen concentration, a residual mass of 20% was observed at the same temperature. Similarly, a residual mass of 40% was observed at 700 °C when the oxygen concentration was further reduced to 5%. The residual mass observed in the latter cases was due to the presence of soot resulting from incomplete PM combustion. The effect of oxygen concentration on the combustion of light VOCs was found to be insignificant, while the combustion of heavy VOCs and soot was significantly affected by the oxygen concentration.

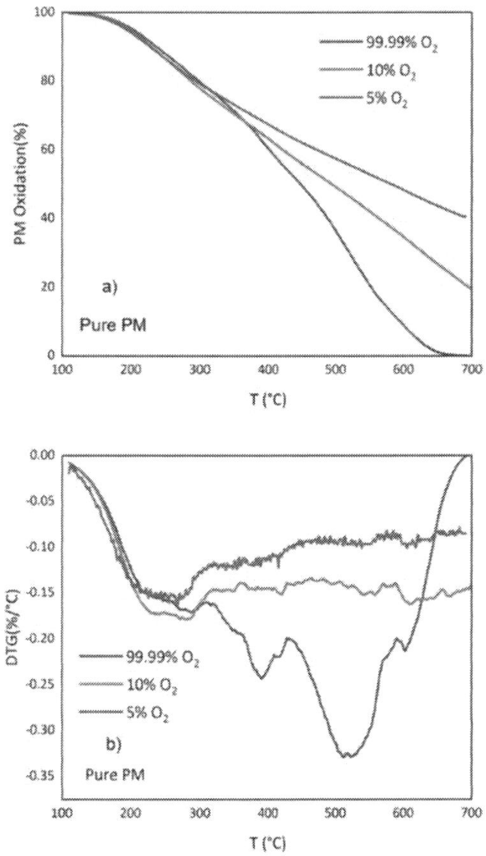

Fig. 4. Pure PM oxidation (a) and DTG of PM oxidation(b); using O_2 concentration 99.99% ,10% and 5 %.

3.2.2 PM with Ag/Al$_2$O$_3$

Figure 5 illustrates the PM oxidation activity of the Ag/Al_2O_3 catalyst. The weight loss percentage and the DTG curves are presented in figures 5a and 5b, respectively. The DTG peak of Ag/Al_2O_3 reveals two peaks at 251 °C and 313 °C in the presence of 99.99% O_2, while the presence of 10 vol% O_2 demonstrates peaks of DTG at 231 °C and 341 °C. The concentration of 5% oxygen exhibits the DTG peak at 215 °C and 365°C. The results of DTG indicate two phases of combustion. The first peak of DTG signifies the oxidation of light VOCs, while the second peak indicates the combustion of heavy VOCs and soot. Although the Ag/Al_2O_3 catalyst promotes active oxygen by Ag^0 after reaching a temperature of 300 °C, the oxidation of light VOCs is not enhanced by the catalyst.

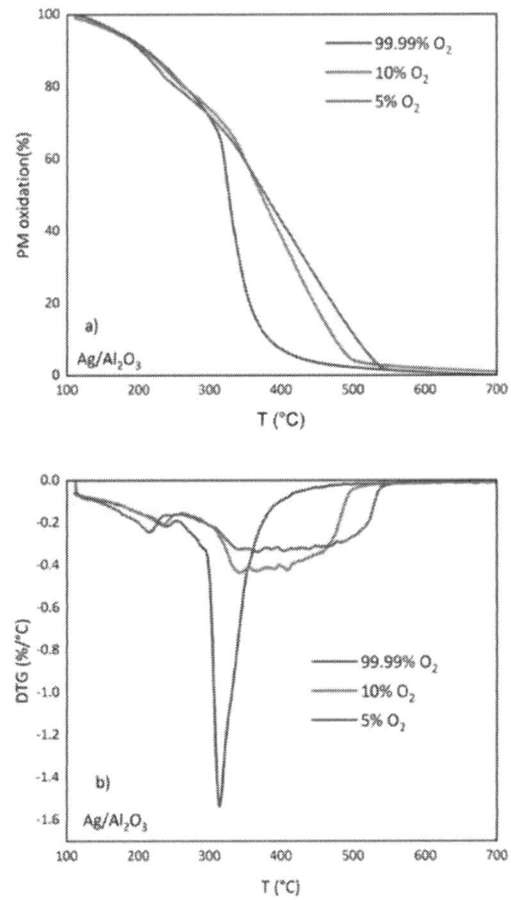

Fig. 5. a) PM oxidation b) DTG of PM oxidation; PM with Ag/Al_2O_3 and tight contact

In contrast, the combustion of heavy VOCs and soot is substantially promoted by Ag/Al_2O_3. The T_{20} values for Ag/Al_2O_3 when using 99.99%, 10%, and 5 vol % O_2 are 256, 264, and 253 °C, respectively. The T_{20} value reflects the performance of the oxidation of light VOCs. The results of T_{20} demonstrate nuances of temperature, indicating that the concentration of oxygen has a low impact on the oxidation of light VOCs. The T_{55} values for Ag/Al_2O_3 when using 99.99%, 10%, and 5 vol % O_2 are 331, 385, and 394 °C, respectively. The T_{55} value indicates the temperature required for the complete combustion of VOCs (heavy VOCs), which reflects the performance of VOCs combustion. It is observed that the reduction in oxygen concentration leads to an increase in the temperature required for the complete combustion of VOCs, implying that the VOCs combustion performance decreases as the oxygen concentration decreases in Ag/Al_2O_3 case. The T_{90} values for Ag/Al_2O_3 when using 99.99%, 10%, and 5 vol % O_2 are 384, 476, and 506 °C, respectively. The T_{90} value represents the temperature required for the combustion of soot and reflects the performance of soot combustion. Similar to the trend observed for T_{55}, the results indicate that decreasing the oxygen concentration leads to a decrease in the performance of soot combustion in the case of the Ag/Al_2O_3 catalyst.

3.2.3 PM with Ag/TiO₂

Figure 6 shows the PM oxidation activity of Ag/TiO_2, where the percentage of weight loss and DTG are displayed in figures 6a and 6b, respectively. The DTG of Ag/TiO_2 reveals two peaks at 197 °C and 425 °C in the presence of 99.99% O_2, while the presence of 10 vol% O_2 demonstrates peaks of DTG at 180 °C and 604 °C. Similarly, the concentration of 5% oxygen exhibits the DTG peak at 207 °C and 604°C. The results of DTG indicate two distinct phases of combustion, like Ag/Al_2O_3. Specifically, the first peak of DTG signifies the combustion of light VOCs, while the second peak indicates the combustion of heavy VOCs and soot. The Ag/TiO_2 catalyst promotes the combustion of light VOCs through the active oxygen generated by Ag_2O, as observed in the H_2-TPR results. This promotion of active oxygen leads to a lower temperature of oxidation of light VOCs compared to Ag/Al_2O_3.

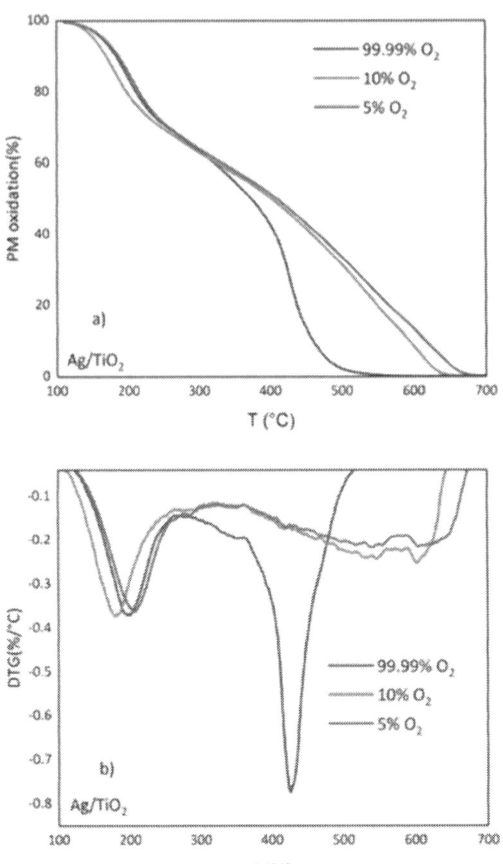

Fig. 6. a) PM oxidation b) DGT of PM oxidation: PM with Ag/TiO_2 and tight contact

Furthermore, the combustion of heavy VOCs and soot is promoted by Ag^0 after the temperature reaches 300 °C, resulting in a decrease in the temperature required for the combustion of heavy VOCs and soot. The T_{20} values for Ag/TiO_2 when using 99.99%, 10%, and 5 vol % O_2 are 212, 199, and 216 °C, respectively. The T_{20} values show a similar trend across different oxygen concentrations, indicating a weaker effect of varying oxygen concentration on the promotion of the combustion of light VOCs by Ag/TiO_2 T_{55} values for Ag/TiO_2 when using 99.99%, 10%, and 5 vol % O_2 are 394,432 and 440 °C, respectively. T_{55} in the case of Ag/TiO_2 shows a clear difference in temperature with a lower oxygen concentration. With this result, it can be implied that the performance of VOCs combustion decreases with less oxygen concentration. Furthermore, the effect of oxygen concentration on the activation of Ag/TiO_2 in promoting soot combustion is evident when considering T_{90}. The decrease in oxygen concentration from 99.99% to 10% results in a significant increase in the temperature required for soot combustion, with a difference of 133°C. The T_{90} values for Ag/TiO_2 when using 99.99%, 10%, and 5 vol % O_2 are 461, 594, and 616 °C, respectively. These results further emphasize the importance of oxygen concentration in promoting soot combustion using Ag/TiO_2.

3.2.4 PM with Ag/ZnO

Figure 7 illustrates the PM oxidation activity of Ag/ZnO, where figure 7a and 7b display the percentage of weight loss and DTG, respectively. In the presence of 99.99% O_2, Ag/ZnO displays three peaks of DTG at 174 °C, 350 °C and 414 °C. Conversely, the presence of 10 vol% O_2 demonstrates peaks of DTG at 174 °C, 415 °C, and 495 °C. Likewise, the concentration of 5% oxygen exhibits the DTG peak at 174 °C, 415 °C, and 542 °C. The results of the DTG analysis for Ag/ZnO showed three peaks. indicating the oxidation of light and heavy VOCs, as well as soot. The reduction of Ag_2O on Ag/ZnO was observed through H_2-TPR, which occurred at 150-400 °C, and suggested that the active oxygen from Ag_2O was responsible for the oxidation of light and heavy VOCs. The combustion of soot was found to occur after the oxidation of VOCs at temperatures between 450-550 °C. Additionally, lattice oxygen was released from ZnO at 400-700 °C, serving as an oxidizer. The reduction of Ag_2O by VOCs generated metallic silver, which acted as an active site for gas-phase oxygen to adsorb on Ag^0, facilitating the oxidation of soot on Ag/ZnO through either lattice or gas-phase oxygen. The T_{20} values of Ag/ZnO for different oxygen concentrations (99.99%, 10%, and 5 vol % O_2) were 172, 172, and 173°C, respectively. The almost similar T_{20} results for different oxygen concentrations indicate that oxygen concentration has a comparably smaller impact on mild VOC combustion by Ag/ZnO. T_{55} values for Ag/ZnO when using 99.99%, 10%, and 5 vol % O_2 are 377,406 and 409, respectively. The value of T_{55} in the case of oxygen consumption at a concentration of 99.99% shows a smaller value. in the case of 10% and 5% oxygen concentrations. This result shows a significant effect on oxygen in the complete combustion of VOCs when Ag/ZnO is used as a catalyst.

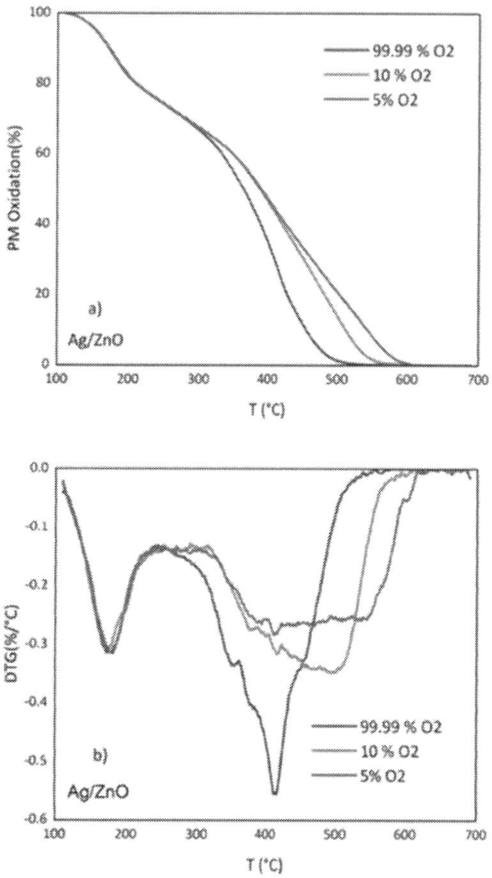

Fig. 7. a) PM oxidation b) DTG of PM oxidation; PM with Ag/ZnO and tight contact

It is of interest that in the case of Ag/ZnO shows similar performance of VOC oxidation in the case of 10 % and 5 % oxygen. concentrations. The T_{55} values for Ag/ZnO at oxygen concentrations of 99.99%, 10%, and 5 vol % are 377, 406, and 409, respectively. The T_{55} value at 99.99% oxygen concentration is smaller than those at 10% and 5% oxygen concentrations, indicating the significant effect of oxygen on the complete combustion of VOCs with Ag/ZnO catalyst. Notably, Ag/ZnO demonstrates comparable performance in VOC oxidation at 10% and 5% oxygen concentrations. The T_{90} values for Ag/ZnO under different oxygen concentrations were investigated, and the results show that the T_{90} values for 99.99%, 10%, and 5 vol % O_2 are 457°, 512°, and 543 °C, respectively. The T_{90} value is a measure of the temperature required for soot combustion and reflects the performance of the Ag/ZnO catalyst in promoting soot combustion. The trend observed for T_{90} is like that observed for T_{55}, indicating that a decrease in oxygen concentration leads to a decrease in the performance of soot combustion when using Ag/ZnO.

3.2.5 PM with Ag/CeO$_2$

Figure 8 presents the oxidation activity of Ag/CeO_2, with the weight loss percentage and the first derivative of weight loss (DTG) displayed in figures 8a and 8b, respectively. When exposed to a 99.99% O_2 atmosphere, Ag/CeO_2 exhibits three distinct DTG peaks at 180 °C, 317 °C, and 418 °C. Conversely, the presence of 10 vol% O_2 demonstrates peaks of DTG at 180 °C, 410 °C, and 497 °C. Likewise, the concentration of 5% oxygen exhibits the DTG peak at 180 °C, 416 °C, and 545 °C. DTG analysis revealed three distinct peaks corresponding to the oxidation of light and heavy VOCs, as well as soot, on Ag/CeO_2. H_2-TPR results indicated that active oxygen is removed from the Ag/CeO_2 surface at temperatures below 200 °C, while VOCs combustion occurs at higher temperatures. This suggests that active oxygen migrates from the catalyst surface to the particulate matter first, with catalytic burnout of VOCs occurring subsequently. Soot oxidation, on the other hand, is promoted by active values of Ag/CeO_2 were determined for different oxygen concentrations (99.99%, 10%, and 5 vol % O_2) were found to be 168, 171, and 169, respectively.

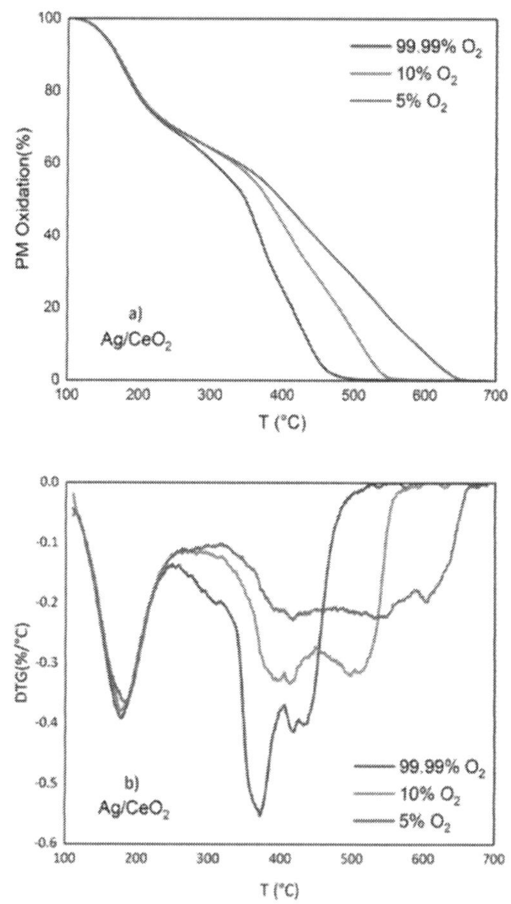

Fig. 8. a) PM oxidation b) DTG of PM oxidation; PM with Ag/CeO_2 and tight contact

The results of T_{20} show a nuanced temperature dependency. These findings suggest that changes in oxygen concentration have a low impact on the oxidation of light VOCs. T_{55} values for Ag/CeO_2 when using 99.99%, 10%, and 5 vol % O_2 are 359, 395 and 422 °C, respectively. The T_{55} value of the case of Ag/CeO_2 shows an increase in the temperature with decreasing oxygen concentration, which affects the performance of the combustion of VOCs. Similarly, the T_{90} result indicates a decrease in soot oxidation performance for Ag/CeO_2 at low O_2 concentrations. The T_{90} values for 99.99%, 10%, and 5 vol % O_2 are 438, 511, and 588 °C, respectively.

3.3 PM oxidation performance

3.3.1 the VOCs oxidation performances

Figure 9 illustrates the performance of VOC oxidation using Ag supported on different oxide materials and under different O_2 concentrations (99.99%, 10%, and 5%). When comparing the promotion effects of silver catalysts supported by different materials and utilizing a 99.99% oxygen concentration, the cumulative performance of VOCs (volatile organic compounds) combustion, in comparison to the pure PM case, can be summarized as follows: Ag/TiO_2 (7%), Ag/ZnO (11%), Ag/CeO_2 (15%), and Ag/Al_2O_3 (22%). Similarly, when employing a 10% oxygen concentration, the cumulative performance of VOCs combustion, relative to the pure PM case, for silver catalysts with different supporters can be summarized as: Ag/TiO_2 (6%), Ag/ZnO (11%), Ag/CeO_2 (14%), and Ag/Al_2O_3 (16%). Furthermore, when utilizing a 5% oxygen concentration, the comparative promotion effects of silver catalysts with different supporters on VOCs combustion, in relation to the pure PM case, can be summarized as: Ag/TiO_2 (17%), Ag/CeO_2 (20%), Ag/ZnO (22%), and Ag/Al_2O_3 (25%).

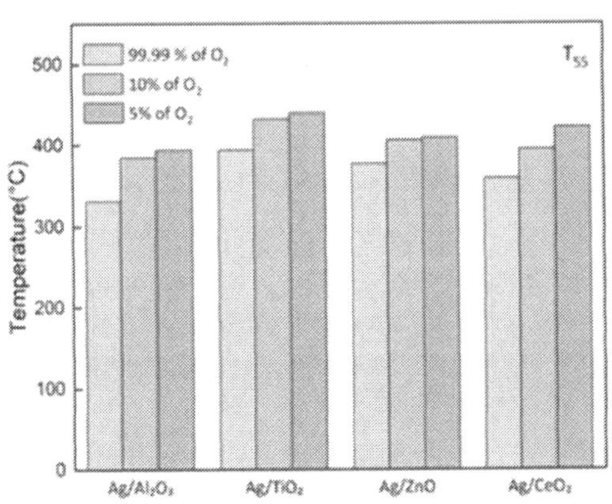

Fig. 9. The comparison of the VOCs oxidation performances.

3.3.2 the soot oxidation performances

In figure 10, the performance of soot oxidation using Ag supported on various oxide materials and subjected to different O_2 concentrations (99.99%, 10%, and 5%) is depicted. When comparing the promotional effects of silver catalysts supported by various materials and employing a 99.99% oxygen concentration, the overall performance of soot combustion, in relation to the pure PM case, can be succinctly summarized as follows: Ag/TiO_2 (23%), Ag/ZnO (23%), Ag/CeO_2 (26%), and Ag/Al_2O_3 (35%). Likewise, by utilizing a 10% oxygen concentration, the cumulative promotion of VOCs combustion, relative to the pure PM case, for silver catalysts with distinct supporters can be summarized as: Ag/TiO_2 (23%), Ag/ZnO (34%), Ag/CeO_2 (34%), and Ag/Al_2O_3 (38%). Furthermore, when employing a 5% oxygen concentration, the comparative effects of silver catalysts with diverse supporters on VOCs combustion, in relation to the pure PM case, can be concisely summarized as: Ag/TiO_2 (32%), Ag/CeO_2 (35%), Ag/ZnO (40%), and Ag/Al_2O_3 (44%). The results obtained using 99.99% O_2 show that Ag/Al_2O_3 exhibits the highest performance of soot oxidation, whereas Ag/TiO_2, Ag/ZnO, and Ag/CeO_2 demonstrate similar soot oxidation performances. When 10% and 5% O_2 are employed, the order of soot oxidation performance is Ag/Al_2O_3 > Ag/ZnO > Ag/CeO_2 > Ag/TiO_2.

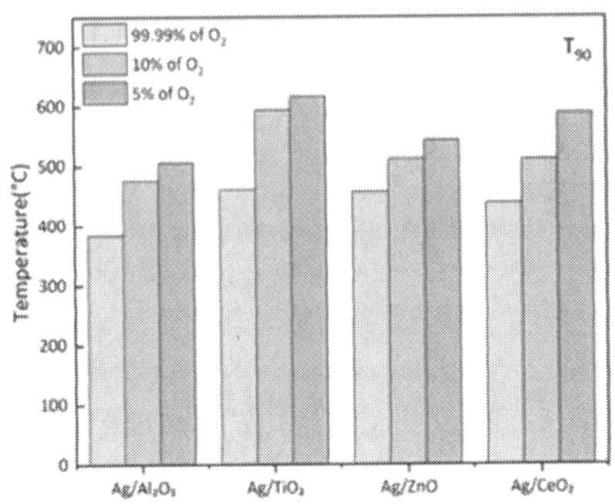

Fig. 10. The comparison of the soot oxidation performances.

4 Conclusions

The aim of this study was to investigate the impact of different oxygen concentrations (99.99%, 10%, and 5%) on the performance of PM oxidation using silver catalysts on various oxide supports. The results showed that the various oxygen concentrations had a minor effect on the combustion performance of light VOCs when compared to using no catalyst or the same catalyst. However, the combustion of heavy VOCs and soot, which require a higher oxygen concentration, significantly reduced the combustion performance. These findings indicate the importance of considering the oxygen concentration when selecting a catalyst for PM oxidation.

Acknowledgements

This research was funded by National Science, Research and Innovation Fund (NSRF), and King Mongkut's University of Technology North Bangkok with Contract no. KMUTNB-FF-66-19. P.Promhouad thanks King Mongkut's University of Technology, North Bangkok, and the National Science and Technology Development Agency, Thailand. Contract No. Grad 018/2563, for supporting his scholarship.

References

1. P.K. Wong, M.A. Ghadikolaei, S.H. Chen, A.A. Fadairo, K.W. Ng, S.M.Y. Lee, J.C. Xu, Z.D. Lian L. Li, H.C. Wong, Z. Ning, Physical, chemical, and cell toxicity properties of mature/aged particulate matter (PM) trapped in a diesel particulate filter (DPF) along with the results from freshly produced PM of a diesel engine, Journal of Hazardous Materials, **434** (2022): 128855
2. Q. Zhang, X. Meng, S. Shi, L. Kan, R. Chen, H. Kan, Overview of particulate air pollution and human health in China: Evidence, challenges, and opportunities, The Innovation, **3**,6 (2022): 0312
3. M. Lapuerta, J. Rodríguez-Fernández, J. Sánchez-Valdepeñas, Soot reactivity analysis and implications on diesel filter regeneration, Progress in Energy and Combustion Science, **78** (2020): 100833
4. L. Xiaowei, R. Jean-Charles, Y. Suyuan, Effect of temperature on graphite oxidation behavior, Nuclear Engineering and design, **227**,3 (2004): 273-280
5. Z. Li, W. Zhang, Z. Chen, Q. Jiang, Mechanism of accelerating soot oxidation by NO2 from diesel engine exhaust, Environmental Pollution, **264** (2020): 114708
6. M. Abián, C. Martín, P. Nogueras, J. Sánchez-Valdepeñas, J. Rodríguez-Fernández, M Lapuerta, M.U. Alzueta, Interaction of diesel engine soot with NO2 and O2 at diesel exhaust conditions. Effect of fuel and engine operation mode, Fuel, **212** (2018): 455-461
7. T.Y. Kim, S.H. LEE, Combustion and Emission Characteristics of Wood Pyrolysis Oil-Butanol Blended Fuels in a Di Diesel Engine, International Journal of Automotive Technology, **16** (2015): 903-912
8. F. Diehl, J. Barbier, D. Duprez, I. Guibard, G. Mabilon, Catalytic oxidation of heavy hydrocarbons over Pt/Al2O3. Oxidation of C10+ solid hydrocarbons representative of soluble organic fraction of Diesel soots, Applied Catalysis A: General, **504** (2015): 37-43
9. A.M. Gänzler, M. Casapu, F. Maurer, H. Störmer, D. Gerthsen, G. Ferre, P. Vernoux, B. Bornmann, R. Frahm, V. Murzin, M. Nachtegaal, Tuning the Pt/CeO2 Interface by in Situ Variation of the Pt Particle Size, Acs Catalysis, **8**,6 (2018): 4800-4811
10. X. Liang, X. Lv, Y. Wang, L. He, Y. Wang, K. Fu, Q. Liu, K. Wang, Experimental investigation of diesel soot oxidation reactivity along the exhaust after-treatment system components, Fuel, **302** (2021): 121047
11. B. Sawatmongkhon, K. Theinnoi, T. Wongchang, C. Haoharn, C. Wongkhorsub, E. Sukjit, A. Tsolakis, Catalytic oxidation of diesel particulate matter by using silver and ceria supported on alumina as the oxidation catalyst, Applied Catalysis A: General, **574** (2019): 33-40
12. J.H. Lee, D.Y. Jo, J.W. Choung, C.H. Kim, H.C. Ham, K.Y. Lee, Roles of noble metals (M = Ag, Au, Pd, Pt and Rh) on CeO2 in enhancing activity toward soot oxidation: Active oxygen species and DFT calculations, Journal of hazardous materials, **403** (2021): 124085
13. J.H. Lee, S.H. Lee, J.W. Choung, C.H. Kim, K.Y. Lee, Ag-incorporated macroporous CeO2 catalysts for soot oxidation: Effects of Ag amount on the generation of active oxygen species, Applied Catalysis B: Environmental, **246** (2019): 356-366
14. L. Zeng, L. Cui, C. Wang, W. Guo, C. Gong, Ag-assisted CeO2 catalyst for soot oxidation, Frontiers of Materials Science, **13** (2019): 288-295
15. C.M. Álvarez-Docio, R. Portela, J.J. Reinosa, F. Rubio-Marcos, J.F. Fernández, Pt mechanical dispersion on non-porous alumina for soot oxidation, Catalysis Communications, **140** (2020): 105999
16. H. Wang, S. Luo, X. Li, W. Liu, X. Wu, D. Weng, S. Liu, Thermally stable Ag/Al 2 O 3 confined catalysts with high diffusion-induced oxidation activity, Catalysis Today, **332** (2019): 189-194
17. E. Aneggi, J. Llorca, C. de Leitenburg, G. Dolcetti, A. Trovarelli, Soot combustion over silver-supported catalysts, **91**,1-2 (2009): 489-498
18. R. Camposeco, S. Castillo, M. Hinojosa-Reyes, N. Nava, R. Zanella, Manganese promoted TiO2 and ZrO2 nanostructures for soot combustion with boosted efficiency, Surface and Coatings Technology, **384** (2020): 125305
19. H.F. Wang, H.Y. Li, X.Q. Gong, Y.L. Guo, G.Z. Lu, P. Hu, Oxygen vacancy formation in CeO 2 and Ce 1-xZr xO 2 solid solutions: Electron localization, electrostatic potential and structural relaxation, Physical Chemistry Chemical Physics, **14**,48 (2012): 16521-16535
20. M. Wang, Y. Zhang, Y. Yu, W. Shan, H. He, Surface oxygen species essential for the catalytic activity of Ce-M-Sn (M = Mn or Fe) in soot oxidation, Catalysis Science & Technology, **11**,3 (2021): 895-903
21. E. Aneggi, C. de Leitenburg, G. Dolcetti, A. Trovarelli, Promotional effect of rare earths and transition metals in the combustion of diesel soot over CeO2 and CeO2-ZrO2, Catalysis Today, **114**,1 (2006): 40-47
22. K.I. Shimizu, H. Kawachi, A. Satsuma, Study of active sites and mechanism for soot oxidation by

silver-loaded ceria catalyst, Applied Catalysis B: Environmental, **96**,1-2 (2010): 169-175

23. X. Zhao, J. Jiang, H. Zuo, G. Jia, Soot combustion characteristics of oxygen concentration and regeneration temperature effect on continuous pulsation regeneration in diesel particulate filter for heavy-duty truck, Energy, **264** (2023): 126265
24. M. Debia, C. Couture, P.E. Njanga, E. Neesham-Grenon, G. Lachapelle, H. Coulombe, S. Hallé, S. Aubin, Diesel engine exhaust exposures in two underground mines, International Journal of Mining Science and Technology, **27**, 4 (2017): 641-645
25. H. Kopseak, Z. Pandur, M. Bačić, Ž. Zečić, H. Nevečerel, K. Lepoglavec, M. Šušnjar, Exhaust Gases from Skidder ECOTRAC 140 V Diesel Engine, Forests, **13**, 2 (2022): 272
26. B. Aliyu, D. Shitanda, S. Walker, B. Agnew, S. Masheiti, R. Atan, Performance and exhaust emissions of a diesel engine fuelled with Croton megalocarpus (musine) methyl ester, Applied Thermal Engineering, **31**,1 (2011): 36-41
27. I. A. Reşitoılu, K. Altinişik, A. Keskin, The pollutant emissions from diesel-engine vehicles and exhaust aftertreatment systems, Clean Technologies and Environmental Policy, **17** (2015): 15-27
28. G. Corro, E. Vidal, S. Cebada, U. Pal, F. Bañuelos, D. Vargas, E. Guilleminot, Electronic state of silver in Ag/SiO2 and Ag/ZnO catalysts and its effect on diesel particulate matter oxidation: An XPS study, Applied Catalysis B: Environmental, **216** (2017): 1-10
29. R. Prasad, S.V. Singh, A review on catalytic oxidation of soot emitted from diesel fuelled engines, Journal of Environmental Chemical Engineering, **8**,4 (2020): 103945
30. M. Skaf, S. Aouad, S. Hany, R. Cousin, E. Abi-Aad, A. Aboukaïs, Physicochemical characterization and catalytic performance of 10% Ag/CeO2 catalysts prepared by impregnation and deposition-precipitation, Journal of catalysis, **320** (2014): 137-146
31. H. Ruan, Soot oxidation performance with a HZSM-5 supported Ag nanoparticles catalyst and the characterization of Ag species, Rsc Advances, **7**,69 (2017): 43789-43797
32. G. Corro, S. Cebada, U. Pal, J.L.G. Fierro, J. Alvarado, Hydrogen-reduced Cu/ZnO composite as efficient reusable catalyst for diesel particulate matter oxidation, Applied Catalysis B: Environmental, **165** (2015): 555-565
33. L. Zhao, Y. Zhang, S. Bi, Q. Liu, Metal-organic framework-derived CeO2-ZnO catalysts for C3H6-SCR of NO: An: in situ DRIFTS study, RSC advances, **9**,33 (2019): 19236-19242
34. M. J. Kim, CeO2 promoted Ag/TiO2 catalyst for soot oxidation with improved active oxygen generation and delivery abilities, Journal of hazardous materials, **384** (2020): 121341
35. R. Ousji, Z. Ksibi, A. Ghorbel, C. Fontaine, Ag-Based Catalysts in Different Supports: Activity for Formaldehyde Oxidation, Advances in Materials Physics and Chemistry, **12**,08 (2022): 163-176

The Influence of Direct Non-Thermal Plasma Treatment on Soot Characteristics under Low Exhaust Gas Temperature

Teerapong Iamcheerangkoon[1,4], *Nuwong* Chollacoop[2], *Boonlue* Sawatmongkhon[1,4], *Thawatchai* Wongchang[3,4], *Kampanart* Theinnoi[1,4,*] and *Ekachai* Juntasaro[5]

[1] Department of Power Engineering Technology, College of Industrial Technology, King Mongkut's University of Technology North Bangkok., Thailand
[2] Renewable Energy and Energy Efficiency Research Team, National Energy Technology Center (ENTEC), National Science and Technology Development Agency
[3] Department of Mechanical and Automotive Engineering Technology, Faculty of Engineering and Technology, King Mongkut's University of Technology North Bangkok (Rayong Campus), Rayong, Thailand.
[4] Research Centre for Combustion Technology and Alternative Energy (CTAE), Science and Technology Research Institute, King Mongkut's University of Technology North Bangkok, Thailand
[5] The Sirindhorn International Thai-German Graduate School of Engineering (TGGS), King Mongkut's University of Technology North Bangkok, 1518 Pracharat 1 Road, Wongsawang, Bangsue, Bangkok 10800, Thailand.

Abstract. This study aimed to assess the effectiveness of nonthermal plasma (NTP) technology utilizing a dielectric barrier discharge (DBD) reactor, both with and without exhaust gas recirculation (EGR), in reducing soot particles and their impact on nitrogen oxides (NO_x). The experiment involved maintaining a constant flue gas flow rate of 10 l/min, employing high voltage values of 0, 6, and 10 kV, fixed frequency of 500 Hz and setting the various IMEP of 5, 6, and 7 bar and the engine speed at 2,000 rpm. The findings demonstrated that NTP was successful in removing NO_x by approximately 16.84% and 17.01%, achieving particle matter (PM) removal efficiencies of around 60.79% and 81.13%, and effectively reducing activation energy by approximately 18.34% and 31.5% (with and without EGR, respectively) at a high voltage of 10 kV. These results highlight the potential of NTP technology in mitigating emissions and reducing the environmental impact associated with diesel engines.

Keyword. Diesel engine, EGR, Nonthermal plasma, Soot

1 Introduction

Diesel engines are more efficient than gasoline engines in terms of torque, stability, and fuel economy. However, the primary pollutants of diesel exhaust gas emissions are nitrogen oxides (NO_x) (NO_x is the sum of nitrogen monoxide; NO and nitrogen dioxide; NO_2) and particulate matter (PM), which seriously impact public health. Because PM exposure has been associated with respiratory and cardiovascular conditions [1,2]. This issue is to meet these more stringent standard requirements. Therefore, many research and technological developments in advanced diesel engines have been concerned and developed high-performance after-treatment systems.

The primary PM emission from diesel engines is carbon black. The accumulation mode encompasses the predominant distribution of particle size and particle mass, with concentrations between 10 nm to 30 μm [3]. The particles in this mode exhibit diverse shapes, including individual particles, long chains, or aggregated masses of larger particles [4]. The specific shape of a particle is two parameters according to its generation time and the range of sizes it falls into [3,4]. Describes the particle size division into the following modes: Nucleation mode (5–50 nm); this mode often consists of volatile organic compounds (VOCs), sulphur compounds, and solid carbon that develop during exhaust dilution and cooling. More than 90% of the particle number and 1–20% of the particle mass are frequently found in the nucleation mode. Accumulation mode (50–500 nm); consists of particles in accumulation mode that have been restrained after being deposited on the surfaces of the cylinder and exhaust system, and coarse mode (above 500 nm); the particle mass in the coarse mode ranges from 5–20% [5].

Diesel particulate filters (DPF) are widely acknowledged as the most effective method to reduce PM emissions. Its capture efficiency is more than 95% [6,7], which has become the usual arrangement for post-treatment systems. The DPF has a honeycomb structure consisting of an open square at one end of the DPF, thus forcing the engine exhaust gases through the porous wall of the DPF, causing the PM particles to be filtered through a porous wall. The filtered exhaust gas, without PM, then flows out of the DPF from the outlet channel. However, the mechanism of diffuse deposition, flow interception, inertial collision, and gravity precipitation was used to explain PM accumulation on the surface and inside of

* Corresponding author: kampanart.t@cit.kmutnb.ac.th

porous walls [2]; In this process, the continuously accumulated PM blocks in inlet channels of the DPF, which increased back pressure and fuel consumption, decreased engine performance compared to the regular engine operation.

Therefore, it is necessary to rapidly remove PM from the channel to regenerate the DPF [8]. The most often used active regeneration technique method increasing the exhaust temperature up to 550 °C [9], by injecting fuel upstream of the Diesel Oxidation Catalyst (DOC), electric heating, microwave heating, etc. [10]; thus oxidizing soot with oxygen (O_2) in a DPF [2]. However, excessive soot loading or fuel injection might result in high temperatures and uncontrolled regeneration from surface oxidation of PM, causing different thermal expansion cracks or melting of the porous supports may occur, causing irreparable damage [7].

The exhaust gas recirculated (EGR), and these exhaust gas and soot particles were once more oxidised inside the cylinder. After using EGR, the Air/Fuel (A/F) ratio decreases [3,11]. Consequently, the oxidation process of polycyclic aromatic precursors and other chemical compounds becomes incomplete when EGR is utilized, increasing the density of primary nuclear-modal particulate matter. Meanwhile, the combustion process also generates active free radicals and intermediate by-products of small molecule combustion, which enter the cylinder with hydrocarbons and aromatic hydrocarbons in the exhaust gas [12]. EGR efficiently reduces NO_x emissions from diesel engines by decreasing cylinder oxygen concentration along with the flame temperature [11,13]. Furthermore, the addition of EGR increased particulate matter emissions [14].

Plasma is the fourth state of matter [15,16], usually combining electrons, ions, and excited and neutral species. An amount of ionic and excited species in plasma with sufficient energy to collide and break the stable molecular structure of the particles passing through it [17]. However, in the nonthermal plasma system, which occurs when the kinetic energy of electrons or temperature is higher than the kinetic energy of gas molecules outside (around ambient temperature) [18-20], electrical energy is transmitted to the electrons, causing the production of free radicals such as N, O, HO_2, and OH [21]. Due to this characteristic, nonthermal plasma (NTP) has a high energy efficiency [22]. Dielectric barrier discharge (DBD) operates between two electrodes. A dielectric layer is present over at least one electrode to prevent spark discharge [23]. In which the dielectric layer restricts the intensity of current accessing the system and distributes the discharge approximately across the entirety of the electrode surface, DBD production typically employs high voltage alternating current (AC), with a typical frequency of 0.05 to 60 kHz [16]. Okubo *et al.*, conducted a study on ozone generation from the air using a DBD-NTP reactor [24]. It was found that this promotes NO to NO_2 for improving DPF regeneration at low oxidation temperatures to the soot reduction mechanism proposed by O, OH, O_3 and NO_2 [25,26]. According to Xu (2001), DBD can offer the optimum energy electrons (1 - 10 eV) with a high density to produce low-excited atomic and molecular species, free radicals, and excimers [27].

As a result of the problems encountered above, this research aimed to investigate soot composition from NTP treatment with and without EGR under low exhaust temperature conditions in diesel engines to develop alternative strategies for removing particulate matter.

2 Experimental Setup

2.1 Engine Specifications

A schematic diagram of the experimental design is shown in Figure 1 The diesel engine was used for generating actual exhaust emissions in this research. This experimental study used a common-rail direct injection (DI) diesel engine to meet the Euro Stage V emissions standards specified in Table 1 to simulate the engine load. The engine was connected to an eddy current dynamometer test stand (AVL; EMCON 400). The crankshaft angle and engine speed (rpm) were measured by a high-resolution crankshaft encoder (model 2614C) with a resolution of 0.1 crank angle (CA). Additionally, a pressure transducer (Kitsler; model 6052b1) was mounted inside the cylinder head for real-time analysis of combustion parameters. The Kitsler system (KiBox® To Go; model 2893A121) was used to calculate engine efficiency and measure cylinder pressure. The engine speed was set at a constant of 2,000 rpm, while the Indicated Mean Effective Pressures (IMEP) were compared at 5, 6, and 7 bar (corresponding to 16.3, 25.2, and 32.6 Nm, respectively).

The back pressure valve maintained constant exhaust gas under all conditions. to confirm that other factors did not influence the number, mass, and volume. In conditions without EGR, it was fitted with a flange on the inlet pipe at the EGR valve to prevent the swirling of exhaust gas into the air intake system. All testing conditions were sampled accordingly. A 10 litres per min vacuum pump then transported the exhaust gases to the DBD-NTP treatment system; engine exhaust emissions were analysed using an exhaust gas analyser (TESTO; model 350) and particle size and quantity were measured by Engine Exhaust Particle Spectrometer (EEPS; model TSI 3090).

Table 1. Engine specifications.

Models	Common rail diesel engine Euro Stage V
Displacement volume	2499 cm^3
Combustion system	Direct injection
Bore	95.4 mm.
Stroke	87.4 mm.
Maximum torque	280 N.m. at 1,800 – 2,200 rpm
Maximum power	8.7 kW at 1,800 – 2,200 rpm

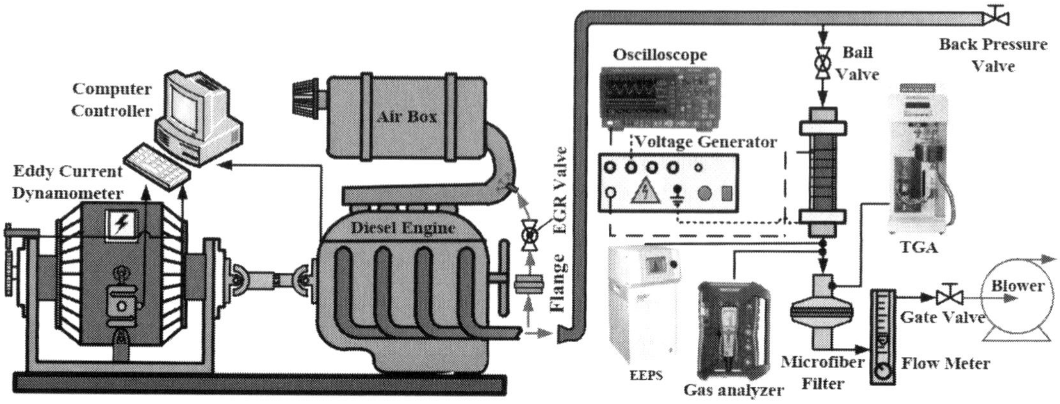

Fig. 1. Schematic diagram of the experimental design.

2.2 Nonthermal Plasma Setup

The dielectric barrier discharge (DBD) for nonthermal plasma (NTP) reactor consists of a metal rod as a high-voltage electrode core with a diameter of 10 mm and a quartz glass tube as a dielectric barrier discharge with an inner diameter of 17 mm. The discharge gap was set at a constant of 3.5 mm. The ground electrode was a stainless steel tube, and the effective discharge length (was 100 mm). The alternating current (AC) voltage in the DBD-NTP system is adjustable at 6 kV (1.152 watts) and 10kV (3.2 watts) with an Oscilloscope (KEYSIGHT; model DSOX 1204G) to determine the voltage of an alternating current (AC), were sent to amplify the High Voltages Power Supply: HVPS (TREK; model 10/10B-HS) with a voltage gain ratio of (1:1,000 voltage and 1 V/4 mA) and constant frequency fixed at 500 Hz according to all conditions. The transformer used in the experiment contains a conversion ratio of 1 V input to 4 mA output, which is used to determine the current. The voltage was the conversion ratio of Voltage (peak to peak) input per 1:1,000 V output.

The DBD-NTP system's exhaust flow rate is then controlled at 10 litres per min after some engine exhaust gases are drawn from the vacuum pump and treated before being released back into the gas treatment system again. Maintain the exhaust gas components in a gaseous condition in the exhaust gas derived from the diesel engine's combustion. The DBD-NTP system is temperature controlled to match the engine exhaust gas temperature. The heating tape was installed in the piping system before the DBD-NTP reactor and microfiber filter sampling; this prevents condensation in the exhaust system and results in more efficient control of the voltage supply at the DBD-NTP reactor.

2.3 Thermogravimetric analysis (TGA)

In analysing different components of combustion-related soot, the soot is captured by glass microfiber filter papers (Whatman Grade GF/C with 1.2μm pore size). The results were analysed by a Thermogravimetric Analyzer (TGA; PerkinElmer model Pyris1), which can identify the composition of soot particles, moisture (H_2O), VOCs and carbon (Element Carbon) [9,21] obtained from the microfiber filter. Table 2 contains a list of the TGA heating programme. The procedure was created to estimate the concentrations of H_2O, VOCs, and carbon soot at established weight loss temperatures [28].

Table 2. TGA temperature program.

Step	Temperature Program	Period (min)	Atmosphere
1	Isothermal at 40 °C	10	N_2 (50 ml/min)
2	Heating to 110 °C (10 °C/min)	7	N_2 (50 ml/min)
3	Isothermal at 110°C	30	N_2 (50 ml/min)
4	Heating to 400 °C (10 °C/min)	29	N_2 (50 ml/min)
5	Isothermal at 400 °C	30	N_2 (50 ml/min)
6	Cooling to 300 °C (10 °C/min)	10	N_2 (50 ml/min)
7	Heating to 600 °C (10 °C/min)	30	O_2 (50 ml/min)
8	Isothermal at 600 °C	30	O_2 (50 ml/min)

3 Results and discussion

3.1 The combustion characteristic

Firstly, monitoring the In-cylinder pressure and HRR to describe engine performance of operating conditions is necessary. As shown in Figure 2, the differences between with and without EGR are based on a B7 diesel. Selecting the low load condition, three selected IMEPs were 5, 6 and 7 bar. The combustion parameters were checked as follows based on the cylinder pressure data.

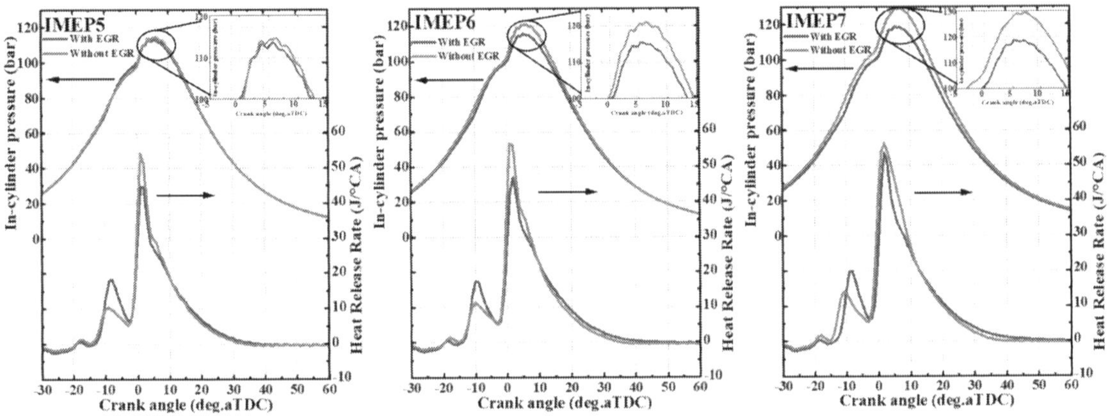

Fig. 2. Comparison graph between the in-cylinder pressure and the heat release rate at IMEP of (Left) 5, (Middle) 6 and (Right) 7 bar under conditions with and without EGR.

It was determined that pilot and primary injections were at -8 °Ca before TDC and 1 °Ca after TDC, respectively. Based on the cylinder pressure measurements, the in-cylinder pressure was somewhat higher at IMEP 5 bar. Nevertheless, it increases at IMEP 6 and 7 bar (4.84% and 8.98%, respectively) [29]. During the main combustion processes (in black line), The engine operated without EGR show higher in-cylinder pressures compare to the engine operating with EGR (in red line) Due to exhaust gas being introduced to the intake manifold [11,13], which reduced oxygen concentration and increased the specific heat capacity of intake, resulting in lower effective fuel/air mixing and worse in-cylinder combustion performance [12]. At the pilot injection, EGR usage was applied in all IMEPs, and the effect of the HRR was increased when compared to that without EGR due to the exhaust gas being recirculated at a higher temperature than intake air [13].

3.2 Exhaust gas emissions

The engine load 6 bar IMEP has been selected for the in-cylinder pressure to analyse the effect of starting to change in the cylinder pressure. Figure 3 illustrates the O_2 concentration in the exhaust gas. It was found that combustion with EGR requires a higher O_2 than without EGR leading to the reduced amount of O_2 used in EGR combustion in a cylinder to keep engine stability [11-14]. On the other hand, when DBD-NTP was activated, the O_2 content was slightly insignificantly altered in both conditions. DBD-NTP results in free electrons reacting with oxygen bonds until breaking down to active oxygen (O*). Then, it interacts with O_2 to produce O_3, as demonstrated in equations (3) and (8).

Figure 4 illustrates the impact of DBD-NTP on NO and NO_2 between conditions with and without EGR. It was found that in the conditions where EGR was applied, a significant (71.78 %) reduction in NO_x content was observed as a result of EGR, which contributes to NO_x reduction [11,13]. Under EGR conditions, there is a slight increase in NO_2 at a voltage of 6 kV (3.31 %). On the other hand, at a voltage of 10 kV, the amount of NO_2 increases by 5.99%. However, the amount of NO decreases by 100%, which is in the same direction as in non-EGR conditions, when increasing the voltage to 10 kV, due to the voltage can transmit energy to electrons, causing free radicals [21,22] from the amount of NO_2 that increases significantly by 59.3%. Moreover, the total NO_x has reduced by approximately 16.84% and 17.01% (with and without EGR, respectively) at a high voltage of 10 kV. [16, 30-33] describes the reactions of DBD-NTP to NO_x removal, dividing them into two main groups.

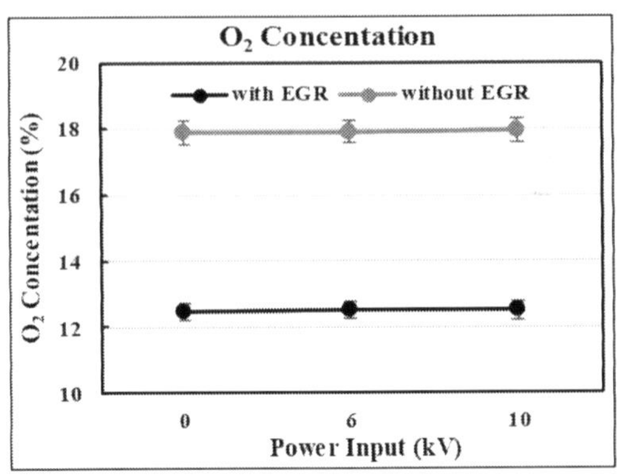

Fig. 3. Effect of DBD-NTP on O_2 concentration under conditions with and without EGR.

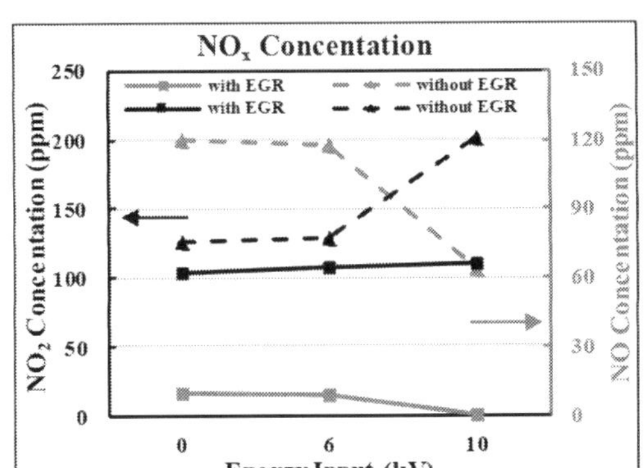

Fig. 4. Effect of DBD-NTP on NO and NO_2 concentration under engine operated with and without EGR.

The first group, the primary and principal of NO_x elimination reactions may be found in Equations (1) - (7):

$$N_2 + e^* \rightarrow N + N + e \quad (1)$$

$$NO + N \rightarrow N_2 + O \quad (2)$$

$$O_2 + O^* \rightarrow O_3 \quad (3)$$

$$N_2 + e \rightarrow e + N_2 (A) \quad (4)$$

$$N_2 (A) + NO \rightarrow N_2 + N + O \quad (5)$$

$$N_2 (A) + N_2O \rightarrow 2N_2 + O \quad (6)$$

$$NO_2 + N \rightarrow N_2 + O_2 \quad (7)$$

where N_2 (A) represents the N_2 metastable state.

Equations (8) - (10) provide a summary of the second group of processes (which includes the reactions oxidising NO to NO_2):

$$O_2 + e^* \rightarrow O^* + O^* + e \quad (8)$$

$$NO + O^* \rightarrow NO_2 \quad (9)$$

$$NO + O_3 \rightarrow NO_2 + O_2 \quad (10)$$

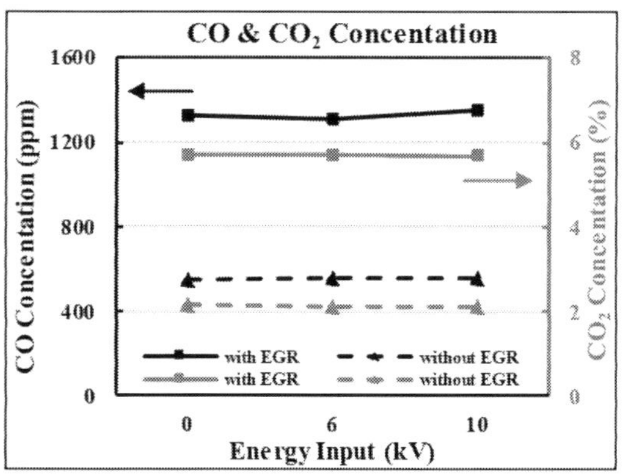

Fig. 5. Effect of DBD-NTP on CO and CO_2 concentration under conditions with and without EGR.

Figure 5 illustrates the effect of DBD-NTP on CO and CO_2 concentrations. The use of EGR increases CO and CO_2 by approximately 58.2% and 62.98%, respectively, when compared with the inactivity of EGR. The CO_2 concentration in the exhaust gas is slightly reduced by 0.13% and 2.67% (with and without EGR, respectively) at a high voltage of 10 kV. The CO concentration has a small and insignificant change in the same direction. The electrical field can be sufficiently strong to excite carbon dioxide molecules due to the more significant electric field and discharge power, which provide electrons more energy to begin their impact reactions [18,34]. Equations (11) - (15) describe regular reaction processes for breaking down CO_2 molecules in plasma [18].

$$CO_2 + O \rightarrow CO + O_2 \quad (11)$$

$$CO_2 + O_2 \rightarrow CO + O_3 \quad (12)$$

$$e + CO_2 \rightarrow CO + O + e \quad (13)$$

$$e + CO^*_2 \rightarrow CO + O \quad (14)$$

$$2CO_2 + 2N^*_2 \rightarrow 2CO + O_2 + 2N_2 \quad (15)$$

The equations (16) can reduce CO_2 concentration by including electron impact reactions and multiple active oxygen species: Where CO_2 and N_2 are, respectively, the excited types of the CO_2 and N_2 molecules, and CO generated through various processes have different amounts of energy [15].

$$C + O_3 \rightarrow CO + O_2 \quad (16)$$

On the other hand, the DBD-NTP system reacts with CO and active oxygen as in equations 17-18, which is a reverse entanglement reaction. As a result, the amount of CO and CO_2 was slightly converted [35].

$$CO + O \rightarrow CO_2 \quad (17)$$

$$CO + O_3 \rightarrow CO_2 + O_2 \quad (18)$$

3.3 Particulate size distribution and Soot compositions

Effect of DBD-NTP with different power inputs on the particle size distribution of PM under with and without EGR conditions. As shown in Figure 6a), PM showed that the particle size distribution was mainly concentrated in the areas between 22.5 - 165 nm and 7 - 45 nm with and without EGR application, respectively. When the engine load increases, the particle quantitative concentration curve's peak value and size gradually increase.

Under the EGR applied condition, it was found that most of the particle size distributions were concentrated in the region between 22.1 - 165.5 nm. In the presence of DBD-NTP at 6 kV, the particle content was reduced by 37.41% (at IMEP 6 bar) from when particles flowing through the DBD-NTP reaction phase have free electrons colliding [27], causing PM particles to split to a small size. The voltage was increased by 10 kV, the PM particle content effectively decreased by 57.49% (at IMEP 6 bar), and PM particles were increased in the particle size distribution range of 8.06 - 22.1 nm. However, the plasma treatment was an increase in the ultrafine particulate matter (8.06 - 22.1 nm). The energy being delivered is sufficient to break up large particles into smaller particles. These phenomena could be clarified by the fact that the plasma zone was produced by the discharge of large-scale particles, which were classified as accumulating and primarily composed of electrically conductive carbon spheres [3]. This indicates that the decrease in large-size particles was effective [9]. In addition, when EGR is disabled shows multi-peak distribution remaining within the nucleation mode range. The highest peak is in the range of 6.98 - 14.3 nm and the second peak is in the range of 14.3 - 45.3 nm. This is primarily caused by the cylinder's decreased oxygen concentration in the application of EGR, which promotes the mass synthesis of carbon core particles and, consequently, increases the number of nuclear mode particles [3]. However, the appearance of NTP can reduce the particulate number distribution by 4.86% (6kV) and 55.81% (10kV) as shown in Figure 6a.

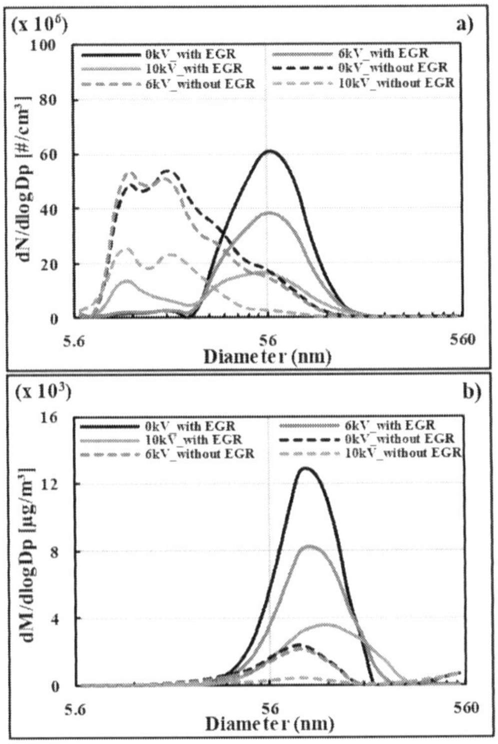

Fig. 6. Effect of DBD-NTP on the a) particulate number distribution and b) particulate mass distribution under conditions with and without EGR.

The relation between particle mass and particulate number, as shown in Figure 6b, is attributed to the fact that particulates in the accumulation mode contribute significantly to the particle mass. Although Kittelson's suggests that particles in the nuclei mode account for more than 90% of the total particle number [36], the data collected indicates that particles in the nuclei mode exhibit a relatively low particle number. Moreover, the observed increase in ultrafine particulate matter (as shown in Figure 6a) has a minimal influence on the mass distribution due to the slight increase in the ultrafine particulate matter mass compared to the mass distribution represented by dN [9]. In the EGR-active condition, the presence of DBD-NTP resulted in a reduction in particle mass of 37.02% and 60.79% at power inputs of 6 and 10 kV, respectively. These findings are consistent with the conditions without EGR, where the particle mass decreased by 9.92% and 81.13% at power inputs of 6 and 10 kV, respectively. These results indicate that DBD-NTP is effective in reducing particulate mass.

Figure 7 shows the results of the analysis conducted with EGR; Figure 7a) illustrates the weight loss penetration of soot oxidation, while Figure 7b demonstrates the derivative weight loss of soot oxidation. The derivative weight loss outcomes obtained from utilising DBD-NTP at 0,6 and 10 kV demonstrate an expected peak at approximately 500 - 550 °C, indicating the presence of the same carbon type in the soot composition. The derivative weight loss result from TGA analysis provides information about the slope of the TGA spectra, which reflects the activity of soot oxidation and its impact on the activation energy of soot combustion. The amplitude of derivative weight loss follows the order of 0 kV > 6 kV > 10 kV, indicating the activation energy of soot combustion.

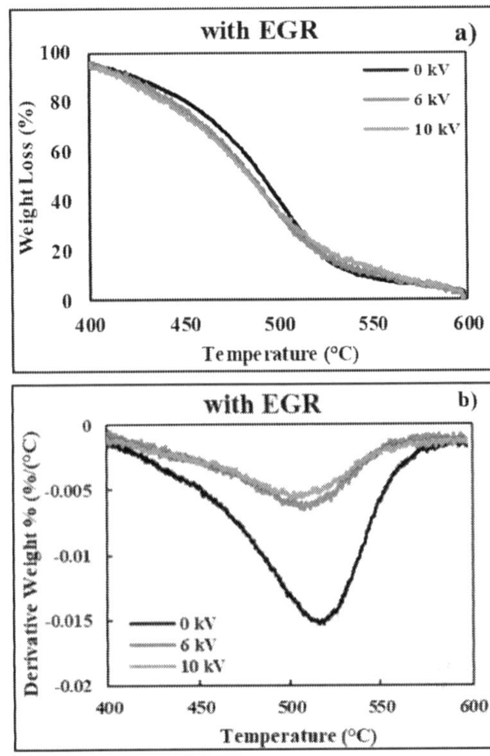

Fig. 7. Effect of DBD-NTP a) weight loss and b) Derivative weight on temperature with EGR conditions.

In this case, the analysis was performed without EGR, and the obtained results are presented in Figure 8. The weight loss penetration of soot oxidation, while the derivative weight loss of soot oxidation was shown in Figure 8b. The results agreed with those obtained when DBD-NTP was paired with EGR, showing the same carbon in the soot composition, as demonstrated by the derivative peak at 500 - 550 °C. The exact order of amplitude of derivative weight loss was observed in the case without EGR. The results obtained from the analysis conducted without EGR agreed with those obtained with EGR, demonstrating the presence of the same type of carbon in the soot composition.

3.4 Activation Energy (Ea)

The activation energy (Ea) analysis is a crucial method to investigate the oxidation kinetics of soot samples. The value of Ea determines the energy required to initiate the oxidation process of elemental carbon. A lower value of Ea indicates that less energy is needed to start the oxidation process, resulting in faster oxidation kinetics. The Arrhenius equation calculates the value of Ea, which describes the relationship between the rate of a chemical reaction and the temperature at which it occurs. The activation energy of soot samples obtained from raw and DBD-NTP exhaust was analyzed by constructing scatter plots of Ln(-dm/dt) against 1/T, as shown in Figure 9. To ensure the accuracy and reliability of the findings, linear regression analysis was conducted, with correlation coefficients (R^2) exceeding 0.85. The plot's fitted straight-line slope corresponded to the activation energy.

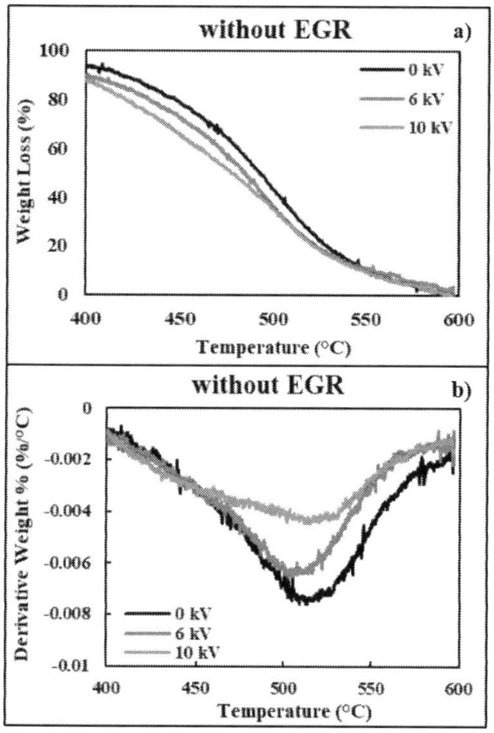

Fig. 8. Effect of DBD-NTP a) weight loss and b) Derivative weight on temperature without EGR conditions.

Figure 10 compares the Ea between the cases of DBD-NTP combined with and without EGR, utilizing energy inputs of 0, 6, and 10 kV. In the DBD-NTP combination with EGR, an increase in energy input leads to a decrease in Ea. Specifically, the Ea at 6 kV is reduced by 7.83% compared to that at 0 kV. Similarly, in the case of 10 kV, the Ea is reduced by 18.34% compared to 0 kV. These findings indicate that higher energy inputs in the DBD-NTP EGR configuration result in lower activation energy values, suggesting enhanced oxidation kinetics and improved effectiveness in soot removal.

In the DBD-NTP without EGR, it has been observed that an increase in energy input results in a decrease in Ea. More precisely, at an energy input of 6 kV, the Ea is found to be reduced by 18.66% compared to its value at 0 kV. Similarly, at an energy input of 10 kV, the Ea is reduced by 31.5% compared to its value at 0 kV. These findings suggest that increasing the energy input can lead to a more efficient and effective DBD-NTP process, enabling the development of novel applications in various fields. However, a comparison between DBD-NTP was combined with and without EGR reveals distinct activation energy (Ea) values. The case of DBD-NTP without EGR demonstrates lower Ea values than DBD-NTP combined with EGR. These findings indicate that utilizing DBD-NTP alone exhibits a higher degree of soot oxidation promotion than when DBD-NTP is combined with EGR.

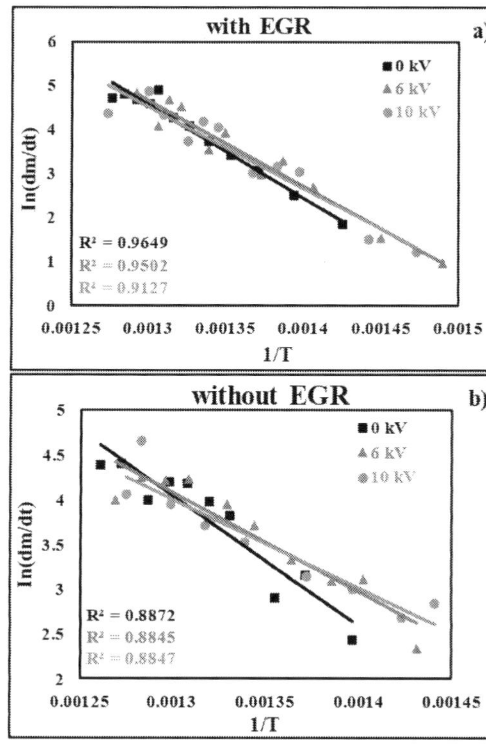

Fig. 9. The Arrhenius equation plots, a) with EGR and b) without EGR

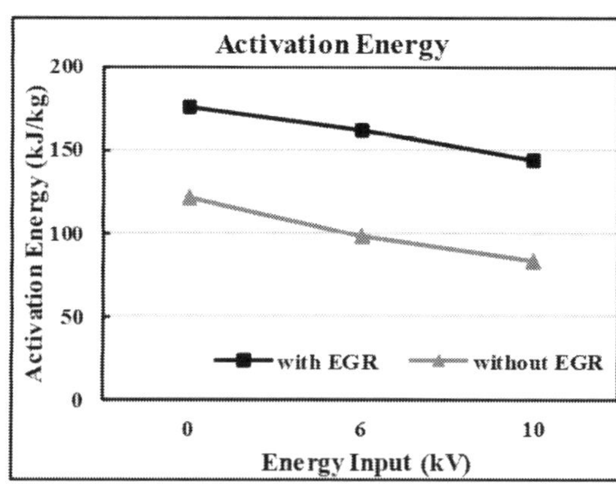

Fig. 10. Effect of DBD-NTP to Activation Energy on the power input under conditions with and without EGR.

4 Conclusion

This research investigates the composition of soot generated by NTP treatment in diesel engines, specifically focusing on examining the impact of EGR under low exhaust temperature conditions. The aim is to explore alternative methods for effectively reducing PM emissions. The DBD-NTP technique and EGR are conducted using a DBD reactor in the real diesel exhaust gas while the effects of EGR are evaluated. The results indicate that DBD-NTP treatment reduces NO_x by approximately 16.84% and 17.01% when using EGR and without EGR, respectively. Additionally, the experiments demonstrate the generation of significant free radicals due to efficient energy transmission from high voltage. Moreover, NTP treatment exhibits effective removal of PM, with removal efficiencies of approximately 60.79% and 81.13% (with and without EGR, respectively). Increasing the voltage level leads to a continuous reduction in PM concentration. NTP treatment also enhances the oxidative activity of PM and reduces the activation energy required for PM dispersion by 18.34% (with EGR) and 31.5% (without EGR) at a high voltage of 10 kV. These findings underscore the promising potential of NTP technology in reducing emissions and improving the environmental impact of diesel engines.

Acknowledgements

This research was funded by the National Science, Research, and Innovation Fund (NSRF), and King Mongkut's University of Technology, North Bangkok, with Contract no. KMUTNB-FF-66-19. T. Iamcheerangkoon thanks King Mongkut's University of Technology, North Bangkok, and the National Science and Technology Development Agency, Thailand. Contract No. Grad 017/2563, for supporting his scholarship.

References

1. K.S. Martirosyan, K. Chen, D. Luss, Behavior features of soot combustion in diesel particulate filter, Chemical Engineering Science, **65**,1 (2010): 42-46
2. S.S. Gill, G.S. Chatha, A. Tsolakis, Analysis of reformed EGR on the performance of a diesel particulate filter, International Journal of Hydrogen Energy, **36**,16 (2011): 10089-10099
3. Z. Wang, X. Zhang, J. Guo, C. Hao, Y. Feng, Particle emissions from a marine diesel engine burning two kinds of sulphur diesel oils with an EGR & scrubber system :Size, number & mass, Process Safety and Environmental Protection, **163** (2022): 94-104
4. N. Ladommatos, S.M. Abdelhalim, H. Zhao, Z. Hu, The dilution, chemical, and thermal effects of exhaust gas recirculation on diesel engine emissions-Part 4: effects of carbon dioxide and water vapour, SAE transactions, (1997): 1844-1862
5. D.B. Kittelson, Engines and nanoparticles: a review, Journal of aerosol science, **29**,5-6 (1998): 575-588
6. Z. Meng, J. Li, J. Fang, J. Tan, Y. Qin, Y. Jiang, Z. Qin, W. Bai, K. Liang, Experimental study on regeneration performance and particle emission characteristics of DPF with different inlet transition section lengths, Fuel, **262** (2020): 116487
7. Y. Shi, Y. Lu, Y. Cai, Y. He, Y. Zhou, J. Fang, Evolution of particulate matter deposited in the DPF channel during low-temperature regeneration by non-thermal plasma, Fuel, **318** (2022): 123552
8. S. Choi, K.C. Oh, C.B. Lee, The effects of filter porosity and flow conditions on soot deposition/oxidation and pressure drop in particulate filters, Energy, **77** (2014): 327-337
9. T. Iamcheerangkoon, N. Chollacoop, B. Sawatmongkhon, T. Wongchang, S. Sittichompoo, S. Chuepeng, K. Theinnoi, Promotion of the NO-to-NO2 conversion of a biofueled diesel engine with nonthermal plasma-assisted low-temperature soot incineration of a diesel particulate filter, Energies, **15**,24 (2022): 9330
10. J. Rodríguez-Fernández, J.J. Hernández, J. Sánchez-Valdepeñas, Effect of oxygenated and paraffinic alternative diesel fuels on soot reactivity and implications on DPF regeneration, Fuel, **185** (2016): 460-467
11. A. Jain, A.P. Singh, A.K. Agarwal, Effect of split fuel injection and EGR on NOx and PM emission reduction in a low temperature combustion (LTC) mode diesel engine, Energy, **122** (2017): 249-264
12. B. Zhao, X. Liang, K. Wang, X. Lv, Y. Wang, Soot particles undergo in-cylinder oxidation again via EGR recirculated gas: Analysis of exhaust soot particle characteristics, Journal of Aerosol Science, **172** (2023): 106190
13. M.M. Abdelaal, A.H. Hegab, Combustion and emission characteristics of a natural gas-fueled diesel engine with EGR, Energy conversion and management, **64** (2012): 301-312
14. A. Abu-Jrai, A. Tsolakis, K. Theinnoi, R. Cracknell, A. Megaritis, M.L. Wyszynski, S.E. Golunski, Effect of gas-to-liquid diesel fuels on combustion characteristics, engine emissions, and exhaust gas fuel reforming, Comparative study, Energy & fuels, **20**,6 (2006): 2377-2384
15. M. Keidar, I. Beilis, Plasma engineering: applications from aerospace to bio and nanotechnology, Academic Press, (2013): 3-100
16. P. Talebizadeh, M. Babaie, R. Brown, H. Rahimzadeh, Z. Ristovski, M. Arai, The role of non-thermal plasma technique in NOx treatment: A review, Renewable and Sustainable Energy Reviews, **40** (2014): 886-901
17. S. Meng, W. Li, Z. Li, H. Song, Non-thermal plasma assisted catalytic thiophene removal from fuel under different atmospheres, Journal of Cleaner Production, **369** (2022): 133282
18. M. Babaie, P. Davari, P. Talebizadeh, F. Zare, H. Rahimzadeh, Z. Ristovski, R. Brown, Performance

evaluation of non-thermal plasma on particulate matter, ozone and CO2 correlation for diesel exhaust emission reduction, Chemical Engineering Journal, **276** (2015): 240-248

19. S. Mohapatro, N.K. Sharma, A. Madhukar, Abatement of NOX using compact high voltage pulse power supply: Towards retrofitting to automobile vehicle, IEEE Transactions on Dielectrics and Electrical Insulation, **24**,5 (2017): 2738-2745
20. A. Fridman, A. Chirokov, A. Gutsol, Non-thermal atmospheric pressure discharges, Journal of Physics D: Applied Physics, **38**,2 (2005): R1
21. T. Wongchang, S. Sittichompoo, K. Theinnoi, B. Sawatmongkhon, S. Jugjai, Impact of high-voltage discharge after-treatment technology on diesel engine particulate matter composition and gaseous emissions, ACS omega, **6**,32 (2021): 21181-21192
22. B. Huang, C. Zhang, H. Bai, S. Zhang, K.K. Ostrikov, T. Shao, Energy pooling mechanism for catalyst-free methane activation in nanosecond pulsed non-thermal plasmas, Chemical Engineering Journal, **396** (2020): 125185
23. S. Yao, Plasma reactors for diesel particulate matter removal, Recent patents on chemical engineering, **2**,1 (2009): 67-75
24. M. Okubo, N. Arita, T. Kuroki, T. Yamamoto, Total diesel emission control system using ozone injection and plasma desorption, In Fourtieth IAS Annual Meeting. Conference Record of the 2005 Industry Applications Conference, **4** (2005): 2924-2931
25. P. Wang, W. Gu, L. Lei, Y. Cai, Z. Li, Micro-structural and components evolution mechanism of particular matter from diesel engines with non-thermal plasma technology, Applied thermal engineering, **91** (2015): 1-10
26. M. Okubo, T. Kuroki, S. Kawasaki, K. Yoshida, T. Yamamoto, Continuous regeneration of ceramic particulate filter in stationary diesel engine by nonthermal-plasma-induced ozone injection, IEEE Transactions on Industry Applications, **45**,5 (2009): 1568-1574
27. X. Xu, Dielectric barrier discharge-properties and applications, Thin solid films, **390**,1-2 (2001): 237-242
28. J. Rodríguez-Fernández, F. Oliva, R.A. Vázquez, Characterization of the diesel soot oxidation process through an optimized thermogravimetric method, Energy & Fuels, **25**,5 (2011): 2039-2048
29. M. Elkelawy, E.A. El Shenawy, S.A. Mohamed, M.M. Elarabi, H.A.E. Bastawissi, Impacts of EGR on RCCI engines management: A comprehensive review, Energy Conversion and Management: X, **14** (2022): 100216
30. Y. Miao, A. Yokochi, G. Jovanovic, S. Zhang, A. von Jouanne, Application-oriented non-thermal plasma in chemical reaction engineering: A review, Green Energy and Resources, (2023): 100004
31. T. Aka-Ngnui, A. Beroual, Non-thermal plasmas for NOx treatment, In IMETI, (2009): sur-CD
32. G.B. Zhao, X. Hu, M.C. Yeung, O.A. Plumb, M. Radosz, Nonthermal Plasma Reactions of Dilute Nitrogen Oxide Mixtures: NO x in Nitrogen, Industrial & engineering chemistry research, **43**,10 (2004): 2315-2323
33. G. Sathiamoorthy, S. Kalyana, W.C. Finney, R.J. Clark, B.R. Locke, Chemical reaction kinetics and reactor modeling of NO x removal in a pulsed streamer corona discharge reactor, Industrial & engineering chemistry research, **38**,5 (1999): 1844-1855
34. X. Pu, Y. Cai, Y. Shi, J. Wang, L. Gu, J. Tian, and W. Li, Diesel particulate filter (DPF) regeneration using non-thermal plasma induced by dielectric barrier discharge, Journal of the Energy Institute, **91**,5 (2018): 655-667
35. M.R. Khani, E. Barzideh Pour, S. Rashnoo, X. Tu, B. Ghobadian, B. Shokri, A. Khadem, S.I. Hosseini, Real diesel engine exhaust emission control: indirect non-thermal plasma and comparison to direct plasma for NO x, THC, CO, and CO 2, Journal of Environmental Health Science and Engineering, **18** (2020): 743-754
36. D.B. Kittelson, Engines and nanoparticles: a review, Journal of aerosol science, **29**,5-6 (1998): 575-588

Nano-particle Characteristic Emitted from Gasoline Direct Injection Engine Equipped with Non-Thermal Plasma Device

Pichitpon Neamyou[1,2], *Kampanart* Theinnoi[1,2,*], *Boonlue* Sawatmongkhon[1,2], and *Sak* Sittichompoo[1,2]

[1] College of Industrial Technology, King Mongkut's University of Technology North Bangkok, 1518 Pracharat 1 Road, Wongsawang, Bangsue, Bangkok 10800, Thailand.
[2] Research Centre for Combustion Technology and Alternative Energy (CTAE), Science and Technology Research Institute, King Mongkut's University of Technology North Bangkok, Bangkok 10800, Thailand.

Abstract. The impact of non-thermal plasma (NTP) on particulate matter (PM) removal, nitrogen oxide (NOx) reduction, and hydrocarbon species in exhaust gases from gasoline direct injection (GDI) engines using gasoline E20 fuel and a mean effective pressure (IMEP) of 6 bar. The experiments were conducted with an exhaust gas flow rate of 20 L/min, applying high voltage in the range of 0 to 10 kV (2 kV per step) at a frequency of 500 Hz. The results show that NTP reduces PM concentrations, particularly in the nucleation mode (10 nm particles). Maximum PM removal of approximately 83% However, with experimental results, compared to 0 kV, the production of particulate matter Aitken mode increased up to 19 times for a voltage increase of 10 kV, and NOx removal has been at a maximum of about 9.5%, with an energy density of 5 J/L at 10 kV. The effects of NTP on hydrocarbon species such as ethylene, propylene, acetylene, 1.3 butadiene, methane, and ethane have been slightly affected by increased high voltages.

Keyword. Exhaust Gas Emissions, GDI Engines, Non-Thermal Plasma, Particulate Matter

1 Introduction

Gasoline Direct Injection (GDI) engines are becoming increasingly popular due to their improved fuel efficiency and performance [1-4]. However, the diffusion combustion in GDI engines leads to emitting high levels of particulate matter (PM) and nitrogen oxides (NO_x), which are harmful pollutants that can have negative impacts on human health and the environment. PM is made up of tiny particles that can penetrate deep into the lungs, causing respiratory problems, and can also contribute to heart disease and other health issues [5-8]. NO_x is a group of gases that can react with other chemicals in the atmosphere to form smog and acid rain, which can harm crops and ecosystems. In addition, GDI engines can also emit other pollutants such as carbon monoxide (CO), volatile organic compounds (VOCs), and sulfur dioxide (SO_2) [9-10]. These pollutants can contribute to air pollution and have negative impacts on air quality and human health. Overall, while GDI engines offer improved fuel efficiency and performance compared to traditional port fuel injection engines, they do emit higher levels of pollutants that can have negative impacts on human health and the environment [11-14]. As such, there is ongoing research and development aimed at reducing the emissions from GDI engines and improving their environmental performance. PM emissions from GDI engines can be a significant concern due to the potential health impacts of these tiny particles.

GDI engines produce PM as a by-product of the combustion process, which can include a range of materials such as carbon, unburned hydrocarbons, and metal compounds. Studies have shown that GDI engines can produce higher levels of PM compared to traditional port fuel injection engines. Fuel is injected directly into the combustion chamber under high pressure, which can cause the fuel to atomize and mix poorly with the air, leading to incomplete combustion and high PM emissions [15-18]. The PM emissions from GDI engines are generally classified into two categories: solid particle emissions and soluble organic fraction (SOF) emissions. Solid particle emissions are composed of tiny particles that can be inhaled deep into the lungs and can cause health problems, such as respiratory issues and heart disease [19-20]. SOF emissions are composed of organic compounds that are soluble in water, which can have negative impacts on water quality and aquatic ecosystems [18].

To control the PM emissions from GDI engines, manufacturers are exploring a range of solutions, such as optimizing fuel injection timing and pressure, using particulate filters, and developing new combustion strategies. In addition, the emission regulators are implementing stricter standards to encourage the development and adoption of cleaner engine technologies [21-23]. Soot is composed of a complex mixture of carbonaceous particles and other materials. The exact composition of soot can vary depending on factors, such as the engine operating conditions, the fuel properties, and

* Corresponding author: kampanart.t@cit.kmutnb.ac.th

the combustion process [24-26]. In general, soot particles from GDI engines can contain a range of materials, including elemental carbon, organic compounds, and trace metals, such as lead, cadmium, and nickel [27-28]. The organic compounds in soot can include polycyclic aromatic hydrocarbons (PAHs), which are known to have negative health impacts, as well as other oxygenated and nitrogen-containing compounds. The formation of soot in GDI engines is influenced by a range of factors, including the fuel-air mixing, the combustion chamber design, and the injection timing and pressure. Soot formation tends to increase at higher engine loads and speeds, and at lean air-to-fuel ratios, where incomplete combustion can occur [29-30]. However, direct injection engines are emitted higher levels of PM emissions compared to conventional port fuel injection engines.

PM emissions from GDI engines can be reduced using after-treatment technologies, such as Diesel particulate filters (DPFs): DPFs can trap and remove PM emissions from the engine exhaust. Selective catalytic reduction (SCR): SCR uses a catalyst to reduce nitrogen oxide (NOx) emissions, which can, in turn, reduce the formation of PM. Exhaust gas recirculation (EGR): EGR reduces the formation of NOx emissions, which can also reduce the formation of PM. Gasoline particulate filters (GPFs): GPFs are like DPFs but are designed specifically for gasoline engines and can trap and remove PM emissions [31-33]. NO_x emissions from GDI engines can also emit NOx because of the high combustion temperatures and pressures. NOx is a term used to describe a group of gases that includes nitrogen oxide (NO) and nitrogen dioxide (NO_2). NO_x emissions can have negative impacts on human health, including respiratory problems, heart disease, and other health issues. Additionally, NOx emissions can contribute to air pollution and have negative impacts on air quality, visibility, and climate change. The formation of NO_x in GDI engines is influenced by factors, such as the fuel-air mixture, combustion chamber design, and engine operating conditions. To reduce NO_x emissions from GDI engines, manufacturers are exploring a range of strategies, such as optimizing fuel injection timing and pressure, using EGR systems, and developing new combustion strategies that promote lower combustion temperatures. Regulations are also being implemented to encourage the development and adoption of cleaner engine technologies that can reduce. the emissions of NOx and other harmful pollutants [34-36].

Nonthermal plasma (NTP) is a technology that uses electrical discharges to produce reactive species, such as ions, radicals, and photons, which can oxidize or reduce pollutants present in exhaust gases. It operates at relatively low temperatures compared to conventional thermal plasma [37-38]. The reactive species produced by NTP can interact with and break down pollutants, including particulate matter (PM), nitrogen oxides (NOx), and volatile organic compounds (VOCs), into smaller and less harmful components. The use of NTP is a promising approach to reduce emissions in different applications, including automotive exhaust after-treatment systems. NTP has been shown to be effective in reducing PM emissions in various types of engines, including GDI engines. In addition to reducing the overall PM mass emissions, NTP has been found to be effective in reducing the number of ultrafine particles (<100 nm) and nanoparticles (<50 nm) emitted from GDI engines. These smaller particles have been shown to have a greater impact on human health than larger PM particles, as they can penetrate deeper into the lungs and even enter the bloodstream. Studies have shown that NTP can reduce PM number emissions from GDI engines by up to 90%. [39]. NTP has also been found to be effective in reducing nitrogen oxide (NOx) emissions from GDI engines. NOx is a major contributor to air pollution and has been linked to a range of health problems. NTP can selectively reduce NOx emissions by converting NOx to nitrogen and oxygen through chemical reactions in the plasma.

The research aimed to investigate the effect of non-thermal plasma technologies on nanoparticle characteristics in exhaust gas emissions from GDI engines fuelled with gasohol E20 fuel. The effect of NTP operating parameters is also investigated in order to improve PM reduction over the different engine operating conditions.

2 Experimental Apparatus

A schematic diagram of the experimental setup is shown in Figure 1. Experiments were conducted on a 1.3 L, four-cylinder, four-stroke, gasoline direct injection engine (Mazda 2, P3-VPS). The engine specifications are detailed in Table 1. The engine operating conditions are engine load was maintained constant at 6 bar indicated mean effective pressure (IMEP), engine speed at 2000 rpm, gasoline E20 fuel in all the experiments. The constant exhaust gas flow rate through the NTP reactor was kept at 20 L/min. the water trap is used to cool exhaust gas to ambient temperature before entering the reactor. In order to prevent blockage and the risk of electrocution, condensate water.

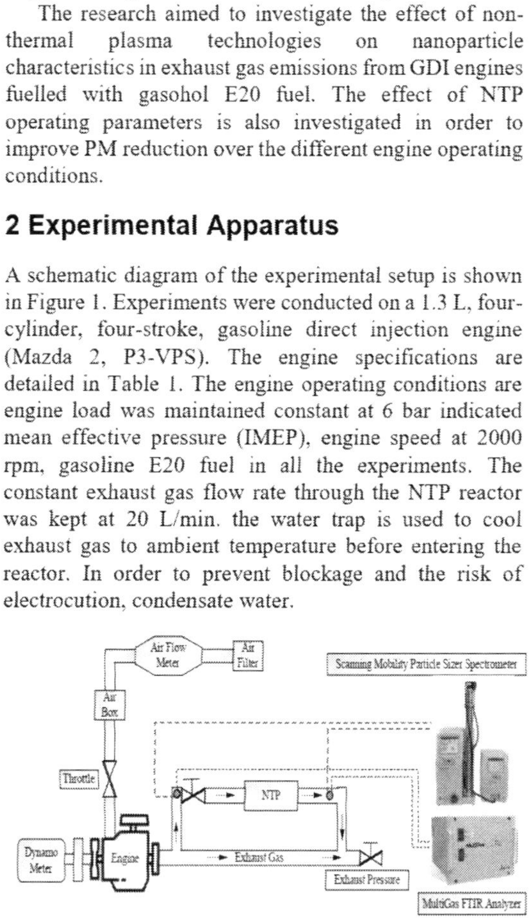

Fig. 1. Schematic diagram of the experimental setup

Table 1. Engine specification of the P3-VPS model.

Engine Parameter	Specifications
No of cylinder	4
Fuel injection	Direct Injection
volume (cm^3)	1298
Bore × Stroke (mm)	82 × 71
Compression ratio	14:1
Maximum power (kW)	62@5400 rpm
Maximum torque (Nm)	112@4000 rpm
Fuel	Gasohol E20

 https://doi.org/10.1051/e3sconf/202342801003

Applying a dielectric barrier discharge (DBD) reactor, plasma was created within the exhaust. DBD is an excellent source of electrons with high energy and density [1]. It consists of an internal and external electrode barrier as shown in Figure 2. Plasma high-voltage amplifier source obtained by Trek 10/10B-HS, Advanced Energy Industries, Inc. Output Voltage: 0 to ±10 kV and Peak AC adjustable from a Digital Oscilloscope DSOX1204G, Keysight Technologies, California, USA. The high-voltage amplifier was used to provide power to the NTP system, while the oscilloscope was utilized to monitor the discharge conditions with applied voltages of 0, 2, 4, 6, 8 and 10 kV at 500 Hz.

In the scanning mobility particle sizer (TSI, SMPS-3082), the size distributions of particles collected before and after the NTP reactor are measured. The particle deposition rate inside the reactor was determined by measuring the PM size distribution at the reactor inlet and reactor exhaust without applying any voltage. The plasma was then introduced into the NTP reactor at the previously described voltage levels. Moreover, the effect of NTP on different nitrogen oxides and hydrocarbon species has been considered. To find out the impact of NTP on NOx concentration, NO, NO2, N2O, and hydrocarbons, which promoted the soot particle, have been measured by the Fourier transform infrared (FTIR) MKS Instruments MultiGas 2030 Gas Analyzers in the reactor with and without High voltage differences.

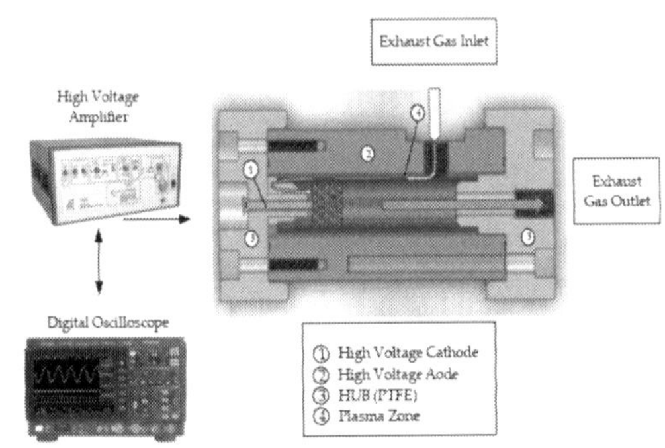

Fig. 2. Schematic diagram of Non-thermal plasma (NTP) system.

3 Results and discussion

3.1 Plasma Discharge power characteristics

The alternating current (AC) voltage generated by increasing the output of the Trek 10/10B-HS transformer (Advanced Energy Industries, Inc.,) at a frequency of 500Hz, was utilized to create a plasma reaction within the DBD reactor by applying it between two electrodes. The transformer converts the input voltage into high voltage in the range from 0 kV to 10 kV (high voltage, ratio 1:1000). A high-voltage and current probe are built into the transformer (Figure 2) with a ratio of 1 V/1000 V for voltage and 1 V/4 mA for electric current and they are inserted into the circuit to minimize load on the oscilloscope. A digital oscilloscope is used to measure, and data log the discharge power in the NTP reactor (Figure 3). The condition example of 6kV for voltage and 30 mA for voltage amperes is shown in Figure 3. The voltage was 0 kV for the first experiment, and it increased up to 10 kV. The power discharge under different voltages is shown in Figure 4. The experiment found that the low discharge power (0.148 joules) at 2 kV. However, when the higher voltage shown the discharge power steeply increases, especially after 10 kV. At this point, plasma can be maintained. This can be confirmed high free radicals' ions and electron impact reactions inside the reactor.

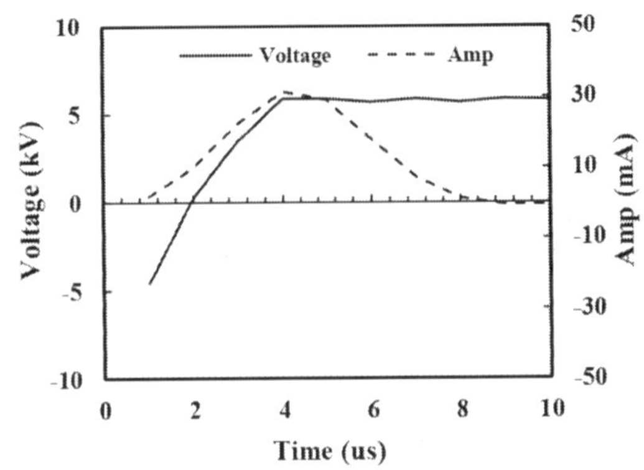

Fig. 3. Voltage and Current signal on oscilloscope

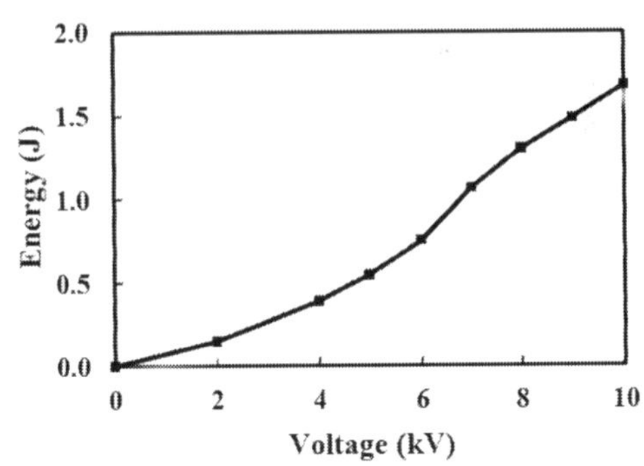

Fig. 4. The effect of voltage on Power discharge for NTP

3.2 Effect of plasma discharge on Particle size distribution

The effect of NTP at different voltage levels is shown in Figure 5. The particle size distribution was measured at the downstream of reactor for all conditions. The result showed that the voltage increases to 2 kV and there is a decline in particle number in nucleation mode (NM) compared to PM numbers from engine out (0 kV). For particles with a diameter range of 10 nm, The NTP reactor exhibited a particle number removal efficiency of 40%. The voltage between 4 kV to 6 kV, the result obtained the particle number removal efficiency of 59% to 65%. After 8 kV, the small particles (<10 nm) have been removed about 80-83% (Figure 6).

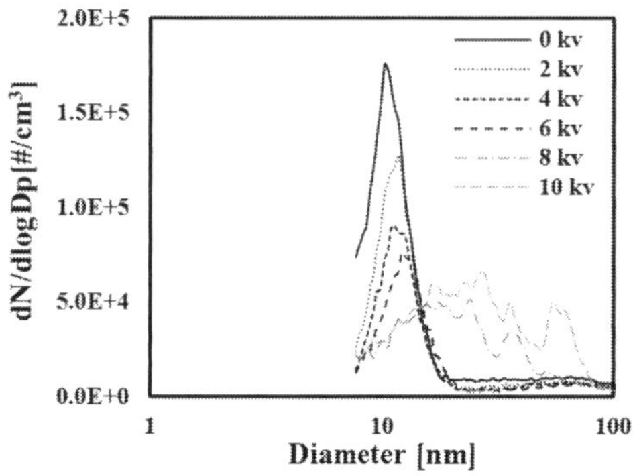

Fig. 5. SMPS particle size distribution at different voltage levels.

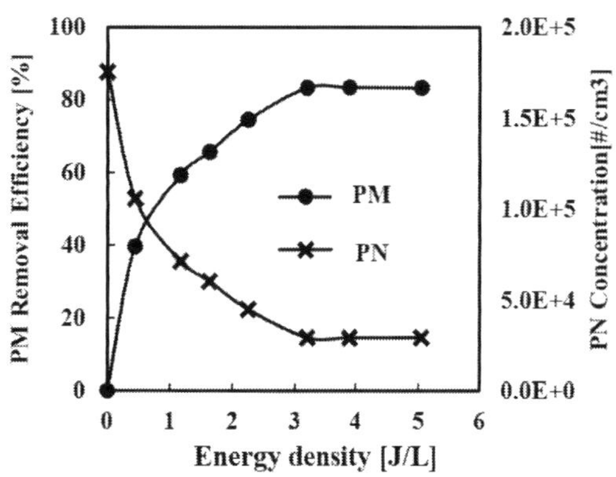

Fig. 6. Effect of energy density on PM removal efficiency and PN concentration.

However, high numbers of particle concentrations in Aitken mode (AKM), particle specific size range of atmospheric aerosol particles with diameters typically ranging from 10 to 100 nanometres, were found at this voltage level. PM size distribution peaks to 6.34 x 10^4 particles, which is 19.5 times greater than the maximum particle number in engine out exhaust gas. In the experiment, it was found that the total PN concentration was in the range of 8 to 10 kV, with a significant increase in nucleation mode and Aitken mode, as shown in Figure 7. In addition, Aitken mode particles are generated through the condensation of SOF that originates from the nucleation mode particles, after the oxidation of their embedded elemental carbons. These particles can also be formed through condensation from the gas phase. The result showed that the main acetylene gas from the NTP reactor had a higher content (Figure 13), when the voltage got to 8 and 10 kV, which was the precursor of soot formation. Subsequently, acetylene gas condenses and combines with small dust particles in the exhaust gases, resulting in the soot formation. The production of acetylene from methane is categorized as a plasma-chemical process, as proposed by Stijn Heijkers and Annemie Bogaerts [46]. In their work, the authors developed a comprehensive chemical kinetics model to investigate the primary conversion mechanisms involved in transforming CH_4 into crucial hydrocarbons, namely C_2H_2, C_2H_4, and C_2H_6, as well as H_2. This analysis encompassed the three prevalent plasma reactors, namely dielectric barrier discharge (DBD), microwave (MW), and gliding arc plasma (GAP) reactors.

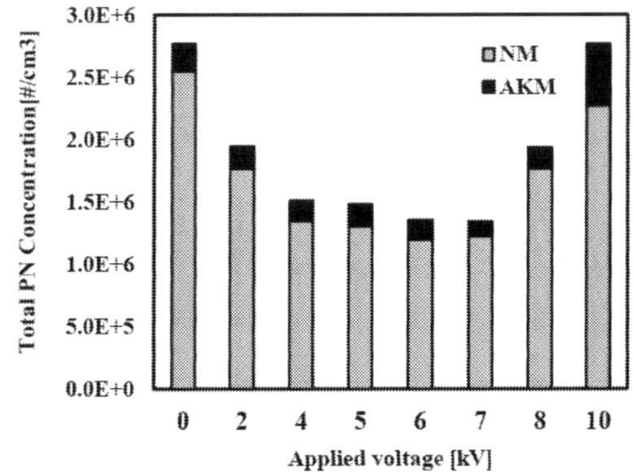

Fig. 7. Comparison of particle distribution of nucleation mode and Aitken mode at different voltage

3.3 Effect of NTP on NOx concentration

The effect of non-thermal plasma on nitrogen oxides has been investigated. The research included adjusting the applied voltages from 2 kV to 10 kV, consistent with previous experimental conditions. The concentrations of NO, NO_2, N_2O, and total NOx ($NO+NO_2$) were considered as shown in Figure 8. The initiation of concentration alteration occurred after applying a voltage of 6 kV. Therefore, plasma beam has low power to handle variations in nitrogen oxide concentrations before this point. The oxidation of NO to NO_2 is explained by the presence of different active oxygen species and ozone. Using a maximum voltage of 10 kV during the experiments resulted in a decrease of approximately 11% in NO concentration and an increase of approximately 48% in NO_2 concentration as shown in Figure 8, similar to previous research that used diesel exhaust gas [44-45].

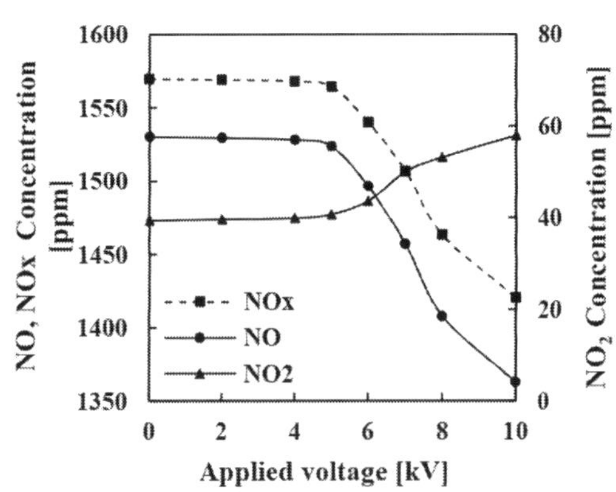

Fig. 8. Effect of non-thermal plasma on nitrogen oxides.

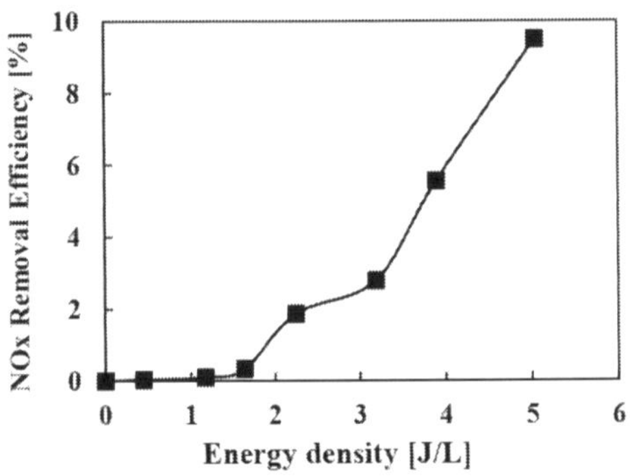

Fig. 9. NO_x removal efficiency at different energy densities.

Figure 9 shows the impact of non-thermal plasma on the NO_x reduction. The maximum value of energy density is constrained by the applied voltage at 10 kV. The discovery has been made that increasing the energy density results in a continuous improvement in the efficiency of NOx removal. In addition, the higher NOx reduction has been observed by increasing the energy density to 5 J/L. For the given configuration, the maximum NOx removal efficiency achieved 9.5% with the energy density was about 5 J/L. The effects of NTP on the different NO_x emissions are shown in Fig 8. The total concentration of NO_x is reduced as the applied voltage is increased. Due to the occurrence of a series of reactions in a plasma state. NO can be removed through equations Eq. (1) and Eq. (2), and it can be oxidized to NO_2 through equations Eq. (3) and Eq. (4), The NO_2 is increased by reaction as shown in equations Eq. (3) and Eq. (4). Moreover, the reduction in NOx concentration can be attributed to the decrease in NO concentration as per equations Eq. (1) and Eq. (2) owing to the significant concentration of NO in the exhaust emission.

$$NO + N \rightarrow N_2 + O \quad (1)$$

$$N_2(A) + NO \rightarrow N_2 + N + O \quad (2)$$

$$NO + O \rightarrow NO_2 \quad (3)$$

$$NO + O_3 \rightarrow NO_2 + O_2 \quad (4)$$

3.4 Effects of NTP on total hydrocarbons (THC) and CO emissions

The NTP effect on total hydrocarbons (THC) concentrations was shown in Figure 10. In this chart, the total concentration of hydrocarbons constantly decreases as the applied voltage increases at 10 kV, and the concentration of THC decreases by around 7%. The reduction of THC can be explained by reaction Eq. (5) to Eq. (8).

$$C_xH_yO_z + O_2 \rightarrow CO_2 + H_2O \quad (5)$$

$$C_2H_4 + e \rightarrow C_2H_2 + H_2 + e \rightarrow C_2H_2 + 2H + e \quad (6)$$

$$C_2H_4 + O \rightarrow CH_3 + HCO \quad (7)$$

$$C_2H_4 + OH \rightarrow HOCH_2CH_2 \quad (8)$$

The higher voltages cause the concentration of CO to increase as shown in Figure10, but the concentration of CO_2 is not different (Figure11). With respect to the amount of oxygen content in the exhaust, hydrocarbons and soot were converted to CO more than CO_2. This is due to the presence of the OH radical in ethanol-blended fuel (E20) as well as the increase in free radicals (OH) resulting from the dissociation of H_2O in Eq. (9). This free radical promotes the conversion of CO through reaction Eq. (10)

$$H_2O + e^- \rightarrow OH + H \quad (9)$$

$$CO + OH \rightarrow CO_2 + H \quad (10)$$

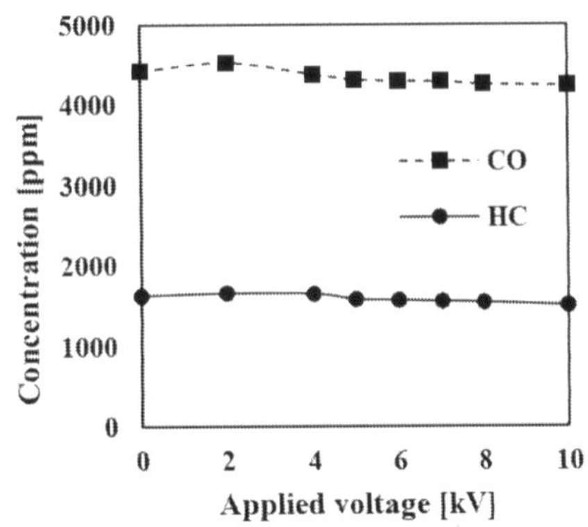

Fig. 10. Effect of NTP on HC and CO Emissions.

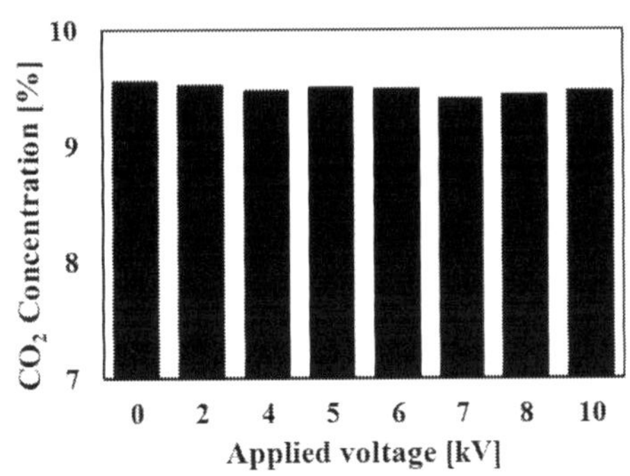

Fig. 11. Effect of NTP on CO_2 Emissions.

3.5 Effects of NTP on hydrocarbon speciation

The hydrocarbon species group can be divided into the following: carbonyl group (formaldehyde and acetaldehyde), unsaturated group (ethylene, propylene, acetylene and 1,3 butadiene), and saturated group (methane and ethane). The effects of NTP on these HCs groups are shown in Figure 12 - 14. In the conditions of a 6-10 kV applied voltage, the carbonyl group exhibits an increase in acetaldehyde (C_2H_4O). The impact of NTP on formaldehyde (CH_2O) is negligible as shown in Figure 12. This mechanism can be explained as follows: the plasma-generated O, OH, and O_3 species have reactions with hydrocarbons, allowing the formation of alkyl (R), alkoxy (RO), and acyl (RCO) radicals. Then, the alkoxy radicals, such as CH_3O, react with oxygen and produce formaldehyde [40]. When the NTP is applied at 6-10 kV, it appears that ethylene, propylene, and 1,3-butadiene show a trend toward decreasing. The reduction of ethylene (C_2H_4) is caused by the oxygen atoms, which are produced by NTP. The NTP also enhances the decomposition of ethylene to CH_3 through Eq. (11) and then CH_3 can be oxidized to CH_3O_2 through Eq. (12), which helps the reduction of NO via Eq. (13), as shown in Figure 8.

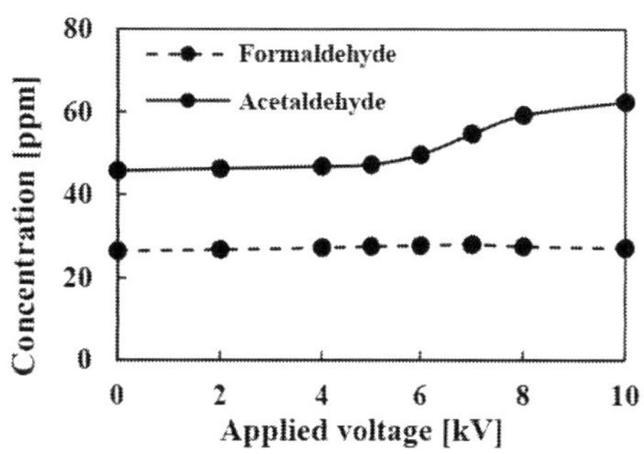

Fig. 12. Effect of NTP on the carbonyl HCs group

However, acetylene exhibits a slight decrease when the NTP voltage is between 0 - 6 kV, followed by an increase when the applied voltage is between 6 - 10 kV, as shown in Figure 13. The increase of acetylene due to the decomposition of ethylene to acetylene (C_2H_2) with NTP by Eq. (14).

$$C_2H_4 + O \rightarrow CH_3 + CHO \quad (11)$$

$$CH_3 + O_2 \rightarrow CH_3O_2 \quad (12)$$

$$CH_3O_2 + NO \rightarrow CH_3O + NO_2 \quad (13)$$

$$C_2H_4 + e \rightarrow C_2H_2 + H_2 + e \quad (14)$$

The effect of NTP saturated HCs group is shown in Figure 14. The NTP has no impact on methane and ethane conversion, because the energy of NTP in the range of 2-10 kV utilized in this study is insufficient to activate transformation of methane and ethane. However, the influence of NTP on the types of hydrocarbons is contingent upon various factors, including the nature of the hydrocarbon, the configuration of the plasma parameters (comprising power, frequency, and gas residence time), and the reactor design. [41-42]. The reactivity of hydrocarbons towards plasma is known to vary depending on their chemical composition, and the reaction could be influenced by a mixture of the different gases in the exhaust gas [43].

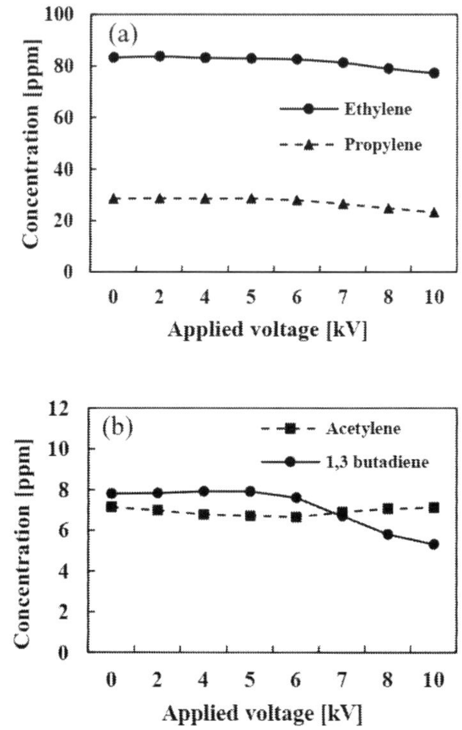

Fig. 13. Effect of NTP on the unsaturated HCs group (a) Ethylene and propylene (b) acetylene and 1,3 butadiene.

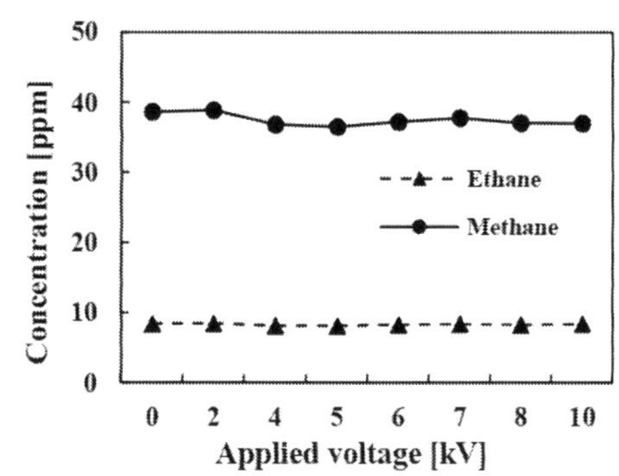

Fig. 14. Effect of NTP on the saturated HCs Group.

4 Conclusion

The effect of non-thermal plasma treatment (NPT) on the distribution of particulate matter (PM) size has been conducted to enhance comprehension of the mechanism of PM removal. NTP can reduce 83% of small particle size (<10 nm), a maximum of 83% with an energy density of 5 J/L. However, the production of particulate matter from 10 nm to 100 nm (Aitken mode) increased up to 19 times for a voltage increase from 10 kV compared with an engine out. Therefore, operating the DBD reactor at 6 kV may be regarded as the ideal operating condition for this design in terms of PM size distribution removal efficiency and energy consumption in nucleation mode and Aitken mode when considering only the removal of small particulate matter. The effect of non-thermal plasma (NTP) on the size distribution of particulate matter (PM) and nitrogen oxide (NOx) discharge in real exhaust from gasoline direct injection under different voltage conditions. Experimental results show the oxidation of nitrogen monoxide (NO) resulted in the formation of nitrogen dioxide (NO_2). The efficiency of NO_x removal has been shown to be increased with the higher discharge power, reaching a maximum percentage of about 9.5 and the energy density about 5 J/L has been measured. In addition, the different effects of applied voltage on hydrocarbon species, such as ethylene, propylene, acetylene, 1.3 butadiene, methane, and ethane are observed.

Acknowledgements

This research was funded by the National Science, Research and Innovation Fund (NSRF), and King Mongkut's University of Technology, North Bangkok, with Contract no. KMUTNB−FF−66−19.

References

1. A.N. Bukkapatnam, R. Sriramula, Y.J. Kim, Gasoline direct injection engines: Advancements, challenges, and future perspectives, Journal of Energy Resources Technology, **142**,6, (2020): 061201
2. S. Singh, M.R. Golovitchev, A.S.G. Wijewardane, Impact of fuel properties on the spray characteristics and combustion of a gasoline direct injection engine, Energy Conversion and Management, **215** (2020): 112996
3. J. Guo, Y. Hu, Z. Liu, Effect of gasoline direct injection timing on mixture formation, combustion, and emissions in a gasoline direct injection engine, **266** (2020): 117088
4. Y. Zhang, C. Chen, Z. Wang, X. Han, An experimental investigation on the combustion and emission characteristics of a gasoline direct injection engine fueled with hydrogen-enriched gasoline, **246** (2019): 78-86
5. K. Min, M.Y. Kim, D. Kim, S. Kwon, Evaluation of particulate matter emissions from gasoline direct injection vehicles under various driving conditions, Environmental Pollution, **269** (2021): 116180
6. K.H. Kim M.Y. Kim, Emissions characteristics of nanoparticles from gasoline direct injection engines, Science of The Total Environment, **725** (2020): 138293
7. T.D. Durbin, C.R. Bartoli, J.M. Norbeck, Impact of ethanol and aromatic hydrocarbon content on particulate matter emissions from a GDI engine, Energy & Fuels, **33**,3, (2019): 2483-2491
8. F. Yang, C. Xu, Y. Li, H. Xu, L. Li, Influence of gasoline composition and operating parameters on the formation of particulate matter in gasoline direct injection engines, **291** (2021): 120029
9. M. Zheng, G.T. Reader, Nitrogen oxide emissions from gasoline direct injection engines: Mechanisms, control strategies, and future perspectives, Applied Energy, **291** (2021): 116857
10. C.P. Kolodziej, T.D. Durbin, J.M. Norbeck, Impact of fuel composition on the formation and emissions of PM from a gasoline direct injection engine, Environmental Science & Technology, **54**,9 (2020): 5732-5740
11. M. Cheng, L. Hao, L. Li, S. Li, H. Liu, K. Cen, Real-world emissions of non-methane volatile organic compounds from gasoline direct injection vehicles, Science of The Total Environment, **773** (2021): 145565
12. P. Přikryl, M. Vojtíšek-Lom, M. Pohořelý, Particle emissions from internal combustion engines: A review, Atmospheric Environment, **259** (2021): 118482
13. H. Zhang, M. Yao, H. Liu, M. Zheng, Emissions and characteristics of particulate matter from a gasoline direct injection engine at different operating conditions, Journal of Environmental Sciences, **90** (2020): 372-381
14. X. Song, H. Liu, Q. Zhang, Experimental investigation of particulate emissions from a gasoline direct injection engine fueled with gasoline-ethanol blends, **241** (2019): 1056-1062
15. H. Zhang, M. Yao, H. Liu, Investigation of the formation and evolution of particulate matter in a gasoline direct injection engine, **261** (2020): 116433
16. M. Zheng, G.T. Reader, Experimental investigation of particulate emissions from a gasoline direct injection engine during cold-start, **253** (2019): 189-198
17. X. Ma, Y. Xue, H. Zhang, S. Wu, Z. Huang, Effect of injection timing on particulate matter emissions from gasoline direct injection engine under cold-start conditions, **285** (2021): 119023
18. Y. Qiao, J. Cai, J. Lv, B. Liu, Z. Huang, Effect of ethanol blending on the morphology and nanostructure of soot particles emitted from a gasoline direct injection engine, **273** (2020): 117779
19. J. Chen, M. Mousazadeh, A. Sarathy, Characterization of particulate emissions from a gasoline direct injection engine: Influence of operating conditions and fuel components, **261** (2020): 116385
20. G. Zhang, Y. Zhang, Z. Wang, H. Yao, Z. Huang, Effect of engine operating conditions on particulate matter emissions from a gasoline direct injection engine, **260** (2020): 116208
21. A.A. Omidvarborna, A. Ahmed, D.A. Nguyen, G.K. Anderson, In-cylinder particle number evolution in a gasoline direct injection engine, **269** (2020): 117457-117457
22. Y. Qiao, J. Cai, J. Lv, B. Liu, Z. Huang, Effect of ethanol blending on the morphology and

nanostructure of soot particles emitted from a gasoline direct injection engine, **273** (2020): 117779-117779

23. L. Li, C. Huang, Y. Lu, M. Liu, J. Peng, C. Zheng, Effects of fuel injection strategy on soot emissions in a gasoline direct injection engine, Energy Conversion and Management, **242** (2021): 114276
24. S. Zhang, G. Song, X. Huang, Z. Zhang, J. Zhang, Effects of injection strategy on soot emissions from a gasoline direct injection engine during start-up, **233** (2018): 445-454
25. K. Borkar, S.W. King, R.R. Steeper, C.A. Gabrys, Effect of injection timing on soot formation in a gasoline direct-injection engine using in-cylinder imaging, SAE International Journal of Engines, **8**,2 (2015): 1020-1032
26. H. Wu, H. Wang, W. Zhang, Y. Zhang, M. Wei, Effect of injection timing on soot emission and combustion process in a GDI engine, **156** (2015): 97-105
27. J.H. Lee, S. Choi, K. Lee, C.S. Lee, Characterization of particle emissions from a gasoline direct injection engine fueled with ethanol-gasoline blends, IEEE Transactions on Transportation Electrification, **7**,4 (2021): 1516-1523
28. J. Kim, C. Yoo, S. Jeon, H. Bae, Impact of ethanol blend ratio on particulate matter emissions from a gasoline direct injection engine, IEEE Transactions on Transportation Electrification, **6**,3 (2020): 1005-1012
29. S. Shamsudeen, P. Bharath,A. Sivakumar, Influence of fuel-air mixing on soot formation in a gasoline direct injection engine, IEEE Access, **8** (2020): 23756-23764
30. P. Prikhodko, S. Kozlov, D. Kosarev, Effect of injection timing on soot formation in a gasoline direct injection engine, in Proceedings of the 21st International Scientific-Technical Conference on Actual Problems of Electronics Instrument Engineering (APEIE), Novosibirsk, Russia, (2020): 253-258
31. S. Song, S. Gao, W. Yan, J. Zheng, Study on the effect of gasoline particulate filters on particulate matter emissions from gasoline direct injection engines, in Proceedings of the 2021 IEEE Vehicle Power and Propulsion Conference (VPPC), Chengdu, China, (2021): 1-6
32. Y. Lee, S. Kim, S. Han, Investigation of the effect of gasoline direct injection on particulate emissions and after-treatment system performance, in Proceedings of the 2020 IEEE Transportation Electrification Conference and Expo (ITEC), Chicago, IL, USA, (2020): 1-6
33. C. Liu, J. Li, Y. Li, J. Wang, Effect of exhaust gas recirculation on particulate matter emissions from a gasoline direct injection engine, in Proceedings of the 2019 IEEE Vehicle Power and Propulsion Conference (VPPC), Hanoi, Vietnam, (2019): 1-6
34. Y. Liu, Q. Wang, Y. Xu, Z. Li, Experimental investigation on particulate matter reduction by non-thermal plasma in a gasoline direct injection engine, in Proceedings of the 2020 IEEE Transportation Electrification Conference and Expo (ITEC), Novi, MI, USA, (2020): 1-5
35. H. Zhao, S. Yuan, H. Li, Y. Zhang, Experimental study on NOx reduction using non-thermal plasma in a gasoline direct injection engine, in Proceedings of the 2020 IEEE International Conference on Automation, Electronics and Electrical Engineering (AUTEEE), Taiyuan, China, (2020): 1-4
36. W. Zhang, H. Zhao, C. Geng, Experimental investigation on non-thermal plasma assisted NOx reduction in a gasoline direct injection engine, in Proceedings of the 2019 IEEE Transportation Electrification Conference and Expo (ITEC), Novi, MI, USA, (2019): 1-6
37. X. Chen, M. Liu, Y. Zhao, X. Wang, Non-thermal plasma technology for diesel engine exhaust gas treatment: A review, in Proceedings of the 2020 IEEE International Conference on Mechatronics and Automation (ICMA), Xi'an, China, (2020): 1-6
38. S. Park, S. Lee, J. Oh, J. Kim, Evaluation of non-thermal plasma on NOx removal for diesel engine exhaust gas, in Proceedings of the 2020 IEEE International Conference on Plasma Science (ICOPS), Chicago, IL, USA, (2020): 1-4
39. K. Park, J. Kim, J. Lee, Y. Kim, Reduction of ultrafine particles using a non-thermal plasma system for GDI engine exhaust, in Proceedings of the 2020 IEEE International Power Electronics and Application Conference and Exposition (PEAC), Nanjing, China, (2020): 1-5
40. A.D. Srinivasan B.S. Rajanikanth, Pulsed plasma treatment for NOx reduction from filtered/unfiltered stationary diesel engine exhaust, in Proceedings of the 2007b IEEE Industry Applications Conference, New Orleans, LA, (2007): 1893-190
41. E. Delikonstantis, M. Scapinello, G.D. Stefanidis, Low energy cost conversion of methane to ethylene in a hybrid plasma-catalytic reactor system, Fuel Processing Technology, **177** (2018): 26-36
42. T. Nozaki, A. Hattori, K. Okazaki, Partial oxidation of methane using a microscale non-equilibrium plasma reactor, Catalysis Today, **98**,4 (2004): 607-616
43. J. Benedikt, Plasma-chemical reactions: low pressure acetylene plasmas, Journal of Physics D: Applied Physics, **43**,4 (2010): 043001
44. T. Iamcheerangkoon, N. Chollacoop, B. Sawatmongkhon, T. Wongchang, S. Sittichompoo, S. Chuepeng, K. Theinnoi, Promotion of the NO-to-NO2 Conversion of a Biofueled Diesel Engine with Nonthermal Plasma-Assisted Low-Temperature Soot Incineration of a Diesel Particulate Filter, Energies, **15**,24 (2022): 9330
45. K. Yoshida, Diesel NOx aftertreatment by combined process using temperature swing adsorption, nonthermal plasma, and NOx recirculation: NOx removal accelerated by conversion of NO to NO2, Journal of the Taiwan Institute of Chemical Engineers, **44**,6 (2013): 1054-1059

https://doi.org/10.1051/e3sconf/202342801003

46. S. Heijkers, M. Aghaei, A. Bogaerts, Plasma-Based CH4 Conversion into Higher Hydrocarbons and H2: Modeling to Reveal the Reaction Mechanisms of Different Plasma Sources, The Journal of Physical Chemistry C, **124**,13 (2020): 7016-7030

Performance Analysis of Integral Process of Bio-Oil Production, Bio-Oil Upgrading, and Hydrogen Production from Sewage Sludge

Lida Simasatitkul[1,*] *Apiwat* Lakkhanasombut [1], *Worawit* Morin [1], *Supachai* Jedsadajerm[1], *Suksun* Amornraksa[2], *Karittha* Im-orb[3]

[1]Department of Industrial Chemistry, Faculty of Applied Science, King Mongkut's University of Technology North Bangkok, Thailand.
[2]The Sirindhorn International Thai-German Graduate School of Engineering (TGGS), King Mongkut's University of Technology North Bangkok, Thailand.
[3]Program in Food Process Engineering, Faculty of Food-Industry, King Mongkut's Institute of Technology Ladkrabang, Thailand.

Abstract. This research investigated the production of bio-oil through the hydrothermal liquefaction (HTL) process using sewage sludge from wastewater, along with the hydrotreating of the bio-oil. The simulation process began with a wastewater flow rate of 460 tonnes/day, where the feedstock was divided into two streams. The first stream underwent the HTL process, while the other was directed towards hydrogen production. The resulting products included gaseous products, crude bio-oil, and heavy liquid. The crude bio-oil was further upgraded by introducing hydrogen, which was obtained through gasification and purified by gas separation using a palladium membrane. The primary product mainly comprised alkane, with a carbon content of 85.89% and hydrogen content of 14.11%. For the purification of gasoline, kerosene, diesel, and fuel oil, a fractionation distillation tower arrangement was designed. In addition, Additionally, the gaseous products underwent fractionation distillation to obtain 98% nitrogen and 99.9% liquid carbon dioxide. Considering the carbon footprint, it was observed that the bio-oil production process resulted in the highest greenhouse gas (GHG) emissions.

Keyword. Bio-oil, Hydrothermal liquefaction, Process design, Sewage, Upgrading

1 Introduction

Nowadays, daily wastewater in Thailand reaches 9.5 million cubic meters; however, the management capacity is limited to only 3 million cubic meters per day. The sewage sludge generated from industrial wastewater contributes to water pollution through odor and chemical contamination. Traditionally, sewage sludge is disposed of through landfilling and combustion. Nevertheless, there is potential to harness energy from sewage sludge through thermochemical processes like pyrolysis or liquefaction [1].

Hydrothermal liquefaction in a batch reactor typically operates at temperatures of 250-375 °C and pressure of 4-22 MPa, utilizing catalysts, such as $NiMo/Al_2O_3$, $CoMo/Al_2O_3$, and Pd/Al_2O_3 [2]. The resulting product is crude bio-oil with a yield of 27.5 wt% and an energy content of 40 MJ/kg [4]. The chemical components include fatty acid methyl esters, alkanes, ketones, amines, amides, and aromatic hydrocarbons [3]. Gaseous compounds like CO_2, NH_3 and CH_4 are also produced. However, the crude bio-oil requires upgrading through hydrotreating processes such as hydrogenation, hydrodeoxygenation (HDO), decarboxylation (DCO_2), decarbonylation (DCO) and hydrocracking. For example, bio-oil can be hydrogenated using an H_2/oil ratio of 2100 L/L, a temperature of 420 °C, and a pressure of 12.4 MPa in the presence of NiMo catalyst to enhance the bio-oil properties for its intended applications [4].

It is well-established that hydrogen plays a crucial role in the hydrotreating process. Traditionally, hydrogen is obtained from refineries or steam reforming of natural gas. However, green hydrogen production from processes, such as steam reforming of bio-oil, biomass gasification, and fermentation should be given attention [5]. A gasification process operated at a high temperature of 500-1400 °C, and a pressure of 33 bar resulted in a hydrogen yield of 25 vol.% [7]. Furthermore, integrated processes like the coupling of bio-oil upgrading with bio-oil steam reforming have been explored [6].

While literature reviews have covered bio-oil production, bio-oil upgrading, and hydrogen production. They are mostly separate processes. Moreover, the specific sources of hydrogen for bio-oil upgrading have not been mentioned. The biomass-based hydrogen was developed by pyrolysis combined with bio-oil steam reforming and biochar steam reforming [7]. Bio-oil was divided into two parts (i.e., upgrading and steam reforming for hydrogen); however, renewable resources were not mentioned [8]. Thus, this research aims to

* Corresponding author: lida.s@sci.kmutnb.ac.th

address this gap by proposing a combined process of bio-oil production and hydrogen production from sewage sludge, along with bio-oil upgrading. This process is developed by process simulation via Aspen Plus. The optimal conditions are determined and, the carbon footprint of the process will be evaluated to justify its worthiness.

2 Methodology

In this research, the design was based on a wastewater quantity of 460 ton/day from the Netherlands, as comprehensive data was available [9]. This quantity was divided into 2 streams: 400 ton/day for bio-oil production and 60 ton/day for hydrogen production. Material and energy balance were conducted using the Aspen Plus process simulator. Soave-Redlich-Kwong model was chosen for bio-oil production, while Peng-Robinson model was chosen for hydrogen production. The ultimate analysis and proximate analysis data are shown in Table 1. The bio-oil consisted of hydrocarbons, esters, aldehydes, ketones, and aromatic hydrocarbons. While some components were conventional, complex components were treated as pseudo-components, requiring their chemical structures to be incorporated into the program.

Table 1. Ultimate analysis and proximate analysis of sewage sludge in wastewater.

Ultimate analysis (wt.%)					Proximate analysis (wt.%)		
C	H	O	N	Ash	FC*	VM*	Ash
38.2	6.6	23.9	6.4	24.9	6.2	68.9	24.9

*FC = Fixed carbon, VM = Volatile matter.

A block flow diagram of the conceptual design process was generated as shown in Figure 1. Based on the diagram, the main products are gasoline, kerosene, diesel, and fuel oil, while the by-products are nitrogen, hydrogen and dry ice. The unit model consists of pump, compressor, valve, mixer, reactor, flash separator, distillation column, heater and cooler. The reactor model of Hydrothermal liquefaction (HTL) is RYield, which sets the mass yield. The upgrading reactor is modeled using a conversion reactor, which specifies the fractional conversion. The distillation model used is Radfrac model.

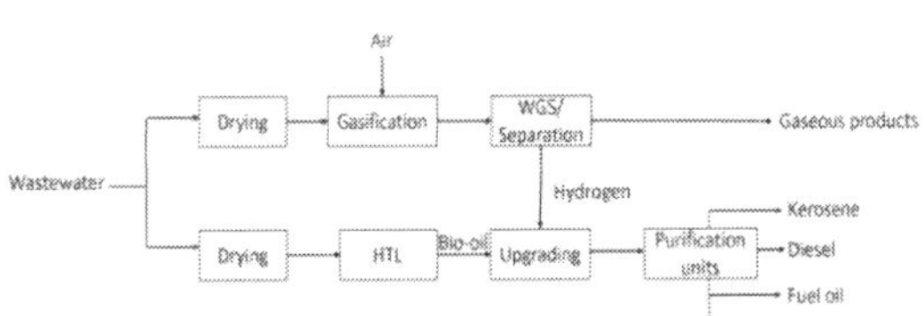

Fig. 1. Conceptual design of the integrated process.

3 Process design

The integrated processes for bio-oil production, bio-oil upgrading, and hydrogen production from sewage sludge are illustrated in Figure 2. The overall process can be divided into 3 distinct sub-processes: bio-oil production process, hydrogen production process, and bio-oil upgrading process.

3.1 Bio-oil production process

A steady-state model for the bio-oil production process was developed and depicted in Figure 2. The wastewater underwent pressurization using a pump to achieve a pressure of 200 bar and was then heated to 350 °C. The preheated stream was directed into the HTL reactor, where the mass yield was determined. The effluent from the reactor underwent a pressure reduction via a valve and was subsequently passed through a three-phase separator to separate the gaseous products, light products, and heavy products. The gaseous products included hydrogen, nitrogen, carbon dioxide, carbon monoxide, methane, ethane, propane, butane, ammonia, and ethylene. The light product obtained is known as crude bio-oil while the heavy product is wastewater. The crude bio-oil was subjected to centrifugation when the liquid-to-solid mass ratio reached 0.103.

3.2 Hydrogen production process

In the hydrogen production process depicted in Figure 2, it starts with the wastewater being passed through a dryer at 1 bar and 100 °C. Then, a separator is used to remove water and sludge. The sludge is then sent to the gasification reactor. To determine the yields of water, ash, carbon, hydrogen, nitrogen, chlorine, sulfur, and oxygen, a calculator block integrated into the process simulator is utilized. The separator is used to remove the ash. The gaseous product obtained from the separator is then conveyed to the gasification reactor, which is modeled by the Gibb reactor. Finally, the effluent from the reactor is passed through a membrane [10].

3.3 Bio-oil upgrading process

In the bio-oil upgrade process depicted in Figure 2, the crude bio-oil obtained from bio-oil production undergoes pumping to increase the pressure to 120 bar, followed by preheating at 400 °C. The preheated stream, along with hydrogen from the hydrogen production section, is then directed to the upgrading reactor. The reactions (i.e. hydrogenation, decarboxylation, desulfurization, decarbonylation) are defined. The composition and flow rate of the products are performed after the fractional conversion of the reactions is assumed according to Table 2. Then, the product stream is sent for separation into gaseous products, an oil stream, and water. The oil stream is directed to the first distillation column to remove any remaining gaseous products before being transferred to the second distillation column for the separation of crude gasoline from crude oil. To ensure high purity, the crude gasoline is further purified using an additional distillation column to remove ethyl diamine. Consequently, highly pure gasoline, consisting of 92 wt% hydrocarbon compounds (C6-C9), is obtained. The crude oil from the first distillation column is introduced to another distillation column for the purification of kerosene (hydrocarbon compounds C11-C14), achieving a purity of 99 wt%. The crude oil collected from the bottom of the second distillation column mainly consists of hydrocarbon compounds. Thus, it is directed to the final distillation column, resulting in the production of highly pure diesel (hydrocarbon compounds C15-C16) at the overhead column, while fuel oil (hydrocarbon compounds C17) is obtained at the bottom of the distillation column.

The gaseous products obtained from the 3-phase separator in the bio-oil production section are combined with the gaseous products from the first distillation column in the bio-oil upgrading section before entering the distillation column to eliminate waste. To purify the gaseous products, they are sent to a compressor, followed by a cooler, and then sent to the distillation column. As a result, nitrogen, with a purity of 98 wt%, is obtained, while CH_4 and CO are obtained in another distillation column. After removing CH_4 and CO, the bottom stream of the distillation column is passed through a reducing valve, cooler and the distillation column, respectively. Through this process, a high-purity CO_2, with a purity of 99 wt%, is obtained.

Table 2. Fractional conversion of the reaction in the conversion reactor

Reaction	Fractional conversion
Formic acid → CO_2 + H_2	1
Acetic acid → CH_4 + CO_2	1
Glycerol + $3H_2$ → Propane + 3 H_2O	1
Phenol + $5H_2$ → Hexane + H_2O	1
Vinylcyclohexane + $2H_2$ → Ethylcyclohexane	1
1-Ethyl-2,5-Pyrrolidinedione + $6H_2$ → Butane + Ethyleneamine + $2H_2O$	1
2,3-Xylenol + $4H_2$ → 1,2-Dimethylcyclohexane + H_2O	1
2,6-Diethylcyclohexanone + H_2 → nonane + CO	1
5-Hydroxymethylfurfural + $7H_2$ → Hexane + $3H_2O$	1
Hexadecanoic acid + $3H_2$ → Hexadecane + $2H_2O$	0.05
Hexadecanoic acid → Pentadecane + CO_2	0.65
Hexadecanoic acid + H_2 → Pentadecane + H_2O + CO	0.3
Tetradecanoic acid + $3H_2$ → Tetradecane + $2H_2O$	0.05
Tetradecanoic acid → Tridecane + CO_2	0.65
Tetradecanoic acid + H_2 → Tridecane + CO + H_2O	0.3
Octadecanoic acid + $3H_2$ → Octadecane + $2H_2O$	0.05
Octadecanoic acid → Heptadecane + CO_2	0.65
Octadecanoic acid + H_2 → Heptadecane + CO + H_2O	0.3
2-Methyl-pyrimidine + $5H_2$ → Propane + Ethylenediamine	1
3-Hydroxy-dodecanoic acid + H_2 → Undecane + CO_2 +H_2O	0.65
3-Hydroxy-dodecanoic acid + $2H_2$ → Undecane + CO + $2H_2O$	0.3
3-Hydroxy-dodecanoic acid + $4H_2$ → Dodecane + $3H_2O$	0.05
1-Ethyl-2-pyrrolidinone + $4H_2$ → Butane + Ethylamine + H_2O	1
Methylthiopyrrolidone → Butane + Methylamine + H_2S	1
Ethylbenzene + $3H_2$ → Ethylcyclohexane	1
5,6,7-Trimethyl-indole + $6H_2$ → 1-Methyl-ethylcyclohexane + Ammonia	1
Tetradecanamide + H_2 → CO + Ammonia + Tridecane	0.9
Tetradecanamide + 3H2 → H_2O + Ammonia + Tetradecane	0.1
Hexadecanamide + H_2 → CO + Ammonia + Heptadecane	0.9
Hexadecanamide + $3H_2$ → H_2O + Ammonia + Hexadecane	0.1
Octadecanamide + H_2 → CO + Ammonia + Heptadecane	0.9
Octadecanamide + $3H_2$ → H_2O + Ammonia + Octadecane	0.1
Diundecyl phthalate + $7H_2$ → 2Undecane + $2H_2O$ + Cyclohexane + 2CO	1

Reaction	Fractional conversion
Diphenyl-1,4-phenylenediamine + $13H_2$ → 2Ammonia + 3Cyclohexane	1
Cholesterol + $2H_2$ → Cholestane + H_2O	1

4 Results and Discussions

The simulation results in the bio-oil production have been validated using literature data. In the hydrogen production section, the equivalence ratio between air and sludge was determined to maximize the yield of hydrogen. In the upgrading production, the effect of design parameters of distillation columns was studied.

4.1 Validation of simulation results

According to the previous section, the yield of products in an HTL reactor is specified because the HTL reactions are quite complex. In addition, the literature has provided information on the mass fraction of 44 compounds. A comparison between the simulation results and the literature data is presented in Table 3, which demonstrates the accuracy of the simulation results with a low percentage deviation. However, the deviation of heptane is high. This is because the significant figures of the literature are 4. While the significant figures of the simulation are 6. In this research, 4 significant digits are reported. For the bio-oil upgrading reactor, it is assumed that 35 reactions and fractional conversion govern the percentages of C, H, O, N content. The comparison of the percentages of C, H, O, N content, as shown in Table 4, further confirms the accuracy of the simulation results, with a low percentage deviation observed.

4.2 Effect of equivalence ratio (ER)

In this section, the effect of the equivalence ratio in the Gibb reactor is studied by sensitivity analysis. The composition and flow rate of products are computed. Thus, the production yields from literatures are not required. Figure 3 illustrates the relationship between gas yields of H_2, CO and CO_2 and the equivalence ratio, which represents the ratio of wastewater to air. The temperature of the Gibb reactor is fixed at 620 °C. The possible reactions in the Gibb reactor include reforming, cracking, and combustion. Hydrogen is formed by reforming and cracking, while CO and CO_2 are formed by combustion of fuel. However, the ER ratio should not be too high due to the increased formation of CO_2. Thus, the optimal ER ratio is crucial. Considering an air flow rate of 2500 kmol/h, the maximum yield of H_2 amounts to 76.8 kg/h (82.8 kmol/h). Subsequently, the gaseous product mixture is sent to the membrane to purify and produce hydrogen of 99 wt% [8]. The hydrogen yield after purification is 76.05 kg/h.

Table 3. The comparison of composition in HTL reactor between literatures and simulation results

Composition	Mass fraction		
	Reported literature	Simulation	% deviation
Water	0.8466	0.8465	0.01181
Hydrogen	0.0000	1.466×10^{-5}	1.466×10^{-5}
Nitrogen	0.0001	1.085×10^{-4}	0
Carbon dioxide	0.0285	0.0285	0
Carbon monoxide	0.0002	2.082×10^{-4}	0
Methane	0.0003	3.108×10^{-4}	0
Ethane	0.0002	1.525×10^{-4}	0
Ammonia	0.0084	8.372×10^{-3}	0
Ethylene	0.0001	8.907×10^{-5}	10.93
Propane	0.0002	2.672×10^{-4}	0
n-Butane	0.0010	9.797×10^{-4}	2.030
Formic acid	0.0087	8.729×10^{-3}	0.3333
Acetic acid	0.0022	2.226×10^{-3}	0.9090
Glycerol	0.0015	1.425×10^{-3}	5
Phenol	0.0014	1.389×10^{-3}	0.7857
Vinyl cyclohexene	0.0002	1.998×10^{-4}	0.055
o-Cresol	0	0	0
p-Cresol	0	0	0
2,5-Pyrrolidinedione, 1-ethyl-	0.0001	7.196×10^{-5}	28.04
2,3-Xylenol	0.0004	3.678×10^{-4}	8.25
Cyclohexanone, 2,6-diethyl-	0.0000	7.995×10^{-6}	7.995×10^{-6}
n-Hexane	0.0000	2.398×10^{-5}	2.398×10^{-5}

Composition	Mass fraction		
	Reported literature	Simulation	% deviation
n-Heptane	0.0001	1.439×10^{-4}	43.9
n-Octane	0.0000	7.995×10^{-6}	7.995×10^{-6}
5-Hydroxymethylfurfural	0.0012	1.175×10^{-3}	2.051
n-Hexadecanoic acid	0.0048	4.813×10^{-3}	0.2708
n-Tetradecanoic acid	0.0036	3.622×10^{-3}	0.6111
Stearic acid	0.0076	7.603×10^{-3}	0.0394
Pyrimidine, 2-methyl-	0.0188	1.879×10^{-2}	0.0218
Dodecanoic acid, 3-hydroxy-	0.0015	1.514×10^{-3}	0.9480
1-Ethyl-2-Pyrrolidinone	0.0011	1.108×10^{-3}	0.7272
n-Methylythipyrrolidone	0.0019	1.959×10^{-3}	2.6315
Ethylbenzene	0.0001	1.199×10^{-4}	10
p-EthylPhenol	0	0	0
Indole	0	0	0
7-Methylindole	0.0088	8.803×10^{-3}	0.0340
Myristic amide	0.0049	4.861×10^{-3}	0.8163
Palmitic acid amide [Hexadecanamide]	0.0096	9.554×10^{-3}	0.4697
Octadecamide	0.0082	8.203×10^{-3}	0.0365
n-Hexadecanoic acid	0.0030	2.966×10^{-3}	1.3333
Naphthalene	0.0008	7.995×10^{-4}	0.1250
β-Cholesterol	0.0166	1.655×10^{-2}	0.3012
N,N′-Diphenyl-p-phenylenediamine	0.0072	7.236×10^{-3}	0.4167
Di-n-Undecyl-Phthalate	0.0001	1×10^{-4}	0

4.3 Effect of design parameters of distillation column of the liquid products

The purification section comprises 10 distillation columns. Although flash separation effectively removes a significant portion of gaseous products, some residual gases remain due to the presence of numerous components. The first distillation column (B21) employs three stages to ensure the complete removal of gases, employing a reflux ratio of 0.06. Key components targeted for separation in this column are butane and hexane. Components with lower boiling points than butane are removed overhead, resulting in gaseous products such as carbon dioxide, ammonia, methane, ethylene, propane, butane, hydrogen sulfide and ethylamine.

The remaining distillation columns are designed to separate key components based on the fuel type, taking into account their respective quantities and boiling points. For instance, distillation column B25 is dedicated to gasoline separation. Thus, 1-methyl-ethylcyclohexane is represented as a light key component while undecane is a heavy key component. In distillation column B27, cyclohexane is the designated light key component, while ethylenediamine is the heavy key component. The distillation column B33 focuses on kerosene separation, with kerosene itself acting as the light key component, while hydrocarbon compounds above C15 serve as the heavy key component. Finally, the distillation column B35 is employed for the purification of diesel and fuel oil. Diesel is considered the light key component in this column, while fuel oil takes the role of the heavy key component. The effect of various parameters such as the number of stages, reflux ratio, and distillation conditions on all distillation columns is investigated.

The effect of the number of stages on the purity of gasoline is shown in Figure 4. It can be seen that the specification of gasoline is not achieved with 20 stages. The presence of ethylenediamine in the gasoline mixture results in a lower high heating value. To solve this issue, the distillation columns B27 and B30 are used. It was found that the distillation column B27 effectively removes ethylenediamine from the gasoline stream.

Table 4. The comparison of composition in bio-oil upgrading reactor between literatures and simulation results

%wt	Literature	Simulation	% deviation
C	86.1	85.89	0.22
H	13.89	14.11	C
O	0	0	0
N	0	0	0

 https://doi.org/10.1051/e3sconf/202342801004

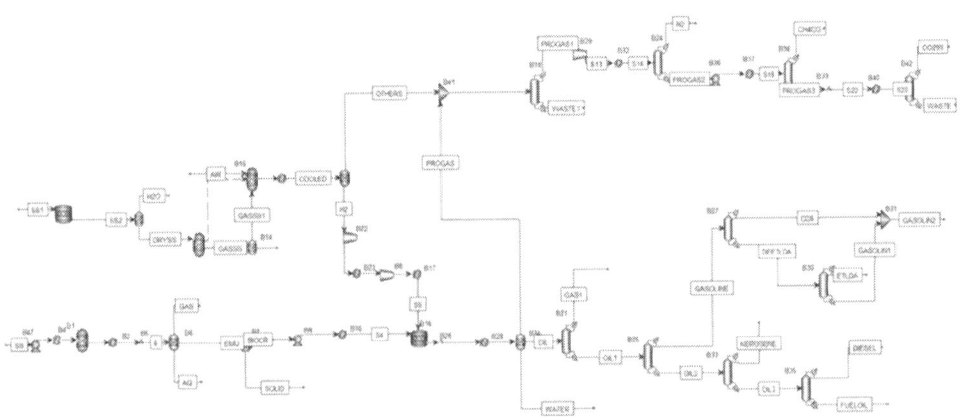

Fig. 2. Conceptual design of the integrated process.

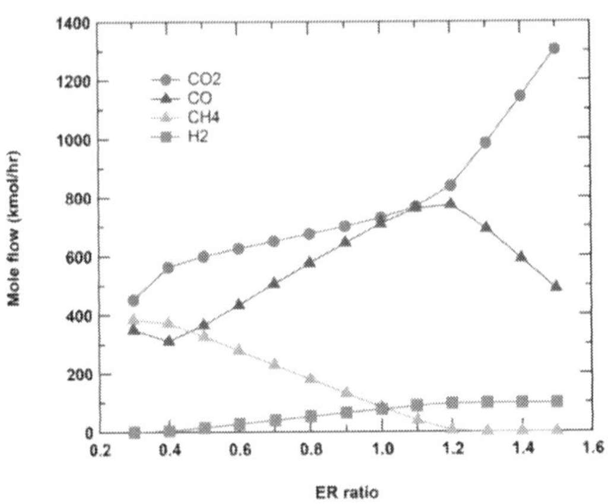

Fig. 3. Effect of ER ratio of mole flow of H_2, CO, CO_2, CH_4.

Figures 5 and 6 demonstrate that by increasing the distillate rate and reflux ratio, can be successfully separated from the lighter components. Consequently, the components with lower boiling points than cyclohexane are collected at the overhead of the distillation column. A distillate rate of 1.15 kmol/h and a reflux ratio of 2 are selected. Furthermore, considering the number of stages, an increased number of stages leads to the removal of gasoline at the overhead of the column, as depicted in Figure 7. Due to the close similarity in boiling points of hydrocarbon compounds (C6-C7), a higher number of stages, specifically 20 stages, is required. The main components in the gasoline stream (CC6) primarily consist of hexane and heptane. However, the effluent stream at the bottom of the distillation column still contains a mixture of gasoline and ethylenediamine.

The distillation column (B30) is used to remove ethylenediamine at the top of the column. However, this distillation allows octane, ethyl cyclohexane to be collected at the top of the column. This is because the boiling point of ethylenediamine, octane, ethyl cyclohexane are close. Consequently, a small amount of octane and ethyl cyclohexane may mix with ethylenediamine.

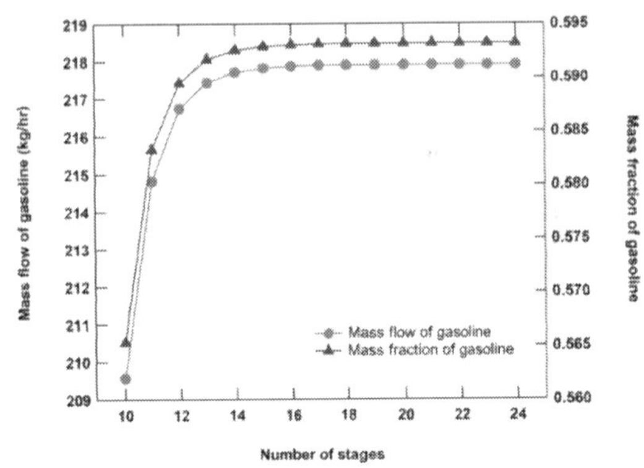

Fig. 4. Number of stages of the distillation (B27)

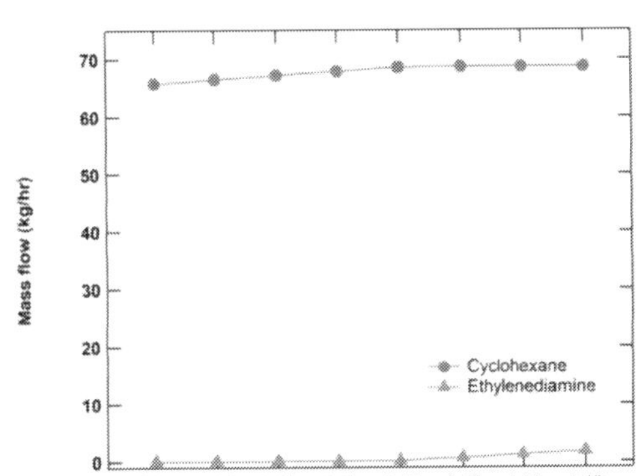

Fig. 5. Effect of distillate rate of the distillation (B27)

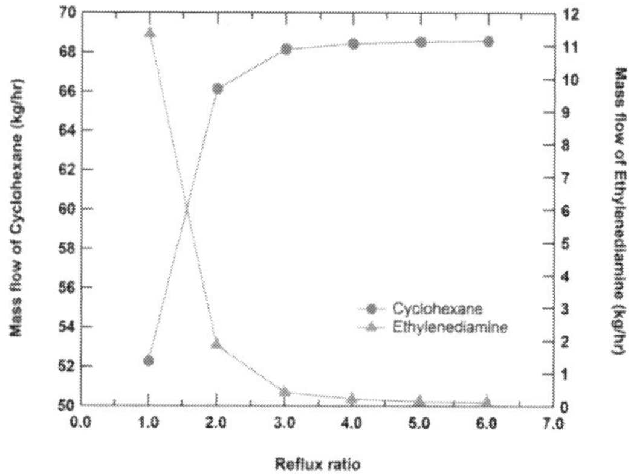

Fig. 6. Effect of reflux ratio of the distillation (B27)

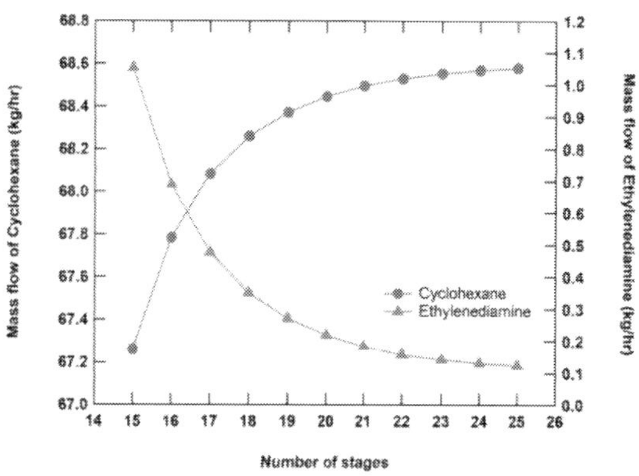

Fig. 7. Effect of the numbers of stages of the distillation (B27)

Figure 8 shows that 1-methyl-ethyl cyclohexane is separated at the bottom of the column as the reflux ratio increases. However, an increase in the reflux ratio also raises the reboiler heat duty. Hence, the reflux ratio of 3 is chosen when the number of stages is 25 stages. Increasing of the number of stages can decrease mole flow of 1-methyl, ethyl cyclohexane at the top of the column as shown in Figure 9. This implies that the distillation (B30) can separate ethylenediamine. Finally, the purified gasoline is a combination of the overhead stream from the distillation column (B27) and the bottom of the distillation column (B30). The quantity of gasoline obtained is 205.07 kg/h. This gasoline meets the product specification in terms of specific gravity, which is 0.7813. However, the simulated gasoline has a higher flash point (-10°C) compared to standard gasoline (-43°C). This is due to the presence of additional components, such as aromatic hydrocarbons, in standard gasoline.

The distillation column (B33) is responsible for purifying kerosene. The reflux ratio and number of stages play crucial roles in achieving the desired purity of kerosene. By increasing the reflux ratio, the purity of kerosene can meet the specification. As a result, kerosene can be collected at the top of the column, while diesel and fuel oil are obtained from the bottom. Figure 10 demonstrates that a reflux ratio of 5 yields a mass fraction of kerosene of 0.99. Moreover, an increase in the number of stages enhances the mole flow and mass fraction of kerosene at the top of the column, as depicted in Figure 11. The quantity of kerosene produced is 134.08 kg/h. The specific gravity of the simulated kerosene is 0.7832, slightly lower than the standard kerosene's specific gravity of 0.79. This variation arises from the presence of paraffins and cycloalkanes in this work's kerosene, while the standard kerosene typically contains paraffins and aromatic hydrocarbons.

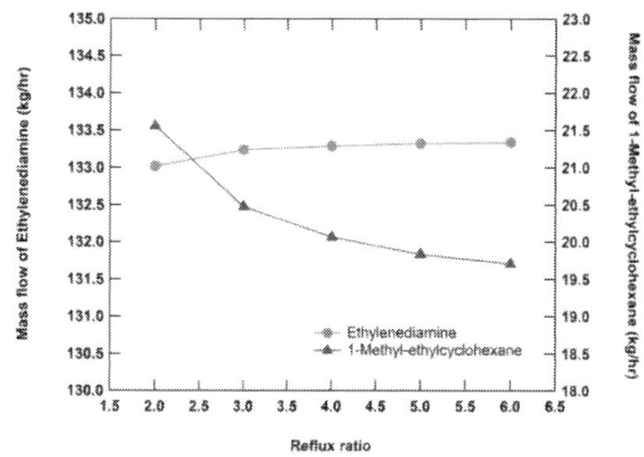

Fig. 8. Effect of reflux ratio of the distillation (B30)

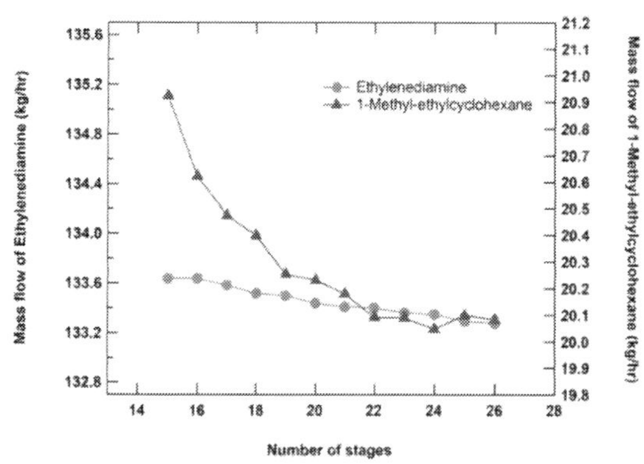

Fig. 9. Effect of number of stages of the distillation (B30)

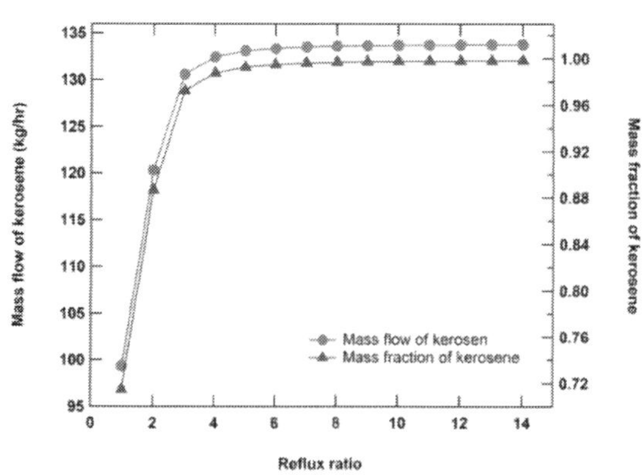

Fig. 10. Effect of reflux ratio of the distillation (B33)

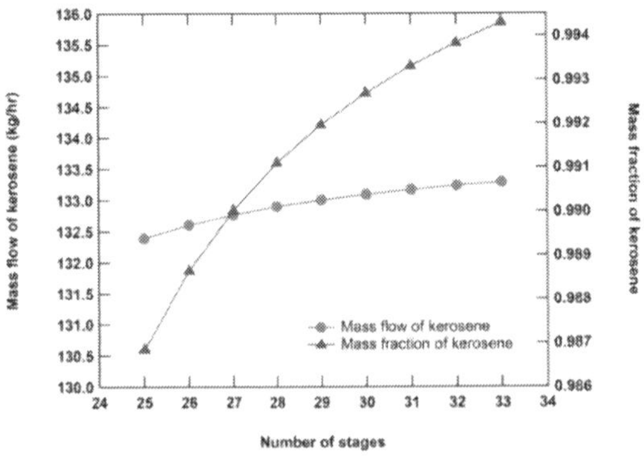

Fig. 11. Effect of number of stages of the distillation (B33)

The distillation column (B35) effectively separates diesel from fuel oil. The mole flow and mass fraction of diesel remain unchanged with varying reflux ratios, so a fixed reflux ratio of 0.5 is chosen. On the other hand, the number of stages plays a crucial role, as illustrated in Figure 12. Optimal performance is achieved with 30 stages, ensuring that both diesel (with a mass fraction of 0.99) and fuel oil (with a mass fraction of 0.99) meet the specification, as depicted in Figure 13. The quantity of diesel obtained is 424.899 kg/h, while the amount of fuel oil is 242.496 kg/h.

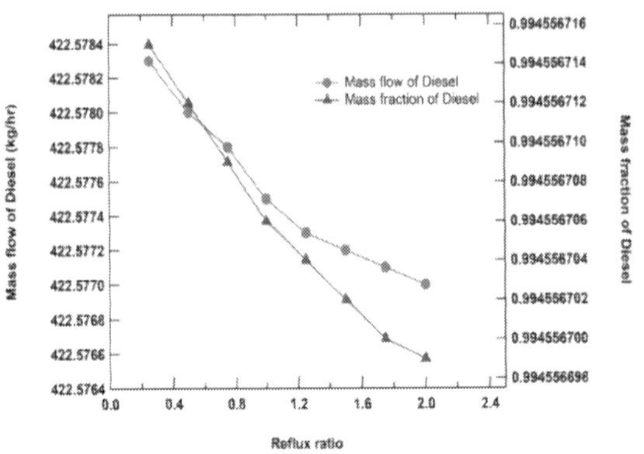

Fig. 12. Effect of reflux ratio of the distillation (B35)

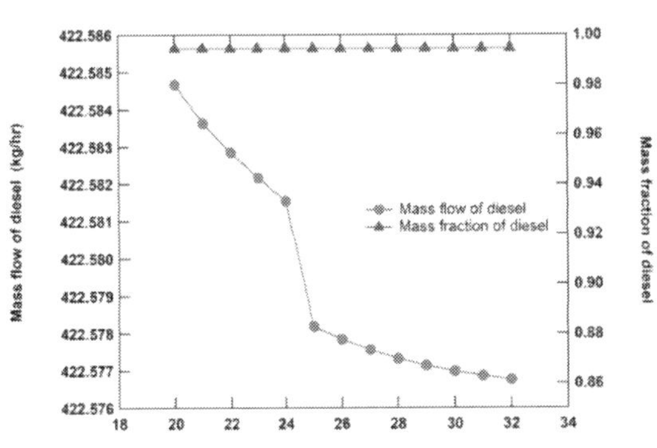

Fig. 13. Effect of number of stages of the distillation (B35)

In terms of the purification sequence for gaseous products, a direct sequence of distillation columns is employed. The first distillation column (B18) is utilized to remove waste gases such as Ethylenediamine, Cyclohexane, Cis-1-Methyl-3-Ethylcyclohexane, Methyl amine, Ethylamine, and hexane. Subsequently, the distillation columns (B24), (B38), and (B42) are arranged to further purify the gaseous products. The resulting sequence involves the separation of nitrogen as the first product, followed by the mixture of methane and carbon monoxide, and finally carbon dioxide. These gaseous products can attain a high purity level of 0.99 wt%. The specific impact of the distillation column parameters is not discussed in this work.

4.4 Carbon footprint

In this work, the carbon footprint refers to the total greenhouse gas (GHG) emissions generated by the activities in the process. The unit of measurement used is kg CO_2 equivalent, which provides a metric measure for comparing different greenhouse gas emissions. The emissions are caused by heating, cooling, and pumping, which involve various heat and cooling sources. Specifically, the heating process utilizes natural gas combustion in industrial equipment, while cooling requires chill water.

Figure 14 illustrates that certain unit operations contribute to GHG emissions, particularly the heater (B4), the cooler (B2), and the HTL reactor (B1). This indicates that the bio-oil production process through hydrothermal liquefaction (HTL) results in higher GHG emissions compared to the hydrogen production process and the upgrading process. The elevated emissions can be attributed to the high operating temperature of 350 °C and the high operating pressure of 200 bar associated with the HTL reactor.

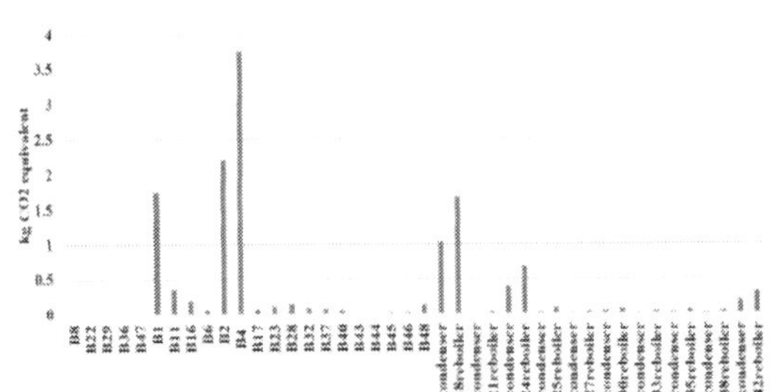

Fig. 14. GHG emissions contributed by unit operations

5 Conclusion

This work proposed an integrated process for bio-oil production and hydrogen production using sewage sludge from wastewater. The bio-oil is further upgraded through hydrogenation processes, utilizing hydrogen obtained from the hydrogen production stage. The performance analysis highlights the significance of the distillation arrangement in the separation process. This integrated process serves as a preliminary guideline for wastewater pretreatment and enables the production of various fuel oil types, including gasoline, kerosene, diesel, and fuel oil. Furthermore, the process generates gaseous byproducts such as nitrogen gas with a purity of 99% and liquid carbon dioxide with a purity of 99%. It is important to note that the bio-oil production process exhibits the highest greenhouse gas (GHG) emissions compared to the hydrogen production and upgrading processes. However, the adverse environmental impact can be mitigated through the design of a heat exchanger network.

Acknowledgements

The authors would like to acknowledge the support of LCSoft program from PSE for SPEED. This research was funded by Faculty of Applied Science, King Mongkut's University of Technology North Bangkok, Thailand contact Number 642067.

References

1. T.X. Do, H. Prajitno, Y. Lim, J. Kim, Process modelling and economic analysis for bio-heavy-oil production from sewage sludge using supercritical ethanol and methanol, The Journal of Supercritical Fluid, **150** (2019): 137-146
2. D. Catello, M.S. Haider, L.A. Rosendahl, Catalytic upgrading of hydrothermal liquefaction biocrudes: Different challenges for different feedstocks, Renewable Energy, **141** (2019): 420-430
3. H. Bayat, M. Dehghanizadeh, J.M. Jarvis, C.E. Brewer, U. Jena, Hydrothermal liquefaction of food waste : Effect of process parameters on product yields and chemistry, Frontiers in Sustainable Food Systems, **5** (2021)
4. H. Wang, P.A. Meyer, D.M. Santosa, C. Zhu, M.V. Olarte, S.B. Jones, A.H. Zacher, Performance and techno-economic evaluations of co-processing residual heavy fraction in bio-oil hydrotreating, Catalysis Today, **365** (2021): 357-364
5. R. Kumar, V. Stezov, Thermochemical production of bio-oil : A review of downstream processing technologies for bio-oil upgrading, production of hydrogen and high value - added products, Renewable and Sustainable Energy Reviews, **135** (2021): 110152
6. J.S. dos Passos, P. Straka, M. Auersvald, P. Biller, Upgrading hydrothermal liquefaction biocrudes from mono- and co-liquefaction of cow manure and wheat straw through hydrotreating and distillation, Chemical Engineering Journal, **452** (2023): 139636
7. Y.A. Situmorang, Z. Zhao, P. An, T. Yu, J. Rizkiana, A. Abudula, G. Guan, A novel system of biomass-based hydrogen production by combining steam bio-oil reforming and chemical looping process, Applied Energy, **268** (2020): 115122
8. R. Kumar, V. Strezov, Thermochemical production of bio-oil : A review of downstream processing technologies for bio-oil upgrading, production of hydrogen and high value-added product, Renewable and Sustainable Energy Review, **135** (2021): 110152
9. E.M. Lozano, S. Lokke, L.A. Rosendahl, T.H. Pedersen, Production of marine biofuels from hydrothermal liquefaction of sewage sludge : Preliminary techno-economic analysis and life-cycle GHG emissions assessment of Dutch case study, Energy Conversion and Management : X, **14** (2022): 100178
10. B. Li, G. He, X. Jiang, Y. Dai, X. Ruan, Pressure swing adsorption/membrane hybrid processes for hydrogen purification with a high recovery, Frontiers of Chemical Science and Engineering, **10** (2016): 255-264

Spirulina Cultivation Using Biogas CO_2 as the Carbon Source: Preliminary Study on Biomass Growth and Productivity

Raj Kumar Oruganti[1], *Madhu* Kumar Kumara[1], *Rakesh* Tejavath[1], *Malinee* Sriariyanun[2], and *Debraj* Bhattacharyya[1,*]

[1] Department of Civil Engineering, Indian Institute of Technology Hyderabad, Sangareddy, Telangana, India
[2] Biorefinery and Process Automation Engineering Center, Department of Chemical and Process Engineering, The Sirindhorn Thai-German International Graduate School of Engineering, King Mongkut's University of Technology North Bangkok, Thailand

Abstract. Anthropogenic activities are causing a rapid increase in global carbon dioxide (CO_2) emissions, which significantly contribute to global warming. Microalgae can be a sustainable solution for simultaneous wastewater treatment and sequestering CO_2 through photosynthesis. The current study reports a comparative evaluation of *Spirulina* sp. microalgal biomass growth and lipid productivity during its cultivation supplied with air and biogas from an anaerobic digester. It was observed that there was a 4-fold increase in biomass productivity in the reactor sparged with biogas compared to air supply. The reactor sparged with biogas showed a significant increase in lipid content. This increase in biomass productivity could be attributed to the increased availability of CO_2, favoring algal growth.

Keywords. Biogas, Biomass productivity, CO_2 sequestration, Lipid content, *Spirulina*

1 Introduction

Anaerobic digestion presents an economically viable and environmentally sustainable approach to organic waste management. Also, it plays a significant role in satisfying global renewable energy demands through biogas production [1]. Conventionally, the biogas generated from anaerobic digestors is used for heat/electricity production due to its methane concentration (55-65%). However, it also contains significant amounts of other gases, such as carbon dioxide (30-40%), nitrogen (0-3%), water vapor (5-10%), oxygen (0-1%), and hydrogen sulfide (0-10,000 ppmv) [2]. For the commercial utilization of biogas in combustion engines or natural gas grids, the biogas needs to undergo partial or complete purification and the high levels of CO_2 in biogas result in a decrease in its heating value. When used in internal combustion engines, this elevated CO_2 concentration leads to increased emissions of carbon monoxide and hydrocarbons [3]. The national or regional standards regulations stipulate that methane content should be ≥ 90-95%, carbon dioxide content of ≤ 2-4%, and minimal traces of oxygen and hydrogen sulfide in the upgraded biomethane [4]. Biogas purification using physio-chemical technologies such as chemical scrubbing and adsorption requires significant chemical and energy consumption, adversely affecting the economic and environmental sustainability of the process [5]. Moreover, the carbon dioxide that was separated during the upgrading process is emitted into the atmosphere. CO_2 accounts for around 68% of the total atmospheric Green House Gas (GHG) emissions [6]. The continuous increase in its atmospheric concentration is contributing to global warming. Hence, there is an increased interest in alternative technologies that minimize carbon emissions.

Microalgae have recently gained significant attention due to their remarkable ability to fix CO_2 through biomass production and their low operational costs and environmental consequences [7]. Microalgae have a greater CO_2 fixation rate than terrestrial plants, and the CO_2 could be effectively utilized for increased biomass productivity [8]. It was reported that 1 kg of algae could fix approximately 1.83 kg of CO_2 [9]. The produced biomass during CO_2 sequestration can be converted into various value-added products such as biodiesel [10], bioethanol [11], and biohydrogen [12]. Microalgae perform photosynthesis in the presence of light and uptakes CO_2 for their growth. Microalgal biomass is also carbon negative and considered as the third-generation biofuel feedstock [13]. Integrating biogas upgrading using microalgae with simultaneous wastewater treatment can increase the economic and environmental sustainability of the process. The liquid digestate from the anaerobic digesters or the domestic wastewater could be used as a source of nutrients for microalgal growth [14]. For instance, Posadas *et. al.*, [15] have employed microalgae for simultaneous biogas upgrading and nutrient removal from a digester centrate in an outdoor high-rate algal pond. Also, it was reported that compared with air sparing, biogas sparging could significantly increase biomass productivity because of high CO_2 availability [16]. The atmospheric level of CO_2 is very low (0.0387% (v/v)) and is insufficient to achieve a high

* Corresponding author: debrajb@ce.iith.ac.in

rate microalgal biorefinery [17]. The carbon constitutes approximately 60% of the microalgal dry weight, thereby accounting for a significant portion of the associated costs with it during microalgal cultivation [18]. Iamtham *et. al.*, [19] have reported a carbon cost saving of 47.6% by utilizing flue gas CO_2 for microalgal cultivation. Hence, employing biogas CO_2 as the carbon source for microalgal cultivation reduces its costs and simultaneously results in biogas with high methane content having a high heating value. Also, several economic value products can be synthesized from the produced algal biomass. Therefore, leveraging biogas as a carbon source for algae cultivation offers significant advantages and holds great potential in sustainable and efficient algae production systems. The present study reports preliminary investigation studies on the comparative microalgal biomass productivity in open-air photobioreactors sparged with air supply and biogas from an anaerobic digester.

2 Materials and methods

2.1 Seed culture

The microalgae used in this study is the *Spirulina* species. The culture was collected from a commercial farm near Hyderabad city, Telangana. The obtained seed culture was transferred to a 2 L conical flask with nutrient media and an air supply of 3 L/min. Table 1 shows the nutrient media composition used in this study.

Table 1. Media composition.

Chemical	Quantity
$NaHCO_3$	8.0 g/L
NaCl	5.0 g/L
Urea	0.2 g/L
K_2SO_4	0.5 g/L
$MgSO_4$	0.16 g/L
H_3PO_4	0.052 mL/L
$FeSO_4$*	0.05 mL/L
Seed Culture	1.0 mL/L

*- $FeSO_4$- 10 g of $FeSO_4$ was dissolved in 100 mL of DI water, and 10 mL of was acid was added to $FeSO_4$

2.2 Experimental setup

Two duplicate sets of identical glass reactors were fabricated, with dimensions measuring 37 x 33.5 x 25 cm. The total volume of reactors was 30.99 liters with a working volume of 25 liters. Figure 1 (A) and Figure 1 (B) show the experimental reactor setups sparged with air and biogas, respectively. The air supply was provided through sparging, using aerators. The reactors with air supply were considered as the control to monitor *Spirulina* sp. growth under normal conditions.

Similarly, other reactors were sparged with biogas during day time and with air during night time. Diffusers with a surface area of 81.0732 cm^2 were used to distribute air and biogas in the reactors. The biogas flow rate of 0.8 L/min was maintained throughout the study period, while the reactors sparged with air were kept at an airflow rate of 1.5 L/min. The reactors were covered with transparent acrylic sheets to prevent dust or debris deposition. The reactors were kept in open-air conditions under natural sunlight. The average day time during the study period was around 13 h 30 min.

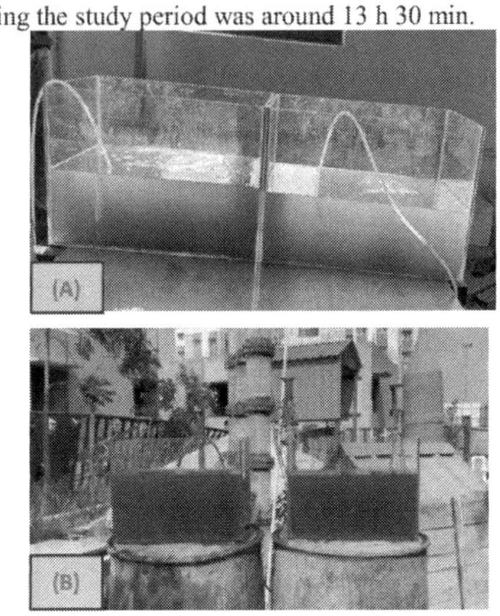

Fig. 1. Microalgal reactor setup used in the study, A- Reactors with aeration, B- Reactors with biogas sparging

2.3 Microalgal growth determination

The microalgal samples were collected daily from all the reactors and analyzed for optical density and chlorophyll content. The optical density was measured at 685 nm wavelength using a UV-Visible spectrophotometer (Make: LAB INDIA, Model: 3000+). The chlorophyll was estimated using method 10, 200 H of the *Standard Methods for Water and Wastewater Examination* [20]. The concentrations of chlorophyll pigments a, b, and c were estimated using the following equations (1-4). Total chlorophyll is calculated by the summation of pigment a, b, and c concentrations.

$$Chl_a\left(\frac{mg}{L}\right) = 11.58 \times (OD_{664}) - 1.54 \times (OD_{647}) - 0.08 \times (OD_{630}) \quad (1)$$

$$Chl_b\left(\frac{mg}{L}\right) = 21.03 \times (OD_{647}) - 5.43 \times (OD_{664}) - 2.66 \times (OD_{630}) \quad (2)$$

$$Chl_c\left(\frac{mg}{L}\right) = 24.52 \times (OD_{630}) - 7.60 \times (OD_{647}) - 1.67 \times (OD_{664}) \quad (3)$$

$$Total\ chlorophyll = Chl_a + Chl_b + Chl_c \quad (4)$$

The correlation between optical density versus dry biomass weight was used to estimate biomass growth. The microalgal biomass productivity (g/L/day) and specific growth rate (1/day) were determined using equations (5) and (6), respectively. N_t and N_i represent the biomass concentration corresponding to the time T_t and T_i, respectively. N_m represents the maximum biomass concentration, whereas N_0 is the initial biomass concentration.

$$Biomass\ productivity = \frac{N_t - N_i}{T_t - T_i} \quad (5)$$

$$Specific\ growth\ rate = \frac{\ln(N_m/N_0)}{T_m - T_0} \quad (6)$$

2.4 Estimation of Lipid Content

The biomass was collected at the end of the study and centrifuged at 5000 rpm for 15 min. The supernatant was disposed of, and the microalgal biomass was kept for drying at 60 °C in a hot air oven until a constant weight was achieved. The dried biomass was powdered using a mortar and pestle. The lipid content of the powered biomass was estimated by following the modified Bligh and Dyer method [21]. The lipid content was estimated according to the following equation (7).

$$Lipid\ (\%)_{dry\ basis} = \frac{Total\ oil\ extracted}{Dry\ biomass} \times 100 \quad (7)$$

3 Results and discussion

The change in the optical density with time for microalgal reactors with air and biogas supply is shown in Figure 2. The figure shows that the reactors sparged with biogas showed a significant growth rate compared to the control reactors with air sparging.

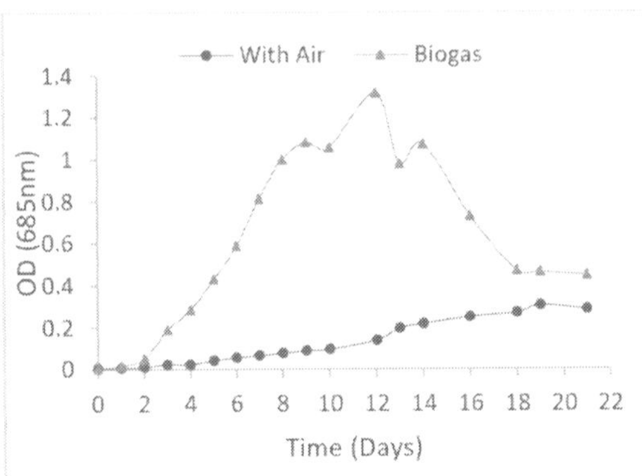

Fig. 2. Change in optical density during the study period.

It is observed from Figure 2 that OD, which is considered the parameter to observe microalgae growth, was found to vary throughout the study period for reactors sparged with biogas. A steep increase in OD was observed during the initial days of reactor operation. OD was found to be increasing up to the 12th day of reactor operation. On saturation of OD on the 12th day of reactor operation, OD declined until the 18th day. Later constant OD was observed up to the 21st day of reactor operation. While there was a rapid change in the OD over the study period in biogas-sparged reactors, air-sparged reactors showed a steady-slow increase in OD was observed until the 18th day of reactor operation. Further, the reactor OD was stable until the 21st day of the reactor operation. Change in the total chlorophyll over the reactor operation period is presented in Figure 3. The overall chlorophyll content was found to be higher in the reactors sparged with biogas throughout the reactor operation period when compared to that of reactors sparged with air. However, in biogas-sparged reactors, chlorophyll values increased steadily until the 12th day and further reduced till the 18th day. It can be observed from Figure 2 that chlorophyll contents variation in both the air and biogas-sparged reactors followed the same trend as that of OD. From Figure 2 and 3, it can be observed that there is a decrease in biomass growth after the 12th day in biogas sparged reactors. This decrease in OD and chlorophyll values could be attributed to a higher biomass growth rate, resulting in nutrient exhaustion leading to cell decay. In the current study, the reactors were operated in batch mode, meaning no additional media or substrate was added during reactor operation. In batch cultures, the cells go through four different phases of the growth cycle: lag phase, log or exponential phase, stationary phase, followed by decay or death phase. In the present study, the lag phase is reduced in biogas sparged reactors, and the exponential growth rate is significantly higher than in the control reactors with air supply. The cultures in the biogas sparged reactors reached the saturation phase earlier than the air sparged reactors, resulting in a limitation of the nutrients (nitrogen and phosphorus). After the 12th day, the culture in biogas sparged reactors might have entered the decay phase due to limited nutrient availability.

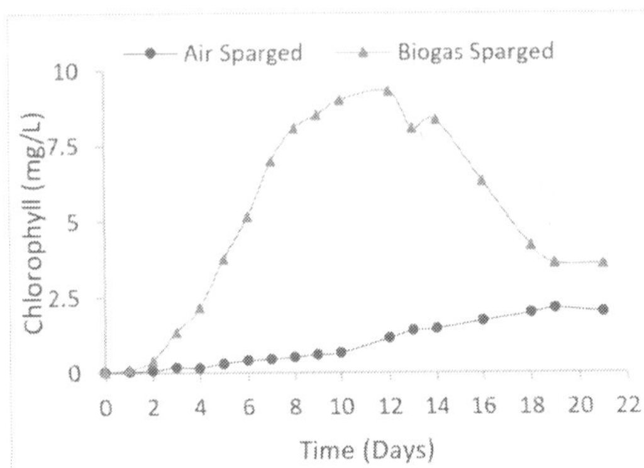

Fig. 3. Change in the Total Chlorophyll during the study period.

Figure 4 shows the correlation plot between dry biomass weight and the optical density. The correlation equation of Y= 476.68x with R^2 of 0.9903 was obtained, depicting a linear relation between dry-weight (Y) and OD (x). The correlation equation was used to estimate the growth rate on dry biomass basis. The maximum biomass productivity of 0.123 g/L/day and specific growth rate of 0.48 per day was observed for the reactor sparged with biogas. Whereas, in control reactors with only air sparging, the maximum biomass productivity and the specific growth rate were observed to be 0.027 g/L/day and 0.23 per day, respectively. Previous studies have reported similar observations for different algal species [22-24]. Jiang *et. al.,* [25] have reported the biomass productivity of *Nannochloropsis sp.* (sea algae) in the range of 0.161-0.212 g/L. Zhu *et. al.,* [26] have reported the *Spirulina* biomass productivity of 0.195 g/L/day with air supply, which increased to 0.259 g/L/day with increasing the CO_2 concentration to 15%. Also, the specific growth increased from 0.19 per day to 0.26 per day with CO_2 supplementation [26]. In the present study, the biomass productivity rate of reactors sparged with biogas CO_2 was 4-fold higher than that of air-sparged reactors indicating the advantages of biogas application in cultivating *Spirulina* species. In the case of biogas-sparged reactors, biomass productivity was found to be increasing until the 8th day of reactors operation. Further, it decreased, which was negative at the end of the 21st day. This is possibly due to cell death in the reactors, which is also evident from reduced OD and chlorophyll contents. In the case of air-sparged reactors, the biomass productivity was slowly increasing until the 13th day of the reactor run. Further, it slightly decreased until the 18th day of the reactor operation.

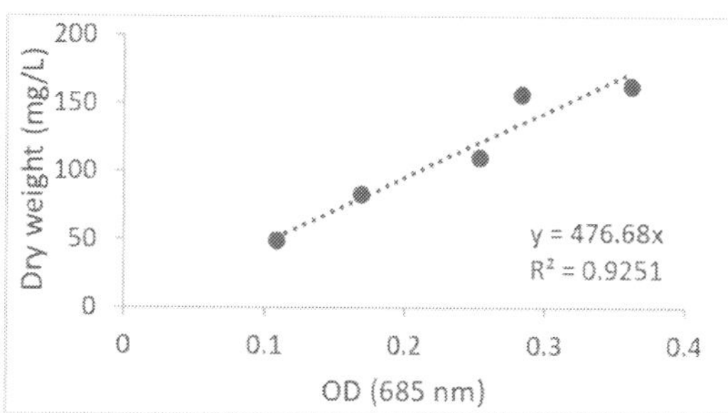

Fig. 4. Correlation between OD and dry-weight.

Microalgae are the photosynthetic microorganisms responsible for more than half of global CO_2 fixation. Microalgae perform photosynthesis in the presence of light by uptaking the dissolved inorganic carbon present in different forms, such as H_2CO_3, HCO_3^-, CO_2, and CO_3^{2-}. This metabolic process is facilitated by the Calvin-Benson cycle, in which the Rubisco enzyme plays a critical role in converting CO_2 into organic compounds. Photosynthesis in microalgae can be categorized into a light-dependent phase and a light-independent or dark phase. In the light-dependent phase, light energy converts NADP+ and ADP into energy-rich NADPH and ATP molecules [27]. The dark phase involves CO_2 fixation and assimilation through the Calvin-Benson cycle by Rubisco enzyme activity, utilizing the NADPH and ATP generated in the light-dependent phase to produce organic compounds like glucose [28]. However, due to its oxygenase activity, Rubisco has a limited affinity for CO_2, resulting in inefficient CO_2 fixation [29]. To overcome this, microalgae employ CO_2 concentrating mechanisms (CCMs) that enhance the localized concentration of CO_2 near Rubisco [30]. CO_2 is one of the limiting substrates in aquatic systems [31]. In the current study, the significant biomass growth rate observed in the photobioreactors supplied with biogas could be attributed to the higher availability of CO_2 for fixation by microalgae. Similar observations have been reported by Miyawaki *et. al.,* [3] during simultaneous biogas purification and wastewater treatment by airlift photobioreactors. They have reported a 70% increase in biomass productivity and lipid content by four times compared with reactors having only an air supply [3]. Jiang *et. al.,* [25] also reported a biomass increase from 0.72 g/L to 2.23 g/L in *Nannochloropsis* sp. cultivated with 15% CO_2 flue gas compared with air supply [25].

The lipids content (dry basis) was estimated using Eq-7. The estimated lipid content for the photobioreactors sparged with air was observed to be 21.2 ± 0.57%. While in the case of photobioreactors sparged with biogas, the lipid content was found to be 28.2 ± 1.41% on a dry basis. The lipid content was found to be 1.4 times more in the photobioreactors sparged with biogas when compared to that of photobioreactors sparged with air. The increase in percentage lipid content was significant. Similar observations have been reported in the literature for different algal species cultivated with CO_2 supply [18,32]. For instance, Saifuddin *et al.,* [33] have reported an increase in lipid productivity from 7.8 mg/L/day to 18.93 mg/L/day by increasing the CO_2 supply from 1% to 15% during *Nannochloropsis* sp. cultivation using CO_2 as the carbon source [33]. El Baky *et. al.,* [34] have also reported that the lipid content was increased from 2.33% to 40.65% by rising CO_2 levels from 0.01% to 12.0%, respectively, during the cultivation of marine microalgae species *Dunaliella salina* [34]. At elevated CO_2 concentrations, the microalgae may prioritize the synthesis of lipids over other components, specifically proteins. This preference is attributed to the mechanism by which the algae capture and utilize extra carbon as an energy reserve to support their growth. Also, increased lipid accumulation in many algal species could be attributed to their adaptive approach to the availability of CO_2 levels within their natural habitat.

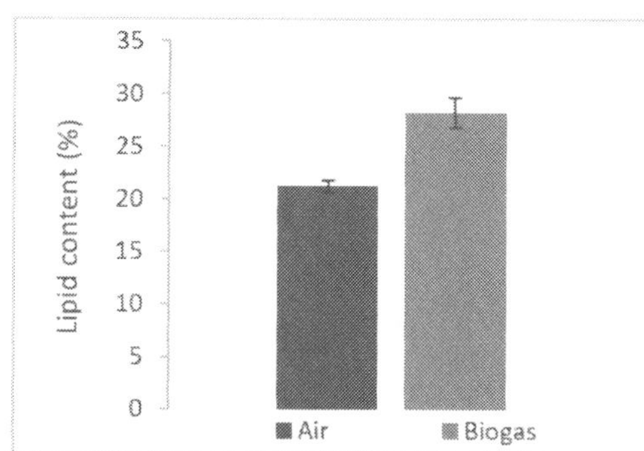

Fig. 5. Lipid contents in the photobioreactor with air and biogas supply.

4 Conclusion

Microalgae has a significant potential for biogas CO_2 uptake. The present study evaluated the growth of *Spirulina* sp. with the supply of biogas CO_2 as the carbon source. This study also investigated biomass growth and lipid productivity in open-air algal photobioreactors with air supply and biogas sparging. The results demonstrate that the microalgal photobioreactors provided with biogas sparging have shown a 4-fold increase in maximum biomass productivity and higher specific growth rate than reactors with only air supply. The biogas sparging significantly increased lipid content compared to the air sparging. Further studies are needed to optimize the biogas sparging rate and reactor configuration, quantifying the microalgal CO_2 absorption rate and the effect of other environmental factors for an efficient microalgal biorefinery.

Acknowledgment

This work was supported by NSL Sugars Limited.

References

1. A. Toledo-Cervantes, M.L. Serejo, S. Blanco, R. Pérez, R. Lebrero, R. Muñoz, Photosynthetic biogas upgrading to bio-methane: Boosting nutrient recovery via biomass productivity control, Algal Research, **17** (2016): 46-52
2. L. Méndez, D. García, E. Perez, S. Blanco, R. Muñoz, Photosynthetic upgrading of biogas from anaerobic digestion of mixed sludge in an outdoors algal-bacterial photobioreactor at pilot scale, Journal of Water Process Engineering, **48** (2022): 102891
3. B. Miyawaki, A.B. Mariano, J.V.C. Vargas, W. Balmant, A.C. Defrancheschi, D.O. Corrêa, B. Santos, N.F.H. Selesu, J.C. Ordonez, V.M. Kava, Microalgae derived biomass and bioenergy production enhancement through biogas purification and wastewater treatment, Renewable Energy, **163** (2021): 1153-1165
4. D. Marín, A. A. Carmona-Martínez, R. Lebrero, R. Muñoz, Influence of the diffuser type and liquid-to-biogas ratio on biogas upgrading performance in an outdoor pilot scale high rate algal pond, Fuel, **275** (2020): 117999
5. R. Muñoz, L. Meier, I. Diaz, D. Jeison, Rev. Environ. A review on the state-of-the-art of physical/chemical and biological technologies for biogas upgrading, Reviews in Environmental Science and Bio/Technology, **14** (2015): 727-759
6. V. Bhola, F. Swalaha, R. Ranjith Kumar, M. Singh, F. Bux, Overview of the potential of microalgae for CO 2 sequestration, International Journal of Environmental Science and Technology, **11** (2014): 2103-2118
7. J.O. Ighalo, K. Dulta, S.B. Kurniawan, F.O. Omoarukhe, U. Ewuzie, S.O. Eshiemogie, A.U. Ojo, S.R.S. Abdullah, Progress in microalgae application for CO2 sequestration, Cleaner Chemical Engineering, (2022): 100044
8. J. Alberto, V. Costa, G. A. Linde, D. Ibraim, P. Atala, Modelling of growth conditions for cyanobacterium Spirulina platensis in microcosms, World Journal of Microbiology and Biotechnology, **16** (2000): 15-18
9. T.S. Gendy, S.A. El-Temtamy, Commercialization potential aspects of microalgae for biofuel production: an overview, Egyptian Journal of Petroleum, **22**,1 (2013): 43-51
10. Y. Chisti, Biodiesel from microalgae, Biotechnology advances, **25**,3 (2007): 294-306
11. W.J. Fu, Z. Chi, Z.C. Ma, H.X. Zhou, G.L. Liu, C.F. Lee, Z.M. Chi, Hydrocarbons, the advanced biofuels produced by different organisms, the evidence that alkanes in petroleum can be renewable, Applied microbiology and biotechnology, **99** (2015): 7481-7494
12. J.V.C. Vargas, A.B. Mariano, D.O. Corrêa, J.C. Ordonez, The microalgae derived hydrogen process in compact photobioreactors, international journal of hydrogen energy, **39**,18 (2014): 9588-9598
13. J.P. Maity, J. Bundschuh, C.Y. Chen, P. Bhattacharya, Microalgae for third generation biofuel production, mitigation of greenhouse gas emissions and wastewater treatment: Present and future perspectives-A mini review, Energy, **78** (2014): 104-113
14. M. del R. Rodero, E. Posadas, A. Toledo-Cervantes, R. Lebrero, R. Muñoz, Influence of alkalinity and temperature on photosynthetic biogas upgrading efficiency in high rate algal ponds, Algal research, **33** (2018): 284-290
15. E. Posadas, D. Marín, S. Blanco, R. Lebrero, R. Muñoz, Simultaneous biogas upgrading and centrate treatment in an outdoors pilot scale high rate algal pond, Bioresource Technology, **232** (2017): 133-141
16. X. Li, Y. Lu, N. Li, Y. Wang, R. Yu, G. Zhu, R. J. Zeng, Mixotrophic cultivation of microalgae using biogas as the substrate, Environmental Science & Technology, **56**,6 (2022): 3669-3677
17. A. Kumar, S. Ergas, X. Yuan, A. Sahu, Q. Zhang, J. Dewulf, F.X. Malcata, H. van Langenhove, Enhanced CO2 fixation and biofuel production via microalgae: recent developments and future directions, Trends in biotechnology, **28**,7 (2010): 371-380
18. A.C. Eloka-Eboka, F.L. Inambao, Effects of CO2 sequestration on lipid and biomass productivity in microalgal biomass production, Applied Energy, **195** (2017): 1100-1111
19. S. Iamtham, P. Sornchai, Biofixation of CO2 from a power plant through large-scale cultivation of Spirulina maxima, South African Journal of Botany, **147** (2022): 840-851

20. J.A. Siegel, P.J. Saukko, Encyclopedia of forensic sciences: Second edition, Encyclopedia of Forensic Sciences: Second Edition, (2012): 1-2250
21. E.G. Bligh, W.J. Dyer, Can. J. Biochem. Physiol. A Can. J. Biochem. Physiol, **37** (1959): 911-917
22. D. Tang, W. Han, P. Li, X. Miao, J. Zhong, CO2 biofixation and fatty acid composition of Scenedesmus obliquus and Chlorella pyrenoidosa in response to different CO2 levels. Bioresource technology, **102**,3 (2011): 3071-3076
23. W. Thiansathit, T. C. Keener, S. Khang, The kinetics of Scenedesmus obliquus microalgae growth utilizing carbon dioxide gas from biogas, Biomass and bioenergy, **76** (2015): 79-85
24. B. Hu, M. Min, W. Zhou, Y. Li, M. Mohr, Y. Cheng, H. Lei, Y. Liu, X. Lin, P. Chen, R. Ruan, Influence of exogenous CO 2 on biomass and lipid accumulation of microalgae Auxenochlorella protothecoides cultivated in concentrated municipal wastewater, Applied biochemistry and biotechnology, **166** (2012): 1661-1673
25. L. Jiang, S. Luo, X. Fan, Z. Yang, R. Guo, Biomass and lipid production of marine microalgae using municipal wastewater and high concentration of CO2, Applied energy, **88**,10 (2011): 3336-3341
26. B. Zhu, T. Xiao, H. Shen, Y. Li, X. Ma, Y. Zhao, K. Pan, Effects of CO2 concentration on carbon fixation capability and production of valuable substances by Spirulina in a columnar photobioreactor, Algal Research, **56** (2021): 102310
27. R. Prasad, S.K. Gupta, N. Shabnam, C.Y.B. Oliveira, A.K. Nema, F.A. Ansari, F. Bux, Role of microalgae in global CO2 sequestration: Physiological mechanism, recent development, challenges, and future prospective, Sustainability, **13**,23 (2021): 13061
28. J.A. Bassham, The path of carbon in photosynthesis, Scientific American, **206**,6 (1962): 88-104
29. P.J.B. Williams, L.M.L. Laurens, Microalgae as biodiesel & biomass feedstocks: Review & analysis of the biochemistry, energetics & economics, Energy & environmental science, **3**,5 (2010): 554-590
30. J.V Moroney, N. Jungnick, R.J. Dimario, D.J. Longstreth, Photorespiration and carbon concentrating mechanisms: two adaptations to high O 2, low CO 2 conditions, Photosynthesis research, **117** (2013): 121-131
31. C. Durall, P. Lindblad, Mechanisms of carbon fixation and engineering for increased carbon fixation in cyanobacteria, Algal Research, **11** (2015): 263-270
32. H. Zheng, Z. Gao, F. Yin, X. Ji, H. Huang, Effect of CO2 supply conditions on lipid production of Chlorella vulgaris from enzymatic hydrolysates of lipid-extracted microalgal biomass residues, Bioresource technology, **126** (2012): 24-30
33. N. Saifuddin, K. Aisswarya, Y.P. Juan, P. Priatharsini, Sequestration of high carbon dioxide concentration for induction of lipids in microalgae for biodiesel production, Journal of Applied Sciences, **15**,8 (2015): 1045
34. H.H. Abd El Baky, G.S. El-baroty, A. Bouaid, Lipid induction in Dunaliella salina culture aerated with various levels CO2 and its biodiesel production, Journal of Aquaculture Research and Development, 5 (2014): 1-6

Design and Development of Performance Rating Apparatus for Cold Room Refrigeration Unit Using Cooling-Load Balance Method

Arruck Tragangoon[1], *Khemapat* Tontiwattanakul[1], *Montri* Ngamprukvanit[2], and *Chayanon* Serttikul[1,*]

[1]King Mongkut's University of Technology North Bangkok, Department of Mechanical and Aerospace Engineering, Bangkok, Thailand
[2]Songserm Cooltech Industry Co., Ltd., Samutsakorn, Thailand

Abstract. Refrigeration systems are composed of many components working together, and their refrigerating capacity depends upon these components constituting the refrigeration system. The design of the refrigeration system does not only consider cooling loads from products but also the operating conditions that change from time to time, especially the ambient temperatures due to global warming and climate change. Therefore, this work aims to develop the apparatus for performance rating of the cold room's refrigeration unit according to the ASHRAE standard test methods as well as the Eurovent certification programs. The principle of enthalpy change is used to determine the system performance, in general. In this work, the cooling-load balanced method is proposed, which shows a good refrigeration capacity estimation by balancing the cooling load with refrigeration capacity. In addition, the use of an ultrasonic flow meter for refrigerant flow rate measurement is also discussed for additional validation in future works.

Keyword. ASHRAE, Cooling-load balance, Cold room, Eurovent, HVAC, Ultrasonic flow meter

1 Introduction

Refrigeration is essentially a part of many supply chains as it is used in preservation of products; for example, perishable products like food and pharmaceutical products, which require low temperature to slow down the rate of spoiling and oxidizing. In the distribution process of these products from manufacturers until the last mile delivery, a cold room is a facility used to preserve these products. As different products require different storage temperatures, this facility is usually designed for specific products or compromised between a group of products.

The design of a cold room, in terms of refrigeration capacity, should consider the cooling load handled by the cold room, which is a function of the product to be stored, the environmental condition, etc. Since global warming and climate change affect the design parameters for cold room refrigeration unit selection, some design criteria used in practice are no longer valid. The refrigeration unit is composed of many components and the resulting refrigeration capacity is derived from them. At present, manufacturers of these components propose a selection software to mitigate the complexity of matching up these components. However, to avoid insufficient refrigeration capacity, many designers overdesign the system resulting in unnecessary first costs as well as an increase in operating costs of up to 50% due to higher energy consumption. The increase in unit energy consumption is primarily due to the power surges to turn the unit on or off, which can happen more often when the unit has greater refrigeration capacity than required. This compressor short-cycling problem also reduces the unit lifespan as it causes wear and tear on many components of the unit, i.e., more maintenance cost is expected.

The performance of the cold room has been studied in different aspects by many researchers, including the uniformity of temperature throughout the cold room [1–3], and heat and moisture transfers between the products and cold air inside the cold room [4–6]. The results from these studies reveal that the products had excessive weight loss, reduced shelf life or product quality. The temperature-time history within a cold room has been predicted by mathematical models [7] Furthermore, the CFD models are used to study the temperature and velocity distributions in the chamber [8].

Besides designing the refrigeration system to obtain the desired system capacity, selection of the components making up the refrigeration system is another issue. Some manufacturers overclaim their product performance, such as the heating or cooling coils. The small-size coils are claimed to have high capacity than the larger coils. This results in a competitive cost, but their performance remains unprovable.

* Corresponding author: chayanon.s@eng.kmutnb.ac.th

The design of this type of facility should then be verified by means of experiments to assure the system performance. In this work, the design of the apparatus used to determine the refrigeration unit performance is proposed, and the standard test methods of ASHRAE 33 and the European standard EN 328 used in the Eurovent certification program for coil performance rating are used as guidelines to ensure the measurement result reliability. The proposed method provides another alternative to determine the unit performance with lower-cost instruments.

2 Refrigeration Capacity Determination

The apparatus developed in this work is designed using the measurement principle proposed in the standard test methods for coil performance rating, where some instructions are followed, e.g., instrument accuracy, mounting, calculation method. The standards used mainly in this work are 1) ANISI/ASHRAE 33 – Methods of Testing Forced-Circulation Air-Cooling and Air-Heating Coils [9], 2) BS EN 328 Heat Exchanger – Forced Convection Unit Air Coolers for Refrigeration – Test Procedures for Establishing Performance [10]. There are other standards used as complements in measurements [11,12]. The refrigeration capacity from the refrigerant side according to the standard test method is determined from the product of the refrigerant mass flow rate and the difference in specific enthalpy between coil inlet and let, as follows:

$$Q = m \times (h_i - h_o) \quad (1)$$

where Q is the refrigeration capacity in kW, m is the refrigerant mass flow rate in kg/s, and h_i and h_o are the refrigerant specific enthalpy at the coil inlet and outlet, respectively.

The enthalpy of the refrigerant entering the coil h_i used in the calculation of the refrigeration capacity is the refrigerant enthalpy at the evaporator inlet, which is equal to the enthalpy at the condenser exit as in the ideal vapor compression cycle.

By following the standard test method, the instruments for measuring temperature, pressure, and refrigerant flow rate are required to assess the system capacity. On the other hand, the proposed method requires mainly the instrument used in the determination of the test chamber cooling load, i.e., the temperature sensor. Therefore, the cost of the instrument is greatly reduced.

2.1 Cooling load simulation

The cooling-load balance method proposed in this work is to balance the cooling load handled by the refrigeration system with the system refrigeration capacity. Once the thermal steady operation is established, the system capacity is equal to the cooling load handled by the system. This way, the additional cooling load is generated by heaters on top of the cooling load of an empty test chamber.

Therefore, the cooling load of this empty cold room is first estimated, then subtracted from the system refrigeration capacity to determine the additional cooling load generated by heaters. The parameters used to estimate the cooling load of this empty cold room are shown in Table 1.

Table 1. Parameters for empty cold room cooling load estimation.

Inside room dimension (width x length x height, m)	3.35 × 4.58 × 2.58
PU panel thickness (m)	0.1
PU thermal conductivity (W/m•K)	0.025
Room temperature (°C)	-18
Ambient air temperature (°C)	25
Air specific heat (J/kg•K)	1005
Heat from unit cooler fans (W)	293.33

Note that the parameters in Table 1 were chosen to determine the maximum heater capacity. Thus, the ambient air temperature as low as 25 °C was used. The heat from unit cooler fans was calculated from 2 160-W fans operating 22 h a day. Note also that only transmission and equipment loads were taken into account since there were no loads from air change and products as the room was empty and kept closed during the test. The transmission load to the empty chamber can be calculated using the Fourier's law, as follows.

$$Q_{tran} = kA_s(T_{amb} - T_{room})/L \quad (2)$$

where Q_{tran} is the heat conduction through the chamber walls, k is the thermal conductivity of the wall panel, A_s is the cross-sectional area perpendicular to the heat conduction direction, L is the chamber wall thickness, and T_{amb} and T_{room} are the ambient and room temperatures, respectively. The room and ambient temperatures used in transmission load calculation can be measured in real-time in order to monitor the current cooling load.

The resulting cooling load of this empty test chamber was 1.29 kW. From the system refrigeration capacity of 5.12 kW, the additional cooling to be generated by heaters was 3.63 kW. In this work, 3 1.5-kW heaters were used as they were in stock of the industrial sponsor. Consequently, 4 cooling load configurations are available on this apparatus, as shown in Table 2.

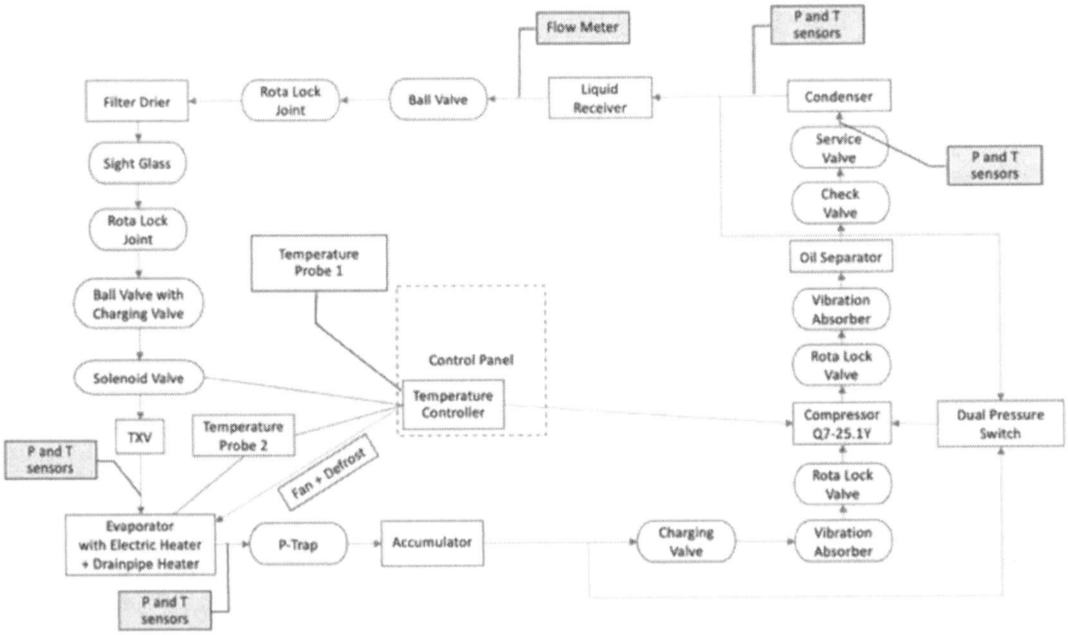

Fig. 1. Refrigeration system diagram.

Table 2. Cooling load configurations.

Configuration	Number of active heaters	Cooling load (kW)
1	0	1.29
2	1	2.79
3	2	4.29
4	3	5.79

2.2 Test chamber

The test chamber used in this work is developed in the cold room with the dimension of 3.2 × 4.8 × 2.4 m. The walls of this chamber are 4-inch PU panels, which are suitable for applications with low temperatures up to -20 °C.

Fig. 2. Test chamber constituted from 4-inch PU panels.

2.3 Refrigeration unit

The refrigeration system using R404a has been designed, and the room temperature under test is -18 °C, where the evaporating and condensing temperatures are -25 °C and 48 °C, respectively. The compressor used in this system is the Frascold Q7-25.1Y, which provides 5.12 kW of refrigeration capacity at the previously mentioned operating condition as estimated by the Frascold Selection Software.

In order to monitor the state of the refrigerant, additional instruments were installed in the refrigerant circuit, as shown by the blue balloons in the system diagram in Figure 1.

2.4 Instruments and measurements

The calculation of refrigeration capacity according to the standard test method is calculated as shown in equation (1) as a function of refrigerant mass flow rate and refrigerant enthalpies. These quantities are measured as instructed in the standards [9,10], where the flow rate is directly measured by an instrument and the refrigerant enthalpy is determined from the measured temperatures and pressures. Although the proposed method does not require the pressure and flow meter instruments, these instruments were installed in this apparatus for more validation in future works. The details of each measurement are covered in the following subsections.

2.4.1 Temperature measurement

The temperature sensors used in measurements must be in direct contact with the refrigerant and have a minimum accuracy of ±0.6 °C. The guidelines for sensor calibration and consistency check must be followed as stated in [9,11].

The temperature measuring sensor used in this work is the ifm TT9281 with the accuracy of ±0.15 °C installed with the thermowell E37603, as shown in Figure 2. There were 4 temperature sensors in total installed in the positions as shown in Figure 3; at the condenser inlet and exit and the evaporator inlet and exit. The connecting pipe between the sensors and refrigerant line has no size requirements and is the same size as the refrigerant line pipeline was used. The refrigerant lines shall be insulated adjacent to the temperature sensors. Moreover, before any test run, all temperature sensors should be checked for equivalent readings at static conditions. In the case where equivalent reading cannot be attained, the reading positions should be arranged to allow a single sensor to be interchanged between the inlet and outlet positions.

2.4.2 Pressure measurement

The pressure sensors must be in direct contact with the refrigerant and have a minimum accuracy of ±0.1 °C equivalent to a change in saturation pressure. The guidelines for sensor calibration and consistency check must be followed as stated in [9,12].

The pressure measuring sensors used in this work is the Gems Sensors 3100 series with an accuracy of ±0.25%, as illustrated in Figure 4. There were 4 pressure sensors installed in the positions as shown in Figure 3; at the condenser inlet and exit and at the evaporator inlet and exit. The connecting pipe between the sensors and the refrigerant line has no size requirements and is the same size as the refrigerant line pipeline was used.

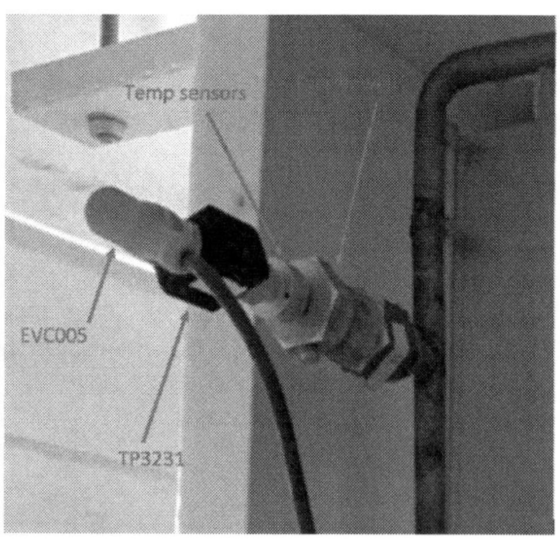

Fig. 3. Temperature measurements using ifm TT9281 coupled with thermowell E37603, transducer TP3231, and cable EVC005.

2.4.3 Refrigerant flow rate measurement

According to the ASHRAE 33 [9], there are 3 methods used to measure the flow rate of refrigerant, i.e., 1) liquid flow meter with an accuracy of ±1% of the quantity measured, such as colioris mass flow meter or similar, 2) water condenser method, and 3) calibrated compressor method.

Fig. 4. The Gems Sensors 3100 series are used to measure refrigerant pressure intrusively.

The flow meter position should be between a liquid receiver and a refrigerant control device. Sight glasses at the upstream and downstream of the flow meter should be used to observe the state of refrigerant for any undesirable flashing of liquid refrigerant into vapor. If the vapor exists downstream of the flow meter due to the pressure drops across measurement instrument, a subcooler ahead of the flow meter should be used. The liquid line subcooling entering the flow meter should not be less than 2.8 °C. Moreover, the standard also suggests measuring the temperature of the liquid refrigerant at the flow meter exit for the degree of subcooling and the oil separator at the compressor discharge to return the oil to the crankcase.

The use of liquid flow meter seems practical for industrial application since it is ready to use after appropriate installation. However, the instrument types proposed by ASHRAE are expensive. The more cost-effective approach using an ultrasonic flow meter for refrigerant flow rate measurement will be discussed later in future works.

2.4.4 Data logging and monitoring system

The software interface developed on Matlab is used to record data from measurement instruments, where the National Instrument USB-6211 was used as a multifunction DAQ device, which provides sufficient settling times at high scanning rates. It also offers high-speed streaming of data across USB. The measured data from all sensors are shown on the software interface and used in post-processing for enthalpy calculation, real-time cooling load, etc. The refrigeration system control box with indicator lights for active devices, the load heater switch, and the emergency stop button are shown in Figure 5.

The software interface developed in this work was intentionally focused on the refrigeration capacity determination. However, the apparatus was equipped with instruments for measuring temperature, pressure, humidity, and flow rate of the refrigerant. Thus, various indexes, such as time-based rate of energy consumption, compressor running time, deviation of the system P-h diagram from the design point, and so on, can be shown for system enhancement benefits.

The data recording system box, and the software interface are as shown in Figures 6, and 7, respectively.

Fig. 5. The refrigeration system control box.

Fig. 6. The data recording system with NI USB-6211.

2.5 Refrigerant enthalpy determination

The thermophysical properties of volatile refrigerants can be obtained from ASHRAE Handbook-Fundamentals [13], REF PROP database from NIST, or the refrigerant manufacturer. However, in the case where these properties are monitored in real time, they should be calculated from mathematical models as a function of the measured temperatures and pressures.

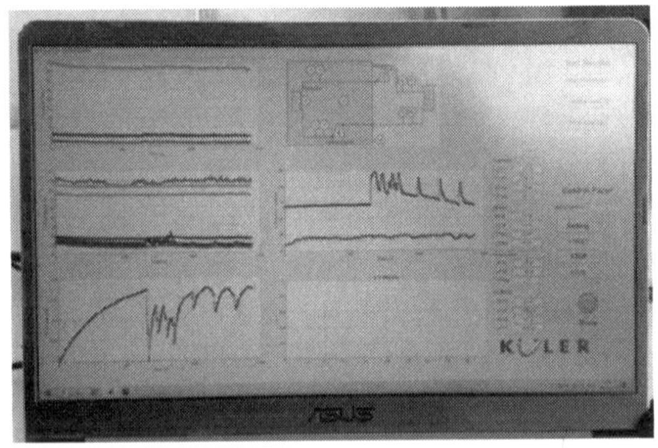

Fig. 7. The software interface developed on Matlab.

Many mathematical models for determining thermophysical properties of refrigerants have been developed and published, but the one that is used by the REF PROP software from NIST is the model proposed by Lemmon *et. al.* [14–17], which works well for the refrigerant mixture used in this work.

The property calculation using the mentioned models could be time and resource consuming due to the equation complexity, and could not be appropriate for real-time monitoring, where many properties need to be recalculated. The remedy for this problem is to pre-calculate the properties for specific working temperatures and pressures and use linear regression from these pre-calculated values.

3 Results and discussions

After the refrigeration system has been charged by R404a, the refrigeration unit was turned on for a day in order to remove heat from the air inside the test chamber as well as heat from the chamber itself. Once the cold room was ready, the cooling loads have been applied to the system starting with the configuration 3 in Table 2. In this case, the cooling load was estimated to be 4.29 kW, which is less than the system refrigeration capacity of 5.12 kW. The system was cycling between on and off cycles as the room temperature varied between the cut in and cut off temperatures. At this cooling load condition, the results showed that the system refrigeration capacity is greater than 4.29 kW.

Then, the configuration 4 for cooling load of 5.79 kW was applied. This time, the system was overloaded, and could not reach the setpoint temperature of -18 °C. Moreover, the room temperature kept rising. From this cooling load configuration, the system refrigeration capacity is less than 5.79 kW.

From the obtained results, we can conclude that the system refrigeration capacity lies between 4.29 kW and

5.79 kW, which is in good agreement with the value predicted by the software from the compressor manufacturer of 5.12 kW. The difference between these upper and lower limits is too large, and the results can be refined by reducing the cooling load increment. For the cooling-load balance method proposed in this work to determine the refrigeration capacity, the relevant error from this method could be originated from the empty cold room cooling load estimation due to the actual thermal conductivity of the chamber panels, which is able to degrade over time, and the estimation of transmission load from the floor of the test chamber.

In the future works, the adjustable load heater can be coupled with the temperature controller to establish the thermal steady operation. Furthermore, the cooling load of the empty cold room could be improved by calculating the real time transmission load from the measured room and ambient temperatures. The outer surface temperature of the test chamber floor can be measured to estimate more reasonable transmission load from the floor.

To measure the refrigeration capacity following the standard test method, the transit-time ultrasonic flow meter can be used to measure the refrigerant volume flow rate. The commercially available ultrasonic flow meters are easy to use and not an intrusive measurement. Despite its sufficient accuracy of about ±1%, the measurement accuracy could be lower if the flow is biphasic, as in the case of refrigerant flow. Thus, the measurement positions should be where the refrigerant is subcooled liquid or superheated vapor, for instance, at the condenser exit or the compressor exit. However, for the refrigerant flow, the speed of sound could be low, and the flow usually occurs in a small pipe. This could lead to an error on commercial ultrasonic flow meters, in which the traveling distance of the ultrasonic wave is pre-calculated and cannot be adjusted by the user. This leads to the wrong results and needs some post-processing for correction, which will be studied in the future work.

The use of an ultrasonic flow meter can also be used to determine the actual vapor quality of the refrigerant entering the evaporator, since it is the volume flow rate measurement. In conjunction with a mass flow meter, e.g., a colioris flow meter, the vapor quality of refrigerant can be calculated from the ratio of the volume flow rate to the mass flow rate, which is the specific volume of the liquid-vapor refrigerant mixture [18]. This information about the vapor quality at the evaporator inlet can be used to determine more accurate enthalpy of the refrigerant entering the evaporator, which will result in more accurate refrigeration capacity determination.

4 Conclusions

The cooling-load balance method has been proposed in this work, where the cooling load was additionally generated by heaters inside the test chamber to match the refrigeration capacity of the system under test. Once the thermal steady operation is established, the refrigeration capacity of the system is equal to the heat generated by heaters plus the cooling load of the empty test chamber. The cooling load generated in this work was incrementally adjusted, and thus the resulting refrigeration capacity was obtained in the form of a range, which is in agreement with the value predicted by the software from the compressor manufacturer. The result obtained from the proposed method can be refined by using the adjustable load heater in conjunction with a temperature controller to establish the thermal steady operation as proposed in the previous section. From this study, the proposed method showed a good potential in refrigeration capacity determination with a lower cost of measuring instruments compared with instruments suggested by ASHRAE and EN standard test methods. In addition, the use of an ultrasonic flow meter in the refrigeration capacity determination is also reviewed and compared with the refrigerant flow rate measurement requirements of the standard test method.

Acknowledgements

This study is funded by Songserm Cooltech Industry Co., Ltd. and the National Science and Technology Development and Agency (NSTDA).

References

1. P.S. Mirade, J.D. Daudin, Computational fluid dynamics prediction and validation of gas circulation in a cheese-ripening room, International Dairy Journal, **16**,8 (2006): 920-930
2. M.K. Chourasia, T.K. Goswami, Steady state CFD modeling of airflow, heat transfer and moisture loss in a commercial potato cold store, International Journal of Refrigeration, **30**,4 (2007): 672-689
3. M. Kolodziejczyk, D. Butrymowicz, CFD modelling of vegetable cold storage chamber, Intelligent Character Recognition, (2011)
4. D. Flick, G. Alvarez, C. Doursat, J. Moureh, Modélisation des écoulements et des transferts lors du refroidissement de fruits et légumes conditionnés en palettes, 20th International Congress of Refrigeration IIR-IIF, (1999): 6
5. N.J. Smale, J. Moureh, G. Cortella, A review of numerical models of airflow in refrigerated food applications, International Journal of Refrigeration, **29**,6 (2006): 911-930
6. P.S. Mirade, *Computational Fluid Dynamics in Food Processing* (CRC Press, 2007)
7. H. Wang, S. Touber, Distributed dynamic modelling of a refrigerated room, International Journal of Refrigeration, **13**,4 (1990): 214-222
8. M.A. Delele, E. Tijskens, Y.T. Atalay, Q.T. Ho, H. Ramon, B.M. Nicolaï, P. Verboven, Combined discrete element and CFD modelling of airflow through random stacking of horticultural products in vented boxes, Journal of food engineering, **89**,1 (2008): 33-41
9. ASHRAE Standard 33-78 Project Committee, Methods of testing forced-circulation air-cooling

and air-heating coils, American Society of Heating, Refrigerating and Air-Conditioning Engineers, (1978)
10. BS EN 328, Heat exchangers-Forced convection unit air coolers for refrigeration - Test procedures for establishing the performance, (2014)
11. ANSI/ASHRAE Standard 41.1-2013, Standard method for temperature measurement, webstore.ansi.org
12. ANSI/ASHRAE Standard 41.3-2014, Standard method for pressure measurement, webstore.ansi.org
13. *ASHRAE Handbook - Fundamentals* (2013)
14. E.W. Lemmon, R.T. Jacobsen, S.G. Penoncello, D.G. Friend, Thermodynamic properties of air and mixtures of nitrogen, argon, and oxygen from 60 to 2000 K at pressures to 2000 MPa, Journal of physical and chemical reference data, **29**,3 (2000): 331-385
15. E.W. Lemmon, Pseudo-pure fluid equations of state for the refrigerant blends R-410A, R404A, R507A, and R-407C, International Journal of Thermophysics, **24**, (2003): 991-1006
16. V.Z. Geller, D. Bivens, A. Yokozeki, Viscosity of mixed refrigerants, R404A, R407C, R410A, and R507C, International refrigeration and air conditioning conference, (2000)
17. V.Z. Geller, B.V. Nemzer, U.V. Cheremnykh, Thermal conductivity of the refrigerant mixtures R404A, R407C, R410A, and R507A, International journal of thermophysics, **22**, (2001): 1035-1043
18. C.T. Tran, P. Rivière, D. Marchio, C. Arzano-Daurelle, M. Coevoet, On side refrigerant measurement of heat pump seasonal performances, 10th International Energy Agency Heat Pump Conference, (2011)

Performance Evaluation of Solar Radiation for Food and Agriculture Dryer

Sriwichai Susuk[1]*, *Weerayuth* Promjan[1], *Natsacha* Inchoorun[1], *Rewadee* Meesat[1], *Wannee* Suttivattanavet[1], *Kusol* Iamsub[2], and *Soravit* Jamjumroon[2]

[1]Expert Center of Innovative Health Food (innoFood), Research and Development Group for Bio-Industries, Thailand Institute of Scientific and Technological Research (TISTR), Pathumtani, Thailand
[2]Expert Center of innovative Agriculture (innoAg), Research and Development Group for Bio-Industries, Thailand Institute of Scientific and Technological Research (TISTR), Pathumtani, Thailand

Abstract. This paper is attempt to utilize the solar radiation in a solar dryer for saving the day-light, energy, and environment. Solar dryer was designed based on thermal analysis heat transfer equations, then it was constructed and tested in Thailand (on a latitude 14°N. and longitude of 100°E). The main three stages were carried out in order to test solar dryer performance. Initially, solar energy consumption data was recorded from 8:00 a.m. to 5:00 p.m., then thermal analysis without load condition was conducted and and tested with fresh fruit sample. In the final stage, the data was compared with an electrical oven. Recording results for the system showed that the solar energy consumption was 313 W/m^2 - 493 W/m^2 (horizontal irradiance), ambient temperature was at 29.5 °C - 40.3 °C, and relative humidity was at 36.2% - 52.2%, respectively. The calculated thermal energy of solar dryer was approximately 41 m^3/h with the rate to remove moisture content out of the system at 0.21 kg/h in average. The average temperature inside the dryer is 47.4 °C. According to the Psychrometric chart, the constant volume is approximately 0.92 m^3/kg. Experimental drying test with fresh fruit in the solar dryer showed that a moisture content of fresh fruit was recorded to be at 81.2% and reduced to 8.4%. Comparatively, under the similar temperature condition, drying with electrical oven is faster for dehumidifying than solar dryer about 21%. However, solar dryer is considered to be more environmentally-friendly than electrical oven. It is also found that the result showed no more differences in dehumidity when testing with the other agricultural samples at the similar drying rate. The results also revealed CO_2 mitigation through a solar dryer system was 2.6 kg/day, energy-saving was 5.63 kWh/day. Therefore, solar dryer system is demonstrated to be an alternative saving sustainable method for all.

Keyword. CO_2 mitigation, Dry-air, Electricity-oven, Environmentally-friendly, Heat transfer coefficient, Solar dryer

1 Introduction

Concerns over climate change energy and food security are among the current major challenges in the global perspective. The need to minimize the utilization of fossil fuels as a mitigation measure in curbing the extent of greenhouse gas emission has brought about extensive research on renewable energy applications [1]. Solar energy is a clean energy source that is very popular, especially in drying process. The sun is the primal energy producer of our solar system and energy is generated. A small fraction of the energy produced by radiation causes all natural cycles and activities such as photosynthesis. The solar surface temperature of the sun is 6,000 celsius, which corresponds to 70,000 - 80,000 kW/m^2 radiation intensity. Earth receives only a very small portion of this energy. Despite this, the incoming solar radiation energy in a year is 2x10^{17} kWh; this is more than 10,000 times of the yearly energy demand of the whole world. The solar radiation intensity outside the atmosphere is nearly 1,360 kW/m^2. When solar radiation penetrates through the atmosphere, some of the radiation is lost. On a clear sky sunny day in summer, 800 - 1,000 W/m^2 (global radiation) can be obtained on the ground [2]. The global radiation and the path length of the beams through the atmosphere. Duration of the sunshine as well as its intensity depend on the time of the year, weather conditions and naturally also on the geographical position as shown in Figure 1. Solar energy is a highly attractive and renewable source of energy as compared to other fossil fuels that pollute the environment [3].

The sun is the central energy producer of our solar system. It has the form of a ball and nuclear fusion takes place continuously in its center. A small fraction of the energy produced in the sun hits the earth and makes life possible on our planet. Solar radiation drives all natural cycles and processes, such as rain, wind, photosynthesis, ocean currents, and several others, which are important for life. The world's energy need has been based from the very beginning on solar energy. All fossil fuels (oil gas and coal) are converted indirectly from solar energy. Among food preservation technologies, cold storage is the best way to conserve its nutritional value, on the contrary, drying is the most suitable option to preserve fruit and

* Corresponding author: sriwichai@tisir.or.th

vegetable for a long time and reduced postharvest loss, increase shelf life, preserve its quality attributes, and reduce transport weight and cost [4]. Drying process is comprised of a heat and mass transfer occurrence where moisture leaves the inside of the product to be dried on to the exterior surface from which it evaporates (mass transfer). Heat energy transfers from the hot drying air into the exterior surface of the food and agricultural product, and the remaining amount of heat energy is functioned in the evaporation of the water from the exterior surface of the product, constituting water vapor. The moisture from the inside migrates into the outside surface in order to restore the loss of moisture occurred by evaporation [5].

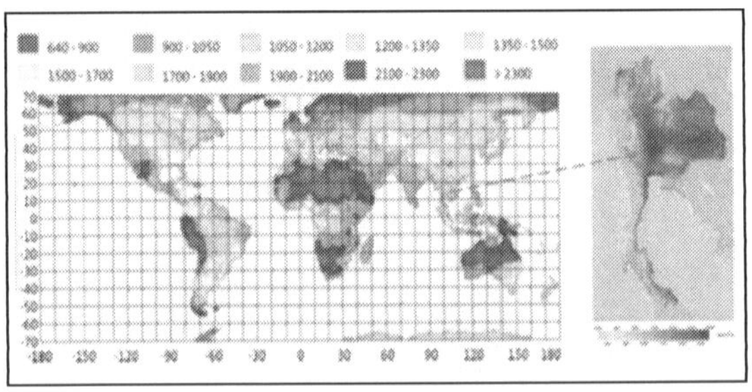

Fig. 1. Global solar radiation[6,7].

The food chain is one of the major contributors to greenhouse gas (GHG) emissions, and global food waste accounts for one-third of produced food. For drying agricultural and marine products, several types of dryers are also being developed. They require a large amount of energy supplied conventionally from pollutant energy sources. The environmental concerns and depletion risks of fossil fuels persuade researchers and developers to seek alternative solutions. Greenhouse dryers (GHDs) are simple facilities that can provide large capacities for drying agricultural products.

The experiment using Particle Image Velocimetry (PIV) technique results were obtained. Fresh apples of moisture content 81.2% (wet basis) were dried to moisture content 8.4% (wet basis) for 8 h 40 min, overall efficiency 16.49% [1]. Recent advancements in the technical design of solar greenhouse dryers are demonstrated as follows;

- Greenhouse dryer includes solar air collector. Efficiency of the solar thermal collector was reported between 29.36% and 88.52% during the drying process. Drying air temperature was reported between 28.08 °C and 55.94 °C during the experiments. Moisture content was reduced from 5.5 g water/g of dry matter to 0.22 g water/of dry matter during 128 h. The product was Grape (Sultana).
- Greenhouse dryer includes photovoltaic (PV) modules (including Flate-plate solar air collector for dried Tomato product). Best efficiency was obtained at a maximum drying period of 28 h. Useful heat gain was ranged between 6.45% and 26.62%. Average overall was between 6.14% and 17.96%.
- Greenhouse dryer includes solar thermal collector. Three drying air's mass flow rates (0.0275, 0.0551 and 0.0826 kg/s) were used. Drying process took 17 h with the optimum airflow rate of 0.0551 kg/s. The average efficiency of the GHD was 19.7% when the air mass flow rate was 0.0551 kg/s. The product was Bitter gourd flakes [8].

Another experiment involving a natural convection solar dryer was conducted at location of 17.115°N. and 74.33°E, India. the environmental parameters taken into consideration during the analysis covered energy, energy payback time and CO_2 emissions, mitigation and carbon credits earned by the dryer. The embodied energy of the solar greenhouse dryer consideration all components of the dryer is 238.137 kWh, the energy payback is 0.588 years and CO_2 emissions are 24.327 kg per year, the carbon dioxide mitigation is 2.024 kg/kWh [9].

2 Equations and mathematics

Determination of convective heat transfer (h). The present focus on evaluating the convective heat transfer coefficient was investigated for the convection flow on the ambient air and moisture content. The convective heat transfer calculations, air moisture and temperature are always a constant in convective drying, and mean convective heat transfer coefficient values are calculated for the lamina flow Figure 2 [10,11].

Reynolds Number (Re)

$$R_e = \frac{D\bar{V}\rho}{\mu} \tag{1}$$

Nusselt Number (Nu)

$$N_u = h\frac{d}{k} \tag{2}$$

$$N_u = 0.68 + \frac{0.67R_a^{1/4}}{\left(1+\left(0.492/\mathrm{Pr}^{9/16}\right)\right)^{4/9}} \tag{3}$$

; For vertical plate analysis

$$R_a = P_r \times G_r \ ; \leq \ 10^9 \tag{4}$$

Prandtl Number (Pr)

$$P_r = \frac{C_p\mu}{k} \tag{5}$$

Grashof Number (Gr)

$$G_r = \frac{d^3 g\beta\rho^2\Delta T}{\mu^2} \tag{6}$$

Heat transfer coefficients in free convection from water or air

$$h_c = C\left(\frac{\Delta T}{L}\right)^{0.25} ;C_{air} = 1.3683, C_{water} = 217.1 \tag{7}$$

Heat transfer by convection and energy required

$$q = h_c A\Delta T \tag{8}$$

$$\dot{q} = \dot{m}\times h_{fg} \tag{9}$$

https://doi.org/10.1051/e3sconf/202342801007

The Re, Pr, Gr and Nu numbers used in the drying process to calculate the heat transfer coefficient of the product were calculated as a result of the different physical properties of the humid air determined by the formula No.1 - No.6 and all equation analyses shown in scenario according to Figure 2 and Figure 3.

$$\rho = \frac{353.44}{(T_{av} + 273.15)} \tag{10}$$

$$k = 0.0244 + 0.6773 \times 10^{-4} T_{av} \tag{11}$$

$$C_p = 999.2 + 0.1434 T_{av} + 1.101 \times 10^{-4} T_{av}^2 - 6.7581 \times 10^{-8} T_{av}^3 \tag{12}$$

$$\mu = 1.718 \times 10^{-5} + 4.620 \times 10^{-8} T_{av} \tag{13}$$

$$\eta_{ad} = \frac{(T_1 - T_2)}{(T_1 - T_a)} \times 100 \tag{14}$$

$$v = \frac{m}{\rho x a} \tag{15}$$

$$V = a \times v \tag{16}$$

$$CO_2 = 0.58 \times Electricity(kWh.) \tag{17}$$

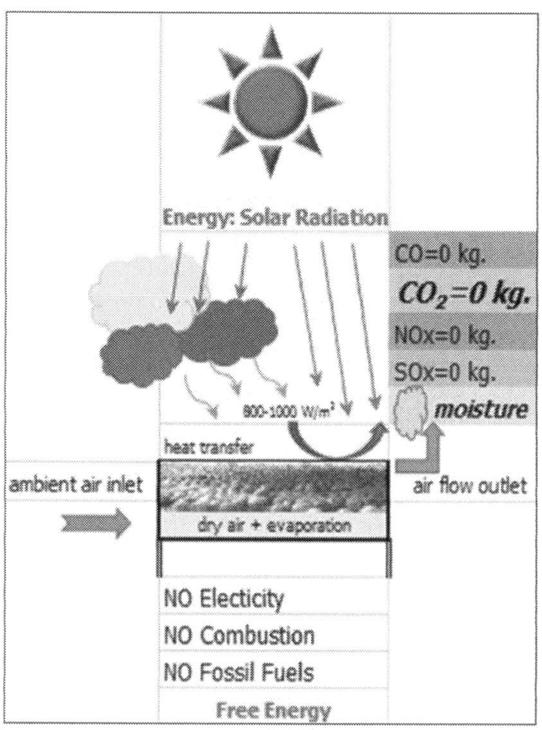

Fig. 2. Illustration chart of global solar radiation, air flow, moisture heat transfer utility and emission (equation analysis).

3 Materials and methods

3.1 Materials

The cross-sectional view of the solar dryer vertical cylindrical shape using materials that are easily obtainable from the local market. Figure 3 shows the schematic of the solar dryer, it consists of main parts, Polycarbonate-bright white color plate (thickness of 8 mm., diameter of 1.5 m., length of 2 m.). Air flows enter the dryer at the lower side and then pass up to the upper side (exhaust). Solar radiation has absorbed by surface areas (cylindrical shape). This process provides effective air heating because airflow passes through all surfaces inside areas.

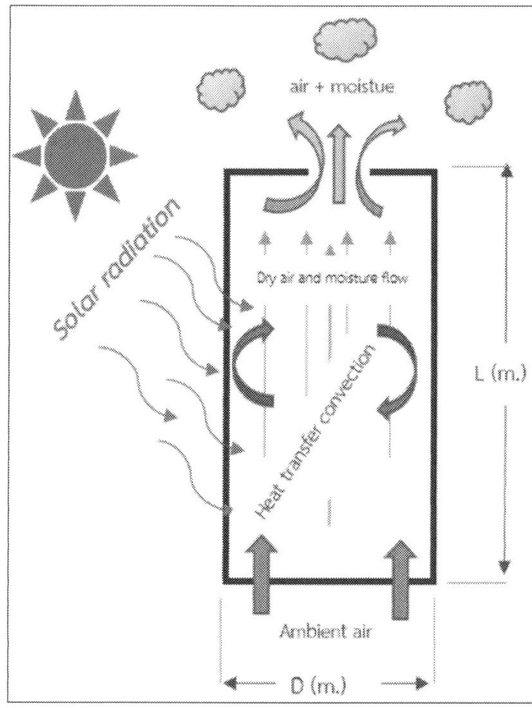

Fig. 3. Illustration of solar dryer diagram.

The external structures can receive sunlight in all directions and helps to distribute heat through all inside areas evenly and thoroughly, internal structure consists of 10 raw material trays (width 1 m., length 1 m) representing a drying area maximum of approximately 10 m². It is made of SUS304 stainless steel mesh material. The upper part of the dryer is equipped with a ventilator, it is rotated by wind and sucked all moisture out of the system. The lower part is equipped with an air vent hole to add up new airflow into the system and circulate within the dryer.

Drying schedule record data from January to June 2023 from 8:00 a.m. to 5:00 p.m. The solar collector was tilted and oriented in such a way that it receives maximum solar radiation during operation. The best stationary orientation is located in Tambon Khlong Ha, Amphoe Khong Luang, Pathum Tani, with a latitude of 14°0'48.46"N and a longitude of 100°31'49.76"E. The angle of tilt (θ) of the solar collector is given by Eq.18 [12].

$$\theta = 10^\circ + Lat\phi \tag{18}$$

Where; $Lat\phi$ = the latitude of the collector location 14° for Thailand, PathumTani Provence.

3.2 Experimental set-up

Most solar energy in the dryer was started by solar radiation at day-light. The main experiment was carried out in three stages, under conditions without load and with load and the final stage compared with utilities electric-oven. In order to evaluate the performance of the solar dryer vertical cylindrical shape, the temperature profile of the dryer was determined by measuring the hourly temperatures of the solar collector, drying and ambient between 8:00 a.m. to 5:00 p.m., a thermometer was placed through the wall dryer (Table 1).

Table 1. Solar radiation and moisture content

Local time (h.)	Energy Solar (W/m²)	Ambient Temp. (°C)	Average dryer Temp. (°C)	Surface of dryer Temp. (°C)	Ambient Relative Humidity (%R.H.)	Average Relative Humidity In dryer (%R.H.)
8:00 a.m.	313	29.5	39.7	43.6	52.2	42.6
9:00 a.m.	371	33.0	43.4	48.8	46.7	38.7
10:00 a.m.	419	35.7	46.4	53.3	44.1	36.8
11:00 a.m.	455	37.6	48.8	56.8	41.0	34.3
12:00 a.m.	477	39.2	50.5	59.0	39.9	33.5
1:00 p.m.	493	40.3	51.8	60.8	36.2	30.5
2:00 p.m.	484	39.6	51.0	59.7	38.0	31.9
3:00 p.m.	456	40.3	50.3	57.8	39.5	33.1
4:00 p.m.	416	39.6	47.9	54.2	42.6	35.4
5:00 p.m.	356	32.8	43.8	48.7	47.3	38.8

The ambient temperature was measured from a maximum and minimum thermometer and the relative humidity was obtained from a psychrometric chart (Figure 4). The heat transfer natural convection, thermal efficiency and dry-air flow rate was calculated as Eq. 1-16 and the carbon dioxide (CO_2) emissions were calculated using Eq. 17. All equations were considered by steady-state for performance evaluation of solar dryer before fruits have tested by drying. The photovoltaic (PV) modules have added up for suitable dry-air flow rate. In the final experiments, solar dryers are compared with utility electric-oven and then consider emissions of gas carbon dioxide equivalent.

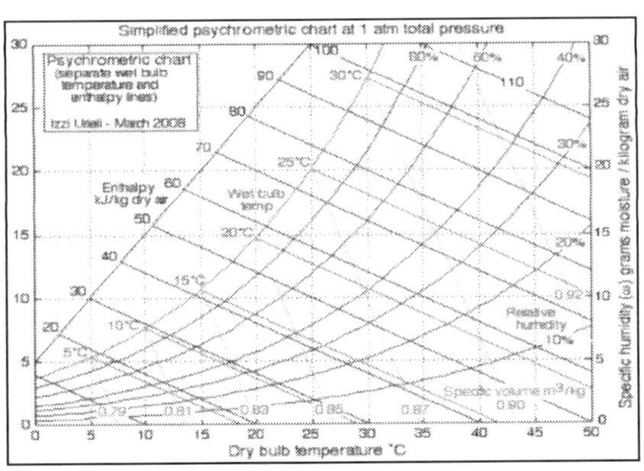

Fig. 4. Illustration of Psychrometric chart [12].

4 Results and Discussion

4.1 Solar radiation and all equations

The solar collector was shown in more detail by the following Table 1 and Figure 5 - Figure 12. Heat is achieved from direct solar radiation through the transparent walls. As shown in Figure 3, the temperature profile of the dryer on the solar collector at 8:00 a.m. to 5:00 p.m. for 6 months (January to June 2023) was shown. All average information was recorded as follows; solar radiation energy maximum of approximately 493 W/m^2 mean 424 W/m^2, ambient temperature maximum of approximately 40.30 °C, mean of 36.34 °C inside dryer temperature maximum of approximately 51.80°C, mean of 47.37 °C, and surface dryer temperature maximum approximately 60.80 °C, mean 54.27 °C, relative humidity maximum approximately 52.23%, mean 42.74%, respectively.

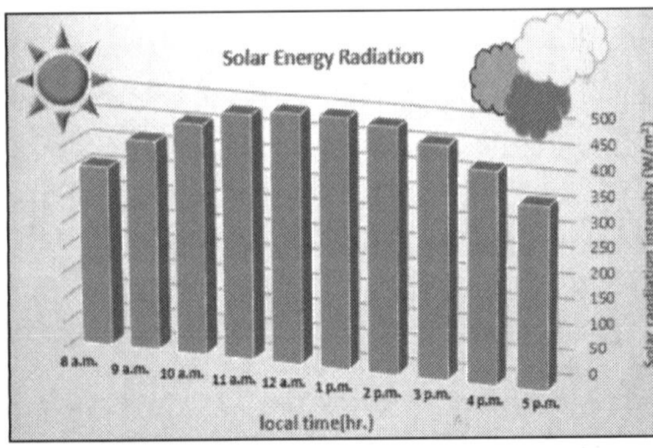

Fig. 5. Solar radiation profile at 8:00 a.m.- 5:00 p.m

Figure 5 shows an hourly variation of the temperatures in solar radiation incidents. In order to evaluate the performance of the solar dryer, the temperatures profile of the dryer was determined by measuring the hourly temperatures of collector between the hours 8:00 to 17:00 solar radiation is hot about mid-day (11.00 a.m.-2.00 p.m.) when the sun is usually overhead, that is highly temperature and energy for good drying process consequently energy saving sustainable and without fossil fuels. However, the performance of solar dryer vertical cylindrical shape has an average of temperature information according to Table 1.

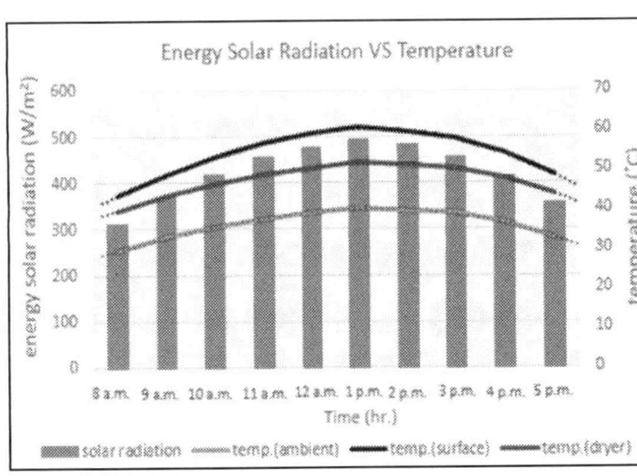

Fig. 6. Profiles of solar energy and temperature.

Figure 6 shows an hourly variation of solar energy and different temperatures. Inside the dryer are much higher than ambient temperatures during day-light. It indicates the prospect of better performance than open sun drying. Additional temperatures are achieved from direct solar radiation incoming through the transparent walls. The higher temperature observed inside the dryer is due to the direct solar radiation. Also, the profiles were recorded as follows; ambient temperature 29.5 °C - 40.3 °C, inside dryer 39.7 °C – 51.8 °C and dryer's surface (inside) 43.6 °C – 60.8 °C, respectively.

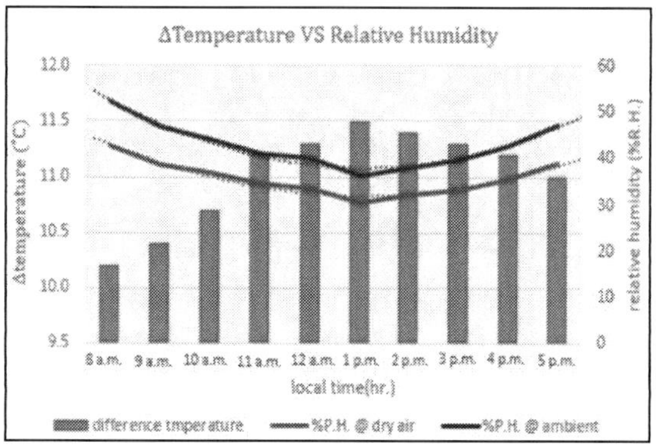

Fig. 7. Profiles of temperature and relative humidity.

Figure 7 shows an hourly variation of difference temperature and relative humidity of dry-air process drying between ambient temperature and inside temperature. Information of recorded temperature is 10.2 °C - 11.5 °C and ambient relative humidity is 36.2% - 52.2%, relative humidity inside dryer is 30.5% - 42.6%, respectively. Information indicated more difference in temperatures (most at 1 p.m.), which means more moisture was removed out of the dryer.

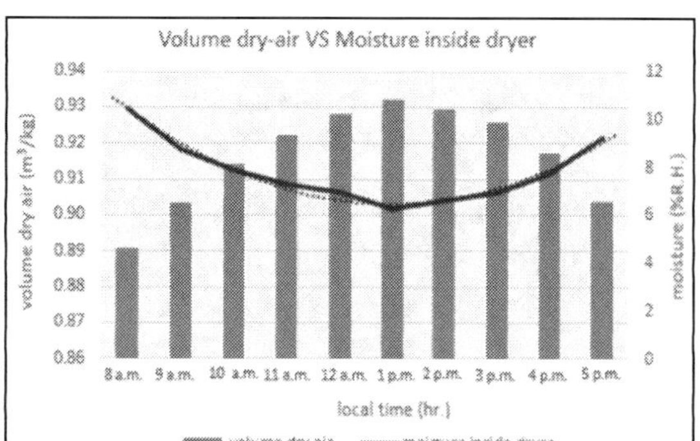

Fig. 8. Profiles of volume dry-air and moisture content.

Figure 8 shows an hourly variation of volume dry-air and moisture content of dry-air process drying between volume dry-air and difference moisture content. The results showed that volume of dry-air flow increase (most is at 1 p.m.) that means dry-air could absorb more moisture. Also, a consequence of moisture inside the dryer decrease. The constant volume of dry-air according to Psychrometric chart Figure 3 and Eq.10 is approximately 0.92 m^3/kg.

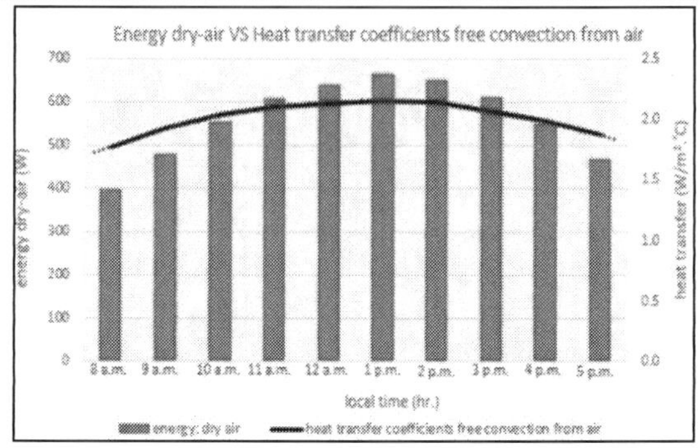

Fig. 9. Profiles of energy and heat transfer coefficients in free convection

Figure 9 showed hourly thermal heat transfer coefficients and free convection values of the dry air process. It can be indicated that the drying system is high or low level. The thermal heat transfer coefficients are high level, which means the energy of dry-air is high level also. The high energy can achieve more volume of dry-air that leads to dehumidification (moisture removed out of the dryer). The value of heat transfer coefficients is the highest that means the highest solar radiation also. Analysis of mathematical equations were solved using suitable initial lamina flow, the heat transfer coefficient natural convection 2.02 W/m^2.°C - 2.15 W/m^2.°C. Simultaneously, energy solar radiation created a dry-air system at 396 W - 666 W.

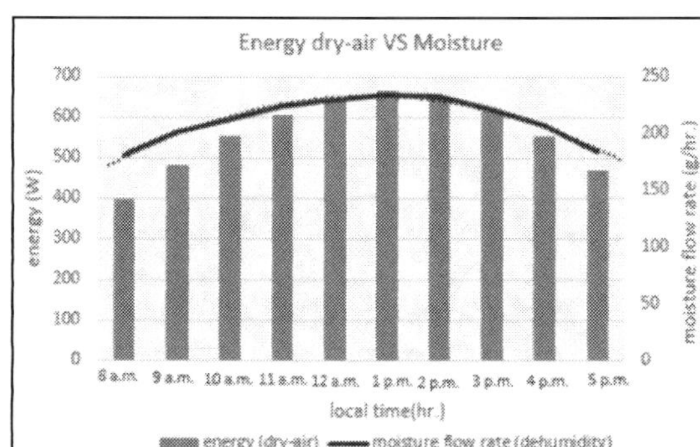

Fig. 10. Profiles of energy transfer to moisture (mass flow rate) or dehumidify

Figure 10. showed hourly energy transfer to moisture (mass flow rate) or dehumidification of the dry air process that is similar to Figure 9. Energy of solar radiation created dry-air system. High energy can remove more moisture out of the dryer also. When the solar radiation or sun's ray is perpendicular to the location between 11 a.m. and 2 p.m. where the highest energy, and highest dry-air lead to removal of moisture at the average of 212.78 g/h.

Figure 11. showed hourly moisture per dry-air and difference of temperatures. The maximum moisture content per dry-air from 8:00 a.m. to 5:00 p.m. is approximately 0.0048 kg$_{.water}$/kg$_{.dry-air}$ according to Psychrometric Chart (Figure 4), and the maximum difference of temperature also is also measured at this point. In this process before the test with drying product, the activation moisture system is increased in the high temperature.

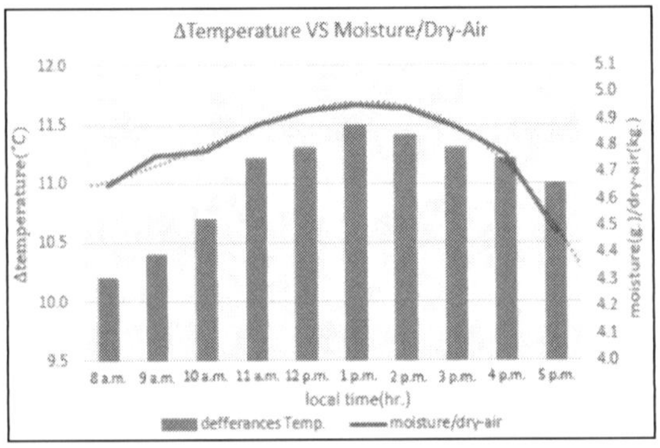

Fig. 11. Profiles of temperature and moisture per dry air ratio

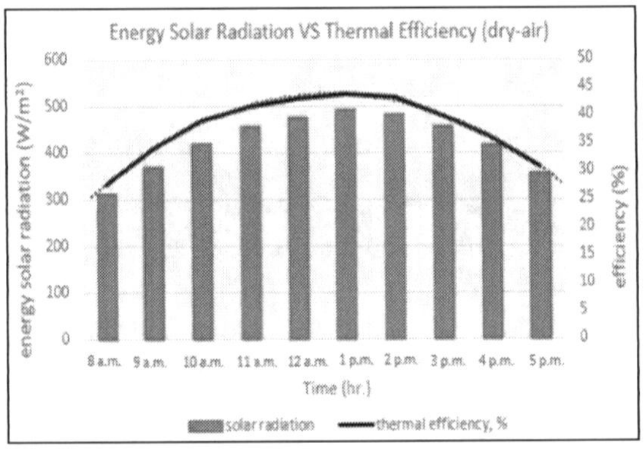

Fig. 12. Profiles of energy solar radiation and thermal efficiency

Figure 12. showed an hourly variation of solar energy and thermal efficiency. Based on the profile of solar radiation from 8:00 a.m. to 5:00 p.m., the maximum of solar energy is approximately 493 W/m^2 at 1 p.m. with the mean at 424 W/m^2, and the maximum thermal efficiency of 44% with the mean of 38%, respectively (Eq.14). The performance of solar dryer can consider at this graph. High efficiency of the solar dryer indicated high moisture removal out of the dryer. Usually, solar dryer systems, the highest performance is observed between 11 a.m. and 2 p.m.

4.2 Experimental drying; fruit (Indian Goosebery) Product compared with electric-oven

The drying test of Indian Goosebery fruit (Figure 13), in a solar dryer, was compared with an electrical oven with the the weight of fruit in the range of 81.2% - 8.4%. Comparatively, the electrical oven showed the better moisture removal out of the dryer than the solar dryer. The electric-oven setup temperature (capacity 3 kWh) was 47 °C (Figure 13). Its drying time was 11 days and solar dryer drying was 14 days. This experiment showed solar dryers spent time more than electrical oven about 36 h and the difference in drying time was 21%. However, drying by solar dryer has not utilized electricity current. Therefore, CO_2 was mitigated throughout the system by approximately 2.6 kg/day (Eq.17) with energy saving approximately 5.63 kWh/day.

The averages moisture removal by electrical oven is at 0.81 kg$_{water}$/h (areas for testing is 5 m^2, 81.2%R.H-8.4%R.H.) and solar average dryer drying rate is 0.58 kg$_{water}$/h (areas for evaporated is 10 m^2, 81.2%R.H-8.4%R.H.). Comparatively, testing results of Indian Gooseberry was compared with other agricultures (Table 2) [13]. It was found that Indian Goosebery as well as Ginger and Butterfly pea have a similar drying rate.

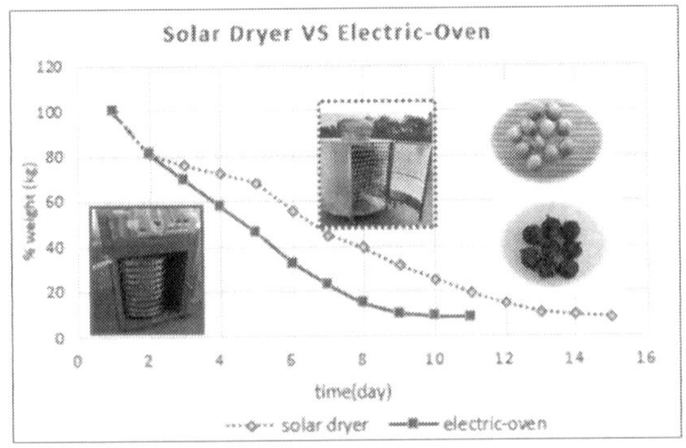

Fig. 13. Demonstration of the relationship between solar dryer vs electrical oven.

Table 2. Example drying test with other agricultures

Products	Ginger	Turmeric	Gotu Kola	Butterfly pea
Initial moisture content (% w. b.)	82.1	86.4	91.5	85.6
Final moisture content (% w .b.)	8.8	7.2	9.1	8.2
Mean ambient temperature (°C)	34.7	36.1	37.2	36.3
Ambient relative humidity (%)	68.4	59.1	57.5	65.2
Average product temperature (°C)	45.5	48.2	49.8	48.4
Drying time (h)	36	27	16	14
Drying rate (kg $_{water}$/h)	0.6	0.7	0.4	0.6

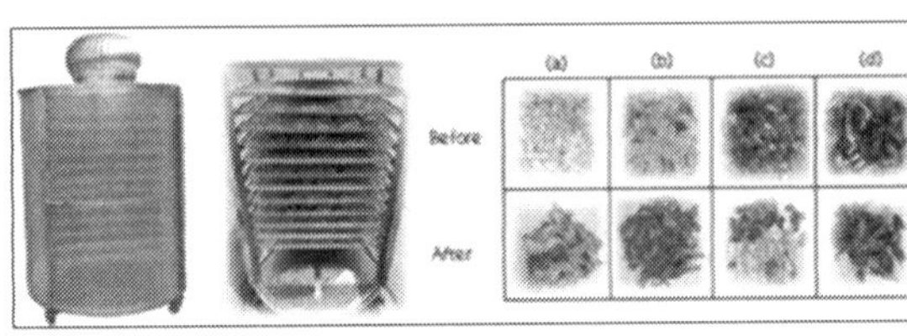

Fig. 14 . Appearances of (a) Ginger (b) Turmeric (c) Gotu Kola and (d) butterfly pea before and after of drying

5 Conclusions

In this research, a practical way of cheap and sanitary preservation of food and agriculture items by using solar dryer (vertical cylindrical shape) is developed. It does not require high technology and electricity current, also the installation and the maintenance cost are low. The drying test results showed that the maximum solar radiation is approximately 493 W/m^2, with the mean of 424 W/m^2, ambient temperature maximum of approximately 40.30 °C, mean of 36.34 °C, average inside dryer temperature maximum of approximately 51.80 °C, mean of 47.37 °C. The relative humidity maximum is approximately 52.23%, mean is 42.74%, respectively. The heat transfer coefficient natural convection maximum is approximately 2.15

W/m^2.°C, mean 2.02 W/m^2.°C. The Reynolds Number is 1,195 < 2,100 (Lamina flow), and velocity of airflow through the dryer is natural convection with flow rate at approximately 0.011 m3/s. The volume of dry-air required approximately 41 m^3/h and moisture removed out of the drying system was at 212.78 g/h. Simultaneously, energy solar radiation created dry-air system was 563 W and maximum air-drying thermal efficiency was approximately 44%. Analysis of Psychrometric chart according to dry-bulb constant temperature line against constant humidity relationship curve line can be found at absolute humidity at 4.8 kg$_{\text{-water}}$/kg$_{\text{-dry-air}}$ and constant volume approximately at 0.92 m^3/kg. Carbon dioxide (CO_2) mitigation is approximately 5.51 kg/day and dryer systems without electricity current. Therefore, solar dryer was environmentally friendly. The solar drying performance was compared with electrical oven by using agricultural items. Comparatively, drying with the solar dryer showed better results than electrical oven in terms of saving electricity current and without release of carbon dioxide (CO_2). When other samples were tested in this solar drying system, the similar drying rate for dehumidification were observed.

Nomenclature

Re	=	Reynolds Number
Nu	=	Nusselt Number
Pr	=	Prandtl Number
Gr	=	Grashof Number
L	=	Length, m.
ΔT	=	Temperature difference,°C
μ	=	Dynamic viscosity, kg/m.s
ρ	=	Density, kg/m^3
β	=	Temperature difference,°C
k	=	Thermal conductivity, W/m°C
v	=	Velocity, m/s
η_{ad}	=	Air-drying efficiency, %
D,d	=	Diameter, m.
h_{fg}	=	Enthalpy, kJ/kg
C	=	Constant value
V	=	Volume of the material m^3/h.
m	=	Mass, g.
A	=	Area, m^2
E	=	Energy, W or J/s
T_1	=	Inside dryer surface Temperature, °C
T_2	=	Inside dryer center Teperature, °C
T_a	=	Ambient Teperature, °C
T_{av}	=	Average dryer Temperature, °C
CO_2	=	Carbon dioxide, kg.

Acknowledgements

The research team would like to thank the Expert Center of Innovative Health Food, [innoFood] Thailand Institute of Scientific and Technological Research (TISTR) for supporting the budget, place, tools, and equipments for this research.

References

1. N.M. Maundu, K.S. Kiptoo, K. Eliud, D. Kindole, Y. Nakajo, Air-flow distribution study and performance analysis of a natural convection solar dryer, American Journal of Energy Research, **5**,1 (2017): 12-22
2. A. Tiwari, A review on solar drying of agricultural produce, Journal of Food Processing & Technology, **7**,9 (2016): 1-12
3. E. Getahun, M.A. Delele, N. Gabbiye, S.W. Fanta, P. Demissie, M. Vanierschot, Importance of integrated CFD and product quality modeling of solar dryers for fruits and vegetables: a review, Solar Energy, **220** (2021): 88-110
4. Aee Intec, www.aee-intec.at
5. S. Abdellatif, Y.M. El-Hadidi, G. Abdell Razik, D. EL-Sayed, Comparative study for two types of solar dryers (Modified-Quonset and Lean-to) for drying stevia plants (Rebaudiana bertoni), Journal of Soil Sciences and Agricultural Engineering, **9**,8 (2018): 313-320
6. Sigma tec, Systemes & installations photovoltaic ques, www.sigma-tec.fr
7. Department of Alternative Energy Development and Efficency Ministry of Energy, Areas with solar power potential, www.weben.dede.go.th
8. S. Gorjian, B. Hosseingholilou, L.D. Jathar, H. Samadi, S. Samanta, A.A. Sagade, K. Kant, R. Sathyamurthy, Recent advancements in technical design and thermal performance enhancement of solar greenhouse dryers, Sustainability, **13**,13 (2021): 7025
9. A.A. Yadav, P.A. Prabhu, J.S. Bagi, Life cycle assessment and economical valuation of a natural convection solar greenhouse dryer in Western Maharashtra, India, Journal of Mechanical and Energy Engineering, **6**,1 (2022): 99-106
10. R.T. Toledo, R.K. Singh, F. Kong, *Fundamentals of food process engineering* (Springer, New York, 2007)
11. M. Daş, E. Alıç, E.K. Akpinar, Numerical and experimental analysis of heat and mass transfer in the drying process of the solar drying system, Engineering Science and Technology, an International Journal, **24**,1 (2021): 236-246
12. Chapter 10: Air - Water Vapor Mixtures, www.ohio.edu
13. N. Inchurat., Drying Herbs with Vertical Cylindrical Solar Incubator. 14th National Science Research Conference, 25-26 May 2023, Bangkok, Thailand.

Oxalic Acid Pretreatment on Enhancement of Enzymatic Saccharification from Napier Grass for Biofuel Production

Danipa Panyarachun[1], *Elizabeth Jayex* Panakkal[2], *Atthasit* Tawai[2], *Wawat* Rodiahwati[3], *Baranitharan* Paramasivam[4], *Suvaluk* Asavasanti[5], *Kraipat* Cheenkachorn[1]*

[1] Department of Chemical Engineering, Faculty of Engineering, King Mongkut's University of Technology North Bangkok, Bangkok, Thailand
[2] Biorefinery and Process Automation Engineering Center, The Sirindhorn International Thai-German Graduate School of Engineering, King Mongkut's University of Technology North Bangkok, Bangkok, Thailand
[3] Department of Chemistry, University of New England: Armidale, New South Wales, Australia
[4] Department of Mechanical Engineering, Saveetha School of Engineering, SIMATS, Chennai, India
[5] Food Technology & Engineering Laboratory, Pilot Plant Development & Training Institute, King Mongkut's University of Technology Thonburi, Bangkok, Thailand

Abstract. Thailand as an agricultural country faces significant challenges in managing the abundant biomass waste generated from agricultural activities. Conventional disposal methods such as incineration contribute to pollution and limited availability of landfill space. To mitigate these issues valorization of this biomass waste has been a solution. This study focuses on the utilization of Napier grass as a renewable energy source. In this experiment, the Napier grass samples were pretreated using oxalic acid with temperature variations (50 – 100 °C), time (30 - 180 min), and oxalic acid concentration (2 - 10%w/v) to determine the limit of these three factors for optimization studies. The utilization of Box-Behnken Design (BBD) within Response Surface Methodology (RSM) enabled the determination of optimal pretreatment conditions and the exploration of the correlation between pretreatment factors and reducing sugar content. The model predicted pretreatment with an oxalic acid concentration of 6% w/v, pretreated at 100 °C for 105 min as the optimal pretreatment condition to produce a maximum reducing sugar concentration of 10.65 mg/ml. Therefore, the sample was pretreated at optimum conditions and the results revealed the amount of reducing sugar obtained was 10.67 mg/ml, which differed from the predicted value with an error of 0.22%. Thus, this study provides insight for future researchers on the optimum condition that can be applied for pretreating biomass with oxalic acid to maximize the sugar yield.

Keyword. Bioethanol, Biorefinery, Enzymatic hydrolysis, Organic acid, Oxalic acid, Pretreatment

1 Introduction

The global population explosion has led to a surge in energy demand across the world. This surge in energy demand is posing a significant challenge to global energy security. The energy production from fossil fuels is hence limited and has facilitated the research on alternative sources for energy production from renewable resources [1]. Thailand is a country with agriculture in all regions, resulting in a large amount of biomass waste from agriculture. These waste materials are mostly used as household heat sources by combustion. Some of these waste materials are either incinerated or dumped in landfills [2]. Apart from its agricultural sector, Thailand is also recognized as an industrial nation, particularly in the food production industry [3]. Consequently, there is a generation of waste materials following the completion of mass production processes. Examples of such waste materials include fruit pulp from juice factories, vegetable waste from food or snack manufacturing facilities, and various byproducts from sugar factories, such as sugarcane residues. These industrial waste materials pose environmental challenges and require proper management. These agro-wastes are often sold cheaply to farmers to produce animal feed [4]. Therefore, biomass energy is considered a renewable energy alternative to fossil fuels to increase the energy supply to meet the demand. Since fossils are an exhaustive source of energy, the utilization of biomass helps reduce global warming caused by the combustion of fossil fuels.

Napier grass is classified as lignocellulose biomass material. Its main components are cellulose, classified as a polysaccharide carbohydrate with glucose molecules connected in a long chain; hemicellulose, a heterologous polymer composed of pentose and hexose subunits, and lignin, an aromatic polymer [5]. These components are interconnected in a complex manner providing recalcitrance to the plant cell. The amount of these components varies in each plant [6]. Previous studies have already identified cellulose and hemicellulose to have the potential to be used as feedstock for energy production from biomass to produce bioethanol from it [7].

* Corresponding author: kraipat.c@eng.kmutnb.ac.th

The complexity of biomass structure has resulted in the application of advanced technology such as a pretreatment process to break down its structure to a simpler form. This step will help in breaking down the polymers into monomers and oligomers that can be taken to the downstream processing steps and finally converted to bioethanol [8]. Among various types of pretreatment methods, including physical, chemical, physicochemical, and biological approaches, chemical pretreatment is extensively employed for biomass utilization. [9,10]. Among the various types of chemical pretreatment, acid pretreatment, and alkaline pretreatment are commonly used techniques [8, 11, 12]. Acid pretreatment can be done with both organic and inorganic acids, however, the use of inorganic acid generates more inhibitors and can cause corrosion to the equipment than the organic acids [13] and it has the benefit of environmental protection [14]. The selection of the pretreatment technique will depend on the purpose of biomass pretreatment.

Oxalic acid is an organic acid that has been applied for the pretreatment of various types of biomass. Pretreatment of olive tree biomass was performed using oxalic acid for production of biohydrogen based on Response Surface Methodology (RSM). A dark fermentation process was carried out using an OTB hydrolysate to maximize the yield of reducing sugar. The independent variables considered in the experiment were time (30–90 min), temperature (100–140 °C), and acid concentration (5–10% w/w for oxalic acid). Under the optimal pretreatment conditions, the maximum reducing sugar obtained was 28 g/L. Furthermore, the highest hydrogen yield achieved through oxalic acid pretreatment was 0.83 mol H2/mol reducing sugar. [15]. Waste lignocellulose medium after cauliflower mushroom (*Sparassis crispa*) cultivation was pretreated by using diluted oxalic acid. The pretreatment was conducted by using the total solids/liquid ratio of 1:4 by weight and the glucose yield was obtained at 44.662 g/l [16]. Corn cob pellets were pretreated with 3% oxalic acid and a solid loading ratio of 1:6. The pretreatment was conducted in a vacuum reactor at 168 °C for 26 min. The main products obtained after saccharification were 2.74 g/L of glucose, 32.55 g/L of xylose, and 1.71 g/L of arabinose. However, just a small fraction of lignin was removed by oxalic acid pretreatment [17]. Yellow poplar (*Liriodendron tulipifera*) stems were pretreated with 3.7% oxalic acid at a loading ratio of 1:4 and 160 °C, and total sugars were obtained at 33.7 g/L [18]. These studies demonstrated the potential of oxalic acid for the pretreatment of lignocellulose.

In this study, Napier grass will be pretreated with organic acid as it is less toxic and causes no corrosion to the equipment. Moreover, it also generates less inhibitory compounds that can interfere with the enzyme in the hydrolysis process causing a decrease in the yields of the reducing sugar that can be converted to bioethanol. The organic acid used in this research is oxalic acid. Response surface methodology (RSM) was employed to optimize the pretreatment conditions and enhance the sugar yield from the biomass. The concentration of reducing sugar was determined using the 3,5-dinitro salicylic acid (DNS) assay.

2 Material and Methods

2.1. Preparation of Raw Material

The Napier grass used in this study was sourced from Kanchanaburi province in Thailand. To remove moisture, the biomass was dried at 60 °C in a hot air oven. Subsequently, the biomass underwent size reduction by using a household blender and was sieved through a 20 mesh-sized aluminum sieve to achieve a uniform particle size. Finally, the sample was stored in a sealed plastic container.

2.2 Acid Pretreatment

Napier grass was pretreated with 2 - 10% w/v of oxalic acid concentration at 50 - 100 °C for 30 - 180 min with 10% biomass loading to determine the limits of the test factors. After the pretreatment, the pretreated slurry was centrifuged to separate the solid fraction from the slurry. The pretreated solids were washed with distilled water and neutralized with 1 M of sodium hydroxide. Further, the solids were separated by vacuum filtration with Whatman filter paper No. 1 and dried at 60 °C for 12 h. The Samples were stored in a desiccant jar until further use.

2.3 RSM Experimental Design

The response surface methodology was chosen in the experiment to identify the optimal conditions for pretreatment based on three factors: time, temperature, and oxalic acid concentration. Each factor was set to three different levels, consisting of low, medium, and high levels, denoted by the symbols -1, 0, and +1 respectively (Table 1). All 17 experiments of pretreatment (Table 2) were derived from RSM design and will be hydrolyzed to determine the reducing sugar after pretreated based on the ANOVA analysis (p–value < 0.05) to find the correlation of pretreatment parameters. Based on the coefficient of determination (R^2), the significance of the condition test in ANOVA, and the lack of fit, the multiple regression analysis will enable the prediction of the optimal condition that yields the highest amount of reducing sugar. Additionally, a second-order model was generated for this purpose.

2.4 Enzymatic Hydrolysis

The pretreated and untreated Napier grass samples were enzymatically hydrolyzed using a commercial enzyme, CTec2. The hydrolysis reaction was performed using 1 g of biomass and a hydrolysis buffer solution consisting of 40 ml of 50 mM citrate buffer, 400 µl of 2M sodium azide, and 200 µl of CTec2. The reaction was conducted at 50 °C and 150 rpm for a duration of 72 hours [19,20].

2.5 Analysis of Reducing Sugar

The concentrations of reducing sugars in the enzymatic hydrolysate were analyzed by the DNS assay [21]. Briefly, a total of 50 µl of hydrolyzed supernatant was combined with 150 µl of DNS solution. The resulting mixture was incubated at 95 °C in a water bath for 5 min. To halt the reaction, the mixture was promptly cooled on ice for 5 min. Subsequently, 1 mL of distilled water was added to the mixture. The concentration of reducing sugars was determined by measuring the absorbance at 540 nm using a UV/vis spectrophotometer. The concentration was calculated using a glucose standard curve (Figure 1).

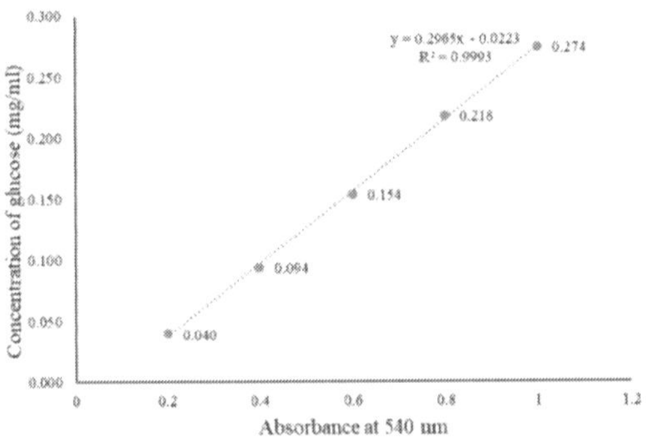

Fig. 1. Standard curve of glucose.

2.6 FTIR Analysis

Fourier Transform Infrared (FTIR) spectroscopy was carried out on both untreated and pretreated Napier grass samples to determine the chemical structures and chemical bonding arrangements using BRUKER, INVENIO S with a resolution of 4 cm^{-1} from 400 cm^{-1} to 4000 cm^{-1}[22].

3 Results and Discussion

3.1 Acid Pretreatment of Napier Grass

In order to assess the range of the test factors used in the RSM investigation, a comparative analysis was conducted, encompassing three variables: pretreatment temperature (ranging from 50 to 100 °C), pretreatment time (ranging from 30 to 180 min), and oxalic acid concentration (ranging from 2 to 6% w/v). This experiment was carried out to determine the boundaries of the variables used in the RSM design. The boundaries of each variable were selected based on the maximum reducing sugar concentration. To determine the temperature boundary, Napier grass samples underwent pretreatment with 6% (w/v) oxalic acid for 105 min, with the temperature ranging from 50 °C to 100 °C (Figure 2A). The experiment demonstrated that pretreatment at 100 °C yielded the highest amount of reducing sugar, producing 12.556 mg/ml. Increasing the temperature further to 120 °C did not have a significant impact on the concentration of reduced sugar. Therefore, the upper limit for the pretreatment temperature was established as 100°C.

Determination of boundary for the time was carried out by pretreating Napier grass samples with oxalic acid at 6%w/v at 100 °C, for durations varying from 30 to 180 min (Figure 2B.). The result shows an increase in the sugar concentration when the duration was extended from 30 min to 105 min. In Figure 2B, the error bands overlap between the pretreatment for 105 and 108 min, indicating that pretreatment with such different duration is not a factor that affects the concentration of reducing sugars. However, further extending the time to 180 min led to a reduction in the sugar concentration, suggesting limiting the pretreatment time to 105 min. The boundary limit for oxalic acid concentration was determined by pretreating the biomass with varying concentrations of oxalic acid from 2-10% w/v at 100 °C for 105 min (Figure 2C). Increase in the oxalic acid concentration initially showed an increase in the sugar concentration. A further increase to 10%w/v showed a decrease in the sugar concentration.

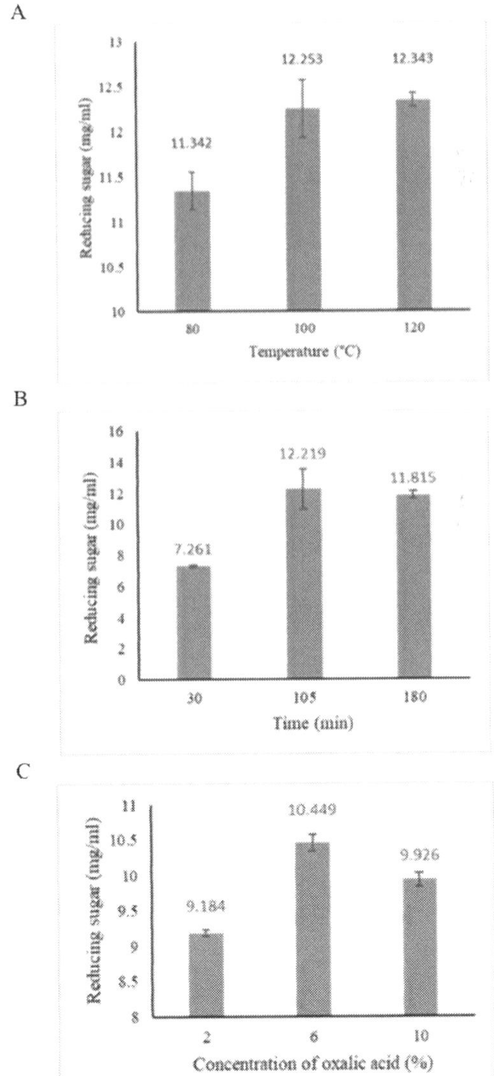

Fig. 2. Effect of pretreatment temperature(A), time(B), and 2 - 6% of Oxalic concentration(C) on the enzymatic hydrolysis of Napier grass. A; the pretreatment was using 6% of Oxalic acid for 105 min, B; the pretreatment was using 6% of Oxalic acid and 100 °C, C; the pretreatment was conducted at 100 °C for 105 min.

Therefore, for this pretreatment, the boundary of factors used in the RSM design was selected as follows: temperature ranging from 50 to 100 °C, time varying from 60 to 105 min, and oxalic acid concentration between 2 and 6% (w/v). These 3 factors were further used to design experiments with RSM (Table 1 and Table 2) by using the Design - expert software (version 7.0.0).

Table 1. Pretreatment factors obtained from RSM with BB design.

Variable factors	Coded symbols	Levels -1	Levels 0	Levels +1
Temperature (c)	X_1	50	75	100
Time (min)	X_2	60	82.5	105
Oxalic acid concentration (%)	X_3	2	4	6

Table 2. 17 Experimental runs from RSM design.

Run	Pretreatment condition: Temp (°C)	Time (min)	Conc (%,w/v)	Reducing Sugar concentration (mg/ml)
1	50	82.50	6	5.98
2	75	60	2	8.07
3	75	82.50	4	7.23
4	50	60	4	7.13
5	50	82.50	2	7.56
6	75	82.50	4	7.06
7	75	82.50	4	7.09
8	75	105	2	7.70
9	100	82.50	6	8.07
10	100	105	4	11.24
11	100	60	4	7.70
12	75	82.50	4	7.16
13	75	82.50	4	7.19
14	75	60	6	7.94
15	100	82.50	2	7.26
16	50	105	4	5.98
17	75	105	6	7.63

3.2 RSM Design and Experimental Testing

Response Surface Methodology (RSM) is a practical application of mathematical and statistical techniques that prove valuable in the modeling and analysis of problems. The response of interest depends on many variables and the objective is to find the best value of the response [23]. Therefore, RSM is an effective technique for complex processes. It reduces the cost and time spent on experiments, which makes it easier to manage and explain the results when compared with other methods [24, 25, 26]. Among the various designs in RSM, Box-Behnken Design was chosen to design the experiment. The Box-Behnken Design is a three-level design for the rebound surface fit. This design is built on combining the 2^K factorial design with an incomplete block design [27,28]. Analysis of variance (ANOVA) is a method to test the difference between the mean of samples from 3 or more groups. This will analyze the ratio of the variance between groups and within the group. The least - Squared method was used to find the experimental coefficient (β) by generating the second-order model from the experimental data. The optimal condition for pretreatment was determined by analyzing the highest yield of reducing sugar concentrations obtained from the multiple regression analysis of the second-order model. [29].

Table 3. ANOVA analysis for the mathematical model.

Source	Sum of Squares	df	Mean Squares	F Value	p-value Prob>F
Model	16.54	4	4.14	12.93	0.0003
A-Temp	7.26	1	7.26	22.70	0.0005
AB	5.50	1	5.50	17.20	0.0014
AC	1.43	1	1.43	4.47	0.0562
B^2	2.36	1	2.36	7.37	0.0188
Residual	3.84	12	0.32		
Lack of Fit	3.82	8	0.48	96.79	0.0003
Pure Error	0.020	4	4.930E-0.03		
Cor Total	20.38	16			

The ANOVA analysis of the model was found to have an F value of 12.93 with a p - value <0.05 and the chance of the model F - value noise is 0.03%. The lack of fit is 96.79 with a 0.03% chance of noise. The ANOVA analysis suggests the significance of the model (p-value = 0.0003). From the data shown in Table 3, The relationship between AC (A: temperature and C: oxalic acid concentration) had a p-value of 0.056, which was over 0.05, indicating that this relationship was not statistically significant. Therefore, it was not used to generate a mathematical model.

3.3 Influence of Pretreatment Parameters on the Enzymatic Hydrolysis of Mathematical Models

Based on the analysis of variance (ANOVA), the influence of temperature, time, and oxalic acid concentration on the amount of reducing sugar was examined in the sample pretreatment. The mathematical model representing the relationship between pretreatment factors and sugar yield was generated and visualized in the 3D model (Figure 3 and Figure 4). It was found that the red-shaded region represents the increasing amount of reducing sugar, which is proportional to the increase of temperature and time. Additionally, it is found that the red-shaded represents the increasing amount of reducing sugar which is proportional to the increasing temperature and concentration of oxalic acid. However, it was observed that the concentration of reducing sugar was not affected by the oxalic acid concentration unless the pretreatment temperature was increased. Hence, oxalic acid concentration alone has no effect on the increase in the concentration of reducing sugars (Figure 2).

A

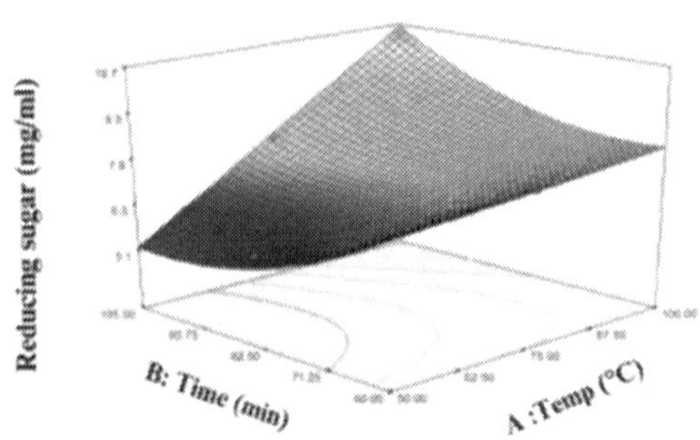

B

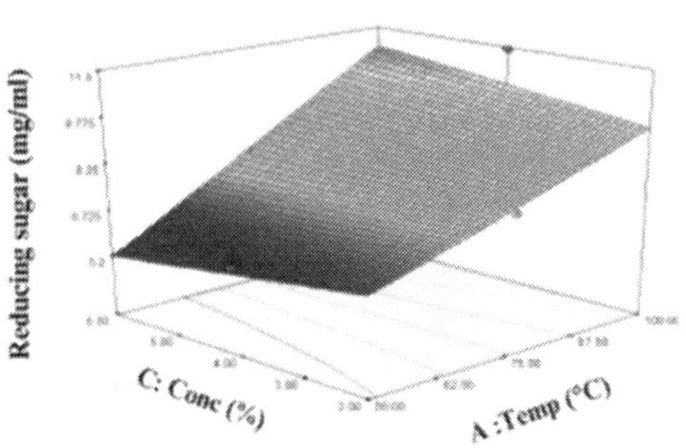

Fig. 3. 3D Response surface plot represents the effect of pretreatment factors on reducing sugar concentration (mg/ml). A; pretreatment time vs pretreatment temperature. B; the oxalic acid concentration vs pretreatment temperature.

The mathematical model and predicted optimal parameters for the pretreatment were simulated by ANOVA analysis, which suggested an oxalic acid concentration of 6%(w/v), pretreated at 100 °C for 105 min as the optimum pretreatment conditions to obtain 10.646 mg/ml of reducing sugar concentration as a maximum yield according to the predicted model. To validate the prediction, the pretreatment of Napier grass samples was conducted under the optimal pretreatment conditions suggested by the mathematical model (Table 4). To confirm the prediction, the pretreatment of the Napier grass samples was then performed again under the optimum pretreated condition suggested by the mathematical model (Table 4).

Mathematical Model: Final equation in terms of coded factors :

$$\text{Reducing sugar} = +7.18 + (0.95*A) + (1.17*A*B) + (0.75*B^2) \quad (1)$$

A

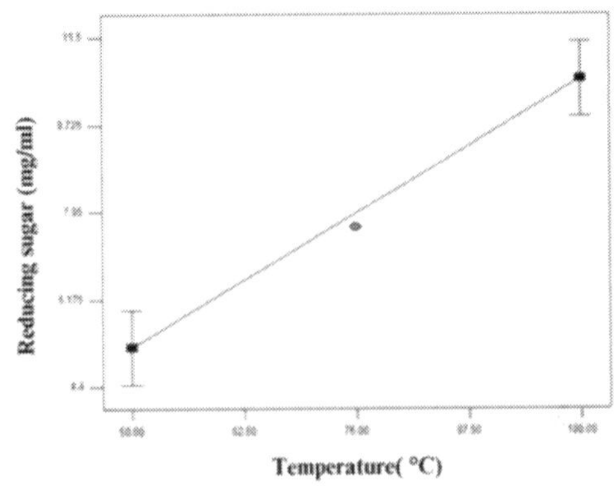

B

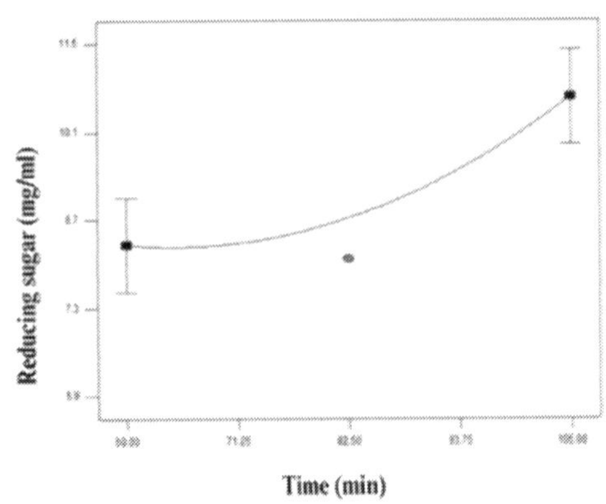

Fig. 4. Relationship between each pretreatment factor, A; pretreatment temperature (°C), B;Pretreatment time (min) and Y - axis is a concentration of reducing sugar (mg/ml).

Table 4. The optimal condition of pretreatment was obtained from RSM.

Predicted optimal condition			**Reducing Sugar concentration (mg/ml)**		
Temp (°C)	Time (min)	Acid (%,w/v)	Predict	Experimental	%Error
100	105	6	10.65	10.67	0.22

3.4 FTIR Analysis

The FT-IR technique was employed to analyze the chemical structure changes of biomass before and after pretreatment. Figure 5 shows the FT-IR graphs of untreated and pretreated Napier grass. The FT-IR analysis of both untreated and pretreated biomass revealed similar peaks at different intensities across various wavenumbers. In Figure 5, the broad peak between 3000 and 3500 cm^{-1}

corresponds to the O–H stretching vibrations of hydrogen bonds associated with cellulose [30]. The peak around 1627 cm^{-1} indicates the presence of C=C and C=O bonds in the aromatic rings of lignin [31] (Figure 5). These peaks were observed in both the untreated and pretreated biomass; however, their intensities were reduced in the pretreated Napier grass. Another peak at 1034 cm^{-1} is attributed to the C–OH bending in hemicellulose [31,32]. Overall, the FT-IR analysis confirms that the oxalic acid pretreatment resulted in delignification, exposing more cellulose for hydrolysis. Consequently, the FT-IR analysis provides evidence that the pretreatment with oxalic acid effectively delignified the biomass, making more cellulose accessible for hydrolysis.

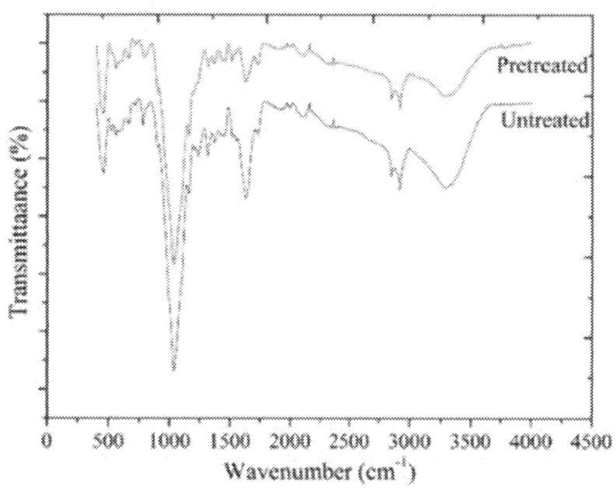

Fig. 5. FTIR analysis of untreated and pretreated of Napier grass.

4 Conclusion

The present study aims to investigate the pretreatment of Napier grass in order to identify the optimal conditions for maximizing the conversion of reducing sugars into biofuel products. This research was carried out to identify the optimum conditions based on the Box - Behnken design of the response surface methodology. The RSM design predicted the maximum yield of reducing sugar concentration with pretreatment using 6% oxalic acid, at 100 °C for 105 min as the optimum pretreatment condition. The Box - Behnken design along with ANOVA analysis predicted 10.65 mg/ml as a maximum yield of reducing sugar concentration when biomass was pretreated at the optimum predicted pretreatment condition. Hence, this research offers valuable insights to future investigators regarding the optimal conditions for pretreating biomass with oxalic acid to maximize sugar yield. In addition to this, further studies can be conducted to recycle oxalic acid from the pretreatment to make the process more economical.

Acknowledgements

The authors would like to thank King Mongkut's University of Technology North Bangkok, Bangkok, Thailand (Grant contract no: KMUTNB-PHD-64-02) for financial support of this work.

References

1. S. Keeratianant, S. Chirarattananon, A. Nathakaranakule, P. Rakkwamsuk, Cost-effectiveness of solar cooling for office and hypermarket, Applied Science and Engineering Progress, **14**, 1 (2021): 31-43 doi: 10.14416/j.asep.2019.09.004
2. A. Martsri, N. Yod, M. Jongprasithpornpijit, S. Junsupasen, Energy economic and environmental (3e) analysis for sustainable development: a case study of a 9.9 mw biomass power plant in Thailand, Applied Science and Engineering Progress, **14**, 3 (2020): 378-386 doi: 10.14416/j.asep.2020.07.002
3. A. Kengpol, T. Pichitkarnkar, K. Elfvengren, A decision support system for consumer behavior of chinese in - bound tourists on functional beverage: an empirical study during covid - 19 with Thailand sandbox, Applied Science and Engineering Progress **15**, 1 (2022) doi: 10.14416/j.asep.2021.09.001
4. I.O. Oladele, T.F. Omotosho, G.S. Ogunwande, F.A. Owa, A review on the philosophies for the advancement of polymer - based composites: past present and future perspective, Applied Science and Engineering Progress, **14**, 4 (2022): 553–579 doi: 10.14416/j.asep.2021.08.003
5. F. Norrahim, R.A. Ilyas, N.M. Nurazzi, M.S.A. Rani, M.S.N Atikah, S.S. Shazleen, Chemical pretreatment of lignocellulosic biomass for the production of bioproducts: an overview, Applied Science and Engineering Progress, **14**, 4 (2021): 588–605 doi: 10.14416/j.asep.2021.07.004
6. N. Raina. M. Sriariyanun, S. Areeya, A.K. Pathak, G. Slathia, H. Saraswat, Trends in harnessing energy from waste biomass: pathways & future potential, E3s Web of Conferences, **355** (2020): 01001 doi: 10.1051/E3sconf/202235501001
7. Y.S. Cheng, Z.Y. Wu, M. Sriariyanun, Evaluation of macaranga tanarius as a biomass feedstock for fermentable sugars production, Bioresource Technology, **294**(2019): 122195 doi: 10.1016/J.Biortech.2019.122195
8. C. Chatkaew, E.J. Panakkal, W. Rodiahwati, S. Kirdponpattara1, S.Chuetor1, M. Sriariyanun, K. Cheenkachorn, Effect of sodium hydroxide pretreatment on released sugar yields from pomelo peels for biofuel production, E3s Web of Conferences, **302** (2021): 02015 doi: 10.1051/E3sconf/202130202015
9. S. Areeya, E. J. Panakkal, M. Sriariyanun, T. Kangsadan, A. Tawai, S. Amornraksa, U.W. Hartley, P. Yasurin, A review on chemical pretreatment of lignocellulosic biomass for the production of bioproducts: mechanisms, challenges and applications, Applied Science and Engineering Progress, **16**, 3 (2023): 6767 doi: 10.14416/j.asep.2023.02.008
10. D. Jose, N. Kitiborwornkul, M.Sriariyanun, K. Keerthi, A review on chemical pretreatment methods

of lignocellulosic biomass : recent advances and progress, Applied Science and Engineering Progress, **15**, 4 (2022): 6210 doi: 10.14416/j.asep.2022.08.001

11. B. Paramasivam, R.Q. Mensah, M. Sriariyanun, advantages and significance of acid and alkali pretreatment of lignocellulose biomass in biorefining process, Applied Science and Engineering Progress, **17**, 1 (2023): 6913 doi: 10.14416/j.asep.2023.05.004
12. M.P. Gundupalli, M. Sriariyanun, Recent trends and updates for chemical pretreatment of lignocellulosic biomass, Applied Science and Engineering Progress, **16**, 1 (2023): 5842 doi: 10.14416/j.asep.2022.03.002
13. Y. Yan, C. Zhang, Q. Lin, X. Wang, B. Cheng, H. Li, J. Ren, Microwave - Assisted oxalic acid pretreatment for the enhancing of enzyme hydrolysis in the production of xylose and arabinose from bagasse, Molecules, **10**, 23 (2018): 862 doi: 10.3390/molecules23040862
14. L. Liu, B. Liu, X. Li, Z. Wang, L. Mu, C. Qin, C. Liang, C. Huang, S. Yao, Mannitol assisted oxalic acid pretreatment of poplar for the deconstruction and separation of hemicellulose, Industrial Crops and Products, **200** (2023): 116811 doi: 10.1016/J.Indcrop.2023.116811
15. O. Yildirim, D. Tunay, B. Ozkaya, A. Demir, Optimization of oxalic and sulphuric acid pretreatment conditions to produce bio - hydrogen from Olive tree biomass, International Journal Of Hydrogen Energy, **47**, 62 (2022): 26316 - 26325 doi: 10.1016/J.Ijhydene.2021.11.017
16. H.J. Lee, Y.J. Seo, J.W. Lee, Characterization of oxalic acid pretreatment on lignocellulosic biomass using oxalic acid recovered by electrodialysis, Bioresource Technology ,**133** (2023): 87-91 doi: 10.1016/J.Biortech.2013.01.051
17. J.W. Lee, C. J Houtman, H.Y. Kim, I.G. Choi, T.W. Jeffries, Scale - up study of oxalic acid pretreatment of lignocellulosic biomass for the production of bioethanol, Bioresource Technology, **102**, 16 (2011): 7451-7456 doi: 10.1016/J.Biortech.2011.05.022
18. H.Y. Kim, J.W. Lee, T.W. Jeffries, I.G. Choi, Response Surface Optimization of oxalic acid pretreatment of yellow poplar (*liriodendron tulipifera*) for production of glucose and xylose monosaccharides, Bioresource Technology, **102**, 2 (2011): 1440-1446 doi: 10.1016/J.Biortech.2010.09.075
19. P. Mutrakulcharoen, P. Pornwongthong, S.T.A. Sahithi, T. Phusantisampan, A. Tawai and M. Sriariyanun, Improvement of potassium permanganate pretreatment by enzymatic saccharification of rice straw for production of biofuels, E3s Web of Conferences, **302** (2011): 02013 doi: 10.1051/E3sconf/202130202013
20. M. Sriariyanun, N. Kitiborwornkul, P. Tantayotai, K. Rattanaporn, P.L. Show, One - pot ionic liquid - mediated bioprocess for pretreatment and enzymatic hydrolysis of rice straw with ionic liquid - tolerance bacterial cellulase, Bioengineering, **9** (2022): 17 doi: 10.3390/Bioengineering9010017
21. G.L. Miller, Use of dinitrosalicylic acid reagent for determination of reducing sugar, Analytical Chemistry, **31**, 3 (1959): 426-428 doi: 10.1021/Ac60147a030
22. Science Instrument center of Ubonrajthani university. Fourier Transform Infrared Spectrometer (FT - IR). www.ubu.ac.th. Access on 12 July 2023
23. L.A. Sarabia, M.C. Ortiz, Response Surface methodology, comprehensive chemometrics, (2009): 345-390 doi: 10.1016/B978-044452701-1.00083-1
24. M.C. Macawile, J. Auresenia, Utilization of supercritical carbon dioxide and co - solvent n - hexane to optimize oil extraction from *gliricidia sepium* seeds for biodiesel production, Applied Science and Engineering Progress, **15**, 1 (2022): 5404 doi: 10.14416/J.Asep.2021.09.003.
25. L.K. Akula, R.K. Oruganti, D. Bhattacharyya, K.K. Kurilla, Treatment of marigold flower processing wastewater using a sequential biological - electrochemical process, Applied Science and Engineering Progress, **14**, 3 (2021): 525–542 doi: 10.14416/J.Asep.2021.04.001
26. T. Ruensodsai, E.J. Panakkal, P. Teerapornnarong, W. Rodiahwati, M. Sriariyanun, K. Rattanaporn, Optimization of enzyme assisted extraction of chondroitin sulfate from bohadschia argus by response surface methodology, E3s Web of Conferences, **302** (2021): 02012 doi: 10.1051/E3sconf/202130202012
27. P. Tantayotai, S.P. Gundupalli, K. Katam, K.N. Rattanaporn, K. Cheenkachorn, M. Sriariyanun, In - depth investigation of the bioethanol and biogas production from organic and mineral acid pretreated sugarcane bagasse: comparative and optimization studies, Biocatalysis and Agricultural Biotechnology, **45** (2022): 102499 doi: 10.1016/J.Bcab.2022.102499
28. M.P. Gundupalli, P. Tantayotai, S. Chuetor, K. Cheenkachorn, S. Joshi, D. Bhattacharyya, M. Sriariyanun, Improvement of water hyacinth bioconversion by different organic and mineral acid pretreatment and the effect of post - pretreatment washing, Bioenergy Research, (2022) doi: 10.1007/S12155-022-10528-9
29. CMUL Online Public Access Catalog. Optimal Composition of Mixed Material for Thermoforming Mould of Plastic Plate. www. search.lib.cmu.ac.th.Access on 12 July 2323
30. W. Song, L. Peng, D. Bakhshyar, L. He, J. Zhang, Mild O_2 - aided alkaline pretreatment effectively improves fractionated efficiency and enzymatic digestibility of Napier grass stem towards a sustainable biorefinery, Bioresource Technology, **319** (2021): 124162 doi: 10.1016/J.Biortech.2020.124162
31. E.J. Panakkal, K. Cheenkachorn, S. Chuetor, P. Tantayotai, N. Raina, Y.S. Cheng, M. Sriariyanun,

Optimization of deep eutectic solvent pretreatment for bioethanol production from Napier grass, Sustainable Energy Technologies and Assessments, **54** (2022): 102856 doi: 10.1016/J.Seta.2022.102856

32. O. Somseemee, P. Saeoui, F.T. Schevenels, C. Siriwong, Enhanced interfacial interaction between modified cellulose nanocrystals and epoxidized natural rubber via ultraviolet irradiation, Scientific Reports, **12** (2022): 6682 doi: 10.1038/S41598-022-10558-5

Optimization of Organosolv Pretreatment with Acid Catalyst to Enhance Enzymatic Saccharification of Corn Husk

Engkarat Buakeaw[1], *Diana* Jose[2], *Wawat* Rodiahwati[3], *Marttin* Paulraj Gundupalli[4], *Keerthi* Katam[5], *Prapakorn* Tantatotai[6], *Malinee* Sriariyanun[2], and *Kraipat* Cheenkachorn[1,*]

[1] Department of Chemical Engineering, Faculty of Engineering, King Mongkut's University of Technology North Bangkok, Bangkok, Thailand
[2] Biorefinery and Process Automation Engineering Center, Department of Chemical and Process Engineering, The Sirindhorn International Thai-German Graduate School of Engineering, King Mongkut's University of Technology North Bangkok, Bangkok, Thailand
[3] Department of Chemistry, University of New England, New South Wales, Australia
[4] Department of Food and Nutrition Science, Faculty of Agricultural, Life and Environmental Science, University of Alberta, Canada
[5] Department of Civil Engineering, Ecole Centrale School of Engineering, Mahindra University, Telangana, India
[6] Department of Microbiology, Faculty of Science, Srinakharinwirot University, Bangkok, Thailand

Abstract. Due to awareness of global warming and the devastation of environmental resources, the management of agricultural residues after each harvesting season has been integrated into the biorefining process to increase its value and mitigate environmental pollution caused by burning or combustion. This research focuses on the process development to utilize agricultural biomass residues for renewable energy production in the form of bioethanol. The study employed organosolv pretreatment with sulfuric acid as a catalyst to promote the enzymatic conversion of corn husk into reducing sugars. To determine the optimal conditions for the process, a one-factor-at-a-time method was initially employed to assess the influence of temperature (80-140 °C), time (40-60 min), and sulfuric acid concentration (0.01-0.5% w/w). Subsequently, Response Surface Methodology (RSM) was conducted based on the Box-Behnken design (BBD) to identify the optimal pretreatment conditions. The predicted optimal pretreatment conditions were found to be 135.4 °C, 57 min, and 0.46% w/w, resulting in a reducing sugar yield of 20.69% with a margin of error of 1.2%. Additionally, biomass composition analysis and Fourier Transform Infrared spectroscopy (FTIR) were performed to decipher the mechanism of organosolv pretreatment on enzymatic saccharification. This study demonstrated the potential of corn husk as an alternative raw material for the production of value-added products like bioethanol. The obtained reducing sugars serve as vital substrates for the fermentation process required to produce bioethanol as an alternative fuel to meet the target of sustainable development goals (SDGs).

Keyword. Bioethanol, Biorefinery, Enzymatic saccharification, Organosolv pretreatment, Sulfuric acid

1 Introduction

As a result of the global COVID-19 pandemic and the implementation of lockdown measures by several nations in 2020 [1,2], the worldwide production of ethanol experienced a decline. The production volume dropped from 113.7 billion liters in the previous year to 101.7 billion liters, falling short of the target of 114.3 billion liters. This decrease was primarily due to production cuts in countries such as Brazil, the United States, and the European Union. Consequently, ethanol factories reduced fuel ethanol production and instead focused on manufacturing industrial-grade ethanol for cleaning and disinfection purposes. However, the trade volume of industrial-grade ethanol remained relatively small and could not fully substitute the trade of fuel ethanol. Additionally, in 2020, the average retail price for ethanol rose by 5.2% to approximately 23.2 baht per liter, reaching its highest point in the second cycle year (with the average price ranging from 24 to 25 baht per liter) due to the increase in sugarcane and molasses prices as in Figure 1.

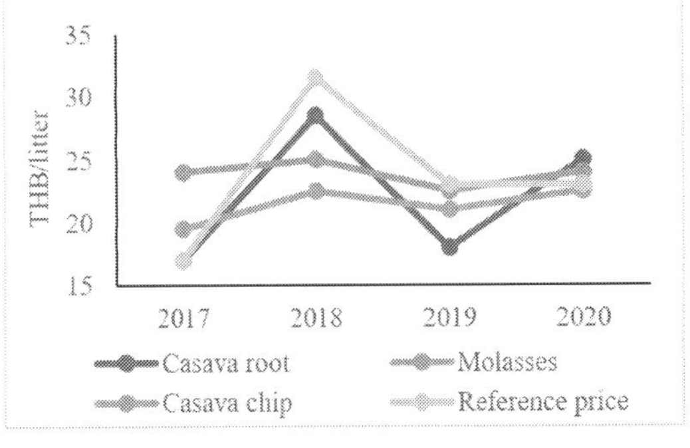

Fig 1. Price chart of ethanol obtained from different raw materials [3].

* Corresponding author: kraipat@gmail.com

The production of industrial-grade ethanol in Thailand has witnessed a significant surge due to the high demand for pure alcohol and hand sanitizers. Production of ethanol in Thailand relies on molasses, cassava, and sugarcane juice as its primary raw materials. As of April 2023, ethanol derived from molasses constituted 65.7% of the total ethanol output, while cassava and sugarcane juice accounted for 28.75% and 5.55%, respectively [4]. Thailand, being rich in agricultural resources, generates substantial amounts of waste materials from its agricultural industry, including straw, rice husks, coconut shells, sawdust, leaf scraps, tree bark, fruit peels, corn cobs, and bagasse. Research conducted earlier has revealed that the agro-industrial sector in Thailand produced an enormous 62 million tons of residual biomass in 2020, which is equivalent to 13,348 thousand tons of crude oil [5]. The amount of this waste biomass material shows the possibility to utilize these biomass residues for the production of alternative energy to increase the energy security of the country. This practice enhances the value of agricultural products, meeting the demands of both local and international consumers. Moreover, it serves the purpose of maximizing the utilization of natural resources, thereby minimizing agricultural waste and reducing pollution [6].

Corn is a significant economic crop grown in various regions of Thailand, but its husks are not widely utilized compared to other agricultural waste. These wastes are often burned directly to generate heat and electricity. This research focuses on assessing the potential of corn husks as a source of lignocellulosic biomass for the production of bioethanol. The husks contain abundant cellulose and hemicellulose, which can be hydrolyzed into monomeric sugars and converted into ethanol. The bioethanol production process typically involves four essential stages: pretreatment, hydrolysis, fermentation, and product recovery/extraction [7, 8]. Due to the natural recalcitrant structure of lignocellulose, the efficiency of the cellulase enzyme that hydrolyzes biomass to sugars is low [9,10]. To improve the enzymatic hydrolysis, pretreatment is necessary. Pretreatment can be performed in several ways, such as physical, chemical, biological, and physicochemical pretreatment [11,12], each of which is suitable for different applications. However, these pretreatment methods affect the arrangements of lignocellulose-type materials, which increases the surface area and porosity, which is beneficial to enzymatic digestion [13,14]. After pretreatment, cellulose components are subjected to enzymatic hydrolysis to produce sugars that are subsequently converted to value-added products, such as biofuels, biochemicals, platform chemicals, and biopolymers [15, 16, 17].

Organosolv solutions are used in the pretreatment of lignocellulose to remove lignin, inhibitors of cellulase, and reorganize the lignocellulose structure, ultimately enhancing the efficiency of bioethanol production [18]. The most commonly used solvents for lignin extraction are acetic acid, formic acid, ethanol and glycerol [19]. In general, organosolv solutions have been applied in the production of kraft and alkali lignin from the fiber pulp industry to obtain high-purity lignin. Several organosolv solutions are considered to be green solvents as they are derived from natural sources and are environmentally friendly chemicals. Glycerol is one of the solvents to be used in organosolv pretreatment. Crude glycerol is produced as a by-product of biodiesel production with low purity [20]. Therefore, using glycerol is a way to meet the circular economy concept.

Previously, the pretreatment of rice straw using the organosolv method was investigated. Glycerol was utilized as the solvent with a concentration of 70% in the reactor, and the process was carried out at a temperature of 220 °C. The researchers employed an X-ray diffraction (XRD) technique to examine the structural changes in lignocellulose, and the results demonstrated that glycerol pretreatment effectively reorganized the cellulose structure. The amorphous components, including lignin and hemicellulose, were effectively removed during the process which could potentially enhance the efficiency of hydrolysis, as observed through the use of infrared wavelength and chemical structural analyzers. These tools identified crucial bonding structures, such as β-ethers, β-esters, and hydrogen bonds [21]. Similarly, the pretreatment of sugarcane bagasse with Lewis acid-mediated glycerol (80 wt%) combined with 1.0 wt% $AlCl_3$ was studied. Under pretreatment conditions of 150 °C for 1 hour, excellent results were obtained with a glucan recovery rate of 98.47%, xylan removal rate of 95.31%, and delignification rate of 49.69%. The efficiency of acidified glycerol pretreatment remained relatively stable during four consecutive cycles, as demonstrated in reutilization experiments. When subjected to in situ enzymatic saccharification after pretreatment, the bagasse yielded approximately 50% glucose at a glycerol concentration of 16 wt%. Following pretreatment, the lignin was solubilized in the pretreated hydrolysate, resulting in two types of lignin: organosolv lignin (OL) and cellulolytic enzyme lignin (CEL), present in the solubilized form and the solid residue, respectively. Further examination of the structure and molecular weights of these two lignin samples revealed their significant potential for being converted into valuable products [22].

Hence, this study aims to optimize the pretreatment method by using a combination of glycerol and acid catalyst to convert corn husks to sugars. The optimization experiments were designed using the Response Surface Methodology (RSM) with Box-Behnken design to identify pretreatment parameters and levels promoting the maximum conversion of corn husk to sugars. This approach aims to add value to the corn husks and minimize environmental pollution, rather than allowing them to be decomposed or wasted. This optimization process is conducted to facilitate bioethanol production from the corn husks by the biorefining process.

2 Material and methods

2.1 Raw materials

Corn husks were obtained from urban markets in Bangkok, Thailand. Corn husks were washed with distilled water and dried at 60 °C for 12 h in a hot air oven to remove moisture. After drying, it is crushed using a grinder and filtered through an aluminium sieve of 40 mesh and 20 mesh, respectively to obtain a uniform sample. The biomass was kept in a plastic bag, tightly sealed, and stored at room temperature until it was needed for future use. Commercial cellulase Ctec2 from *Trichoderma reesei* was purchased from Sigma-Aldrich (aqueous solution of 700 units /ml).

2.2 Organosolv pretreatment

Pretreatment was performed by soaking 3 g of ground corn husk in 30 g of glycerol solution mixed with sulfuric acid at a solid loading ratio of 10% w/w. The treatment was carried out in a hot air oven. Heat treatment using 70% glycerol concentration mixed with sulfuric acid (at different concentrations from 0.01% to 0.5% w/w), temperature (80 to 140 °C) and time (40 to 60 minutes). Following the pretreatment process, the liquid fraction and solid residue were separated using a Whatman No. 1 filter paper through filtration. The solid residue underwent additional washing with distilled water until reaching a neutral pH. Subsequently, the solid was dried in a hot air oven at 60°C for a duration of 8 hours. The treated samples were then stored in a desiccator in preparation for the subsequent enzymatic saccharification step.

2.3 RSM Experiment design

To determine the ideal pretreatment conditions (X) for maximizing sugar yield (Y), an optimization experiment using the Box-Behnken Design (BBD) with Response Surface Methodology (RSM) was conducted. Experimental data was collected and analyzed using Design Expert software version 7.0.0. Three factors, namely pretreatment temperature (X_1), time (X_2), and sulfuric acid concentrations (X_3), were varied across three levels as shown in Table 1. The pretreatment process was carried out within the ranges of 80 - 140 °C (X_1), 40 - 60 minutes (X_2), and sulfuric acid concentrations of 0.01%wt - 0.5%wt (X_3). Each factor was assigned levels of -1, 0, and +1 as indicated in Table 1. A total of 17 experimental runs were conducted according to the RSM design outlined in Table 2.

Table 1. Independent variable factors in pretreatment condition of corn husk on RSM.

Independent variable factors	Coded symbols	Levels		
		-1	0	-1
Temperature (°C)	X_1	80	139.66	140
Time (min)	X_2	40	44.27	60
Sulfuric acid concentration (%wt)	X_3	0.01	0.41	0.50

After pretreatment, the treated biomass underwent hydrolysis using cellulase enzymes, and the resulting liquid hydrolysates were analyzed to determine the quantity of reducing sugars produced. The amounts of reducing sugars obtained from each experiment were subjected to analysis of variance (ANOVA) to establish the correlation between the pretreatment parameters (model p-value < 0.05). Through multiple regression analysis, the optimal pretreatment conditions that would yield the highest sugar content were predicted. The generated second-order model was evaluated based on the coefficient of determination (R^2), the significance of the test conditions in the ANOVA, and the lack of fit test.

Table 2. RSM experimental design for organosolv pretreatment of corn husk

Run	Pretreatment condition			Sugar yield (%)
	X1: Temperature (°C)	X2: Time (min)	X3: Sulfuric concentration (%w/w)	
1	110.00	50.00	0.26	13.41
2	110.00	40.00	0.01	6.45
3	140.00	50.00	0.50	19.88
4	80.00	40.00	0.26	4.14
5	140.00	50.00	0.01	5.95
6	110.00	60.00	0.01	5.32
7	80.00	60.00	0.26	9.00
8	110.00	50.00	0.26	12.94
9	110.00	60.00	0.50	15.37
10	80.00	50.00	0.01	4.46
11	110.00	50.00	0.26	11.62
12	140.00	40.00	0.26	18.32
13	140.00	60.00	0.26	19.38
14	80.00	50.00	0.50	8.56
15	110.00	50.00	0.26	12.21
16	110.00	40.00	0.50	12.07
17	110.00	50.00	0.26	13.74

2.4 Enzymatic hydrolysis

Commercial Ctec2 was used to enzymatically hydrolyze both untreated and pretreated corn husks. The hydrolysis reaction was conducted with 0.5 g of biomass in 20 mL of 50 mM citrate buffer, supplemented with 200 µl of 2 M sodium azide solution and 10 µl of Cellic CTec2 (20 FPU/g-biomass) [23,24,25]. The reaction mixture was then incubated at 50 °C and 150 rpm for a duration of 72 hours [6]. The mixture was incubated at 100 °C for 10 minutes to stop the reaction. The liquid hydrolysate fraction was obtained by centrifuging the mixture at 6000 rpm for 10 minutes. The concentrations of reducing sugars in the liquid hydrolysate were then determined using the dinitrosalicylic acid (DNS) method [26,27].

In brief, 50 mL of the enzymatic hydrolysis supernatant was mixed with 150 mL of the DNS solution. The mixture was then incubated in a water bath at 95°C for 5 minutes. The mixture was subsequently placed on ice for 5 minutes to stop the reaction. After incubation, 1 mL of distilled water was added to the mixture and thoroughly mixed using a vortex shaker. The absorbance of each sample was measured at 540 nm using a UV/VIS spectrophotometer. The concentration of reducing sugar was determined by comparing the absorbance values to a glucose standard curve, which established the correlation between sugar concentration and absorbance.

2.5 Composition analytical methods

The compositions of corn husk, including cellulose, hemicellulose and lignin before and after pretreatment were determined by using the Van Soet method [28,29].

The chemical structures and chemical bonding arrangements of corn husk samples were analyzed by Fourier transform infrared analyzer (FTIR) (Nicolet Is50) by scanning the wavenumbers between 400-4000 cm^{-1}.

3 Result and discussion

3.1 Screening of pretreatment parameters by OFAT method

Before RSM optimization, the tested ranges of pretreatment parameters were determined by using the one factor at a time (OFAT) method. Preconditioning with different pretreatment temperatures was varied at 80, 110 and 140 °C, while using a constant sulfuric acid concentration of 0.1 wt% and a pretreatment time of 20 min. After the range of pretreatment temperature was screened and selected, the concentration of sulfuric acid was tested at 0.02, 0.1 and 0.5%wt, while the pretreatment temperature and pretreatment time were fixed at one condition. Lastly, after the selection of the ranges of pretreatment temperature and acid concentration, the pretreatment time was varied at 20, 40 and 60 min, respectively.

In Figure 2, the results clearly showed that the yield of the reducing sugar at 80 °C has the highest yield of reducing sugar (13.72 g per 100 g corn husk). For the pretreatment time, the highest yield of reducing sugars at 10.22 g per 100 g corn husk was obtained at 60 min of pretreatment time. Furthermore, the maximum yield of reducing sugar at 22.10 g per 100 g corn husk was obtained when using 0.5%wt of sulfuric acid concentration.

3.2 Optimization of pretreatment based on RSM

RSM is used for determining the optimum state for independent factors (i.e. pretreatment factor) to obtain the minimum or maximum points of dependent factors (i.e. sugar yield). Furthermore, it assesses the impact of each independent variable and its interactions with the RSM-dependent variable, minimizing the need for excessive experimental trials, thus saving time and reducing trial costs. Additionally, RSM has the capability to predict outcomes and generate surface models based on various conditions of the independent variables. Several studies have applied RSM to optimize and develop processes in various areas [30,31,32,33].

In this study, after 17 runs of pretreatments were conducted by using the condition shown in Table 2, the reducing sugar yield obtained from all runs was analyzed by using ANOVA (Table 3). The predicted model was suggested to be the second-order model with a p-value of 0.0012 suggesting the model significance (p-value < 0.05). Also, the R^2 value of the predicted model was determined to be 0.9456 indicating a low variance between experiments and demonstrating the reliability of the model. Generally, an R^2 value above 0.9 is considered significant [34].

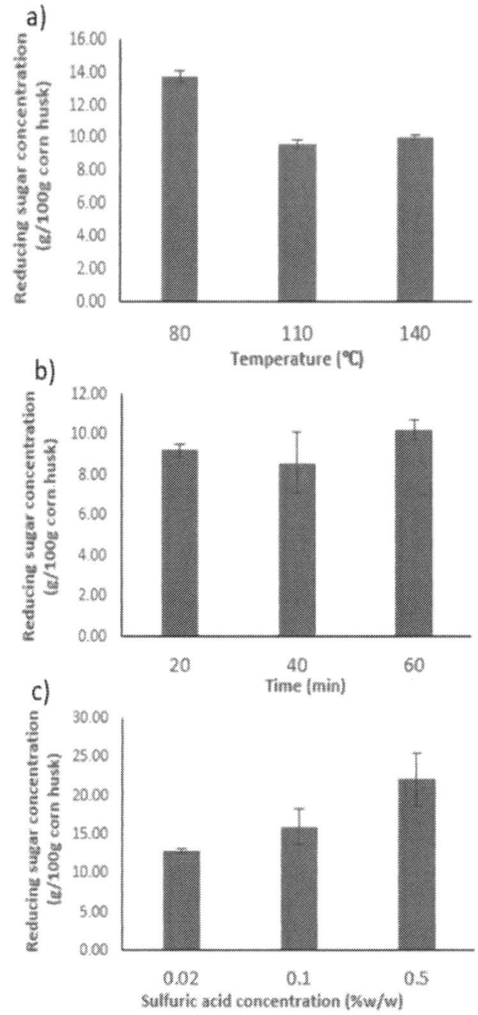

Fig 2. Effect of (a) pretreatment temperature, (b) time and (c) sulfuric acid concentration on the reducing sugar yields based on OFAT method.

Table 3. Analysis of variance (ANOVA) for the predicted model of pretreatment optimization. The significance of each parameter was justified at a p-value < 0.05.

Source	Squares	df	Mean square	F Value	p-value
Model	395.29	9	43.92	13.53	**0.0012**
A-Temp	174.55	1	174.55	53.76	**0.0002**
B-Time	8.16	1	8.16	2.51	0.1568
C-conc	141.92	1	141.92	43.71	**0.0003**
AB	3.62	1	3.62	1.12	0.3259
AC	24.15	1	24.15	7.44	**0.0295**
BC	4.91	1	4.91	1.51	0.2587
A^2	0.03	1	0.03	0.01	0.9267
B^2	0.00	1	0.00	0.00	0.9929
C^2	37.62	1	37.62	11.59	**0.0114**
Residual	22.73	7	3.25		
Lack of Fit	19.70	3	6.57	8.67	0.0318
Pure Error	3.03	4	0.76		

From the ANOVA analysis of the model (Table 3), it was found that the F value was 13.53 with statistical significance (p-value < 0.05) and there was a 0.01% chance of interference of themodel F value. Pretreatment parameters, such as temperature and the concentration of sulfuric acid were the important normalization factor according to the ANOVA analysis. The effect of each pretreatment factor, temperature, time, and sulfuric acid concentration on sugar yield was visualized as shown in Figure 4. Furthermore, the interaction effects of two pretreatment factors at a time were observed in the form of 3D-contour plots (Figure 5). The data showed that the yield of the reducing sugars increased when temperature, time and acid concentration were increased. This observation could be explained that this pretreatment condition may lead to swelling in the cellulose structure and a change in the structural organization of hemicellulose and lignin, which leads to an increase in the surface area of biomass to cellulase. As a result, this allows the enzymes to have better access to cellulose and reactivity leading to increased sugar production accordingly [35,36].

From the ANOVA analysis, the generated mathematical model predicted the optimal levels of pretreatment parameters to be at 135.46 °C for 57 min and at a sulfuric acid concentration of 0.46 (%w/w) to achieve the maximum sugar yield at 20.69% (Table 4). To confirm the reliability of this predicted model, the pretreatment experiment was performed again at the predicted optimum pretreatment conditions. The sugar yield obtained from the experiment was 20.43% with a deviation of only 1.2% from the predicted model value. When comparing the yield of reducing sugar, it can be inferred that the model from ANOVA prediction has high accuracy.

Table 4. Optimal pretreatment condition obtained from RSM experiment.

Optimal pretreatment parameter		
Temperature(°C)	Time (min)	Sulfuric acid concentration (%w/w)
135.4	57	0.46
Predicted sugar yield (%)	Experimental sugar yield (%)	Difference (%)
20.69	20.43	1.2

The effects of pretreatment factors for the organosolv method in this study were in good agreement with the previous studies. Razi *et. al.*, (2020) studied the organosolv pretreatment of peanut shells under various conditions of time, biomass loading and sulfuric acid concentration using Central Composite Design in RSM to determine the correlation of the variables associated with lignin content after pretreatment [37]. Izzi *et. al.*, (2020) conducted sodium hydroxide pretreatment using under reaction time, temperature, and concentration based on BBD in RSM [38]. This study reported a similar relationship between the content of the reducing sugar and the pretreatment parameters. It was found that these parameters significantly correlated with the reduction of sugar.

3.3 Effect of organosolv pretreatment with acid catalyst on the chemical composition of corn husk.

To understand the mechanism of how glycerol with acid can enhance enzymatic saccharification, the compositions of untreated and pretreated corn husks were analyzed (Table 5). The cellulose content of corn husk was increased from 36% to 77.5% after pretreatment with optimal conditions at 135.46 °C for 57 min and at a sulfuric acid concentration of 0.46 (%w/w). The hemicellulose content of corn husk decreased after pretreatment from 49.7% to 4.6%. Additionally, lignin content was removed from biomass due to organosolv pretreatment. Due to these changes in lignocellulose compositions, the hemicellulose and lignin were removed allowing more accessibility of cellulose to cellulase [39,40]. Therefore, the release of reducing sugars of pretreated biomass was increased during enzymatic saccharification.

Table 5. Composition analysis of pretreated corn husk as an optimal parameter and untreated corn husk.

Sample	Untreated	Pretreated
Cellulose (%)	36	77.5
Hemicellulose (%)	49.7	4.6
Lignin (%)	3.07	8.87

3.4 FTIR characterization of the raw and pretreated samples.

To observe the influence of pretreatment on the chemical arrangement and bonding, FTIR analysis was done by using the wave number range 40-4000 cm^{-1}. The Infrared absorption spectra were shown in Figure 3. The stretching mode of the OH bond in cellulose, representing the chemical bond, was observed as peak intensity within the range of 3300 cm^{-1} to 3600 cm^{-1}. Additionally, signals in the wave number range of approximately 2800-2900 cm^{-1} were detected, corresponding to the stretching mode of CH bonds in cellulose [38]. In the wavelength range of 1715-1765 cm^{-1}, the presence of C=O groups in hemicellulose was identified [41]. The organosolv pretreatment effectively dissolved hemicellulose, as evidenced by the peak at 1100-1000 cm^{-1} corresponding to the bending of the C-OH functional group in hemicellulose disappeared [41]. Moreover, a peak observed at 1032 cm^{-1} indicated the C-O vibration of carbon C_2, while the 1632 cm^{-1} band represented carbonyl groups [41]. The presence of lignin was detected in the natural state within the wavelength range of 1315-1942 cm^{-1}. Comparatively, the pretreated corn husk exhibited lignin at this wavelength, distinguishing it from the untreated corn husk. Altogether, the FTIR results were well agreed to composition analysis (Table 5).

4 Conclusion

This study demonstrates the potential of corn husk as a feedstock for biorefining processes. It also provides an alternative to reducing agricultural waste and air pollution. The maximum yield of reducing sugars was obtained from optimally pretreated corn husks by the organosolv method. These sugars have the potential to be converted into various products, such as biogas and bioethanol. Initially, the pretreatment process was conducted using the one factor at a time method to determine the optimal range for testing the pretreatment conditions. Then, the pretreatment condition was optimized by using RSM. The predicted condition of pretreatment was suggested to be at a temperature of 135.4 °C, a time of 57 min and a sulfuric acid concentration of 0.46 (%w/w). The yield of reducing sugar was 20.69%, which was the highest yield of reducing sugar under the best conditions.

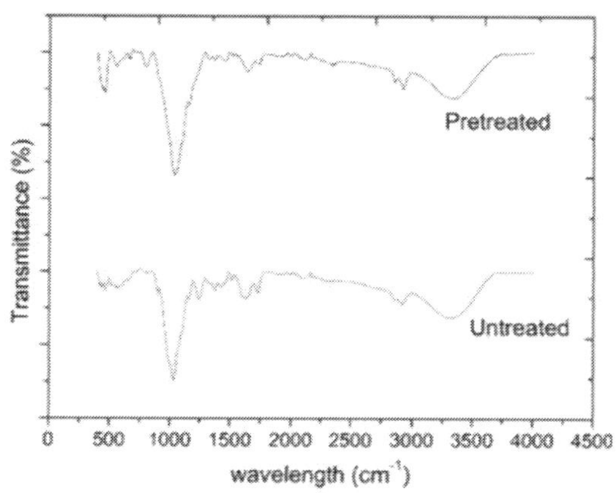

Fig. 3. FTIR spectra of untreated and pretreated corn husk.

Acknowledgment

The authors would like to thank King Mongkut's University of Technology, North Bangkok (Research Grant No. KMUTNB-PHD-66-03) and Srinakharinwirot University (Grant contract no: 036/2566-SWU) for the financial support of this work.

References

1. A. Kengpol, K. Elfvengren, Avoiding covid-19 using a 3D digital mock up and augmented reality with Cobot in Digital Factory, Applied Science and Engineering Progress, **15**,3 (2022): 5624-5624
2. A. Kengpol, T. Pichitkarnkar, K. Elfvengren, A decision support system for consumer behavior of Chinese in-bound tourists on functional beverage: An empirical study during COVID-19 with Thailand Sandbox, Applied Science and Engineering Progress, **15**,1 (2022)
3. M. Sriariyanun, M.P. Gundupalli, V. Phakeenuya, T. Phusamtisampan, Y.S. Cheng, P. Venkatachalam, Biorefinery approaches for production of cellulosic ethanol fuel using recombinant engineered microorganisms, Journal of Applied Science and Engineering, **27**,2 (1985)
4. Ministry of Energy Annual Report, www.dede.go.th (2022)
5. Office of the Cane and Sugar Board, www.ocsb.go.th
6. V. Menon, M. Rao, Trends in bioconversion of lignocellulose: Biofuels, platform chemicals & biorefinery concept, Progress in energy and combustion science, **38**,4 (2012): 522-550
7. C. Chatkaew, E. Panakkal, W. Rodiahwati, S. Kirdponpattara, S. Chuetor, M. Sriariyanun, S. Cheenkachorn, effect of sodium hydroxide pretreatment on released sugar yields from Pomelo peels for biofuel production, E3S Web of Conferences, **302** (2021): 02015
8. S. Areeya, E.J. Panakkal, M. Sriariyanun, T. Kangsadan, A. Tawai, S. Amornraksa, U. Hartley, P. Yasurin, A review on chemical pretreatment of lignocellulosic biomass for the production of bioproducts: Mechanisms, challenges and applications, Applied Science and Engineering Progress, **16**,3 (2023):6767
9. M.P. Gundupalli, M. Sriariyanun, Recent trends and updates for chemical pretreatment of lignocellulosic biomass, Applied Science and Engineering Progress, **16** (2022): 5842
10. M. Sriariyanun, K. Kitsubthawee, Trends in lignocellulosic biorefinery for production of value-added biochemicals, Applied Science and Engineering Progress, **13**,2 (2020)
11. Y. Zheng, J. Zhao, F. Xu, Y. Li, Pretreatment of lignocellulosic biomass for enhanced biogas production, Progress in Energy and Combustion Science, **42** (2014): 35-53
12. N. Raina, M. Sriariyanun, S. Areeya, A. Pathak, G. Slathia, H. Saraswat, Trends in harnessing energy from waste biomass: Pathways & Future potential, E3S Web of Conferences, **355** (2022): 01001
13. W. Siri-anusornsak, N. Sinbuathong, Chemical pretreatment of rice straw for a raw material in the production of renewable energy, Proceedings of 51st Kasetsart University Annual Conference: Science, Natural Resources and Environment, (2014)
14. E.J. Panakkal, M. Sriariyanun, J. Ratanapoompinyo, P. Yasurin, K. Cheenkachorn, W. Rodiahwati, P. Tantayotai, Influence of Sulfuric Acid Pretreatment and inhibitor of sugarcane bagasse on the production of fermentable sugar and ethanol, Applied Science and Engineering Progress, **15**,1 (2022)
15. M. Sriariyanun, J.H. Heitz, P. Yasurin, S. Asavasanti, and P. Tantayotai, Itaconic acid: A promising and sustainable platform chemical?, Applied Science and Engineering Progress, **12**,2 (2019): 75-82
16. Y.S. Cheng, P. Mutrakulcharoen, S. Chuctor, K. Cheenkachorn, P. Tantayotai, E.J. Panakkal, M. Sriariyanun, Recent situation and progress in biorefining process of lignocellulosic biomass: Toward green economy, Applied Science and Engineering Progress, **13**,4 (2020): 299-311
17. E.J. Panakkal. N. Kitiborwornkul, M. Sriariyanun, J. Ratanapoompinyo, P. Yasurin, S. Asavasanti, Production of food flavouring agents by enzymatic

reaction and microbial fermentation, Applied Science and Engineering Progress, **14**,3 (2021): 297-312
18. W. Kingkeaw, Optimization of Lignin production from agricultural waste, 58 Kasetsart University Annual Conference, (2020)
19. T. Kim, D. Im, K. Oh, Effects of Organosolv pretreatment using temperature-controlled bench-scale ball milling on enzymatic saccharification of miscanthus × giganteus, Energies, **11**,10 (2018): 2657
20. M.N.F. Norrahim, R.A. Ilyas, N.M. Nurazzi, M.S. A. Rani, M.S.N. Atikah, S.S. Shazleen, Chemical pretreatment of lignocellulosic biomass for the production of bioproducts: An overview, Applied Science and Engineering Progress, **14**,4 (2021): 588-605
21. F.F. Sun, L. Wang, J. Hong, J. Ren, F. Du, J. Hu, Z. Zhang, B. Zhou, The impact of glycerol organosolv pretreatment on the chemistry and enzymatic hydrolyzability of Wheat Straw, Bioresource Technology, **187** (2015): 354-361
22. Y. Zhu, B. Qi, X. Liang, J. Luo, Y. Wan, Lewis acid-mediated Aqueous Glycerol Pretreatment of Sugarcane Bagasse: Pretreatment Recycling, one-pot hydrolysis and lignin properties, Renewable Energy, **178** (2021): 1456-1465
23. M.P. Gundupalli, S.A. Sahithi, E.P. Jayex, S. Asavasanti, P. Yasurin, Y.S. Cheng, M. Sriariyanun, Combined effect of hot water and deep eutectic solvent (DES) pretreatment on a lignocellulosic biomass mixture for improved saccharification efficiency, Bioresource Technology Reports, **17** (2022): 100986
24. M.P. Gundupalli, P. Tantayotai, E.J. Panakkal, S. Chuetor, S. Kirdponpattara, A.S.S. Thomas, B.K. Sharma, M. Sriariyanun, Hydrothermal pretreatment optimization and deep eutectic solvent pretreatment of lignocellulosic biomass: An integrated approach, Bioresource Technology Reports, **17** (2022): 100957
25. P. Mutrakulcharoen, P. Pornwongthong, S.A. Sahithi, T. Phusantisampan, A. Tawai, M. Sriariyanun, Improvement of potassium permanganate pretreatment by enzymatic saccharification of rice straw for production of biofuels, E3S Web of Conferences, **302** (2021): 02013
26. G.L. Miller, Use of dinitrosalicylic acid reagent for determination of reducing sugar, Analytical Chemistry, **31**,3 (1959): 426-428
27. I.P. Wood, A. Elliston, P. Ryden, I. Bancroft, I.N. Roberts, K.W. Waldron, Rapid quantification of reducing sugars in biomass hydrolysates: Improving the speed and precision of the dinitrosalicylic acid assay, Biomass and Bioenergy, **44** (2012): 117-121
28. I.K. Hindrichsen, M. Kreuzer, J. Madsen, K.B. Knudsen, Fiber and lignin analysis in concentrate, forage, and faeces: Detergent versus enzymatic-chemical method, Journal of Dairy Science, **89**,6 (2006): 2168-2176
29. Y.D. Singh, Determination of carbohydrate composition in lignocellulosic biomass for biofuel production, (2018)
30. D.D. Tran, H.H. Pham, V.M. Phan, Effects of supercritical carbon dioxide extraction (SC-CO2) on the content of triterpenoids in the extracts from Ganoderma lucidum, Applied Science and Engineering Progress, (2022)
31. S. Pumkrachang, Multi-objective optimization of UV spot curing technique of slider - suspension attachment process using response surface methodology approach, Applied Science and Engineering Progress, **15**,4 (2022): 5512-5512
32. K. Rattanaporn, S. Roddecha, M. Sriariyanun, K. Cheenkachorn, Improving saccharification of oil palm shell by acetic acid pretreatment for biofuel production, Energy Procedia, **141** (2017): 146-149
33. T. Ruensodsai, E.J. Panakkal, P. Teerapornnarong, W. Rodiahwati, M. Sriariyanun, K. Rattanaporn, Optimization of enzyme assisted extraction of chondroitin sulfate from Bohadschia argus by response surface methodology, E3S Web of Conferences, **302** (2021): 02012
34. F. Arshad, H.A. Shakir, F. Tabbsum, J.I. Qazi, Optimization of dilute sulphuric acid pretreatment of peanut shells through Box- Bhenken design for cellulase production by Bacillus subtilis K-18, Punjab University Journal of Zoology, **32**,1 (2017): 81-90
35. M.P. Gundupalli, Y.S. Cheng, S. Chuetor, D. Bhattacharyya, M. Sriariyanun, Effect of dewaxing on saccharification and ethanol production from different lignocellulosic biomass, Bioresource Technology, **339** (2021): 125596
36. M. Sriariyanun N. Kitiborwornkul, P. Tantayotai, K. Rattanaporn, P.L. Show, One-pot ionic liquid-mediated bioprocess for pretreatment and enzymatic hydrolysis of rice straw with ionic liquid-tolerance bacterial cellulase, Bioengineering, **9**,1 (2022): 17
37. M.O. Razi, S. Sasmal, Organosolv pre-treatment of Groundnut (arachis hypogaea) shell and its Upshot, Biomass Conversion and Biorefinery, **12**,11 (2020): 5221-5228
38. A. Izzi, N.N. Yusuf, W.F. Ishak, H. Kim, Box-Behnken-design based Optimization Strategy for alkaline pretreatment of palm oil mill effluent for producing reducing sugar, IOP Conference Series: Earth and Environmental Science, **596**,1 (2020): 012024
39. E.J. Panakkal, K. Cheenkachorn, M.P. Gundupalli, N. Kitiborwornkul, M. Sriariyanun, Impact of sulfuric acid pretreatment of Durian Peel on the production of fermentable sugar and ethanol, Journal of the Indian Chemical Society, **98**,12 (2021): 100264
40. E.J. Panakkal, K. Cheenkachorn, S. Chuetor, P. Tantayotai, N. Raina, Y.S. Cheng, M. Sriariyanun, Optimization of deep eutectic solvent pretreatment for bioethanol production from Napier Grass, Sustainable Energy Technologies and Assessments, **54** (2022): 102856
41. M.O. Razi, S. Sasmal, Organosolv pre-treatment of Groundnut (arachis hypogaea) shell and its Upshot, Biomass Conversion and Biorefinery, **12**,11 (2020): 5221-5228

Process Optimization of Deep Eutectic Solvent Pretreatment of Coffee Husk Biomass

Sukunya Areeya[1], *Marttin Paulraj* Gundupalli[2], *Babu* Dharmalingam[3], *Baranitharan* Paramasivam[4], *Prapakorn* Tantayotai[5], *Patchanee* Yasurin[6], and *Elizabeth Jayex* Panakkal[1,*]

[1] Biorefinery and Process Automation Engineering Center, Department of Chemical and Process Engineering, The Sirindhorn International Thai-German Graduate School of Engineering, King Mongkut's University of Technology North Bangkok Bangkok, Thailand
[2] Food and Nutritional Science Department, Faculty of Agricultural, Life and Environmental, Sciences, Agricultural, University of Alberta, Edmonton, AB, Canada
[3] College of Engineering Guindy, Anna University, Chennai, India
[4] Department of Mechanical Engineering, Saveetha School of Engineering, SIMATS, Chennai, India
[5] Department of Microbiology, Faculty of Science, Srinakharinwirot University, Bangkok, Thailand
[6] Department of Food Biotechnology, Faculty of Biotechnology, Assumption University, Bangkok, Thailand

Abstract. The increased processing of coffee beans has generated huge amount of coffee husk, which are improperly disposed. Inappropriate disposal of coffee husk has led to release of toxic compounds to the environment causing serious environmental concerns. To mitigate the impact of improperly disposed coffee husk, it is suggested for valorisation of the coffee husk. Hence, this study has focussed on identifying the potential of coffee husk in maximizing the sugar yield from it which can be converted to value added product. Deep eutectic solvent (DES) involving choline chloride and lactic acid (ChCl:LA) mixed at 1:4 molar ratio was studied to investigate the effect of DES pretreatment on coffee husk to produce reducing sugar in the hydrolysis process. Pretreatment conditions of the biomass were optimized for biomass loading (5-20%, w/w), temperature (70-120 °C), and duration (60-240 min) using Response Surface Methodology (RSM) for obtaining maximum yield of reducing sugar. The RSM model predicted an optimal pretreatment condition of biomass loading with 20% (w/w), pretreated at 120 °C for 231.80 min to achieve maximum sugar yield (30.522%). The pretreatment effect on biomass composition was analyzed using the Van Soest method, which showed an increase in the cellulose content along with the hemicellulose removal when compared with the native biomass. Moreover, evaluation of chemical structural changes also confirmed the effectiveness of DES pretreatment. Thus, the current study would illustrate the potential of coffee husk to produce value-added compounds from it.

Keyword. Biofuels, Biorefinery, Coffee husk, DES pretreatment, Lignocellulosic biomass

1 Introduction

Coffee husk is the major residual produced during coffee bean processing because a major portion of the coffee fruit accounts for its husk (43.2%) and the bean contributes 38.9% of its weight [1]. After the coffee processing, the coffee husk is mostly inappropriately disposed, leading to severe environmental problems due to the presence of various harmful organic compounds like caffeine, tannins, and polyphenols. Furthermore, the burning of the coffee husk will lead to the release of greenhouse gases and particulate matter [2]. Via the wet processing method, a lower heating value (LHV) of 16.60 MJ kg^{-1} was noted in coffee husks, which was closer to the LHV of sugarcane bagasse (17.70 MJ kg^{-1}). However, it was higher than LHV reported from the rice husk (13.39 MJ kg^{-1}) [3]. In addition, coffee husks have high volatile content, low ash content, and high carbon content, which is suitable for their thermochemical conversion processes [1]. Hence, valorization of this agro-waste to valuable products like biofuels and other platform chemicals, would reduce the negative environmental impact and follows the concept of circular economy [4,5].

However, the complex structure of coffee husk, composed of amorphous polymers with complicated interactions between cellulose, hemicellulose, and lignin, presents recalcitrance to the biomass, thereby preventing chemical and biological degradation [6]. Primarily, the drying process is carried out to reduce the costs of storage and transportation and since the drying process prevents the deterioration of materials, it expands the life of coffee husk biomass [1]. Subsequently, the particles are reduced in size to attain a standard size for the densification step that can probably increase the energy density of biomass and its calorific value [1].

The primary purpose of pretreatment is disaggregating or disrupting interactions within the

* Corresponding author: elizabeth.jayex@gmail.com

lignocellulosic complex structure [7]. The method of thermochemical conversion used in the pretreatment determines the efficiency of the pretreatment. Moreover, it also helps in reducing the particle size of lignin and the crystallinity of cellulose, thus increasing the surface area and pore volume to facilitate enzymatic accessibility and microbiological digestibility [8].

Owing to the unique characteristic of deep eutectic solvents (DES) as a green and environment-benign solvent, along with its other properties of low volatility, non-toxicity, high thermal stability, and less inhibitor generation has led to prefer DES over other pretreatment methods [9]. DES is formed by mixing a hydrogen bond acceptor (HBA) and a hydrogen bond donor (HBD) [10]. It is well known for its ability to dissolve lignin from the lignocellulosic biomass as the chloride ions cause the disruption of β-O-4 aryl ether bonds resulting in delignification [11]. Besides, DES can also remove hemicellulose because of the proton dissociation while cellulose is retained in biomass [10,12]. Choline chloride (ChCl) as HBD, especially combined with organic acid (as HBA) has higher lignin removal capability and cheaper cost than other HBA [9]. In addition, it is also reported in pretreatment of various types of biomasses [13].

Previously reported studies have used ChCl combined with lactic acid (LA) in different molar ratios. ChCl/LA in a ratio of 1:10 has reported the high recovered lignin (72.3%) for pretreated masson pine [14]. A glucose yield of 87.09% was achieved by ChCl/LA (1:4) pretreatment for Napier grass [15]. Moreover, ChCl as HBD was also investigated to pretreat Bambara groundnut haulm by combining with various HBA, namely acetic acid, formic acid, LA, glycerol, and urea. The highest sugar recovery (94.8%) was achieved by ChCl/LA pretreatment [16]. Consequently, this study has used ChCl as HBD and LA as HBA.

A study on Ethiopian Arabica coffee husk has carried out pretreatment with NaOH (10% w/w) to determine the influence of alkaline pretreatment on coffee husk [17]. The study showed that the alkaline pretreatment could decrease the recalcitrant polymer, hemicellulose, and lignin, and slightly increase the cellulose content. Another study on the pretreatment of coffee husk with ozone utilized the hydrolysate for production of biogas and preserved the solid phase rich in cellulose for 2G ethanol production [8]. The study revealed that two-stage anaerobic digestion (AD) could produce more methane than single-stage AD. Moreover, the addition of activated carbon in powder form significantly increased the methane yield and energy recovery. The physical pretreatment, namely steam explosion, of coffee husk was also carried out for biogas production through anaerobic digestion [6]. The energy production of methane and electricity from the pretreated coffee husk, using a combined heat and power co-generation system (CHP) was more when compared with the untreated coffee husk. The combination of biological pretreatment and physical pretreatment, with white-rot fungi *Pleurotus ostreatus* (PL) and steam explosion on coffee husk revealed that the combined pretreatment could achieve the highest overall yield of 26.93 g reducing sugars/100 g biomass [2].

The present study has focused to investigate the effectiveness of DES pretreatment on coffee husk under the determination of the optimal pretreatment conditions via Box-Behnken design from the Response Surface Methodology (RSM). The experimental data were used to analyze the prediction of pretreatment condition and response variables by using multiple regression analysis based on maximized sugar yield. The effectiveness of pretreatment in the structural changes was further analyzed by Fourier Transform Infrared (FTIR) spectroscopy and the Van Soest methods.

2 Materials and methods

2.1 Raw materials

Coffee husk was obtained from Chiang Mai Province, Thailand. To remove the moisture content, the coffee husk was dried at 60 °C overnight. In the subsequent process, it was pulverized by a blender to reduce the particle sizes and screened by a 20 mesh-sized aluminum sieve to obtain coffee husk with uniform size.

Deep eutectic solvent (DES) for pretreatment was prepared by mixing Chlorine chloride (ChCl) and Lactic acid (LA) in a ratio of 1:4 w/w and heating at 60 °C, with continuous stirring at 100 rpm for 10 min. The transparent DES formed was stored within a desiccator to prevent moisture absorption.

2.2 RSM experiment design

Box-Behnken design from the Response Surface Methodology (RSM) was applied via design-expert 7.0.0 to achieve the objective of the optimization [18-20]. The model used three boundary conditions consisting of biomass loading (X_1) varying between 5-20% (w/w), temperature (X_2) from 70-120 °C, and time (X_3) between 60-240 min. The design has suggested 17 runs varying the boundary conditions at different levels (Table 1). The model was further optimized depending on the maximum sugar yield (Y) obtained from the model. The pretreated samples were hence enzymatically hydrolyzed to evaluate the sugar yield (%) for prediction of the optimal pretreatment condition.

2.3 Deep eutectic solvents pretreatment

DES pretreatment was performed according to the conditions depicted in Table 1 using a stirring mantle. The pretreated solids were washed with distilled water several times until the pH of wash liquid was neutral. The pretreated solids were separated from the wash liquid by using Whatman No. 1 filter paper through vacuum filtration. The pretreated solids were then dried in a hot-air oven at 60 °C overnight and further stored in desiccator for future use.

2.4 Enzymatic hydrolysis

The untreated and pretreated coffee husks were hydrolyzed with a solid loading of 2.5% (w/v) in 50 mM citrate buffer along with the commercial CTec2 enzyme (20 FPU/g biomass) [21,22]. The hydrolysis reaction was done at 50°C, in an orbital shaker with 150 rpm for 72 h. The reaction in the mixture was stopped by heating the mixture at 95 °C for 10 min in a water bath. The liquid fraction was separated by filtration with Whatman No. 1 filter paper and further taken to analyze the reducing sugar using high-performance liquid chromatography (HPLC) [15].

2.5 Determinations of reducing sugar and biomass composition

Reducing sugar analysis was performed using high-performance liquid chromatography (HPLC) (Perkin Elmer Flexar LC) equipped with Brownlee Amino 5 µm column (150×4.6 mm) and a refractive index detector (RID). The mobile phase used for the analysis was water and acetonitrile (25:75) at a flow rate of 1 mL/min. The biomass composition for both untreated and pretreated coffee husks was analyzed by using the Van Soest method [23,24] to calculate cellulose, hemicellulose, and lignin composition in the sample. All experiments were repeated at least three times.

2.6 Fourier Transform Infrared (FTIR) spectroscopy analysis

FTIR spectroscopy was performed on both untreated and pretreated coffee husk samples using Spectrum 2000, Perkin-Elmer, USA with a resolution of 4 cm^{-1} from 400 cm^{-1} to 4000 cm^{-1}.

3 Results and discussions

3.1 Optimization of DES pretreatment by Box Behnken Design (BBD)

RSM is an important method in the Design of Experiments (DoE) for achieving the optimization of experimental conditions. It is a dependable optimization technique by applying both mathematical and statistical tools, which can demonstrate the correlation between the independent variables and the response variables [25]. Interpreting the interactions of these variables in an optimization approach with the RSM method consumes less time than experimental trials [26,27]. Box-Behnken design [28] is one of the RSM to achieve an appropriate response variable. It is integrating the 2^k Factorial Design and the incomplete block design, moreover, the Analysis of Variance (ANOVA) technique and the Lack-of-Fit test are used to estimate the accuracy of the fitted model [29]. Seventeen experimental conditions of DES pretreatment for coffee husk were conducted through RSM based on Box-Behnken design using design-expert 7.0.0 trial with reducing sugar yield (Y) as response variables. The reduced sugar yield obtained for each run is depicted in Table 1.

Table 1. Experimental design using BBD for pretreated coffee husk biomass.

Run	Biomass loading (%, w/w)	Temperature (°C)	Time (min)	Sugar yield (%)
1	5	120	150	22.494
2	20	120	150	26.628
3	12.5	95	150	26.265
4	5	70	150	23.769
5	20	95	240	28.778
6	12.5	70	240	25.055
7	12.5	70	60	17.352
8	12.5	95	150	29.165
9	12.5	120	60	20.488
10	5	95	240	18.371
11	12.5	95	150	24.350
12	20	95	60	21.771
13	20	70	150	32.126
14	5	95	60	26.191
15	12.5	120	240	25.722
16	12.5	95	150	25.970
17	12.5	95	150	21.794

The release of maximum reducing sugar is optimized by using multiple regression analysis to experimental data. ANOVA based on the backward quadratic model, which is most fit in this study, is shown in Table 2. The ANOVA analysis revealed the significance of the model with an F-value of 5.28 (p-value <0.05). Figure 1 depicts a three-dimensional plot of the effects of three independent variables, such as biomass loading, temperature, and time, on sugar yield for the saccharification process of pretreated coffee husk. The figure shows that the reducing sugar yield increased according to the increase of biomass loading and time, but the temperature is not affected on reducing sugar yield. The results of RSM based on the Box-Behnken design indicated that optimal pretreatment conditions are 20% biomass loading, pretreated at a temperature of 120 °C for a time period of 231.80 min to achieve the predicted reducing sugar yield (30.522%). The regression equation describing the relation between predicted reducing sugar yield (Y) and three independent variables consisting of biomass loading (X_1), temperature (X_2), and time (X_3) is shown as follows.

https://doi.org/10.1051/e3sconf/202342801010

$$Y = 21.77782 + 0.054643X_3 - 0.51577X_1 + 5.49149\times 10^{-3}X_3X_1 - 3.54826\times 10^{-3}X_3^2 \quad (1)$$

Table 2. ANOVA analysis from RSM experiments.

Source	Sum of square	DF	Mean square	F value	Prob > F
Model	151.00	4	37.75	5.28	0.0109
B-Time	18.37	1	18.37	2.57	0.1349
C-BL	42.68	1	42.68	5.97	0.0310
BC	54.96	1	54.96	7.69	0.0169
B2	34.99	1	34.99	4.89	0.0471
Residual	85.79	12	7.15		
Lack of Fit	56.50	8	7.06	0.96	0.5550
Pure Error	29.29	4	7.32		
Cor Total	236.76	16			0.0109

*BL = %Biomass loading

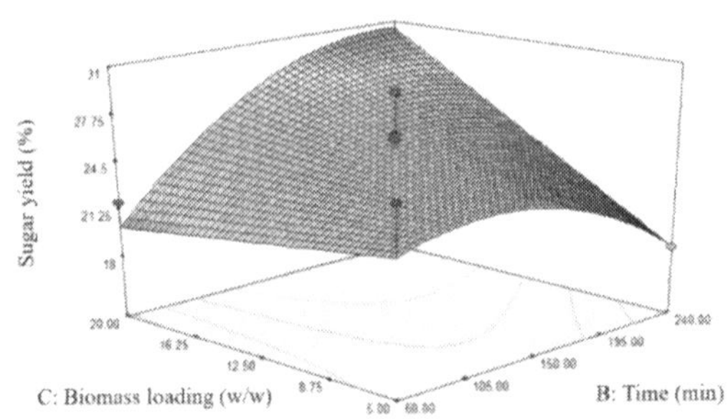

(a)

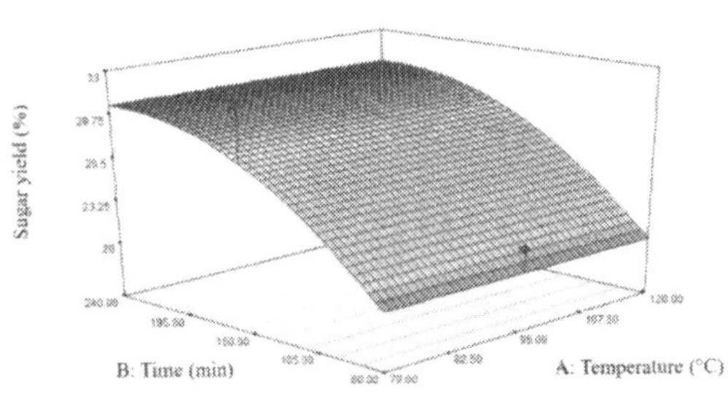

(b)

Fig. 1. Three-dimensional plot of the effects of (a) biomass loading and time on sugar yield at optimal temperature (120 °C) and (b) temperature and time on sugar yield at optimal biomass loading (20%).

3.2 Effect of DES Pretreatment on coffee husk compositions

Van Soest and Wine method [8,24] is used to estimate the cell wall components of cellulose, hemicellulose, and lignin [30]. The components of both native and pretreated coffee husk are shown in Table 3. In this study, DES pretreatment has resulted in increasing the cellulose content from 39.91% to 43.16% in addition to the increased lignin content. It could be the acidic DES pretreatment at a higher temperature for a prolonged time that could have led the lignin to redeposit onto the biomass surface, leading to increased lignin content in the pretreated coffee husk [31]. Furthermore, the results also show that the hemicellulose in the untreated coffee husk was completely removed after pretreatment with DES. With the DES pretreatment process, cellulose increased as same as lignin, but lignin was inconsistent with the FTIR results. A previous study on the pretreatment of Ethiopian Arabica coffee husk with alkali (NaOH) has enhanced the cellulose content from 53.2% to 56.58% along with hemicellulose and lignin removal [12]. Another study on the H_2SO_4 pretreatment of coffee husk has also resulted in enhanced cellulose content coupled with hemicellulose removal [27]. A similar trend was observed in the present study which had enhanced cellulose content with removal of hemicellulose.

Table 3. The components of untreated coffee husk and pretreated coffee husk.

Biomass composition (%)	Untreated coffee husk	Pretreated coffee husk
Cellulose	39.91	43.16
Hemicellulose	4.04	0.00
Lignin	21.51	33.09

3.3 Biophysical Characterization of Coffee husk biomass

FTIR analysis generally demonstrates the bond rupture and the stretching vibrations which correlate with the structural integrity of lignocellulosic biomass [32]. Generally, the components of biomass are the compounds of esters, alkene, aromatics, alcohol, and ketones [33]. The FTIR results of untreated and pretreated coffee husk are represented in Figure 2. The peak near 3337 cm^{-1} presents in both untreated and pretreated biomass was ascribed to –OH stretching of hydrogen bonds, mainly assigned to the cellulose [26,34]. The peak of 2355 cm^{-1} was attributed to the aliphatic and alkyl groups within the cellulose and the methyl, methoxy groups in hemicellulose and lignin respectively [2]. The intensity of this peak has been decreased in the pretreated biomass, which may be due to the hemicellulose removal. The sharp peak at 1727 cm^{-1} denoted the C=O stretching of acetyl or carboxylic acid that was associated with hemicellulose, which decreased after the pretreatment process [26,35]. The peak of 1610 cm^{-1} is assigned to the C=C stretching vibration together with the asymmetric-stretching vibration in the aromatic ring of COOH that refers to the relation of cellulose, hemicellulose, and lignin [36,37]. The sharp peak at 1155 cm^{-1} implies the presence of β-O-4 linkages referred to as an entry point for lignin valorization [38]. FTIR study implies that the pretreatment with ChCl:LA (1:4) has caused significant changes in the chemical structure of coffee husk.

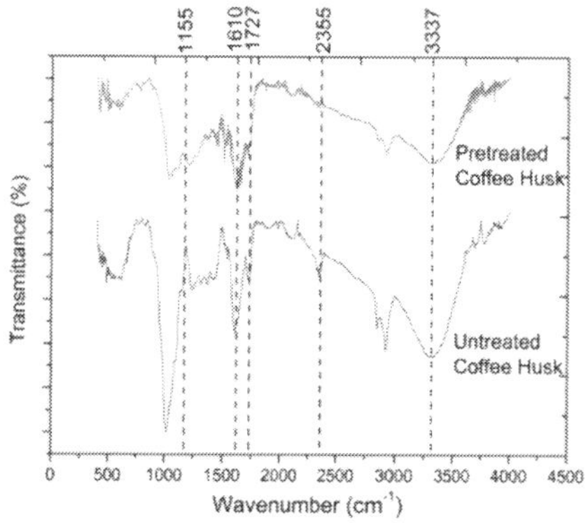

Fig. 2. Fourier-transform infrared spectroscopy (FTIR) spectra of untreated and pretreated coffee husk biomass.

4 Conclusion

The present study has focused on the optimization of pretreatment conditions for coffee husk using RSM. The mathematical model has predicted the optimal pretreatment conditions to be biomass loading of 20% (w/w), pretreatment at a temperature of 120 °C, for a duration of 231.80 min to obtain the maximum sugar yield. Under this optimal condition, the pretreatment was able to remove hemicellulose from the biomass thereby exposing more cellulose for the enzymatic hydrolysis. The chemical structural changes in biomass after pretreatment also confirm the effectiveness of DES pretreatment on the coffee husk. Thus, this study suggests an optimal pretreatment condition for the acidic DES pretreatment of coffee husk that can further ease the valorization of coffee waste to produce value-added products in the biorefinery industry.

Acknowledgments

The authors would like to thank King Mongkut's University of Technology North Bangkok, Bangkok, Thailand (Grant contract no: KMUTNB-PHD-64-02) and Srinakharinwirot University (Grant contract no: 036/2566-SWU) for financial support of this work.

References

1. A.D.O. e Silva, F.P. Garcia, M.T.B. Perazzini, H. Perazzini, Design and economic analysis of a pre-treatment process of coffee husks biomass for an integrated bioenergy plant, Environmental Technology & Innovation, **30** (2023): 103131
2. A.M. Sabogal-Otálora, L.F. Palomo-Hernández, Y. Piñeros-Castro, Sugar production from husk coffee using combined pretreatments, Chemical Engineering and Processing-Process Intensification, **176** (2022): 108966
3. V. Dal-Bó, T. Lira, L. Arrieche, M. Bacelos, Process synthesis for coffee husks to energy using hierarchical approaches, Renewable Energy, **142** (2019): 195–206
4. M. Sriariyanun, K. Kitsubthawee, Trends in lignocellulosic biorefinery for production of value-added biochemicals, Applied Science and Engineering Progress, **13**, 4 (2020): 283-284
5. Y.S. Cheng, P. Mutrakulcharoen, S. Chuetor, K. Cheenkachorn, P. Tantayotai, E.J. Panakkal, M. Sriariyanun, Recent situation and progress in biorefining process of lignocellulosic biomass: toward green economy, Applied Science and Engineering Progress, **13**, 4 (2020): 299-311
6. B.E.L. Baêta, P.H. de Miranda Cordeiro, F. Passosa, L.V.A. Gurgel, S.F. de Aquino, F. Fdz-Polanco, Steam explosion pretreatment improved the biomethanization of coffee husks, Bioresource Technology, **245**, (2017): 66-72
7. D. Jose, N. Kitiborwornkul, M. Sriariyanun, K. Keerthi, A review on chemical pretreatment methods of lignocellulosic biomass: recent advances and progress, Applied Science and Engineering Progress, **15**, 4 (2022): 6210
8. L.C. dos Santos, O.F.H. Adarme, B.E.L. Baêta, L.V.A. Gurgel, S.F. de Aquino, Production of biogas (methane and hydrogen) from anaerobic digestion of hemicellulosic hydrolysate generated in the oxidative pretreatment of coffee husks, Bioresource Technology, **263** (2018): 601-612
9. M. del Mar Contreras-Gamez, A. Galan-Martin, N. Seixas, A.M. da Costa Lopes, A. Silvestre, E. Castro, Deep eutectic solvents for improved biomass pretreatment : Current status and future prospective towards sustainable processes, Bioresource Technology, **369** (2022): 128396
10. M.P. Gundupalli, S.A. Sahithi, E.P. Jayex, S. Asavasanti, P. Yasurin, Y.S. Cheng, M. Sriariyanun, Combined effect of hot water and deep eutectic solvent (DES) pretreatment on a lignocellulosic biomass mixture for improved saccharification efficiency, Bioresource Technology Reports, **17** (2022): 100986
11. M.P. Gundupalli, P. Tantayotai, E.J. Panakkal, S. Chuetor, S. Kirdponpattara, A.S.S. Thomas, B.K. Sharma, M. Sriariyanun, Hydrothermal pretreatment optimization and deep eutectic solvent pretreatment of lignocellulosic biomass: an integrated approach, Bioresource Technology Reports, **17** (2022): 100957
12. S. Areeya, E.J. Panakkal, M. Sriariyanun, T. Kangsadan, S. Amornraksa, U.W. Hartley, A. Tawai, A Review on chemical pretreatment of lignocellulosic biomass for the production of bioproducts: mechanisms, challenges and Applications, Applied Science and Engineering Progress, **16**, 3 (2023): 6767
13. C.L. Yiin, K.L. Yap, A.Z.E. Ku, B.L.F. Chin, S.S.M. Lock, K.W. Cheah, A.C.M. Loy, Y.H. Chan, Recent advances in green solvents for

lignocellulosic biomass pretreatment: Potential of choline chloride (ChCl) based solvents, Bioresource Technology, **333** (2021): 125195

14. L. Yang, T. Zheng, C. Huang, J. Yao, Using deep eutectic solvent pretreatment for enhanced enzymatic saccharification and lignin utilization of masson pine, Renewable Energy, **195** (2022): 681-687
15. E. J. Panakkal, K. Cheenkachorn, S. Chuetor, P. Tantayotai, N. Raina, Y. S. Cheng, M. Sriariyanun, Optimization of deep eutectic solvent pretreatment for bioethanol production from Napier grass, Sustainable Energy Technologies and Assessments, **54** (2022): 102856
16. S.I. Okuofu, A.S. Gerrano, S. Singh, S. Pillai, Deep eutectic solvent pretreatment of bambara groundnut haulm for enhanced saccharification and bioethanol production. Biomass Conversion and Biorefinery, 12, 8 (2020): 3525-3533
17. B.T. Amena, H. Altenbach, G.S. Tibba, N. Hossain, Physico-chemical characterization of alkali-treated Ethiopian Arabica coffee husk fiber for composite materials production, Journal of Composites Science, **6**, 8 (2022): 233
18. E. J. Panakkal, M. Sriariyanun, J. Ratanapoompinyo, P. Yasurin, K. Cheenkachorn, W. Rodiahwati, P. Tantayotai, Influence of sulfuric acid pretreatment and inhibitor of sugarcane bagasse on the production of fermentable sugar and ethanol, Applied Science and Engineering Progress, **15**, 1 (2022): 5238
19. M.C. Macawile, J. Auresenia, Utilization of supercritical carbon dioxide and co-solvent n-hexane to optimize oil extraction from gliricidia sepium seeds for biodiesel production, Applied Science and Engineering Progress, **15**, 1 (2022): 5404
20. P. Pangsri, T. Wuttipornpun, W. Songserm, Mannanase and cellulase enzyme production from the agricultural wastes by the Bacillus subtilis p2-5 strain, Applied Science and Engineering Progress, **14**, 3 (2021): 425-434
21. M.P. Gundupalli, Y. S. Cheng, S. Chuetor, D. Bhattacharyya, M. Sriariyanun, Effect of dewaxing on saccharification and ethanol production from different lignocellulosic biomass, Bioresource Technology, **339** (2021): 125596
22. E.J. Panakkal, K. Cheenkachorn, M.P. Gundupalli, N. Kitiborwornkul, M. Sriariyanun, Impact of sulfuric acid pretreatment of durian peel on the production of fermentable sugar and ethanol, Journal of the Indian Chemical Society, **98**, 12 (2021): 100264
23. P.V. Soest, R.H.Wine, Use of detergents in the analysis of fibrious feeds. IV. Determination of plant cell wall constituents, Journal of the Association of Official Analytical Chemists, **50**, 1 (1967): 50–55
24. P.J. Van Soest, R.H. Wine, Determination of lignin and cellulose in acid detergent fiber with permanganate, Journal of the association of official analytical chemists, **51**, 4 (1968): 780–785
25. A. Lawong, S. Sergsiri, A study of optimal values with pid controller using response surface method, Udon Thani Rajabhat University Journal of Sciences and Technology, **8**, 2 (2020): 105-117
26. K. Anil, K.K. Jain, S. Bijender, Process optimization for chemical pretreatment of rice straw for bioethanol production, Renewable Energy, **156** (2020): 1233-1243
27. A.S. Thomareis, G. Dimitreli, Techniques used for processed cheese characterization, In *Processed Cheese Science and Technology* (Woodhead Publishing, 2022)
28. G.E. Box, D.W. Behnken, Some new three level designs for the study of quantitative variables, Technometrics **2**, 4 (1960): 455–475
29. A.H. Serafín Muñoz, C.E. Molina Guerrero, N.L. Gutierrez Ortega, J.C. Leal Vaca, A. Alvarez Vargas, C. Cano Canchola, Characterization and integrated process of pretreatment and enzymatic hydrolysis of corn straw, Waste and Biomass Valorization **10** (2019): 1857-1871
30. V. Vandenbossche, J. Brault, G. Vilarem, Ó. Hernández-Meléndez, E. Vivaldo-Lima, M. Hernández-Luna, E. Bárzana, A. Duque, P. Manzanares, M. Ballesteros, J. Mata, E. Castellón, L. Riga, A new lignocellulosic biomass deconstruction process combining thermo-mechano chemical action and bio-catalytic enzymatic hydrolysis in a twin-screw extruder, Industrial Crops and Products, **55**, (2014): 258-266
31. M.J. Selig, S. Viamajala, S.R. Decker, M.P. Tucker, M.E. Himmel, T.B. Vinzant, Deposition of lignin droplets produced during dilute acid pretreatment of maize stems retards enzymatic hydrolysis of cellulose, Biotechnol Prog, **23**, 6 (2007) : 1333-1339
32. J.L. Morales-Martínez, M.G. Aguilar-Uscanga, E. Bolaños-Reynoso, L. López-Zamora, Optimization of chemical pretreatments using response surface methodology for second-generation ethanol production from coffee husk waste, BioEnergy Research, **14**,3 (2021):815–827
33. S.W. Suciyati1, P. Manurung, S. Sembiring, R. Situmeang, Comparative study of Cladophora sp. cellulose by using FTIR and XRD, Journal of Physics, Conference Series, **1751**(2021): 012075
34. X. Xian, L. Fang, Y. Zhou, B. Li, X. Zheng, Y. Liu, X. Lin, Integrated bioprocess for cellulosic ethanol production from wheat straw: New ternary deep-eutectic-solvent pretreatment, enzymatic saccharification, and fermentation, Fermentation, **8**, 8 (2022): 371
35. A. Azizan, N.S.M. Shafaei, N.S Sidek, F. Hanafi, N. Mokti, S. Zaharudin, Fourier Transform infrared spectroscopy interpretation on pretreated Acacia Auriculiformis, Melastoma Malabathricum and

Leucaeana Leucocephala, International Journal of Applied Engineering Research, **11**, 20 (2016): 10048-10051

36. X. Li, Y. Wei, J. Xu, N. Xu, Y. He, Quantitative visualization of lignocellulose components in transverse sections of moso bamboo based on FTIR macro- and micro-spectroscopy coupled with chemometrics, Biotechnology for Biofuels, **11**, 1 (2018): 1-16
37. A.M. da Costa Lopes, K.G. João, D.F. Rubik, E. Bogel-Łukasik, L.C. Duarte, J. Andreaus, R. Bogel-Łukasik, Pre-treatment of lignocellulosic biomass using ionic liquids: Wheat straw fractionation, Bioresource Technology, **142** (2013): 198-208
38. R. Ahorsu, M. Constanti, P.D. de María, F. Medina, Synergy of ball milling, microwave irradiation, and deep eutectic solvents for a rapid and selective delignification: walnut shells as model for lignin-enriched recalcitrant biomass, Biomass Conversion and Biorefinery, (2022): 1-13

Conversion of lignocellulose residue obtained from biorefinery stream to electricity by microbial fuel cell

Keerthi Katam[1], *Maythee* Saisriyoot[2], *Supacharee* Roddecha[2], *Peerapong* Pornwongthong[3], and *Malinee* Sriariyanun[4,*]

[1]Department of Civil Engineering, Ecole Centrale School of Engineering, Mahindra University, Telangana, India
[2]Department of Chemical Engineering, Faculty of Engineering, Kasetsart University, Bangkok, Thailand
[3]Department of Agro-Industrial, Food, and Environmental Technology, Faculty of Applied Science, King Mongkut's University of Technology North Bangkok, Bangkok, Thailand
[4]Biorefinery and Process Automation Engineering Center, Department of Chemical and Process Engineering, The Sirindhorn International Thai-German Graduate School of Engineering, King Mongkut's University of Technology North Bangkok, Bangkok, Thailand

Abstract. In general, lignocellulose biorefinery has the main functions to fractionate biomass compositions and convert them to value-added products. However, leftover organic compounds in output streams are mixed with large amounts of wastewater becoming the cost and burden for treatment. Therefore, to close the loop of circular economy, this review paper explores the potential of microbial fuel cells (MFCs) as a sustainable and efficient way to convert lignocellulose residue, a byproduct of biorefinery processes, into electricity. Lignocellulose residue is a complex mixture of carbohydrates and lignin that is often difficult to dispose of properly. By using MFCs, this waste material can be converted into valuable energy while reducing the environmental impact of its disposal. The paper covers the different types of MFCs, their working principles, and their potential application in lignocellulose residue conversion. It also discusses the factors that affect the performance of MFCs, including substrate availability, electrode material, and reactor design. Additionally, the paper reviews the current state of research in this area, highlighting recent advances and identifying areas for future exploration. Overall, this review paper demonstrates the promise of MFCs as a sustainable and innovative approach to converting lignocellulose residue into electricity.

Keyword. Circular economy, Lignocellulose biomass, Microbial fuel cell, Wastewater

1 Introduction

Lignocellulose is the fundamental structural component of plant biomass and is comprised of cellulose, hemicellulose and lignin. It is the most abundant organic material on Earth and it is estimated to be produced globally more than 1.3 billion tons per year. Engaged with agricultural activities, improper management of lignocellulose residues, which are discarded with no use after harvesting season, can lead to the emission of greenhouse gases, the depletion of soil quality, and the contamination of water resources [1]. Therefore, the circular economy model is proposed to be a solution by converting lignocellulose residues to be the raw materials for productions of value-added products to motivate the social and industrial movement to this campaign. Biorefining process adapts to the circular economy model by converting lignocellulose biomass to various types of products such as biofuels, bioenergy, platform chemicals, biochemical and biopolymers [2].

On one hand, lignocellulose biorefinery is a solution to reduce the release of biomass waste to environment in manageable facility or process, on another hand, this process generates large amounts of wastewaters containing organic and inorganic residues. For example, after pretreatment of mixed vegetable waste with organic acids, such as citric acid, oxalic acid, and acetic acid, about 5-6 liters of water needed to be used for washing organic acids from 5 g biomass to remove inhibitors for enzymatic saccharification and microbial fermentation [3]. It is estimated that a typical biorefinery process requires input water about 4−10 times more than the amount of generated biofuel [4]. Therefore, several attempts have been done to close the loop of circular economy model of lignocellulose biorefinery by integrate various technologies or units, such as anaerobic digester, photocatalytic, and microbial fuel cell.

The use of microbial fuel cells (MFCs) is a promising technology for converting lignocellulose residue into electricity, thereby providing a sustainable and efficient way to utilize this waste material. By harnessing the natural abilities of microorganisms to oxidize organic matter and produce electrical energy, MFCs offer a novel approach to the management of lignocellulose residue [5]. The use of MFCs is not limited to the conversion of lignocellulose residue, they have also been applied in other areas, such as wastewater treatment, bioremediation, and biosensors. Furthermore, their potential applications extend beyond the production of electricity, with some researchers exploring the use of

* Corresponding author: macintous@gmail.com

MFCs for the production of chemicals and fuels [6]. Due to these wide ranges of applications, the numbers of publications related to MFCs indexed in SCOPUS are doubling-increased from 701 papers in 2013 to 1417 papers in 2022 (Figure 1). In the same period of time, the trend of biorefinery research with application of MFCs has been growing significantly from 10 to 198 papers suggesting the potential of MFC technology. This review paper aims to explore the current state of research on the use of MFCs for lignocellulose residue conversion, covering the different types of MFCs, their working principles, and their potential application in this area. The paper also discusses the factors that affect the performance of MFCs, such as substrate availability, electrode material, and reactor design. Finally, the paper highlights recent advances in this field and identifies areas for future exploration.

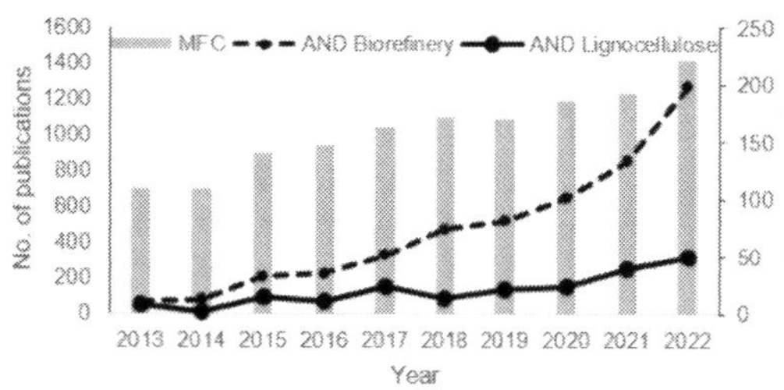

Fig. 1. Numbers of publications indexed in SCOPUS database during 2013 – 2022 related to MFCs, biorefinery and lignocellulose.

2 Lignocellulosic biorefining process and its output streams

Lignocellulose is a complex material that is resistant to degradation, and its disposal can lead to environmental and economic issues. Additionally, the transportation and disposal of lignocellulose residue can be costly and can consume significant amounts of energy due to its bulky shape and low-density characteristic. The biorefinery process of lignocellulose biomass typically involves four main steps, including pretreatment, hydrolysis, fermentation and product separation (Figure 2) [7]. The bottleneck of the process to convert lignocellulose biomass to value-added products, such as biofuels and biochemical, is the hydrolysis due to the recalcitrant structure of biomass that functions as the protector of plants in nature from environmental stresses and pathogen attacks [8].

Pretreatment involves breaking down the lignocellulosic material into smaller components to increase their accessibility for downstream processes, especially enzymatic hydrolysis by cellulase enzyme. Currently, there are many pretreatment methods that are categorized as chemical, biological, physical and combined methods. The most common pretreatment methods include steam explosion, acid hydrolysis, and alkaline treatment [9]. It is estimated that the pretreatment cost could be 40-60% of the whole process. Hydrolysis uses enzymes or acid catalysts to break down the cellulose and hemicellulose into simple sugars, such as glucose and xylose, which can be used as feedstocks for productions of various chemical and biological processes (e.g. fermentation). The final step in the biorefinery process involves separating and purifying the desired products from the fermentation broth using various physical and chemical processes [10].

In production process of cellulosic ethanol or second generation ethanol (Figure 2), the combination of fractionation and reaction in each step produce various output streams containing different products, which are influenced by the conditions of each biorefining step. For example, strong acid pretreatment, such as hydrochloric or sulfuric acid, leads to the degradation of glucose and dehydration of xylose to 5-Hydroxymethylfurfural (HMF) and furfural, respectively. The harsh condition of pretreatment can further promote productions of various degraded chemicals from hemicellulose, such as organic acids (e.g. acetic acid, formic acid, levulinic acid, furoic acid), aldehydes, uronic acids. The lignin could be also degraded to various phenolic compounds, for example, coniferyl aldehyde, ferulic acid, benzoic acid [11]. Although many of these by-products are conceptually proved to be candidates for productions of platform chemicals or potential intermediates compounds for downstream industries [12]. Nevertheless, considered to maximize the cellulosic ethanol yield, the more by-product formation, the less ethanol yield. Based on this scheme of biorefining process, these pretreatment by-products are mostly fractionated to be the liquid fractor, or mostly called "pretreatment liquor". Additionally, pretreated biomass in solid fraction is usually needed to be washed to remove the chemical residues used in pretreatment. In a previous study, it is demonstrated that

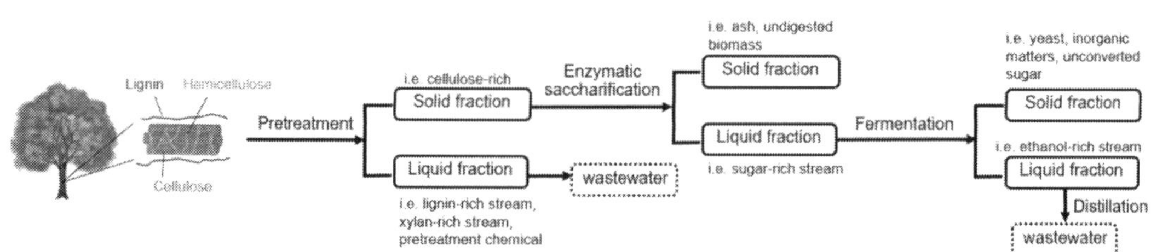

Fig. 2. Process diagram of lignocellulose biorefinery and ethanol production

the remaining pretreatment chemicals, such as ionic liquid, reduce the cellulase activities up to more than 60% when about 10-20% concentration of ionic liquid remains [13-14]. Therefore, a large volume of wastewater is generated during biomass solid washing (Figure 2). In the next step, pretreated biomass is hydrolyzed by cellulase enzyme, and the liquid fraction stream of hydrolysate is enriched with sugar monomers, especially hexose and pentose, which are further fermented by *Saccharomyces cerevisiae* to produce ethanol. The ethanol stream as an output from fermenter is proceeded to distillation column and spent liquid of distillates is enriched with organic compounds. Collectively, the output liquid streams of cellulosic ethanol contain various chemical by-products that are the sources of Chemical oxygen demand (COD) and Biochemical Oxygen Demand (BOD) values when they are released to environment.

3 MFC: components and design

The use of microbial fuel cells (MFCs) has been growing rapidly in recent years due to their potential as a sustainable and efficient technology for the production of electricity from organic waste materials. Comparing to the traditional treatment method for wastewater face several challenges that limit their effectiveness. One of the main challenges is the high energy consumption required for the treatment process. Traditional methods rely on aeration and mixing to promote microbial growth and degradation of pollutants, which requires significant amounts of electricity and power. In addition, traditional treatment methods are limited in their ability to remove certain types of pollutants such as microplastics, pharmaceuticals, and other emerging contaminants [15]. Another challenge of traditional treatment is the production of large volumes of sludge, which can pose challenges for disposal and management. The sludge contains high levels of nutrients and organic matter, which can contribute to eutrophication and other environmental problems if not properly managed. In addition, traditional methods are susceptible to operational issues, such as clogging, odors, and corrosion, which can lead to decreased efficiency and increased maintenance costs [16].

MFCs use microorganisms to catalyze the oxidation of organic matter and generate electrical energy, making them an attractive option for the treatment of organic waste and the generation of renewable energy. In an MFC, microorganisms are attached to an electrode and consume organic matter in the wastewater, producing electrons that flow through an external circuit to produce electrical power. The potential of MFCs for wastewater treatment lies in their ability to not only treat the wastewater but also generate electricity as a byproduct. MFCs have demonstrated high removal efficiencies for pollutants such as organic matter, nutrients, and heavy metals, and have been shown to remove emerging contaminants, such as pharmaceuticals and microplastics [17]. One of the main advantages of MFCs over traditional treatment methods is their lower energy consumption. Unlike traditional treatment methods that require significant amounts of electricity for aeration and mixing, MFCs rely on microbial metabolism to drive the treatment process. This reduces the energy demand of the treatment process and makes MFCs more sustainable and cost-effective. Additionally, MFCs produce lower volumes of sludge compared to traditional methods, which can reduce the costs and environmental impacts associated with sludge disposal [18].

The MFC system consists of two compartments, an anode and a cathode, separated by a proton exchange membrane (Figure 3). Microorganisms, especially

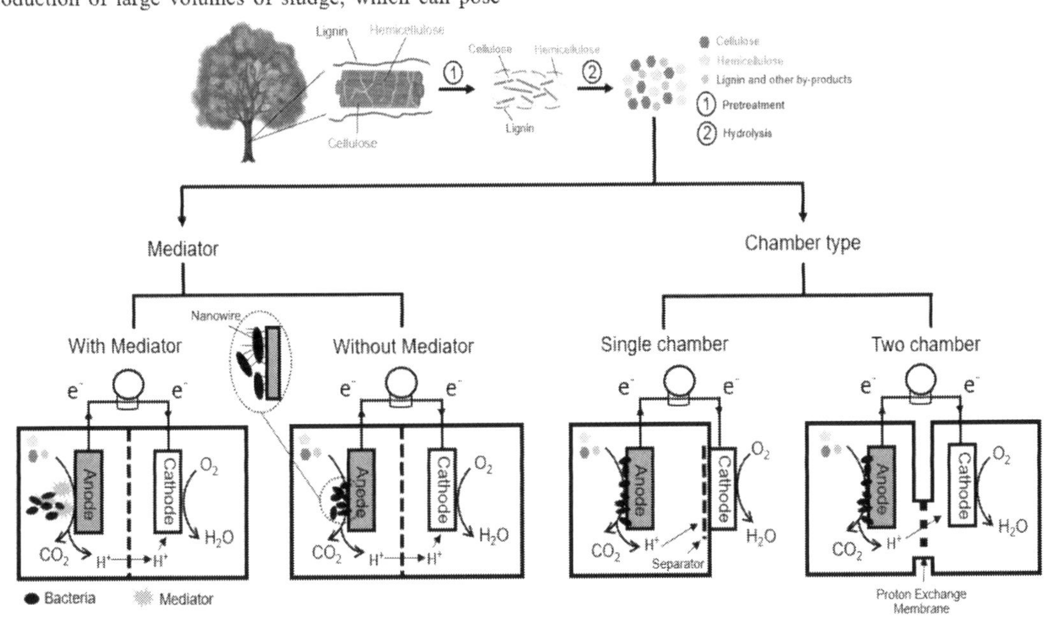

Fig. 3. Various MFC design for application in lignocellulose biorefinery

bacteria, are attached to the anode, where they oxidize organic matter and produce electrons and protons. The electrons flow from the anode through an external circuit to the cathode, where they combine with protons and oxygen to form water [17]. The conversion of organic matter into electrical energy in an MFC involves two main processes: microbial metabolism and electron transfer. Microbial metabolism is the process by which microorganisms break down organic matter into simpler compounds, releasing energy in the form of electrons and protons. The electrons and protons produced by microbial metabolism are then transferred to the anode and the cathode, respectively, through electron transfer mechanisms. Electron transfer in MFCs occurs through two main pathways: direct transfer and mediated transfer (Figure 3). In a direct transfer, electrons are transferred from the microbial cells to the anode through conductive pili or other extracellular electron transfer structures, so-called nanowire. This process is often facilitated by excreted electron shuttles such as flavins, quinones, and humic substances. Mediated transfer, on the other hand, involves the use of a mediator that acts as an intermediate electron carrier between the microbial cells and the anode. The mediator accepts electrons from the microbial cells and then transfers them to the anode, however, these mediator chemicals have high cost and toxicity, such as thionine, methyl viologen, methyl blue, humic acid and neutral red [19].

Currently, MFCs can be configured in various ways to optimize their performance for specific applications. The most common configurations of MFCs are the single-chamber MFC (SC-MFC) and the two-chamber MFC (TC-MFC) (Figure 3). The SC-MFC is a simple and compact design that consists of a single chamber containing the anode and the cathode. The chamber is filled with wastewater that serves as the substrates for the microorganism metabolisms. The anode and cathode are usually separated by a proton exchange membrane (PEM) to prevent direct contact between the electrodes and to maintain the electrochemical potential difference between the anode and cathode. The main advantage of the SC-MFC is its simplicity and low cost. However, its performance is often limited by the low power output and relatively low treatment efficiency compared to the TC-MFC [20]. On the other hand, the TC-MFC consists of two separate chambers, one for the anode and one for the cathode. The chambers are connected by a salt bridge or a PEM that allows for the transfer of ions and maintains the electrochemical potential difference between the anode and cathode. The wastewater or nutrient solution is fed into the anode chamber, and air or oxygen is fed into the cathode chamber to provide the necessary electron acceptor for the reduction of protons and electrons. The TC-MFC has several advantages over the SC-MFC, including higher power output, improved treatment efficiency, and better control over the operating conditions. The separation of the anode and cathode also allows for the recovery of valuable byproducts, such as hydrogen gas and organic acids [21].

The choice of MFC configuration depends on the specific application and the desired performance properties, such as power output, treatment efficiency, and cost-effectiveness. As MFC technology continues to advance, new configurations and designs are likely to emerge, further expanding the potential applications of this promising technology. The performance of MFCs is affected by several factors that need to be carefully optimized to achieve optimal treatment efficiency and power output. The main factors that affect MFC performance are its electrode. The anode material is an essential component of the MFC and can significantly affect its performance. The choice of anode material depends on its conductivity, surface area, and biocompatibility with the microbial community. Common anode materials include carbon-based materials, metal oxides, and conductive polymers. Additionally, the cathode material also affects the reduction of oxygen or other electron acceptors. Common cathode materials include graphite, carbon cloth, and metal catalysts such as platinum. In addition to the electrode, the microbial community in MFCs plays a critical role in the degradation of pollutants and the generation of electrical power. The selection of the appropriate microbial community depends on the wastewater composition and the desired treatment efficiency and power output [22]. Different microbial communities, such as bacteria, archaea, and fungi, have been used in MFCs for wastewater treatment.

The operating conditions of MFCs can significantly affect their performance, including temperature, pH, hydraulic retention time, and external resistance. The optimal operating conditions depend on the specific application and wastewater composition. The characteristics of the wastewater, such as its chemical composition, organic loading rate, and nutrient content, can affect MFC performance. The optimal design and operation of MFCs need to consider the specific wastewater characteristics to achieve optimal treatment efficiency and power output. The spacing between the anode and cathode electrodes can significantly affect MFC performance, with smaller electrode spacing generally leading to higher power output and treatment efficiency. Another important concern is related to substrate composition in wastewater. Inhibitors and toxic compounds, such as heavy metals and antibiotics, can affect the microbial community and reduce MFC performance [23]. Therefore, strategies to mitigate the effects of inhibitors and toxicants should be included, especially pretreatment of the wastewater or using a robust microbial community that can tolerate these substances.

4 Integration of MFC in biorefinery

Lignocellulose is abundant with the compositions of polymeric carbohydrate compounds, especially cellulose and hemicellulose. Following the process scheme of lignocellulose biorefinery (Figure 2), lignocellulose biomass is needed to be hydrolyzed by cellulase enzymes. However, based on the design of MFCs, a cellulose-degrading microbial strain or a consortium, such as *Clostridium cellulolyticum*, could be primary catalysts to convert polymeric lignocellulose substrates to oligomeric or monomeric sugars, which are subsequently catabolized by other microbes to CO_2 or small organic acids. Several bacterial strains that possess extracellular electron transfer structures, or nanowire, such as *Geobacter sulfurreducens*, *Geobacter metallireducens*, *Enterobacter ludwigii*, *Enterobacter cloacae*, *Shewanella oneidensis* and *Shewanella marisflavi*, are co-culture to improve the electrotransfer capacity to anode and cathode, respectively [24].

The bacterial strains that can function as mediators in MFC could be co-cultured with other microbial consortiums, such as wastewater sludge from food processing industries, wastewater from municipal waste, soil, ruminal secrets. It is reported that when *Geobacter metallireducens* were co-cultured with ruminal contents and pasteurized soil in the FWA-Fe(III)-citrate medium to enrich cellulolytic bacteria. This bacterial culture was filled in anode chamber equipped with graphite anode air-type carbon cloth cathode [25]. The solid form of corncob biomass was used as the substrate for MFC, which continuously produced the current of 0.15 mA and 0.15V for 1300 h. After the addition of pasteurized soil and rumen fluid, the generated maximum currents were increased to 1.38 mA/m^3 ad 770 mA/m^3, respectively. When the bacterial culture in the anode chamber was augmented by *Geobacter metallireducens*, the power density was maximized to 1170 mA/m^3, suggesting that the cellulase-producing bacteria and anode-respiring bacteria can coexist in the presence of solid form lignocellulose substrates [25].

Lignocellulose hydrolysate enriched with sugars could be also used as a substrate for MFC to produce electricity. As a case study, rapeseed straw was pretreated by hydrothermal process and enzymatic hydrolyzed, and its liquid hydrolysate fraction was input in a two-chamber MFC (H-type) for electricity generation [26]. The hydrolysate was fed in an anode chamber equipped with graphite felt anode and mixed with the post-fermentation sludge from the wastewater treatment facility and various formulas of hydrolysis media. The highest electricity was obtained at 58 mW/m^2 from the utilization of hydrolysate substrate at 150 mg/m^3 and the highest COD removal rate was 0.602 g COD/m^2.d [26]. Another study using wheat straw hydrolysate as the substrate for yeast-type MFC was conducted in a two-chamber type by adding two strains of cellulase- and laccase-producing microbes, *Phlebia floridensis* and *Phlebia brevispora*, in cathode chamber and *Pichia fermentans* in anode chamber [27]. The reducing sugars and phenolic compounds derived from wheat straw were degraded and converted to electricity with a maximum power density of 33.19 mW/m^2. Combinations of banana peels and wetland sediments (as microbial inoculum) were tested as substrates for MFC using a membrane-less single chamber. When anaerobically fermented banana peels were added into the MFC, the highest current density was obtained at 91.3 mW/m^2 with the maximum voltage at 146 mV, which is equivalent to the substrate conversion of 13.5 j/g of banana peels. However, this scale of electricity production per gram of substrate was much less than MFC with membrane type [28].

In addition to be used as a substrate for MFC, lignocellulose biomass is also applied as the electrode for MFC reactors. Water hyacinth biochar was previously produced and applied as an air-type cathode in a single chamber MFC [29]. Water hyacinth biochar was prepared by pyrolysis and its electrochemical property was analyzed to function as a cathode. This biochar cathode was installed in a single chamber MFC that operated in anaerobic condition. The artificial wastewater medium was supplemented with trace element solution and inoculated by sewage sludge, and the maximum power density was obtained at 12.3 mW/m^2 [29]. Likewise, silver grass-derived activated carbon was prepared to be used as anode in a H-type two-chamber MFC [30]. Silver grass biomass was acid-pretreated and enzymatically hydrolyzed. The anode was prepared on carbon cloth support by adding biomass slurry with a PTFE binder. The anode chamber was inoculated with *Escherichia coli* in the fresh media. Using silver grass activated carbon anode, the maximum voltage reached 790 mV and power density at 963 mW/m^2, which are much higher than the electricity reported previously for biomass-derived activated carbon [30]. Altogether, these reports suggested the potential of lignocellulose biomass as the substrates and electrodes for MFC. The lists of lignocellulose-based MFC research are shown in Table 1.

Table 1. Integrations of MFCs in different LCB biomass.

Lignocellulose biomass	MFC design	Maximum voltage (mV)	Power generation (mW/m^2)	References
Corn stover powder	Single chamber	380	331	[31]
Corn cob powder	Tubular single chamber	672	7.18	[25]
Corn stover hydrolysate	Single chamber	~500	952	[32]
Rapeseed hydrolysate	Two chamber (H-type)	~470	58	[28]
Wheat straw hydrolysate	Two chamber	504	33.19	[27]
Rice straw compost	Single chamber with air cathode	277	112	[33]
Wheat straw hydrolysate and wastewater	Two chamber	240	123	[34]
Banana peel extracts and wetland sediments	Single chamber	146	91.3	[35]
Bamboo	Two chamber	760	578	[36]
Cashew apple juice	Two chamber	400	31.58	[37]

Although MFCs have been developed and well established in wastewater treatment as a green technology for electricity production. Aforementioned, various types of MFCs are designed and applied to lignocellulose biorefinery by using direct solid biomass, biomass hydrolysate or biomass by-products as substrates. Several limitations of MFCs were discussed, especially low power density and voltage instability. MFCs typically produce low power densities compared to other energy sources. This is due to the slow rate at which microorganisms oxidize organic matter, limiting the amount of electricity that can be generated. This slow metabolism rate of microorganisms could be the result of their sensitivity to changes in environmental conditions, such as temperature, pH, and salinity. Any changes in these conditions can affect the activity of microorganisms and reduce the efficiency of the MFC. Also, due to the activities of microorganisms, the lifespan of microbial cultures is limited due to the saturation of microbial growth. Its lifespan is also limited by the formation of biofilms on electrode and PEM (biofouling) that inhibit the electron transfer between electrodes [38-39]. Specifically, MFC application in lignocellulose biorefinery has the main bottleneck in the hydrolysis of lignocellulose biomass, therefore the bioaugmentation of lignocellulose-degrading microorganisms is necessary. However, most hydrolysis reactions of lignocellulose prefer higher temperatures, especially at 50 °C, whereas most MFCs were operated at room temperature. Therefore, process optimization is needed to be conducted to increase the efficiency of MFCs. Similarly, process integration with other technology, such as hydrogen production, could also increase the feasibility of MFC for further application. However, the prime benefit of lignocellulose-based MFC is the minimization of lignocellulose waste and wastewater produced from biorefinery to release to the environment. Lastly, lignocellulose-based MFC implements the circular economy, which leads toward a sustainable development goal

5 Conclusion

Lignocellulose biomass is an abundant resource for biorefining process to produce various value-added products, especially biofuels and biochemicals. The lignocellulose biorefinery is a multi-step process, which is composed of fractionation and catalytic conversion processes. Based on the process scheme of lignocellulose biorefinery, wastewater and liquid streams containing high organic compounds are produced in large volumes that require treatment before release to the environment. MFCs are a promising technology for the conversion of lignocellulose biomass into electricity as well as a practical method for wastewater treatment. Different MFC designs have been developed and applied to lignocellulose biorefinery, especially single-chamber type and two-chamber type. Based on the production scale of electricity generated from reported MFCs, it is recommended to be used for treatment of liquid streams of lignocellulose biorefinery, which could further produce value-added by-products, especially organic acid, alcohol and hydrogen to complete the circular economy model.

Acknowledgements

Authors would like to thank for the financial support from National Science, Research and Innovation Fund (NSRF) and King Mongkut's University of Technology North Bangkok (Grant No. KMUTNB-FF-66-50).

References

1. M.P. Gundupalli, M. Sriariyanun, Recent trends and updates for chemical pretreatment of lignocellulosic biomass, Applied Science and Engineering Progress, **16**,1 (2023): 5842
2. M. Sriariyanun, K. Kitsubthawee, Trends in lignocellulosic biorefinery for production of value-added biochemicals, Applied Science and Engineering Progress, **13**,4 (2020): 283-284
3. B. Dharmalingam, P. Tantayotai, E.J. Panakkal, K. Cheenkachorn, S. Kirdponpattara, M.P. Gundupalli, Y.S. Cheng, M. Sriariyanun, Organic acid pretreatments and optimization techniques for mixed vegetable waste biomass conversion into biofuel production, BioEnergy Research, **26** (2022): 1-6
4. A.P. Borole, C.Y. Hamilton, D.J. Schell, Conversion of residual organics in corn stover-derived biorefinery stream to bioenergy via a microbial fuel cell, Environmental Science & Technology, **47**,1 (2013): 642-8
5. S. Manikandan, S. Vickram, R. Sirohi, R. Subbaiya, R.Y. Krishnan, N. Karmegam, C. Sumathijones, R. Rajagopal, S.W. Chang, B. Ravindran, M.K. Awasthi, Critical review of biochemical pathways to transformation of waste and biomass into bioenergy, Bioresource technology, **372** (2023): 128679
6. J.Wang, K. Ren, Y. Zhu, J. Huang, S. Liu, A review of recent advances in microbial fuel cells: preparation, operation, and application, BioTech (Basel) , **11**,4 (2022): 44
7. D. Jose, A. Tawai, D. Divakaran, D.j Bhattacharyya, P. Venkatachalam, P. Tantayotai, M. Sriariyanun, Integration of deep eutectic solvent in biorefining process of lignocellulosic biomass valorization, Bioresource Technology Reports, **21** (2023): 101365
8. M. Broda, D.J. Yelle, K. Serwańska, Bioethanol production from lignocellulosic biomass-challenges and solutions, Molecules, **27**,24 (2022): 8717
9. D. Jose, N. Kitiborwornkul, M. Sriariyanun, K. Keerthi, A review on chemical pretreatment methods of lignocellulosic biomass: recent advances and progress, Applied Science and Engineering Progress, **15**,4 (2022): 6210
10. S. Areeya, E.J. Panakkal, M. Sriariyanun, T. Kangsadan, A. Tawai, S. Amornraksa, U.W. Hartley, P. Yasurin, A review on chemical pretreatment of lignocellulosic biomass for the

production of bioproducts: mechanisms, challenges and applications. Applied Science and Engineering Progress, **16**,3 (2023): 6767

11. L.J. Jönsson, C. Martín, Pretreatment of lignocellulose: Formation of inhibitory by-products and strategies for minimizing their effects, Bioresource Technology, **199** (2016): 103-112
12. Y.S. Cheng, P. Mutrakulcharoen, S. Chuetor, K. Cheenkachorn, P. Tantayotai, E.J. Panakkal, M. Sriariyanun, Recent situation and progress in biorefining process of lignocellulosic biomass: toward green economy. Applied Science and Engineering Progress, **13**,4 (2020): 299-311
13. M. Sriariyanun, N. Kitiborwornkul, P. Tantayotai, K. Rattanaporn, P.L. Show, One-Pot ionic liquid-mediated bioprocess for pretreatment and enzymatic hydrolysis of rice straw with ionic liquid-tolerance bacterial cellulase, Bioengineering, **9** (2022): 17
14. S. Chuetor, E.J. Panakkal, T. Ruensodsai, K. Cheenkachorn, S. Kirdponpattara, Y.S. Cheng, M. Sriariyanun, Improvement of enzymatic saccharification and ethanol production from rice straw by recycled ionic liquid: Effect of anti-solvent mixture, Bioengineering, **9**,3 (2022): 115
15. S. Maddalwar, K. Kumar Nayak, M. Kumar, L. Singh, Plant microbial fuel cell: Opportunities, challenges, and prospects, Bioresource technology, **341** (2021): 125772
16. A.S. Jatoi, F. Akhter, S.A. Mazari, N. Sabzoi, S. Aziz, S.A. Soomro, N.M. Mubarak, H. Baloch, A.Q. Memon, S. Ahmed, Advanced microbial fuel cell for waste water treatment-a review, Environmental Science and Pollution Research, **28**,5 (2021): 5005-5019
17. J. Greenman, B.A. Mendis, I. Gajda, I.A. Ieropoulos, Microbial fuel cell compared to a chemostat, Chemosphere, **296**,5 (2022): 133967.
18. D. Vidhyeswari, A. Surendhar, S. Bhuvaneshwari, General aspects and novel PEMss in microbial fuel cell technology: A review, Chemosphere, **309** (2022): 136454.
19. C. Munoz-Cupa, Y. Hu, C. Xu, A. Bassi, An overview of microbial fuel cell usage in wastewater treatment, resource recovery and energy production, Science of the Total Environment, **1**,754 (2021): 142429.
20. M. Al-Sahari, A.A. Al-Gheethi, R.M.S. Radin Mohamed, G. Yashni, D.N. Vo, N. Ismail, Microbial fuel cell systems; developments, designs, efficiencies, and trends: A comparative study between the conventional and innovative systems, Chemosphere, **298** (2022): 134244
21. G. Dattatraya Saratale, J. Rajesh Banu, R.A. Nastro, A. Kadier, V. Ashokkumar, C.H. Lay, J.H. Jung, H. Seung Shin, R. Ganesh Saratale, K. Chandrasekhar, Bioelectrochemical systems in aid of sustainable biorefineries for the production of value-added products and resource recovery from wastewater: A critical review and future perspectives, Bioresource technology, **359** (2022): 127435.
22. K.A. Dwivedi, S.J. Huang, C.T. Wang, Integration of various technology-based approaches for enhancing the performance of microbial fuel cell technology: A review. Chemosphere, Chemosphere, **287** (2022): 132248
23. C. Saran, D. Purchase, G.D. Saratale, R.G. Saratale, L.F. Romanholo Ferreira, M. Bilal, H.M.N. Iqbal, C.M. Hussain, S.I. Mulla, R.N. Bharagava, Microbial fuel cell: A green eco-friendly agent for tannery wastewater treatment and simultaneous bioelectricity/power generation, Chemosphere, **312** (2023): 137072
24. A. Shrivastava, R. Kumar Sharma, Lignocellulosic biomass based microbial fuel cells: Performance and applications, Journal of Cleaner Production , **361** (2022): 132269
25. K.P. Gregoire, J.G. Becker, Design and characterization of a microbial fuel cell for the conversion of a lignocellulosic crop residue to electricity, Bioresource Technology, **119** (2012): 208-215
26. M.A. Jablonska, M.K. Rybarczyk, M. Lieder, Electricity generation from rapeseed straw hydrolysates using microbial fuel cells, Bioresource Technology, **208** (2016): 117-122
27. M. Pal, R.K. Sharma, Development of wheat straw based catholyte for power generation in microbial fuel cell, Biomass Bioenergy, **138** (2020): 105591
28. M. Sjöblom, L. Matsakas, A. Krige, U. Rova, P. Christakopoulos, Direct electricity generation from sweet sorghum stalks and anaerobic sludge, Industrial Crops and Products, **108** (2017): 505-511
29. F.Allam, M. Elnouby, K.M. El-Khatib, D.E. El-Badan, S.A. Sabry, Water hyacinth (Eichhornia crassipes) biochar as an alternative cathode electrocatalyst in an air-cathode single chamber microbial fuel cell, International Journal of Hydrogen Energy, **45** (2020): 5911–5927
30. M. Rethinasabapathy, J.H. Lee, K.C. Roh, S.M. Kang, S.Y. Oh, B. Park, G.W. Lee, Y.L. Cha, Y.S. Huh, Silver grass-derived activated carbon with coexisting micro-, meso- and macropores as excellent bioanodes for microbial colonization and power generation in sustainable microbial fuel cells, Bioresource technology, **300** (2020): 122646
31. X. Wang, Y.J. Feng, H.M. Wang, Y.P. Qu, Y.L. Yu, N.Q. Ren, N. Li, E. Wang, H. Lee, B.E. Logan, Bioaugmentation for electricity generation from corn stover biomass using microbial fuel cells, Environmental Science & Technology, **43** (2009): 6088–6093
32. Y. Zuo, P.C. Maness, B.E. Logan, Electricity production from steam-exploded corn stover biomass, Energy Fuels, **20** (2006): 1716–1721
33. C.Y. Ma, C.H. Wu, C.W. Lin, A novel V-shaped microbial fuel cell for electricity generation in

biodegrading rice straw compost, Journal of advanced agricultural technologies, **2** (2015): 57-62

34. Y. Zhang, B. Min, L. Huang, I. Angelidaki, Generation of electricity and analysis of microbial communities in wheat straw biomass-powered microbial fuel cells, Applied and Environmental Microbiology, **75** (2009): 3389
35. Y. Yang, E. Lin, S. Sun, H. Chen, A.T. Chow, Direct electricity production from subaqueous wetland sediments and banana peels using membrane-less microbial fuel cells, Industrial Crops and Products, **128** (2019): 70–79
36. H.N. Dai, T.A. Nguyen, L.P. LE, M. Van Tran, T.H. Lan, C.T. Wang, Power generation of Shewanella oneidensis MR-1 microbial fuel cells in bamboo fermentation effluent, International Journal of Hydrogen Energy, **46**, 31 (2019): 16612–16621
37. A. Divya Priya, Y. Pydi Setty, Cashew apple juice as substrate for microbial fuel cell, Fuel, **246** (2019): , 75–78
38. F. Wang, D. Ouyang, Z. Zhou, S.J. Page, D. Liu, X. Zhao, Lignocellulosic biomass as sustainable feedstock and materials for power generation and energy storage, Journal of Energy Chemistry, **57** (2021): 247–280
39. H. Chang, Y. Zou, R. Hu, H. Feng, H. Wu, N. Zhong, J. Hu, Membrane applications for microbial energy conversion: a review, Environmental chemistry letters, **18** (2020): 1581–1592

The Relationship Between Environmental Technology Patenting and Environmental Performance Index in Countries: What Does It Mean and How Can We Measure It

Tatyana Maximova[1], *Dmitry* Verzilin[2,3], and *Min* Zhang[1]

[1] UTMO University, St. Petersburg, Russia
[2] St. Petersburg Federal Research Center of the Russian Academy of Sciences, St. Petersburg, Russia
[3] Lesgaft University, St. Petersburg, Petersburg, Russia

Abstract. National governments need to make informed decisions to ensure sustainable development and the use of new technologies. Thus, two major problems emerge: how to evaluate governments' success in encouraging companies to invest in environmental technologies, and how to measure the efficiency of technology diffusion in terms of environmental well-being. The knowledge about the relationship between environmental performance and environmental technologies at the country level enables decision-makers in the field of sustainable development to more rationally plan the costs of developing new technologies, as well as track the return on their implementation. As a result, society and industry will receive signals about the effectiveness of the implemented sustainable development policy. The main goal of the research was to overcome the gap in the field of environmental wellbeing: how to measure at the macro level the dependence of countries' success in environmental performance on how developed they are in environmental technologies. The specific objective of the study was to quantify the relationship between the integral indicator of environmental well-being Environmental Performance Index (EPI) and innovative activity in the field of environmental technology at the cross-country level. To evaluate the development of environmental technologies, the platform solution Orbit Intelligence was used, specifically, the FamPat worldwide patent database. It was confirmed that the more developed the economy, the higher EPI and the level of development of environmental technology. At the same time, no relationship was found between the 10-year change in EPI and the 10-year change in the patent activity index. The hypothesis about the statistical significance of the relationship between the integral indicators of patent activity in the field of environmental technology and the current value of EPI was confirmed. A regression dependence was determined, which was well approximated by the linear regression of EPI on the logarithm of the country's patent activity index in the field of environmental technology. The dependence can be interpreted as a slowdown in the growth of EPI when a certain level of patenting is reached. The novelty of the research lies in the fact that a framework has been proposed and implemented for assessing the relationship between environmental well-being and environmental technology. This framework can be used to study individual environmental problems in countries in more detail and to identify the level of available technologies for solving these problems.

Keywords. Environmental performance, Environmental well-being, Patent activity, Patent landscapes, Regression

1 Introduction

1.1 Problem statement

In the 21st century, the population, scientists, and leaders of many countries are aware of the importance of sustainable development and the effective solution to environmental problems, the most significant of which are global warming, a decrease in clean drinking water supplies, pollution of the world's oceans and a decrease in biodiversity. Companies need constant efforts to create innovative technologies that help neutralize the anthropogenic impact on the environment and increase the rational use of natural resources. National governments need to make informed decisions to ensure sustainable development and the use of new technologies. Thus, two major problems emerge: how to evaluate governments' successfulness in encouraging companies to invest in environmental technologies, and how to measure efficiency of technology diffusion in the terms of environmental well-being.

If we examine the relationship between environmental performance and environmental technologies at the country level, then we can identify those countries in which the development of technology is accompanied by an increase in environmental performance and those countries that, despite the high level of technological development, have not achieved success in environmental performance. In addition, we can identify countries where technology development in companies is not sufficiently stimulated and those countries where technology is not being used effectively enough. We can also identify a trend and predict some average level of environmental performance for a fixed level of technology development and identify countries with good and bad practices in the use of technologies. This knowledge will enable decision-makers in the field of sustainable development to more rationally plan the costs of developing new technologies, as well as track the return on their implementation at the macro level. As a result, society and industry will receive signals about the effectiveness of the implemented sustainable development policy. Today, the importance of data-driven insights to improve environmental decision-making and ensure a sustainable future is widely recognized. For countries to make evidence-based sustainable development decisions based on data, it is necessary to assess the current state of environmental performance and existing resources that can improve this state.

Environmental technologies are a key resource that provides environmental well-being. The significance of these technologies lies, firstly, in the fact that they are a sharable resource. Second, an environmental technology can be seen as a resource that enhances the efficiency of other resources. Overall, there is a research gap in the field of environmental well-being: how to measure at the macro level the dependence of countries' success in environmental performance on how developed they are in environmental technologies.

1.2 Current solution

The Environmental Performance Index (EPI), based on 40 environmental indicators, is widely used to assess the effectiveness of countries' environmental policies [1]. These indicators are grouped into three groups with corresponding sub-indices: Climate Change, Environmental Health, Ecosystem Vitality. Each of these sub-indices consists of individual components, which in turn are calculated based on the transformed values of statistical indicators of the country's ecological state. Each sub-index is calculated as a linear convolution of its constituent components with different weights [1]. The Climate Change sub-index is represented by one component, Climate Change Mitigation. The Environmental Health sub-index consists of components: Air Quality, Sanitation & Drinking Water, Heavy Metals, Waste Management. The Ecosystem Vitality sub-index includes components: Biodiversity & Habitat, Ecosystem Services, Fisheries, Acid Rain, Agriculture, Water Resources.

The individual components make it possible to assess the effectiveness of countries in mitigating the consequences of climate change, increasing the viability of ecosystems, and protecting the environment. The composition of these individual components allows us to say that with the help of EPI, we indirectly measure not only environmental performance but also environmental well-being. The integrated indicator EPI makes it possible to identify leaders and outsiders in the field of sustainable development. EPI-2022 shows the progress countries have made in sustainable development. For 180 observed countries, the value of the integrated EPI index is on average higher for countries with a higher level of development in terms of GDP per capita: "EPI scores are correlated with country wealth" [1]. It should be noted that this regression dependence is linear on the logarithm of GDP per capita [1]. The study [2] offers a quantitative description of the relationship between globalization and environmental indicators that are part of the EPI. Panel data for 148 countries from 2001 to 2018 confirmed that social and political globalization contributes to the improvement of environmental performance, while economic globalization has no impact on environmental performance.

Social studies of the influence of the environmental concern of the population of various countries upon the level of economic development often demonstrate polar points of view: from the denial of such dependence to the confirmation of its existence with a positive or negative sign [3]. In the study [3], conducted using panel data for 82 countries over seven years, the following variables were identified as predictors of environmental concern: exposure to environmental degradation (positive relationship), economic abundance (negative relationship). The volume of exports as a percentage of GDP has a negative impact on concern, and the percentage of exports to highly developed countries has a positive effect.

We have proved [4] that data on search queries on the Internet for keywords related to environmental pollution reflect the degree of public concern about the environmental situation in a region and can be used as an indirect indicator of environmental trouble. On an intuitive level, one can assume that there is a relationship between the success of countries in achieving sustainable development goals and the development of technologies to achieve these goals.

Patent analytics methods have been developed to analyze technological trends and the level of technology development, including trends in the field of sustainable development. Scientific research in this area is usually aimed at evaluating the development of certain groups of technologies and identifying technological trends in eco-innovations [5,6].

In [7,8] the impact of patent activity on environmental indicators was estimated. In the study [7], on the example of Spain, a statistically significant negative impact of patent activity in the field of environmental technologies on the volume of CO_2 Emissions was confirmed: as all factors held constant, an increase in environmental technology patents leads to a decrease in carbon emissions. The findings of the study [8] show that the number of patent applications in the field of environmental technologies is an important predictor of the ecological footprint in the United States, causing a decrease in environmental deprivation in the long term. These results show that the use of technological innovations in the field of ecology can contribute to the sustainable development of countries.

1.3 Proposed solution

Since the level of environmental well-being can be representatively assessed using the EPI index, we, firstly, were faced with the task of identifying the main trends in the development of environmental technologies at the macro level. Secondly, we were faced with the task of determining at the macro level for a sample of countries' regression dependencies, in which the indicator of technology development is an independent variable, and the integral indicator of environmental wellbeing is a dependent variable. Additionally, regressions may be evaluated for the change of these indicators over some period. As a quantitative characteristic of environmental well-being, we used an integral indicator of the ecological state, the Environmental Performance Index (EPI) [1].

Patenting indicators for the technological area "Environmental technologies" were used as characteristics of technology availability for sustainable development. There are several reasons for the choice of these indicators:

- the traditional use of the characteristics of patenting as the results of the effectiveness of research and development;
- the possibility of interpreting indicators as characteristics of shared resources;
- openness and reliability of patent data;
- the ability to fine-tune queries to patent databases.

At the same time, it is difficult to talk about clear causal relationships between patenting and the level of environmental well-being. However, such an analysis makes it possible to clarify the mutual influence of technological development and the ecological state.

1.4 Research novelty and objective

Overall, the main goal is to overcome the research gap in the field of environmental well-being: how to measure at the macro level the dependence of countries' success in environmental performance on how developed they are in environmental technologies.

The specific objective of the study was to quantify the relationship between the integral indicator of environmental well-being Environmental Performance Index and innovative activity in the field of environmental technology at the cross-country level, as well as between the growth of these indicators over a 10-year period. To achieve this goal, we have formed a sample of countries that are currently the most active in patenting solutions in the field of environmental technologies. To form the sample, we used the patent database and analytical tools of platform solutions Orbit Intelligence [9]. For the same countries, the EPI values were taken from the report for 2022 [1]. Next, we used correlation and regression analysis of the obtained data. As a result, we confirmed the hypothesis about the statistical significance of the relationship between the value of the Environmental Performance Index and the indicator of patent activity in the field of environmental technology. A linear regression of the Environmental Performance Index from the logarithm of the country's patent activity index in the field of environmental technology was determined. This can be interpreted as a slowdown in the growth of the Environmental Performance Index when a certain level of patenting is reached. In addition, it was confirmed that the more developed the economy, the higher its Environmental Performance Index and the higher the level of development of environmental technology. We failed to establish the relationship between the 10-year change in the Environmental Performance Index and the 10-year change in the patent activity index.

2 Materials and Methods

The methodology for constructing the Environmental Performance Index based on statistical indicators of the ecological state of countries has been developed over the past two decades and was presented in the report [1]. We used country summary data on EPI score for 2022 and EPI 10-year change presented in [1].

To assess the level of development of environmental technologies, one of the leading platform solutions Orbit Intelligence [9] was used, specifically, the FamPat worldwide patent database and software for patent research and analysis. The data sources for FamPat include 110 patent-issuing authorities with up to date 66 million patent families.

The time depth of the search was from 2003 to 2023. The unit of observation was a patent family, i.e. all patents describing one invention. Only data on valid patents and pending applications were analyzed. The geographical scope of patenting was not limited.

The visualization tools QUESTEL - ORBIT were used to build diagrams. Some of the diagrams were built by the authors using analytical data obtained from the QUESTEL-ORBIT system.

We analyzed data on submitted applications and registered patents for the technology domain "Environmental technology". The selection of technological areas available only in Orbit Intelligence [8, 9] was used as groups of classes and subclasses of the International Patent Classification (IPC). In total, 35 technological domains are distinguished, which are combined into groups: Chemistry, Electrical Engineering, Instruments, Mechanical Engineering, and Others. The technological area investigated in the work is part of the Chemistry group.

We used the queries as, for example, (("ENVIRONMENTAL TECHNOLOGY")/TECT AND (EPD < 2023-01-01) AND (STATE/ACT=ALIVE)) or (("ENVIRONMENTAL TECHNOLOGY")/TECT AND (EPD < 2013-01-01) AND (STATE/ACT=ALIVE)).

Similar patterns can probably be obtained using other patent databases, such as those of the World Intellectual Property Organization, the European Patent Office,

Goggle, national patent offices and others, using International Patent Classification codes and corresponding keywords. Note that the classification into technological domains is unique for Orbit Intelligence [8, 9].

Promising areas of research in the analyzed technological area were determined by:

- by the ratio of active patents and applications under consideration (Technology domain "Environmental technology", Status Alive, Granted / Pending);

- by year-to-year growth in the number of pending applications.

The dynamics of patent activity, which also indicates interest in the technological field and its prospects, was estimated by the number of patent families in the 1st year of filing an application. In addition, an analysis was made of the distribution of patent families in the technological field by the main concepts and by related technological fields, which are most often found in patents.

World leaders in the analyzed technological field were determined by the number of active patent families published in the country's patent office. Expansion into markets indicating the demand for technology, was estimated by the number of active patent families from right holders in various patent offices of countries. The prevalence of technology, that is, the expansion of world leaders in subject areas, was estimated by the number of active patent families from right holders by application area.

To identify the mutual influence of Environmental technology on EPI, the distribution of existing patent families for the technological area "Environmental technology" was analyzed by countries of protection (countries in which inventions are protected by a patent). The top 30 patent offices of countries have been identified. The European Patent Office (EP), the patent office of the World Intellectual Property Organization (WO), as well as patent offices of European countries, were excluded from the list, since many patent holders in these countries, do not register applications directed to the European Patent Office (EP) and the Patent Office of the World Intellectual Property Organization (WO) in national patent offices. For selected countries, an index of patent activity in the field of "Environmental technology" was proposed and determined as the ratio of the number of active patent families in this field to the volume of GDP, expressed in US dollars at purchasing power parity. A similar normalization of the total number of patent families is used in the methodology for constructing the components of the global innovation index [10].

Next, a pairwise regression was built and analyzed between the values of EPI and the index of patent activity in the technological area "Environmental technology". We used the logarithmic transformation of the independent variable. To assess the statistical significance of the regression dependence, p-values were calculated to test the hypotheses of non-zero regression coefficients. In addition, the relationship between the growth values of these indicators over a 10-year period was considered.

3 Results and discussion

3.1 Prospects for the development of environmental technology

The ratio of patent applications under consideration and approved applications characterizes the intensity of patenting. The intensity of patenting in the technological field indirectly characterizes the development prospects and the demand for new technologies in this field by the economy and society. To understand the data in Table 1, the following features of application counting should be considered. Not individual patent applications are counted, but patent families. Each active patent family (Alive) can be represented by both pending applications and already approved applications. The family with the status "approved" necessarily includes approved applications. There are no approved applications in families with the status "pending".

Table 1. The ratio of filed and approved patent applications (only valid patents in the technological field "Environmental technology", built according to [9]), the number of patent families.

Legal status	Before 01.01.2023	Before 01.01.2013
Alive	1 046 707 (100%)	71 083 (100%)
Granted	860 942 (82%)	67 445 (95%)
Pending	185 765 (18%)	3638 (5%)

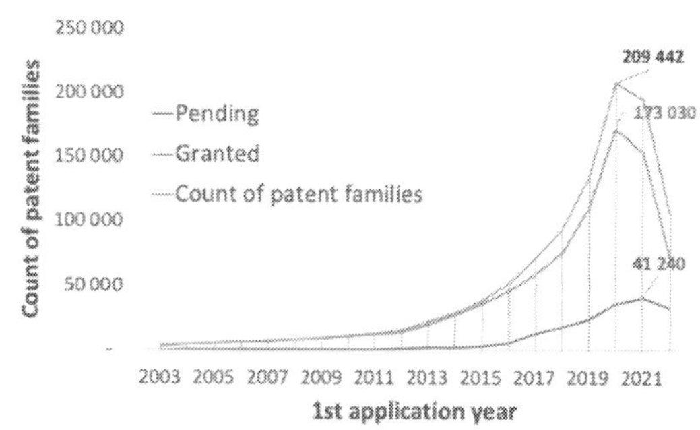

Fig. 1. Dynamics of patent activity for technological area "Environmental technology": the distribution of the number of patent families for the 1st application year, according to [9].

We compared the number of patent families for the technological area "Environmental technology" at two points in time, separated by 10 years. There is a significant increase in the number of active patents, as well as an increase in the share of pending applications. An analysis of the ratio of patent families under consideration and patent families with applications approved by 2013 and by 2023 showed that the proportion of patent families under consideration has increased. This happened because of a combination of two factors - the increase in patent activity and the increase in time for consideration of applications. When analyzing the dynamics of patent activity in the technological field "Environmental technology", the data were grouped by the year of filing the first application in the patent family (Figure 1). The reduction in patent families in 2021 and 2022 is explained by the fact that not all applications are included in the database yet.

3.2 Concepts and related areas for the Environmental technology area

To determine the main concepts used in the patent families of the technological field "Environmental technology", the Questel Orbit service was used, which makes it possible to build clusters of jointly used keywords that are interconnected in meaning (Figure 2). The concept represents the theme that characterizes the cluster. Some concepts are most common, for example - Water Inlet, Air Outlet, and Purification.

Another Questel-Orbit service made it possible to determine the number of patent families that simultaneously belong to the "Environmental technology" technology area and the remaining 34 patent areas (Figure 3).

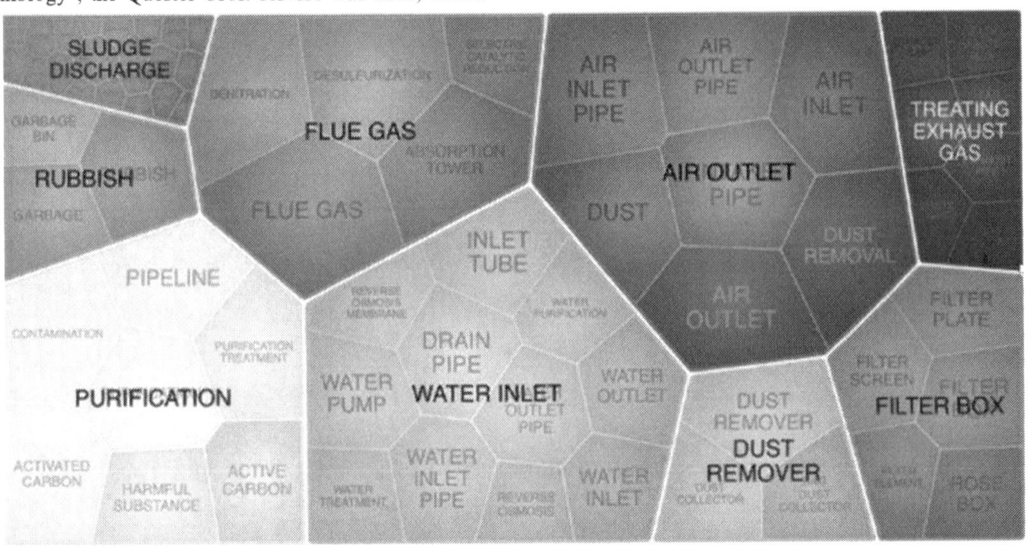

Fig. 2. Basic concepts for the technological area "Environmental technology": the distribution of patent families of the technological area "Environmental technology" by thematic areas most often found in patents, built according to [9].

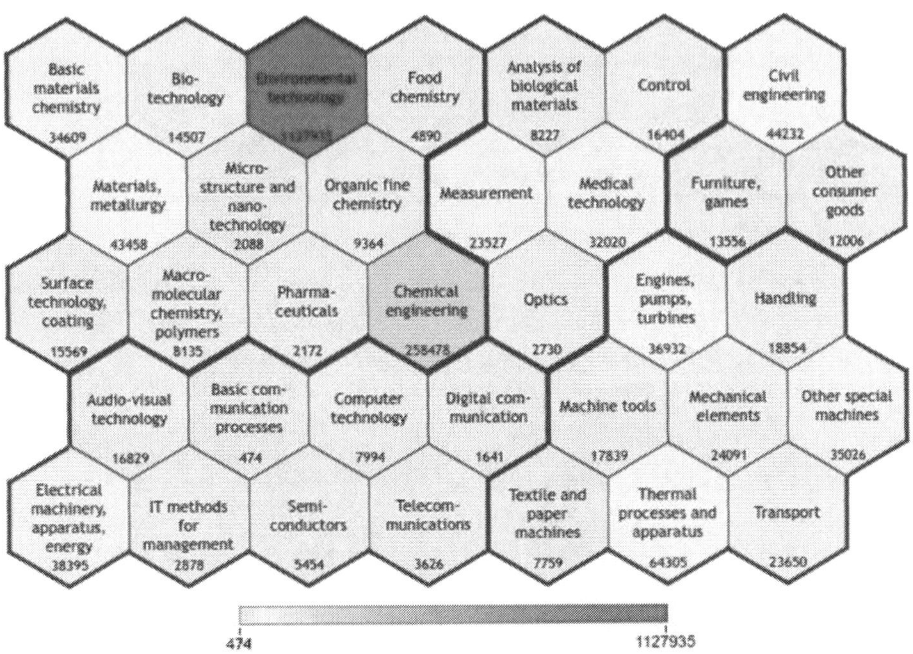

Fig. 3. Related technological areas for patent families from the technological area "Environmental technology", built according to [9], the number of active patent families, before 2023.

3.3 Leading countries and companies for the environmental technology area

In total, as of January 1, 2023, 1,046,707 valid patents in this area have been identified. China is a leader as a patent publishing country. The Chinese office accumulates 89% of patents, the US, and Japan 7% each, and Korea 6%. At WIPO and European Patent Offices 1% and 4% respectively. It should be noted that the total number of patents for the top 20 countries across all patent offices is 1.32 times greater than the total number of patents, since some patents are registered simultaneously in several patent offices (Figure 4).

Fig. 4. World leaders (top 20) in terms of the number of active patent families published in the country's patent office for the technological field "Environmental technology", built according to [9].

It is widely known that China is the world leader in the total number of patents. At the same time, one must consider that China publishes fewer patents in other countries than other countries do in the China patent office (Figure 5). This indicates the importance of the Chinese market for the global economy.

	CN	JP	US	KR	EP	DE	IN	FR	GB	CA
CHINA PETROLEUM & CHEMIC	4340	31	60	24	44	9	27	7	6	14
TOYOTA MOTOR	995	2526	1314	198	598	799	272	390	288	24
GREE ELECTRIC APPLIANCES	1929	3	10	1	17	4	5	3	4	0
SINOPEC	1846	1	9	1	8	2	2	0	1	1
TSINGHUA UNIVERSITY	1644	31	114	9	45	33	6	20	33	6
TPRI	1648	4	0	0	0	0	0	0	0	0
MIDEA GROUP	1578	12	39	11	42	15	9	5	8	6
HYUNDAI MOTOR	373	74	546	1426	42	355	17	32	29	2
BEIJING UNIVERSITY OF TECHN	1411	0	23	0	16	0	0	0	0	0
WEICHAI POWER	1229	0	10	0	18	4	4	3	3	2

Fig. 5. Market Expansion: Distribution rights holders by offices of countries for filing applications and registering patents for the technological field "IT "Environmental technology", built according to [9].

3.4 Relationship between Environmental technology patents and Environmental Performance Index

When forming a sample of countries to identify dependence, we excluded European countries from the top 30 leading countries that are under the jurisdiction of the European Patent Office (EP). Also excluded are data on the number of patent families, registered with the patent office of the World Intellectual Property Organization (WO).

Figure 6 illustrates the validity of our hypothesis about the possibility of quantitative confirmation of the relationship between the EPI score and patent activity in the technological field "Environmental technology". We have identified a statistically significant regression dependence for a group of 11 countries that are in the top countries in terms of the number of active patent families published in the country's patent office in the technological field "Environmental technology".

We found a similar logarithmic dependence on the index of patent activity of countries for the integral indicator of intellectual capital [11]. Thus, we can suggest that technologies are not only a resource for sustainable development, but also for the development of intellectual capital and the knowledge economy.

A study on patent data on water conservation and supply technologies [12] showed that even those technologies that are more needed in underdeveloped countries are being more actively used in highly developed countries. Therefore, the dissemination of technologies as a shared resource to less developed countries that need these technologies is of great social, economic and environmental importance.

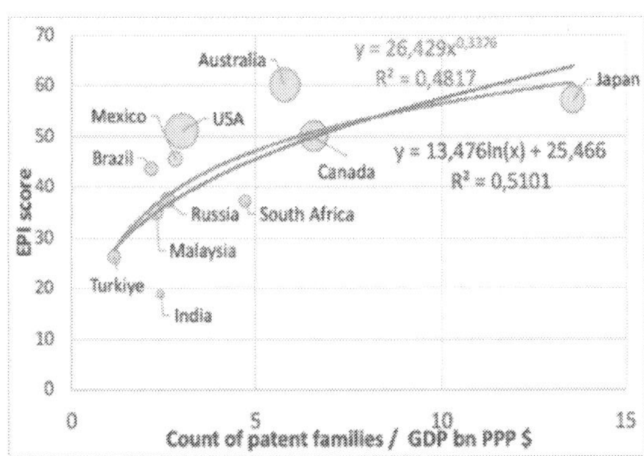

Fig. 6. Positive relationship between EPI score and patent activity in the technological area "Environmental technology". The size of the bubble is proportional to GDP per capita in US dollars, plotted according to [1, 9].

A power regression was added to illustrate some similarities of our results to those obtained in [13]. In [13] patenting was considered as an activity resulting in new innovative products rather than an output of R&D. Linear regressions linked the log number of new innovative products belonging to firms and product categories to the log number of patent applications filled in some previous year. For all regressions obtained in [12], the value of the power parameter is <0.1, which means that there is a noticeable slowdown in the growth of the dependent variable with an increase in the independent variable characterizing patent activity.

Logarithmic regression:

$$y = 13,476\ ln(x) + 25,466;\ R^2 = 0,5101, \quad (1)$$

where y is EPI score,

x is a patent activity index, count of patent families / GDP bn PPP $.

Logarithmic regression gives the correct interpretation for the coefficient of determination as a proportion of the explained variance of the dependent variable.

Power regression:

$$y = 26,429\ x^{0,3376};\ R^2 = 0,4817, \quad (2)$$

where y is EPI score,

x is count of patent families / GDP bn PPP $.

The power regression is like that obtained in [13]. The value of the exponent at x can be interpreted as the elasticity of the EPI score with respect to the patent activity index. Elasticity is calculated as the relative change in the dependent variable per unit relative change in the independent variable. In other words, with an increase in the patent activity index by 10 times, the EPI score will change by 10 * 0.3376 = 3.376 times.

The more developed the economy (GDP per capita in US dollars), the higher the level of EPI score and the higher the level of development of environmental technology. The regression line in figure 6 illustrates this rather predictable relationship. However, for China and the Republic of Korea, this dependence is not fair. The reason for this may be that these countries show much more patent activity than the rest of the top countries. For the Republic of Korea, the patent activity indicator is 27 (Count of patent families / GDP bn PPP $), and for China, it is equal to 34.

At the same time, we were unable to identify cross-country patterns between the 10-year change in the patent activity indicator and the 10-year change in EPI score (Figure 7).

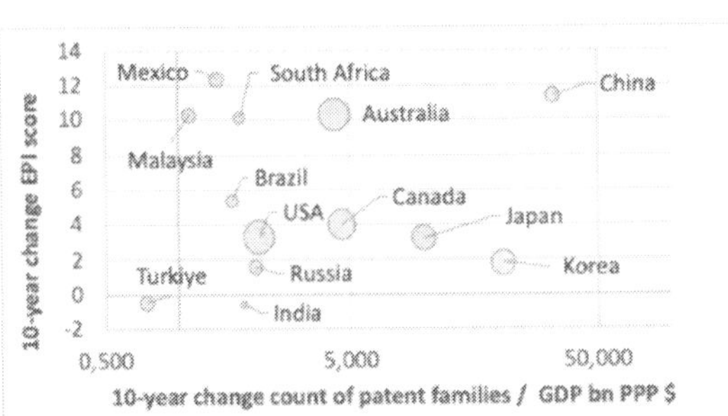

Fig. 7. 10-year change EPI score and 10-year change count of patent families / GDP bn PPP $ in the Environmental technology area. The size of the bubble is proportional to GDP per capita in US dollars, plotted according to [1, 9].

This fact may evidence a significant time lag between the moment a technology is patented and its widespread use, which contributes to sustainable development and is reflected in statistical indicators. Currently the greatest achievements in sustainable development, driven using innovative environmental technologies, have countries that are consistently focused on innovation in the field of environmental technology. Countries such as China and Korea will see a return on patent activity after a certain period.

4 Conclusion

The relationship between the integral indicator of environmental well-being (Environmental Performance Index) and innovative activity in the field of environmental technology at the cross-country level was studied.

The hypothesis about the statistical significance of the relationship between the integral indicators of patent activity in the field of environmental technology and the current value of the Environmental Performance Index was confirmed. A regression dependence was determined, which was well approximated by the linear regression of the Environmental Performance Index on the logarithm of the country's patent activity index in the field of environmental technology and with the power dependence. Regressions can be interpreted as growth retardation of the Environmental Performance Index upon reaching a certain level of patenting in environmental technology.

It was confirmed that the more developed the economy, the higher the Environmental Performance Index and the higher the level of development of environmental technology. At the same time, no relationship was found between the 10-year change in the Environmental Performance Index and the 10-year change in the patent activity index.

This study contains useful methodological recommendations. The novelty of the research lies in the fact that a framework has been proposed and implemented for assessing the relationship between environmental well-being and environmental technology. This framework can be used to study individual environmental problems in countries in more detail and to identify the level technology availability for solving these problems. For such purposes, it is promising to refine the index of patent activity by IPC (International Patent Classification) codes for technological domain environmental technology and identify its statistically significant impact on individual components of the Environmental Performance Index. The main value of the study is that the proposed framework can be used to enable policymakers to make evidence-based decisions in the field of sustainable development based on data on the current state of environmental performance and existing technologies that can improve this state.

This study contains several generalizations about the relationship between patent activity and environmental well-being, although there are some limitations. As a quantitative indicator of environmental well-being, we used the EPI score, as an integral indicator, thus, it does not allow us to measure which of the environmental problems is more acute for the country. Therefore, when using the proposed framework for assessing the ecological state of a country caused by the most acute problems and its relationship with the level of technology development, it is necessary to use EPI components that are more sensitive to the analyzed problem instead of the EPI score. The approach used to evaluate patent activity assumed a selection of patents for the technological domain "Environmental technology", the formation of which by IPC codes and keywords is the know-how of Questel, which provides Orbit Intelligence platform solutions [9]. We used the FAMPAT patent database. When using other patent databases, the composition of patent families may be different.

Acknowledgements

The study was financially supported by ITMO University, N 622150.

References

1. M.J. Wolf, J.W. Emerson, D.C. Esty, A.D. Sherbinin, Z.A. Wendling, Environmental performance index (EPI) results, New Haven, CT: Yale Center for Environmental Law & Policy, (2022)
2. Q.J. Wang, Y. Geng, X.Q. Xia, Revisited globalization's impact on total environment: evidence based on overall environmental performance index, International Journal of Environmental Research and Public Health, **18**,21 (2021): 11419
3. F. Hao, A panel regression study on multiple predictors of environmental concern for 82 countries across seven years, Social Science Quarterly, **97**,5 (2016): 991-1004
4. D. Verzilin, T. Maximova, I. Sokolova, S. Skorykh, Digital society as a driving force for sustainable manufacturing, IFAC-PapersOnLine, **52**,13 (2019): 2261-2266
5. I. Haščič, M. Migotto, Measuring environmental innovation using patent data, OECD Environment Working Papers (2015): 89
6. M. Urbaniec, J. Tomala, S. Martinez, Measurements and trends in technological eco-innovation: evidence from environment-related patents. Resources, **10**,7 (2021): 68
7. M.O. Oyebanji, R.A. Castanho, S.Y. Genc, D. Kirikkaleli, Patents on environmental technologies and environmental sustainability in Spain, Sustainability, **14**,11 (2022): 6670
8. D. Kirikkaleli, E. Sofuoflu, O. Ojekemi. Does patents on environmental technologies matter for the ecological footprint in the USA? Evidence from the novel Fourier ARDL approach, Geoscience Frontiers, **14**,4 (2023): 101564
9. Technologies, https://static.orbit.com/orbit/help/1.9.8/en/index.html#!Documents/technologies.htm, access on 18 July 2023
10. S. Dutta, Br. Lanvin, L.R. León, S. Wunsch-Vincent , What is the future of innovation-driven growth: Productivity stagnation or revival? (15th Edition., WIPO, 2022), Global Innovation Index (2022)
11. T.G. Maximova, M. Zhang, Regression Models of the Relationship Between Innovation Activity and Intellectual Capital, Ekonomika. Pravo. Innovacii, **1** (2023): 15-26
12. A. Dechezleprêtre, I. Haščič, N. Johnstone, Invention and international diffusion of water conservation and availability technologies: evidence from patent data, OECD Environment Working Papers, (2015): 82
13. D. Argente, S. Baslandze, D. Hanley, S. Moreira, Patents to products: Product innovation and firm dynamics, Federal reserve bank of Atlanta, Working Paper, (2020): 4

Economic Assessment of Medium and Large-Scale Landfill Mining Business: Case Study Thailand

Anupong Muttaraid[1,2], *Sirintornthep* Towprayoon[1,2], *Chart* Chiemchaisri[3], *Thapat* Silalertruksa[4], and *Komsilp* Wangyao[1,2,*]

[1] The Joint Graduate School of Energy and Environment (JGSEE), King Mongkut's University of Technology Thonburi, Bangkok, Thailand
[2] Center of Excellence on Energy Technology and Environment (CEE), Ministry of Higher Education, Science, Research and Innovation (MHESI), Bangkok, Thailand
[3] Department of Environmental Engineering, Faculty of Engineering, Kasetsart University, Bangkok, Thailand
[4] Department of Environmental Engineering, Faculty of Engineering, King Mongkut's University of Technology Thonburi, Bangkok, Thailand

Abstract. Thailand produces over 25 million tons of waste yearly, while only a third is utilized. The waste disposed of in the landfill is rarely utilized, and research on the utilization of landfill waste in Thailand is limited. The information regarding the business model and the profitability rate of landfill mining is limited and generally was not displayed to the public. This paper examined the landfill mining business of medium and large-scale businesses in Thailand. Both sites' business operations were analyzed, and the net present value was presented. The NPV results show that landfill mining is profitable and gives more sustainable waste management. The large scale is highly profitable but requires more investment extensively, while the medium scale is easily adopted and still provides a reasonable profit. Furthermore, to understand the business operation and sensitivity of the operation, this paper uses sensitivity analysis to analyze the factors influencing business profitability. Even though the result displays that both projects are easily profitable, the large-scale operation tends to be simpler as the expense has a lower influence on the business.

Keyword. Landfill mining, Municipal solid waste, Net-present value, Refuse-derived fuel, Sensitivity analysis

1 Introduction

In recent years, the circular economy has been closely linked to the concepts of zero waste and waste utilization. The circular economy aims to create a closed-loop ecosystem where resources are effectively consumed and utilized through the principles of reduce, reuse, and recycle [1]. This paradigm challenges the traditional linear economy and emphasizes the need to minimize waste generation and maximize resource efficiency [2]. Zero waste is a key objective of the circular economy, aiming to eliminate waste by recirculating it back into production and consumption processes [3]. By adopting circular economy principles, waste can be transformed into valuable resources, contributing to the sustainable management of resources and reducing environmental impacts [4]. Waste utilization plays a crucial role in the circular economy. It involves finding innovative ways to repurpose and extract value from waste materials.

Over the past decade, municipal solid waste (MSW) management has become increasingly concerning for many countries, including Thailand. Thailand's solid waste has been increasing by an average of 10% annually. According to studies, the country generated 27.8 million tons of waste in 2018, with approximately 20.8 million tons disposed of in landfills. The overreliance on disposal in landfills has led to a shortage of landfill space [5], which has led to the government encouraging the adoption of waste-to-energy facilities to address waste challenges. As a result, Thailand has experienced growth in incineration plants and waste-to-energy facilities in recent years. Increasing solid waste has created the need to explore more efficient and sustainable management approaches, such as landfill mining (LFM). To mitigate the strain on landfill space and reduce environmental impacts, LFM has been proposed as a potential solution.

LFM is a process that involves the excavation and sorting of waste materials in landfills to recover valuable resources. The concept of LFM was initially introduced in Tel Aviv, Israel, in 1953, where it was primarily used to mine soil-like materials for fertilizer in orchards. In the 1990s, LFM gained attention as a strategy for material recovery and received a significant promotion in the United States [6,7]. However, it gained little popularity due to the challenges associated with extracting valuable materials from the mined waste. Optimizing the excavation of waste is a key consideration in LFM. Since waste in landfills consists of diverse materials, each with its characteristics, researchers are actively exploring various processes and

* Corresponding author: komsilp.wan@kmutt.ac.th

technologies to enhance the profitability of LFM projects. The goal is to identify efficient methods for extracting valuable materials and maximizing their recovery. By optimizing the excavation and sorting processes, LFM has the potential to reduce the environmental impact of landfills, contribute to resource recovery, and promote a more sustainable approach to waste management. Ongoing research and development efforts are focused on improving the efficiency and effectiveness of LFM techniques to maximize this approach's economic and environmental benefits.

LFM has been defined as an environmentally friendly technology that combines material recycling and sustainable waste management [8]. The key advantage of LFM is the potential for materials recycling and the reclamation of land [9]. LFM is a concept that is gaining popularity globally due to its potential to provide resources and minimize waste in landfills. LFM involves excavating materials when the landfill is still operational or after it has been filled and capped with a protective layer. Materials that can be reused are sorted and processed, while the remainder is disposed of in a regulated landfill. This translates to a reduction in landfill waste and its associated problems.

LFM has many benefits, which make it a viable solution to the problem of solid waste management in Thailand. LFM creates space and reduces the amount of waste in landfills, serves as a source of recycling materials, reduces greenhouse gas emissions, and can contribute to the restoration of the land. LFM enables waste to become a resource, which can be used to generate energy and minimize the need for natural resources. In addition, LFM can also create job opportunities for communities surrounding landfill sites.

However, research on LFM in Thailand is limited, and only a few studies are on the subject. One of the methods used to evaluate the feasibility of LFM projects is the net present value (NPV) analysis [10]. The NPV is the sum of the present value of cash inflows and outflows over a defined period using a predetermined discount rate. The NPV determines the feasibility and profitability of investments and can be implemented in other LFM projects [11]. The discounted cash flow technique is employed in NPV, which accounts for the time value of money. NPV is used to evaluate long-term investments in diverse industries, including LFM. The application of NPV in waste management involves forecasting future cash flows, including revenue stream, discount rate, and capital expenditure for the project. It can be useful in conducting feasibility studies and assessing the potential profitability of an LFM project [12 -14].

Several studies have utilized NPV analysis to evaluate the economic viability of landfill mining projects. For example, research conducted in Belgium examined the NPV values of different landfills, with some demonstrating economic viability while others had negative NPV values [10]. Similarly, a study in China assessed the NPV of a landfill mining project and found that it could yield positive net benefits, although the NPV was sensitive to factors such as land reuse and financial support [5]. In landfill mining research, NPV analysis is often used with other assessment methods to provide a comprehensive evaluation. For instance, a holistic assessment method was developed to evaluate landfill mining projects, incorporating both monetary factors (such as costs and proceeds) and non-monetary factors (such as environmental impact and stakeholder concerns) [15]. This integrated approach allows for a more robust evaluation of landfill mining projects' economic and environmental performance.

Sensitivity analysis is a valuable tool in assessing the financial viability and risk associated with landfill mining (LFM) businesses. It allows for the examination of how changes in key variables and assumptions impact the financial outcomes of the project. By conducting sensitivity analysis, researchers and stakeholders can gain insights into the robustness of the financial model and identify the factors that have the most significant influence on the profitability of LFM projects. In the context of LFM, sensitivity analysis can be applied to various financial aspects of the business. For example, it can explore the sensitivity of the net present value (NPV) to changes in factors such as waste composition, market prices of recovered materials, operational costs, and discount rates. By varying these parameters within a range of plausible values, sensitivity analysis can provide a comprehensive understanding of the financial risks and opportunities associated with LFM. A case study conducted on enhanced landfill mining at the Mont-Saint-Guibert landfill in Belgium highlighted the importance of valorization routes for the outputs of LFM [8]. Sensitivity analysis can be used to assess the impact of different valorization routes on the financial performance of the LFM business. It can help identify the most profitable and sustainable pathways for material and energy recovery from landfill-mined materials.

Furthermore, sensitivity analysis can also be applied to evaluate the financial feasibility of energy production from landfill-mined materials. The financial viability of energy recovery from landfill-mined materials can be assessed by conducting a sensitivity analysis on factors such as energy conversion efficiency, electricity prices, and operational costs.

This research compares the NPV of two LFM projects in Thailand: large-scale and mid-scale.

2 Materials and methods

This research collected data from two waste disposal sites that engage in landfill mining and produce refuse-derived fuel (RDF) from old waste. Site A's first site is the Integrated Solid Waste Management Centre in Phraek Sa Mai Subdistrict, Samutprakarn province.

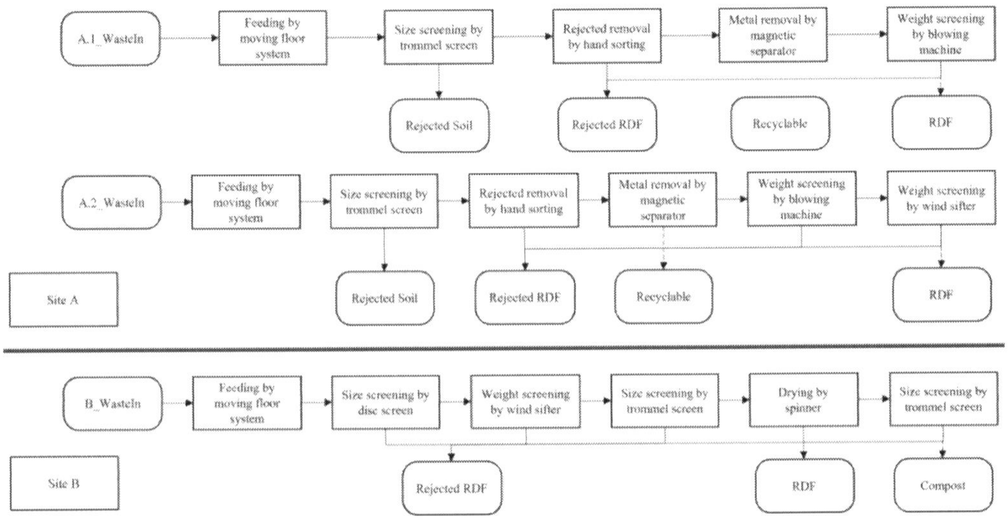

Fig. 1. The process of sorting landfill waste of study sites A (top) and B (bottom).

Operated by Eastern Energy Plus Company Limited, this site receives over 2,500 tons of municipal solid waste daily and deposits it into landfills. Old waste is excavated and used to produce RDF, which is then transported to a waste-to-energy (WtE) power plant operated by Ratchaburi Renewable Energy Company Limited. The plant generates 9.9 megawatts of electricity and sells eight megawatts to the Metropolitan Electricity Authority. This large-scale project has an investment of THB 2.3 billion (USD 66.26 million).

The second site, Site B, is the Sanitary Landfill Solid Waste Disposal Site in Chanthaburi Municipality, Chanthaburi province. This site manages 250 tons of municipal solid waste daily and disposes of it in a sanitary landfill. Old waste separation occurs at this site, producing RDF that is sold to a cement company as a substitute for coal. A private company was given the right to operate by the Chanthaburi Municipality, which manages the sanitary landfill and old waste separation process. Therefore, the municipality has invested in the landfill and part of the structure. Compared to Site A, Site B only consisted of THB 163 million (USD 4.7 million).

2.1 Process description

At both Site A and Site B, landfill mining involves using excavators to extract waste from the landfill. The excavated waste is transported to an in-house sorting facility using 10-wheel trucks. To determine the mining area, both sites rely on historical data on waste disposal, specifically targeting landfill waste over five years old. At site A, the sorting facility is equipped with a range of sorting machines, most of which are designed and fabricated in-house. The facility consists of six sorting lines divided into two sets. The first set comprises two sorting lines, while the second set comprises four sorting lines. Figure 1 illustrates the process of the first set. The process begins with the excavation machines feeding the landfill waste into the sorting lines. The waste then undergoes a screening process using a Trommel screen with a screening size of two inches. This process separates the waste into different fractions. The heavy fraction, "rejected soil," is collected and set aside. Next, the waste goes through a hand sorting process, where employees manually remove plastic bags larger than 50 cm x 50 cm and recyclable materials such as tires and wood. The removed plastic bags are considered rejected refuse-derived fuel (RDF). Metal materials are separated using a magnetic separator called the "recyclable." After the hand sorting process, the waste is passed through a blower to remove the heavy fraction mixed with the rejected RDF. The final product obtained from this process is known as refuse-derived fuel (RDF), utilized in the power plant. The process of the second set of sorting lines is like that of the first set, with one additional step. In the final step of the second set, a wind sifter is introduced to remove smaller heavy fractions from the product.

Overall, Sites A and B employ similar methods for landfill mining, utilizing excavators and in-house sorting facilities. However, there are slight variations in the sorting processes, particularly in the final steps of the second set at site A, where a wind sifter is used to refine the product further.

Figure 1 presents the sorting process at site B's landfill. In contrast to site A, the components of the sorting machine are purchased abroad and imported. While the operations at the two sites are similar, the second site's process is more concise, featuring a single sorting line that involves size screening using a disc-screening machine, removal of the heavy fraction through a wind sifter, another round of size screening using a trommel screen, a drying process utilizing a spinner, and a small trommel screen. The screening and wind-sifting processes yield rejected RDF as a by-product, while the product generated from the spinner process is RDF. Additionally, the small trommel screen produces compost. Personal communication with waste management company officials. Diagram created based on observations and site visits to the waste disposal facilities.

The major difference between sites A and B is the utilization of their products. Site A operates as a full cycle waste management having its waste-to-energy power plant, with a production capacity of 9.9 MW and export capacity of 8 MW. The RDF produced in site A is transported to their power plant facility 100 meters from the sorting plant. This helps generate more revenue streams for site A. In contrast, site B's RDFs are sold and transported to another third-party facility. Thus, making the revenue stream of site B is much less than that of site A.

2.2 Net-present value

Net Present Value (NPV) is an analytical method used to assess the financial viability of a project or investment by calculating the present value of its projected cash flows. NPV considers both the timing and magnitude of these cash flows and discounts them back to the present using an appropriate discount rate. The result is a single value, either positive or negative, that represents the net value or profitability of the project. To calculate NPV, the project's future cash flows are estimated, including income and expenses, over the project's lifespan. These cash flows are then adjusted for the time value of money by discounting them back to the present using the chosen discount rate. The discount rate represents the required rate of return or the opportunity cost of investing in the project. It considers factors such as inflation, risk, and the cost of capital. The formula for NPV is as follows:

$$NPV = \frac{R_t}{(1+i)^t} \quad (1)$$

Thus, NPV is net present value; n is the calculated duration of the project (20 years for this research); t is the year; R_t is the net cash flow at time t; and i is the social discount rate. The conservative discount rate of 9% was used in the model. In addition, an inflation rate of 3% per year was selected.

The NPV calculation considers all cash flows associated with the project, including initial investment costs, regular income or savings, and any additional one-time costs or benefits. By summing up the discounted cash flows and subtracting the initial investment, we obtain the NPV. If the NPV is positive, it indicates that the project is expected to generate more value than the cost of investment and may be considered financially viable. Conversely, a negative NPV suggests that the project may need to deliver more returns to justify the investment.

In this research, the operational data of both sites was collected using the 2022 data. This research classification distinguishes capital investments and operating expenses, with operating expenses further categorized into cash flows relating to investment and operational expenses. Operational expenses can be further divided into process and material flow-related cash flows. Table 1 provides an overview of the relevant economic parameters for LFM based on this classification, including an additional "liquidation" category. The table differentiates between fixed and variable parameters to indicate their dependency on the amount of material being mined.

Capital investments in LFM encompass the costs associated with establishing the landfill mining process, such as purchasing machinery, plants, or buildings. They also include one-time expenditures incurred before the project commences, such as planning facilities or the entire LFM project. Regular maintenance, repair, insurance, taxes, and administration expenses are necessary for purchased machinery or facilities, with their amounts directly linked to the corresponding capital investment. Liquidations refer to one-time cash flows at the end of an LFM project. Positive liquidation cash flows can arise from the sale of used machinery or plants and the marketing of recovered land or landfill airspace. Conversely, negative cash flows may be incurred for removing plants and infrastructure used for landfill closure and aftercare.

The variable terms in LFM are influenced by the quantity and quality of the material, as well as the intensity of the process. Positive cash flows related to material flow result from product sales, while negative cash flows arise from purchasing operating supplies and energy, residue disposal, material transport, and storage. Negative cash flows dependent on process intensity include repair and maintenance costs (linked to material throughput), wages, and aftercare for landfill segments that have not yet been excavated

Table 1. Economic Parameters for economic assessment.

Fixed parameters	Variable parameters
Capital investment - Project development	*Capital investment* - Machines, plants, buildings, etc.
Investment-related cash flows - Insurance, taxes - Administration	*Process-related cash flows* - Repair and maintenance - Salary expense - Recover space value - Diesel expense
Liquidation - Value of the capital injection - Site preparation and aftercare	*Material flow-related cash flows* - Sales of products (RDF and electricity) - Tipping fees

2.3 Sensitivity analysis

Sensitivity analysis plays a crucial role in evaluating and assessing the factors and parameters influencing landfill mining businesses' financial viability and environmental impact. By conducting sensitivity analysis, researchers and practitioners can gain insights into the key variables that significantly affect the outcomes and make informed decisions based on this information.

One study applied scenario modeling and sensitivity analysis to assess the critical factors for the climate impact of landfill mining [7]. The research identified four factors, including landfill gas management, background energy system, excavated waste composition, and waste combustion technology, that significantly influenced the net contributions to global warming. Furthermore, sensitivity analysis can also examine landfill mining projects' economic feasibility and profitability. Research conducted a cost-benefit analysis of China's landfill mining project and found that the net present value (NPV) was sensitive to factors such as the mode of land reuse, availability of energy recovery facilities, and financial support [5].

A cost simulation model for landfill mining could be developed using a sensitivity analysis to assess the economic feasibility of recovering secondary raw materials from landfills [16]. The results indicated that the profitability of landfill mining projects depended on factors such as the amount of recoverable secondary raw materials. Sensitivity analysis can also aid in decision-making regarding landfill site selection in the context of waste management.

This research conducted a sensitivity analysis using the capital investment, salary, RDF expense, diesel consumption, income from tipping fees, the recovered space, and the RDF income to conduct the sensitivity analysis and determine the factor with the highest impact on each site.

3 Results and discussions

NPV results show that both sites are currently profitable. The large-scale operation has extensively more investment but also has a higher NPV at THB 3 billion, compared to the medium scale of THB 224 million. The major difference in their profitability is from the large-scale income from the WtE powerplant and the tipping fees of up to 3,000 tons per day. In contrast, the medium-scale site has income from only 250 tons of MSW per day and no income from the WtE powerplant.

Income from the WtE powerplant consisted of THB 243 million per year on average, while Site B can only gain an average of 31 million per year from RDF. Moreover, as Site B is further away from the capital city, their tipping fee is approximately two-thirds of Site A, and the waste is only one-tenth of Site A. The tipping fee of Site A generates an average income of THB 580.4 million per year over the course of 20 years and only THB 36.3 million per year for Site B. Furthermore, as Site A is closer to the capital city of Thailand and is within the developed area of their province, the recovered space value is higher than Site B.

Furthermore, the landfill operation expense does not increase proportionally to the waste amount or income. Figure 2 depicts the profit and expense allocation of landfill operations of Site A and B. Site A spent an average of THB 67.7 million per year on their landfill operation, which is 11.66% of their income from landfill operation. Compared to site B's spending of THB 20.8 million per year, which is 57.26% of their income from landfill operation.

The sensitivity analysis results of sites A and B, as depicted in Figures Figure 3 and Figure 4, provide valuable insights into the profitability and risk factors associated with the respective landfill mining projects. The sensitivity of 8 factors is analyzed: capital expense (CAPEX), salary expense, diesel expense, MSW income, space recovery value gained, RDF income, RDF expense, and kHw income. Each factor is selected following the economic parameters mentioned in Table 1.

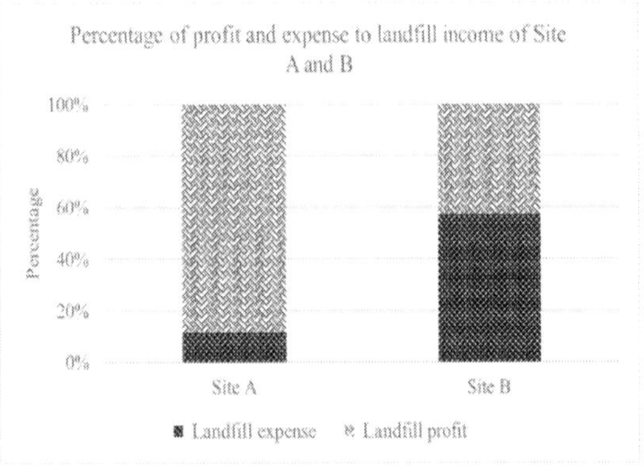

Fig. 2. Graph displaying the expense allocation to income for Site A and B landfill operation.

In the case of Site A, a large-scale landfill mining project, the income generated from municipal solid waste (MSW) tipping fees emerges as a significant driver of project profitability. This finding suggests that the project's financial success is highly dependent on the revenue generated from waste disposal. Following MSW tipping fees, the factors influencing profitability in descending order are kWh income, capital expenditure (CAPEX), space recovery value, salary, RDF (refuse-derived fuel) expense, RDF income, and diesel consumption.

The sensitivity analysis reveals that operating a large-scale landfill mining project with a waste-to-energy (WtE) power plant is particularly sensitive to the income derived from waste disposal and the power plant's performance. Conversely, the impact of normal operating expenses is relatively less significant. These findings highlight the importance of effectively managing waste disposal income and optimizing the power plant's performance to ensure the financial viability of the large-scale project.

In contrast, Site B, a medium-scale landfill mining project, exhibits a different sensitivity profile. Interestingly, both the income from MSW tipping fees and RDF income demonstrate similar levels of sensitivity. The project at Site B is highly sensitive to all factors considered in the analysis, with the sensitivity ranking as follows: MSW tipping fee, RDF income, space recovery value, CAPEX, diesel consumption, and salary. Given that the operator's primary income sources are the tipping fee and the sale of RDF, the diesel consumption rate becomes a critical factor. Additionally, due to the smaller scale of the project compared to Site A, the investment demonstrates a higher rate of effectiveness in terms of project feasibility.

The results indicate that despite differences in business scaling and the amount of incoming waste, both Site A and Site B have the potential to generate positive revenue. However, due to the lower volume of incoming waste, Site B needs to focus more on managing operating expenses than Site A. Furthermore, as Site B relies on only two sources of income, namely RDF sales and tipping fees, both revenue streams are equally important and require careful consideration. In comparing both sites, if Site B adopted a WtE power plant, the income generated would be more secure, and the effective rate of diesel consumption would be significantly reduced. This highlights the potential benefits of incorporating a WtE power plant in Site B's operations, as it would enhance revenue stability and improve overall project feasibility.

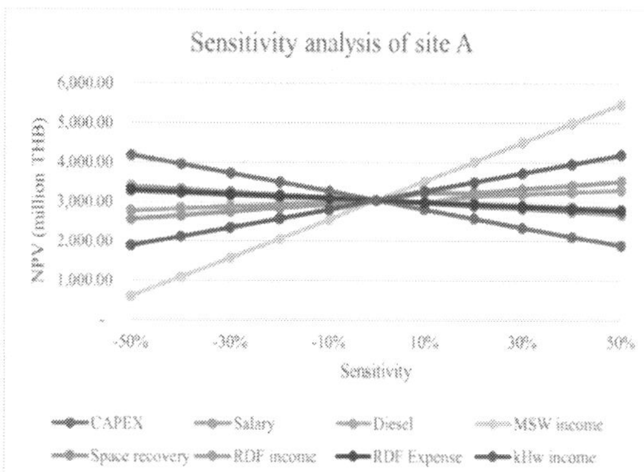

Fig. 3. Sensitivity analysis of Site A, including the WtE power plant on site.

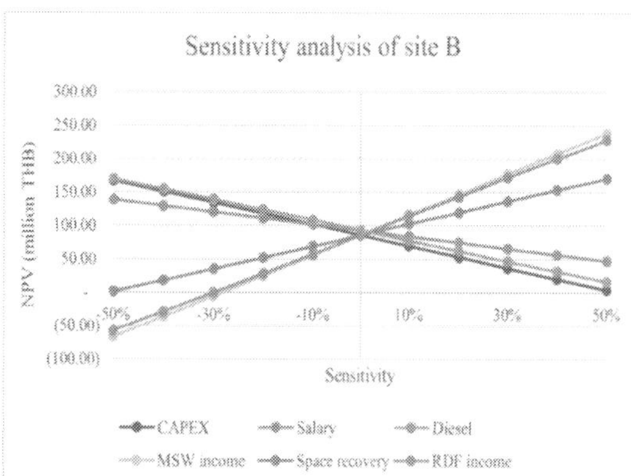

Fig. 4. Sensitivity analysis of Site B, having no WtE power plant, RDF is sold to a cement plant.

It is important to note that these findings are based on the sensitivity analysis conducted, and actual results may vary. However, the analysis provides valuable insights into the key factors influencing the profitability and risk of the landfill mining projects at both sites, aiding decision-making and strategic planning for the successful implementation of such ventures.

4 Conclusion

This study utilized the Net Present Value (NPV) and sensitivity analysis to examine the profitability of two landfill mining projects, one of medium scale and the other of large scale. The objective was to identify the key factors that influence the financial viability of these projects and assess their vulnerability to operational factors. The findings of the study indicate that both medium-scale and large-scale landfill mining projects are profitable. However, the large-scale project is more likely to be profitable and less susceptible to operational factors. This suggests that scaling up the project size can enhance its profitability and reduce the risks associated with operational challenges. The sensitivity analysis conducted in this study shed light on the specific factors that significantly impact the profitability of each project. For Site A, waste disposal income emerged as a highly influential factor. This implies that any changes in the income generated from waste disposal activities can substantially affect the project's profitability.

However, due to the operation of their own waste-to-energy (WtE) power plant, Site A is unlikely to incur losses. The presence of the WtE power plant provides an additional revenue stream and mitigates the financial risks associated with waste disposal income fluctuations. On the other hand, as a smaller-scale project, Site B is also highly affected by waste disposal income. However, the sensitivity analysis revealed that all factors examined in the study significantly influence the project's profitability. This suggests that, due to its smaller scale, Site B is more sensitive to changes in various operational factors, including waste disposal income, operating expenses, and other project-related costs.

In summary, the results of this study indicate that landfill mining projects, whether medium or large-scale, have a high probability of being profitable. However, the profitability of a large-scale project with a WtE power plant is expected to be higher than a medium-scale project. The presence of a WtE power plant provides a stable revenue source and reduces the project's vulnerability to operational factors. These findings highlight the potential financial benefits of landfill mining projects and emphasize the importance of considering project scale and additional revenue streams, such as WtE power generation, to enhance profitability and mitigate risks.

It is worth noting that the profitability and sensitivity analysis results presented in this study are specific to the examined medium and large-scale landfill mining projects. The findings may vary for different projects depending on their unique characteristics, waste composition, market conditions, and other relevant factors. Further research and analysis are necessary to validate these findings and provide a more comprehensive understanding of the financial aspects of landfill mining projects.

Acknowledgments

The authors would like to express their gratitude to the Joint Graduate School of Energy and Environment (JGSEE), the King Mongkut's University of Technology Thonburi (KMUTT) and the Center of Excellence on Energy Technology and Environment (CEE), the Ministry of Higher Education, Science, Research, and Innovation (MHEISI) for the financial support provided to conduct this study. Also, special gratitude must be given to Eastern Energy Plus Co., Ltd. (Site A) and Choakchai Environment Co., Ltd. (Site B) for their support, advice, and information in conducting this study.

References

1. M.L. Manca, E. Casula, F. Marongu, From waste to health: sustainable exploitation of grape pomace seed extract to manufacture antioxidant, regenerative and prebiotic nanovesicles within circular economy, Scientific reports, **10**,1 (2020): 14184
2. A.I. Hălmaciu, I. Ionel, M.R. Wächter, The circular economy in the agro-zootechnical industry, Editorial Board, **58** (2021)
3. A. Zaman, Zero-waste: a new sustainability paradigm for addressing the global waste problem, In The Vision Zero Handbook: Theory, Technology and Management for a Zero Casualty Policy, Cham: Springer International Publishing, (2020): 1-24
4. S. Maina, V. Kachrimanidou, A. Koutinas, A roadmap towards a circular and sustainable bioeconomy through waste valorization, Current Opinion in Green and Sustainable Chemistry, **8**, (2017): 18-23
5. C. Zhou, Z. Gong, J. Hu, A. Cao, H. Liang, A cost-benefit analysis of landfill mining and material recycling in China, Waste Management, **35** (2015): 191-198
6. N. Sutthasil, C. Chiemchaisri, W. Chiemchaisri, K. Wangyao, K. Endo, T. Ishigaki, M. Yamada, The effectiveness of passive gas ventilation on methane emission reduction in a semi-aerobic test cell operated in the tropics, Waste Management, **87**, (2019): 954-964
7. D. Laner, O. Cencic, N. Svensson, J. Krook, Quantitative analysis of critical factors for the climate impact of landfill mining, Environmental Science & Technology, **50**,13 (2016): 6882-6891
8. J.C.H. Parrodi, D. Vollprecht, R. Pomberger, Case study on enhanced landfill mining at mont-saint-guibert landfill in belgium: Physico-chemical characterization and valorization potential of combustibles and inert fractions recovered from fine fractions, Detritus, **10** (2020): 44-61
9. J. Burlakovs, M. Kriipsalu, M. Klavins, A. Bhatnagar, Z. Vincevica-Gaile, J. Stenis, W. Hogland, Paradigms on landfill mining: From dump site scavenging to ecosystem services revitalization, Resour Conserv Recycl, **123** (2017): 73-84
10. M. Hadiwidodo, E. Sutrisno, S. Hartini, M.A. Budihardjo, B.S. Ramadan, A.S. Puspita, F.R. Efriani, Feasibility study for mining waste materials as sustainable compost raw material toward enhanced landfill mining, Polish Journal of Environmental Studies, **32**,3 (2013)
11. J. Lin, What is the better investment rule for investing in the financial markets-NPV or IRR? Why? Are there alternatives we should consider instead?, (2023)
12. R. Rosendal, Landfill mining-process, feasibility, economy, benefits, and limitations, Copenhagen: RenoSam, (2009)
13. P.H. Brunner, H. Handbook of material flow analysis: For environmental, resource, and waste engineers, CRC press, (2016)
14. E. Van Eygen, D. Laner, J. Fellner, Integrating high-resolution material flow data into the environmental assessment of waste management system scenarios: The case of plastic packaging in Austria, Environmental science & technology, **52**,19 (2018): 10934-10945
15. R. Hermann, T. Wolfsberger, R. Pomberger, R. Sarc, Landfill mining: Developing a comprehensive assessment method, Waste management & research, **34**,11 (2016): 1157-1163
16. T. Wolfsberger, A. Aldrian, R. Sarc, R. Hermann, D. Höllen, A. Budischowsky, R. Pomberger, Landfill mining: Resource potential of Austrian landfills - Evaluation and quality assessment of recovered municipal solid waste by chemical analyses, Waste Management & Research, **33**,11 (2015): 962-974

Immobilization of Cellulase on Zinc Oxide Deposited on Zeolite Pellets for Enzymatic Saccharification of Cellulose

Tokla EOM[1], *Jantiya* Isanapong[1], *Pisist* Kumnorkaew[2], *Krisanavej* Songthanasak[1] and *Peerapong* Pornwongthong[1,3,4,*]

[1] Department of Agro-Industrial, Food and Environmental Technology, Faculty of Applied Science, King Mongkut's University of Technology North Bangkok, Bangkok, Thailand
[2] Innovative Nanocoating Research Team, National Nanotechnology Center, National Science and Technology Development Agency, Pathum Thani, Thailand
[3] Food and Agro-Industry Research Center, King Mongkut's University of Technology North Bangkok, Bangkok, Thailand
[4] Agritech and Innovation Center, King Mongkut's University of Technology North Bangkok Techno Park, Bangkok, Thailand

Abstract. The consumption of fossil fuels to fulfill the global energy demand can cause global warming issues. Renewable energy, i.e., bioethanol, from lignocellulosic biomass, is a promising source of alternative energy to fossil fuels. The conversion of lignocellulosic biomass into bioethanol requires the release of fermentable sugars during the saccharification process using cellulase. However, the utilization of this enzyme on an industrial scale is not feasible due to its difficult separation, instability, and high cost. Here, we present a method for cellulase immobilization on functionalized zinc oxide prepared from either zinc nitrate hexahydrate (ZnO(I)) or zinc acetate dihydrate (ZnO(II)) solutions on zeolite (ZEO) pellets. The immobilized cellulase on ZnO-ZEO structures was characterized by scanning electron microscopy, X-ray diffraction spectroscopy, and Fourier transform infrared spectroscopy. The immobilization efficiencies of immobilized cellulase either on ZnO(I)-ZEO or ZnO(II)-ZEO were determined as 58.17 ± 0.75% and 55.51 ± 0.81%, respectively. The immobilized cellulase on ZnO-ZEO was capable of catalyzing microcrystalline cellulose breakdown, releasing reducing sugars. The immobilized cellulase on these structures could be recycled up to four repetitive runs. Based on kinetic data, both the Michaelis constants (K_m) and maximum reaction velocity (V_{max}) of the immobilized cellulase on the ZnO-ZEO structures were lower than those of free cellulase. This suggests that immobilized cellulase has a higher affinity toward the substrate, but a lower reaction rate than the free enzyme.

Keywords. Biocatalysis, Enzymatic hydrolysis, Enzyme kinetics, Reusability

1 Introduction

Environmental concerns about oil supply shortages have encouraged researchers to develop innovative and cost-effective technologies for the effective production of renewable energy, including biodiesel, biohydrogen, biobutanol, bioethanol, and biomethane [1,2]. These alternative and environmentally friendly fuels are usually produced from lignocellulosic biomass, which is widely distributed throughout the world [3]. Lignocellulosic biomass is typically composed of 40-60% cellulose, 20-30% hemicellulose, and 15-20% lignin. It is considered the most abundant material for the generation of biobased fuels and value-added chemicals [4-7]. Additionally, the utilization of lignocellulosic biomass for the production of these products can reduce open combustion, mitigating global warming [4,8].

In the process of lignocellulosic biomass conversion, a hydrolysis step is required to break the long-chain polysaccharides, especially cellulose, in the biomass into a simple monosaccharide (sugar). Chemical, physical, and biological techniques have been applied for the hydrolysis of polysaccharide structures in biomass [9-11]. Both chemical and physical technologies are frequently operated using strong acids at high temperatures and pressure. Under these extreme conditions, the process not only generates fermentable sugars, but also undesired products, which require further purification. On the other hand, enzymatic saccharification of cellulose is commonly used in industries for fermentable sugar production due to its mild hydrolysis conditions, high efficiency, and high specificity [9,12]. However, the saccharification process requires the use of hydrolytic enzymes to catalyze the breakdown of cellulose structures.

Cellulases are hydrolytic enzymes used in various industries, including animal feed, bioenergy, food, textile, agriculture, and so on [13,14]. Cellulase is considered a key enzyme for decomposing the long-chain structural carbohydrates of biomass into simple reducing sugars. However, the direct application of cellulase as a catalyst for achieving an efficient hydrolyzing cellulose substrate can be an expensive process because of its limited recovery and reuse [13,15]. This causes impurity of the products due to the cellulase remaining in the enzymatic hydrolysate [16]. To overcome this drawback, the immobilization of cellulase is one of the most powerful and simple

* Corresponding author: peerapong.p@sci.kmutnb.ac.th

techniques for making the process stable, recyclable, and cost-effective [16-18]. Immobilization can be conducted using various approaches, including covalent binding, encapsulation, entrapment, physical absorption, and cross-linked aggregates [19].

Covalent binding is considered to have the most potential, and provides reliable results due to the strong interaction between the enzyme and the support material, leading to difficulty in the carrier dissociating from the enzyme [20]. Also, the stability of the covalent bond allows immobilized cellulase to be reused a number of times, meaning the covalent bond process has attracted much attention at an industrial level [21]. The factor affecting the covalent binding in immobilization is the surface-functionalization and cross-linking that connects an active group of the support with the enzyme. Zhang *et. al.*, [21] reported that 3-aminopropyltriethoxysilance (APTES) is an essential reagent used to modify the support surface and form an active amino group, while glutaraldehyde (GA) plays the role of a cross-linker that binds between the functional group of the support and the cellulase [21, 22]. Choosing a support is an important step in the process of cellulase immobilization; thus, physical strength, chemical stability, and cost-effectiveness are the preferred characteristics of an immobilized support [21].

Many studies have immobilized cellulase on various types of supports, including functionalized magnetic Fe_2O_3/Fe_3O_4 nanocomposites [22], sodium alginate-polyethylene glycol-chitosan [16], magnetic gold mesoporous silica nanoparticles core shell [23], magnetic nanoparticles [24], metal-organic frameworks [25], and hydrogel microspheres [26]. Recently, researchers have reported on glucose oxidase immobilized on zinc oxide nanowires [27], laccase immobilized on a zinc oxide nanoarray [28], a chitinolytic enzyme immobilized on a polyurethane/nano ZnO matrix [29], and glucose oxidase immobilized on zinc oxide nanoparticles [30].

Among these supports, zinc oxide (ZnO) nanoarrays have attracted much attention due to their specific benefits compared to other nanometal oxides, including a large specific surface area, great biocompatibility, nontoxicity, stabilized properties, and low cost [28, 31, 32]. ZnO has a variety of structures such as nanoparticles, nanotubes, nanowires, nanorods, and nanoflowers; these structural variations can provide large specific surface areas with potential applications in several specific fields of nanotechnology [31]. Immobilization of α-amylase on nano ZnO [32] and laccase on a ZnO nanoarray [28] has been reported. Interestingly, no report on the application of ZnO as a support for the immobilization of cellulase was found in the literature review, although a number of other types of supports have been successfully synthesized and applied for the immobilization of cellulase [33,34].

This study aims to develop a novel strategy for cellulase immobilization on functionalized ZnO deposited on spherical zeolite (ZnO-ZEO). The biocatalysis of immobilized cellulase was evaluated by hydrolyzing microcrystalline cellulose (MCC) to release simple fermentable sugars. The kinetic reaction of free and immobilized cellulase was experimentally compared using a series of MCC concentrations as the substrate, and the Michaelis-Menten constant (K_m) and maximum velocity (V_{max}) were determined from the Lineweaver-Burk plot. Furthermore, the reusability of the immobilized cellulase was also investigated.

2 Materials and methods

2.1 Materials

Reagents such as APTES (98%), GA (50% in H_2O), and cellulase (enzyme blend) were purchased from Sigma-Aldrich (Saint Louis, MO, USA). MCC and 3,5-dinitrosalilcylic acid (DNS; 98%) were obtained from Loba Chemie Pvt Ltd. (Mumbai, India); zinc nitrate hexahydrate, zinc acetate dihydrate, citric acid monohydrate, and sodium hydroxide pellets were procured from Kemaus (NSW, Australia). Commercial ZEO in spherical pellets (ZEO-4A, size 1.7-2.5 mm, 99.9% purity) was bought from Zibo Yinghe Chemical Co., Ltd. (Shandong, China).

2.2 Fabrication of ZnO on ZEO pellets

Commercial ZEO pellets were used as a support for zinc oxide deposition. Briefly, 7 g of zinc nitrate hexahydrate (ZNH) and zinc acetate dihydrate (ZAD) were separately dissolved in 30 ml of distilled water with constant stirring until clear and homogenous solutions were obtained. Then, 20 g of ultrasonically cleaned (in isopropanol and deionized water for 15 min each) ZEO were added into both prepared Zn^{2+} solutions (solution ZNH → ZnO(I) and ZAD → ZnO(II)); they were then incubated at 50 °C for 2 h. The products were then cooled to room temperature and aged overnight. The obtained ZnO(I)-ZEO and ZnO(II)-ZEO were dried at 105 °C for 1 h and calcinated at 350 °C for 30 min.

2.3 Surface modification of ZnO-ZEO

The surface of the ZnO-ZEO was modified by APTES and glutaraldehyde, as reported by Isanapong and Pornwongthong [28]. Briefly, 15 ml of freshly prepared 2% (v/v) 3-APTES in acetone was added to 10 g of ZnO(I)-ZEO and ZnO(II)-ZEO and then incubated at 50 °C while being stirred at 150 rpm. Upon completion of the reaction, the obtained APTES-ZnO(I)-ZEO and APTES-ZnO(II)-ZEO were washed several times with acetone and deionized water to remove the unbounded APTES. Then, the obtained APTES-ZnO-ZEO supports were placed into 15 ml of 5% GA in a sodium phosphate buffer (0.1 M, pH 7.4) at room temperature. After aging for 4 h, the obtained functionalized ZnO-ZEO supports were washed with a sodium phosphate buffer solution to clean the unbounded GA. The obtained functionalized ZnO-ZEO supports were dried at 105 °C for 30 min and were finally kept at room temperature before being used in the immobilization of cellulase.

2.4 Immobilization of cellulase

Briefly, 5 g of each functionalized ZnO-ZEO support was soaked in 30 ml of 50% cellulase solution in a sodium citrate buffer (0.05 M, pH 5.0). The mixture was reacted at 22 °C overnight under constant shaking at 120 rpm. Cellulase was immobilized on each functionalized ZnO-ZEO support by covalent binding. Finally, the immobilized cellulase on ZnO-ZEO was obtained simply via filtration. The immobilized cellulase on ZnO-ZEO was further washed with 5 ml of sodium citrate buffer two times to remove noncovalently attached cellulase. The supernatant and washing solution were used to determine the protein by the Lowry method [35], and bovine serum albumin (BSA) was used as the standard. The absorption was read at 750 nm. Binding efficiency and immobilization efficiency were calculated according to Eq. (1) and (2) [24],

Binding efficiency (%) = (Total protein bound/Total protein added) × 100 (1)

$$\textit{Immobilization efficiency (\%)} = [(C_i - C_s)/C_i] \times 100 \quad (2)$$

where C_i and C_s are the initial cellulase concentration and cellulase concentration in the supernatant after immobilization, respectively. The immobilized cellulase on ZnO-ZEO was further confirmed by Fourier transform infrared (FTIR) spectroscopy. Additionally, the immobilized enzyme was also characterized by X-ray diffraction (XRD) and scanning electron microscopy (SEM).

2.5 Stability of immobilized cellulase at different pH values and temperatures

The effect of different pH values (3, 4, 5, 6, 7, and 8) on the biocatalytic activities of free and immobilized cellulase, prior to MCC hydrolysis, was investigated using a sodium citrate buffer and heating at 50 °C for 1 h in a water bath without shaking. The effect of temperature was evaluated at various temperatures (30, 40, 50, 60, and 70 °C) at pH 5.0 while being incubated in a water bath without shaking. The residual biocatalytic activities of cellulase at different pH values and temperatures were determined; pH 5.0 and 50 °C were considered the reference for determining the relative biocatalytic activity of free and immobilized cellulase.

2.6 Estimation of enzyme kinetics

The enzyme kinetics of free and immobilized cellulase were experimentally compared in this study. Hydrolysis reaction assays using either free cellulase (2.99 Filter paper unit (FPU)/g MCC) or 3 pieces of immobilized cellulase on ZnO-ZEO in triplicate were performed at 50 °C with constant stirring (150 rpm) for 48 h using MCC as the substrate to calculate the cellulase biocatalytic activity. A series of substrate concentrations were prepared from 0.05 to 0.30 mg/ml in a sodium citrate buffer (0.05 M, pH 5). A Lineweaver-Burk plot was used to estimate the Michaelis-Menten constant (K_m) and maximum velocity (V_{max}) of free and immobilized cellulases.

2.7 Reusability assay

The recovery and recycling stability of the immobilized cellulase were determined by employing MCC as the raw material. Briefly, free cellulase (6.5 FPU/g MCC) and 12 pieces of immobilized cellulase on ZnO-ZEO were experimentally compared by hydrolyzing 2% (w/v) MCC at 50 °C with constant stirring (150 rpm). After one batch of hydrolysis, the immobilized cellulase was collected by simple filtration, washed several times with distilled water, and reused in the subsequent batch of hydrolysis. The hydrolysis was experimentally repeated for up to four cycles. The enzymatic activity was considered as 100% for the original activity at the first cycle, and the activities in subsequent batches of hydrolysis were determined relative to the first cycle. In this work, all experiments were conducted in triplicate and the average value is reported.

2.8 Statistical analysis

The obtained data were statistically compared using analysis of variance (ANOVA) through a post hoc t-test. A pair was considered statistically significant when the p-value was less than 0.05.

3 Results and discussion

3.1 Characterization of immobilized cellulase on ZnO-ZEO

ZnO particles were successfully deposited on the ZEO pellets. According to the SEM images, the particle size of the ZnO on the surface of the ZEO samples appears to increase with a large aggregate, making it difficult to determine the particle size (Figure 1(a) and 1(b)). It was found the morphology of ZnO did not alter after the immobilization of cellulase (Figure 1(c) and 1(d)). From this observation, it is impossible to illustrate the presence of the immobilized cellulase on ZnO-ZEO structures. This may be due to a very small amount of enzyme.

In this study, an X-ray diffractometer in plane mode was employed to characterize the crystal structure of the ZnO on the surface of the ZEO. Figure 2 depicts the XRD patterns of ZnO, ZnO(I)-ZEO, ZnO(II)-ZEO, immobilized cellulase on ZnO(I)-ZEO, and immobilized cellulase on ZnO(II)-ZEO. Based on the standard XRD pattern of ZnO, it was found that the XRD pattern of all ZnO samples matched well with the hexagonal ZnO wurtzite (ICSD Collection Code: 290,322). This finding

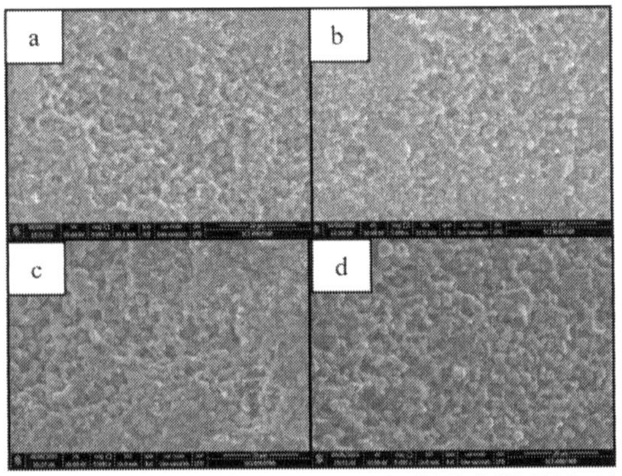

Fig. 1. SEM images of (a) ZnO(I)-ZEO, (b) ZnO(II)-ZEO, (c) immobilized cellulase on ZnO(I)-ZEO, and (d) immobilized cellulase on ZnO(II)-ZEO

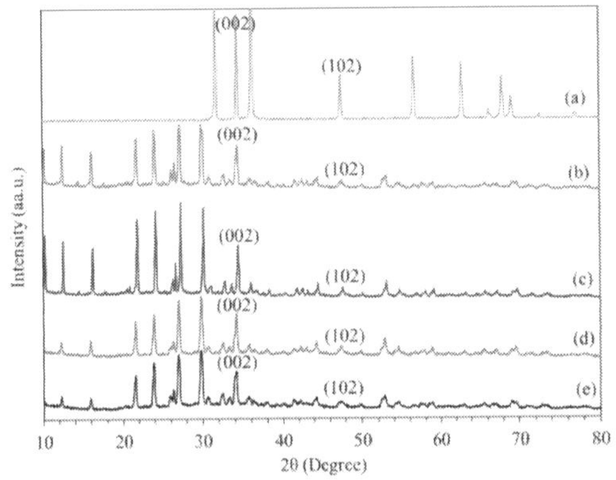

Fig. 2. XRD patterns of (a) ZnO, (b) ZnO(I)-ZEO, (c) ZnO(II)-ZEO, (d) immobilized cellulase on ZnO(I)-ZEO, and (e) immobilized cellulase on ZnO(II)-ZEO.

is in good agreement with Isanapong and Pornwongthong's study [28]. Therefore, the XRD pattern confirmed the presence of spherical ZnO on the surface of the ZEO pellets. The XRD patterns also exhibited a slight decrease in the intensity of the diffraction peak after the immobilization of cellulase on the ZnO-ZEO support. This reduction could possibly exist during the two successive processes, i.e. surface modification and immobilization. Note that the diffraction peaks starting from 10° to 30° result from the ZEO pellets.

To acquire more information, FTIR analysis of ZnO(I)-ZEO, ZnO(II)-ZEO, immobilized cellulase on ZnO(I)-ZEO, immobilized cellulase on ZnO(II)-ZEO, and free cellulase was conducted. As illustrated in Figure 3, the FTIR spectra of the ZnO-ZEO supports display the characteristic bands of a hydroxyl group at 3445 cm^{-1} and 1654 cm^{-1}. These bands were involved in the stretching and bending vibrations of the OH groups, resulting from the presence of absorbed water [32]. The vibrational band observed in the range of 674 cm^{-1} and 554 cm^{-1} represents the stretching mode of the Zn-O bond [28,29]. In the case of the immobilization of cellulase, no additional peak was observed. The FTIR spectra of immobilized cellulase on ZnO(I)-ZEO and immobilized cellulase on ZnO(II)-ZEO were similar to those of the ZnO(I)-ZEO and ZnO(II)-ZEO supports. It was observed that the peak intensity dramatically decreased at around 1652 cm^{-1} in the immobilized cellulase on ZnO(I)-ZEO and immobilized cellulase on ZnO(II)-ZEO compared to the ZnO(I)-ZEO and ZnO(II)-ZEO supports. This finding was attributed to a decrease in the amide bond from the attached cellulase to the ZnO-ZEO supports.

In addition, the binding efficiency and immobilization efficiency were investigated using BSA as the standard and were measured at 750 nm. The immobilization efficiency was found to be 58.57 ± 0.75% and 55.51 ± 0.81% for immobilized cellulase on ZnO(I)-ZEO and immobilized cellulase on ZnO(II)-ZEO, respectively, indicating a medium binding efficiency. Therefore, the surface of the ZnO-ZEO support was not completely covered by cellulase, and the

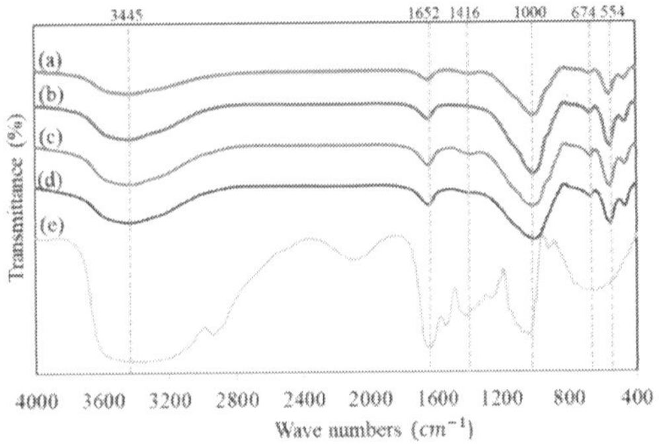

Fig. 3. FTIR spectra of (a) ZnO(I)-ZEO, (b) ZnO(II)-ZEO, (c) immobilized cellulase on ZnO(I)-ZEO, (d) immobilized cellulase on ZnO(II)-ZEO, and (e) free cellulase.

obtained results agree well with the SEM, XRD, and FTIR results. This study suggests that ZnO-ZEO can be considered as an alternative support for the effective immobilization of cellulase.

3.2 Biocatalytic activity assay

The biocatalytic activity of free and immobilized cellulase was experimentally compared by hydrolyzing the MCC substrate to release fermentable sugars. The effect of different pH values and temperatures on the hydrolysis was also investigated, as these two main factors affect the molecular structure of enzymes and cause their biocatalytic activity to decrease [17,32]. First, the effect of different pH values ranging from 3 to 7 on the hydrolysis reactions at 50 °C for 1 h was studied, and the results are presented in Figure 4(a). Both free and immobilized cellulase showed the maximum biocatalytic activity at pH 5. It was noted that immobilized cellulase showed low activity in the pH range from 6 to 7 compared to free cellulase. On the other hand, when the hydrolyzed solution's pH value was 8, the biocatalytic activity of immobilized cellulase

https://doi.org/10.1051/e3sconf/202342802003

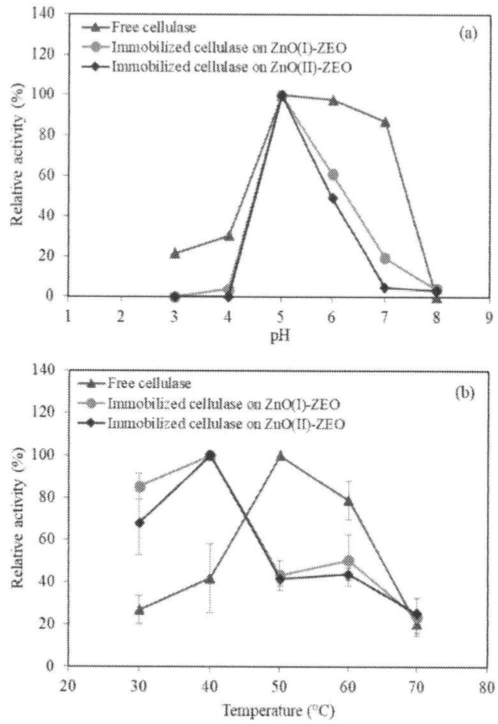

Fig. 4. Effect of hydrolysis pH (a) and hydrolysis temperature (b) on the immobilized cellulases and free cellulase.

on ZnO(I)-ZEO and immobilized cellulase on ZnO(II)-ZEO retained 3.90% and 3.05%, respectively, while that of free cellulase was absent. Hence, the immobilization process ineffectively protected the cellulase from the severe acidic and alkaline hydrolysis media. Moreover, the isoelectric point of cellulase was 4.8 and ZnO was about 9.5 [32]. This could be attributed to the wide range of instability of cellulase and the supports, thereby resulting in less resistance of immobilized cellulase toward pH change compared to the free enzyme.

The effect of different temperatures ranging from 30 °C to 70 °C on the biocatalytic activity of free and immobilized cellulase was also assessed at pH 5. As illustrated in Figure 4(b), the temperature strongly affected the biocatalytic activity of both free and immobilized cellulase. The maximum activity of free cellulase was found at 50 °C; after that, its activity decreased considerably between 50 °C and 70 °C. A significant decline in biocatalytic activity of free cellulase above 50 °C was attributed to the structurally thermal denaturation of cellulase as it was exposed directly to a highly hydrolyzed temperature [36]. Both immobilized cellulase on ZnO(I)-ZEO and immobilized cellulase on ZnO(II)- ZEO showed the best performance at 40 °C, and this was set to be 100% of activity at this maximum hydrolysis temperature. When the hydrolysis temperature was at 30 °C, the immobilized cellulase on ZnO(I)-ZEO and immobilized cellulase on ZnO(II)-ZEO exhibited activities of 85.32% and 67.95%, respectively, while that of the free cellulase was only 26.89%. This finding demonstrates that, after immobilization, both immobilized cellulases performed well at a low temperature. The decrease in temperature along with an increase in stability of the immobilized cellulase might be due to the modification of the conformational integrity between the molecular structure of the cellulase and the support, making immobilized cellulase suitable to perform at a low temperature with a slight structural change. As depicted in Figure 4 (b), the hydrolysis temperature may be affected not only by the molecular structure of cellulase but also by the surface of the support due to the biocatalytic activity of immobilized cellulase decreasing when the temperature increases. Interestingly, the biocatalytic activity of immobilized cellulase was stable when the temperature was between 50 °C and 60 °C. Finally, when the hydrolysis temperature was 70 °C, the activities were only 23.70% and 25.26% for immobilized cellulase on ZnO(I)-ZEO and immobilized cellulase on ZnO(II)-ZEO, respectively, while free cellulase was only 20.43%. This observation simply demonstrates that immobilized cellulases possess high thermal stability. Improved thermal stability of cellulase after immobilization might be because of the existence of covalent binding between the amino functionalized ZnO-ZEO and cellulase enzyme molecules, thus resulting in conformational stabilization of cellulase on the support.

3.3 Enzyme kinetics study

The efficiency of the cellulase immobilization method on MCC substrate hydrolysis was assessed by investigating the shifts in kinetic parameters. The Michaelis constant (K_m) and maximum velocity (V_{max}) were determined by a Lineweaver-Burk plot, as depicted in Figure 5 and Table 1. The K_m reflects the affinity of the enzyme on the substrate; thus, a lower value of K_m demonstrates that the enzyme displays a significant substrate affinity [9,16]. The K_m value can be changed during enzyme immobilization; this may be due to a modification in activation energy, pH profile, as well as the orientation that existed as a consequence of the immobilization technique [32,37].

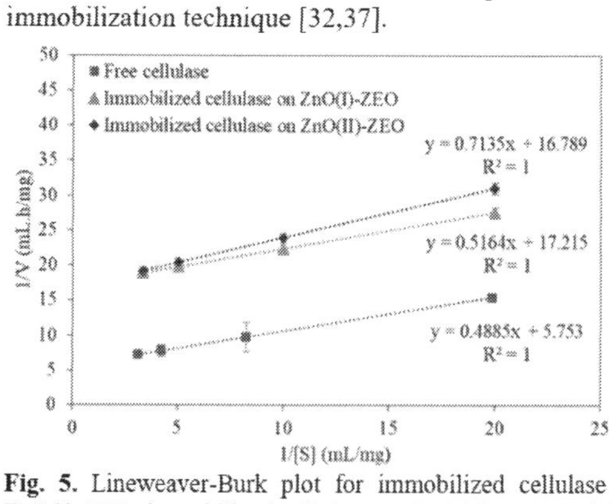

Fig. 5. Lineweaver-Burk plot for immobilized cellulase on ZnO(I)-ZEO, immobilized cellulase on ZnO(II)-ZEO, and free cellulase.

As presented in Table 1, the immobilized cellulase on ZnO(I)-ZEO and immobilized cellulase on ZnO(II)-ZEO showed lower K_m and V_{max} values than those of free cellulase. This finding indicates that the immobilized cellulases were more hydrophilic than free cellulase. Thus, in an aqueous hydrolyzed reaction solution, immobilized cellulase can more easily access the substrate. A decrease in the K_m value indicates significant hydrophilicity of both immobilized cellulases. Moreover, a decline in the V_{max} value was found for immobilized cellulase, which may possibly be due to the decrease in active sites of cellulase and the restriction of cellulase flexibility. Another study also investigated the decrease of both the K_m and V_{max} of immobilized cellulase [9].

Table 1. The kinetic parameters of free and immobilized cellulases

Types of cellulase	Kinetic parameters	
	V_{max} (mg/mL/h)	K_m (mg/mL)
Free cellulase	0.17 ± 0.00	0.09 ± 0.00
Immobilized cellulase on ZnO(I)-ZEO	0.06 ± 0.00	0.03 ± 0.00
Immobilized cellulase on ZnO(II)-ZEO	0.06 ± 0.00	0.04 ± 0.00

3.4 Reusability assay

Free cellulase can only be used once because of its strong reaction with the substrate and difficulty in separation after use. Thus, the aim of immobilization is to enhance stability, reduce production costs, and enable reuse in practical applications. The reusability of immobilized cellulase on ZnO(I)-ZEO and immobilized cellulase on ZnO(II)-ZEO was tested by hydrolyzing MCC at 50 °C for 1 h by keeping a constant pH at 5. Upon completion of each reaction bath, the immobilized cellulases were collected by a simple filtration technique; they were then thoroughly washed with deionized water and reused in the next hydrolysis batch. A total of four cycles was performed to observe the reusability of the immobilized cellulases. As illustrated in Figure 6, the biocatalytic activity of immobilized cellulase on ZnO(I)-ZEO and immobilized cellulase on ZnO(II)-ZEO in the second cycle was 52.56% and 47.38%, respectively. The loss of cellulase biocatalytic activity in the second and subsequent cycles was observed due to the insufficient binding efficiency between the cellulase and the support, thereby causing the cellulase to leach [22,36]. The fourth cycle test for immobilized cellulase on ZnO(I)-ZEO and immobilized cellulase on ZnO(II)-ZEO showed biocatalytic activity of about 19.29% and 10.88%, respectively. In summary, the biocatalytic activity of the immobilized cellulase on ZnO(I)-ZEO and Zn(II)-ZEO reduced up to 80.71% and 89.12%, respectively. The sudden decrease of biocatalytic activity after the third and fourth hydrolysis cycles may be due to the structural changes of the support in the successive runs and the forceful shaking during each hydrolysis cycle [32].

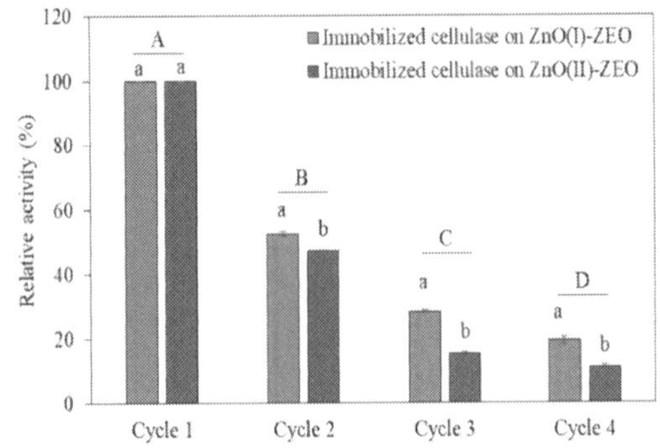

Fig. 6. Reusability and recyclability of immobilized cellulase on ZnO(I)-ZEO and immobilized cellulase on ZnO(II)-ZEO. Note that A, B, C, and D and a and b show significant difference between cycles and samples, respectively ($p < 0.05$; n =3).

3.5 Cumulative yield of reducing sugar

The hydrolysis efficiency of immobilized cellulase on MCC was experimentally compared to free cellulase. Although free cellulase has a strong interaction with a substrate and speedily releases by-products, it is difficult to separate after use. Immobilized cellulase can be used to overcome this drawback. In this work, cellulase immobilized on ZnO(I)-ZEO and ZnO(II)-ZEO could be repeatedly used for as many as four successive runs. As illustrated in Figure 7, a total reducing sugar (TRS) yield of 291.42 ± 1.76 mg/g MCC, 329.57 ± 1.96 mg/g MCC, and 420.96 ± 23.30 mg/g MCC were obtained from the first cycle of MCC hydrolyzed by immobilized cellulase on ZnO(I)-ZEO, immobilized cellulase on ZnO(II)-ZEO, and free cellulase, respectively. The TRS yields obtained from immobilized cellulase on ZnO(I)-ZEO and immobilized cellulase on ZnO(II)-ZEO were 1.44 and 1.28 times lower than the free cellulase. On the other hand, after four cycles, the overall reducing sugar yield obtained from immobilized cellulase on ZnO(I)-ZEO and immobilized cellulase on ZnO(II)-ZEO were 556.61 ± 3.63 mg/g MCC and 552.84 ± 5.14 mg/g MCC, respectively, which were 1.32 and 1.31 times higher than that of free cellulase. Similarly, the cumulative TRS yield obtained from biocatalytic reaction of immobilized cellulase on sodium alginate-polyethylene glycol-chitosan (SA-PEG-CS) was 22.68% higher than that of free cellulase [16]. Therefore, immobilized cellulase can be used as an alternative enzyme for enhanced reducing sugar production.

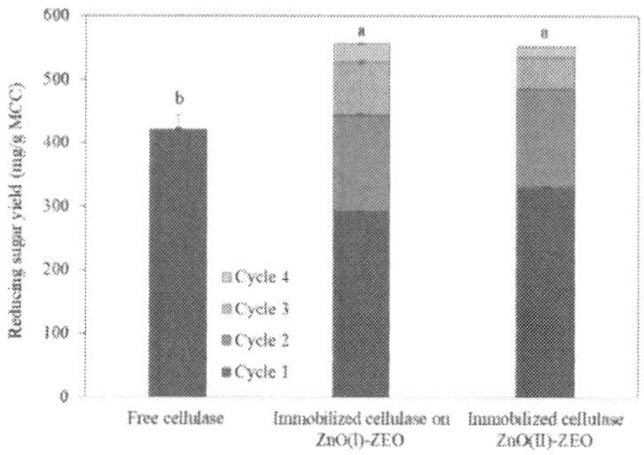

Fig. 7. Results comparing the cumulative reducing sugar yield of enzymatic hydrolysis on MCC. Note that a and b illustrate significant differences between samples ($p < 0.05$; n = 3).

4 Conclusion

This study demonstrated a method for the immobilization of cellulase on a ZnO-ZEO support. The successfully immobilized cellulase was confirmed by SEM, XRD, and FTIR. The immobilization efficiencies of the immobilized cellulase on ZnO(I)-ZEO and immobilized cellulase on ZnO(II)-ZEO was 58.17 ± 0.75% and 55.51 ± 0.81%, respectively. Based on kinetic data, lower values of K_m and V_{max} were observed for the immobilized cellulases, which indicates better hydrophilicity along with a decline in active sites and a reduction of cellulase flexibility after immobilization. Thus, both immobilized cellulases exhibited good performance in the process of simple fermentable sugars production, and can be reused for up to four successive recycle runs.

Acknowledgements

The authors are grateful for the financial support from the King Mongkut's University of Technology North Bangkok and National Science and Technology Development Agency, Thailand. Contract no. Grad 007/2564. XRD and SEM analyses were performed using equipment and facilities in the Scientific Instrument and High Performance Computing Center (SICC), Faculty of Applied Science, KMUTNB. We acknowledge the support of Pranee Preecha of the Department of Industrial Chemistry, Faculty of Applied Science, KMUTNB, who assisted in carrying out the FTIR analysis.

References

1. J.E. Hyeon, S.K. Shin, S.O. Han, Design of nanoscale enzyme complexes based on various scaffolding materials for biomass conversion and immobilization, Biotechnology journal, **11**,11 (2016): 1386-1396
2. S. Ariaeenejad, E. Motamedi, G. Hosseini Salekdeh, Stable cellulase immobilized on graphene oxide@CMC-g-poly(AMPS-co-AAm) hydrogel for enhanced enzymatic hydrolysis of lignocellulosic biomass, Carbohydrate Polymers, **230** (2020): 115661
3. M. Alexandri, R. Schneider, H. Papapostolou, D. Ladakis, A. Koutinas, J. Venus, Restructuring the conventional sugar beet industry into a novel biorefinery: fractionation and bioconversion of sugar beet pulp into succinic acid and value-added coproducts, ACS Sustainable Chemistry & Engineering, **7**,7 (2019): 6569-6579
4. R. Alayoubi, N. Mehmood, E. Husson, A. Kouzayha, M. Tabcheh, L. Chaveriat, C. Sarazin, I. Gosselin, Low temperature ionic liquid pretreatment of lignocellulosic biomass to enhance bioethanol yield, Renewable Energy, **145** (2020): 1808-1816
5. Z. Ziaei-Rad, J. Fooladi, M. Pazouki, S.N. Gummadi, Lignocellulosic biomass pre-treatment using low-cost ionic liquid for bioethanol production: An economically viable method for wheat straw fractionation, Biomass and Bioenergy, **151** (2021): 106140
6. M. Balat, Production of bioethanol from lignocellulosic materials via the biochemical pathway: A review, Energy Conversion and Management, **52**,2 (2011): 858-875
7. A. Limayem, S.C. Ricke, Lignocellulosic biomass for bioethanol production: Current perspectives, potential issues and future prospects, Progress in Energy and Combustion Science, **38**,4 (2012): 449-467
8. A. Stark, Ionic liquids in the biorefinery: a critical assessment of their potential, Energy & Environmental Science, **4**,1 (2011): 19-32
9. Y. Sui, Y. Cui, G. Xia, X. Peng, G. Yuan, G. Sun, A facile route to preparation of immobilized cellulase on polyurea microspheres for improving catalytic activity and stability, Process Biochemistry, **87** (2019): 73-82
10. T. Eom, S. Chaiprapat, B. Charnnok, Enhanced enzymatic hydrolysis and methane production from rubber wood waste using steam explosion, Journal of Environmental Management, **235** (2019): 231-239
11. Z. Qiu, G.M. Aita, M.S. Walker, Effect of ionic liquid pretreatment on the chemical composition, structure and enzymatic hydrolysis of energy cane bagasse, Bioresource Technology, **117** (2012): 251-256
12. R.H.Y. Chang, J. Jang, K.C.W. Wu, Cellulase immobilized mesoporous silica nanocatalysts for efficient cellulose-to-glucose conversion, Green Chemistry, **13**,10 (2011): 2844-2850
13. W. Huang, S. Pan, Y. Li, L. Yu, R. Liu, Immobilization and characterization of cellulase on hydroxy and aldehyde functionalized magnetic Fe_2O_3/Fe_3O_4 nanocomposites prepared via a novel rapid combustion process, International Journal of Biological Macromolecules, **162** (2020): 845-852
14. M. Abbaszadeh, P. Hejazi, Metal affinity immobilization of cellulase on Fe3O4 nanoparticles with copper as ligand for biocatalytic applications, Food Chemistry, **290** (2019): 47-55

15. O.C. Amadi, I.P. Awodiran, A.N. Moneke, T.N. Nwagu, J.E. Egong, G.C. Chukwu, Concurrent production of cellulase, xylanase, pectinase and immobilization by combined Cross-linked enzyme aggregate strategy- advancing tri-enzyme biocatalysis, Bioresource Technology Reports, **18** (2022): 101019
16. Y. Wang, C. Feng, R. Guo, Y. Ma, Y. Yuan, Y. Liu, Cellulase immobilized by sodium alginate-polyethylene glycol-chitosan for hydrolysis enhancement of microcrystalline cellulose, Process Biochemistry, **107** (2021): 38-47
17. S. Raza, X. Yong, J. Deng, Immobilizing cellulase on multi-layered magnetic hollow particles: Preparation, bio-catalysis and adsorption performances, Microporous and Mesoporous Materials, **285** (2019): 112-119
18. B. Qi, J. Luo, Y. Wan, Immobilization of cellulase on a core-shell structured metal-organic framework composites: Better inhibitors tolerance and easier recycling, Bioresource Technology, **268** (2018): 577-582
19. E.C. Lau, H.H. Yiu, Chapter 11 - Enzyme immobilization on magnetic nanoparticle supports for enhanced separation and recycling of catalysts, In Nanomaterials for Biocatalysis, (2022): 301-321
20. Q. Li, Y. Chen, S. Bai, X. Shao, L. Jiang, Q. Li, Immobilized lipase in bio-based metal-organic frameworks constructed by biomimetic mineralization: A sustainable biocatalyst for biodiesel synthesis, Colloids and Surfaces B: Biointerfaces, **188** (2020): 110812
21. D. Zhang, H.E. Hegab, Y. Lvov, L. Dale Snow, J. Palmer, Immobilization of cellulase on a silica gel substrate modified using a 3-APTES self-assembled monolayer, SpringerPlus, **5**,1 (2016): 1-20
22. F.R. Paz-Cedeno, J.M. Carceller, S. Iborra, R.K. Donato, A.P. Godoy, A.V. de Paula, R. Monti, A. Corma, F. Masarin, Magnetic graphene oxide as a platform for the immobilization of cellulases and xylanases: Ultrastructural characterization and assessment of lignocellulosic biomass hydrolysis, Renewable Energy, **164** (2021): 491-501
23. E. Poorakbar, A. Shafiee, A.A. Saboury, B.L. Rad, K. Khoshnevisan, L. Ma'mani, H. Derakhshankhah, M.R. Ganjali, M. Hosseini, Synthesis of magnetic gold mesoporous silica nanoparticles core shell for cellulase enzyme immobilization: Improvement of enzymatic activity and thermal stability, Process Biochemistry, **71** (2018): 92-100
24. M.P. Desai, K.D. Pawar, Immobilization of cellulase on iron tolerant Pseudomonas stutzeri biosynthesized photocatalytically active magnetic nanoparticles for increased thermal stability, Materials Science and Engineering: C, **106** (2020): 110169
25. M. Zhou, L. Yan, H. Chen, X. Ju, Z. Zhou, L. Li, Development of functionalized metal-organic frameworks immobilized cellulase with enhanced tolerance of aqueous-ionic liquid media for in situ saccharification of bagasse, Fuel, **304** (2021): 121484
26. Z. Zhou, X. Ju, M. Zhou, X. Xu, J. Fu, L. Li, An enhanced ionic liquid-tolerant immobilized cellulase system via hydrogel microsphere for improving in situ saccharification of biomass, Bioresource Technology, **294** (2019): 122146
27. F. Miao, X. Lu, B. Tao, R. Li, P.K. Chu, Glucose oxidase immobilization platform based on ZnO nanowires supported by silicon nanowires for glucose biosensing, Microelectronic Engineering, **149** (2016): 153-158
28. J. Isanapong, P. Pornwongthong, Immobilized laccase on zinc oxide nanoarray for catalytic degradation of tertiary butyl alcohol, Journal of hazardous materials, **411** (2021): 125104
29. V. Hooda, A novel polyurethane/nano ZnO matrix for immobilization of chitinolytic enzymes and optical sensing of chitin, International Journal of Biological Macromolecules, **106** (2018): 1173-1183
30. R. Batool, S.A. Kazmi, S. Khurshid, M. Saeed, S. Ali, A. Adnan, F. Altaf, A. Hameed, F. Batool, N. Fatima, Postharvest shelf life enhancement of peach fruit treated with glucose oxidase immobilized on ZnO nanoparticles, Food Chemistry, **366** (2022): 130591
31. S. Adesoye, K. Dellinger, ZnO and TiO2 nanostructures for surface-enhanced Raman scattering-based bio-sensing: A review, Sensing and Bio-Sensing Research, **37** (2022): 100499
32. N. Antony, S. Balachandran, P.V. Mohanan, Immobilization of diastase alpha-amylase on nano zinc oxide, Food chemistry, **211** (2016): 624-630
33. K.N. Rajnish, M.S. Samuel, S. Datta, N. Chandrasekar, R. Balaji, S. Jose, E. Selvarajan, Immobilization of cellulase enzymes on nano and micro-materials for breakdown of cellulose for biofuel production-a narrative review, International Journal of Biological Macromolecules, **182** (2021): 1793-1802
34. K. Khoshnevisan, F. Vakhshiteh, M. Barkhi, H. Baharifar, E. Poor-Akbar, N. Zari, H. Stamatis, A.K. Bordbar, Immobilization of cellulase enzyme onto magnetic nanoparticles: Applications and recent advances, Molecular Catalysis, **442** (2017): 66-73
35. O. Classics Lowry, N. Rosebrough, A. Farr, R. Randall, Protein measurement with the folin phenol reagent, Journal of Biological Chemistry, **193**,1 (1951): 265-75
36. K. Saha, P. Verma, J. Sikder, S. Chakraborty, S. Curcio, Synthesis of chitosan-cellulase nanohybrid and immobilization on alginate beads for hydrolysis of ionic liquid pretreated sugarcane bagasse, Renewable Energy, **133** (2019): 66-76
37. D. Tanyolaç, B.I. Yürüksoy, A.R. Özdural, Immobilization of a thermostable α-amylase, Termamyl®, onto nitrocellulose membrane by

Cibacron Blue F3GA dye binding, Biochemical Engineering Journal, **2**,3 (1998): 179-186

Climate-Conscious Food Preserving Technologies for Food Waste Prevention

Yousif Alhammadi [1], *Doris Ying Ying* Tang [2], *Kit Wayne* Chew [3], *Suksun* Amornraksa[4], and *Pau Loke* Show [5,*]

[1] Department of Civil Infrastructure and Environmental Engineering, Khalifa University of Science and Technology, P.O. Box 127788, Abu Dhabi, United Arab Emirates

[2] Department of Chemical and Environmental Engineering, University of Nottingham Malaysia, Jalan Broga, Selangor 43500, Malaysia

[3] School of Chemistry, Chemical Engineering and Biotechnology, Nanyang Technological University, 62 Nanyang Drive, Singapore, 637459 Singapore.

[4] Department of Chemical and Process Engineering, The Sirindhorn International Thai-German Graduate School of Engineering, King Mongkut's University of Technology North Bangkok Bangkok, Thailand

[5] Department of Chemical Engineering, Khalifa University of Science and Technology, P.O. Box 127788, Abu Dhabi, United Arab Emirates

Abstract. Global food production is responsible for around 26% of greenhouse gas emissions caused by human activities. Notably, 6% of these emissions are caused by unconsumed food. Both traditional and current climate-conscious technologies for food preservatives that assure food waste reduction are discussed. This review investigates the potential of smart packaging biosensors and natural antimicrobial agents in fostering environmentally friendly, cutting-edge food systems. Specifically, it highlights the studies that explore the use of natural antimicrobial agents of calcined corals in active packaging systems for storing milk. The finding revealed that this method had a significant impact on maximizing the shelf life of fresh food. Furthermore, this review discusses the concept of smart packaging of food, focusing on biopolymer-based nanocomposites and biosensors, which have gained increasing attention in the food industry due to concerns about food safety and quality. The review also examines the efforts of the United Arab Emirates (UAE) to combat food waste through the initiatives such as UAE Food Bank, Winnow, and Ne'ma which is the national food loss and waste project. These technologies and practices have the potential to guarantee food safety, preserve quality, and reduce waste, but there are still issues with cost, biocompatibility, and consumer acceptance.

Keyword. Climate-conscious food, Food preservatives, Natural antimicrobial agents, Smart Packaging, UAE food safety.

1 Introduction

Globally, food production accounts for approximately 26% of the human-caused greenhouse gas emissions, with 6% is from unconsumed food [1]. Food that is produced does not reach consumers due to various reasons, such as spoilage or inefficiencies in the supply chain which results in the loss or waste of resources, time, energy, and effort. This decreases the effective yield of the food production system and thus reduces the amount of food accessible for consumption [2]. Unsustainable production and consumption habits are largely responsible for the three major problems of biodiversity loss, pollution, and climate change. Goal 12 of SDGs [3] strives to address this issue by fostering sustainable consumption and production practices, which are critical for supporting the livelihoods of both present and future generations. Moreover, food waste due to the supply chain is mainly caused by traditional food technologies. For a considerable time, conventional meat production has been associated with high greenhouse gas emissions due to manure and enteric fermentation. Practical difficulties such as resource-intensive operations, pollution, the prevalence of antibiotics in animal products, and the advent of Zoonotic illnesses have afflicted the industry. Diet that primarily consists of meat has also faced criticism for using inefficient production techniques and generating substantial carbon footprint [4].

Furthermore, traditional food preservation and processing techniques frequently necessitate substantial amounts of energy and may contribute to greenhouse gas emissions due to fuel consumption.

* Corresponding author: PauLoke.Show@ku.ac.ae

These traditional methods may increase food spoilage and waste, resulting in additional carbon emissions [5]. In addition to food preservation and processing techniques, conventional irrigation and transportation practices have a huge negative environmental impact. Using conventional irrigation techniques, like flood irrigation, could cause a considerable loss of water and may add to soil erosion and damage. Such consequences might cause a decrease in the amount of carbon that is stored in the soil and lead to reduced carbon sequestration, thereby contributing to climate change. When water supplies are uncertain, irrigation cannot be considered sustainable. This is particularly true in regions that suffer from water scarcity. In such locations, the primary focus of irrigation development should be on reducing water consumption to the minimum amount needed for crops [6]. Furthermore, due to fuel consumption, conventional methods of shipping and delivering food can result in significant emissions of greenhouse gases, especially when long-distance transportation is required. Conventional transportation practices might also cause food spoilage during transit, resulting in food waste [7].

The effects of climate change have been the major threat to global food security in recent years. Climate change reduces food production, leading to increased food prices. Climate change hazards are also exacerbated by the expanding global population [8]. Therefore, we need to explore new advancements in food production systems to minimize the environmental impacts and food waste. Meat substitutes are foods that imitate the visual, texture, and chemical properties of traditional meat products. Numerous customer testimonials have praised contemporary meat replacements for their ability to satisfy consumer desires by mimicking the look, flavor, and texture of traditional meat. Addressing customer concerns about the environmental effect, food waste, and animal welfare issues associated with conventional meat production is another important goal [9]. Precision agriculture is an advanced technique that utilizes a variety of devices, such as sensors, drones, and other tools, to gather information regarding weather conditions, soil conditions, and crop growth. This technology enables farmers to enhance resource management, minimize waste, and boost crop productivity [10]. Plastic packaging used for many food products is a major source of pollution in the food processing industry. Biodegradable packaging produced from natural materials such as plant fibers or starch can be a significant step toward waste reduction [11]. In terms of packaging, advancements in packaging design have the potential to decrease the weight and size of food items, resulting in lower transportation costs and emissions [12].

This review paper is to provide a detailed overview of climate-conscious food technologies for preventing food waste and various technologies available to address this critical challenge. However, these technologies were focused on food preservation. This review paper will fill up the gap by assisting researchers, policymakers, and industry professionals in better understanding the latest advancements in this field and identifying areas where further research is required. The following part will address historical, present, and recent innovations methods and technologies in climate-conscious food preservatives for preventing food waste. Additionally, the limitations and current challenges for each perspective, as well as food safety concerns in UAE, will be reviewed and defined.

2 Traditional food waste prevention technologies

Climate-conscious techniques have been used for millennia to prolong the shelf life of food and decrease food waste. The approaches, such as fermentation, drying, smoking, and canning, delay or prevent food from spoiling, hence prolonging its shelf life and availability. Traditional fermentation is a food preservation method that helps to reduce food waste. This time-honored technique of food preservation employs naturally occurring microorganisms to convert sugars within foodstuffs, generating lactic acid, alcohol, and other compounds that contribute to food preservation. As a result, the life span, taste, and nutritional content of the food are enhanced. Fermented foods like kimchi, sauerkraut, kefir, and yogurt have been essential to human nutrition for ages and will likely continue to be consumed frequently [13]. Traditional drying is another food preserving method that can aid in preventing food waste. By removing moisture from food products, drying stops the growth of bacteria and other microbes that cause spoilage. This method has been utilized for centuries to preserve various foods, such as fruits, vegetables, meats, and grains [14].

Traditional smoking is also a food preservation method that can assist in reducing food waste. For millennia, smoking has been used as a food preservation technique, particularly for meats and fish. Food is exposed to smoke from the combustion of wood or other plant resources, which provides a barrier that prevents bacteria and other microbes from replicating on the food's surface. Additionally, the smoke bestows a distinct flavor to the food, making it a preferred option for a variety of culinary applications [15]. Traditional canning is the fourth environmentally friendly food preservation method that aids in minimizing food waste. In canning process, food is sterilized by heating it to a high temperature and sealing it in airtight containers to prevent bacteria and other germs from causing food to spoil. The sealed containers restrict oxygen access, preventing food spoilage and enabling long-term storage at room temperature [16].

Traditional food preservation methods have several benefits, including reducing food waste, less energy consumption than modern techniques, and increasing food security by providing a more stable supply during times when fresh food is unavailable. However, these methods have limitations, such as the inability to accommodate mass production and distribution, potential inconsistencies in results due to environmental factors, and health hazards associated with improper execution, for instance the risk of botulism in improperly canned foods. Consequently, traditional existing technologies had to be updated and replaced by modern food waste prevention technologies.

3 Emerging food waste prevention technologies

Techniques for managing food waste focus primarily on reducing waste. Thus, it is critical to draw attention to recent developments in food waste management. The conventional food waste management techniques are as follows [17].

a. Insect-based bioconversion: Break down of food waste by insects (mealworms, crickets, black soldier flies) and turning it into high value products from their excrement
b. Incineration: It can recover resources, generate electricity, and minimize the quantity of waste that needs to be disposed of, but because of the high nitrogen dioxide emissions and the abundance of produced dioxins, it will also exacerbate acidification, eutrophication and be hazardous to human health.
c. Landfill: Low-cost, but it will pollute the environment, cause climate change because of greenhouse gases, take up a lot of space, contaminate groundwater sources, and deteriorate soil quality.
d. Composting: Prevents the leaching of waste underground and aids in the production of field-ready manure. It can cause carcinogens if improperly handled.
e. Anaerobic digestion: Low environmental impact.
f. Animal Feeding: Direct feeding or the conversion of food waste into animal feed. Animals may be harmed by the variance in food waste and food contamination found in different batches.

3.1 General emerging food waste prevention technologies

High-pressure processing (HPP) is a current food preserving technology that can help to prevent food waste. HPP includes exposing food to high pressure, which kills microorganisms that cause spoilage while preserving the nutritional value and flavor of the food. This technology is effective for perishable foods such as meats, seafood, and juices, to prolong their shelf life while maintaining the quality [18]. Modified atmosphere packaging (MAP) is another recent food preservation technology that can assist reduce food waste by modifying the atmosphere inside the food package, typically by increasing the amount of carbon dioxide or nitrogen and decreasing the amount of oxygen. The growth of microorganisms that lead to food spoiling can be slowed down by this altered environment, extending the shelf life of the food. MAP is especially useful for fresh vegetables and fruits, meats, and bakery products [19].

Next, vacuum packaging is a food preservation technology that works by eliminating air from the food package, generating a vacuum, and then sealing the box. This procedure can slow down the growth of the microorganism that led to food spoilage. Vacuum packaging is very useful for fresh meats, fish, and cheese, as well as processed foods such as snacks and coffee [20]. Moreover, irradiation is a recent food preservation technology, but its climate-consciousness is still being debated due to some environmental concerns. Irradiation is exposing food to ionizing radiation, which destroys bacteria and other germs that cause deterioration. This method has the potential to prevent foodborne illness while also extending the shelf life of food. Irradiation is especially beneficial for fresh fruits and vegetables, meats, poultry, and spices [21]. Current food preservation methods have several advantages, including increased food safety by neutralizing harmful microorganisms and enzymes, extending shelf life to minimize waste, and improving food quality, thereby enhancing its value. However, the drawbacks of these methods are potential adverse effects on the environment due to the production of radioactive waste from irradiation, high energy consumption that contributes to greenhouse gas emissions, and high costs for small-scale food producers. Therefore, it is necessary to upgrade current existing technologies and replaced them with newly developed food waste prevention technologies that prioritize climate consciousness such as incorporation with natural antimicrobial agents and biosensors for smart packaging, which aim to reduce the environmental impact of preservation methods while also promoting food industry sustainability.

3.2 Food packaging

In addition to food waste, food packaging materials are also regarded as municipal solid waste, particularly plastics-based packaging materials that are difficult to degrade and cannot be composted. The widespread use of plastic in food packaging considerably increases environmental pollution because the plastic can break down into smaller fragments (micro- and nano-plastics), which can infiltrate the food chain and have an impact on all trophic levels, including humans [22]. Consumer awareness and safety concerns drive the evolution of food packaging applications due to the migration of packaging material into the food. For instance, when using materials like paper and plastic for food packaging, additives including plasticizers, antioxidants, UV stabilizers, colors, and printing inks may contaminate the packed food. In addition, monomers, and oligomers of the materials as well as additives needed for polymerization may migrate into the food. The usage of metal packaging, such as food and beverage cans, raises the risk of corrosion from high-salt or acidic food items. Heavy metals can also be found in food packaging materials. In short, Food safety is impacted by packaging materials due to chemical migration, inadequate barrier qualities, packaging failure, and loss of seal integrity [23].

Thus, package optimization enters the picture, which is the use of smart packaging to contain, communicate, and protect your items as they are moved from a manufacturing plant, warehouse, or fulfillment center to their destination. Biodegradable packaging materials are preferred because they decompose and can be degraded by soil microbes. This resulted in the development of intelligent packaging, active packaging, and smart packaging, as well as their corresponding applications on the global market. An intelligent packaging system monitors environmental conditions and provides information on the quality of packed goods, whereas an active packaging system includes active components into packaging to increase food quality and shelf life. The usage of "smart packaging" systems can keep track of physicochemical factors like environmental conditions and prevent microbial changes. With the use of cutting-edge technology, active packaging systems can incorporate active ingredients, such as antioxidants, antimicrobials, carbon dioxide scavengers, ethylene scavengers and oxygen scavengers, into the polymeric packaging matrix to maintain and extend the shelf life of food. Active food packaging offers significant promise for maintaining the quality and safety of food products, particularly oxidation-sensitive foods. Next, the level of freshness of the product and its environmental influences, such as temperature, pH level, and gas, are indicated and tracked by an intelligent packaging system during transportation and storage. When there are any internal or exterior changes, the packaging's sensor can detect them and alert the consumer to the situation by giving audio and visual data. Integrating sensors (biosensor, gas sensor), indications (temperature, leakage freshness, pathogen, color), or radio frequency identification systems is the core component of intelligent packaging. All the packaging materials mentioned must be affordable in relation to the value of the product, consumer-acceptable, and environmentally friendly [24].

3.2.1 Natural antimicrobial agents

Food spoilage is largely caused by microbial contamination throughout the food chain, which in turn contributes to food waste, economic losses, and food insecurity. Synthetic chemical preservatives are routinely used to prevent microbial spoilage and prolong the shelf life of food products. However, due to concerns about their negative health effects, consumers and researchers are not recommending their use. As a result, naturally occurring antimicrobials have piqued the interest of food manufacturers and researchers because of their non-toxic nature. These preservatives are naturally derived from numerous sources, such as plants, animals, and microbes, and can be extracted using advanced techniques. Nisin, essential oils, and natamycin are a few examples of natural preservatives with potent antibacterial activity. However, some developing nations have not yet regulated these natural preservatives [25].

The introduction of antimicrobial compounds into food packaging materials is gaining popularity in the packaging industry due to its ability to reduce microbial surface contamination, improve food safety, and prolong shelf life. Different types of packaging materials can be combined with various antimicrobial compounds. However, due to scarcity and safety concerns, there has been an increase in the demand for natural food ingredients, resulting in the substitution of chemical additives with observed safer natural compounds. Current research is mostly focused on utilizing natural antimicrobials obtained from biological sources in food packaging, like bacteriocins, phytochemicals, and enzymes. These natural antimicrobials can be added to packaging materials to provide antimicrobial properties [26].

Natural substances that are biologically produced, such as enzymes, plant extracts, and bacteriocins, can be used in antimicrobial packaging. Table 1 lists a few examples of natural antimicrobials that could be used for food packaging [26]. A study was conducted to investigate the incorporation of natural antibacterial compounds of calcined corals in an active packaging system for storing milk [27].

Table 1. Possible natural antimicrobial agents and biopolymers that could be used in food packaging [26].

Types	Biopolymers and antimicrobial agents
Lipid based coatings	Carnauba wax, beeswax, sugar cane wax, bay berry wax, rice bran wax.
Derivatives of polysaccharides	Chitosan, starch, pullulan, cellulose based paper, natural gums, fatty acids, carrageenan, chitosan, alginate.
Plant/ spice extracts and plant volatiles	Cinnamaldehyde, allyl-isothiocyanate, eugenol, terpineol, linalool, thymol, pinene, carvacrol, allicin, grape seed extract, grapefruit seed extract, hop beta acid, rosemary oil, brassica erucic acid oil, oregano oil, basil oil.
Chelating agents	Ethylenediaminetetraacetic acid (EDTA)
Enzymes/ bacteriocins/ proteins	Soy-protein isolate, corn-zein, whey-protein isolates, peanut-protein, wheat-gluten, collagen/gelatin, milk-proteins.

The study produced a variety of composite films made of low-density polyethylene/ nylon that contain calcined corals (LL/ NY-CORALS). The aim was to investigate the relationship between the number of calcined corals and the physical characteristics as well as the antibacterial properties, particularly the suitability for milk storage. The findings revealed that increasing the number of calcined corals decreased the crystallinity of the composite films without affecting thermal stability or permeability. Notably, LL/NY-CORALS packaging greatly increased the time it took for bacteria to begin growing while slowing down the growth cycle of bacteria in the stored milk with the LL/NY-CORALS 0% film having the highest number of surviving microorganisms of all analyzed composite films. The number of surviving microorganisms decreased as the content of composite films calcined corals increased. Therefore, LL/NY-CORALS composite films have the potential to be employed as food packaging material, potentially extending the shelf life of fresh foods [27].

3.2.2 Biosensors for Smart packaging

Smart packaging is a comprehensive concept that encompasses both intelligent and active packaging. Intelligent packaging can detect external and internal changes in a product and communicate with an external interface, whereas active packaging can respond to these changes by releasing or absorbing substances to extend the shelf life and preserve the freshness of the product. The ultimate purpose of smart packaging is to increase product safety, and traceability throughout the supply chain, and provide quality information to consumers. Active packaging is an alternative to traditional packaging and can maintain the high quality and freshness of food products by embedding different components that can release or absorb substances to prevent spoilage [28].

The idea of intelligent food packaging, which utilizes biosensors and biopolymer-based nanocomposites, has been gaining traction in the industrial sector due to concerns about food quality and safety. The detection layer in biosensors consists of biological materials like antibodies, enzymes, antigens, nucleic acids, and phages. There are a few examples of food packaging integrated biosensor systems [29]. Despite the fact that many biosensors have uses in the health and environmental sciences, not all of them are appropriate for food packaging due to factors such as sensitivity, microstructure, specificity, processing cost, and stability. Several biosensors have been documented and tested specifically for food-related uses, including gas detection sensors, microfluidics and fluorescent sensors, electrochemical/imprinted biosensors, thermal biosensors, and immunosensors. Table 2 summarizes the most often discussed biosensors for intelligent food packaging [30].

Prompt detection of foodborne pathogens is critical for ensuring food safety. A microfluidic biosensor was studied for real-time and precise *Salmonella* detection in a study [30]. The biosensor integrated fluorescence labeling, smartphone video processing, and immunomagnetic separation. The target bacteria, which produced magnetic bacteria, were initially concentrated and separated using immune magnetic nanoparticles. Subsequently, immune microspheres fluorescently labeled magnetic bacteria, resulting in fluorescent bacteria. Lastly, fluorescent bacteria were continually fed into the microfluidic chip using a microscopic smartphone-based fluorescent system, and an app using an inter-frame difference algorithm calculated the desired bacteria number by counting the fluorescent spots online. This proposed biosensor could detect *Salmonella typhimurium* concentrations quantitatively under optimal conditions, with a lower detection limit of 58 CFU/mL. The modification of this could detect different foodborne infections by using various fluorescent materials.

The development of eco-friendly food systems has been considerably aided by recent research on the biosensors in smart packaging and natural antibacterial agents. These innovative techniques contribute to a greener food industry by encouraging sustainability, reducing waste, and guaranteeing food safety. However, there are some difficulties in implementing biosensors in smart packaging and natural antimicrobial agents to promote sustainable food systems. Obstacles for biosensors include the high costs of development and implementation, potential issues with sensor accuracy and precision, and the integration of these sensors into the existing supply chain. Moreover, the biocompatibility and biodegradability of these sensors remain major concerns. As for natural antimicrobial agents, their limitations include their varied effectiveness depending on origin and concentration, potential interactions with food components that could affect their performance, and regulatory issues regarding their safe incorporation into food products. Furthermore, the likelihood of scaling up the production of these natural agents as well as consumer acceptance must be considered. In summary, while these technologies hold great promise for environmentally responsible food systems, overcoming these hurdles will be essential for their widespread adoption and long-term success.

3.2.3 Nanocomposites in food packaging

As the applications of nanotechnology have grown, it has been discovered to be a promising technology for the food packaging business. With its increased barriers, mechanical, thermal, and biodegradable qualities, as well as applications in active and intelligent food packaging, it has demonstrated satisfactory abilities as food packaging materials. Silver, zinc oxide, and magnesium oxide are a few nanofillers that exhibit antibacterial or antioxidant properties. These nanofillers inhibit or delay the growth of microbes in polymer or biopolymer matrices, which lowers the risk of food deterioration [31]. Gold nanoparticles (AuNPs) are employed as the novel materials for the nanopackaging industry due to their medicinal and antibacterial properties as well as their inert nature. [32]

Table 2. Types of biosensors or sensors for intelligent food packaging [30].

Type of biosensor	Types of Biosensors	Analytes	Detection limit	Detection time
Microfluidic and fluorescent biosensor	The fluorescent biosensor of Magnetic type	*E. coli* 0157:H7	14 CFU/mL	2 h
	Nanoclusters of fluorescent Ag +	Ammonia	336 nM	60 min
	Microfluidic sensor poly(dimethylsiloxane) coated	H_2O_2	5 nM	30 min
	Fluorescence biosensor iron coated	*Shigella* spp.	10^2 CFU/mL	20 min
	Microfluidic biosensor	*Salmonella typhimurium*	10^5 CFU/mL	15 min
Electrochemical biosensor	Xanthanin biosensor	Xanthanin	0.1 μM	–
	Electronic transistor CNT	*Salmonella Infantis*	10^2 CFU/mL	1 h
	SWCNT-based biosensor	*Y. enterocolitica*	10^5 CFU/mL	30 min
	Potentiometric aptasensor	*Salmonella typhimurium*	10^1 CFU/mL	10 min
	Amperometric biosensor	L-malic acid	2.9×10^2 g/L	2 min
Gas biosensor	Microcantilever sensor	H_2S	1 ppm	2 h
	Field-effect transistor poly(3-hexyl thiophene) organic	NH_3	100 ppm	6 min
	FET-type sensor	SO_2	10 ppm	3 min
	Pd coated SnO2 nanofiber	H_2	0.25 ppm	40 s
	Carbon codoped acetone sensor	Acetone	10 ppm	100 s

Numerous Gram-positive and Gram-negative microorganisms have been studied, with *E. coli* being the most contentious. Thus, the use of AuNPs as antibacterial agents for high-end, luxurious goods like caviar is strongly advised. *et. al.* [33] employed polystyrene and active agents to fabricate active antifungal packaging material. Thyme extract was used as a reducing agent in the manufacture of zinc oxide nanoparticles. Zinc oxide nanoparticles were impregnated in polystyrene to create the nanocomposite film. According to the findings, nanocomposite films were extremely resistant to the fungus such as *Pencillum* spp., *Nigrospora oryzae*, and *Chaetomium oryzae*. Besides, Jayakumar *et. al.*, [34] created a composite polymeric film made of starch and PVA with the addition of ZnO nanoparticles, jamun (*Syzygium cumini*) and nutmeg (*Myristica fragrans*) extracts to provide it additional desirable qualities for use in food packaging. It was discovered that the nanocomposite film changed color in response to pH changes. Additionally, to preserve the quality of raw meat, biopolymer films based on chitosan, potato protein, linseed oil, and ZnO NPs were produced [35]. Results showed that the film demonstrated good tensile strength, elasticity and moisture barrier [35]. Throughout history, various types of packaging materials have been used, but bio-nano composite materials have proven to be the most effective because they have been developed with vital properties like biocompatibility, antimicrobial activity, biodegradability, and barrier properties. Sensory components can be included into the bio-nanocomposite material to advance active and intelligent packaging, which is a type of packaging utilised particularly for long transportation and massive packing.

4 Food waste prevention in the UAE

As the UAE will host COP28 in Abu Dhabi at the end of 2023, preventing food waste in the country is crucial to promoting sustainability and responsible consumption. The country has been actively working to reduce food waste, including implementing public awareness campaigns, supporting food redistribution programs, and promoting sustainable corporate practices [36, 37]. The UAE hopes to contribute to worldwide efforts to reduce food waste and improve environmental conservation by focusing on minimizing waste in the food supply chain and developing a culture of mindful consumption [38].

4.1 The UAE food bank

The UAE Food Bank was established on 4th January 2017 as part of the Mohammed bin Rashid Al Maktoum Global Initiatives (MBRGI). Providing food to those in need and minimizing food waste are two of its main objectives. The Food Bank collaborates with local authorities, and both local and international NGOs, to establish an efficient system for packaging, distributing, and storing surplus fresh food from restaurants, hotels, and other food institutions. The goals of minimizing food waste include saving money on the high expenses of discarded food, which total AED 282 million per year in Dubai and about 13 billion AED across the UAE.

Additionally, the UAE contributes to sustainable development for a variety of purposes, including energy production, by recycling inedible food [36]. Efforts to repurpose food instead of discarding it help to minimize carbon emissions, pollution, and climate change. These initiatives also aim to save the UAE's natural resources for future generations by conserving soil and water. Moreover, by encouraging the use of organic fertilizers made from surplus food, they contribute to reduce chemical pollution caused by chemical fertilizers [36].

4.2 Winnow

The hospitality industry confronts yearly food waste expenditures of more than $100 billion, with kitchens squandering up to 20% of the food they purchase, frequently equalling their whole net profits [37]. The root of this problem is chefs lacking the necessary tools to precisely monitor, measure and manage waste. Better management results from accurate measurement, and smart data use can increase kitchen productivity. Winnow creates technology that gives chefs more visibility in their kitchens, allowing them to make more educated decisions that decrease food waste and costs. This allows chefs all around the world to focus on cuisine inventiveness. By enabling smarter kitchens, Winnow helps the hospitality and food service industries reduce food waste. Winnow allows kitchens to properly track their waste. Winnow Vision, our AI-enabled solution, enables kitchens to automatically track food waste, saving time and money. In order for the computer to learn and recognize foods dumped in the trash, the system takes photos of wasted food as it is thrown out. As food is thrown away over time, this leads to automatic data capture, improving data accuracy and usability. The process is streamlined by the Winnow Waste Monitor, which is user-friendly and has a digital scale and connected iPad. Staff employees dispose of food in any bin as usual, with the weight noted. The user then selects the reason for disposal and recognizes the item or dish on the tablet [37].

4.3 UAE future directions through food waste prevention

By launching the National Food Loss and Waste Initiative, Ne'ma, the UAE has taken a big step towards addressing the issue of food loss and waste. By implementing sustainable practices in the food industry and raising consumer awareness, the initiative seeks to reduce food loss and waste throughout the UAE. According to the Ministry of Climate Change and Environment, food waste in the UAE is estimated to be around 3.27 million tons per year, which is equivalent to around 13% of the total food produced in the country [39]. The Ne'ma program entails cooperation between public and private sector organizations as well as consumers to develop a sustainable food system in the UAE. The project is designed to benefit the environment and the economy by lowering greenhouse gas emissions, conserving natural resources, and improving food security in the country. The UAE's National Food Loss and Waste Initiative, Ne'ma, serves as a model for other countries to follow in their efforts to tackle food waste.

5 Conclusion and future directions

The use of smart packaging biosensors and natural antimicrobial agents has shown promising results in the development of sustainable and ecologically friendly food systems. The United Arab Emirates' attempts to eliminate food waste through numerous projects demonstrate the country's commitment to sustainability and ethical consumption. Nonetheless, issues such as cost, biocompatibility, and consumer acceptance must be addressed before these technologies and practices can be widely adopted. To achieve a more sustainable and ecologically responsible future, government agencies, the commercial sector, and consumers must continue to collaborate on research, development, and collaboration. To that aim, ongoing research into emerging technologies, as well as the dedication of all stakeholders, will be critical in overcoming obstacles and realizing the full potential of these innovative solutions.

Acknowledgements

I would like to extend my heartfelt gratitude to Prof. Show Pau-Loke and Dr. Doris for their invaluable guidance and suggestions throughout the writing process. The authors would also like to thank Khalifa University for the facilities and resources provided for the completion of this work.

References

1. J. Poore, T. Nemecek, Reducing food's environmental impacts through producers and consumers, Journal of Scienc, **360** (2018): 987-992

2. G.L. Galford, O. Peña, A.K. Sullivan, J. Nash, N. Gurwick, G. Pirolli, M. Richards, J. White, E. Wollenberg, Agricultural development addresses food loss and waste while reducing greenhouse gas emissions, Science Total Environment, **699** (2020): 134318.
3. J. Sachs, C. Kroll, G. Lafortune, G. Fuller , F. Woelm, Sustainable development report, Cambridge University Press, (2022)
4. C. Zhang, X. Guan, S. Yu, J. Zhou, J. Chen, Production of meat alternatives using live cells, cultures and plant proteins. Current Opinion Food Science, **43** (2022): 43-52
5. I. Djekic, I. Djekic, N. Sanjuán, G. Clemente, A.R. Jambrak, A. Djukić-Vuković, U.V. Brodnjak, E. Pop, R. Thomopoulos, A. Tonda, Review on environmental models in the food chain - Current status and future perspectives, Journal of Cleaner Production, **176** (2018): 1012-1025
6. K. Chartzoulakis, M. Bertaki, Sustainable Water Management in Agriculture under Climate Change, Agriculture and Agricultural Science Procedia, **4** (2015): 88-98
7. A. Malak-Rawlikowska, E. Majewski, A. Wąs, S.O. Borgen, P. Csillag, M. Donati, R. Freeman, V. Hoàng, J. Lecoeur, M.C. Mancini, A. Nguyen, M. Saïdi, B. Tocco, A. Török, M. Veneziani, G. Vittersø, P. Wavresky, Measuring the Economic, Environmental, and Social Sustainability of Short Food Supply Chains. Sustainability, **11** (2019)
8. R. Singh, G.S. Singh, Traditional agriculture: a climate-smart approach for sustainable food production. Energy, Ecology and Environ, **2** (2017): 296-316
9. B.M. Bohrer, An investigation of the formulation and nutritional composition of modern meat analogue products. Food Science and Human Wellness, **8** (2019): 320-329
10. I. Cisternas, I Velásquez, A. Caro, A. Rodríguez, Systematic literature review of implementations of precision agriculture, Computers and Electronics in Agriculture, **176** (2020): 105626
11. J. Nilsen-Nygaard, E.N. Fernández, T. Radusin, B.T. Rotabakk, J. Sarfraz, N. Sharmin, M. Sivertsvik, I. Sone, M.K. Pettersen, Current status of biobased and biodegradable food packaging materials: Impact on food quality and effect of innovative processing technologies, Comprehensive Reviews in Food Science and Food Safety (CRFSFS), **20** (2021): 1333-1380
12. J. Bahlau, A Molded Paper Pulp Packaging Design Using Topology Optimization Method, Michigan State University, (2021)
13. J.P. Tamang, J.P. Tamang, P.D. Cotter, A. Endo, N.S. Han, R. Kort, S.Q. Liu, B. Mayo, N. Westerik, R. Hutkins, Fermented foods in a global age: East meets West, Comprehensive Reviews in Food Science and Food Safety (CRFSFS), **19** (2020): 184-217
14. V.R. Sagar, P. Suresh Kumar, Recent advances in drying and dehydration of fruits and vegetables, Journal of Food Science and Technology, **47** (2010): 15-26
15. S.T. McDonald, Comparison of health risks of smoked foods as compared to smoke flavorings: are smoke flavors healthier, Advances in Food Technology and Nutritional Sciences - Open Journal, **1** (2015): 130-134
16. S. Featherstone, A Complete Course in Canning and Related Processed ,Processing Procedures for Canned Food Products. Woodhead Publishing Series in Food Science, Technology and Nutritio, **3** (2016)
17. M. Al-Obadi, H Ayad, S. Pokharel, M.A. Ayari , Perspectives on food waste management: Prevention and social innovations, Sustainable Production and Consumption, **31** (2022): 190-208.
18. D.G. Yordanov, G.V. Angelova, High Pressure Processing for Foods Preserving Biotechnol, Biotechnology, biotechnological equipment, **24** (2010): 1940-1945.
19. U.L. Opara, O.J. Caleb, Z.A. Belay, 7 - Modified atmosphere packaging for food preservation, in Food Quality and Shelf Life, C.M. Galanakis, Editor, Academic Press, (2019): 235-259
20. M.L. Hernández-Macedo, G.V. Barancelli, and C.J. Contreras-Castillo, Microbial deterioration of vacuum-packaged chilled beef cuts and techniques for microbiota detection and characterization, Brazilian journal of microbiology, **42** (2011)
21. M.R. Yousefi, A.M. Razdari, Irradiation and its potential to food preservation, International journal of advanced biological and biomedical research, **3** (2015): 51-54
22. J.I. Castro, J.I. Castro, D.P. Navia-Porras , J.A. Arbeláez Cortés, J.H. Mina Hernández , C.D. Grande-Tovar , synthesis, characterization, and optimization studies of starch/chicken gelatin composites for food-packaging applications. Molecules, **27** (2022)
23. V. Mishra, Safety Issues in Food Packaging Material, www.pmg.engineering
24. M.R. Yan, S. Hsieh, N. Ricacho, Innovative food packaging, food quality and safety, and consumer perspectives. Processes, **10** (2022)
25. F. Saeed, F. Saeed, M. Afzaal, T. Tufail, A. Ahmad, Use of natural antimicrobial agents: a safe preservation approach, Active antimicrobial food packaging, **18** (2019)
26. R. Irkin, O.K. Esmer, Novel food packaging systems with natural antimicrobial agents, Journal of Food Science and Technology, **52** (2015): 6095-6111
27. S. Thanakkasaranee, S. Thanakkasaranee, K. Sadeghi, I. Lim, J. seo, Effects of incorporating calcined corals as natural antimicrobial agent into active packaging system for milk storage,

Materials Science and Engineering C, **111** (2020): 110781
28. S. Chen, S. Brahma, J. Mackay, C. Cao, B. Aliakbarian, The role of smart packaging system in food supply chain, Journal of Food Science, **85** (2020): 517-525
29. M. Ghaani, C.A. Cozzolino, G. Castelli, S. Farris, An overview of the intelligent packaging technologies in the food sector, Trends in Food Science and Technology, **51** (2016): 1-11
30. A. Sobhan, K. Muthukumarappan, L. Wei, Biosensors and biopolymer-based nanocomposites for smart food packaging: Challenges and opportunities, Food Packaging and Shelf Life, **30** (2021): 100745
31. Z. Honarvar, Z. Hadian, M. Mashayekh, Nanocomposites in food packaging applications and their risk assessment for health, Electronic Physician, **8** (2016): 2531-8
32. S. Paidari, S.A. Ibrahim, Potential application of gold nanoparticles in food packaging, Gold Bulletin, **54** (2021): 31-36
33. T. Thirugnanasambandan, S.M. Kumar Thiagamani, H. Natarajan, S. Siengchin, S.M. Rangappa, Fabrication and characterization of an active nanocomposite film based on polystyrene/thyme/nano ZnO for food packaging, Applied Science and Engineering Progress, (2022)
34. A. Jayakumar, H. K.V., S. T.S., M. Joseph, S. Mathew, P. G., I.C. Nair, R. E.K., Starch-PVA composite films with zinc-oxide nanoparticles and phytochemicals as intelligent pH sensing wraps for food packaging application, International Journal of Biological Macromolecules, **136** (2019): 395-403
35. C. Wang, T. Chang, S. Dong, D. Zhang, C. Ma, S. Chen, H. Li, Biopolymer films based on chitosan/potato protein/linseed oil/ZnO NPs to maintain the storage quality of raw meat, Food Chemistry, **332** (2020): 127375
36. D. Municipality, UAE Food Bank, www.dm.gov, (2022)
37. Winnow. Sustainable commercial food waste solutions, www.winnowsolutions, (2023)
38. Winnow. UAE Food Waste Pledge, www.foodwastepledge, (2023)
39. K.L. Tim Ramsey, A. Hanna-Amodio, J. Reynolds, J. Farrington, D. Perera, New Results: Reducing food waste in the UAE's cafeterias, (2023)

Levan Production in Shake Flask and Fermenter - Influence of Feeding Strategy on Levan Yield and Molecular Weight Distribution

Bhuvaneshwari Veerapandian[1], *Saravanan* Ramiah Shanmugam[1,2], *Srividhya* Krishnan[1], *Subramaniyasharma* Sivaraman[1], *Malinee* Sriariyanun[3], and *Ponnusami* Venkatachalam[1,*]

[1] Biomass conversion and Bioproducts Laboratory, Center for Bioenergy, School of Chemical & Biotechnology, SASTRA Deemed University, Thirumalaisamudram, Tamil Nadu, India
[2] Department of Biosystems Engineering, Auburn University, Auburn, AL, USA 36849
[3] Biorefinery and Process Automation Engineering Center, Department of Chemical and Process Engineering, The Sirindhorn Thai-German International Graduate School of Engineering, King Mongkut's University of Technology North Bangkok, Thailand

Abstract. Effect of feeding strategy on levan production was studied in a shake flask and a 5 L lab scale fermenter. In a shake flask, levan specific substrate yield ($Y_{P/S}$) increased from 0.35 g levan/g sucrose to 0.48 g levan/g sucrose with repeated batch feeding. In a 3 L reactor, levan productivity of 7.18 g/L h was obtained with the fed-batch mode of fermentation. The gel permeation chromatography results indicate that higher initial sucrose concentration under the fed-batch mode operation resulted in the formation of low molecular weight fractions (4 and 10 kDa). Thus, fed-batch fermentation favors levan production resulting in higher yield and productivity and also affects the molecular weight distribution of the biopolymer.

Keyword. Circular economy, Feeding strategy, Levan, Levan type fructooligosaccharide, Molecular weight distribution

1 Introduction

Levan is a fructose based biopolymer produced by both microorganisms and plants. Levan is produced by a variety of microorganisms from sucrose via the action of the enzyme levansucrase. It consists of two fructan molecules linked by β-(2, 6) and β-(2, 1) linkages within the core and branch chains, respectively, and carry D-glucosyl residues at its terminal end. Levan has been widely produced by the microorganisms belonging to genera viz., *Pseudomonas, Bacillus, Halomonas, Erwinia, Paenibacillus, Streptococcus, Zymomonas, and Acetobacter* [1]. The physicochemical properties, degree of polymerization, and molecular weight of levan strongly influence biological activities as well as biotechnological applications. It is considered that the size and molecular weight of levan differ on the microbial source and substrate concentration maintained during fermentation [2].

Levan is solely produced using sucrose as substrate, which is obtained from agricultural activities. Thus, it is considered as a value addition to agricultural processing industry to boost its economy. In our recent study, we have demonstrated that levan could be directly obtained from sugarcane juice without need for refining it. Thus, the process is suitable for the circular economy model [3]. Levan, oligolevan, and levan-type fructooligosaccharides (LFOS) find their application in the consumer sector ranging from food industries, cosmetic industries, pharmaceutical industries, etc. It has also gained increased research focus over the last few years due to its anti-tumor, immuno-modulating, and prebiotic activities. Low viscosity, strong adhesivity, high water, and chemical holding capacity, self-assembling ability, high water-solubility, non-toxicity, and biodegradability make the polymer very attractive in the food and biomedical sectors [4]. About 60% of the theoretical yield (0.31 g levan/g sucrose) has been obtained so far using *Bacillus subtilis* [5]. In comparison, Shih *et al.*, (2005)[6] reported a yield of 0.247 g levan/g sucrose using *Bacillus subtilis* (Natto) at a concentration of 200 g sucrose/L. When the initial concentration of sucrose during batch fermentation was increased further to 250 g sucrose/L, the yield of levan obtained using different strains of *Bacillus subtilis* (*Bacillus subtilis* var. natto, *Bacillus lentus* V8 strain, and *Bacillus subtilis* (Natto) Takahashi) reported were 0.166, 0.224 and 0.230 g levan/g sucrose, respectively [7-9]. These results suggest that increased substrate concentration, results in low yield and productivity which could probably be due to substrate inhibition. To overcome the issue of inhibition at high substrate concentration, fermentation using fed-batch mode of operation could be a promising alternative to traditional batch fermentation to increase the levan yield and productivity.

Fed-batch fermentation is one of the most popular methods used to attain high cell density, product concentration, and production rate [10]. This mode of operation helps to overcome substrate inhibition and catabolite repression. During fed-batch fermentation, the

* Corresponding author: vponnu@chem.sastra.edu

concentrations of the substrate in the medium are varied by adjusting the frequency of substrate feeding intervals. The main success of the fed-batch process is the designing of a feeding strategy that satisfies the demands of cells to production of the desired product [11]. The most efficient feeding strategy is determined by considering specific product formation rates as a criterion to eventually achieve increased production levels. On comparing the production process with the conventional batch fermentation process, the fed-batch fermentation along with substrate inhibition significantly promotes the productivity of various products such as lactic acid, formic acid, lipid and PHB [12-15]. A repeated batch fermentation strategy is a constructive production route that has several advantages, such as short separation time, higher substrate consumption, and increased biomass and product productivity. The effect of levan molecular weight distribution at different modes of reactor operation- batch is not reported to date to the best of our knowledge. Also, data on feeding strategy on levan yield and molecular weight distribution are sparingly available in the literature. Hence, the current study aims to evaluate the effect of feeding strategy on levan specific yield and its molecular weight distribution.

2 Materials and Methods

2.1 Reagents and microorganisms for culture medium

The strain *Bacillus subtilis* MTCC441 was purchased from MTCC-Microbial Type Culture Collection, Chandigarh, India was used in this study. Isopropanol used for levan recovery was obtained from SRL chemicals, India. All other reagents including sucrose used in this study were of analytical grade (HiMedia, India). The seed culture was prepared using Luria Bertani (LB) broth and incubated at 37 °C overnight in an orbital shaker at 150 RPM. The glycerol stock of this strain of *Bacillus subtilis* was maintained at -80 °C.

2.2 Repeated fed-batch in shake flask

Batch production of levan was carried out in 250 mL Erlenmeyer's flask using 10% (v/v) of overnight culture as inoculum. The composition of production media was as follows (in g/L): sucrose - 100, yeast extract - 2, ammonium sulphate ($(NH_4)_2SO_4$) - 3, potassium dihydrogen phosphate (KH_2PO_4) - 1, manganese sulphate ($MnSO_4$) - 0.2, and magnesium sulphate ($MgSO_4.7H_2O$) - 0.6. The initial pH of the medium was set to 7.0 by the addition of 1.0 N HCl or 1.0 N NaOH before the start of the sterilization process. Batch fermentation is carried out under previously optimized conditions 37 °C, 150 RPM, and 20 h [16, 17].

Repeated fed-batch studies were conducted out in 500 mL Erlenmeyer's flask with a 100 mL working volume. The same fermentation conditions as mentioned above were used in the fed-batch mode also. The process was started with 100 mL production medium with an initial sucrose content of 100 g/L. Subsequently, at the late exponential phase (after 24 h), 50 mL culture broth was withdrawn and the flask was topped up with an equal amount of fresh substrate containing 200 g/L sucrose. The remaining cells in the flask serve as inoculum for the next batch. The pH of the culture was set to 7.0 using 1N NaOH. This procedure was repeated every 24 h for 5 days. Throughout the study, the culture was maintained at 37 °C, and 150 RPM. The concentrations of residual sugar, levan, and biomass in the harvested culture were estimated. Experiments were conducted in triplicates and the means were compared using Tukey's test at $\alpha = 0.05$.

2.3 Fermenter studies

After completing shake flask studies, fermentation studies were performed in a 5 L bench-scale fermenter with a working volume of 3 L (Make : M/s Lark Biotech, India). The fermenter was fitted with two six-bladed Rushton impellers. The agitation speed, aeration rate, and temperature were maintained at 250 rpm, 1 LPM, and 37 °C, respectively. The fermentation pH was maintained at 6.0 by the addition of 2M NaOH/2N HCl solution as required. Fermentation was carried out for three different sucrose feeding modes viz:
(1) batch mode - initial sucrose concentration 100 g/L
(2) batch mode - initial sucrose concentration 250 g/L and
(3) fed batch mode - here initial sucrose content of 100 g/L was taken and after 12 h a pulse addition was made to raise the concentration to 250 g/L. That is after 12 h (late exponential phase), when the residual sugar concentration drop below ~10 g sucrose/L, 1 L of culture broth was removed from the reactor and an equal volume of fresh feed containing approximately 75% sucrose concentration was added to increase the residual sugar concentration in the reactor to 250 g sucrose/L.

Considering the scale of operation, for 5 L reactor studies an inoculum size of 5% was used. Fermentation was carried out at 37 °C and 250 RPM. The samples were taken after, every 4 h, until 48 h to estimate biomass concentration, levan production, and residual sugar concentration.

2.4 Biomass recovery and levan isolation

For biomass recovery, the culture samples were centrifuged at 8000 RPM for 10 min and the pellets were collected. The pellet was dried overnight at 60 °C for biomass determination. Levan was precipitated from the cell-free supernatant following a pH adjustment to 9.0. After adjusting pH, the supernatant was added to ice-cold isopropanol in a 1:3 ratio to precipitate the levan biopolymer. The precipitate was then centrifuged at 8000 RPM for 10 minutes and the obtained pellet was dried at 60 °C to obtain crude levan. Purification of levan was carried out by re-precipitation using IPA (1:3) followed by centrifugation. Reprecipitation was repeated twice to ensure maximum removal of impurities. The pellet was then re-suspended in hot water and purified using dialysis. The water was changed two times a day for 3 days. This purified levan was freeze-dried and stored at 4 °C for future use [16, 17].

2.5 Determination of intrinsic viscosity

The intrinsic viscosity [η] of the levan solution (0.25-10 g/dL) was determined in triplicates using a Brookfield Viscometer (LV DV 2+ pro deployed with extra S18 spindle). 10 mL of the levan solutions were placed to a sample holder in a viscometer and at different shear rates, apparent viscosity was measured at room temperature. The apparent viscosity (η) of the sample was changed to relative viscosity (η_{rel}) and specific viscosity (η_{sp}) using eq. (1) and eq. (2).

$$\eta_{rel} = \frac{\eta}{\eta_s} \quad (1)$$

$$\eta_{sp} = \eta_{rel} - 1 \quad (2)$$

where η_s is the solvent viscosity.

The intrinsic viscosity of the diluted levan solutions was calculated using Huggins model (eq. 3) and Kraemer model (eq. 4) [18] where solutions were prepared to give relative viscosity ranging from 1.2 to 2, and the corresponding specific viscosity range from 0.2 to1.0.

$$\frac{\eta_{sp}}{C} = [\eta] + K_H[\eta]^2 C \quad (3)$$

$$\frac{\ln \eta_{rel}}{C} = [\eta] + K_K[\eta]^2 C \quad (4)$$

Where K_H is Huggins constant, K_K is Kraemer constant, and C is solute concentration.

Intrinsic viscosity can also be determined using Tanglertpaibul - Rao model (eq. 5), Higiro model (eq. 6 and eq. 7) [19, 20].

$$\eta_{rel} = 1 + [\eta]C \quad (5)$$

$$\eta_{rel} = e^{[\eta]C} \quad (6)$$

$$\eta_{rel} = 1/(1 - [\eta]C \quad (7)$$

The conformation of polysaccharides was elucidated from the power law (eq. 8) model parameters [20, 21].

$$\eta_{sp} = aC^b \quad (8)$$

3 RESULTS AND DISCUSSION

3.1 Effect of repeated fed-batch on levan production

The results for levan production using a repeated feeding strategy are shown in Figure 1. We hypothesized that levan production can be improved by increasing the biomass and levansucrase enzyme concentration from the first batch. Upon successive substrate feeding in pulse, the concentration of levansucrase enzyme can be maintained at a relatively higher level and this will enhance the production of levan. The results obtained from this study show that more than 95% of the initial sucrose concentration was consumed within an initial 24 h (Figure 1).

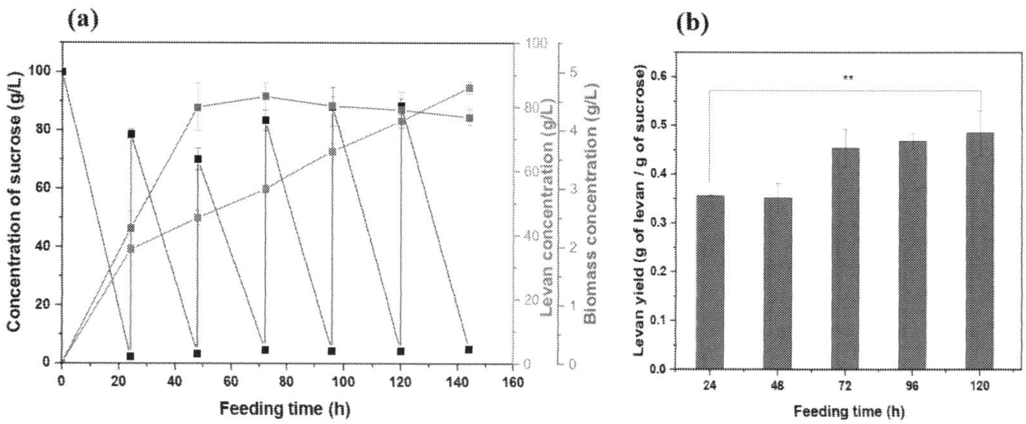

Fig. 1. Effect of cyclic feeding strategy for levan production (a) Time profile for levan concentration, Biomass concentration & Concentration of sucrose (b) Time profile for levan yield on successive feeding of sucrose.

Table 1. Molecular weight distributions of levan from repeated fed-batch fermentation.

Feeding time (h)	F1 (kDa)	F2 (kDa)	F3 (kDa)	F4 (kDa)	F5 (kDa)	F6 (kDa)	F7 (kDa)
24 (Batch 1)	2652.54	ND*	ND	9.16	5.54	3.36	1.56
48 (Batch 2)	2699.57	552.72	ND	8.69	6.25	3.91	1.74
72 (Batch 3)	2891.92	ND	10.65	ND	6.22	3.84	1.80
96 (Batch 4)	2463.45	ND	ND	ND	6.09	3.79	1.81
120 (Batch 5)	2456.25	223.92	ND	ND	6.26	3.83	1.78

* ND- Not determined; F1, F2, F3….F7 = Fraction 1, Fraction 2, Fraction 3…Fraction 7, respectively

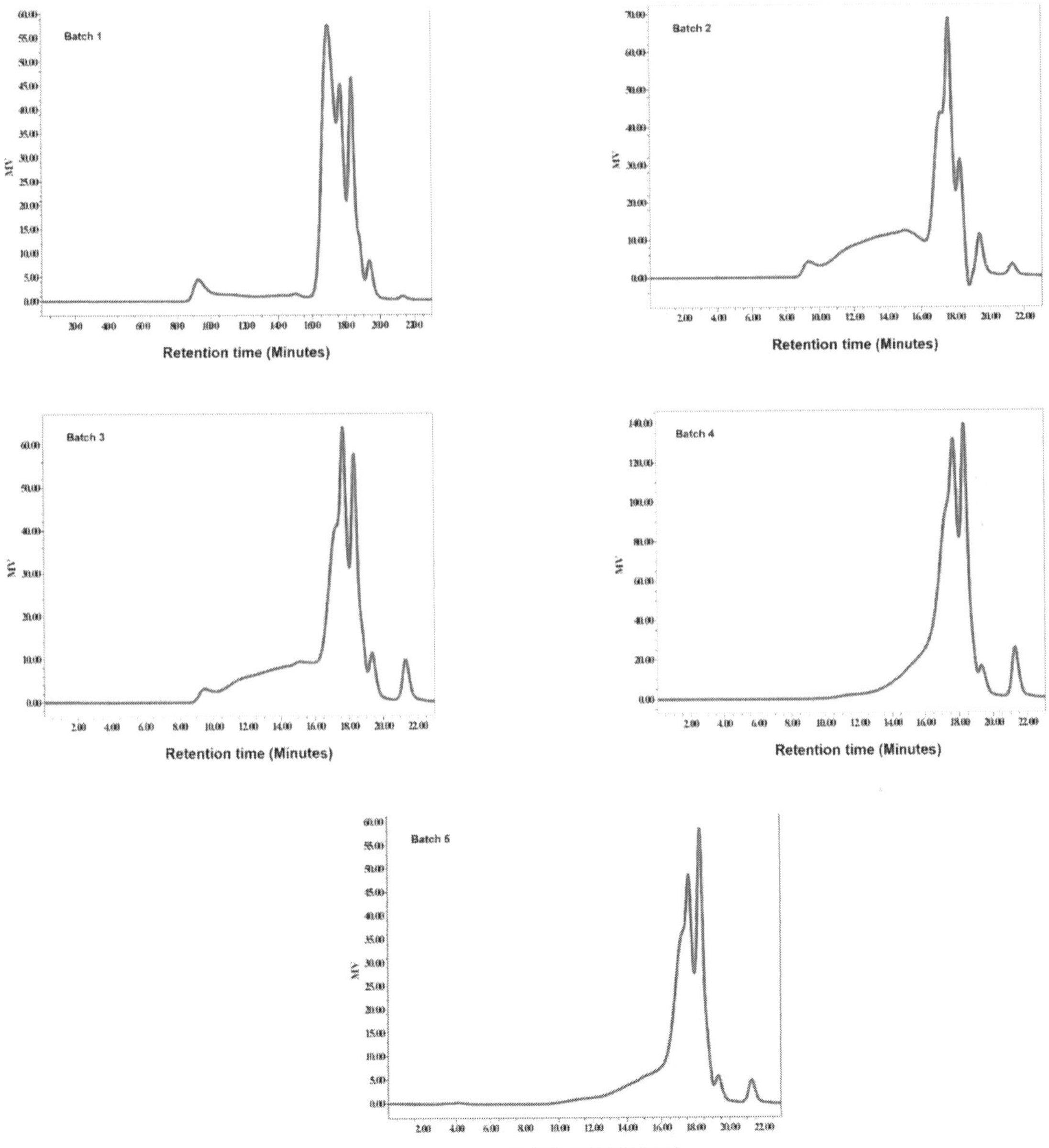

Fig. 2. Gel permeation chromatogram of levan produced from cyclic fed-batch fermentation.

Repeated feeding increased the specific levan yield significantly from 0.35 g/g sucrose (at 24 h) to 0.48 g /g sucrose (at 120 h). This is almost 96% of the maximum theoretical yield (0.50 g levan/g sucrose) possible from sucrose. The levan yields obtained after 96 h and 120 h were statistically the same. Thus, four-step additions could result in maximum specific yield. Similarly, previous reports in the literature on different biopolymers (Poly-Ɛ-lysine, poly-γ-glutamic acid, dextran, EPS) have shown increased yield during repeated feeding of the substrate [22-24] and the results obtained in this study are consistent with previous literature reports.

From the GPC results shown in Figure 2, we can observe that both high molecular (2400 - 2800 kDa) and low molecular (2 - 11 kDa) weight fractions were obtained in repeated fed-batch (Table 1). Results from GPC analysis of levan from batches 1st - 5th indicate that there is no significant change observed in the low and high molecular weight fractions obtained. Whereas levan from the 2nd- 5th batches shows intermediate molecular weight fractions, which could be due to the chain length increase in low molecular weight fractions from the previous batches. The nonprocessive synthesis of low molecular weight levan is mainly due to the oligosaccharide interaction with at least four acceptor binding sites. Due to increasing concentration of levansucrase in the late batches leads to the occurrence of non-processive mechanism resulting in a reduction of molecular weight

[25]. Both levan and LFOS produced can be further fractionated based on their molecular weight as low and high molecular weight levan. Levan biopolymer with a high degree of polymerization (high molecular weight) finds its applications in tissue engineering such as wound dressing. For example, biocompatible levan based hydrogels were formed as drug delivery systems for tissue engineering applications and various medicinal applications [26, 27]. Whereas the low molecular weight fraction of levan i.e., LFOS can be used as a prebiotic in food industries. It has been reported that the intestinal adhesion capacity of probiotic bacteria (*Lactobacillus reuteri* JN101) was improved by levan biopolymer from *Bacillus amyloliquefaciens* JN4 [28]. Also, these types of polysaccharides have gained noticeable importance, such as the ability to enhance the activity of gut microbiota, low caloric sweeteners, non-toxic, and improve the intestinal immune response [29-31].

3.2 Scalability of levan production in bench-scale bioreactor

Results of fermentor studies are shown in Figure 3. Figure 3a shows the sucrose consumption profile at different initial sucrose concentrations. At 100 g/L initial sucrose concentration, about 93.7 % of sucrose consumption was observed within 12 h. In comparison, when the initial sucrose concentration was 250 g/L, similar levels of sucrose consumption (94.8 %) were observed only after 44 h. At an initial sucrose concentration of 100 g/L, the levan yield obtained at the end of fermentation at 12 h is 0.35 g levan/ g sucrose. This indicates that levan results obtained after scaling up from the shake flask to the bench bioreactor showed similar levels of levan yield when operated under batch fermentation. As the initial sucrose concentration was increased to 250 g/L, levan yield increased to 0.46 g levan/g sucrose with less productivity of 2.97 g/ L h at 28 h of fermentation. These results show that substrate inhibition might play a huge role in biomass growth and levan production. To address this issue, a feeding strategy using fed-batch cultivation was devised for reactor studies.

The results obtained from batch fermentation of 100 g/L initial sucrose concentration show, nearly 95 % of sucrose was consumed by *Bacillus subtilis* MTCC441 after 12 h of fermentation. Therefore, at the end of 12 h, about 1.0 L of the fermentation broth was withdrawn and replaced with 1.0 L of 750 g/L (75% w/v) to attain a final sucrose concentration of 250 g/L (25% w/v). Sucrose solution during fed-batch cultivation was added at a feed rate of 30 mL/min. The biomass concentration was increased from 2.67 g/L (12 h) to 5.5 g/L (28 h) Figure 3b.

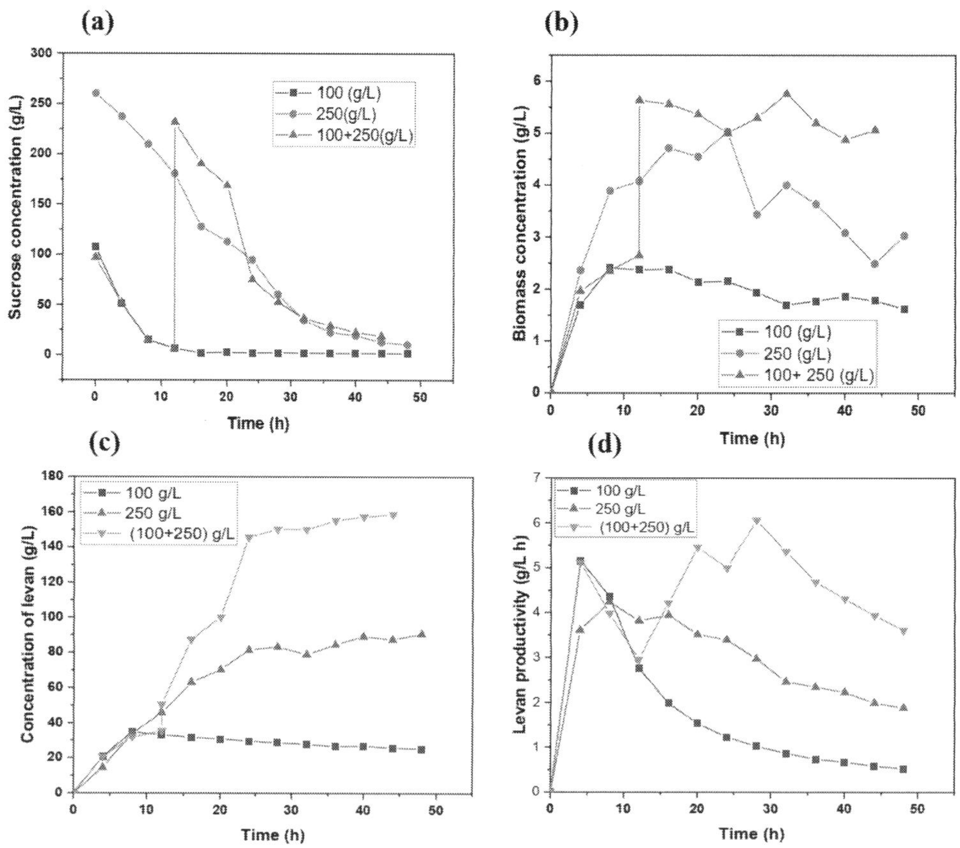

Fig. 3. Effect of feeding strategy on sucrose concentration using batch and fed-batch fermentation. (a) Sucrose consumption rate (b) Biomass concentration (c) Concentration of levan (d) Levan productivity.

 https://doi.org/10.1051/e3sconf/202342802005

After 48 h of the fed-batch mode of fermentation, about 94.8 % of the sucrose consumption was observed for a total sucrose concentration of 350 g/L. Figure 3c shows that levan production follows a similar trend observed in sucrose consumption rate. On comparing batch with fed-batch mode of operation, levan concentration reached 150.03 g/L at 28 h to a total sucrose concentration of 350 g/L with high productivity of 7.18 g/L h. This may be attributed to the presence of biomass and levansucrase enzyme at sufficient levels after 12 h of initial fermentation, which helps in the conversion of sucrose to levan and, in turn, results in higher productivity (Figure 3d). Based on the results obtained from two-stage fermentation, it is evident that the fed-batch fermentation mode not only results in higher productivity but also aids in the cost-effective process [32]. Obtained results also provide an opportunity for developing a cost-effective fermentation process where sucrose-rich renewable substrates could be used for levan production as a less expensive process. In addition, the fed-batch mode of fermentation has a high scope of improving levan productivity which is the need of the hour for industrial-scale production.

Results from GPC analysis indicate the appearance of high and low molecular weight fractions for 100 g/L initial sucrose concentration and upon increasing the sucrose concentration to 250 g/L, only low molecular weight fractions were observed. Raga-carbajal *et al.*, (2015) have investigated the mechanism of high and low molecular weight levan synthesis from *Bacillus* spp [33]. The non-processive synthesis of low molecular weight levan is mainly due to the oligosaccharide interaction with at least four acceptor binding sites. Raga-carbajal *et al.*, (2015) have also done a structural comparison of different levansucrase *Bacillaceae* families and found that differences in low molecular weight fractions synthesized are due to the structural changes in the upper receptor binding site [33]. However, the processive synthesis of levan with a high degree of polymerization remains unclear to date. A secondary site for oligosaccharide binding site in the vicinity of the catalytic pocket might be in the elongation of a high molecular weight fraction or could be responsible for the formation of branches during levan formation. The exact role of this ancillary site is currently under investigation [25]. When the initial sucrose concentration was increased to 100 and 250 g/L, a predominantly low molecular weight fraction was observed (Figure 4).

This type of levan-fructooligosaccharides (LFOS) could be used for various food applications. Fructooligosaccharide (FOS) consists of short chains of fructose with glucose at the terminal end. LFOS exhibits various health benefits for humans if ingested in appropriate quantities. They have low-calorie values and are non-carcinogenic in nature. FOS has been demonstrated to improve the absorption of Ca and Mg in the gastrointestinal tract, provide resistance to infections, bolster the immune system, and encourage overall nutrient utilization [34]. It has been reported that FOS kindles the growth and activity of gut bacteria, such as *Bifidobacteria* spp. and *Lactobacilli* spp. [35]. Studies conducted on FOS have indicated that FOS improves the memory and cognitive abilities of Alzheimer's patients [36] and helps to reduce blood plasma phospholipid, cholesterol, and triglyceride levels [37]. Hence, there is an increased demand for FOS production in the industry[38]. The production of LFOS by two-stage fed fermentation could be an efficient approach to maximize the production level of levan and LFOS for food industry applications.

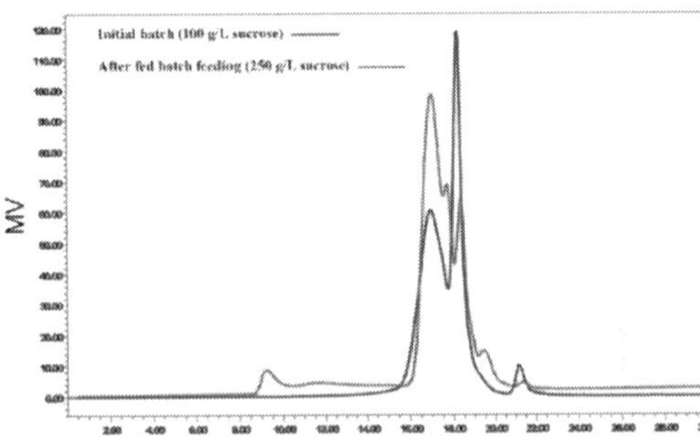

Fig. 4. Gel permeation chromatogram of levan produced from fed-batch fermentation.

3.3 Intrinsic viscosity and molecular conformation

Discussion of the concentration of levan solution (c) is impossible without knowledge of [η]. The intrinsic viscosity of the solutions also provides an idea of the fundamental molecular properties of the molecules in the solution. Based on the calculated coefficient of determination, the linear fittings were weighed (R^2). The most common models used to compute the [η] of polysaccharides are Huggins (Eq. (4)) and Kraemer (Eq. (5)). However, both models failed to predict the when fitting levan solution. Lack of application to solutions with concentrations below the critical value (c), which reduces the number of accessible experimental points, may be the cause of a poor fit. However, the better fit provided by the Tanglertpaibul Rao and Higiro models shows higher efficiency to determine intrinsic viscosity based on slope. Huggins and Kraemer's approaches were improved upon by this method, which is also unrestricted by the shear spectrum. This may be due to fewer experimental points available due to the model's restricted applicability to levan solutions with concentrations below the critical value (c). Therefore, the finding of the intrinsic viscosity from the slope of the dilute region seems to give a more reliable range even at different shear rates. The finding of [η] based on the slopes of the plots gives higher correlation coefficients and smaller standard errors than the intercept values of the plots [39-41]. Additionally, further dilution during sample preparation increases η_{sp}/C inaccuracy [42]. Literature shows that the Huggins equation is applicable only at $\eta_{sp} < 0.7$. In the present study, η_{sp} varied from 0.2 and 1.0.

Table 2. Intrinsic viscosity of the levan solutions.

Shear rate (s^{-1})	Tanglertpaibul Rao		Higiro-1		Higiro-2	
	R^2	η(dl/g)	R^2	η(dl/g)	R^2	η(dl/g)
132	0.9939	0.491	0.9915	0.3093	0.973	0.202
198	0.9788	0.473	0.9919	0.2972	0.998	0.198
264	0.9805	0.471	0.9928	0.2865	0.9991	0.1797

Table 3. The values of exponent b using power law and Berry number (C*η)

Shear rate (s^{-1})	R^2	b	Tanglertpaibul Rao (C*η)	Higiro-1 (C*η)	Higiro-2 (C*η)
132	0.9637	1.1514	0.1-1.22	0.077-0.77	0.051-0.505
198	0.9616	1.0227	0.12-1.2	0.07-0.74	0.05-0.49
264	0.9281	0.8584	0.12-1.18	0.07-0.72	0.04-0.45

The intrinsic viscosities determined by equations 5 to 7 at different shear rates are shown in Table 2. The [η] of the levan solution obtained from the Tanglertpaibul Rao plot is higher than the value from Higiro plots at different shear rates. Similar results were obtained when estimated for sage seed gum, Cress seed gum, and Xanthan gum [41, 43]. Even at higher concentrations of levan solutions, it showed low intrinsic viscosity, and also it exhibited a decrease in viscosity on increasing shear rate [44].

The plot of log (η_{sp}) vs. log (C[η]) was used to find the dilute Newtonian domain and the coil overlap parameter. The slope of the curve at a different rate and [η] from Tanglertpaibul Rao was in the range of 0.8 - 1.15 and all the samples were also in the dilute regime. The molecular entanglement of the levan solution at different concentrations can be observed using the Berry number (C[η]) if this dimensionless concentration exceeds one and the semi-dilute regime is determined to be in the range of 1.0-10.0. But in the current study, it was in the range 0.01- 1.2 for the concentration from 0.25 to 2.5 g/dl and believed to be free of coil overlap and molecule entanglement (Table 3). While the concentration between 5 to 10 g/dL exhibits a semi-diluted regime and is thought to be the result of molecule entanglement and coil overlap. The exponent b value derived from the power law equation (eq. 8) is shown in Table 3. The random coil conformation in a diluted regime is associated with the value $b > 1$, but the rod-like conformation is associated with $b < 1$. For levan solutions of different concentrations at different rates show the b value was in the range of 0.9 to 1.2 indicating that the molecular conformation of rod-like structure to random coil conformation upon changing shear rate. At a lower shear rate, it exhibited random coil conformation whereas at a higher shear rate exhibits a rod-like structure.

4 Conclusions

The current work investigated on levan production using different feeding strategies by *Bacillus subtilis* MTCC441 in batch and fed-batch modes of operation. A repeated feeding strategy on levan production resulted in an increased yield from 70 % to 96 % of the theoretical maximum on levan production. Scaling up of levan production from shake flask to bench scale fermenter was successfully implemented with increasing levan productivity from 1.75 g/L h (shake flask) to 4.38 g/L h (bioreactor) with 94 % of sucrose consumption within 8h of fermentation. On the fed-batch mode of fermentation, levan yield increased to 7.18 g/L h within 28 h. This is the first systematic study of this strain *Bacillus subtilis* MTCC441 in a fermenter that was reported with a higher yield. The results from this study help us to produce the levan on an industrial scale. The molecular weight distribution of levan depends on the initial sucrose of the medium. Feeding higher sucrose concentration in fed-batch fermentation, results in producing low molecular weight levan (4 and 10 kDa). This type of low molecular weight levan or fructooligosaccharides could be used as a prebiotic in food applications.

Acknowledgment

The first author Mrs. Bhuvaneshwari Veerapandian sincerely thanks CSIR for the financial support through the SRF fellowship (Direct SRF/09/1095(0061)/2020 EMR-I).

References

1. F. Freitas, C.A. Torres, M.A. Reis, Engineering aspects of microbial exopolysaccharide production, Bioresour Technol, **245** (2017): 1674-1683.
2. Á. González-Garcinuño, A. Tabernero, J.M. Sánchez-Álvarez, M.A. Galán, E.M. Martin del Valle, Effect of bacteria type and sucrose concentration on levan yield and its molecular weight, Microbial Cell Factories, **16**,1 (2017): 1-11
3. B. Veerapandian, S.R. Shanmugam, S. Sivaraman, M. Sriariyanun, S. Karuppiah, P. Venkatachalam, Production and characterization of microbial levan using sugarcane (Saccharum spp.) juice and chicken feather peptone as a low-cost alternate medium, Heliyon, (2023)
4. E.T. Öner, L. Hernández, J. Combie, Review of Levan polysaccharide: From a century of past experiences to future prospects, Biotechnology advances, **34**,5 (2016): 827-844
5. N.B. Laddha, M.P. Chitanand, Screening of levan producing bacteria from soil collected from jaggery

field, International Journal of Pharmaceutical, Chemical & Biological Sciences, **7**,3 (2017): 195-203

6. I.L. Shih, Y.T. Yu, C.J. Shieh, C.Y. Hsieh, Selective production and characterization of levan by Bacillus subtilis (Natto) Takahashi, Journal of Agricultural and Food Chemistry, **53**,21 (2005): 8211-8215
7. A.M. Vieira, F. Zahed, A.C. Crispim, E. de Souza Bento, R.D.F.O. França, I.O. Pinheiro, B.M. Carvalho, Production of levan from Bacillus subtilis var. natto and apoptotic effect on SH-SY5Y neuroblastoma cells, Carbohydrate Polymers, **273** (2021): 118613
8. K.A. Abou-Taleb, M.O. Abdel-Monem, M.H. Yassin, A.A. Draz, Production, purification and characterization of levan polymer from Bacillus lentus V8 Strain, British Microbiology Research Journal, **5**,1 (2015): 22-32
9. L. Shih, L.D. Chen, J.Y. Wu, Levan production using Bacillus subtilis natto cells immobilized on alginate, Carbohydrate Polymers, **82**,1 (2010): 111-117
10. S. Öztürk, P. Calik, T.H. Özdamar, Fed-Batch biomolecule production by Bacillus subtilis : a state of the art review, Trends in biotechnology, **34**,4 (2016): 329-345
11. R. Poontawee, S. Limtong, Feeding strategies of two-stage fed-batch cultivation processes for microbial lipid production from sugarcane top hydrolysate and crude glycerol by the oleaginous red yeast Rhodosporidiobolus fluvialis, Microorganisms **8**,2 (2020): 151
12. F. Zhang, J. Liu, X. Han, C. Gao, C. Ma, F. Tao, P. Xu, Kinetic characteristics of long-term repeated fed-batch (LtRFb) l-lactic acid fermentation by a Bacillus coagulans strain, Engineering in Life Sciences, **20**,12 (2020): 562-570
13. M.G. Dashti, P. Abdeshahian, Batch culture and repeated-batch culture of Cunninghamella bainieri 2A1 for lipid production as a comparative study, Saudi journal of biological sciences, **23**,2 (2016): 172-180
14. S. Grunwald, A. Mottet, E. Grousseau, J.K. Plassmeier, M.K. Popović, J.L. Uribelarrea, A. Sinskey, Kinetic and stoichiometric characterization of organoautotrophic growth of Ralstonia eutropha on formic acid in fed-batch and continuous cultures, (2014)
15. S. Srisuddee, M. Sriariyanun, A. Tawai, Enhancement of PHB production process in a fed-batch bioreactor using input-output linearization technique with optimal setpoints, Applied Science and Engineering Progress, **14**,2 (2021): 196-205
16. J.S.C. Chidambaram, B. Veerapandian, K.K. Sarwareddy, K.P. Mani, S.R. Shanmugam, P. Venkatachalam, Studies on solvent precipitation of levan synthesized using Bacillus subtilis MTCC 441, Heliyon, **5**,9 (2019)
17. B. Veerapandian, S.R. Shanmugam, S. Varadhan, K.K. Sarwareddy, K.P. Mani, V. Ponnusami, Levan production from sucrose using chicken feather peptone as a low cost supplemental nutrient source, Carbohydrate polymers, **227** (2020): 115361
18. E.O. Kraemer, Molecular weights of celluloses and cellulose derivates, Industrial & Engineering Chemistry, **30**,10 (1938): 1200-1203
19. T. Tanglertpaibul, M.A. Rao, Intrinsic viscosity of tomato serum as affected by methods of determination and methods of processing concentrates, Journal of Food Science, **52**,6 (1987): 1642-1645.
20. J. Higiro, T.J. Herald, S. Alavi, S. Bean, Rheological study of xanthan and locust bean gum interaction in dilute solution: Effect of salt, Food Research International, **40**,4 (2007): 435-447
21. L.S. Lai, J. Tung, P.S. Lin, Solution properties of hsian-tsao (Mesona procumbens Hemsl) leaf gum, Food Hydrocolloids, **14**,4 (2000): 287-294
22. R. Baruah, B. Deka, N. Kashyap, A. Goyal, Dextran utilization during its synthesis by weissella cibaria RBA12 can be overcome by fed-batch fermentation in a bioreactor, Applied biochemistry and biotechnology, **184** (2018): 1-11
23. L. Shih, M.H. Shen, Optimization of cell growth and poly (ε-lysine) production in batch and fed-batch cultures by Streptomyces albulus IFO 14147, Process Biochemistry, **41**,7 (2006): 1644-1649
24. S.H. Yoon, J. Hwan Do, S. Yup Lee, H. Nam Chang, Production of poly- γ -glutamic acid by fed-batch culture of Bacillus licheniformis, Biotechnology Letters, **22** (2000): 585-588
25. E. Raga-Carbajal, A. Díaz-Vilchis, S.P. Rojas-Trejo, E. Rudiño-Piñera, C. Olvera, The molecular basis of the nonprocessive elongation mechanism in levansucrases, Journal of Biological Chemistry, **296** (2021)
26. A. Osman, E.T. Oner, M.S. Eroglu, Novel levan and pNIPA temperature sensitive hydrogels for 5-ASA controlled release, Carbohydrate polymers, **165** (2017): 61-70
27. S.S. Selvi, M.E. Hasköylü, S. Genç, E. Toksoy Öner, Synthesis and characterization of levan hydrogels and their use for resveratrol release, Journal of Bioactive and Compatible Polymers, **36**,6 (2021): 464-480
28. G. Cai, D. Wu, X. Li, J. Lu, Levan from Bacillus amyloliquefaciens JN4 acts as a prebiotic for enhancing the intestinal adhesion capacity of Lactobacillus reuteri JN101, International journal of biological macromolecules, **146** (2020): 482-487
29. M. Li, M.H. Monaco, M. Wang, S.S. Comstock, T.B. Kuhlenschmidt, G.C. Fahey Jr, S.M. Donovan, Human milk oligosaccharides shorten rotavirus-induced diarrhea and modulate piglet mucosal immunity and colonic microbiota, The ISME journal, **8**,8 (2014): 1609-1620

30. K. Sivieri, M.L.V. Morales, S.M. Saad, M.A.T. Adorno, I.K. Sakamoto, E.A. Rossi, Prebiotic effect of fructooligosaccharide in the simulator of the human intestinal microbial ecosystem (SHIME® model), Journal of Medicinal Food, **17**,8 (2014): 894-901
31. N. Wiebe, R. Padwal, C. Field, S. Marks, R. Jacobs, M. Tonelli, A systematic review on the effect of sweeteners on glycemic response and clinically relevant outcomes, BMC medicine, **9** (2011): 1-18
32. L. Liu, F. Wang, G. Pei, J. Cui, J. Diao, M. Lv, W. Zhang, Repeated fed-batch strategy and metabolomic analysis to achieve high docosahexaenoic acid productivity in Crypthecodinium cohnii, Microb Cell Fact Microbial Cell Factories, **19** (2020): 1-14
33. E. Raga-Carbajal, E. Carrillo-Nava, M. Costas, J. Porras-Dominguez, A. López-Munguía, C. Olvera, Size product modulation by enzyme concentration reveals two distinct levan elongation mechanisms in bacillus subtilis levansucrase, Glycobiology, **26**,4 (2016): 377-385
34. Y. Wang, T. Zeng, S.E. Wang, W. Wang, Q. Wang, H.X. Yu, Fructo-oligosaccharides enhance the mineral absorption and counteract the adverse effects of phytic acid in mice, Nutrition, **26**,3 (2010): 305-311
35. M. Peng, Z. Tabashsum, M. Anderson, A. Truong, A.K. Houser, J. Padilla, D. Biswas, Effectiveness of probiotics, prebiotics, and prebiotic-like components in common functional foods, Comprehensive reviews in food science and food safety, **19**,4 (2020): 1908-1933
36. D. Chen, X. Yang, J. Yang, G. Lai, T. Yong, X. Tang, Q. Wu, Prebiotic effect of fructooligosaccharides from Morinda officinalis on Alzheimer's disease in rodent models by targeting the microbiota-gut-brain axis, Frontiers in aging neuroscience, **9** (2017): 403
37. P. Markowiak, K. Śliżewska, Effects of probiotics, prebiotics, and synbiotics on human health, Nutrients, **9**,9 (2017): 1021
38. S. Bhadra, D. Chettri, A. K. Verma, Microbes in fructooligosaccharides production, Bioresource Technology Reports, (2022): 101159
39. F. Behrouzian, S.M. Razavi, H. Karazhiyan, Intrinsic viscosity of cress (Lepidium sativum) seed gum: Effect of salts and sugars, Food Hydrocolloids, **35** (2014): 100-105
40. M. Salahi, S.M.A. Razavi, E. Hasanvand, Physicochemical, rheological and functional properties of a novel gum from Eremurus luteus root, Bioactive Carbohydrates and Dietary Fibre, **27** (2022): 100296
41. Z. Zamani, S.M.A. Razavi, Dilute solution properties of nettle seed (Urtica pilulifera) gum as a function of temperature, Letters in Applied NanoBioScience, **12** (2022)
42. B. Launay, G. Cuvelier, S. Martinez-Reyes, Viscosity of locust bean, guar and xanthan gum solutions in the Newtonian domain: A critical examination of the log (ηsp) o-log C[η]o master curves, Carbohydrate Polymers, **34**,4 (1997): 385-395
43. S.M. Razavi, T.M. Moghaddam, B. Emadzadeh, F. Salehi, Dilute solution properties of wild sage (Salvia macrosiphon) seed gum, Food Hydrocolloids, **29**,1 (2012): 205-210
44. E.C. De Siqueira, J. de Souza Rebouças, I.O. Pinheiro, F.R. Formiga, Levan-based nanostructured systems: An overview, International Journal of Pharmaceutics, **580** (2020): 119242

Antidiabetic Activity and Molecular Docking Analysis of Milky Mushroom (*Calocybe indica*) Grown on the Renewable Substrate

Anne Sahithi Somavarapu Thomas[1], *Vijaya* Lakshmi Murugan Kavitha[2], *Jayapriya* Sekar[2], *Mahalakshmi* Velmurugan[2], *Malinee* Sriariyanun[3], and *Vinodhini* Shanmugam[2,*]

[1] Institute of Brain Science (IBS), TICEL Biopark, Chennai, Tamilnadu, India
[2] Department of Biotechnology, D.K.M College for Women, Vellore, Tamilnadu, India
[3] Biorefinery and Process Automation Engineering Center, Department of Chemical and Process Engineering, The Sirindhorn International Thai-German Graduate School of Engineering, King Mongkut's University of Technology North Bangkok, Bangkok, Thailand

Abstract. As part of the circular economy idea, rice straw without additives has been investigated as a way to turn agricultural waste into products with added value. The nutrients in the substrate, *Calocybe indica* yield, and biological effects were all calculated. In this investigation, the methanol extract was used. GC-MS was examined to discover the necessary compounds present in fungi. A surplus of mushrooms was harvested, and it was discovered that the growth of mushrooms on the rice substrate took place in less than five days. At a humidity of 93%, biological efficiency was determined to be in the range of 54.5-130.9%. In vitro and molecular docking results for the antidiabetic showed good inhibitory properties. As a result, rice straw could be a productive and affordable growing medium for milky mushrooms.

Keywords. Antidiabetic property, Bioactive compounds, *Calocybe indica*, Cultivation, Molecular docking

1 Introduction

A large, delicious, milk mushroom (*Calocybe indica*), also known as the summer mushroom, was first discovered in India in 1976. It is typically prized for its flavor, nutritional value, and medicinal properties and is a member of the family Tricholomataceae of the order Agaricaceae [1]. It is an edible food for people with high blood pressure and heart disease because it contains a crucial source of vitamin D and protein, as well as vitamins, carbohydrates, iron, and calcium [2]. It also contains significant amounts of potassium and sodium [3]. This aids in controlling the amount of bad cholesterol and preventing an increase in blood glucose levels. Patients with severe diabetes mellitus have a variety of diseases, including neuropathy, hyperlipemia, and nephropathy, and they can be managed with specific medications. *Calocybe indica* has strong antioxidant properties [4]. Recent years have seen a surge in interest in the natural anti-glycoside compounds found in milk mushrooms because they show promise in lowering the risk of chronic complications in people with diabetes mellitus. Inhibiting the primary enzymes that hydrolyze carbohydrates can control it and lower postprandial hyperglycemia.

Biorefinery is a facility that integrates several technologies from various fields to create a seamless process for converting biomass into different classes of compounds [5]. The most prevalent and promising renewable resource that can be used to produce chemicals and other useful byproducts is biodiversity [6]. Humans can produce food with added value by growing *Calocybe indica* mushrooms with lignocellulose agricultural waste. It is commonly grown all over the world and is referred to as the fruiting body of mushrooms. As a result, it can grow using a variety of lignocelluloses in a wide temperature range. Mushroom farming started in India in the 19th century [7]. Inorganic substances, carbon and nitrogen as a food source, as well as crucial nutrients like cellulose, hemicellulose, and lignin, are needed by milky mushrooms. Agriculture produces rice straw as a byproduct, which is then used as a substrate for mushroom growth. At the moment, rice fields are being destroyed by open-air burning, which causes significant environmental issues. Rice straw has the potential to convert inedible waste into profitable and palatable biomass if it can encourage the growth of milky mushrooms [8]. These mushrooms grow on deeply decomposing organic materials and can be harvested in the wild during the last, wettest part of the rainy season. However, it is said that due to its poor biological value and yield, the use of rice straw in the cultivation of milk mushrooms has not taken off in China. For those who have diabetes or cancer, it also has therapeutic advantages [9].

In particular, the *Calocybe indica* species, which is an edible food for people with high blood pressure and heart disease, contains significant amounts of potassium and sodium [10]. In addition, by lowering the composition of lignocellulose biomass, the practice of

* Corresponding author: shanvinodhini22@gmail.com

mushroom cultivation might enhance the quality of straw [11]. Thus, the primary substrate for growing milk mushrooms in this study is rice straw (also known as paddy straw), and it also aims to look into the in vitro inhibitory activity of the antidiabetic plant *Calocybe indica*.

2 Materials and methods

2.1 Cultivation of mushroom

Milky mushrooms were grown on a substrate of rice straw using protocol-compliant techniques [12]. Bedding preparation was carried out in a polythene bag under sterilized conditions using a 3:1:2 ratio of casein soil, coco-peat, and sand.

2.2 Extraction

The harvested mushrooms were dried in the air in an oven at a temperature of 40 °C, and then a sample of dried mushrooms (5 g) was extracted by mixing with 50 ml of methanol, filtered through Whatman filter paper No. 1. Then, extract of milk mushroom *(C. indica)* was evaporated by rotation at a temperature of 40 °C until drying. The dried extract was stored at a temperature of 4 °C until further use [13].

2.3 Antidiabetic activity: Alpha-amylase

To determine the inhibition assays of pancreatic α-amylase activity were carried out by the standard procedure. The milky mushroom extract was taken in a small amount of 1 mg/ml in different concentrations, and then starch solution was used as a substrate. After starting the reaction by adding 100 ml of a 10 mg/ml starch solution, 20 mm of sodium phosphate buffer (pH 6.9), and 6 mm of sodium chloride, the reaction was carried out at 25 °C for 10 min. A volume of 100 µl of pancreatic α-amylase (0.5 mg/ml) was added to each tube, and all tubes with the mixture were incubated at 25 °C for 10 min the reaction was stopped to count the amount of glucose present by adding 200 µl of the coloring reagent 3,5-dinitro salicylic acid (DNS). The reaction mixture was heated for 5 min at 100 °C and placed in an ice bath to cool the mixture at room temperature; at the end of the reaction, 100 µl of sodium potassium tartrate was added and transferred to 96 well plates. Using acarbose as a standard, the activity of - amylase was measured at 540 nm, and the inhibition of enzyme activity was calculated using the formula below [14].

$$\%\text{Inhibition} = \text{Abs}_{\text{control}} - \text{Abs}_{\text{sample}} / \text{Abs}_{\text{control}} \quad (1)$$

2.4 Alpha-glucosidase

A preliminary study of the activity of α-glucosidase was carried out in the presence of milk mushroom extract: 1 mg/ml of the extract was taken in different concentrations (10-100 mcg/ml). The extract was prepared in a 100 mm sodium phosphate buffer (pH 6.9) and then 50 µl of 5 mm solution of p-nitrophenyl, α-D glucopyranoside in a phosphate buffer were mixed in a 96well microplate. The sample was incubated at 37 °C for 5 min, followed by the addition of 100 ml of phosphate buffer containing 0.1 U/ml. α-glucosidase (from baker's yeast) into each well and using a microplate reader to set the temperature at 37 °C. The reaction mixture was recorded for 30 min and measured the absorbance at 405 nm. The standard drug acarbose was dissolved in 10% DMSO and used as a positive control. The percentage (%) of inhibition was calculated as follows [15].

$$\% \text{ of antioxidant activity} = [(AC-AS)/AC] \times 100 \quad (2)$$

Where: AC- control reaction absorbance; AS- testing specimen absorbance

2.5 Molecular Docking and GC-MS Analysis

Using the AutoDock version, a molecular interaction study was conducted on the chosen phytocompounds from the GC-MS/MS analysis. Alpha-amylase and alpha-glucosidase enzymes were the targets for the interaction study, and the Protein Data Bank (PDB) was used to retrieve the three-dimensional structures of the proteins. The protein target was docked against various ligands using the Autodock and AutoGrid algorithms to examine its inhibitory activity [16].

Alpha-amylase and alpha-glucosidase, which have been used commercially for inhibitory properties, were measured using acarbose as a standard. The employed algorithm forecasts the relationship between ligands and macromolecule (protein) targets. Charges from Kollman and Gasteiger were added. The Lamarckian genetic algorithm's chosen docking parameters are as follows: With a population of 150 and a maximum of 27,000 generations, the number of docking runs was set to 10. The highest binding affinity is demonstrated by the lowest binding energy. Ligplot+ was used to view the hydrogen bonds and hydrophobic interactions of each docked complex.

3 Results and Discussion

Mushrooms are epigenetic macrofungi that have two distinct growth phases, reproductive (fruiting bodies) and vegetative (mycelium), and they have an umbrella-like structure in which spores are produced [4]. There are over 14,000 different types of mushrooms in the world, but only about 2,000 of them are edible. As a result, about 200 species of mushrooms were grown commercially to be used in the creation of food and medication [17]. The growth of milk mushroom species (*Calocybe indicia*), which are high in vitamins and calcium, and have nutraceutical, pharmaceutical, bioremediation and biodegradable properties, has continued and gained momentum in recent years [18]. In addition, mushrooms have more than 100 therapeutic properties, with their primary medical applications being for detoxification, antibacterial, immunomodulation, antifungal, antiviral, antiparasitic, antitumor, antiallergic, antioxidant, and anticholesterolemic effects [19]. In particular, the presence of biologically active substances that inhibit enzymes can contribute to antidiabetic activity. This includes *in vitro* training with noteworthy data on alpha-amylase and alpha-glucosidase inhibitory activity that was comparable to acarbose, a common antidiabetic drug.

To prevent chronic complications, this study focuses on the antidiabetic activity of milk mushrooms for the treatment of patients with diabetes mellitus at the onset of the disease. Researchers are working to identify essential components with a higher margin of safety and promising areas of application after conducting extensive research on mushrooms in the food and pharmaceutical industries over the past few years. Consumption has significantly increased among people of all ages as a result of mushrooms' superior nutritional qualities, desired organoleptic properties, and aroma. Additionally, there is still a lot of interest in mushrooms because of their importance as a staple food item around the world and their use as food and medicine for a variety of illnesses. These benefits include their dietary, antioxidant, and therapeutic properties. The majority of the complications that are currently occurring are with mushrooms, which are regarded as one of the essential and suitable foods for patients suffering from various types of diseases, such as diabetes, obesity, and cancer [20].

Mushrooms are a crucial ingredient in cooking because of their potential immunomodulatory effects, high-quality protein, and low fat and cholesterol content. *Calocybe indica* is advantageous to health as the third most significant commercially grown mushroom after champignons and oyster mushrooms. Studies reported that milky mushrooms are an excellent source of antioxidants and organic substances that can be used to treat diabetes and obesity. Milk-white mushrooms can be consumed nutritionally to help treat this condition [21]. Several studies have used multiple approaches to tackle diabetes mellitus, amongst these inhibiting the enzymes that facilitate the absorption and metabolism of carbohydrates has been one approach. The important enzymes that are involved in glucose absorption from the gut are the pancreatic α-amylase enzyme and α-glucosidase enzyme. Inhibiting these enzymes reduces the absorption of glucose from the gut and thereby controls postprandial blood sugar levels. In the present study, we evaluated the antidiabetic properties of the methanolic extract of *Calocybe indica*, the results suggest that Dioxa-10-thia-4,13- diazacyclopentadeca-5,9,12-trione and Oxacycloheptadec-8-en-2-one compound of Milky mushroom effectively inhibits the activities of α-amylase and α-glucosidase enzymes using molecular docking analysis. These effects were compared with standard drugs. These findings are consistent with the earlier reports on the effect of natural compounds in inhibiting the enzyme activities of α-amylase and α-glucosidase enzymes.

3.1 *In vitro* anti-diabetic activity- alpha-amylase inhibition assay

The methanolic extract's ability to inhibit amylase was assessed, and the results of the inhibition assay are depicted in Figure 1. The percentage inhibitory activity against the alpha-amylase enzyme increased in a dose-dependent manner. The enzyme was most effectively inhibited by the extract concentration at 75.03±0.72. Alpha-amylase inhibitory activity was detected at concentrations of 25-200 µg/ml of the extract, with an IC_{50} value of 44.57 µg/ml. The IC_{50} value of sample is 30.96 µg/ml, and acarbose was used as the standard reference drug (IC_{50} 80.67±1.22 µg/ml).

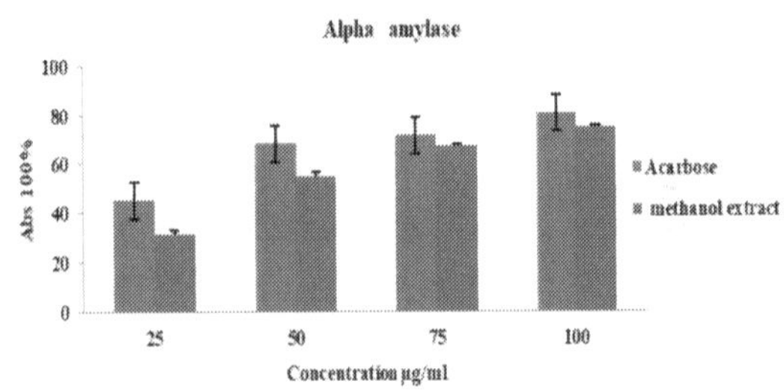

Fig. 1. Inhibitory effects of alpha-amylase in methanolic extract of milky mushroom and acarbose.

3.2 Yeast α-glucosidase activity

The yeast-glucosidase activity was found to be significantly inhibited by a methanol extract of *Calocybe indica*. At concentrations between 25 and 200 µg/ml of the extract, as shown in Figure 2, the percentage inhibition varied from the highest concentration of 59.85±2.41 µg/ml to the lowest concentration of 14.84±1.78 µg/ml. It was determined that 85.91 µg/ml was the IC_{50}—the concentration needed to produce 50% inhibition. When the extract's IC_{50} value was compared to that of the reference drug, acarbose (63.45 µg/ml), it revealed inhibition activity.

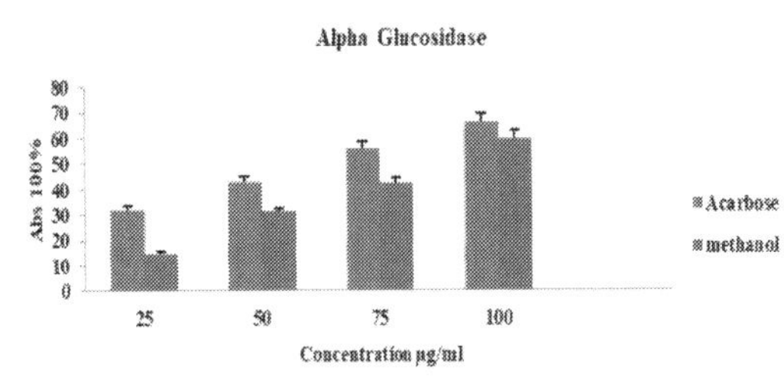

Fig. 2. Inhibition of α-glucosidase in *milky mushroom* extract and acarbose.

3.3 Yeast cell glucose uptake

Studies have been done on how the methanolic extract affects antidiabetic activity. The amount of glucose taken up by yeast cells treated with the methanolic extract was found to rise dose-dependently. The percentage increases in the cell's uptake of glucose at various glucose concentrations are shown in Figure 3 and 4, and are 5 mM and 10 mM, respectively. The extract was most active at glucose concentrations of 5 mM and 10 mM (66.07±1.27 µg/ml and 58.24±1.9 µg/ml, respectively). The values of IC_{50} are 68.0 µg/ml and 89.90 µg/ml for 5 mM and 10 mM, respectively. According to the results, milky mushrooms are more effective than the common drug acarbose (73.34±1.71 µg/ml) and (70.49±1.65) at increasing glucose uptake by yeast cells. The values of 44.6 µg/ml and 61.08 µg/ml are the IC50.

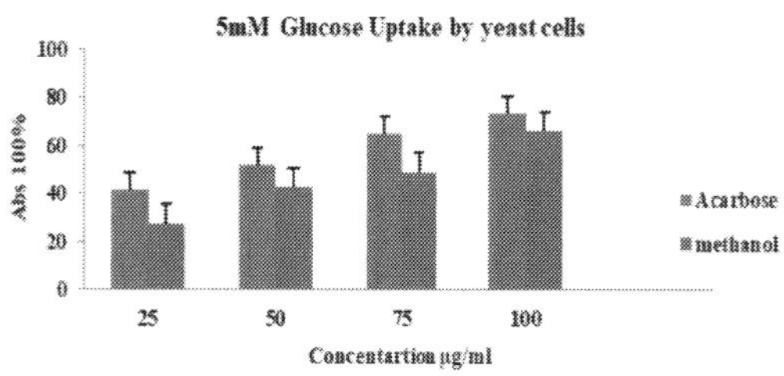

Fig. 3. Methanolic extract effects on milky mushroom and acarbose glucose uptake by yeast cells (5 mM).

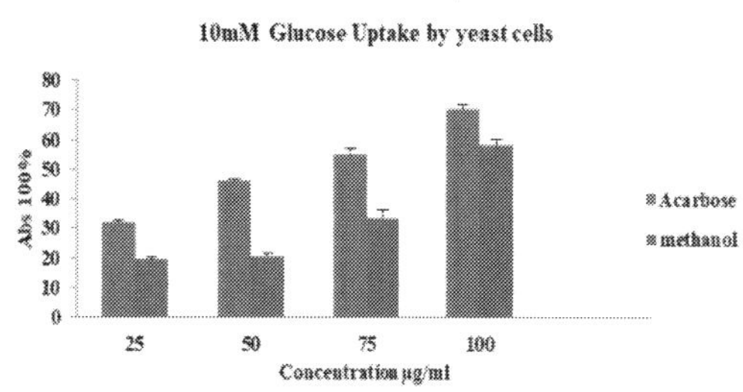

Fig. 4. Methanolic extract effects on milky mushroom and acarbose glucose uptake by yeast cells (10 mM).

3.4 GC-MS analysis of the crude extract

GC-MS analysis for crude extract; GC-MS chromatogram of the crude extract showed the presence of compounds at different retention times and compared with the NIST library seven major compounds were identified at different retention times it shown GC-MS spectra revealed various peaks, the indicated the occurrence of different bioactive compounds in the methanolic extract obtained from the mushroom extract (Figure 5). The spectral fingerprints of compounds were identified using the NIST library and the molecular weight of the bioactive compound. GC-MS chromatogram profile of crude extracts is present while the identified volatile compounds are presented. The major compounds present in the methanolic extract and the compound listed in Table 1.

Table 1. List of GCMS Compounds milky mushroom.

S. No	Compounds	Peaks	
		RT	%
1	1 Methylamine, N-cyclopentylidene	4.823	16.21
2	2 N,N'-Bis(2-hydroxyethyl)-1,7- dioxa-4,10-diazacyclododecane	5.820	2.31
3	3 -Valine, N-propoxycarbonyl-, ethyl ester	5.895	19.97
4	4 Ala-Gly, N-trimethylsilyl-, trimethylsilyl ester	6.056	3.95
5	5 Ethyl 3-[2-methyl-2-mercaptopropylamino]butyrate	6.503	9.82
6	N-Methyldodecanamide	8.149	31.04
7	**1,7-Dioxa-10-thia-4,13-diazacyclopentadeca-5,9,12- trione**	**8.235**	**42.32**
8	Oxacycloheptadec-8-en-2- one	9.589	21.10
9	4-Isoxazoline-4,5-dione, 3- tert-butyl-, 4-oxime	13.521	5.04
10	9,12,15-Octadecatrienoic acid, 2,3-dihydroxypropyl ester, (Z,Z,Z)	13.739	2.72
11	9-Hexadecenoic acid	14.305	9.57
12	6-Octadecynenitrile	16.588	49.90
13	Carnegine	19.847	16.94

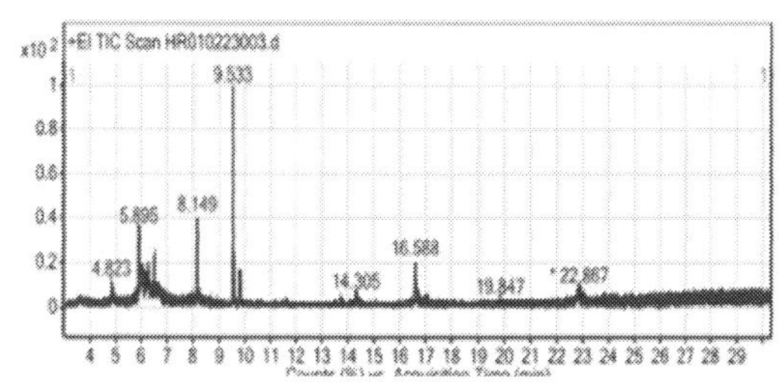

Fig. 5. Chromatogram of milky mushroom.

3.5 Molecular Docking

Molecular docking was performed to predict the antidiabetic compound of (1, 7-Dioxa-10 thia-4, 13-diazacyclopentadeca-5,9,12-trione and Oxacyclohepta dec-8-en-2- one from extract with target enzymes were studied based on their interaction using dockthor version tools. The docking study aims to check the transformation of whether one molecule fits with the other molecule at the optimal level and to identify the binding potential of the compound with the Enzymes using ligplot. In this docking analysis, initially, the PDB structure of the compound was taken from the PubChem database and enzyme structures were taken from the RCSB databank. The structure of the compound was converted to PDB structure format using the auto dock and was docked with target receptors. This study shows the binding energy (kcal/mol) and configuration of hydrogen bonds with active site residues. Based on the binding potential of 1,7-Dioxa-10-thia-4,13-diazacyclopentadeca-5,9,12-trione and oxacyclohepta dec-8-en-2- one against the molecular receptors were observed the interactions of active residue site respectively (Figure 6).

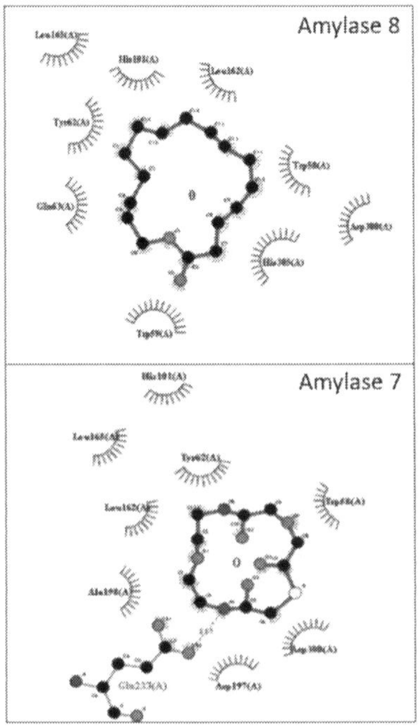

(a)

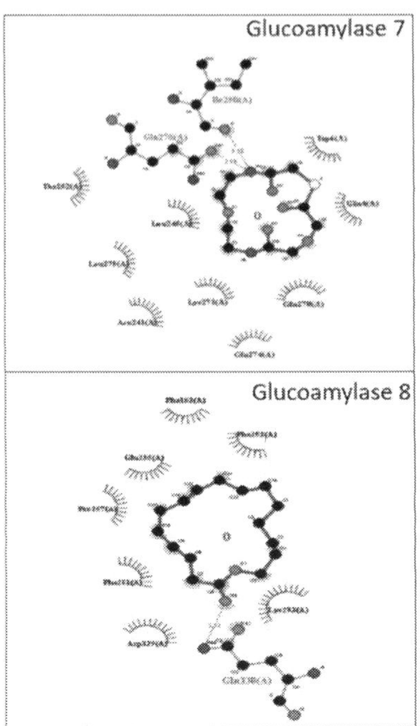

(b)

Fig. 6. Docked pose of enzymes with the ligand complexes of a) alpha-amylase; b) alpha-glucosidase

The results are shown in Table 2 negative scores are obtained, which show good binding affinity with molecular targets. Docking studies showed that compounds have had good binding affinities to all the receptors, which are strongly related to type-2 diabetes and the biding energy are α-amylase, α glucosidase, milky mushrooms are packed with a ton of essential vitamins, and minerals, and boost the anti-inflammatory, and immune system as it is rich sources of vitamin D, vitamin B, essential amino acids, potassium, protein, and fiber. Moreover, researchers have found several benefits in the mushroom as it lowers blood pressure by reducing the negative impact of sodium in our bodies.

Table 2. Molecular docking of enzymes with the ligand complexes of alpha-amylase and alpha-glucosidase.

S. No	Compounds	Binding energy (kCal/mole)	
		Amylase (1HNY)	Glucosidase (1UOK)
1	Methylamine, Ncyclopentylidene	-4.4	-4.2
2	N,N'-Bis(2-hydroxyethyl)-1,7-dioxa-4,10- diazacyclododecane	-5.6	-5.7
3	Valine, N-propoxycarbonyl-, ethyl ester	-3.8	-4.3
4	Ala-Gly, N-trimethylsilyl-, trimethylsilyl ester	-	-
5	Ethyl 3-[2-methyl-2-mercaptopropylamino]butyrate	-4.2	-3.8
6	6 N-Methyldodecanamide	-3.5	-3.4
7	**1,7-Dioxa-10-thia-4,13-diazacyclopentadeca-5,9,12-trione**	**-6.4**	**-7.2**
8	**Oxacycloheptadec-8-en-2- one**	**-7.4**	**-7.4**
9	4-Isoxazoline-4,5-dione, 3- tert-butyl-, 4-oxime	-5.7	-5.1
10	9,12,15-Octadecatrienoic acid, 2,3-dihydroxypropyl ester, (Z,Z,Z)	-5.5	-4.0
11	9-Hexadecenoic acid	-4.8	-4.1
12	6-Octadecynenitrile	-4.3	-4.0
13	Carnegine	-6.1	-5.8
14	Papaveroline, 2'-bromo-2-methyl-, tetramethyl(ester)	-6.2	-6.6

By encouraging macrophages to fight off foreign invaders, the anti-inflammatory effect of mushrooms has been demonstrated to significantly increase the immune system's effectiveness. Additionally, lowering the risk of hypertension and other metabolic diseases, mushrooms' antioxidants. Additionally, it has affected weight loss. It has anticancer, antiviral, antimicrobial, antiallergic, and anticholesterolemic properties and hepatoprotective effects [22]. The use of secondary metabolites as therapeutic agents includes polysaccharides, lectins, lactones, terpenoids, alkaloids, and antibiotics [23].

This study examines extracts and bioactive compounds for their potential anti-obesity and anti-diabetic properties. The maceration method was used to create a methanolic extract of milky mushrooms. The antidiabetic activity of the milky mushroom extract was examined using various assays, including the inhibition of -glucosidase and -amylase, as well as the uptake of glucose by yeast cells. These assays were specifically used in vitro. Similarly, 1,7-Dioxa-10-thia-4,13-diazacyclopentadeca-5,9,12-trione and Oxacyclohepta dec-8-en-2- compounds showed good binding affinity towards receptors. This research also deals with improving phytotherapy to manage diabetes through bioactive compounds as drug delivery. It could potentially be investigated further using cell lines and gene sequencing methods.

Acknowledgements

We are extremely thankful for the opportunity given by DKMCFRI and FIST, DKM.

References

1. H. Sardar, M.A. Anjum, A. Nawaz, S. Naz, S. Ejaz, A. Sajid, S.A. Haider, Effect of different agro-aastes, casing materials and supplements on the growth, yield and nutrition of milky mushroom (Calocybe indica), Folia Horticulturae, **32**,1 (2020): 115–124
2. A.S.S. Thomas, W. Pongprayoon, K. Cheenkachorn, M. Sriariyanun, Plant-microbe interactions - insights and views for applications in sustainable agriculture, Applied Science and Engineering Progress, **15**,1 (2022)
3. K.A. Subbiah, V. Balan, A comprehensive review of tropical milky white mushroom (Calocybe indica P&C), Mycobiology, **43**,3 (2015): 184-194
4. A.K. Maurya, Impact of different substrates for spawn production and production of milky mushroom (Calocybe indica), International Journal of pharma and Bio Sciences, **10**,3 (2019)
5. M. Sriariyanun, K. Kitsubthawee, Trends in lignocellulosic biorefinery for production of value-added biochemicals, Applied Science and Engineering Progress, **13**,4 (2020): 283-284
6. M.P. Gundupalli, M. Sriariyanun, Recent trends and updates for chemical pretreatment of lignocellulosic biomass, Applied Science and Engineering Progress, **16**,1 (2023)
7. S. Selvaraju, M. Vasanth, R. Muralidharan, R.R. Rajan, Yield potential of milky mushroom-Calocybe Indica (Apk-2) with respect to various agricultural wastes, World Journal of Pharmaceutical Research, **4**,11 (2015): 1499-1508
8. Y.S. Cheng, P. Mutrakulcharoen, S. Chuetor, K. Cheenkachorn, P. Tantayotai, E.J. Panakkal, M. Sriariyanun, Recent situation and progress in biorefining process of lignocellulosic biomass: Toward green economy, Applied Science and Engineering Progress, **13**,4 (2020)
9. W. Pongprayoon, T. Siringam, A. Panya, S. Roytrakul, Application of chitosan in plant defense responses to biotic and abiotic stresses, Applied Science and Engineering Progress, **15**,1 (2022)
10. M.F. Ahmed, M.J. Rahman, M.N. Islam, J. Ullah, N. C. Sarker, Effect of casing material management on yield and yield attributes of milky white mushroom (Calocybe Indica), International Journal of Research -GRANTHAALAYAH, **8**,10 (2020): 333-337
11. S. Kumar, V.P. Sharma, M. Shirur, S. Kamal, Status of milky mushroom (Calocybe indica) in India-a review, Mushroom Research, **26**,1 (2017): 21-39
12. A.S.S. Thomas, S. Arivu, V. Shanmugam, M.P. Gundupalli, S. Amornraksa, Paddy straw: An economical substrate for oyster mushroom (Pleurotus ostreatus) cultivation, E3S Web of Conferences, **355** (2022)
13. A.B.D. Nandiyanto, N.N. Azizah, G.C.S. Girsang, Optimal design and techno-economic analysis for corncob particles briquettes: A literature review of the utilization of agricultural waste and analysis calculation, Applied Science and Engineering Progress, **15**,3 (2022)
14. P. Pangsri, T. Wuttipornpun, W. Songserm, Mannanase and cellulase enzyme production from the agricultural wastes by the bacillus subtilis P2-5 strain, Applied Science and Engineering Progress, **14**,3 (2021): 425-434
15. S. Vinodhini, M. Shri Preethi, N. Nusrath Fathima, S.S. Kushwaha, V. Devi Rajeswari, Antioxidant and free radical scavenging activity of punica granatum leaf extracts, Asian Journal of Pharmaceutical and Clinical Research, **9**,6 (2016): 140-146
16. H. Rasyid, R. Armunanto, Molecular docking analysis on epidermal growth factor receptor wild type (EGFR wt) with quinazoline derivative compounds as tyrosine kinase inhibitors, KMUTNB Int J Appl Sci Technol, **10**,4 (2017): 293-299
17. M. Nath, A. Barh, A. Sharma, S. Bijla, R.K. Bairwa, S. Kamal, V. Sharma, Impact of the different casing material on the yield of Calocybe Indica in polyethylene bag and bed system, mushroom research, **31**,2 (2022): 181-186
18. A.G. Niego, S. Rapior, N. Thongklang, O. Raspé, W. Jaidee, S. Lumyong, K.D. Hyde, Macrofungi as a nutraceutical source: Promising bioactive compounds and market value, Journal of Fungi, **7**,5 (2021)
19. A. Das, C.M. Chen, S.C. Mu, S.H. Yang, Y.M. Ju, S.C. Li, Medicinal components in edible mushrooms on diabetes mellitus treatment, Pharmaceutics, **14**,2 (2022)
20. A.K. Maurya, R. Murmu, V. John, D.K. Srivastava, H. Pant, An introduction about milky mushroom: Their Cultivation and Disease Management, (2020)
21. S. Ghosh, K. Acharya, Milky Mushroom: A healthy nutritious diet, Food Research International, **156** (2022)

22. I.S. Mirunalini, G. Dhamodharan, K. Deepalakshmi, Antioxidant potential and current cultivation aspects of an edible milky mushroom-Calocybe, International Journal of Pharmacy and Pharmaceutical Sciences, **4**,1 (2012): 137-143

23. N. Nallathamby, C.W. Phan, S.L.S. Seow, A. Baskaran, H. Lakshmanan, S.N. Abd Malek, V. Sabaratnam, A status review of the bioactive activities of tiger milk mushroom lignosus rhinocerotis (Cooke) ryvarden, Frontiers in Pharmacology, **8** (2018): 998

Cider Production from King Mandarin (*Citrus nobilis* Lour.) and Its Antioxidant Activity

Hao Thien Vo[1], *Bich* Ngoc Thi Bui[1], *Chau* Minh Luu[2], *Thanh* Ngoc Nguyen[2], *Long* Dang Hoang Bui[2], *Nhi* Yen Thi Tran[3,4], *Phat* Tan Dao[3,4], *Phong* Xuan Huynh[2*]

[1] Advanced Program in Biotechnology, Can Tho University, Can Tho City, Vietnam
[2] Institute of Food and Biotechnology, Can Tho University, Can Tho City, Vietnam
[3] Institute of Applied Technology and Sustainable Development, Nguyen Tat Thanh University, Ho Chi Minh City, Vietnam
[4] Faculty of Environmental and Food Engineering, Nguyen Tat Thanh University, Ho Chi Minh City, Vietnam

Abstract. With the necessity of diversifying alcoholic beverages, cider has become a kind of drink that can fulfill this demand. This is because the cider will be diversified depending on the kinds of fruit that are chosen to be used for the cider fermentation. Therefore, this study aims to investigate the effects of dilution ratio, Brix, pH, and yeast concentration on the production of cider from king mandarin (*Citrus nobilis Lour.*), and to evaluate the analytical characteristics and antioxidant activity of the product. After the investigation, it can be claimed that the dilution of the juice causes the ethanol content to decrease, whereas the increase of Brix, pH, and yeast concentration makes the ethanol content increase. However, the proportional increase in the ethanol content with Brix, pH, and yeast concentration has its limitations. Specifically, when the Brix and the yeast concentrations were, respectively, higher than 16°Brix and 0.04%, the ethanol content tended to maintain the same. This is also the same when the pH was lower than 4.5. In addition, by using the DPPH and ABTS•+ methods, the antioxidant activity of cider is estimated to be lower than the one of the juice before fermentation, which is smaller than 3.78 times for the DPPH method and 3.76 times for the ABTS•+ method.

Keyword. Antioxidant activity, Cider, *Citrus nobilis*, King mandarin, *Saccharomyces cerevisiae*

1 Introduction

With the development of modern society, alcoholic beverages have become popular worldwide, but the issue of overusing these beverages has become a major concern in causing many unwanted incidents [1]. However, it still cannot be denied that these beverages have offered many benefits to human life. Many studies have pointed out that consuming these kinds of drinks at low levels of ethanol concentration will enhance the digestive system as well as mental health [2, 3]. Therefore, consuming low-ethanol beverages is an alternative way to obtain the benefit of alcoholic products instead of consuming beverages with higher ethanol concentrations. Cider is a low ethanol concentration beverage that is first fermented from apple juice. In addition, apple is not the only material that is used for cider fermentation, cider can also be fermented from different kinds of fruit depending on the differences in geographical locations and fruit sources.

Vietnam is a tropical country, which is suitable for growing fruit trees. Therefore, in Vietnam, some research has been carried out to investigate cider production from a variety of different kinds of fruit, such as *Docynia indica* fruit [4], strawberry [5], acerola [6], pitaya [7], etc. As many mentioned kinds of fruit, king mandarin, or known as *Citrus nobilis Lour.*, can also be used as the initial material for cider fermentation. This fruit is a cultivar of citrus fruit, which has a balanced flavor between sweetness and sourness, and is also rich in nutrients and health values, which can be included as anti-cancer, anti-inflammatory, antioxidant, cardiovascular protective and neuroprotective [8].

Despite having potential health benefits, studies targeting cider production from king mandarin are insufficient. Therefore, the objectives of this research were to investigate the effects of dilution ratio, initial Brix, pH, and yeast concentrations on the production of cider fermented from king mandarin, and to evaluate the analytical characteristics of the product and its antioxidant activity. Furthermore, this research will indirectly solve the problem of food waste from the excessive product, which is king mandarin. Therefore, this research will play a role in suggesting any beverage developer or company an idea of cider production from king mandarin. From that, the excessive of produced king mandarin will reduce, which also reduces food waste, and partly save the environment.

2 Materials and Methods

2.1 Materials and Chemicals

Materials: King mandarin was collected from Vinh Long province, Vietnam. Yeast *Saccharomyces cerevisiae* BV818 was purchased from Angel Group (distribution by ICFOOD Vietnam Co., Ltd.).

* Corresponding author: hxphong@ctu.edu.vn

Chemicals: Na_2CO_3, vitamin C, pectinase, $NaHSO_3$, tri-n-butyl phosphate (TBP), dinitrosalicylic acid (DNS), $K_2Cr_2O_8$, $KNaC_4H_4O_6.4H_2O$, NaOH 0.1N, H_2SO_4, DPPH (2,2-diphenyl-1-picrylhydrazyl), ABTS (2,2'-azino-bis (3-ethylbenzothiazoline-6-sulfonic acid) are analytical grade chemicals from Xilong Scientific (China) and Merck KGaA (Germany).

2.2 Methods

2.2.1 Investigation of the Effect of Dilution Ratio and Initial Brix on the Cider Fermentation

King mandarin juice after being filtered was investigated with two dilution ratios, which were using pure juice and a ratio of 1:1 between juice and water. In addition, the filtered juice was also added an amount of sucrose to be adjusted to the desired Brix. There were a total of 6 levels of Brix to be investigated, and they were 10, 12, 14, 16, 18, and 20°Brix. After finishing the initial setup, the pH of the juice was also set to 4.5, and the juice will be pasteurized in 2 h by using 140 mg/L of $NaHSO_3$. Then, yeast powder was added to the juice of which the concentration is 0.04% (w/v), and the mixture was left to be fermented in 48 h at 30°C. After the fermentation, the product will be taken to measure ethanol content and reducing sugar content by respectively using TBP and DNS methods.

In the TBP method, a standard ethanol solution will be used to form the standard curve. The ethanol content of the sample will be measured by mixing 1 mL of TBP and 1 mL of the sample. In the mixture, 2 layers will be formed and 500 μL of the upper layer will be continuously mixed with 500 μL $K_2Cr_2O_7$. The mixture continuously forms layers, and the below one having cyan color will be used for the measurement. The measurement will be done with a wavelength of 595 nm (using a UV-Vis spectrophotometer; Genesys 10-S, Thermo Corporation, USA). The result will be compared with the standard curve to calculate the sample ethanol content [9].

In the DNS method, glucose will be used to form the standard curve. The reducing sugar content of the sample will be measured by mixing 2 mL of the sample and 2 mL of DNS solutions. The mixture will be heated in the water bath, and then let cool. Finally, the measurement will be done with a wavelength of 540 nm using a UV-Vis spectrophotometer (Genesys 10-S, Thermo Corporation). The result will be compared with the standard curve to calculate the sample ethanol content [10].

2.2.2 Investigation of the Effect of pH and Yeast Concentration on the Cider Fermentation

After successfully selecting the dilution ratio and initial Brix, the effects of pH and yeast concentration on the juice were spontaneously investigated. The process is similar to the previously described with four pH levels (4.0, 4.5, 5.0, and 5.5) and four yeast inoculations (0.02, 0.03, 0.04, and 0.05% w/v). Finally, the fermentation time was 48 h. After the fermentation, ethanol content and reducing sugar content of the product will be measured by TBP and DNS methods, respectively.

2.2.3 Evaluation of the Analytical Characteristics of the Product

The fermented product was evaluated with the following criteria: Physicochemical characteristics, heavy metals, and microbiological characteristics. All these criteria will be conducted based on the requirements of the regulation in Vietnam, which is regulated in QCVN 6-3:2010/BYT.

2.2.4 Evaluation of the Antioxidant Activity of the Product by Using DPPH Method

The antioxidant activity of the product was evaluated by the IC_{50} value of the product after using the DPPH method. Vitamin C was used as the control sample, and the juice before the fermentation and the product were used as the experimental samples. 0.2 mL of each sample was mixed with 1 mL of 39.4 μg/mL of DPPH and was left to react in the dark for 15 min. Then, the absorbance at 715 nm wavelength was measured by UV-Vis spectrophotometer (Genesys 10-S, Thermo Corporation). In addition, for each sample, a set of concentrations was used for the investigation, which was 8, 10, 12, 14, and 16 μg/mL for vitamin C; 40, 80, 120, 160, and 200 μL/mL for the juice before the fermentation; and 200, 250, 300, 350, 400 μL/mL) for the final product [11].

2.2.5 Evaluation of the Antioxidant Activity of the Product by Using $ABTS^{\bullet+}$ Method

Besides using the DPPH method, the $ABTS^{\bullet+}$ method can also be used to evaluate the antioxidant activity of the product. The overall process of this method is similar to the DPPH method with the same set of concentrations for the juice before fermentation and the product, but instead of using vitamin C, trolox solution is used as the control sample of which the used concentrations is 12.5, 25, 50, 100, 200, and 400 μM. The process started with the preparation of $ABTS^{\bullet+}$ by mixing 2 mL of 7mM of ABTS•+ with 2 mL of 2.45 mM of $K_2S_2O_8$ and letting it react in the dark for 16 h. The wavelength used for the investigation was 734 nm using a UV-Vis spectrophotometer (Genesys 10-S, Thermo Corporation). After that, the mixture of 10 μL of each sample at different concentrations and 990 μL of $ABTS^{\bullet+}$ was left to react in the dark for 6 min [12].

3 Results and Discussions

3.1 The Effect of Dilution Ratio and Initial Brix on the Cider Fermentation

With the differences in the dilution ratio and Brix, the ethanol contents of each combination resulted differently (Table 1). Specifically, among the diluted treatments, the highest ethanol content was recorded to be 6.11% (v/v), which is the result of the combination of using the diluted juice and the adjustment of Brix to 20°Brix. Similarly, the combination of pure juice and 16°Brix yielded the highest ethanol content, which was 6.90% (v/v). In contrast, the smallest ethanol contents when using pure juice and diluted juice were 4.50% and 4.39% (v/v), respectively.

With the results, the range of ethanol contents when using different dilution ratios was estimated to be from 4.39% to 6.11% v/v for using diluted juice and from 4.50% to 6.90% for using pure juice. In order to ensure the product ethanol content will yield in the range of 4-6%, and to reduce the cost of production, the dilution ratio of 1:1 between the juice and the diluted water is more reasonable, which corresponds to the previous study of the investigation of low-alcohol fermented passion fruit juice [13].

With the increase in Brix from 10 to 14°Brix when using the diluted juice, the ethanol content increased from 4.39% to 5.91% (v/v), which was correlated with previous research [4] showing that Brix was proportional to the yields of ethanol contents. Despite an increase in the ethanol content from 4.39 to 5.91% (v/v) when increasing Brix from 14 to 20°Brix, these results were not different from each other in the mean of statistical significance with $p < 0.05$. In addition, the reduced sugar content was also reported to be increased proportionally with Brix, and in the range of Brix from 14 to 20°Brix, the reduced sugar contents were recorded to be 4.66, 6.69, 7.27, and 6.59 g/100 mL. However, only the reduced sugar content of the 14°Brix treatment showed a difference in the mean of statistical significance (p-value < 0.05) with the 3 other treatments. Based on the obtained results, the dilution ratio and the Brix level were chosen to be a ratio of 1:1 and 16°Brix, which was chosen to ensure that the product ethanol content would yield in the range of 4-6% v/v, to yield the highest reduced sugar content and to reduce the cost of production for the next experiments.

Table 1. Results of ethanol content after fermentation with different dilution ratios and Brix values.

Treatment	Factors		Ethanol content (% v/v)	Reduced sugar content (g/100 mL)
	Dilution ratio	Brix		
1	Pure	10	5.19^{d}	0.74^{f}
2	Pure	12	4.50^{e}	0.71^{f}
3	Pure	14	5.83^{bc}	0.80^{f}
4	Pure	16	6.90^{a}	3.14^{d}
5	Pure	18	6.35^{b}	5.83^{c}
6	Pure	20	6.12^{b}	8.02^{a}
7	1:1	10	4.39^{e}	0.76^{f}
8	1:1	12	5.32^{cd}	2.43^{e}
9	1:1	14	5.91^{b}	4.66^{cd}
10	1:1	16	5.89^{b}	6.69^{b}
11	1:1	18	5.95^{b}	7.27^{b}
12	1:1	20	6.11^{b}	6.59^{b}

***Note:** Each result is the average of 3 replicates. Different lowercase letters indicate significantly different values within each column at p-value < 0.05.

3.2 The Effect of pH and Yeast Concentration on the Cider Fermentation

In previous studies, the ethanol content tended to increase proportionally with the increase in pH and the yeast concentration [4,13], which was caused by the higher yeast inoculation accelerated rate of conversion from sucrose into ethanol. Therefore, when more yeast appeared in the juice, the ethanol content increased.

In Table 2, at the same pH, treatment with higher yeast concentrations yielded higher ethanol contents. Specifically, when pH was 4.0, the ethanol contents produced by the treatment with 0.02% to 0.05% of yeast increased from 5.30% to 6.60% (v/v). Hence, this trend was observed similarly in other pH treatments. Despite having an increase when there was an increase in yeast concentration, there was no difference in ethanol content yielded from 0.04% and 0.05% yeast inoculations (v/v). Overall, the data from Table 2 suggested that the ethanol content when adding 0.04% and 0.05% of yeast concentrations were no different in the mean of statistical significance (p-value < 0.05) at every pH level. Similarly, at the same yeast inoculation, the increase in pH led to an improvement in ethanol concentrations. Specifically, with 0.05% yeast concentration, the pH from 4.0, 4.5, 5.0, and 5.5 yielded 6.02%, 6.06%, 7.28%, and 7.63% ethanol contents of each treatment, respectively. From this result, the ethanol contents of the treatments at pH 4.0 and 4.5 were not different from each other in the mean of statistical significance ($p<0.05$). Meaning that the ethanol content only increased when the pH of the treatment was adjusted from 4.5 to 5.5.

Table 2. Results of ethanol content after fermentation with the investigation of pH and yeast concentration.

Treatment	Factors		Ethanol content (% v/v)	Reduced sugar content (g/100 mL)
	pH	Yeast concentration (% w/v)		
1	4.0	0.02	5.30^{k}	10.82^{a}
2	4.0	0.03	5.48^{j}	7.75^{de}
3	4.0	0.04	5.99^{h}	6.93^{f}
4	4.0	0.05	6.02^{h}	6.60^{gf}
5	4.5	0.02	5.39^{jk}	9.00^{c}
6	4.5	0.03	5.62^{i}	7.99^{d}
7	4.5	0.04	6.04^{h}	7.64^{de}
8	4.5	0.05	6.06^{h}	7.30^{e}
9	5.0	0.02	6.49^{g}	9.50^{b}
10	5.0	0.03	6.80^{f}	9.32^{b}
11	5.0	0.04	7.16^{d}	8.91^{c}
12	5.0	0.05	7.28^{c}	8.60^{cd}
13	5.5	0.02	6.99^{e}	9.04^{c}
14	5.5	0.03	7.46^{b}	8.94^{c}
15	5.5	0.04	7.61^{a}	8.07^{d}
16	5.5	0.05	7.63^{a}	8.11^{d}

Note: Each result is the average of 3 replicates. Different lowercase letters indicate significantly different values within each column at p-value < 0.05.

3.3 Evaluation of the Analytical Characteristics of the Product

The analytical characteristics of the product were evaluated based on the regulation in QCVN 6-

3:2010/BYT from the Ministry of Health of Vietnam. The result of the comparison between the product characteristics and regulations is presented in Table 3.

The results in Table 3 indicate that the product is compatible with the requirements of the regulation. Specifically, the product's physicochemical characteristics, which were the methanol, hydrocyanic acid, and sulfur dioxide content, were all smaller than the limitation of the regulation. For heavy metals, such as cadmium, arsenic, mercury, zinc, and copper were not detected in the product. Similarly, some pathogenic bacteria such as *Staphylococcus aureus* and *Pseudomonas aeruginosa* were also not detected in the product. Overall, the product demonstrated that its characteristics were appropriate for the regulation of QCVN 6-3:2010/BYT.

Table 3. Results of analytical characteristics of the product.

Analytical characteristics	Product	QCVN 6-3:2010/BYT
Methanol (mg/L)	657	< 10,000
Sulfur dioxide (mg/L)	36.4	< 150
Hydrocyanic acid (mg/L)	nd	< 70
Volatile acidity (mEq/L)	nd	-
Lead (mg/L)	nd	< 0.2
Cadmium (mg/L)	nd	-
Arsenic (mg/L)	nd	-
Mercury (mg/L)	nd	-
Zinc (mg/L)	nd	-
Copper (mg/L)	nd	-
Total aerobic microorganisms (CFU/mL)	39	$< 10^3$
Fungal (CFU/mL)	< 1	$< 10^2$
E. coli (CFU/mL)	< 1	0
Coliforms (CFU/mL)	< 1	0
Clostridium perfringens (CFU/mL)	< 1	0
Streptococcus feacalis (CFU/mL)	< 1	0
Staphylococcus aureus (CFU/mL)	< 1	-
Pseudomonas aeruginosa (CFU/mL)	< 1	-

***Note**: nd – not determined

3.4 The Antioxidant Activity of the Product by using DPPH Method

Figures 1 and 2 illustrate that the inhibition percentage of all three samples increased when the concentration of each sample increased. Specifically, when the concentration of vitamin C is increased from 8 µg/mL to 16 µg/mL, the percentages are recorded from 31.96% to 75.03%, respectively. Despite using different ranges of concentrations, both the juice and the cider are investigated at the concentration of 100 µL/mL and at this concentration there was a different result between the two samples. The percentage of inhibition of the juice at a concentration of 200 µL/mL is reported to be 87.03%, whereas the cider was only 26%. This means that both samples were investigated at the same concentration, but there was a change in the inhibition percentage before and after fermentation.

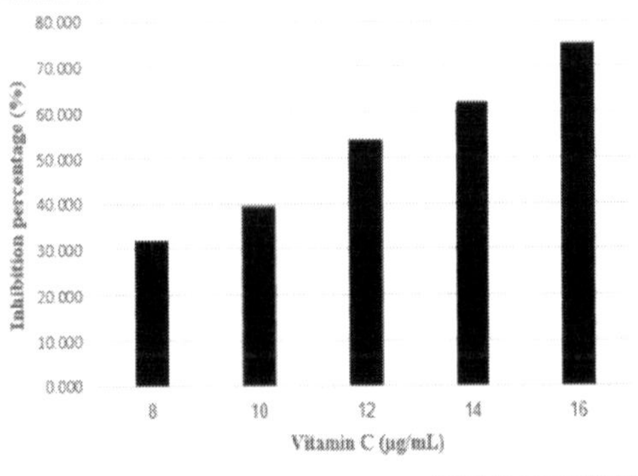

Fig. 1. DPPH free radical inhibition percentage of vitamin C.

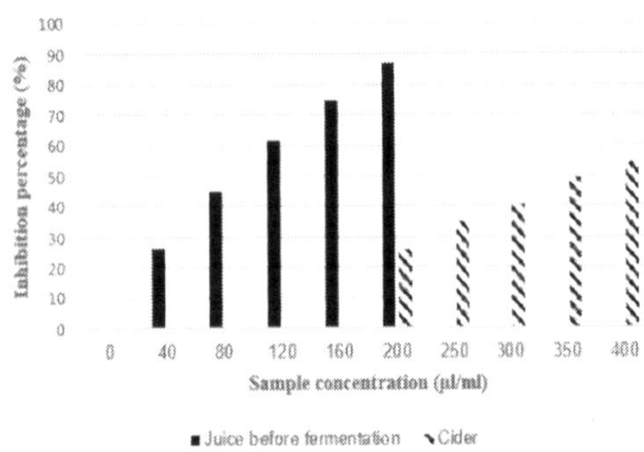

Fig. 2. DPPH free radical inhibition percentage of juice and cider.

As the results shown in Figures 1 and 2, the standard curve as well as the linear equation of each sample is established, and with the formed equation, the IC_{50} value of each sample is calculated. The IC_{50} value of a sample is the required concentration of a sample to inhibit 50% of free radicals in which the smaller the IC_{50} value is, the greater the antioxidant activity of a sample is [14]. The IC_{50} values of all samples are illustrated in Table 4.

Table 4. IC_{50} value of vitamin C, unfermented juice and cider when using DPPH method.

Samples	IC_{50} value
Vitamin C	11.27 µg/mL
Unfermented juice	96.37 µL/mL
Cider	363.94 µL/mL

* **Note:** Each result is the average of 3 replicates.

It can be seen that both the juice and the cider show significant antioxidant activity (Table 4). However, as mentioned, the smaller the IC_{50} value was, the greater the antioxidant activity of the sample. Therefore, the results from Table 4 show that the IC_{50} value of the juice before fermentation was smaller by about 3.78 times than the IC_{50} value of the cider. In addition, with the calculated IC_{50} value of each sample, the needed concentrations of the juice and cider were respectively 96.37 µL/mL and 363.94 µL/mL, which was also equal to 11,27 µg/mL of vitamin C.

3.5 The Antioxidant Activity of the Product by using ABTS$^{•+}$ Method

Figures 3 and 4 illustrate that the inhibition percentage of all three samples increases when the concentration of each sample increases. Specifically, when the concentration of vitamin C was increased from 12.5 µM to 400 µM, the percentages were recorded from 3.71% to 83.98%, respectively.

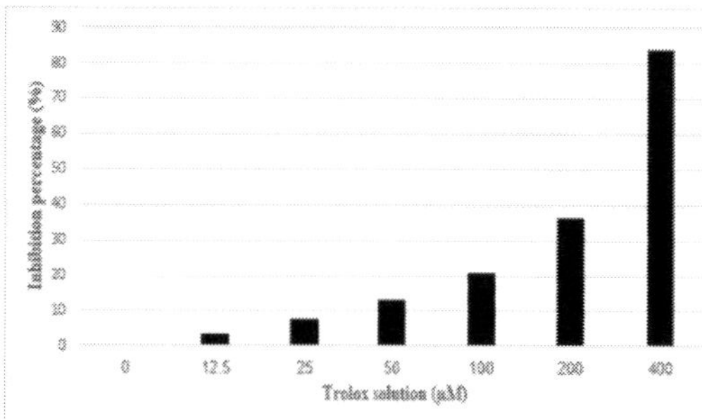

Fig. 3. ABTS$^{•+}$ free radical inhibition percentage of trolox solution.

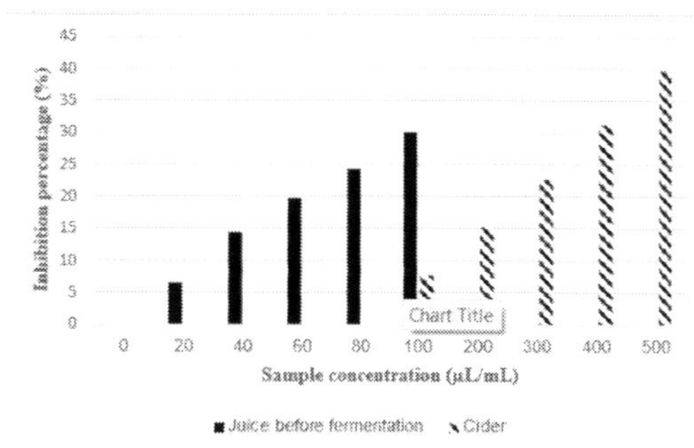

Fig. 4. ABTS$^{•+}$ free radical inhibition percentage of juice and cider.

Despite using different ranges of concentrations, both the juice and the cider were investigated at the concentration of 100 µL/mL and at this concentration, there was a different result between the two samples which was similar to the DPPH method. The percentage of inhibition of the juice at the concentration of 100 µL/mL was reported to be 29.98%, whereas the cider was only 7.75%. This means that both samples were investigated at the same concentration but there was a change in the inhibition percentage before and after fermentation. Similar to the DPPH method, the IC_{50} value of each sample when using ABTS$^{•+}$ was calculated and illustrated in Table 5.

Table 5. IC_{50} value of vitamin C, unfermented juice and cider when using ABTS$^{•+}$ method.

Samples	**IC_{50} value**
Trolox	242.66 µM
Unfermented juice	168.63 µL/mL
Cider	633.86 µL/mL

***Note:** Each result is the average of 3 replicates.

In Table 5, it can be seen that both the juice and the cider show significant antioxidant activity. However, as mentioned, the smaller the IC_{50} value was, the greater the antioxidant activity of the sample. Therefore, the results from Table 5 show that the IC_{50} value of the juice before fermentation was smaller by about 3.76 times than the IC_{50} value of the cider. Meaning that the antioxidant activity of the juice was greater by about 3.76 times than that of cider. In addition, with the calculated IC_{50} value of each sample, it was believed that the needed concentrations of the juice and cider were respectively 168.63 µL/mL and 633.86 µL/mL, which was also equal to 242.66 µM of trolox solution.

It can be claimed that the product shows antioxidant activity after using DPPH and ABTS$^{•+}$ methods. However, the results show that the product performed the antioxidant activity less greatly than the juice before fermentation, in which the ratio was 3.78 times for the DPPH method and 3.76 times for the ABTS$^{•+}$ method. This result corresponded to a previous study on the determination of the antioxidant activity of *Syzygium cumini* fermented juice [15]. Even though there is a decrease in antioxidant activity of the product after fermentation, the product is still having its own benefits compared to only pure juice. Cider is a kind of beverage that can be preserved much longer than fresh juice. Normally, it is recommended to use fresh juice within 24 hours. In contrast, cider can be preserved within several weeks without changing the original flavor when the product is stored at a temperature of 0 – 2 °C [16]. Furthermore, with the need of beverages diversity, cider, specifically fermented from king mandarin, can be considered as a fresh candidate, which will accomplish the demand of brand-new products consumption.

4 Conclusions

The ethanol content of the product increased proportionally with the increase in Brix, pH, and yeast concentration. However, the ethanol content resulted in no difference in the mean of statistical significance ($p < 0.05$) when the Brix and the yeast concentration were, respectively, higher than 16°Brix and 0.04%. In contrast, when pH was lower than 4.5, the ethanol content resulted in no difference in the mean of statistical significance ($p < 0.05$). In addition, it can be claimed that the product is appropriate for the requirements of the regulation. Lastly, cider showed significant antioxidant activity but there was a decrease compared with the juice before fermentation.

Acknowledgements

The authors would like to thank Can Tho University for funding assistance (research project no. TSV2022-163) and partly support from the Advanced Program in Biotechnology, Can Tho University, Vietnam.

References

1. R. Room, T. Babor, J. Rehm, Alcohol and public health, Lancet, 365 (2005): 519–530
2. J. B. German, L. W. Rosemary, The health benefits of wine, Annual Review of Nutrition, **20**, 1 (2000) : 561–593
3. T. Brányik, D. P. Silva, M. Baszczyňski, R. Lehnert, J. B. Almeida E Silva, A review of methods of low alcohol and alcohol-free beer production, Journal of Food Engineering, **108**, 4 (2012): 493–506
4. D. H. Nguyen, T. L. H. Hoang, T. T. M. Hoang, V. L. Nguyen, Study on the use of yeast *Saccharomyces cerevisiae* in cider making from docynia indica fruit, Journal of Vietnam Agricultural Science and Technology, **8**, 69 (2016): 89–93
5. V. T. Bui, Optimizing fermentation beverage cider strawberry by four-factors response surface, Sao Do University Scientific Journal, **2**, 65 (2019): 77–85
6. T. N. M. Tran, Processing of fermented fruit juice from acerola (*Malpighia glabra L.*), The Journal of Agriculture and Development, **19**, 2 (2020): 99–105
7. T. N. M. Huynh, T. K. T. Doan, Fermention of Pitaya (*Selenicereus undatus*) using *Saccharomyces cerevisiae* Rv100, TNU Journal of Science And Technology, **226**, 14 (2021): 137–145
8. L. Xinmiao, Z. Siyu, N. Zhanagchi, Z. Honglian, S. Yisong, T. Ou, X. Cheng, L. Cheng, L. Yuanyan, Citrus fruits as a treasure trove of active natural metabolites that potentially provide benefits for human health, Chemistry Central Journal, **9**, 68 (2015)
9. M. Sriariyanun, P. Mutrakulcharoen, S. Tepaamorndech, K. Cheenkachorn, K. Rattanaporn, A rapid spectrophotometric method for quantitative determination of ethanol in fermentation products, Oriental Journal of Chemistry, **35**, 2(2019): 744–750
10. G. L. Miller, Use of Dinitrosalicylic acid reagent for determination of reducing sugar, Analytical Chemistry, **3**, 3 (1959): 426–428
11. M. Ye, L. Ren, Y. Wu, Y. Wang, Y. Liu, Quality characteristics and antioxidant activity of hickory-black soybean yogurt, LWT - Food Science and Technology, **51** (2013): 314–318
12. N. Loganayaki, P. Siddhuraju, S. Manian, Antioxidant activity and free radical scavenging capacity of phenolic extracts from *Helicteres isora* L. and *Ceiba pentandra* L., Journal of Food Science and Technology, **50** (2013): 687–695
13. P. P. T. Huynh, Study on low-alcohol fermented pasion fruit juice with adding probiotics *Lactobacillus plantarum* Ly-78, The Journal of Food and Science, **16**, 1 (2018): 56–66
14. M. Rezaie, R. Farhoosh, A. Sharif, J. Asili, M. Iranshah, Chemical composition antioxidant and antibacterial properties of bene (*Pistacia atlantica* subsp. *mutica*) hull essential oil, Journal of Food Science and Technology, **52** (2015): 6784–6790
15. N. T. T. Huynh, T. T. Dao, T. M. T. Nguyen, T. H. H. Van, T. M. T. Duong, D. D. Nguyen, Determination of fermentation conditions and antioxidant activity of *Syzygium cumini* L. fermented juice, Can Tho University Journal of Science, **56** (2020): 72–79
16. D. L. Downing, Apple cider, Processed Apple Products, (1989): 169–188

Utilization of Nongkhai Black Jasmine Rice Bran Oils for Development of Functional Drink Emulsion

Ketinun Kittipongpittaya*, *Teerawan* Suwan, *Piyarach* Kullamethee, *Premsak* Puangploy, *Pattaranan* Yimchom, and *Tanyaporn* Intaratul

Department of Agro-industry Technology and Management, Faculty of Agro-industry, KMUTNB, Prachinburi, Thailand

Abstract. Rice bran is a nutritious by-product from rice milling process. It is usually used as animal feed otherwise rejected as waste that could raise environmental issues. This research aims at utilizing oil extracted from Nongkhai black jasmine rice bran to develop an oil-in-water emulsion drink. Oil was extracted from Nongkhai black jasmine rice bran using hexane as a solvent by Soxhlet extraction method. Nongkhai black jasmine rice bran gave an oil yield of 12.38%. The extracted oil contained total phenolic 120.03 ± 1.26 μg GAE/g oil, flavonoid 46.90 ± 0.69 μg QE/g oil and γ-oryzanol 236.73 ± 7.54 μg/g oil. The antioxidant activity of the oil tested by DPPH, ABTS, and FRAP were 1676.63 ± 76.86, 592.75 ± 46.22, 1.31 ± 0.22 μg Trolox equivalent/g oil, respectively. An oil-in-water emulsion beverage was then developed by dispersing 1% (w/w) of Nongkhai black jasmine rice bran oil with 0.1% (w/w) of Tween80/Span80 (1:1 w/w) as emulsifiers in water. The sweetness of the emulsion beverage was adjusted by adding erythritol mixed with stevia extract sweetener at 0.1, 0.2, 0.3, and 0.4 % (w/v). After pasteurization, all emulsion beverages were subjected to Just-about-right and 9-point hedonic sensory tests using a randomized complete block design. The emulsion containing 0.4 % sweetener had the highest overall liking score of 7.0 ± 1.1, representing moderate liking. The emulsion beverage contained γ-oryzanol 13.3 ± 0.3 μg/mL with the antioxidant activity tested by ABTS of 267.0 ± 37.7 μg Trolox equivalent/mL. In conclusion, Nongkhai black jasmine rice bran is a source of bioactive lipids that can be utilized as an ingredient in a plant-based functional drink emulsion.

Keyword. Antioxidant, Functional drink, Nongkhai black jasmine rice bran, Oil-in-water emulsion,

1 Introduction

Rice (*Oryza sativa*) is an important economic crop in Thailand. During the rice milling process, rice bran which is the outer layer of the rice is produced approximately 8-10% of the rice kernel as a by-product. A large amount of rice bran is usually used as a raw material for the production of animal feed otherwise it is discarded as waste that could impact on environmental pollution. The burning of rice bran might release particles related to the PM 2.5 problem that has been a great concern in Thailand [1]. Rice bran possesses high oil content of 18-22%, so it is used as a raw material for rice bran oil processing [2]. Rice bran oil has a ratio of saturated and unsaturated fatty acids similar to the ratio recommended by the World Health Organization for healthy oil consumption [3]. Moreover, rice bran contains lipophilic beneficial substances, including gamma-oryzanol and vitamin E. Pigmented rice bran also contains anthocyanin which is categorized as flavonoid compounds that have antioxidant activity. The types and amounts of these bioactive components vary depending on the varieties of rice. Nongkhai black jasmine rice or RD 83 rice is a variety of rice recently developed in 2019. It has a purple-black seed coat and not sensitive to light. Lasunon *et.al.*, (2022) reported that Nongkhai black jasmine rice possessed total phenolic, total flavonoid and anthocyanin contents in the range of 0.010-0.035 g GAE/100 g, 1.5-3.5 g QE/100 g, and, 0.01-0.03 g/100 g, respectively, which decreased during the cooking process [4]. To our knowledge, the bioactive components and antioxidant activities of Nongkhai black jasmine rice bran oil have not been investigated yet.

Functional beverages have grown in related to health concerns among consumers. Along with hydrophilic compounds, various lipophilic bioactive components, such as fat-soluble vitamins, phytosterols, and ω-3 fatty acids, etc. have been extensively reported for their health benefits [5]. Incorporation of these lipid soluble compounds into a beverage of which mainly composed of water is a challenge for food industry. Lipophilic components cannot be distributed steadily in the water phase. Eventually, these non-polar components will aggregate and separate layers on top of the product. Emulsification is an effective technology that mainly applied for emulsion beverage development. Oil-in-water emulsion consists of an oil phase dispersed in a

* Corresponding author: ketinun.k@agro.kmutnb.ac.th

water phase in the presence of emulsifier that helps to stabilize the emulsion. In the production of emulsified beverages, more than one type of emulsifier is commonly added, such as using Span 80 (S80) in combination with Tween 80 (T80). In addition, the products' taste plays an important role in consumers' acceptance and needs to be considered in the development of emulsion beverages. Currently, natural sweeteners such as stevia extract are widely used as a sugar substitute in the beverage industry in response to health-conscious consumers. However, apart from sweetening, these sweeteners can influence a product's properties such as color, flavor, and texture, thus appropriate types and concentrations of sweeteners need to be evaluated for each product.

There are research studies on the development of beverages made from rice bran oil and their biochemical effect in laboratory animals. The research suggested that emulsion drinks from rice bran oil helped increasing HDL cholesterol levels and significantly reduced blood pressure levels in experimental animals [6]. Moreover, there is a report suggesting that rice bran oil emulsion helped preventing metabolic syndrome and reducing inflammation which is linked to chronic diseases, such as diabetes, coronary artery disease, etc. [7].

From searching for information, there is no report on the use of Nongkhai black jasmine rice bran oil, which is indigenous colored rice for use in functional beverage products. Therefore, this research aims at studying the chemical and biological properties of Nongkhai black jasmine rice bran oil and studying the utilization of rice bran oil to develop an emulsified functional drink product. This could promote the utilization and add value to Nongkhai black jasmine rice bran, as well as, help reducing environmental problems arising from waste materials and lead to sustainability.

2 Materials and methods

2.1 Materials

The Nongkhai black jasmine rice paddy was obtained from a community enterprise in Sakonnakhon province, Thailand. All reagents were of analytical grade. Double-distilled and deionized water was used in the preparation of all solutions. Ingredients for emulsion formulation including erythritol mixed with stevia extract sweetener (Equal®), polysorbate 80 (Tween80), and sorbitan oleate (Span 80) were acquired from a local market in Prachinburi province, Thailand.

2.2 Rice bran preparation and oil extraction

After milling, rice bran was immediately heated at 110 °C in the hot air oven for 10 min in order to inactivate lipase activity. Then, the rice bran was sealed in a plastic bag and kept at -20 °C for further extraction.

Rice bran oil was extracted using hexane as a solvent by Soxhlet extraction method for 6 h. Hexane was removed by using a rotary evaporator at 175 mbar, 45 °C. Then, the oil was heated in a hot air oven at 70 °C to assure that there was no hexane left in the oil. The oil yield was determined by using the following equation;

$$Yield\ (\%) = \frac{Extracted\ oil\ weight\ (g)}{Rice\ bran\ weight\ (g)} \times 100 \quad (1)$$

2.3 Preparation of rice bran oil-in-water emulsion drink

The oil-in-water emulsion was developed by dispersing 1% (w/w) of Nongkhai black jasmine rice bran oil with 0.1% (w/w) of Tween80/Span80 (1:1 w/w) as emulsifiers in water. The mixture was emulsified using a high shear homogenizer (IKA, T-25 basic Ultra-Turrax, Germany) at 16,000 rpm for 2 min followed by a 2-stage homogenizer at 1,000 bars 3 times. After that, all the samples were pasteurized in a water bath at 80 °C for 10 min. The sweetness of the emulsion beverage was adjusted by adding erythritol mixed with stevia extract sweetener at 0.1, 0.2, 0.3, and 0.4 % (w/v) during the pasteurization. The emulsion samples were then packed in amber glass bottles and stored at 10 ± 2 °C for further studies.

2.4 Determination of total phenolic content

The total phenolic content (TPC) of samples was analyzed using Folin Ciocalteu assay [8]. Briefly, 20 μL of the sample was mixed with 100 μL of Folin-Ciocalteu reagent and 80 μL of 20% sodium carbonate. The mixture was incubated for 30 min in the dark at ambient temperature. Then, the absorbance of the samples was determined at 765 nm using a microplate reader (BMG Labtech, SPECTRO star Nano, Germany). The TPC was calculated from the calibration curve of gallic acid (20-100 μg/mL) (R^2 = 0.9909). The results were expressed in μg gallic acid equivalent (GAE)/g oil.

2.5 Determination of total flavonoid content

The total flavonoid contents (TFC) of samples were determined according to aluminum chloride colorimetry assay [9]. Briefly, sample (50 μL) was mixed with 10% aluminum chloride (10 μL), 1 M potassium acetate (50 μL) and 95% ethanol (150 μL). After incubation for 40 min, the absorbance of the samples was determined at 415 nm using a microplate reader (BMG Labtech, SPECTRO star Nano, Germany). The TFC was calculated from the calibration curve of quercetin (20-100 μg /mL) (R^2 = 0.9992) and expressed in μg quercetin equivalent (QE)/ g oil.

2.6 Determination of γ-oryzanol

The γ-oryzanol content was determined using a spectrophotometric method according to the CODEX-STAN 210-1999 method [10]. Sample was dissolved in isopropanol (100 mg/mL) and measured the absorbance at 315 nm using a microplate reader (BMG Labtech, SPECTRO star Nano, Germany). The γ-oryzanol content was calculated from a standard curve of γ-oryzanol (10-50 μg/mL) (R^2 = 0.9994) and expressed in μg/ g oil.

2.7 Determination of antioxidant activity

Antioxidant activities of the samples were investigated using 2,2-diphenyl-1-picrylhydrazyl (DPPH) radical scavenging assay, 2,2'azinobis (3-ethylbenzothaiazoline-6-sulfonic acid (ABTS) cation radical scavenging assay, and ferric reducing antioxidant power assay (FRAP). Brief details for each assay were described as follows.

According to the DPPH assay, DPPH ethanolic solution (100 μL) was mixed with 20 μL of a sample or standard solution and kept in the dark for 30 min [11]. The absorbance was recorded at 517 nm using a microplate reader (BMG Labtech, SPECTRO star Nano, Germany). The DPPH radical scavenging activity was calculated from the calibration curve of trolox (20-200 μg/mL) (R^2 = 0.9907). The results were expressed in μg trolox equivalent (TE)/ g oil.

ABTS assay was performed by following the method of Arnao *et.al.*, (2001) [12]. The ABTS radical solution composing of 4.9 mM ABTS and 14 mM $K_2S_2O_8$ at a ratio of 1:1 (v/v) was prepared and left for 24 h prior use. The ABTS radical solution was diluted with ethanol to achieve an absorbance of 0.7 ± 0.1. The sample (5 μL) was mixed with ABTS radical cation solution (500 μL) and incubated for 10 min. The absorbance was determined at 734 nm using a microplate reader (BMG Labtech, SPECTRO star Nano, Germany). The antioxidant activity was calculated from the calibration curve of trolox (200-1000 μg/mL) (R^2 = 0.9913) and expressed in μg trolox equivalent (TE)/ g oil.

For the FRAP assay, the FRAP reagent was prepared by mixing 300 mM acetate buffer (pH 3.6), 10 mM TPTZ solution (in 40 mM HCl) and 20 mM ferric chloride solution in the proportions of 1:1:10 (v/v), respectively [13]. The sample (50 μL) was mixed with the FRAP reagent (150 μL) and incubated for 10 min. The absorbance at 595 nm was recorded using a microplate reader (BMG Labtech, SPECTRO star Nano, Germany). The antioxidant activity was calculated from the Trolox standard curve (0-50 μg /mL) (R^2 = 0.9957) and expressed in μg trolox equivalent (TE)/g oil.

2.8 Sensory analysis of rice bran oil-in-water emulsion drink

The oil-in-water emulsion drinks were subjected to Just-about-right and 9-point hedonic sensory test by 30 untrained panelists. Testing was done in a sensory laboratory where each panelist was randomly served 4 emulsion drinks (30 mL in a plastic cup) in cold (10 ± 1°C). An unsalted biscuit was used to cleanse the palate between each sample test. Overall liking score was assessed on a 9-point hedonic scale, where 1 = 'dislike extremely' and 9 = 'like extremely'. At the same time, the 5-point just-about-right (JAR) scale was used to determine the appropriateness of sweet intensity of the samples, where 1 = 'Not nearly sweet enough'; 2 = 'somewhat not sweet enough'; 3 = 'just about right'; 4 = 'somewhat too sweet'; 5 = 'much too sweet'.

2.9 Statistical analysis

All data shown in this study represent the mean values ± standard deviation of triplicate measurements. The statistical differences between mean values were analyzed by analysis of variance (ANOVA) using IBM SPSS Statisics 25.0 and compared using Duncan's multiple-range test with a significance level of 0.05.

3 Results and discussion

3.1 % Yield and bioactive compound contents of Nongkhai black jasmine rice bran oil

Nongkhai black jasmine rice bran was extracted by Soxhlet apparatus using hexane as a solvent. Hexane is commonly used in the vegetable oil production industry because of its low polarity and high productivity. Moreover, the solvent extraction process is simple to manage. In this study, the yield of oil from Nongkhai black jasmine rice bran was 12.38%. It's been previously reported that oil yield from other rice cultivars was between 13-22% [14,15]. The yield of rice bran oil depends on the type of solvent, method, extraction time and temperature as well as the varieties of rice used as raw materials.

From Table 1, bioactive compound content of Nongkhai black jasmine rice bran oil was investigated. Among other components, phenolic compounds are substances with antioxidant activity found in rice bran. The major groups of phenolic compounds are phenolic acids (e.g. p-coumaric acid, ferulic acid, gallic acid, protocatechuic acid, and sinapic acid) and flavonoids (quercetin, catechin, rutin, and apigenin). The total phenolic and total flavonoid content of Nongkhai black jasmine rice bran oil were 120.03 ± 1.26 μg GAE/g oil and 46.90 ± 0.69 μg QE/g oil, respectively. Janu and co-workers (2014) revealed that the total phenolic contents of some common vegetable oils were in the range of 0.33-3.09 mg GAE /100 g oil (approximately 3-30 μg GAE /g oil) [16]. In terms of total flavonoid content, Ghasemzadeh *et. al.*, (2018) reported that the total flavonoid contents of Malinin, Sangyod, and Leum Phua black glutinous rice bran were 0.52-0.57 mg QE/g oil (about 520-570 μg QE/g oil) [17].

Table 1. Bioactive compound content and antioxidant activity of Nongkhai black jasmine rice bran oil

Chemical properties	Mean±SD
Total phenolic content (μg GAE/g oil)	120.03 ± 1.26
Flavonoid content (μg QE/g oil)	46.90 ± 0.69
γ-Oryzanol content (μg/g oil)	236.73 ± 7.54
Antioxidant activities	
DPPH assay (μg TE/ g oil)	1676.63 ± 76.86
ABTS assay (μg TE/ g oil)	592.75 ± 46.22
FRAP assay (μg TE/ g oil)	1.31 ± 0.22

γ-oryzanol is a group of ferulate compounds mainly found in rice bran oil. It possesses health benefits as there have been evidences that could help reducing the risk of cardiovascular disease and lowering the levels of low-density lipoprotein cholesterol [18,19]. Thus, it is well known as one of the heart-friendly oils. In this study, the γ-oryzanol content of Nongkhai black jasmine rice bran oil was 236.73 ± 7.54 μg/g oil (Table 1). This is relatively low compared to other Thai rice bran oils of which are reported to contain γ-oryzanols ranging from 1.75-17.54 mg/g oil (1750-17500 μg/g oil). The variation of γ-oryzanols depends on factors such as the extraction technique, rice cultivars, and farming region, etc. [20].

Regarding to antioxidant activity of the extracted oil, different assays were performed including DPPH, ABTS, and FRAP assays. We found that the antioxidant activity of the Nongkhai black jasmine rice bran oil tested by DPPH, ABTS, and FRAP were 1676.63 ± 76.86, 592.75 ± 46.22, 1.31 ± 0.22 μg TE/g oil, respectively (Table 1). It was observed that the antioxidant activities of the extracted oil varied among different assays, which could be a result of the systems and reaction processes occurred in different methods. Thus, it is important to apply different techniques to assess the antioxidant activity of tested samples in order to ensure the accuracy and thoroughness of the findings. A previous study reported that other Thai pigmented rice bran oils possessed the DPPH radical scavenging activity of 12.19-18.80 mg TE/g oil and ABTS radical scavenging activity of 13.05-17.17 mg TE/g oil [20]. Significant variations in the antioxidant capacity of rice bran oil from various cultivars indicated that the phytochemical composition and antioxidant capacity of rice varieties depend on a variety of factors, especially cultivars and extraction techniques. The antioxidant activity of rice bran oil could be owing to lipophilic antioxidants such as tocopherol (vitamin E) or γ-oryzanol, etc.

3.2 Development of rice bran oil-in-water emulsion drink

Due to its unique qualities and nutritional values, rice bran oil has found many uses as a functional oil in food industry and pharmaceuticals. In the present study, the extracted Nongkhai black jasmine rice bran oil was formulated into a functional oil-in-water emulsion beverage. The appearance of emulsion was white and cloudy without creaming separation. The erythritol mixed with stevia extract sweetener was added in the emulsion beverage at 0.1, 0.2, 0.3 and 0.4% (w/w). The hedonic scale was used in combination with just-about-right test to measure the optimum intensity of sweetness of an emulsion beverage. The hedonic score was shown in Table 2. The emulsion beverage with the addition of 0.4% sweetener obtained the significantly highest hedonic score in terms of taste and overall liking. The taste and overall liking score of 6.8 ± 1.1 and 7.0 ± 1.1, respectively, which represent moderate liking.

Table 2. The 9-point hedonic score of Nongkhai black jasmine rice bran oil -in-water emulsion beverage with different concentrations of sweetener

% Sweetener	Mean ± SD	
	Taste	Overall liking
0.1	4.6 ± 1.6^{b}	4.7 ± 1.6^{c}
0.2	4.9 ± 1.4^{b}	5.0 ± 1.3^{bc}
0.3	5.3 ± 1.4^{b}	5.5 ± 1.3^{b}
0.4	6.8 ± 1.1^{a}	7.0 ± 1.1^{a}

Note: Means with different letters within a column are significantly different ($p \leq 0.05$).

The 5-point just about right (JAR) test was performed along with the hedonic test in order to assess whether the sweetness level is appropriate. The results of the JAR evaluation are shown in Table 3. The 96.7% of panellists, which is more than 70% rated the samples with 0.4% sweetener as being the just-about-right level for sweetness. Moreover, the % net effect was less than 10%. This suggests that the addition of 0.4% sweetener into the rice bran oil emulsion was the most appropriate compared with other concentrations in this study.

Table 3. Percentage of panelists based on the 5- point just about right test of Nongkhai black jasmine rice bran oil -in-water emulsion beverage with different concentrations of sweetener

Sweetener (%)	Just about right scale)%(					Net effect (%)
	1	2	3	4	5	
0.1	46.7	40.0	3.3	6.7	3.3	76.7
0.2	33.3	53.3	3.3	6.7	3.3	76.7
0.3	16.7	56.7	10.0	13.3	3.3	56.7
0.4	0.0	3.3	96.7	0.0	0.0	3.3

Note: 1 = Not nearly sweet enough; 2= Somewhat not sweet enough; 3= Just about right ; 4 = Somewhat too sweet; 5= Too much sweet

The Nongkhai black jasmine rice bran oil-in-water emulsion beverage with 0.4% (w/w) sweetener was chosen according to the sensory evaluation and was tested for the bioactive compound content and antioxidant activity as shown in Table 4. The Nongkhai black jasmine rice bran oil-in-water emulsion beverage contained γ-oryzanol of 13.3 ± 0.3 μg/mL and possessed ABTS radical scavenging activity of 267.0 ± 37.7 μg TE/mL.

Table 4. Bioactive compound content and antioxidant activity of Nongkhai black jasmine rice bran oil-in-water emulsion beverage with 0.4% (w/w) sweetener

Chemical properties	Mean±SD
Total phenolic content (μg GAE/mL)	n.d.
Flavonoid content (μg QE/mL)	n.d.
γ-Oryzanol content (μg/mL)	13.3 ± 0.3
Antioxidant activities	
DPPH assay (μg TE/mL)	n.d.
ABTS assay (μg TE/mL)	267.0 ± 37.7
FRAP assay (μg TE/mL)	n.d.

Note: n.d. means not detected.

However, some bioactive compounds including phenolic and flavonoid could be degraded during the process of emulsification and pasteurization which occurred at high pressure and temperature. Nayak *et al.*,

(2020) reported that total phenolic contents, total flavonoid contents, antioxidant activity of elephant apple juice were reduced as affected by pasteurization process [21]. Moreover, the oil content used in this study was low (1% w/w) leading to low content of bioactive compounds. To increase the antioxidant activity of the emulsion beverage, a higher oil content could be added.

4 Conclusions

This study reports the bioactive compound content and the antioxidant activity of Nongkhai black jasmine rice bran oil. The oil contained a significant amount of phenolic 120.03 ± 1.26 µg GAE/g oil, flavonoid 46.90 ± 0.69 µg QE/g oil and γ-oryzanol 236.73 ± 7.54 µg/g oil. The antioxidant activity of the oil tested by DPPH, ABTS, and FRAP were 1676.63 ± 76.86, 592.75 ± 46.22, 1.31 ± 0.22 µg Trolox equivalent/g oil, respectively. The Nongkhai black jasmine rice bran oil - in-water emulsion beverage was successfully developed. The emulsion containing 0.4 % sweetener had the highest overall liking score of 7.0 ± 1.1, representing moderate liking. The emulsion beverage contained γ-oryzanol as a lipophilic bioactive component with the antioxidant activity tested by ABTS of 267.0 ± 37.7 µg Trolox equivalent/mL. This study suggests that Nongkhai black jasmine rice bran oil possesses beneficial components including γ-oryzanol as well as other lipophilic antioxidants such as tocopherol. Hence, it could be used in food products and nutraceuticals for sustainable development.

Acknowledgements

The research was funded by National Science, Research and Innovation Fund (NSRF), and King Mongkut's University of Technology North Bangkok with Contract No. KMUTNB-FF-66-75.

References

1. R. Janta, K. Sekiguchi, R. Yamaguchi, K. Sopajaree, B. Plubin, T. Chetiyanukornkul, Spatial and temporal variations of atmospheric PM10 and air pollutants concentration in upper northern Thailand during 2006-2016, Applied Science and Engineering Progress, **13**,3 (2020): 256-267
2. P. Sookwong, S. Mahatheeranont, Some strategies for utilization of rice bran functional lipids and phytochemicals, Journal of oleo science, **67**,6 (2018): 669-67
3. WHO, Interim summary of conclusions and dietary recommendations on total fat and fatty acids, from the joint FAO, (2008): 1-14
4. P. Lasunon, N. Phonkerd, S. Pariwat, N. Sengkhamparn, Effect of soaking conditions and fuzzy analytical method for producing the quick-cooking black jasmine rice, Molecules, **27**,11 (2022): 3615
5. B. Burlando, L. Cornara, Therapeutic properties of rice constituents and derivatives (Oryza sativa L.): A review update, Trends in Food Science and Technology, **40**,1 (2014): 82-98
6. R. Refdanita, E. Damayanthi, C.M. Dwiriani, C. Sumantri, A.T. Effendi, Effect of intervention with rice bran oil-emulsion beverage on metabolic syndrome markers in men, International journal of sciences: basic and applied research, **32**,2 (2017): 165-173
7. D. Alamsah, E. Damayanthi, C.M. The study of rice bran oil emulsions beverage intervention on inflammation status among metabolic syndrome adult subjects, IOP Conference Series: Earth and Environmental Science, **196** (2018): 012036
8. V. Singleton, J. Rossi, Colorimetry of total phenolic compounds with phosphomolybdic-phosphotungstic acid reagents, American Journal of Enology and Viticulture, **16** (1965): 144-158
9. A.A. Abdelazim, A. Mahmoud, M.F. Ramadan-Hassanien, Oxidative stability of vegetable oils as affected by sesame extracts during accelerated oxidative storage, Journal of Food Science and Technology, **50** (2013): 868-878
10. Codex-Stan 210-1999, Codex standard for named vegetable oils, www.fao.org/fao-who-codexalimentarius, Access on 13 May 2023
11. D. Predner, P.C. Hsieh, P.Y. Lai, A.L. Charles, Evaluation of drying methods on antioxidant activity, total phenolic and total carotenoid contents of sweet potato (Ipomoea batatas (L.) Lam.) var. J., International Cooperation, **3** (2018): 73-86
12. M.B. Arnao, C. Antonio, A. Manuel, The hydrophilic and lipophilic contribution to total antioxidant activity, Food chemistry, **73**,2 (2001): 239-244
13. I.F. Benzie, J.J. Strain, The ferric reducing ability of plasma (FRAP) as a measure of "antioxidant power": the FRAP assay, Analytical biochemistry, **239** (1996): 70-76
14. B.M.W.P.K. Amarasinghe, M.P.M. Kumarasiri, N.C. Gangodavilage, Effect of method of stabilization on aqueous extraction of rice bran oil, Food and Bioproducts Processing, **87** (2009) :108-114
15. B. Pimpa, C. Thongraung, P. Sutthirak, Effect of solvents and extraction conditions on the properties of crude rice bran oil, Walailak Science and Technology, **18**,17 (2021): 9611-9617
16. C. Janu, D.R.S. Kumar, M.V. Reshma, P. Jayamurthy, A. Sundaresan, P. Nisha, Comparative study on the total phenolic content and radical scavenging activity of common edible vegetable oils, Journal of food biochemistry, **38**,1 (2014): 38-49
17. A. Ghasemzadeh, M.T. Karbalaii, H.Z.E. Jaafar, A. Rahmat, Phytochemical constituents, antioxidant activity, and antiproliferative properties of black,

red, and brown rice bran, Chemistry central journal, **12**,17 (2018): 1-13

18. A. Bumrungpert, R. Chongsuwat, C. Phosat, A. Butacnum, Rice-bran oil containing gamma-oryzanol improves lipid profiles and antioxidant status in hyperlipidemic subjects: A randomized double-blind controlled trial, Journal of Alternative and Complementary Medicine, **25**,3 (2019): 353-358
19. H.Y. Park, K.W. Lee, H.D. Choi, Rice-bran constituents: Immunomodulatory and therapeutic activities. Food and Function, **8**,3 (2017): 935-943
20. N. Pengkumsri, C. Chaiyasut, B.S. Sivamaruthi, C. Saenjum, S. Sirilun, S. Peerajan, P. Suwannalert, S. Sirisattha, K. Chaiyasut, P. Kesika, The influence of extraction methods on composition and antioxidant properties of rice bran oil, Food Science and Technology, **35**,3 (2015): 493-501
21. P.K. Nayak, B. Basumatary, C.M. Chandrasekar, D. Seth, R. K. Kesavan. Impact of thermosonication and pasteurization on total phenolic contents, total flavonoid contents, antioxidant activity, and vitamin C levels of elephant apple (Dillenia indica) juice, Journal of food process engineering, **43** (2020): e13447

The Future of Food Preservation: Active Packaging with Controlled Release Systems

Khadija Farousha[1], *Pei En* Tham[2], *Kit Wayne* Chew[3], *Suksun* Amornraksa[4], and *Pau Loke* Show[1,*]

[1] Department of Chemical Engineering, Khalifa University, Shakhbout Bin Sultan St - Zone 1 - Abu Dhabi - United Arab Emirates
[2] Department of Chemical and Environmental Engineering, Faculty of Science and Engineering, University of Nottingham Malaysia, Jalan Broga, 43500 Semenyih, Selangor Darul Ehsan, Malaysia.
[3] School of Chemistry, Chemical Engineering and Biotechnology, Nanyang Technological University, 62 Nanyang Drive, Singapore, 637459 Singapore
[4] Department of Chemical and Process Engineering, The Sirindhorn International Thai-German Graduate School of Engineering, King Mongkut's University of Technology North Bangkok Bangkok, Thailand

Abstract. This report provides an overview of active packaging with a focus on controlled release packaging (CRP) technologies, which have been developed to improve the shelf life of food products. Active packaging systems incorporate various functional components such as antimicrobial agents or oxygen scavengers into package material to maintain product quality during storage. CRP technology involves encapsulating bioactive compounds within a carrier matrix that can be released in a controlled manner over time. The paper compares these two promising technologies and highlights their advantages for extending shelf life while maintaining product quality. While active packaging is more suitable for short-term preservation due to non-controllable active agent release, CRP has potential applications in long-term preservation due to its ability to provide sustained release of bioactive compounds. Future prospects include developing a blend of CRP and intelligent food packaging. However, challenges remain including the sustainable release rate of the active agents from the packaging into the headspace or food surface. Overall, this review provides insights into the current state-of-the-art research on CRP technologies while highlighting future directions for improving food safety through innovative approaches aimed at preserving freshness while minimizing waste generation from expired products.

Keyword. Active agents, Active packaging, Antioxidants, Controlled release, Encapsulation, Polymer matrix

1 Introduction

Before millennia, clay pots and wooden barrels were used to store and transport food products. These traditional methods of packaging are often more expensive compared to modern plastic-based alternatives. However, since it can be reused repeatedly, it is a more sustainable choice in longer-term whereas plastic food packaging is the main source of solid waste [1]. This emphasizes how crucial it is to reduce the use of single-use plastics for food packaging in order to preserve the environment from further contamination driven by plastics ending up in landfills or oceans after being thrown away after a single use. Thus, there are still ways to minimize reliance on single-use plastics when comes to determining the type of material used for food packaging, despite traditional approaches that may not always be feasible or economical.

Recent developments in food packaging have focused on the use and promotion of active or biodegradable food packaging, due to their environmental benefits. Traditional petroleum-based packaging materials are still commonly used because it is convenient and affordable, although it pollutes the environment [2]. Films and coatings made of biopolymers provide an option that is both biodegradable and capable of preserving the quality of food over time. Active packaging regulates the environment inside the packaged material and guards against spoiling brought by external forces such as physical, chemical and biological factors. Some packaging can even assist in keeping nutrients in food products intact for a longer period of time. Overall, incorporating biopolymer-based additives pose a solution for sustainable food packaging with numerous advantages compared to traditional methods [3].

The aim of this report is to showcase the new innovative food packaging technology known as active food packaging (AP) with a focus on controlled release food packaging (CRP). A comprehensive literature review was carried out to compare active and controlled release packaging, as well as review different methods to achieving sustained diffusion of active components and the challenges and future prospects of CRP. The

* Corresponding author: pauloke.show@ku.ac.ae

importance of this research lays in understanding how to prolong the shelf life of food without compromising food safety and human health.

2 Active packaging associated with controlled released

Active packaging (AP) is a novel technology used in food preservation and storage that contains active agents such as antioxidants and antimicrobial components in the film to efficiently combat the build-up of bacteria that lead to food spoilage. This helps limit bacterial growth, food oxidation and decomposition of foods to prolong storage life. The mode of action is dependent on the volatility of the active ingredient, with non-volatile active agents diffusing through the packaging directly to the food surface [4]. Research into this type of AP has progressed through three phases, with the latest involving controlled-release packages that are designed to match up with food deterioration over time. By controlling when and concentration of active ingredients released onto the food surface, it helps maintain optimal concentrations for maximum safety and quality by preventing spoilage or oxidation from occurring. Control release active packaging technology improves numerous properties of packaging, such as gas and moisture permeability, UV protection and mechanical characteristic [5].

It is well understood that the release rate of active compounds from packaging into the food system is the primary factor that influences food quality. For instance, the release rate of antioxidants from packaging into food formulation is rapid, hence exceeding the authorized amount in food, and resulting in the production of pro-oxidants due to high concentrations of antioxidants [6]. Whereas the sustainable release rate of antioxidants has the advantage of inhibiting oxidation, hence resolving the issue of exceeding the authorized concentration level of antioxidants. Besides, the level of antioxidants efficiently diffused into the food is an essential phenomenon for designing CRP [7]. As an organic additive for meat products, edible oils, cereals, bakery goods, and fried meals, bamboo leaf extract (BLE) was permitted in China [8]. Table 1 summarizes the difference between control release packaging and active packaging.

3 Latest development

Active packaging development has been accelerated by incorporating nanocomposites [9]. Nanomaterials present a huge opportunity to overcome the obstacles associated with the production of active packaging. Minimizing the film thickness of polymer-based packaging has been made possible by nanomaterials resulting in cheaper transportation costs due to lower weight [10]. The incorporation of nanomaterials such as nanofibers and particles can serve as stabilizers to enhance the mechanical characteristics of biopolymers, thus eliminating the need for additional additives to achieve high and desirable characterizations [11]. In addition, it improves tensile strength, antioxidant and antibacterial properties [10,12].

Table 1. Comparison between control release packaging (CRP) and active packaging (AP)

Control Release Packaging (CRP)	Active Packaging (AP)
Involves the gradual active components diffusion over a period of time.	Fast release of active agent.
Straightforward addition of agents to the polymer or encapsulating the agents before addition to the polymer to achieve controlled release methods.	May use these same methods but also relies on natural active agents for its functionality
	Designed to respond to certain stimuli or conditions

For active packaging, nanocomposites such as antimicrobial nanocomposites and barrier-enhancing nanocomposites are a potential class of materials to use owing to their distinctive characteristics and activities [13-15]. Antimicrobial nanocomposites emit antibacterial substances or develop physical barriers that stop the spread of microbes [16]. Because of their broad spectrum of antibacterial activity, low cytotoxicity and prolonged shelf life of packaged foods, antimicrobial nanocomposites such as silver nanoparticles and zinc oxide nanoparticles are frequently used in the development of nanopackaging materials [17,18]. However, eco-friendly biological techniques, often known as green techniques, that include microbes, enzymes and plant extracts are becoming more popular at the current stage [19]. For instance, the zinc oxide nanoparticles synthesized via thyme extract demonstrated antifungal properties, making them a suitable alternative for food packaging [20]. While for barrier-enhancing nanocomposites, clay and graphene oxide nanoparticles can be introduced into polymers to improve their barrier performance by restricting oxygen or moisture from penetrating [14].

Recent advances in active food packaging have focused on the exclusive use of biodegradable and biocompatible materials, as well as natural compounds to enhance sustainability and sensory properties [21]. This shift has been driven by consumer preference for natural additives over synthetic ones due to their perceived health benefits. Technologies such as packaging with a controlled atmosphere and vacuum sealing are not effective at eliminating oxygen or moisture or protecting food from light. Active-release packaging technology could overcome this as it involves incorporating an active component within the polymer, which eliminates possible leakage onto packaged food items [12]. Examples of these agents include oxygen scavengers (iron oxidation or glucose oxidase, CO_2 and ethanol emitters), antioxidants agents (extracts, polyphenols and tocopherols) and antimicrobials components (organic acids, essential oils, bacteriocins chitosan derivatives) was the potential alternative agent used [22]. To be effective at preserving food, these components must be released in a controlled and sustained manner when needed [23]. The active agents used in food packaging were chosen based on the specific application, desired functionality, compatibility with the packaging materials and product, regulatory considerations and safety requirements [22].

Table 2. Advantages and disadvantages of control release food packaging

Advantages	Disadvantages
Provides protection from environmental stress like light, oxygen, moisture, etc.	Strict safety regulations must be adhered to when using active agents in packaging materials
Can be tailored to specific needs and conditions	Costly materials may be required for production which can increase the cost of packaging products
Reduces food waste by extending shelf life	

Controlled release (CR) active packaging has recently received wide attention, due to its pro-oxidation and regulatory maximum allowable concentration compliance compared to the traditional packaging [24]. Table 2 summarized the advantages and drawback of control release food packaging. In this regard, the controlled release of antioxidants from the packaging has been widely investigated to sustain food quality during transportation and storage. In addition, CR-based food packaging systems are intended to ensure the effective amount of active agent is disbursed into the food from the polymeric carrier to slow down the deterioration of food [25]. This reduces waste from spoiled foods and decreases reliance on single-use plastics for short-term storage solutions. Additionally, biodegradable polymers used in CRP systems are derived from renewable resources instead of nonrenewable petroleum sources like traditional plastics, making them a more environmentally friendly option with less potential for toxic compounds to be released into the environment.

Figure 1 summarizes 4 different techniques to facilitate the controlled and slower release of active agents. Multilayer active packaging is composed of several layers, including a layer that regulates the release of active agents and another to prevent their loss. Microencapsulation of active agents within a porous carrier material has been effectively developed for controlled-release packaging films [25]. Mesoporous silica materials, MCM-41 silica is an effective carrier material due to its strong textural properties, which can be used to encapsulate a wide range of natural compounds [26]. Reactive extrusion is a process in which two or more polymers are mixed and then heated to form a homogeneous blend. This process can be used to incorporate active substances into the polymer matrix, allowing for better control over release rates [27]. Polymer mixing can be used to provide control release of active packaging by adjusting the ratio of different polymers in a composite film. Nano clay and other particles were added to increase the tortuosity of the antioxidant diffusion path resulting in a slower release rate thus preserving the food for a longer period [28]. Surface coating can be used to control dispersion of active agent. For instance, natural antimicrobial agents encapsulated in fiber carrier was effective at controlling and releasing the agents and could be applied to various types of food applications [29]

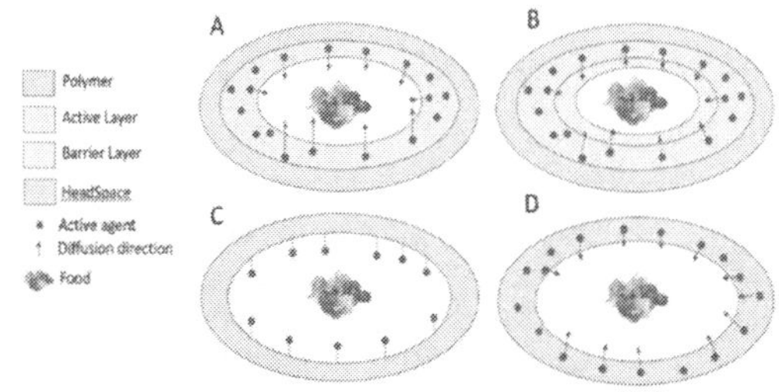

Fig. 1. (A) active layer applied by lamination, (B) Multiple layer Film, (C) covalently attaching molecules to the polymer surface, and (D) incorporating them directly into the polymer matrix which may involve encapsulating them.

The other recent development in packaging which caught the public attention includes edible packaging and intelligent packaging. Edible packaging refers to packaging materials or containers that are safe for consumption along with the product they contain. These materials are designed to be consumed or easily biodegradable, reducing waste and environmental impact. Edible packaging can be made from various natural sources, such as plant-based materials, seaweed, edible films, or even edible coatings [30]. Intelligent or smart packaging integrates technologies like sensors, indicators, and tracking systems to monitor and provide real-time information about product quality, freshness, and integrity. This enables improved quality control, supply chain transparency, and consumer engagement [31].

4 Current challenges and future prospect

CRP can be difficult to control and predict the rate at which active compounds are released from a package, as it differs based on pH levels, moisture content in the air and temperature. This unpredictability in release rates leads to inconsistent performance over time, making it difficult for manufacturers to guarantee food safety standards [32]. To overcome this challenge newly developed method for polymer matrix modification allow more precise control over active compounds released from packages. Testing methods have been developed to better understand how modified polymers interact with different foods and environments with their performance can be accurately assessed before use [23].

The future prospects for controlled release packaging (CRP) are very promising, with research suggesting that it could extend shelf-life up to five times more than traditional methods while also providing additional safety benefits due to its ability to interact with the environment around it [32]. One of the main trends in CRP is the development of intelligent or smart packaging (IOSP), which includes time–temperature indicators (TTIs), gas indicators, radiofrequency identification (RFID), and others which provide further information about handling foods safely and conveniently for consumers [23]. This demonstrates how CRPs can be used not only as a way of preserving food quality but also as a tool for providing useful data on food handling and storage conditions. In short, controlled release packaging offers great potential when it comes to maintain food safety whilst increasing convenience for consumers through extended shelf-life periods.

However, there are still challenges in the current packaging industry that need to be further studied, especially in understanding how nanomaterials interact with living things. It is important to take into account their migration behavior, which is still unknown in the current research field. The use of nanomaterials at a commercial scale in the food technology industry is constrained by conflicting evidence regarding cytotoxicity and a lack of comprehensive risk assessment and management studies. Additionally, the development of a sizable market for food applications based on nanotechnology must take into account customer acceptance.

5 Conclusion

In conclusion, active packaging and controlled release packaging technologies aim to prolong the storage life of food products by incorporating active agents such as antioxidants, antimicrobial components and oxygen scavengers. Future prospects include developing an intelligent food packaging system for better food storage and handling systems that could be beneficial to the community. However, the challenges regarding the release rate of active agents from packages into headspace or onto food surfaces needed to be further studied.

Acknowledgements

The author would like to thank Buhooth scholarship and Khalifa university for providing required resources and facilities.

References

1. X. Zhao, K. Cornish, Y. Vodovotz, Narrowing the gap for bioplastic use in food packaging: an update, Environmental science & technology, **54**, 8 (2020): 4712-4732
2. K.E.K. Vimal, K. Mathiyazhagan, V. Agarwal, S. Luthra, K. Sivakumar, Analysis of barriers that impede the elimination of single-use plastic in developing economy context, Journal of Cleaner Production **272** (2020): 122629
3. J. Jacob, U. Lawal, S. Thomas, R.B. Valapa, Biobased polymer composite from poly (lactic acid): processing, fabrication, and characterization for food packaging, *Processing and development of polysaccharide-based biopolymers for packaging applications* (Elsevier Inc., 2020)
4. A.M. Khaneghah, S.M.B. Hashemi, S. Limbo, Antimicrobial agents and packaging systems in antimicrobial active food packaging: An overview of approaches and interactions, Food and Bioproducts Processing, **111** (2018): 1-19
5. J.R. Westlake, M.W. Tran, Y. Jiang, X. Zhang, A.D. Burrows, M. Xie, Biodegradable active packaging with controlled release: principles, progress, and prospects, ACS Food Science and Technology, **2**, 8 (2022): 1166-1183
6. D. Dutta, N. Sit, Application of natural extracts as active ingredient in biopolymer based packaging systems, Journal of Food Science and Technology (2022): 1-15
7. J. Gómez-Estaca, C. López-de-Dicastillo, P. Hernández-Muñoz, R. Catalá, R. Gavara, Advances in antioxidant active food packaging, Trends in Food Science & Technology, **31**, 1 (2014): 42-51
8. R. Klinjapo, W. Krasaekoopt, Application of microencapsulated bamboo leaf extract powder to control the rancidity in moo yor (vietnamese-style sausage) during refrigerated storage, Applied Science and Engineering Progress, **14**, 1 (2021): 13-18
9. A.L. Brody, B. Bugusu, J.H. Han, C.K. Sand, T.H. McHugh, Innovative food packaging solutions, Journal of food science, **73**, 8 (2008): 107-116
10. J.W. Han, L. Ruiz-Garcia, J.P. Qian, X.T. Yang, Food packaging: A comprehensive review and future trends. Comprehensive Reviews in Food Science and Food Safety, **17**, 4 (2018): 860-877
11. V.G.L. Souza, A.L. Fernando, Nanoparticles in food packaging: biodegradability and potential migration to food—a review. Food Packaging and Shelf Life, **8** (2016): 63-70
12. N. Omerović, M. Djisalov, K. Živojević, M. Mladenović, J. Vunduk, I. Milenković, N. Knežević, I. Gadjanski, J. Vidić, Antimicrobial nanoparticles and biodegradable polymer composites for active food packaging applications. Comprehensive Reviews in Food Science and Food Safety, **20**, 3 (2021): 2428-2454
13. K. Kraśniewska, S. Galus, M. Gniewosz, Biopolymers-based materials containing silver nanoparticles as active packaging for food applications–a review. International Journal of Molecular Sciences, **21**, 3 (2020): 698.
14. D. Nath, R. Santhosh, K. Pal, P. Sarkar, Nanoclay-based active food packaging systems: a review. Food Packaging and Shelf Life, **31** (2022):100803
15. V. Dharini, S.P. Selvam, J. Jayaramudu, R.S. Emmanuel, Functional properties of clay nanofillers used in the biopolymer-based composite films for active food packaging applications-review, Applied Clay Science, **226** (2022): 106555

16. S. Roy, J.W. Rhim, Starch/agar-based functional films integrated with enoki mushroom-mediated silver nanoparticles for active packaging applications, Food Bioscience, **49** (2022): 101867
17. E.O. Simbine, L.D.C. Rodrigues, J. Lapa-Guimarães, E.S. Kamimura, C. H. Corassin, C.A.F.D Oliveira, Application of silver nanoparticles in food packages: a review. Food Science and Technology, **39** (2019): 793-802
18. S. Smaoui, I. Chérif, H. Ben Hlima, M.U. Khan, M. Rebezov, M. Thiruvengadam, T. Sarkar, M.A. Shariati, J.M. Lorenzo, Zinc oxide nanoparticles in meat packaging: a systematic review of recent literature, Food Packag Shelf Life **36** (2023): 101045
19. Ł. Łopusiewicz, S. Macieja, M. Śliwiński, A. Bartkowiak, S. Roy, P. Sobolewski, Alginate biofunctional films modified with melanin from watermelon seeds and zinc oxide/silver nanoparticles, Materials **15**, 7 (2022): 2381
20. T. Theivasanthi, S.M.K. Thiagamani, H. Natarajan, S. Siengchin, S.M. Rangappa, Fabrication and characterization of an active nanocomposite film based on polystyrene/thyme/nano zno for food packaging, Applied Science and Engineering Progress, **16**, 4 (2023): 6440
21. D. Nath, R. Chetri, R. Santhosh, P. Sarkar, Nanocomposites, in food packaging, Food, Medical, and Environmental Applications of Nanomaterials, (2022): 167–203
22. S. Yildirim, B. Röcker, Active packaging, Nanomaterials for Food Packaging, (2018): 173-202
23. M.W. Ahmed, M.A. Haque, M. Mohibbullah, M.S.I. Khan, M.A. Islam, M.H.T. Mondal, R. Ahmmed, A review on active packaging for quality and safety of foods: current trends, applications, prospects and challenges. Food Packaging and Shelf Life, **33** (2022): 100913
24. X. Chen, M. Chen, C. Xu, and K.L. Yam, Critical review of controlled release packaging to improve food safety and quality. Critical Reviews in Food Science and Nutrition, **59**, 15 (2019): 2386-2399
25. C. Vasile, M. Baican, Progresses in food packaging, food quality, and safety—controlled-release antioxidant and/or antimicrobial packaging, Molecules, **26**, 5 (2021): 1263
26. J.A.S. Costa, R.A. de Jesus, D.O. Santos, J.F. Mano, L.P. Romão, C.M. Paranhos, Recent progresses in the adsorption of organic, inorganic, and gas compounds by MCM-41-based mesoporous materials. Microporous and Mesoporous Materials, **291** (2020): 109698
27. J.E. Herskovitz, J.M. Goddard, Reactive extrusion of nonmigratory antioxidant poly (lactic acid) packaging. Journal of agricultural and food chemistry, **68**, 7 (2020): 2164-2173
28. L. Mei, Q. Wang, Advances in using nanotechnology structuring approaches for improving food packaging, Annual Review of Food Science and Technology, **25**, 11 (2020):339-364
29. W. Zhang, X. Li, W. Jiang, Development of antioxidant chitosan film with banana peels extract and its application as coating in maintaining the storage quality of apple. International Journal of Biological Macromolecules, **154** (2020): 1205-1214
30. M.C. Gaspar, M.E.M. Braga, Edible films and coatings based on agrifood residues: a new trend in the food packaging research. Current Opinion in Food Science, **50** (2023): 101006
31. P. Müller, M. Schmid, Intelligent packaging in the food sector: a brief overview. Foods, **8**, 1(2019): 16
32. M. Thirupathi Vasuki, V. Kadirvel, G. Pejavara Narayana, Smart packaging—an overview of concepts and applications in various food industries. Food Bioengineering, **2**, 1 (2023): 25-41

E3S Web of Conferences **428**, 02010 (2023) https://doi.org/10.1051/e3sconf/202342802010
RFC 2023

From Kimchi to Kefir: An Exploration of Probiotics, Benefits, and Future

Malak AbuZaid[1], *Sook Sin* Chan[2], *Kit Wayne* Chew[3], *Atthasit* Tawai[4], and *Pau Loke* Show[1, 5, 6, 7,*]

[1] Department of Chemical Engineering, Khalifa University, P.O. Box 127788, Abu Dhabi, United Arab Emirates
[2] Institut Sains Biologi, Fakulti Sains, Universiti Malaya, 50603, Wilayah Persekutuan Kuala Lumpur, Malaysia.
[3] School of Chemistry, Chemical Engineering and Biotechnology, Nanyang Technological University, 62 Nanyang Drive, Singapore, 637459 Singapore.
[4] Biorefinery and Process Automation Engineering Center, Department of Chemical and Process Engineering, The Sirindhorn International Thai-German Graduate School of Engineering, King Mongkut's University of Technology North Bangkok, Bangkok, Thailand
[5] Zhejiang Provincial Key Laboratory for Subtropical Water Environment and Marine Biological Resources Protection, Wenzhou University, Wenzhou 325035, China
[6] Department of Chemical and Environmental Engineering, Faculty of Science and Engineering, University of Nottingham Malaysia, Jalan Broga, 43500 Semenyih, Selangor Darul Ehsan, Malaysia
[7] Department of Sustainable Engineering, Saveetha School of Engineering, SIMATS, Chennai 602105, India

Abstract. Live microorganisms known as probiotics, which have various beneficial claims, have undergone substantial research and commercial exploration in a wide range of goods across the world. Many scientific studies have demonstrated their advantages for both human and animal health. The two primary probiotic bacterial species are *Lactobacillus* sp. and *Bifidobacterium* sp. The multi-billion health food industry has employed probiotics with a variety of dietary matrices, which are briefly reported. The history of probiotics, their use in food and medicine, and the latest developments in probiotic processes such as microencapsulation and genetically engineered probiotics are all covered in this review.

Keyword. Antibiotics, Engineered probiotics, Fermentation, Freeze-drying, Lactic acid bacteria, Lactobacillus, Microencapsulation.

1 Introduction

Probiotics are essentially living microorganisms that help to maintain a healthy balance of gut bacteria, improving the overall health of the individual [1,2]. *Lactobacillus* and *Bifidobacterium* are the most common types of Gram-positive probiotic bacteria in which their primary roles involve regulating and preserving the health of the intestinal tract [3]. Probiotics are commonly added to a variety of foods, including traditional foods like dairy products and specialized food like yogurt, kombucha, and fermented veggie [4]. Probiotics can also be food and medical supplements [5]. According to Arora and Baldi, probiotics can be classified as pharma-biotics and nutria-biotics as shown in Figure 1 [6].

Pharmabiotics refer to probiotics that have particular health claims and are potentially able to improve physiological functions or treat diseases through pharmacological mechanisms [7]. On the other hand, nutribiotics are in the form of food or supplement to sustain and modify the physiological function to maintain human health [7,8]. With the beneficial properties and high demand for probiotics, this industry has appeared as one of the fastest expansions in food categories in recent years [2].

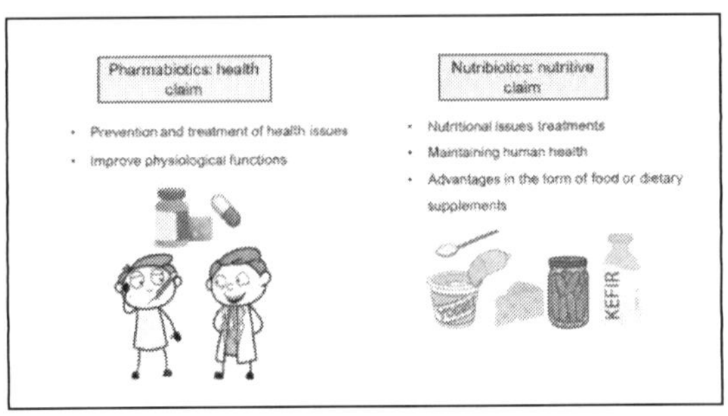

Fig. 1. Difference between pharmabiotics and nutribiotics.

Probiotics serve multiple crucial functions such as digestion and absorption of nutrients. They are also known to decrease the chances of infections and the production of toxins by harmful organisms, thereby reducing the potential for various human diseases [9, 10] and exhibit anticancer, anti-obesity, anti-diabetic, and immunomodulatory [11].

Probiotics contribute considerably to food preservation and enhancement, specifically via the fermentation process. This involvement allows probiotics to improve the taste, texture, and longevity of various food items including fruits, vegetables, baked goods, and meat products [9,12]. By fermentation,

* Corresponding author: PauLoke.Show@ku.ac.ae

carbohydrates are changed into new products by microorganisms in a chemical reaction. In ancient times, people used the natural fermentation process to create a variety of goods, such as meals and medicines [13] as it was known to promote products' safety and preservation [14]. In addition, fermented or preserved food and beverages were associated with particular ethnic practices or cultures without recognizing the science behind utilizing the role of microorganisms. The fermentation processes involved in creating foods such as kimchi and kefir embody principles of sustainability and waste reduction. Fermentation is an ancient technique used to prevent food spoilage, and thus, reduce waste. For example, kimchi is traditionally made using cabbage and other vegetables that might otherwise be discarded due to seasonal overproduction. This process not only minimizes waste but also adds nutritional value to the original product. Kimchi is a common fermented vegetable that originated in Korea and is made primarily from cabbage and seasonings [15]. Kimchi has over 200 types with effective properties in battling cancer, aging, and inflammation [14]. Probiotics are not only limited to food but also cover beverages such as kefir. Similar to yogurt, kefir is a fermented milk generated by lactic acid bacteria and yeast contained in kefir grains [15]. It has antitumor and antiallergic features with the ability to reduce blood pressure [14].

Traditionally, when a scientific background was shaped about the important function of useful bacteria in fermented food, the category of dairy products dominated the probiotic foods in the market. However, nowadays, food industries have introduced several products globally, both dairy and non-dairy, as researchers have explored the beneficial impact of probiotic microbes [16]. Consequently, as illustrated in Figure 2, the probiotics market is predicted to grow from \$66.67 billion in 2022 to \$90.43 billion in 2026 a compound annual growth rate of 7.9% [17].

With the increasing interest in studying probiotics, various developments were achieved, for instance, engineered probiotics to yield products with desired and improved qualities, as well as microencapsulation technologies that intended to enhance the probiotics microbiome's viability during products' manufacturing and storage and within the harsh environment of the human gut. Lately, probiotics are being studied as a friendly antibiotic alternative [18] and to combat COVID-19 infections [11].

To maximize the potential of nutrition in maintaining health and preventing diseases, nutritionists, researchers, pharmacists, regulatory authorities such as the World Health Organization, and food producers are currently working together [19]. Hence, research on the possible positive impacts of probiotics on health has become a central area of study in the fields of nutrition, food, and medical sectors [19,20].

Since eating habits play a major role in people's health, nowadays, consumers have become increasingly aware of what they consume, then, there is a real need for the production of items, which offer extra health advantages beyond those of the original products [21] as well as outlining the work and studies done on such food. This work shed light on providing useful information and exploring probiotics. It particularly aims to discuss types of probiotics, health benefits, latest developments, challenges, limitations, and the future of probiotics.

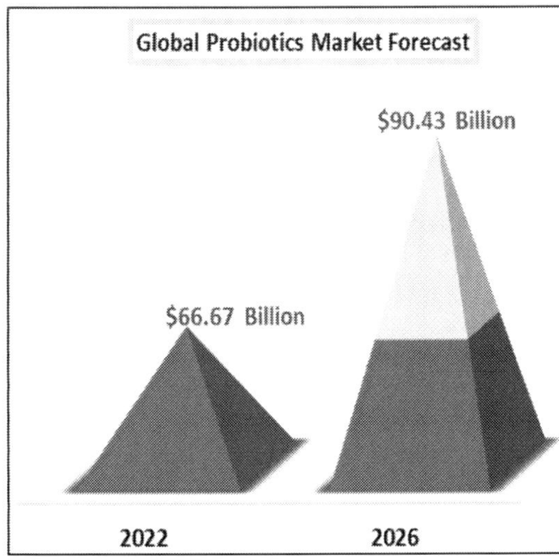

Fig. 2. 2026 forecast of the global probiotics market.

2 Literature Review

The word "probiotics," which means "for life," is a Greek word [22]. The classification of lactic acid-producing bacteria, also known as LAB, comprises genera such as *Lactobacillus*, *Enterococcus*, *Streptococcus*, and *Bifidobacterium*. Traditional fermented dairy products like Maasai milk, kurut, kefir, lassi curd, and buttermilk are the main source of these healthy probiotic microorganisms [23]. Regarding Gutiérrez *et. al.*, [24], probiotics have been linked to a variety of therapeutic benefits, including improved immune defense, lowered cholesterol levels, shielding against gastrointestinal and urinary tract infections, cancer, and assisting in the treatment of atopic dermatitis, atherosclerosis, rheumatoid arthritis, and other conditions.

Table 1. Examples of disorders or diseases and probiotic strains that are used as treatment [14].

Disease or Disorder	Examples of probiotic strains
Acute and antibiotic associated diarrhea	*Lactobacillus rhamnosus*, *L. bulgaricus*, *Enterococcus faecium* W54, *B. bifidum* W23
Urinary or kidney stones	*Oxalobacter formigenes*, *L. acidophilus* LA-14.
Constipation	*L. bulgaricus*, *L. acidophilus* (NCFM), *B. lactis*
Acute viral respiratory infection	*L. acidophilus*, *B. animalis ssp*, *L. rhamnosus*,
Colon cancer	Lactic acid bacteria
Colic	*B. breve*, *L. reuteri*, *L. casei*
Diabetes and Obesity	*L. gasseri*, *L. rhamnosus*

Table 2. Probiotics are tested experimentally for the treatment and management of infections caused by foodborne pathogens [14].

Probiotic	Pathogen	Animal Model	Outcomes
L. acidophilus heat killed	*Salmonella*	Rats	Prevention of *Salmonella* sp. infection
L. acidophilus, L. plantarum, E. faecium, L. casei, and *L. fermentum*	*E. coli* O157: H7	Sheep	Regular probiotic administration to sheep for seven weeks considerably reduced the overall number of pathogens in excreta
Probiotic *E. coli* Nissle *1917*	*Salmonella enteritidis*	Turkey	After two weeks of *Salmonella* sp. exposure, the administration of probiotics dramatically reduced the pathogen load

Around 1900, Elie Metchnikoff proposed that the healthy and long lives of Bulgarian peasants were due to their use of fermented milk, hence, the concept of probiotics was developed. He postulated throughout his research that the probiotics in yogurt shield the host from the negative effects of other pathogenic microbes [25]. It was identified that there are many lactobacilli strains found in yogurt, which gave them the scientific name *Lactobacillus bulgaricus*. In accordance with his research, the pure cultures of *L. bulgaricus* may be used to make fermented milk products. Metchnikoff proposed that pathogenic bacteria that produce toxins are removed from the gut by *Lactobacilli* [14].

In the 1930s, the first clinical studies examining how well probiotics relieve constipation were conducted. Subsequently, a probiotic product was approved by the United States Department of Agriculture as a therapeutic agent for managing *E. coli*-induced scouring in pigs. A variety of probiotic species have been employed in the prevention and treatment of many diseases such as colon cancer, kidney or urinary stones, constipation, acute diarrhea, obesity, diabetes, etc. Table 1 shows several illnesses with examples of probiotic strains used as a cure [14].

As per the data from the Centers for Disease Control and Prevention, foodborne diseases are responsible for around 48 million cases annually, 128 thousand of them requiring hospitalization with 3 thousand fatalities. With the increasing number of moralities, foodborne diseases are becoming a major threat worldwide [26]. Multiple biological, physical, and chemical methods such as antibiotics, thermal treatment, and preservatives, respectively, were used to diminish foodborne diseases. Nevertheless, these approaches were not effective and resulted in side effects including altering the appearance and organoleptic properties of food, antibiotic resistance in foodborne pathogens, as well as chemical intolerance in the body. Thus, alternatives are needed to manage and monitor foodborne illnesses. As demonstrated in Table 2, several studies have proven experimentally the effectiveness of probiotics as an alternative to preventing infectious diseases [14]. These and other studies along with the advantages of probiotics opened the door for many opportunities for further applications in medical fields and food industries.

3. Latest Development

In the past decades, the main focus of scientists and food technologists besides understanding the mechanism of action of probiotic bacteria is developing probiotic food and supplements. As a result, consumers have witnessed a significant increase in probiotic-based products which include pharmaceutical probiotic formulations, fermented dairy products, and non-dairy products as illustrated in Table 3.

A few years ago, the majority of the probiotics on the market were dairy based. However, high demand for non-dairy-based products such as fermented fruits and vegetables, herbs and tea, and cereals, has appeared. This is attributed to consumers with allergies to milk and its products and lactose intolerant or owing to dairy products' high cholesterol and saturated fatty acid content [14].

Table 3. Classification of probiotics [14].

<table>
<tr><td rowspan="11">Probiotic</td><td rowspan="7">Food formulations</td><td>Diary based products</td><td colspan="2">Lassi, Yogurt, Yakult, Cheese, Buttermilk, Kefir, Icecream, Chocolate</td></tr>
<tr><td rowspan="6">Non-diary-based products</td><td>Vegetables</td><td>Pickles</td></tr>
<tr><td>Fruits</td><td>Jam, Puree</td></tr>
<tr><td>Soy and Pulses</td><td>Flour, Soy milk, Tempeh</td></tr>
<tr><td>Cereals</td><td>Koji, Bread, and bakery</td></tr>
<tr><td>Meat and Fish</td><td>Salami, Sausage, Fermented meat</td></tr>
<tr><td>Herbs</td><td>Kombucha, Tea</td></tr>
<tr><td rowspan="4">Pharmaceutical formulations</td><td colspan="3">Tablet</td></tr>
<tr><td colspan="3">Freeze-dried powder</td></tr>
<tr><td colspan="3">Syrup</td></tr>
<tr><td colspan="3">Capsule</td></tr>
</table>

3.1 Microencapsulation

All forms of probiotics including powder, suspensions, capsules, and embedded into food share the same issue of losing their viability upon processing and storing as they contain live bacteria [27]. With the recent explosion of probiotic-based food in the market, ensuring the survival and retention of the probiotics' health-boosting properties throughout the manufacturing process, technological food handling, and storage until the product's expiration date is a crucial precondition for their application. Furthermore, given that probiotics need to be alive and functional when they arrive at their intended site within the host, it's essential that they possess the ability to resist the host body's natural defenses against ingested bacteria. Microencapsulation, a recently developed highly effective technique, has been shown to improve the survival rate of probiotics during food processing and their journey through the upper parts of the digestive system [28]. It refers to enclosing solids, liquids, or gases within tiny, sealed capsules that can be released at predetermined rates in response to particular conditions. The ultimate goal of microencapsulation is to shield the probiotics from unfavorable conditions in the environment. In the food industry, this technique is applied for the following reasons:

1. Protection of the probiotic (core) from degradation caused by environmental factors such as temperature, oxygen, light, and moisture.
2. Reduction of core material evaporation.
3. Improvement of material handling by altering physical characteristics.
4. Masking of flavor, color, or unwanted taste.
5. Achieving even dispersion upon dilution.

The viability and survival of a probiotic cell that is encapsulated rely on the concentration of the wall material, size of the microcapsule, and type of bacteria strain. The encapsulation process involves enclosing cells in a wall material using various processes such as spray-drying, freeze-drying, emulsification, and extrusion. The selection of encapsulation is extremely important. During industrial processing and storage, inadequate encapsulation can expose sensitive probiotics to the external environment, causing cell wall damage and decreased nutritional properties. Commercially, freeze-drying and spry-drying have been successfully employed [29]. Among the encapsulation method, freeze-drying achieved the highest encapsulation efficiency of 98% according to Palanivelu *et. al.*, [30]. Freeze-drying (Figure 3), also known as lyophilization, is a standard method used to maintain probiotics in a dehydrated state for extended periods, however applying to freeze-dry for encapsulation is relatively new [29]. Commonly, water is extracted from probiotic bacterial cells as a standard practice to ensure the stability along the storage period [27].

During World War II, the freeze-drying method was first made commercially available to preserve penicillin and blood plasma. Subsequently, the French virologist Charles Merieux preserved vaccines using the freeze-drying technique. In 1938, the scientist Max Mortgenthaler pioneered the development of freeze-dried coffee, a breakthrough that paved the way for the creation of various powdered food items [27]. Probiotic cells are mixed with an aqueous solution of wall material during the process of this method of microencapsulation.

The mixture is subsequently frozen at low temperatures, and the frozen water is then sublimated under vacuum conditions. The main drawback of this process is the elevated cost and time consumed, and it may damage cell membranes reducing their activity [29]. Despite this, several techniques have been developed to increase the survivability of probiotic cultures using this useful and popular drying process. Pulse-spouted microwave freeze drying is an example that is capable to decrease drying time [27].

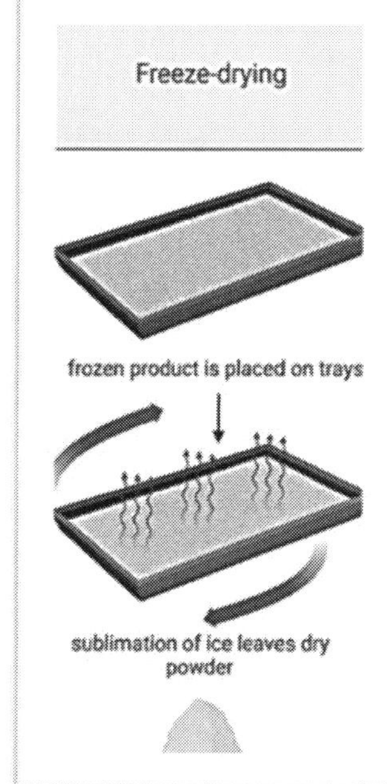

Fig. 3. Schematic of Freeze-drying [27].

3.2 Engineered Probiotics

Although microencapsulation can enhance and protect probiotic microbial strains under harsh conditions, there are other challenges in creating easily accepted probiotic-based foods, determining appropriate doses, and evaluating the effectiveness of different strains. Researchers have recently studied the design of novel probiotics with desired features through genetically modifying probiotics. Genetically engineering bacteria strains can improve their properties, safety, and effectiveness in therapeutic applications [31]. Besides, this process allows further applications like vaccine and drug delivery [32]. There are various applications of genetically modified (GM) probiotics.

One property of probiotics that grabbed the attention of scientists is their antimicrobial activity. Conventionally, infectious diseases are treated using antibiotics. However, antibiotics are known to kill all types of bacteria including the beneficial ones. Moreover, antibiotics can cause adverse side effects at the patient level and allow for the development of antimicrobial-resistant pathogens [18]. Therefore, there is a pressuring need for alternatives in antimicrobial therapy [3], particularly creating novel antimicrobial agents that are risk-free, environmentally benign, and effective against bacteria that are resistant to antibiotics [31]. GM probiotics can generate molecules that are similar to antibiotics. These molecules are called antimicrobial peptides (AMPs) and have antimicrobial action without antibiotic resistance phenomena [33].

Infections caused by *Clostridium difficile* cause traveler's diarrhea which leads to severe clinical issues. In the last decade, probiotics have been proposed probiotic as an effective approach to treating it instead of using antibiotics [34].

Furthermore, engineered probiotics offer anticancer therapeutics. Uncontrolled cell division, or cancer, is usually discovered only when it has progressed to an advanced stage. Once cancerous cells have spread, they eventually require several developmental stages for a tumor to become malignant [35]. According to the World Health Organization (World Health Organization, 2020), it is predicted that by 2040 cancer cases will reach around 30 million. Cancer is typically treated by chemotherapy and multiple drugs supplying. These treatments are found to damage both cancer cells and healthy cells, leading to resistance that affects future treatments of patients [35]. Recently, engineered probiotics have been found to target and replicate within tumor cells, offering a safer and potentially more effective alternative to traditional cancer treatments. Specifically, certain bacteria like *Clostridia* sp. and *Salmonella* sp. have been found to be helpful in treating cancer [31]. The use of these probiotics could also help combat drug resistance and reduce the side effects of chemotherapy. Furthermore, non-pathogenic strains, such as *E. coli*, have the ability to multiply within tumors and nearby tissues, making them valuable in treating melanomas (associated with skin cancer) [36]. As scientists continue to study the mechanisms of these bacteria, it may be possible to explore various combinations of probiotics to treat different types of cancer.

4. Current Challenges and Future Prospects

Despite the facts associated with the health benefits of probiotics, there are still a number of obstacles that could prevent their widespread use [37]. Maintaining probiotics' viability in edible products at the time of consumption and improving bioavailability in the human gut are the two most difficult probiotic delivery steps. Making up food matrices augmented with probiotics is still an interesting research topic, especially regarding their interaction with carbohydrates, proteins, and flavoring agents as they have been shown to alter or change probiotics' efficacy and capability. As much literature has been developed over the years, this is still the case [38]. Although microencapsulation is utilized to assure probiotics' viability during the manufacture, treatment, and storage of food items, it faces some challenges such as developing microencapsulation equipment, creating beads or capsules from polymers, choosing non-toxic materials for encapsulation, and figuring out the proper mechanism for probiotic release. Cost is one of the significant difficulties since finished items that have been encapsulated can be quite expensive. This is due to the requirement of financial resources and time for their development [39].

Even though clinical trials provide us with significant insights, the precise ways in which bacterial probiotics work and their effectiveness in easing different health conditions still pose numerous unanswered questions. In the future, further clinical study is thus required, as foods containing bacterial probiotics have the potential to minimize drug consumption and prevent specific diseases when combined with a balanced diet and lifestyle. Also, as the majority of microencapsulated have been applied to fermented foods, particularly dairy products, more study is required as they can be incorporated into non-diary food. As a result, the food business as well as research in the fields of nutrition, health, and food science are presented with tremendous potential [35]. Future research should also focus on understanding the long-term safety and gastrointestinal tolerance of products containing probiotics, as well as the illnesses that can be caused by certain probiotics, such as opportunistic pathogens like *Lactobacilli* as such information is limited especially in new-borns [39].

There is no doubt that probiotics have various health claims. It is known that premarket safety approval of drugs is necessary; Nonetheless, such requirements are still not mandated for nutritional and dietary supplements. For instance, in the United States, nutritional supplements (capsules or tablets) do not fall under the same manufacturing and quality control testing requirements as medications [40]. As a result, both consumers and healthcare providers lack assurance about the quality standards of probiotic products as well as the safety of their constituents [31,40]. To address probiotic concerns, such as safety, effectiveness, claims, and labeling, it is recommended that probiotic products be given worldwide regulatory status. Moreover, the probiotic formulations that have been demonstrated to provide the host with specific health benefits must describe these benefits in detail, along with an efficient control system for evaluating any negative side effects and tracking the probiotic formulations' overall health benefits. Genetically modified probiotics necessitate a strict safety protocol to prevent the spread of strains and genetic alterations.

5. Conclusion

Probiotics have gained more attention in the food and feed sectors over the past several decades as a result of rising consumer demand for wholesome and functional meals, or foods that do more than just provide essential nutrients for survival. Because of their well-established functional probiotic qualities, LAB strains are the most commonly used probiotics. Nevertheless, there is still a need to find new probiotic strains with superior health-promoting properties compared to the current ones. A plethora of advantages are associated with encapsulation when it comes to preserving live microorganisms. The functional components can be encapsulated using a variety of techniques. The greatest encapsulation efficiency was achieved using conventional freeze-drying methods. Genetically modified probiotics are a promising and novel option for treating infections. Engineered probiotics have the potential to restore health effectively, easily, and with site specificity. Eventually, a detailed safety assessment should be carried out from production reaching the end user consumption.

Acknowledgments

The writer is thankful to Sook Sin Chan for the meticulous correcting and editing of this manuscript. Special thanks to Professor Ir Ts Dr. Show Pau-Loke for his guidance and fruitful feedback and support.

References

1. R. El Jeni, D.K. Dittoe, E.G. Olson, J. Lourenco, N. Corcionivoschi, S.C. Ricke, T.R. Callaway, Probiotics and potential applications for alternative poultry production systems, Poultry Science, **100**, 7 (2021): 101156
2. C. R. Soccol, L.P. de Souza Vandenberghe, M.R. Spier, A.P. Medeiros, C.T. Yamaguishi, J. De Dea Lindner, A. Pandey, V. Thomaz-Soccol, The potential of probiotics: a review, Food Technology and Biotechnology, **48**, 4 (2010): 413-434
3. D.R. Silva, J.D.C.O. Sardi, N. de Souza Pitangui, S.M. Roque, A.C.B. da Silva, P.L. Rosalen, Probiotics as an alternative antimicrobial therapy: current reality and future directions, Journal of Functional Foods, **73** (2020): 104080
4. R.R. Watson, V.R. Preedy, Probiotics, prebiotics, and synbiotics, *Bioactive Foods in Health Promotion* (Elsevier Inc., 2015)
5. Y. Vandenplas, G. Huys, G. Daube, Probiotics: an update, Jornal de Pediatria, **91**, 1 (2015): 6-21
6. M. Arora, A. Baldi, Regulatory categories of probiotics across the globe: a review representing existing and recommended categorization, Indian Journal of Medical Microbiology, **33** (2015): 2-10
7. E.S. Lee, E.J. Song, Y.D. Nam, S.Y. Lee, Probiotics in human health and disease: from nutribiotics to pharmabiotics, Journal of Microbiology, **56** (2018): 773-782
8. L. Das, E. Bhaumik, U. Raychaudhuri, R. Chakraborty, Role of nutraceuticals in human health, Journal of Food Science and Technology, **49**, 2 (2012): 173-83
9. Z. Jiang, M. Li, D.J. McClements, X. Liu, F. Liu, Recent advances in the design and fabrication of probiotic delivery systems to target intestinal inflammation, Food Hydrocolloids, **125** (2022): 107438
10. M.E., Sanders, Probiotics and microbiota composition, BMC Medicine, **14**, 1 (2016): 1-13
11. T.K. Das, S. Pradhan, S. Chakrabarti, K.C. Mondal, K. Ghosh, Current status of probiotic and related health benefits, Applied Food Research, **2**, 2 (2022): 100185
12. Q. Yue, M. Li, C. Liu, L. Li, X. Zheng, K. Bian, Extensional rheological properties in mixed and fermented/rested dough and relationships with steamed bread quality, Journal of Cereal Science, **93**, (2020): 102968
13. I.C. Taveira, K.M.V. Nogueira, D.L.G.D. Oliveira, R. Silva, Fermentation: humanity's oldest biotechnological tool, Frontiers for Young Minds, **9**, (2021): 1-7
14. A. Nadda, *Advances in Probiotics for Sustainable Food and Medicine* (Springer, 2020)
15. S.S. Behera, S.K. Panda, Ethnic and industrial probiotic foods and beverages: efficacy and acceptance, Current Opinion in Food Science, **32**, (2020): 29-36
16. D. Granato, F. Nazzaro, T. Colombo Pimentel, E. Esmerino, E. Gomes da Cruz, *Encyclopedia of Food Security and Sustainability/Ferranti P* (Berry EM, Anderson JR (eds.), 2018)
17. T.B.R. Company, *Probiotics Global Market Report 2022* (2022)
18. R. Ahmad, Y.H. Yu, F.S.H. Hsiao, A. Dybus, I. Ali, H.C. Hsu, Y.H. Cheng, Probiotics as a friendly antibiotic alternative: assessment of their effects on the health and productive performance of poultry, Fermentation, **8**, 12 (2022): 672
19. S. Manzoor, S.M. Wani, S.A. Mir, D. Rizwan, Role of probiotics and prebiotics in mitigation of different diseases, Nutrition, **96**, (2022): 111602
20. O'Toole, P.W., J.R. Marchesi, C. Hill, Next-generation probiotics: the spectrum from probiotics to live biotherapeutics, Nature Microbiology, **2**, 5 (2017): 17057
21. J.T. Guimarães, C.F. Balthazar, R. Silva, R.S. Rocha, J.S. Graça, E.A. Esmerino, M.C. Silva, A.S. Sant'Ana, M.C.K.H. Duarte, M.Q. Freitas, A.G. Cruz, Impact of probiotics and prebiotics on food texture, Current Opinion in Food Science, **33**, (2020): 38-44
22. R. Jobby, Y. Flora, A. Bora, P. Jha, H. Kawalkar, N. Desai, Exploring probiotic activity of lactobacillus sp. isolated from indigenous breeds of cattle milk and fecal samples in bhatan village, MH., IN, Current Microbiol, **77**, 7 (2020): 1184-1190
23. H. Ezzatpanah, Traditional food and practices for health: Iranian dairy foods, In *nutritional and health aspects of food in south Asian countries* (Academic Press, 2020, pp. 275-287)
24. L. Diez-Gutiérrez, L. San Vicente, L.J. R. Barrón, M.del Carmen Villarán, M. Chávarri, Gamma-aminobutyric acid and probiotics: Multiple health benefits and their future in the global functional food and nutraceuticals market, Journal of Functional Foods, **64**, (2020): 103669
25. E. Metchnikoff, *The Prolongation of Life* (Putnam, 1908)
26. Prevention, C.f.D.C.a. *Estimates of Foodborne Illness in the United States*. 2019; Available from: https://www.cdc.gov/foodborneburden/index.html
27. J. Kiepś, R. Dembczyński, Current trends in the production of probiotic formulations, Foods, **11**, 15 (2022): 2330
28. T. Amin, M. Thakur, S.C. Jain, Microencapsulation the future of probiotic cultures. Journal of Microbiology, Biotechnology and Food Sciences, **3**, 1 (2013): 35-43
29. R. Rajam, P. Subramanian, Encapsulation of probiotics: past, present and future, Beni-Suef

University Journal of Basic and Applied Sciences, **11**, 1 (2022): 1-18
30. J. Palanivelu, S. Thanigaivel, S. Vickram, N. Dey, D. Mihaylova, I. Deseva, Probiotics in functional foods: survival assessment and approaches for improved viability, Applied Sciences, **12**, 1 (2022): 455
31. S.F. Mazhar, M. Afzal, A. Almatroudi, S. Munir, U.A. Ashfaq, M. Rasool, H. Raza, H. Munir, M.S. Riaz Rajoka, M. Khurshid, The prospects for the therapeutic implications of genetically engineered probiotics, Journal of Food Quality, (2020): 1-11
32. M.A.R. Amalaradjou, A.K. Bhunia, Bioengineered probiotics, a strategic approach to control enteric infections, Bioengineered, **4**, 6 (2013): 379-387
33. S.M. Mandal, O.N. Silva, O.L. Franco, Recombinant probiotics with antimicrobial peptides: a dual strategy to improve immune response in immunocompromised patients, Drug Discovery Today, **19**, 8 (2014): 1045-1050
34. L. Santacroce, I.A. Charitos, L. Bottalico, A successful history: probiotics and their potential as antimicrobials, Expert Review of Anti-infective Therapy, **17**, 8 (2019): 635-645
35. V.E. Vera-Santander, R.H. Hernández-Figueroa, M.T. Jiménez-Munguía, E. Mani-López, A. López-Malo, Health benefits of consuming foods with bacterial probiotics, postbiotics, and their metabolites: a review, Molecules, **28**, 3 (2023): 1230
36. J. Stritzker, A.A. Szalay, Single-agent combinatorial cancer therapy, Proceedings of the National Academy of Sciences, **110**, 21 (2013): 8325-8326
37. W. Wolfe, Z. Xiang, X. Yu, P. Li, H. Chen, M. Yao, Y. Fei, Y. Huang, Y. Yin, H. Xiao, The challenge of applications of probiotics in gastrointestinal diseases, Advanced Gut & Microbiome Research, (2023): 1-10
38. S. Brahma, M.B. Sadiq, I. Ahmad, Probiotics in Functional Foods, Reference Module in Food Science, (2019): 1-17
39. S. Pramanik, S. Venkatraman, P. Karthik, V.K. Vaidyanathan, A systematic review on selection characterization and implementation of probiotics in human health, Food Science and Biotechnology, **32**, 4 (2023): 423-440
40. M.E. Sanders, D.J. Merenstein, A.C. Ouwehand, G. Reid, S. Salminen, M.D. Cabana, G. Paraskevakos, G. Leyer, Probiotic use in at-risk populations, Journal of the American Pharmacists Association, **56**, 6 (2016): 680-686

Ultrasound-Assisted Food Processing: A Mini Review of Mechanisms, Applications, and Challenges

Mahra Alshehhi[1], *Guowei* Wu[2], *Tawiwan* Kangsadan[3], *Kit Wayne* Chew[4,*], and *Pau Loke* Show[1,*]

[1] Department of Chemical Engineering, Khalifa University, Shakhbout Bin Sultan St - Zone 1 - Abu Dhabi - United Arab Emirates
[2] Department of Chemical and Environmental Engineering, Faculty of Science and Engineering, University of Nottingham Malaysia, Jalan Broga, Semenyih 43500, Malaysia
[3] Program of Chemical and Process Engineering, The Sirindhorn International Thai-German Graduate School of Engineering, King Mongkut's University of Technology North Bangkok, Bangkok, Thailand
[4] Biorefinery and Process Automation Engineering Center, School of Chemistry, Chemical Engineering and Biotechnology, Nanyang Technological University, 62 Nanyang Drive, Singapore 637459, Singapore

Abstract. Ultrasound technology in food processing holds promise in terms of energy efficiency, environmental impact, and sustainability compared to traditional processing methods. These conventional heat-based techniques, such as salting, smoking, and frying, are energy-intensive and time-consuming. Therefore, ultrasound as a promising technology has attracted the interest of scientists and stakeholders in the food processing field. This alternative solution utilizes ultrasound and can achieve similar results with reduced energy input. This not only reduces energy consumption but also contributes to reducing carbon footprint and greenhouse gas emissions. In addition, ultrasound processing technology enhances food safety and quality by inhibiting microbial growth and killing pathogens, leading to longer shelf life and reduced food waste. However, there are also present some limitations of ultrasound in food processing through dense and complex food matrices like protein. Current research and development efforts are expected to address these challenges and expand applications in food processing. Overall, ultrasonic technology could transform the sustainability of food processing in the future.

Keyword. Food processing, Food quality, Ultrasonication, Ultrasound applications, Ultrasound limitations

1 Introduction

Food processing involves using traditional methods, such as drying, frying, smoking, salting, or pickling to transform agricultural products and enhance their appeal, shelf-life, and safety for consumption. These traditional processing methods use heat to limit the growth of microorganisms and destroy pathogens. However, these techniques are limited since they take a long time and a lot of energy [1]. Furthermore, some foods can be impacted by losing a component throughout the traditional process, leading to changes in flavor, texture, and color [2]. As a result, research is being done to find green and innovative ways of assisted processing of food. This includes applying methods like ultrasound assisted processing.

Ultrasound involves using sound waves of high frequency and intensity to modify the physico-chemical and functional properties of food components, such as proteins, polysaccharides, and polyphenols [3]. This can be accomplished by adjusting processing parameters like temperature or pressure. Without affecting their fundamental properties, ultrasonography can also encourage interactions between various natural products. Ultrasound assisted food processing with pressure (monosonication) and thermal treatment (thermosonication), and combination of pressure and heat (Monothermosnication) can be applied to enhance food quality. This method helps to reduce microbial contamination, as well as increase shelf life and nutritional value by preserving vitamins, minerals, and other nutrients in the food [4].

In addition, ultrasound technology in food processing has important environmental implications. Compared to conventional techniques, it provides a more energy-efficient approach, reducing the carbon footprint associated with food production and preservation. This non-thermal ultrasound technique results in reducing energy consumption and less processing time. Furthermore, a research study conducted by Bhargava et al. (2020) demonstrated that ultrasound processing improves food safety and extends shelf life, reducing food waste and its associated environmental impacts [5]. Therefore, the application of ultrasound technology in food processing can contribute to a more environmentally friendly and sustainable food industry.

This review paper discusses several types of transducers used to create ultrasound, ultrasonic processing principles, and the diverse applications of ultrasonic processing in food preparation. Moreover, it also highlights the limitation of ultrasound in food processing through dense and complex food matrix like

* Corresponding authors: kitwayne.chew@ntu.edu.sg, pauloke.show@ku.ac.ae

protein. To sum up, ultrasound technology is an emerging tool for food quality inspection and change with the potential to revolutionize food processing.

2 Generation of Ultrasound-assisted food processing: A Literature Review

The earliest use of ultrasound technology dates back to the late 19th century, when it was used by a German physicist named Christian Doppler for medical imaging [6]. Since then, its applications have expanded into many other fields including food science. Over time, researchers developed more sophisticated methods, such as using higher frequencies or amplifying sound waves in order to improve the accuracy and efficiency of results obtained from ultrasonic analysis [4]. The benefits of ultrasound technology are diverse and lucrative for the food sector and making it an emerging technology for probing and food product enhancement.

Ultrasound may be employed at both high and low power levels in food processing. High power ultrasound, which applies frequencies between 20-100 kHz, can cause cavitation in the material being processed and alter its properties through pressure, shear, and temperature changes [5, 6]. Low power ultrasound applies higher frequencies between 2-10 MHz without altering the material's physical or chemical properties. Several types of transducers, including liquid-driven, magnetostrictive, and piezoelectric transducers (Figure 1), can be applied to generate ultrasound. Liquid-driven transducers use a powerful pump to force process material within a narrow blade, causing the blade to vibrate and produce pressure waves and cavitation. Magnetostrictive transducers utilize electromagnetic devices and ferromagnetic materials that alter size whilst subjected to a magnetic field. Piezoelectric transducers convert electrical energy to acoustic energy by aligning polarized molecules within the material when subjected to an electric field (electrostriction) or mechanical force (piezoelectric effect) [7].

Over 60 years have passed since low-intensity ultrasound was first used to analyze and describe food items, but only recently have researchers started to fully understand its capabilities. In the past, ultrasound was largely employed for non-destructive testing of food quality and making physical and mechanical changes to food items. It was employed, for example, to destroy cell walls and let intracellular materials to be released [8]. Recently, ultrasound has been integrated into various stages of food processing, such as blanching, drying, extraction, freezing, etc., to improve efficiency [9]. Although these technologies demand an initial investment, they can ultimately increase product quality while lowering expenses.

3 Ultrasonic Assisted Food Processing: Food properties modification

Ultrasonic has several principles to improve food processing including acoustic cavitation, mechanical effects, vibration, and agitation [5]. To increase emulsion homogeneity and stability, researchers utilized an ultrasonic agitator. The ultrasonic agitator caused localized high-intensity mixing, which resulted in smaller droplet sizes and improved emulsion stability [10]. Another important principle is a vibration that's useful for delicate and sticky food items like cheese, pastries, and cakes since it lessens the growth of bacteria on the product surface and helps to prevent sticking [5]. Table 1 illustrates other ultrasound principles with instances of how they are applied, including uniform heat, cavitation, and diffusion.

Ultrasound waves are passed through the food product, and the way the waves travel through the product can provide information about its physical and chemical properties, to assess the quality of food products [11]. Jiménez et al. (2017) developed an ultrasound-based monitoring system to measure the properties of raw milk during curdling and found that the ultrasound measurements of temperature and viscosity were highly correlated with traditional methods. The researchers concluded that ultrasound has potential for use in optimizing the curdling process and enhancing dairy products quality [12]. Furthermore, utilizing ultrasound in the meat industry can improve the meat tissue's water dynamics and tenderness. In addition, it

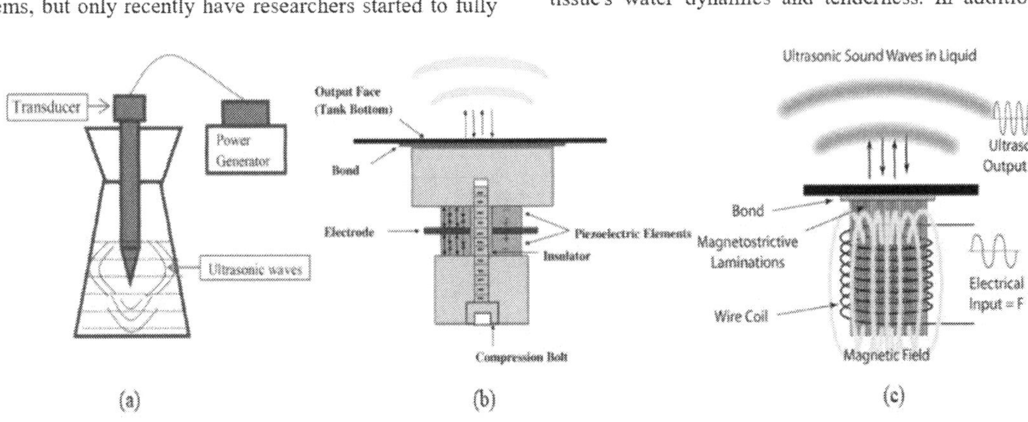

Fig. 1. Several types of transducers used in ultrasonic generation: (a) Ultrasonic probe [8] (b) Piezoelectric transducers (c) Magnetostrictive transducers [5]

can also increase the meat's water holding capacity and enhance its color [13]. These processes create novel methodologies that exceed the potential of traditional techniques in food processing.

Ultrasound technology can also be employed to lessen microbial contamination in food processing. The usage of high-intensity ultrasound can reduce the harmful microorganisms and enzymes present in dairy products. To emphasize, the findings of subjecting ultrasound in dairy products show increased probiotic viability, reduced lactose content, and higher oligosaccharides concentration [14]. Hence, further investigation is required before ultrasound can be scaled up to industrial levels to identify the best application parameters for each type of food. The pros of ultrasound application in food processing include improved physical, and chemical properties, reduced spoilage by microorganisms, and enhanced. However, it can be expensive to implement, as specialized equipment and instrumentation are required [12, 15].

Apart from the applications in food processing, ultrasound is extensively used as a pretreatment technique for lignocellulosic biomass [16]. This process employed high-intensity ultrasound to modify biomass structure and improves the accessibility of enzymes and chemicals to its contents. Ultrasound pretreatment has proven effective in improving enzymatic hydrolysis, increasing sugar release, and enhancing the efficiency of biofuel production from biomass. Moreover, it also assists in the extraction of beneficial bio-chemicals from lignocellulosic biomass, enabling their use in waste valorization and biorefinery processes [17].

4 Ultrasonic Assisted Food Processing: Limitations and Potential Prospect

Ultrasound effectiveness is limited in dense and complex food matrices such as protein-based ones, where it may struggle to penetrate deeply and reach the target region [23]. The influence of ultrasound can vary relying on the food type and whether the proteins are separated or present in the food system [24]. In addition, ultrasound may generate free radicals that can oxidize active compounds in some solid meals, altering the food matrix's properties or even making it unsafe for consumption [25]. Using ultrasound to measure food properties of complex food matrices can also present challenges such as attenuation, lower resolution with lower frequencies, and difficulty in obtaining clear results when multiple variables are changing simultaneously [26]. Thus, it is crucial to select the appropriate frequency, power, and mode of operation, while considering the type of food matrix.

Ultrasound technology has shown considerable promise in the food sector, and its uses are anticipated to expand in the future. Ultrasound, for example, is likely to be integrated with other processing technologies, such as high-pressure processing, pulsed electric fields, and thermal processing, to achieve greater efficiencies and improve food product quality and safety [27]. Furthermore, the operation of ultrasound in food processing is probably going to become more automated and miniaturized with invention of portable and handheld devices [28]. This will make it easier for food processors to apply ultrasonic technology at various phases of the food manufacturing process. Application of

Table 1. Principles of Ultrasound and its application in food processing.

Ultrasound Principle	Ultrasound Specifications	Sample Tested	Application	Observations	References
Uniform heat transfer	High-intensity ultrasound, frequency range between 20 kHz and 1 MHz, with an intensity level of up to 100 W/cm^2	Juice	Pasteurization	Inactivation of microorganisms present in juice, resulting in a 5-log microbial reduction; Shortage of pasteurization time; Reduction of negative impacts on juice organoleptic and nutritional characteristics	[18]
Diffusion	Low-intensity ultrasound, frequency range below 40 kHz	Polyphenols (plant material)	Extraction	Increase extraction yield of polyphenols; Improve phenolic extract biological activity over conventional maceration	[19]
Cavitation	High-intensity ultrasound, frequency of 20 kHz, power output of 500 W, and duty cycle of 50%	Green pepper	Drying	Reduction in drying time; Low energy consumption; Maintain product quality factors such as shrinkage and nutrient content	[20]
	High-intensity ultrasound, frequencies of 30 kHz and 20 kHz, and the power levels ranged from 150 W to 175 W	Broccoli	Freezing	Reduction in overall freezing time as well as pre-cooling, phase transition, and sub-cooling durations for broccoli; Drip loss reduction compared to normal immersion freezing	[21]
	Low-intensity ultrasound, frequency is 20 kHz	Skim milk	Emulsion	High encapsulation yield; Good shelf stability	[22]

the technology will become more targeted and precise as we learn more about how ultrasound impacts various food components, its mode of action, and its influence on the physicochemical qualities of food.

Ultrasound applications have the potential to improve food processing by successfully killing microorganisms and enzymes while maintaining food's sensory and nutritional characteristics. These technologies can complement existing traditional methods and can be combined into various unit operations like blanching, drying, and freezing to improve efficiency. Furthermore, ultrasonic technology in food processing is a sustainable alternative since it may eliminate the usage of chemical preservatives and increase product shelf life, decreasing food waste. Furthermore, the initial investment required for ultrasound equipment and the need for skilled operators could limit its adoption by small-scale food factories or those operating in low-income countries [27]. Therefore, solving this dilemma requires scientists to further explore these technologies in future research to develop safer, more efficient and economical food processing technologies.

5 Conclusions

In conclusion, advances in food processing are being driven by the continued development of ultrasonic technology. These developments improve several areas of food processing, including consistent heat distribution, extraction, emulsion stability, and bacterial control on product surfaces, by using principles including acoustic cavitation, mechanical effects, vibration, and agitation. In addition, there is a growing trend of integrating ultrasound with other technologies such as pulse electric fields, to further improve food safety and quality. As a result, the ongoing advancements in ultrasound-assisted food processing show immense potential to revolutionize the food industry, offering more sustainable and efficient processing techniques.

Acknowledgements

The authors would also like to thank Khalifa University for the facilities and resources provided for the completion of this work.

References

1. F.J. Barba, Microalgae, and seaweeds for food applications: Challenges and perspectives, Food Res. Int, **99**, 3 (2017): 969-970
2. P.S Negi, Plant extracts for the control of bacterial growth: Efficacy, stability and safety issues for food application. Int. J. Food Microbiol, **156**, 1 (2012): 7-17
3. X. Fu, T. Belwal, G. Cravotto, Z. Luo, Sono-physical and sono-chemical effects of ultrasound: Primary applications in extraction and freezing operations and influence on food components, Ultrasonics Sonochemistry, **60** (2020): 104726
4. P. Chavan, P. Sharma, S.R. Sharma, T.C. Mittal, A.k. Jaiswal, Application of high-intensity ultrasound to improve food processing efficiency, **11**, 1 (2022): 122
5. N. Bhargava, R.S. Mor, K. Kumar, V.S. Sharanagat, Advances in application of ultrasound in food processing, Ultrasonics Sonochemistry, **70** (2021): 105293
6. P.G. Newman, G.S. Rozycki, The history of ultrasound, **78**,2(1998): 179-195
7. D. Knorr, M. Zenker, V. Heinz, D.U. Lee, Applications and potential of ultrasonics in food processing, Trends in Food Science and Technology, **15**,5(2004):261-266
8. Z.J. Dolatowski, J. Stadnik, D. Stasiak, Applications of ultrasound in food technology, Acta Scientiarum Polonorum, Technologia Alimentaria, **6**,3(2007):88-99
9. M. Singla, N. Sit, Application of ultrasound in combination with other technologies in food processing, Ultrasonics Sonochemistry, **73**(2021): 105506
10. T. Leong, T.S.H. Leong, T.J. Wooster, S.E. Kentish, M. Ashokkumar, Minimising oil droplet size using ultrasonic emulsification, Ultrasonics Sonochemistry, **16**, 6 (2009): 721-727
11. M.E. Mohammed, M.R. Alhajhoj, Importance and applications of ultrasonic technology to improve food quality, Journal of Food Process Engineering, **9** (2019): 144
12. A. Jiménez, M. Rufo, J.M. Paniagua, A.T. Crespo, M.P. Guerrero, M.J. Riballo, Contributions to ultrasound monitoring of the process of milk curdling, Ultrasonics, **76** (2017): 192-199
13. A. Wang, D. Kang, W. Zhang, C. Zhang, Y. Zou, G. Zhou, Changes in calpain activity, protein degradation and microstructure of beef M. semitendinosus by the application of ultrasound, Food Chemistry, **245** (2018): 724-730
14. J.T. Guimarães, C.F. Balthazar, H. Scudino, T.C. Pimentel, E.A. Esmerino, M. Ashokkumar, M.Q. Freitas, A.G. Cruz, High-intensity ultrasound: A novel technology for the development of probiotic and prebiotic dairy products, Ultrasonics Sonochemistry, **57** (2019): 12-21.
15. M.S. Firouz, A. Farahmandi, S. Hosseinpour, Recent advances in ultrasound application as a novel technique in analysis, processing and quality control of fruits, juices and dairy products industries, Ultrasonics Sonochemistry, **57** (2019): 73-88
16. M.J. Bussemaker, D. Zhang, Effect of ultrasound on lignocellulosic biomass as a pretreatment for biorefinery and biofuel applications, Industrial & Engineering Chemistry Research, **52**, 10 (2013): 3563-3580

17. V.Z. Ong, T.Y. Wu, An application of ultrasonication in lignocellulosic biomass valorisation into bio-energy and bio-based products, Renewable and Sustainable Energy Reviews, **132** (2020): 109924
18. Z.M. Baboli, L. Williams, G. Chen, Design of a batch ultrasonic reactor for rapid pasteurization of juices, Journal of Food Engineering, **268** (2020): 109736
19. C.S. Dzah, Y. Duan, H. Zhang, C. Wen, J. Zhang, G. Chen, H. Ma, The effects of ultrasound assisted extraction on yield, antioxidant, anticancer and antimicrobial activity of polyphenol extracts, Food Bioscience, **35** (2020): 100547
20. J. Szadzińska, J. Łechtańska, S.J. Kowalski, M. Kowalski, The effect of high power airborne ultrasound and microwaves on convective drying effectiveness and quality of green pepper. Ultrason. Sonochem, **34** (2017): 531-539
21. Y. Xin, M. Zhang, B. Adhikari, The effects of ultrasound-assisted freezing on the freezing time and quality of broccoli (Brassica oleracea L. var. botrytis L.) during immersion freezing, International Journal of Refrigeration , **41** (2014): 82-91
22. T.S. Leong, M. Zhou, N. Kukan, M. Ashokkumar, G.J.O. Martin, Preparation of water-in-oil-in-water emulsions by low frequency ultrasound using skim milk and sunflower oil, Food Hydrocolloids, **63** (2017): 685-695
23. J. Chen, X. Cheng, G. Zhou, X. Xu, Ultrasound: A reliable method for regulating food component interactions in protein-based food matrices, Trends in Food Science and Technology, **128** (2022): 316-330
24. N. Wang, X. Zhou, W. Wang, L. Wang, L. Jiang, T. Liu, D. Yu, Effect of high intensity ultrasound on the structure and solubility of soy protein isolate-pectin complex, Ultrasonics Sonochemistry, **80** (2021): 105808
25. T. Wang, K. Chen, X. Zhang, Y. Yu, D. Yu, L. Jiang, L. Wang, Effect of ultrasound on the preparation of soy protein isolate-maltodextrin embedded hemp seed oil microcapsules and the establishment of oxidation kinetics models, Ultrasonics Sonochemistry, **77** (2021): 105700
26. N.K. Rastogi, Opportunities and challenges in application of ultrasound in food processing, Critical Reviews in Food Science and Nutrition, **51**, 8 (2011): 705-722
27. H.A. Khouryieh, Novel and emerging technologies used by the US food processing industry, Innovative Food Science and Emerging Technologies (IFSET), **67**(2021): 102559
28. A. Hassoun, S. Anusha Siddiqui, S. Smaoui, İ. Ucak, R.N. Arshad, Z.F. Bhat, H.F. Bhat, M. Carpena. M.A. Prieto, A. Aït-Kaddour, J.A.M. Pereira, C. Zacometti, A. Tata, S.A. Ibrahim, F. Ozogul, J.S. Camara, Emerging technological advances in improving the safety of muscle foods: framing in the context of the food revolution 4.0., Food reviews international, (2023): 1-42

Manganese Constituent in Stainless Steels Oxidized in Oxygen Containing Water Vapor at 800 °C: High Temperature Oxidation and Volatilization

Methanan Sangsuebsri[1], *Suwijak* Pokwitidkul[1], *Panya* Wiman[1], *Youhei* Tanaka[2] and *Thammaporn* Thublaor[1,*]

[1]High Temperature Corrosion Research Centre, Department of Materials and Production Technology Engineering, Faculty of Engineering, King Mongkut's University of Technology North Bangkok, 1518, Pracharat 1 Road, Bangsue, Bangkok 10800, Thailand
[2]Division of Materials Science and Engineering, Graduate School of Engineering, Muroran Institute of Technology, 27-1 Mizumoto, Muroran 0508585, Japan

Abstract. Many industrial operations, such as solid oxide fuel cells (SOFCs) or combustion processes, have water vapor environments. Stainless steel was applied as part of these applications at high temperatures. The present work investigates high and low manganese content stainless steel that oxidized in an oxygen-containing 5% water vapor at 800 °C. SEM and EDX were performed to analyze oxide formation and ICP-OES was used to detect the volatile species that evaporated from steel surfaces. The results show that manganese in steel increases spallation and reduces Cr volatilization rates in high Mn stainless steel. The average Cr volatilization of high Mn samples is 0.09×10^{-11} g cm^{-2} s^{-1}, which is about 14 times lower than the ones (1.25×10^{-11} g cm^{-2} s^{-1}), while Fe and Mn volatilization rates increase by 10 and 62 times, respectively.

Keyword. High temperature oxidation, Manganese content, Volatilization, Water vapor

1 Introduction

Stainless steel has been extensively used in various industrial applications. This is due to their excellent oxidation resistance and good mechanical properties. Chromium oxide (Cr_2O_3) can form on stainless steel which has a high chromium content (> 10.5-12.0 wt.%) [1]. It provides a dense, continuous, adherent steel substrate and a relatively slow growth rate. The prevention of Cr_2O_3 helps to increase high-temperature corrosion resistance and reduce the maintenance process due to material loss. Stainless steel is substantially more corrosive in the atmosphere containing water vapor than dry air [2,3], and this often arises in many applications. It has been reported that the amount of water vapor important to the hot-rolling process is around 19.5% [4] and can reach up to 40.0% in the combustion process [5]. Including solid oxide fuel cells (SOFCs), which are potential technologies for producing sustainable energy [6]. The water vapor can induce Cr evaporation from the chromium oxide in the form of $CrO_2(OH)_{2(g)}$ at lower temperatures of 1500 °C, as follows: (1) [7].

$$\frac{1}{2}Cr_2O_{3(g)} + \frac{3}{4}O_{2(g)} + H_2O_{(g)} \rightarrow CrO_2(OH)_{2(g)} \qquad (1)$$

As a result of chromia evaporation and inadequate Cr supplied from the steel, the protective Cr-rich oxide transforms into a non-protective Fe-rich oxide, and breakaway oxidation ensues [8]. Besides chromium in stainless steel, manganese is a common constituent element in alloys and affects oxidation resistance. When high content is added to alloys, it can create an austenite phase, which is regarded as a nickel substitute for the production of austenitic stainless steel grades [9,10]. It also is seven times cheaper than nickel at an equivalent weight [11,12]. Indeed, various studies have been conducted on the effect of low-level manganese additions on the oxidation resistance of (Fe, Ni, or Co)-Cr alloys since 1970. The scales created were proportional to the bulk chromium content [13-15]. They observed that adding up to 5% manganese to alloys containing around 20% chromium resulted in the creation of $MnCr_2O_4$.

For SOFCs with metallic interconnects, H. Falk-Windisch *et. al.*, [16] studied Sanergy HT (0.25 wt.%Mn) and Crofer 22 H (0.40 wt.%Mn) stainless steels of chromium content ~23 wt.% in air-3% H_2O at 650, 750 and 850 °C. They found that the presence of manganese in steels at high temperatures with low content contributes to the formation of a duplex-layered oxide scale with an outer layer of $(Mn, Cr)_3O_4$ whereas Cr_2O_3 is underneath. Moreover, the mass gain of Crofer 22 H stainless steel was higher than the others but reduced in chromium volatilization. This is due to the effect of Mn on the production of a continuous top layer of $(Cr,Mn)_3O_4$, which decreases Cr activity at the metal substrate compared to Cr_2O_3. Despite the fact that prior research [13-16] continues to examine the impact of manganese in alloys on oxidation resistance at high temperatures. These studies still lack an investigation of

* Corresponding author: thammaporn.t@eng.kmutnb.ac.th

the volatilized phase that causes mass loss from steel substrates. To better understand, the effect of manganese on chromium volatilization and oxidation resistance was comparable. In the present work, stainless steel with high manganese (Fe-15.3 wt.%Cr-8.9 wt.%Mn) and low content as AISI 430 stainless steel (Fe-16.4 wt.%Cr-0.8 wt.%Mn) were studied. The samples were oxidized in an oxygen atmosphere containing water vapor at 800 °C and then collected chromium, manganese, and iron from volatile species. The oxidation mechanism of the alloy is also discussed through the dependence of manganese content on the alloy.

2 Experimental procedures

2.1 Material

An AISI 430 stainless steel (low Mn) and special grade (high Mn) were cut into rectangular shapes (15 x 15 x 1 mm^3) and its chemical composition was measured using optical emission spectroscopy (Thermo Electron Corporation, ARL 3460) and reported in Table 1. The sample was ground on silicon abrasive papers of 180 up to 1000 grits and cleaned with deionized water and ethanol in an ultrasonic bath, respectively. It was dried by an air dryer.

Table 1. Chemical composition of the studied high and low Mn stainless steel in wt.%.

Element in wt%	Stainless steel	
	Low Mn	High Mn
Cr	16.41	15.32
Mn	0.79	8.94
Si	0.20	0.45
C	0.10	0.12
Ni	0.05	0.90
P	0.03	0.07
Fe	Bal.	Bal.

2.2 Experimental setup

To begin, suspend each specimen one at a time inside a controlled-atmosphere furnace in a vertical direction, as the hottest part of the furnace is in the center. The desired furnace temperature was set at 800 °C for the test and the oxidation times were set at 1, 24, 48, 72, and 96 h. The velocity of argon gas was 1.0 cm s^{-1}. It flowed directly through the specimen in the vertical furnace while waiting for the temperature inside the furnace to rise to 800 °C. When the temperature reaches 800 °C, the oxygen gas is switched from argon with a velocity flow rate at 1.0 cm s^{-1} into a water flask. A 5% H_2O content was controlled by maintaining the water temperature at 31 °C. The temperature was calculated according to the Clausius-Clapeyron equation using the enthalpy of water vaporization, 40,893 J mol^{-1} [17]. The humidified oxygen flowed through the sample surfaces and condensed at the bottom column of the furnace. This condensate was known as a concentration solution. The tube and condenser were cleaned with 0.1 M HCl, and the cleaning solution was added to the concentration solution, which was then used to analyze the number of elements from vaporization using inductively coupled plasma optical emission spectroscopy (ICP-OES). Before and after each test, the samples were weighed using a precision balance.

2.3 Characterization

Scanning electron microscopy (SEM) was performed to provide the surface image of the sample, and SEM equipped with energy-dispersive X-ray spectroscopy (EDS) was used to examine elements. The X-ray diffraction (XRD) technique was utilized at room temperature to characterize the phases present on oxidized stainless steels, and the incident Cu-Kα, α = 1.5406 Å was utilized. XRD patterns obtained from the experiment were matched with the standard patterns by X'Pert HighScore program which was reported as an ICDD number.

3 Results and discussion

The results of the testing were reported in four sections. Firstly, oxidation was tested of both low and high Mn stainless steel oxidized in O_2-5%H_2O for 1 h up to 96 h at 800 °C. Second, the volatilization rates of the samples were measured in O_2-5%H_2O at 800 °C for 96 h. SEM-EDS results of the oxidized sample and the XRD were exhibited in the last section.

3.1 Oxidation test

During the experimental workpieces, measured the weights of the specimens before and after putting the specimen in the furnace with a five-digit weighting machine. It was converted to mass gain which weight change divided by surface area of the specimen. Figure 1 shows mass gain in mg.cm^{-2} as a function of time for both stainless steel samples during the oxidation test in O_2-5%H_2O at 800 °C. We found that the mass gain of the high Mn stainless steel sample has values lower than zero and begins at 4 h. It means that spallation behaviors of the thermal oxide growth occur on the surface of the sample. In contrast, the mass gain of low Mn steel rises with time. The result provides that the Mn content in metal substrates has an impact on the formation of thermal oxide.

3.2 Volatilization rates

For the volatile species phase of the thermal oxide growth on stainless, Table 2 shows Cr, Mn and Fe-species volatilization rates of both low and high Mn stainless steel oxidized in O_2-5%H_2O for 96 h at 800 °C. During the oxidation test, the metal volatile phase was entrapped at the end of the furnace tube in a condenser bottle. The quantitative determination of volatile metal was evaluated by the ICP-OES method. This analytic method can enable the elements in the 0.1 to 50 ppb [18]. The volatilization rate was presented in terms of the mass of volatile metals per surface area and time. It was found that Cr volatilization rates in high Mn stainless steel are 14 times lower than in low Mn stainless steel, while Fe and Mn volatilization rates increase by 10 and 62 times. The dominant volatilization species phases may be hydroxide compounds of Cr Mn and Fe. There were $CrO_2(OH)_2$, $Mn(OH)_2$ and $Fe(OH)_2$, respectively [19].

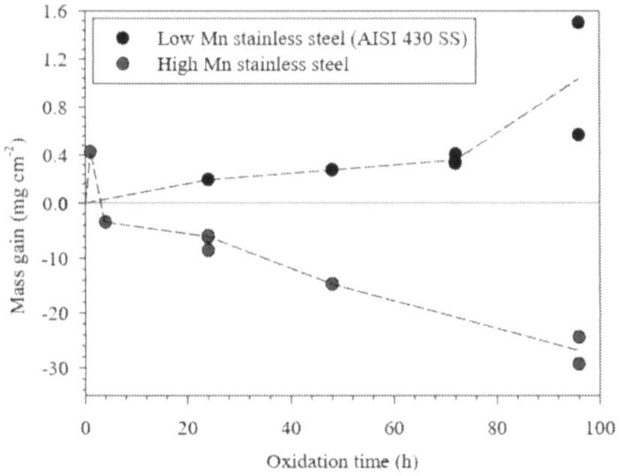

Fig. 1. Mass gain as a function of time of the sample during the oxidation test in O_2 5%H_2O at 800 °C.

Table 2. Cr, Mn and Fe-species volatilization rates of both low and high Mn stainless steel oxidized in O_2-5%H_2O at 800 °C for 96 h.

Stainless steel	Volatilization rates ($\times 10^{-11}$ g cm^{-2} s^{-1})		
	Cr	Mn	Fe
Low Mn	1.25 ± 0.66	0.08 ± 0.03	1.34 ± 0.48
High Mn	0.09 ± 0.01	4.96 ± 1.52	13.66 ± 6.67

3.3 SEM and EDS

Cross-sectional SEM images and EDS mapping results of the oxidized low Mn stainless steel after the test in O_2-5%H_2O at 800 °C for 96 h is revealed as shown in Figure 2 at 170x magnitude image. It can see that the thermally grown oxides on the stainless-steel substrate have two types. There is a large nodule of oxide and a thin continuous oxide layer. For the EDS mapping, the outer part of nodule oxide consists of Fe and O which is the main element distribution in outward growth nodule oxide. Moreover, Mn, Fe, and O were detected covering the outer part of nodule oxide. The inner part of the nodule oxide has Cr, Fe, and O. It was indicated that this oxide is an inward growth to metal substrates. Nearly the nodule oxide, a thin continuous oxide layer is found. Mn, Cr, and O were obtained in this layer. For high Mn stainless steel 96 h shown in Figure 3, it has a thicker oxide layer composed of Cr, Mn, Fe and O which surface of the oxide is covered by a thin oxide layer of Mn, Fe and O but most of the outer oxide layer consists of Cr and O.

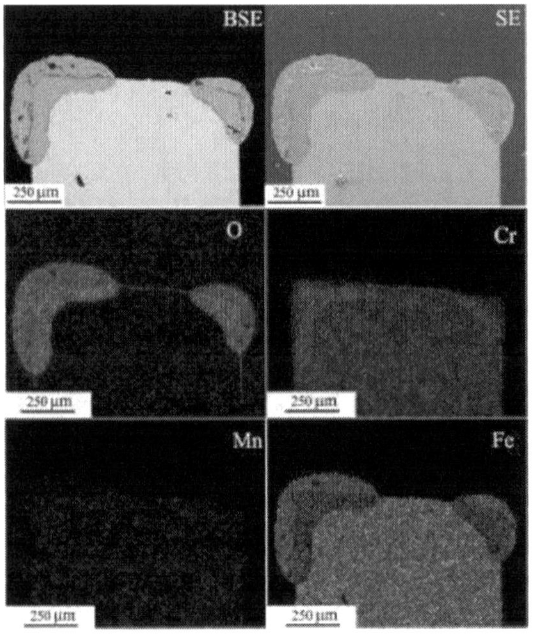

Fig. 2. Cross-sectional micrographs and EDS mapping results of low Mn stainless steel oxidized after 96 h (170x magnitude image).

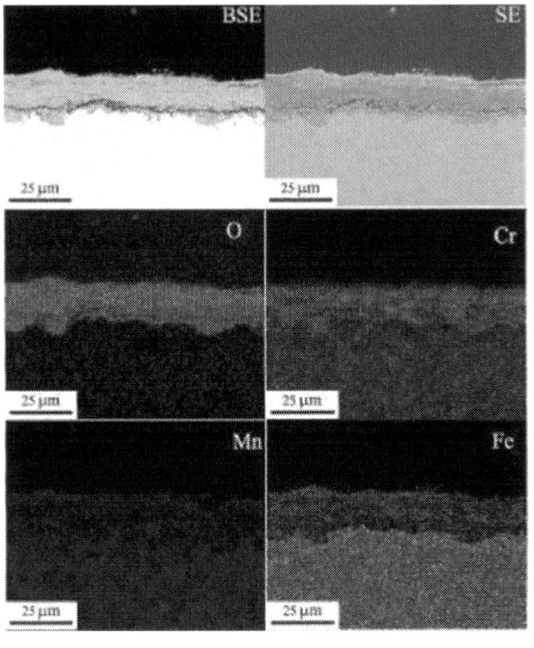

Fig. 3. Cross-sectional micrographs and EDS mapping results of high Mn stainless steel oxidized after 96 h (1,000x magnitude image).

3.4 XRD phase identification

To identify the oxide phases formed after the test, the X-ray diffraction technique was applied to the samples. Figure 4 shows XRD pattern of the oxidized low Mn stainless steel in O_2-5%H_2O at 800 °C for 96 h. The peaks of $MnFe_2O_4$ (ICDD 00-010-0319), Cr_2O_3 (ICDD 00-002-1362), $(Cr, Fe)_2O_3$ (ICDD 00-002-1357) and Fe_2O_3 (ICDD 00-013-0534) were detected on the surface sample. For the oxidized high Mn stainless steel for 1 h at the same oxidation atmosphere and temperature test, peaks $MnCr_2O_4$ (ICDD 01-075-1614) and $Fe_{0.902}O$ (ICDD 01-086-2316). When increasing the oxidation time to 96 h. The sample has peaks of $MnCr_2O_4$ (ICDD 01-075-1614), Mn_2O_3 (ICD 00-001-1061), Cr_2O_3 (ICDD 00-002-1362) and Fe_3O_4 (ICDD 01-074-0748).

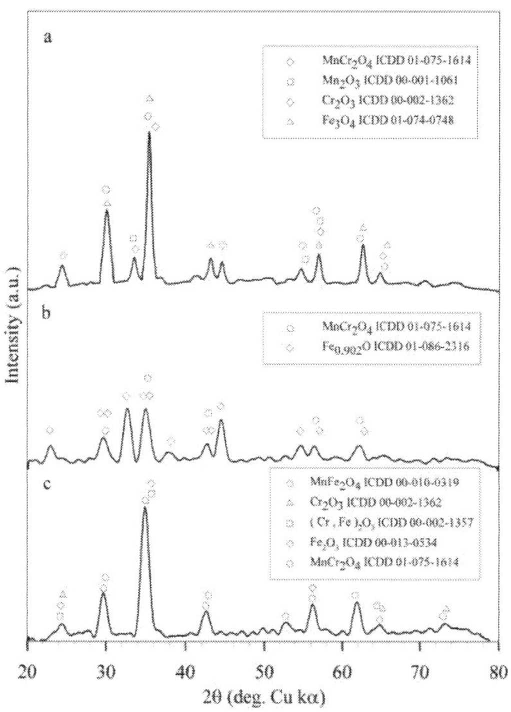

Fig. 4. XRD patterns of high Mn stainless steel oxidized in O_2-5%H_2O at 800 °C for 96 h (a), 1 h (b) and low Mn stainless steel for 96 h (c)

Figure 5 shows the behavior of oxide growth on low Mn stainless steel. The nodule oxide was formed at an angle on the sample. This nodule occurs because of the direction of the gas flow, the angle was turbulent. Nevertheless, the thin oxide layer beside the nodule was covered by Cr_2O_3 and $MnCr_2O_4$. It is close to the SEM-EDS mapping and XRD results. That is why Cr is highly volatile shown in Table 2. According to Asteman *et. al.* [8] found that the nodule oxide formed (Breakaway oxidation) on 304L stainless steel at 500-800 °C in O_2-40%H_2O atmospheres as a result of the flow rate. It was obtained from $(Cr,Fe)_2O_3$ and Fe_2O_3 oxide formation. In this case, the results were similar.

From the results of high Mn stainless steel, it can be inferred that the thermal oxide growth was shown in Figure 6. At the initial time, $MnCr_2O_4$ covering FeO was fabricated by Cr and Mn reacting with O. After that $MnCr_2O_4$ and FeO interdiffusion to create the Mn-Cr-Fe oxide. In the long term, Mn and Fe diffuse through the Mn-Cr-Fe oxide to form $(Mn,Fe)_2O_3$ or $(Mn,Fe)_3O_4$ on the top surface. This phase contributes to the volatile phases of Mn and Fe. It related to volatilization rate results, which are measured. When the sample was cooled down from high temperatures to room temperature. Spallation can occur. Moreover, the results were closed to A.L. Marasco and D.J. Young [20]. They found that the high Mn element in stainless steel oxidized at 900 °C at an oxygen partial pressure of 26.7 kPa, which makes bixbyite-$(Mn, Fe)_2O_3$-and α -Fe_2O_3 oxides and increases the high oxidation rate, then spallation occurs.

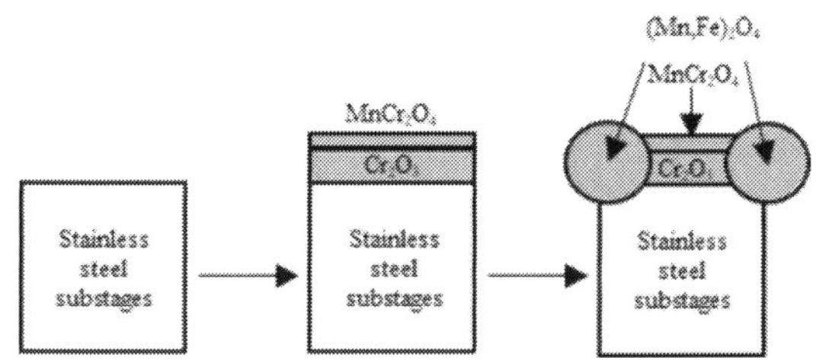

Fig. 5. Schematic sketch behavior of oxide growth on low Mn stainless steel.

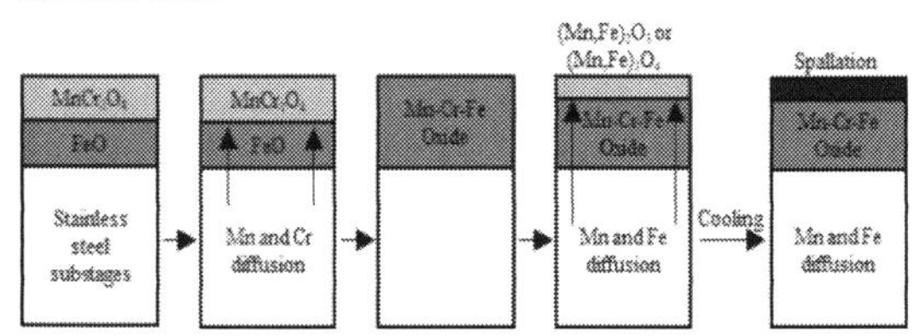

Fig. 6. Schematic sketch behavior of oxide growth on high Mn stainless steel.

4 Conclusion

In the present work, stainless steel with high manganese content (Fe-15.32 wt.% Cr-8.94 wt.% Mn) and low manganese content as AISI 430 stainless steel (Fe-16.41 wt.% Cr-0.79 wt.% Mn) were oxidized in O_2-5%H_2O atmospheres at 800 °C for 1 h up to 96 h. The summary was described as follows.

1) Manganese in stainless steel induces spallation of oxide after oxidization in O_2-5%H_2O at 800 °C as a result of nodule oxide formation.
2) Cr volatilization rates in high Mn stainless steel are lower than the other by a factor of 14, while Fe and Mn volatilization rates increase by 10 and 62 times, respectively. It may be possible that Mn-Fe oxide formed at the outer layer.

As a recommendation, the selection of stainless steel for industrial Mn concentration should be suitable to reduce Cr loss and avoid spallation of the oxide scale.

Acknowledgements

The authors acknowledge the financial support from National Science, Research and Innovation Fund (NSRF) and King Mongkut's University of Technology North Bangkok (Contract no. KMUTNB-FF-66-22).

References

1. S. Chandra-Ambhorn, T. Thublaor, C. Pascal, Thermodynamics and kinetics of the high temperature oxidation of stainless steels, Solid State Phenomena, **300**, (2020): 1-24
2. R. Peraldi, B.A. Pint, Effect of Cr and Ni contents on the oxidation behavior of ferritic and austenitic model alloys in air with water vapor, Oxidation of metals, **61**, (2004): 463-483
3. J. Ehlers, D.J. Young, E.J. Smaardijk, A.K. Tyagi, H. J. Penkalla, L. Singheiser, W.J. Quadakkers, Enhanced oxidation of the 9% Cr steel P91 in water vapour containing environments, Corrosion science, **48**, (2006): 3428-3454
4. D.B. Wei, J.X. Huang, A.W. Zhang, Z.Y. Jiang, A.K. Tieu, X. Shi, S.H. Jiao, X.Y. Qu, Study on the oxidation of stainless steels 304 and 304L in humid air and the friction during hot rolling, Wear, **267** (2009): 1741-1745
5. L. Intiso, L.G. Johansson, J.E. Svensson, M. Halvarsson, Oxidation of Sanicro 25 (42Fe22Cr25NiWCuNbN) in O_2 and O_2+H_2O environments at 600-750 °C, Oxidation of metals, **83**, (2015): 367-391
6. G. Li, Y. Gou, J. Qiao, W. Sun, Z. Wang, K. Sun, Recent progress of tubular solid oxide fuel cell: From materials to applications, Journal of power sources, **477** (2020): 228693
7. W. Wongpromrat, H. Thaikan, W. Chandra-ambhorn, S. Chandra-ambhorn, Chromium vaporisation from AISI 441 stainless steel oxidised in humidified oxygen, Oxidation of metals, **79**, (2013): 529-540
8. H. Asteman, J.E. Svensson, L.G. Johansson, Evidence for chromium evaporation influencing the oxidation of 304L: the effect of temperature and flow rate, Oxidation of metals, **57**, (2002): 193-216
9. M. Kemp, A. van Bennekom, F.P.A. Robinson, Evaluation of the corrosion and mechanical properties of a range of experimental Cr-Mn stainless steels, Structural Materials: Properties, Microstructure and Processing, **199**, (1995): 183-194
10. R.L. Klueh, P.J. Maziasz, E.H. Lee, Manganese as an austenite stabilizer in Fe-Cr-Mn-C steels, Structural Materials: Properties, Microstructure and Processing, **102**, (1988): 115-124
11. F.H. Stott, G.C. Wood, J. Stringer, The influence of alloying elements on the development and maintenance of protective scales, Oxidation of metals, **44**, (1995): 113-145
12. S.N. Basu, G.J. Yurek, Effect of alloy grain size and silicon content on the oxidation of austenitic Fe-Cr-Ni-Mn-Si alloys in pure O_2, Oxidation of metals, **36**, (1991): 281-315
13. D.L. Douglass, J.S. Armijo, The effect of silicon and manganese on the oxidation mechanism of Ni-20 Cr, Oxidation of metals, **2**, (1970): 207-231
14. D.L. Douglass, J.S. Armijo, The influence of manganese and silicon on the oxidation behavior of Co-20Cr, Oxidation of metals, **3**, (1971): 185-202
15. G.N. Irving, J. Stringer, D.P. Whittle, Effect of the possible fcc stabilizers Mn, Fe, and Ni on the high-temperature oxidation of Co-Cr alloys, Oxidation of metals, **8**, (1974): 393-407
16. H. Falk-Windisch, J.E. Svensson, J. Froitzheim, The effect of temperature on chromium vaporization and oxide scale growth on interconnect steels for Solid Oxide Fuel Cells, Journal of power sources, **287**, (2015): 25-35
17. Barin I. Platzki G. *Thermochemical data of pure substances* (Weinheim: VCh, 1989)
18. McMahon G. *Analytical instrumentation: a guide to laboratory, portable and miniaturized instruments* (John Wiley & Sons, 2008)
19. D.L. Myers, N.S. Jacobson, C.W. Bauschlicher, E.J. Opila, Thermochemistry of volatile metal hydroxides and oxyhydroxides at elevated temperatures. Journal of Materials Research, **34**, (2019): 394-407
20. A.L. Marasco, D.J. Young, The oxidation of Iron-Chromium-Manganese alloys at 900 °C, Oxidation of metals, **36**, (1991): 157-174

Machine Learning Techniques for the Design and Optimization of Polymer Composites: A Review

J. Maniraj[1], *Felix Sahayaraj* Arockiasamy *[1], *C. Ram* Kumar[1], *D. Ashok* Kumar[1], *I.* Jenish[2], *Indran* Suyambulingam[3], *Sanjay Mavinkere* Rangappa[3], *Suchart* Siengchin[3]

[1] Department of Mechanical Engineering, KIT-Kalaignarkarunanidhi Institute of Technology, Coimbatore, Tamil Nadu, India.
[2] Department of Applied Mechanics, Seenu Atoll School, Hulhu-medhoo, Addu City, Maldives.
[3] Natural Composites Research Group Lab, Department of Materials and Production Engineering, The Sirindhorn International Thai-German School of Engineering (TGGS), King Mongkut's University of Technology North Bangkok (KMUTNB), Bangkok, Thailand.

Abstract. Polymer composites are employed in a variety of applications due to their distinctive characteristics. Nevertheless, designing and optimizing these materials can be a lengthy and resource-intensive process for low cost and sustainable materials. Machine learning has the potential to simplify this process by offering predictions of the characteristics of novel composite materials based on their microstructures. This review outlines machine learning techniques and highlights the potential of machine learning to improve the design and optimization of polymer composites. This review also examines the difficulties and restrictions of utilizing machine learning in this context and offers insights into potential future research paths in this field.

Keyword. Design, Machine learning, Mechanical properties, Optimization, Physical properties, Polymer composites

1 Introduction

In recent times, the utilization of polymer composites has grown significantly, particularly in high-performance applications like aerospace, automotive, and defense [1]. As an example, the aerospace industry has seen the use of composites in aircraft structures rise from 7% of the total weight in the 1990s to over 50% in some of the most recent commercial airliners [2-3]. This expansion is propelled by the rising demand for lightweight, high-strength materials, as well as the need for more eco-friendly materials that have a lower carbon footprint than traditional materials like metals. When creating polymer composites, it is essential to select the right combination of matrix and reinforcement materials, as well as the right processing conditions, in order to achieve the desired properties. Currently, this is usually done through trial and error, which can be time-consuming and require a lot of resources. Machine learning has the great potential to simplify the process by using algorithms to examine extensive datasets of composite testing outcomes and forecast the characteristics of new composite materials based on their microstructures [4]. Although machine learning is still in its early stages of being used for the design and optimization of polymer composites, its potential advantages are considerable. By utilizing the right data and algorithms, machine learning can significantly enhance the efficiency and efficacy of composite material development, resulting in the production of new materials with superior characteristics and a reduced cost of development.

As the need for high-performance and sustainable materials increases, the effective use of advanced techniques is becoming increasingly significant. By utilizing machine learning algorithms, it is possible to analyze extensive datasets of composite testing outcomes and forecast the characteristics of new composite materials based on their microstructures. This can significantly enhance the speed and precision of the development process, lower the development cost, and enable the creation of new materials with enhanced characteristics [5]. The potential advantages of utilizing machine learning in this context are considerable and can have a beneficial effect on a broad range of industries [6]. Machine learning has the potential to reduce the need for trial-and-error experimentation and enable the creation of new high-performance materials, thus promoting the development of more sustainable materials and helping to build a more sustainable future [7].

Crafting polymer composites is a complex and resource-intensive process that necessitates the selection of a suitable combination of matrix and reinforcement materials, as well as the proper processing conditions, to attain the desired characteristics. Currently, this process is typically done through trial and error, which is both time-consuming and not always successful in producing the desired outcomes. The use of machine learning to design and optimize polymer composites is a rapidly growing field that could greatly accelerate and refine the development process. By utilizing algorithms to analyze extensive datasets of composite testing results, machine

* Corresponding author: indransdesign@gmail.com

learning algorithms predict the characteristics of novel composite materials based on their microstructures, thus enabling the development of novel materials.

The utilization of machine learning to create and enhance polymer composites is an expanding area with great potential. The energy storage and saving materials can be optimized using these novel techniques. The current research in this area seeks to assess recent research works, which apply machine learning techniques to improve the design and optimization of polymer composites. This involves creating and assessing machine-learning algorithms for forecasting the characteristics of polymer composites based on their microstructures and assessing the potential advantages of using machine learning, such as increased efficiency, accuracy, and cost savings. Nevertheless, there are difficulties and restrictions related to using machine learning in this context that must be addressed. To progress in the field, future studies should concentrate on uncovering research possibilities and helping to build a more thorough comprehension of the part of material science.

2 Current state of art

Although the applying machine learning techniques in the creation and optimization of polymer composites is still in its early stages, there is mounting evidence of its potential to improve the development process [8]. Several studies have demonstrated that machine learning algorithms can be employed to forecast the properties of the polymer composites. This has demonstrated encouraging outcomes in terms of enhanced accuracy and efficiency in comparison to traditional trial-and-error methods. For instance, some research has demonstrated that machine learning algorithms can accurately forecast the mechanical properties of composites and that these forecasts can be used to optimize the microstructure of the composites to enhance their performance [9].

Applying machine learning to the design and optimization of polymer composites could bring about numerous advantages. To begin with, machine-learning algorithms can process extensive datasets of combined testing outcomes and detect patterns that are not easily discernible by human specialists [10]. This can result in more precise forecasts of the characteristics of novel composite materials, thereby allowing for the creation of materials with enhanced properties. Secondly, machine learning can drastically reduce development costs by lessening the need for trial-and-error experimentation. Thirdly, machine-learning algorithms can be employed to refine the microstructure of composites for better performance, thereby allowing the production of new composites with enhanced characteristics. Machine learning has the potential to revolutionize the design and optimization of polymer composites, which could have a positive effect on many industries. There is an increasing awareness of the necessity for new, more effective methods for creating polymer composites, and machine learning could be a major factor in satisfying this requirement.

3 Challenges and limitations

Despite the great potential of machine learning in the polymer composites, there are also a number of difficulties and restrictions associated with its application. Figure 1 illustrates the difficulties in using machine learning techniques to optimize polymer composites.

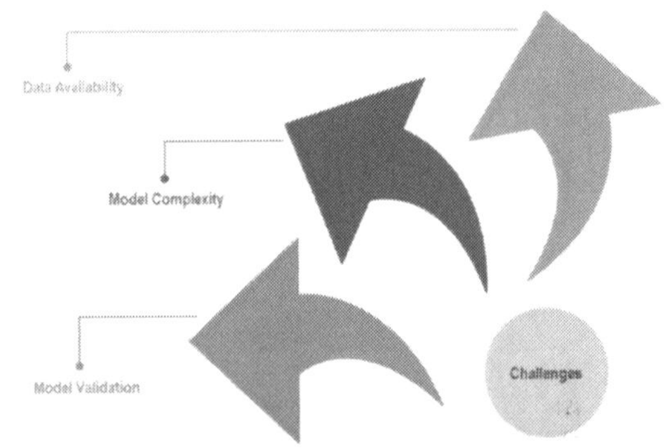

Fig. 1. Challenges of machine learning in the design and optimization of polymer composites.

A major obstacle to using machine learning in this context is the lack of high-quality, pertinent data. Accurate predictions by machine learning algorithms necessitate large datasets of composite testing results, which can be challenging and time-consuming to obtain [11]. Furthermore, the data must be varied and accurately reflect the materials and microstructures of interest. Another issue is that polymer composites are intricate materials and forecasting their characteristics based on their microstructures is a difficult task. [12] was cited. This can make it challenging to create machine-learning algorithms that are both precise and computationally economical. The third challenge is verifying the accuracy of machine learning models. The accuracy of machine learning algorithms must be tested against experimental data, which can be a lengthy and costly process. Despite these difficulties, there is increasing acknowledgment of the potential of machine learning in the development and optimization of polymer composites, and the field is advancing quickly [13].

To make progress in this area and address these issues, future research should concentrate on creating more precise, efficient, and scalable machine-learning algorithms and enhancing the quality and amount of data available for training these algorithms. Furthermore, research should concentrate on creating and confirming machine learning models for a broader selection of polymer composites, as well as investigating novel methods for validating and enhancing the models. Reference number fourteen. To sum up, the application of machine learning in the development and optimization of polymer composites is a burgeoning field with great potential, yet also presents a variety of challenges that must be addressed. Going forward, research in this field should concentrate on refining the accuracy, efficiency, and scalability of machine-learning algorithms, as well as increasing the quality and quantity of data used to train these algorithms. With sustained investment in research and development, machine learning has the potential to revolutionize the design and optimization of polymer composites [14].

4 Machine learning algorithms for predicting the properties of polymer composites based on their microstructure

Developing and testing machine-learning algorithms for predicting the properties of polymer composites based on their microstructures is a critical step in realizing the potential of machine learning in this field. Several steps were involved in this process shown in figure 2.

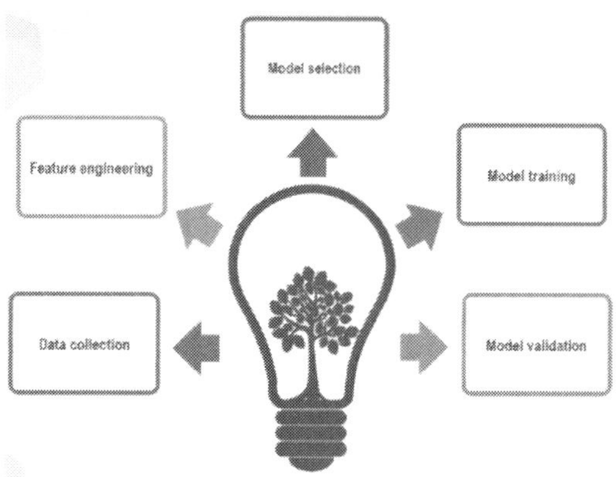

Fig. 2. Steps involved in the machine learning algorithms for predicting the properties of polymer composites.

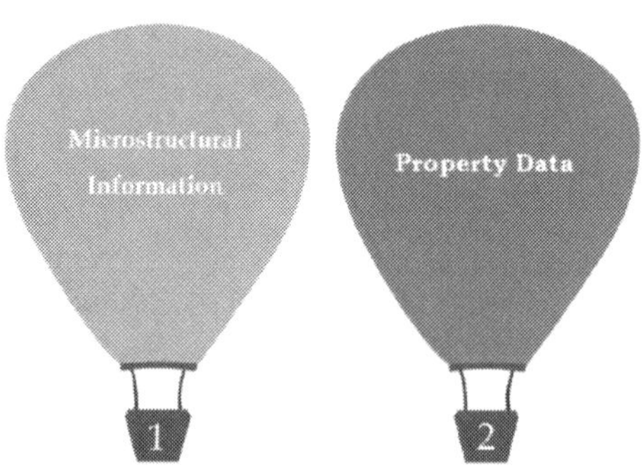

Fig. 3. Steps involved in the data collection.

Gathering data is a critical step in the creation and evaluation of machine-learning algorithms for forecasting the characteristics of polymer composites based on their microstructures [15]. The aim of the data collection was to acquire a comprehensive and representative dataset of composite testing outcomes, encompassing both microstructural details and property data. These data were employed to educate and assess the machine-learning algorithms.

Figure 3 illustrates the steps involved in the data collection process. This includes details about the composition, structure, and geometry of the polymer composites, such as the size, shape, and arrangement of the reinforcement fibers or particles [16]. This data can be acquired through methods such as microscopy, computed tomography (CT), and image processing. This includes data on the physical and mechanical characteristics of polymer composites, such as their strength, rigidity, resilience, and thermal behavior [17]. These data can be acquired through a variety of testing methods, including tensile testing, compression testing, and impact testing. It is essential to guarantee that the gathered data accurately reflects the materials and microstructures of interest and that it is of superior quality. This may necessitate gathering data from multiple sources and in different contexts, as well as filtering or cleaning the data to eliminate any outliers or mistakes [18]. Ultimately, data collection is a key component in the creation and testing of machine learning algorithms for forecasting the characteristics of polymer composites based on their microstructures, and it is imperative to guarantee that the collected data is representative, varied, and of excellent quality.

Feature engineering is an essential step in the creation and evaluation of machine-learning algorithms for forecasting the characteristics of polymer composites based on their microstructures. The aim of feature engineering is to draw out pertinent features from microstructural data that can be used as inputs for machine learning algorithms [19]. The numerical features are numerical values that depict the microstructural characteristics of polymer composites, such as the average fiber diameter, volume fraction of the reinforcement, and orientation of the fibers. These characteristics can be acquired through image analysis or other data processing methods. Textural Features describe the texture of the microstructure, such as the arrangement of the reinforcement fibers or particles, the form of the pores, and the roughness of the surfaces [20]. These characteristics can be acquired through image analysis or other data processing methods. Statistical Features that quantify the statistical distribution of the microstructural characteristics of polymer composites, such as the mean, standard deviation, skewness, and kurtosis. These characteristics can be acquired through statistical analysis or other data-processing methods. Figure 4 illustrates the different types of extraction features used to analyze the composites.

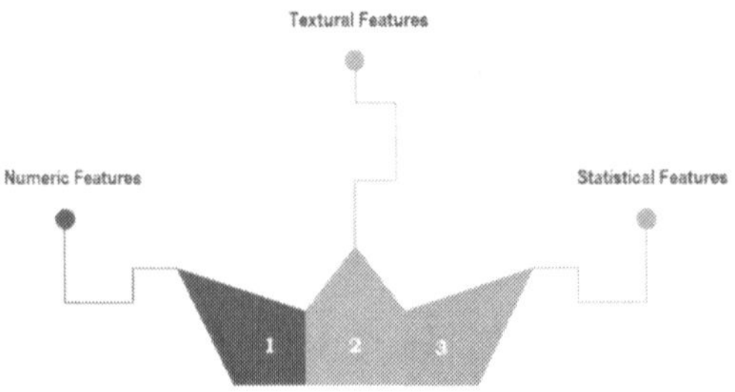

Fig. 4. Types of features extraction for analysis.

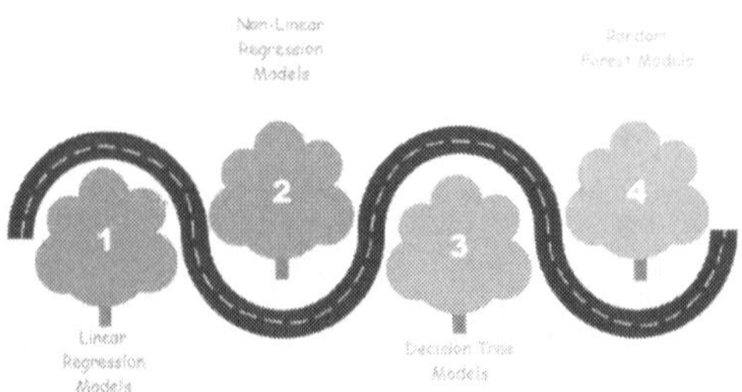

Fig. 5. Types of machine learning models.

It is essential to guarantee that the extracted features are pertinent and significant for the issue being addressed and that they can record the vital connections between the microstructure and characteristics of the polymer composites. This could necessitate transforming the data or combining multiple features to generate new and more informative features. Feature engineering is a key part of creating and evaluating machine learning algorithms for predicting the characteristics of polymer composites based on their microstructures. It is essential to make sure that the extracted features are pertinent, significant, and able to capture the significant connections between the microstructure and properties of the polymer composites.

Selecting the right model is a critical step in creating and assessing machine-learning algorithms for forecasting the characteristics of polymer composites based on their microstructures [21]. The objective of model selection is to identify the most suitable machine learning model to depict the connections between the microstructure and characteristics of the polymer composites [22]

Figure 5 illustrates the various machine learning models used for optimization. Linear Regression Models were employed to forecast continuous output based on a linear combination of input characteristics. These models are straightforward and easy to comprehend, yet they may not be able to accurately depict the intricate connections between the microstructure and properties of polymer composites. Nonlinear regression models are employed to forecast continuous output based on a nonlinear combination of input variables. These are more versatile and can capture more intricate connections between the microstructure and characteristics of polymer composites, though they may be more challenging to comprehend [23]. Decision Tree Models are employed to forecast a categorical output based on a sequence of decisions based on the input characteristics. While these models are straightforward and easy to comprehend, they may not be able to accurately depict the intricate connections between the microstructure and characteristics of polymer composites. Random Forest Models are employed to forecast categorical outcomes based on a combination of multiple decision trees. These models are more flexible and can account for more intricate connections between the microstructure and characteristics of polymer composites, though they may be harder to interpret. It is essential to consider a range of model types and utilize suitable evaluation metrics to compare the effectiveness of various models. The ultimate model selection should be based on its performance on the validation data and its capacity to extrapolate to new, unseen data [24]. To sum up, model selection is a key step in creating and evaluating machine-learning algorithms for forecasting the characteristics of polymer composites based on their microstructures. It is essential to evaluate a range of model types and select the most suitable model based on its performance on validation data and its capacity to extrapolate to new, unseen data.

Model training is an essential step in the creation and evaluation of machine-learning algorithms for estimating the characteristics of polymer composites based on their microstructures [25]. The aim of model training is to calculate the parameters of the machine learning model based on the input and output characteristics of polymer composites. The training process usually involves dividing the available data into training and validation datasets. The training dataset was used to determine the parameters of the machine learning model, and the validation dataset was used to evaluate the model's accuracy and ensure that it can be applied to new, unseen data. The training process typically involves repeatedly modifying the model parameters to minimize the difference between the predicted and actual characteristics of polymer composites [26]. The model parameters can be assessed using a range of metrics, such as mean squared error or mean absolute error, and the model can be further improved by altering the parameters or the features used as inputs. To conclude, model training is a key element in the creation and assessment of machine-learning algorithms to forecast the characteristics of polymer composites based on their microstructures. It is critical to divide the available data into training and validation datasets in order to adjust the model parameters iteratively to reduce the discrepancy between the predicted properties and the actual properties of the polymer composites, and to assess the model's performance using suitable metrics.

Model validation is a critical step in the development and evaluation of machine-learning algorithms for predicting the properties of polymer composites based on their microstructures [27]. The purpose of model validation is to assess the machine learning model's performance on data it has not seen before and to ensure that the model is suitable for different data distributions. The validation process typically involves splitting the existing data into training and validation datasets. The training dataset was used to determine the parameters of the machine learning model, and the validation dataset was used to assess the model's performance on data not seen before. To evaluate the model's accuracy on the validation data, metrics such as mean squared error, mean absolute error, R-squared, and correlation coefficient can be used. These metrics provide insight into the accuracy and reliability of the model and can be used to assess the performance of different models. In addition to metrics, it is also important to visually evaluate the model's performance on the validation data, for instance by plotting the predicted values against the actual values or plotting the discrepancy between the predicted values and the actual values. These plots can provide insight into how the model performs in different parts of the feature space and can help identify any potential outliers or areas where the model does not perform optimally [28]. Briefly, model validation is a critical step in the development and testing of machine learning algorithms for predicting the properties of polymer composites based on their microstructures; it is essential to split the available data into training and validation datasets to evaluate the performance of the model on the validation data using appropriate metrics, and to visually inspect the performance of the model on the validation data to ensure that it generalizes well to different data distributions.

5 Machine learning in the design and optimization of polymer composites can bring several potential benefits, including improved efficiency, accuracy, and cost savings

A key advantage is the enhanced efficiency. Machine learning algorithms can automate the process of forecasting the characteristics of polymer composites based on their microstructures, thereby cutting down the time and effort needed for this task. This can expedite the design and optimization process, potentially leading to greater productivity and efficiency in the production of polymer composites [29]. Another advantage of utilizing machine learning in the engineering and optimization of polymer composites is the increased precision. Machine learning algorithms can detect the intricate connections between the microstructure and properties of these materials, leading to more precise predictions of the properties of polymer composites than traditional empirical models or simulations [30]. This can enhance the dependability and strength of the design and optimization processes, resulting in higher-quality products. Furthermore, machine learning can be employed to create and optimize polymer composites, leading to cost savings. Automating the prediction process can reduce the need for manual labor and experimentation, thereby decreasing labor and material expenses related to testing [31]. Furthermore, more precise predictions can lead to better design and optimization, which can minimize the risk of expensive errors and enhance the overall effectiveness of the development process [32]. To sum up, machine learning has the potential to bring about greater efficiency, accuracy, and cost savings in the design and optimization of polymer composites, making it a field of study and application that is worth exploring.

6 Opportunities for future research in the area of machine learning and the design and optimization of polymer composites

There are numerous possibilities for further research in the field of machine learning and the development and optimization of polymer composites [33]. The current state of the field furnishes a strong basis for further research into creating more sophisticated machine-learning algorithms for forecasting the characteristics of polymer composites based on their microstructures [34]. This could involve the creation of deep learning algorithms that have yielded encouraging outcomes in other contexts [35]. The precision of machine-learning algorithms is largely contingent on the quality and quantity of the dataset used for training [36]. Future studies should concentrate on enlarging the dataset used for training to encompass a broader selection of polymer composites, microstructures, and properties to enhance the precision and applicability of the algorithms. Combining with simulation tools: At present, machine-learning algorithms are employed as standalone tools for forecasting the characteristics of polymer composites [37]. Future studies should strive to combine machine-learning algorithms with simulation tools, enabling a smoother and more effective design and optimization process. Creation of multi-objective optimization algorithms: The fabrication and optimization of polymer composites often necessitate balancing multiple objectives, such as strength, stiffness, and cost [38].

Future studies should concentrate on creating multi-objective optimization algorithms that can take into account multiple objectives when optimizing the design of polymer composites. Despite the advantages of employing machine learning for the design and optimization of polymer composites, there are still a number of restrictions and difficulties that need to be investigated. Future studies should focus on exploring these limitations and difficulties and devising strategies to address them. To sum up, the realm of machine learning and the engineering and optimization of polymer composites present numerous possibilities for future exploration. By building on the existing knowledge base, researchers can help to create a more comprehensive comprehension of the role of machine learning in this domain and promote its progress.

7 Conclusion

The application of machine learning to the fabrication and enhancement of polymer composites is a burgeoning and promising field that offers numerous benefits. Machine-learning algorithms can automate the task of forecasting the properties of polymer composites based on their microstructures, leading to increased efficiency, precision, and cost savings. Despite the difficulties and obstacles associated with applying machine learning in this context, there are numerous possibilities for future research, including the creation of more sophisticated algorithms, enlarging the dataset used for training, combining with simulation tools, and exploring the limitations and challenges. The ongoing advancement of machine learning in this field has the potential to significantly influence the design and optimization of polymer composites, resulting in improved products and more efficient development procedures.

Availability of data and materials

All the data were included within the article.

Competing interest

The authors do not have any conflicts of interest regarding the publication of this paper in this journal.

Funding

The authors have not claimed any funding for this study. All data are interpreted in this paper and have not been discussed in any of the existing journals

Acknowledgements

The authors thank KIT-Kalaignarkarunanidhi Institute of Technology, Coimbatore for providing the facility support to complete this research work.

References

1. J. Zhang, V.S. Chevali, H. Wang, C.H. Wang, Current status of carbon fibre and carbon fibre composites recycling, Composites Part B: Engineering, **193** (2020): 108053
2. A.P. Mouritz, Introduction to aerospace materials, Elsevier, (2012)
3. M. Carus, A. Eder, L. Dammer, H. Korte, L. Scholz, R. Essel, M. Barth, Wood-plastic composites (WPC) and natural fibre composites (NFC), Nova-Institute: Hürth, Germany, **16** (2015)
4. M. Elbadawi, L.E. McCoubrey, F.K. Gavins, J.J. Ong, A. Goyanes, S. Gaisford, A.W. Basit, Disrupting 3D printing of medicines with machine learning, Trends in Pharmacological Sciences, **42**,9 (2021): 745-757
5. O. Faruk, A.K. Bledzki, H.P. Fink, M. Sain, Progress report on natural fiber reinforced composites, Macromolecular Materials and Engineering, **299**,1 (2014): 9-26
6. S. Athmaja, M. Hanumanthappa, V. Kavitha, A survey of machine learning algorithms for big data analytics, In 2017 International conference on innovations in information, embedded and communication systems (ICIIECS), IEEE, (2017): 1-4
7. A. Sharma, T. Mukhopadhyay, S.M. Rangappa, S. Siengchin, V. Kushvaha, Advances in computational intelligence of polymer composite materials: machine learning assisted modeling, analysis and design, Archives of Computational Methods in Engineering, **29**,5 (2022): 3341-3385
8. M.X. Zhu, Q.C. Yu, H.G. Song, T.X. Chen, J.M. Chen, Rational design of high-energy-density polymer composites by machine learning approach, ACS Applied Energy Materials, **4**,2 (2021): 1449-1458
9. Y.K. Hamidi, A. Berrado, M.C. Altan, Machine learning applications in polymer composites. In AIP Conference Proceedings, AIP Publishing, **2205**,1 (2020)
10. P. Pattnaik, A. Sharma, M. Choudhary, V. Singh, P. Agarwal, V. Kukshal, Role of machine learning in the field of Fiber reinforced polymer composites: A preliminary discussion. Materials Today: Proceedings, **44** (2021): 4703-4708
11. M.A. Matos, S.T. Pinho, V.L. Tagarielli, Application of machine learning to predict the multiaxial strain-sensing response of CNT-polymer composites, Carbon, **146**, (2019): 265-275
12. S. Cassola, M. Duhovic, T. Schmidt, D. May, Machine learning for polymer composites process simulation-a review, Composites Part B: Engineering, (2022): 110208
13. P.P. Das, M.M. Rabby, V. Vadlamudi, R. Raihan, Moisture content prediction in polymer composites using machine learning techniques, Polymers, **14**,20 (2022): 4403
14. J. Wang, M.A. Ayari, A. Khandakar, M.E. Chowdhury, S.A. Uz Zaman, T. Rahman, B. Vaferi, Estimating the relative crystallinity of biodegradable polylactic acid and polyglycolide polymer composites by machine learning methodologies, Polymers, **14**,3 (2022): 527
15. H.E. Balcıoğlu, A.Ç. Seçkin, Comparison of machine learning methods and finite element analysis on the fracture behavior of polymer composites, Archive of Applied Mechanics, **91** (2021): 223-239
16. B. Liu, N. Vu-Bac, X. Zhuang, X. Fu, T. Rabczuk, Stochastic integrated machine learning based multiscale approach for the prediction of the thermal conductivity in carbon nanotube reinforced polymeric composites, Composites Science and Technology, **224** (2022): 109425
17. G. Kamath, B. Mishra, S. Tiwari, A. Bhardwaj, S.S. Marar, S. Soni, S.B. Anjappa, Experimental and statistical evaluation of drilling induced damages in glass fiber reinforced polymer composites-Taguchi integrated supervised machine learning approach, Engineered Science, **19** (2022): 312-318

18. C.T. Chen, G.X. Gu, Machine learning for composite materials, MRs Communications, **9**,2 (2019): 556-566
19. A. Sharma, T. Mukhopadhyay, S.M. Rangappa, S. Siengchin, V. Kushvaha, Advances in computational intelligence of polymer composite materials: machine learning assisted modeling, analysis and design, Archives of Computational Methods in Engineering, **29**,5 (2022): 3341-3385
20. G.R. Arpitha, H. Mohit, P. Madhu, A. Verma, Effect of sugarcane bagasse and alumina reinforcements on physical, mechanical, and thermal characteristics of epoxy composites using artificial neural networks and response surface methodology, Biomass Conversion and Biorefinery, (2023): 1-19
21. G. Spathis, E. Kontou, Creep failure time prediction of polymers and polymer composites, Composites Science and Technology, **72**,9 (2012): 959-964
22. P.K. Penumakala, J. Santo, A. Thomas, A critical review on the fused deposition modeling of thermoplastic polymer composites, Composites Part B: Engineering, **201**, (2020): 108336
23. G. Anand, N. Alagumurthi, R. Elansezhian, K. Palanikumar, N. Venkateshwaran, Investigation of drilling parameters on hybrid polymer composites using grey relational analysis, regression, fuzzy logic, and ANN models, Journal of the Brazilian Society of Mechanical Sciences and Engineering, **40** (2018): 1-20
24. M. Noryani, S.M. Sapuan, M.T. Mastura, M.Y.M. Zuhri, E.S. Zainudin, A statistical framework for selecting natural fibre reinforced polymer composites based on regression model. Fibers and Polymers, **19** (2018): 1039-1049
25. H. El Kadi, Modeling the mechanical behavior of fiber-reinforced polymeric composite materials using artificial neural networks-A review, Composite structures, **73**,1 (2006): 1-23
26. S.M. Rangappa, S. Siengchin, H.N. Dhakal, Green-composites: Ecofriendly and sustainability, Applied Science and Engineering Progress, 13,3 (2020): 183-184
27. S.M. Rangappa, S. Siengchin, Natural fibers as perspective materials, Applied Science and Engineering Progress, **11**,4 (2018)
28. S.H. Jang, H. Yin, Effective electrical conductivity of carbon nanotube-polymer composites: a simplified model and its validation, Materials Research Express, **2**,4 (2015): 045602
29. F. Chen, J. Wang, Z. Guo, F. Jiang, R. Ouyang, P. Ding, Machine learning and structural design to optimize the flame retardancy of polymer nanocomposites with graphene oxide hydrogen bonded zinc hydroxystannate, ACS Applied Materials & Interfaces, **13**,45 (2021): 53425-53438
30. M. Puttegowda, H. Pulikkalparambil, S.M. Rangappa, Trends and developments in natural fiber composites, Applied Science and Engineering Progress, **14**,4 (2021): 543-552
31. M.C. de Souza, I. Moroz, I. Cesarino, A.L. Leão, M. Jawaid, O.A.T. Dias, A Review of Natural Fibers Reinforced Composites for Railroad Applications, Applied Science and Engineering Progress, **15**,2 (2022): 5800-5800
32. Y.D. Boon, S.C. Joshi, S.K. Bhudolia, G. Gohel, Recent advances on the design automation for performance-optimized fiber reinforced polymer composite components, Journal of Composites Science, **4**,2 (2020): 61
33. A. Milad, S.H. Hussein, A.R. Khekan, M. Rashid, H. Al-Msari, T.H. Tran, Development of ensemble machine learning approaches for designing fiber-reinforced polymer composite strain prediction model, Engineering with Computers, **38**,4 (2022): 3625-3637
34. D. Yue, Y. Feng, X.X. Liu, J.H. Yin, W.C. Zhang, H. Guo, Q.Q. Lei, Prediction of Energy Storage Performance in Polymer Composites Using High-Throughput Stochastic Breakdown Simulation and Machine Learning, Advanced Science, **9**,17 (2022): 2105773
35. M.X. Zhu, Q.C. Yu, H.G. Song, T.X. Chen, J.M. Chen, Rational design of high-energy-density polymer composites by machine learning approach, ACS Applied Energy Materials, **4**,2 (2021): 1449-1458
36. M. Shi, C.P. Feng, J. Li, S.Y. Guo, Machine learning to optimize nanocomposite materials for electromagnetic interference shielding, Composites Science and Technology, **223** (2022): 109414
37. Z. Liang, Z. Li, S. Zhou, Y. Sun, J. Yuan, C. Zhang, Machine-learning exploration of polymer compatibility, Cell Reports Physical Science, **3**,6 (2022): 100931
38. H. Wei, S. Zhao, Q. Rong, H. Bao, Predicting the effective thermal conductivities of composite materials and porous media by machine learning methods, International Journal of Heat and Mass Transfer, **127** (2018): 908-916

Sustainable Smart Polymer Composite Materials: A Comprehensive Review

A.Felix Sahayaraj*[1], *S.* Dhamotharan[1], *D.* Sandeep[1], *P.* Ramachandran[1], *I.* Jenish[2], *Divya* Divakaran[3], *Indran* Suyambulingam[3], *M. R.* Sanjay[3], *Suchart* Siengchin[3]

[1] Department of Mechanical Engineering, KIT-Kalaignarkarunanidhi Institute of Technology, Coimbatore, Tamil Nadu, India
[2] Department of Applied Mechanics, Seenu Atoll School, Hulhu-medhoo, Addu City, Maldives
[3] Natural Composites Research Group Lab, Department of Materials and Production Engineering, The Sirindhorn International Thai-German School of Engineering (TGGS), King Mongkut's University of Technology North Bangkok (KMUTNB), Bangkok, Thailand

Abstract. This review provides a thorough analysis of the progress made in smart polymer composite materials, which have recently been seen as potential game-changers in areas such as construction, aerospace, biomedical engineering, and energy. This article emphasizes the distinctive characteristics of these materials, including their responsiveness to stimuli like temperature, light, and pressure, and their potential uses in different industries. This paper also examines the difficulties and restrictions associated with the creation and utilization of smart polymer composite materials. This review seeks to provide a thorough understanding of smart polymer composite materials and their potential to offer innovative solutions for a variety of applications.

Keyword. Advanced engineering, Composite technology, Cutting-edge, Futuristic materials, Polymer composites, Smart materials

1 Introduction

The global polymer composite market is anticipated to expand rapidly in the near future, propelled by various factors, including the rising demand from the transportation and aerospace industries [1]. In 2020, the market size was estimated to be USD 73.56 billion and is projected to reach USD 102.79 billion by 2028, increasing at a CAGR of 4.5% [2]. The use of polymer composites in the transportation sector is anticipated to expand at a CAGR of 7.2% from 2020 to 2027, while the aerospace industry is projected to be the main driver of the polymer composite market with an estimated CAGR of 5.9% from 2020 to 2027 [3]. The construction sector is also anticipated to make a substantial contribution, with an estimated compound annual growth rate of 6.7% from 2020 to 2027. The Asia-Pacific region is projected to account for 42.3% of the polymer composite market in 2020. These figures demonstrate the increasing potential of polymer composites, including smart polymer composites, to revolutionize multiple industries around the world [4].

Polymer composites, including smart polymer composites, are essential in many industries due to their durability, lightweight, cost-efficiency, versatility, and eco-friendly characteristics [5]. Polymer composites are renowned for their strength and durability, making them suitable for use in demanding applications, such as aerospace and transportation. Additionally, they are lighter than traditional materials, a key factor for lightweight structures and vehicles. Furthermore, polymer composites can be produced more quickly and in larger amounts, making them more economical than traditional materials. Their versatility makes them suitable for a variety of uses, and many are made from renewable resources and are recyclable, making them eco-friendly. Smart polymer composites go a step further by reacting to environmental stimuli such as temperature, humidity, or pressure fluctuations, leading to improved performance and greater efficiency [6]. In general, the utilization of polymer composites, including smart polymer composites, has the potential to revolutionize a variety of industries and provide lighter, stronger, and more economical materials.

Although there is increasing interest in polymer composites, there is a dearth of thorough research on the capacity of smart polymer composites to revolutionize various industries. This research seeks to bridge this gap by offering a thorough overview of the current status of smart polymer composite materials and their potential to revolutionize the world. The field of smart polymer composite materials is constantly changing, and it is essential to assess the current state of the art to gain a comprehensive understanding of its potential and restrictions. In the last few years, the capacity of these materials to revolutionize industries like transportation, aerospace, and construction has become more and more evident. Despite this, the widespread use of smart polymer composites is impeded by a number of challenges and restrictions. To progress further in this field, it is essential

* Corresponding author: : indransdesign@gmail.com

to recognize these challenges and offer suggestions for future research and development. By conducting a thorough review and assessment of the current state-of-the-art, it is possible to create a platform for the ongoing development and progress of smart polymer composite materials.

2 Current State of the Art

In recent years, the current state-of-the-art smart polymer composite materials have been widely recognized for their various exceptional properties. Smart polymer composites are materials that can react to environmental stimuli like temperature, humidity, or pressure fluctuations and display changes in their mechanical, electrical, or optical properties [7]. The capacity to react to environmental stimuli offers numerous potential advantages, including enhanced performance, enhanced efficiency, and self-healing capabilities. Examples of the most renowned smart polymer composites include shape-memory, conductive, and self-healing polymers. Shape memory polymers can revert to their original form after being deformed, while conductive polymers can conduct electricity, making them useful for applications like sensors and actuators. Self-healing polymers are able to fix damage caused by external factors such as cracks or fractures, thus increasing the material's lifespan [8].

Smart polymer composites have already been employed in a variety of industries, including aerospace, transportation, and construction [9]. In the aerospace industry, they have been utilized to make lightweight and resilient structural components, while in the transportation industry, they have been employed to manufacture fuel-efficient and lightweight vehicles. In the construction sector, they have been employed to create self-healing concrete and structural materials with enhanced durability. In general, the current state-of-the-art smart polymer composite materials are a rapidly expanding field with great potential for use in a variety of industries. Despite this potential, many obstacles still need to be addressed, including the need for further research and development, enhanced processing techniques, and a better comprehension of their characteristics and behavior.

3 Types of Smart Polymer Composites

3.1 Shape Memory Polymers

Shape memory polymers (SMPs) are intelligent polymer composites that can revert to their original form after being subjected to distortion. These materials are activated by fluctuations in temperature, humidity, or pressure, and their capacity to return to their original form is due to a transition temperature or pressure, which determines the temperature or pressure at which the material shifts from a pliable, malleable state to a rigid, shape-maintaining state. SMPs are usually created by combining a polymer with a shape-memory material, such as a shape-memory polymer or shape-memory alloy [10]. The shape memory agent is responsible for enabling the material to revert back to its original shape, while the polymer provides the necessary mechanical strength. The outcome has distinctive characteristics, such as the capacity to be formed into a desired shape, maintain this shape at high temperatures or pressures, and revert to the original shape when the temperature or pressure decreases. Table 1 outlines the characteristics of shape memory polymers.

The potential uses of SMPs are varied, including medical instruments like stents and catheters, which can be inserted into the body in a flexible state and then revert to their original shape to fulfill their purpose [11]. SMPs have been employed in the aerospace sector to manufacture lightweight and resilient structural components, and in the transportation sector to make fuel-efficient and lightweight vehicles. There are a variety of ways to regulate the transition temperature or pressure of SMPs, such as employing different polymers or shape memory agents, adding plasticizers, and utilizing cross-linking agents. Despite this progress, there are still numerous obstacles to be addressed in the development of SMPs, including the need for additional research and development, enhanced processing techniques, and a better comprehension of their characteristics and behavior. In conclusion, shape-memory polymers are a promising type of material with distinctive characteristics and potential applications in a variety of industries. The capacity to return to its original form after being subjected to distortion offers numerous advantages, and the possibility for further growth and enhancement makes SMPs a field with immense potential for future exploration and invention [12]. Figure 1 illustrates the different kinds of smart polymers (SMPs).

Table 1. Shape memory polymer properties.

Shape memory polymers	Properties
Polyurethane	High thermal stability, good recovery force and deformation, good thermal and mechanical stability
Polycaprolactone	Good shape memory properties, biodegradable and biocompatible, good mechanical properties
Polyvinyl alcohol	Good shape memory properties, hydrophilic and biocompatible, low melting temperature
Polyethylene	High shape recovery rate, good dimensional stability, high resistance to oxidation and UV

Table 2. Conductive polymer properties.

Conductive polymers	Electrical Conductivity (S/cm)	Other Properties
Polyaniline	10^{-3} to 10^{-1}	High mechanical strength, good stability and processability, good transparency in the doped form
Polypyrrole	10^{-2} to 10^{1}	Good stability and processability, good thermal stability, good transparency in the doped form
Polythiophene	10^{-3} to 10^{-1}	Good thermal stability, good stability and processability, good transparency in the doped form
Polyacetylene	10^{3} to 10^{5}	High electrical conductivity, good processability, good stability

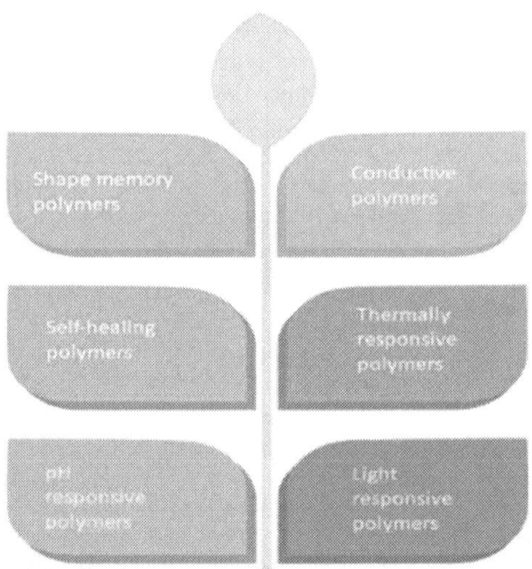

Fig. 1. Types of smart polymers.

3.2 Conductive Polymers

Conductive polymers are a type of polymer that can be used to produce electricity. They are produced by incorporating conductive fillers, such as metals or carbon-based materials, into a polymer matrix, thereby increasing the electrical conductivity of the material [13]. The electrical conductivity of conductive polymers can vary from 10-3 to 103 S/cm, depending on the particular material and how it is prepared [14]. For instance, polyaniline, one of the most renowned conductive polymers, has a conductivity range of 10-3 to 10-1 S/cm [15]. The electrical conductivity of these materials is much lower than that of conventional conductors like copper or silver, yet is adequate for many uses, including electronics and energy storage. Table 2 outlines the characteristics of conductive polymers.

Conductive polymers are extremely versatile and have a multitude of uses, including in electronic devices such as displays, batteries, and sensors [16]. These materials can be processed into various forms, such as films, fibers, and composites, and can be tailored to suit the particular needs of a given application. In terms of durability, conductive polymers are relatively stable, yet they can be impacted by environmental elements such as temperature, humidity, and light exposure. Nevertheless, this can be addressed by utilizing suitable encapsulation techniques or by adding protective layers to the material. Conductive polymers are a promising group of materials that possess exceptional electrical conductivity and versatility. The capacity to incorporate conductive fillers into a polymer matrix offers a variety of possible applications, and the potential for further advancement and enhancement makes conductive polymers an area with immense potential for future exploration and invention.

3.3 Self-Healing Polymers

Self-healing polymers are materials that are able to mend themselves after being damaged. This characteristic is accomplished through the inclusion of a self-healing mechanism, like the presence of microencapsulated healing agents or the formation of covalent bonds between polymer chains [17]. Figure 2 illustrates the features of self-healing polymers.

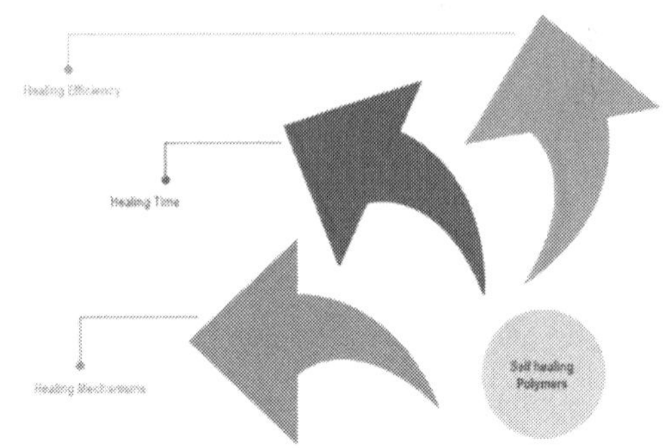

Fig. 2. Characteristics of self-healing polymers.

Depending on the material and the method of preparation, self-healing polymers can reach healing efficiencies of up to 95% [18]. The healing efficiency is defined as the ratio of the mechanical strength regained after the healing process to the original strength. The curing time of self-healing polymers can differ greatly depending on the particular material and method of manufacture. For instance, some self-healing polymers can be fully restored in a matter of minutes, while others may take several hours or even days to complete the healing process. Self-healing in polymers can be accomplished through various methods, such as microencapsulation, covalent bond formation, and supramolecular interactions. The particular mechanism employed depends on the desired characteristics and the particular use of the self-healing polymer. Figure 3 illustrates the categorization of different self-healing polymers. SMP is a field with immense potential for future exploration and invention [12]. Figure 1 illustrates the different kinds of smart polymers.

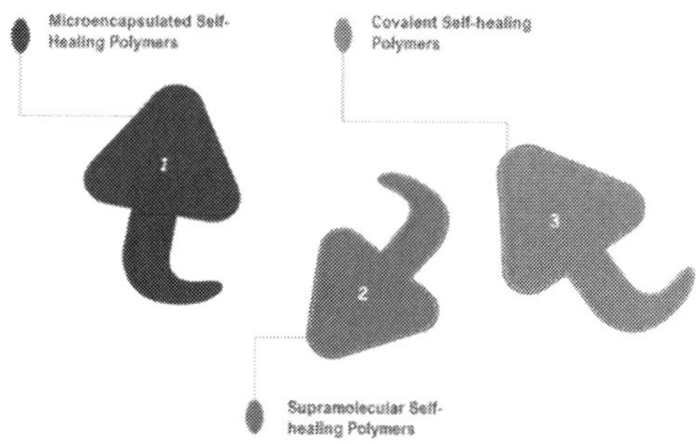

Fig. 3. Classifications of self-healing polymers.

One of the most extensively researched self-healing polymers is the microencapsulated self-healing polymer, which uses microencapsulated healing agents dispersed throughout a polymer matrix [19]. When damage occurs, the capsules break open and release agents that promote healing, which then diffuse and act to fix the damage. Supramolecular Self-healing Polymers are another kind of self-healing polymer that utilizes supramolecular interactions to accomplish self-healing. In these materials, the polymer chains are designed to self-organize into specific configurations that enable them to reconnect when damage occurs. Covalent self-healing polymers gain their self-healing properties through chemical reactions. In these materials, when damage occurs ,the polymer chains interact with each other, forming covalent bonds that mend the damage [20].

3.4 Thermally Responsive Polymers

Thermally responsive polymers are a type of intelligent materials that alter their physical characteristics in response to temperature fluctuations [21]. Examples of thermally responsive polymers include poly(N-isopropylacrylamide) (PNIPAM), poly (ethylene oxide) (PEO), and poly (propylene oxide) (PPO) [22]. PNIPAM is a temperature-sensitive polymer that experiences a volume phase transition at a lower critical solution temperature (LCST) of around 32-34°C [23]. This transformation results in considerable alterations in the hydrophobicity and mechanical characteristics of the polymer. For instance, when temperatures are below the LCST, PNIPAM is hydrophobic and has a low modulus, while when temperatures are above the LCST, it is hydrophilic and has a high modulus. PEO is a temperature-sensitive polymer with a glass transition temperature (Tg) of roughly -120°C [24]. This transformation results in considerable alterations in the mechanical characteristics of the polymer, including its glass transition temperature and mechanical strength. PPO is a temperature-sensitive polymer that has a glass transition temperature (Tg) of roughly -70°C. This transformation results in considerable alterations in the mechanical characteristics of the polymer, including its glass transition temperature and mechanical strength. Generally, thermally responsive polymers are very beneficial in a variety of applications, including drug delivery, cell culture, and tissue engineering. By incorporating these polymers into different materials, scientists and engineers can create materials that can alter their properties in response to temperature fluctuations. Table 3 outlines the characteristics of thermally responsive polymers.

3.5 pH Responsive Polymers

pH-responsive polymers are materials that alter their characteristics in reaction to fluctuations in the pH of the surrounding environment. These polymers have gained significant interest in recent times due to their potential uses in various areas such as drug delivery, bio-separation, and tissue engineering [25]. pH-responsive polymers can alter their characteristics in response to pH fluctuations through a variety of mechanisms, including ionization of acidic or basic groups, protonation/deprotonation of amine or carboxylic groups, or modifications in the charge density of the polymer backbone. Several pH-responsive polymers have been developed, such as poly (acrylic acid) (PAA), poly(2-vinylpyridine) (PVP), poly(ethyleneimine) (PEI), and poly(amidoamine) (PAMAM) dendrimers [26]. The lower critical solution temperature (LCST) or pKa value of a pH-responsive polymer is a critical factor that hydrophobic state when the pH falls below 4.7. PVP has a pKa of 5.5 and changes from a hydrophilic to a hydrophobic state when the pH falls below 5.5. [27]. The pH sensitivity of a polymer can be affected by its molecular weight, concentration, and the presence of other chemical groups. pH-sensitive polymers have numerous uses, including drug delivery, bio-separation, and tissue engineering. As an example, pH-responsive

Table 3. Properties of thermally responsive polymers.

Polymer	LCST/Tg (°C)	Transition	Properties Change
PNIPAM	32-34	Volume	Hydrophobicity, Modulus
PEO	-120	Glass	Glass Transition Temperature, Mechanical Strength
PPO	-70	Glass	Glass Transition Temperature, Mechanical Strength

Table 4. Mechanisms of pH responsive polymers.

Polymer	Mechanism	pKa/LCST	Responsiveness	Applications
Poly(acrylic acid) (PAA)	Ionization	4.7	Hydrophilic to hydrophobic transition below pH 4.7	Drug delivery, bio-separation
Poly(2-vinylpyridine) (PVP)	Protonation	5.5	Hydrophilic to hydrophobic transition below pH 5.5	Drug delivery, bio-separation
Poly(ethyleneimine) (PEI)	Protonation	10.0	Hydrophilic to hydrophobic transition below pH 10.0	Drug delivery, bio-separation
Poly(amidoamine) (PAMAM) dendrimers	Protonation	7.0-8.0	Hydrophilic to hydrophobic transition below pH 7.0-8.0	Drug delivery, bio-separation

polymers can be employed as carriers for drugs that must be released in response to alterations in the body's pH. They can also be employed in separation processes to eliminate impurities based on the pH-induced changes in solubility. The characteristics of the pH-responsive polymer are outlined in Table 4.

3.6 Light Responsive Polymers

Light-responsive polymers, also referred to as photoresponsive polymers, are a type of material that alters its characteristics when exposed to light [28]. These materials have numerous uses in the realms of optics, electronics, and biomedicine. The refractive index of a light-responsive polymer can be modified by exposure to light, leading to alterations in the transmission and reflection of the light. Generally, the alteration in the refractive index is between 0.01 and 0.1. Light-responsive polymers can undergo various shape transformations when exposed to light, such as shrinking, swelling, or bending [29]. Light exposure can alter the conductivity of light-responsive polymers, making them useful for electronics and optoelectronics applications. Depending on the material and intensity of the light, the change in conductivity can vary from several orders of magnitude to several hundred percent. Light-sensitive polymers can display alterations in their optical characteristics, including absorption, fluorescence, and birefringence, when exposed to light. These modifications can be employed in applications such as optical data storage, optical switching, and optical sensing [30]. The temperature and viscosity of light-responsive polymers can be altered by exposure to light, altering their thermal properties. These modifications can be beneficial for applications like energy conversion, thermal management, and biomedical engineering [31]. Table 5 outlines the characteristics of light responsive polymers.

4 Potential of Smart Polymer Composite Materials in Various Industries

4.1 Transportation applications

Smart polymer composites are a type of material made up of a polymer matrix and smart fillers or particles that can react to external stimuli like temperature, light, or pH [32]. By combining a flexible polymer matrix with responsive fillers or particles, materials with adjustable and distinctive characteristics can be produced. Smart polymer composites have the potential to revolutionize the transportation industry due to their capacity to offer enhanced performance characteristics [33]. Smart polymer composites, with their lightweight structure and high strength and stiffness, are perfect for use in lightweight vehicles, aircraft, and marine vessels. Smart polymer composites can be developed to adjust to fluctuating loads and conditions, thereby delivering improved performance in both dynamic and extreme situations [34].

Smart polymer composites can be engineered to possess shape-memory properties, enabling them to revert back to their original form after being exposed to external loads or distortions. Smart polymer composites can be engineered to transform ambient energy from sources like light, heat, or vibration into electrical energy, offering a renewable and self-powered alternative to conventional energy sources [35]. Smart polymer composites can be engineered to incorporate multiple functionalities, such as self-healing, self-lubrication, and self-sensing, into a single material. These special characteristics make smart polymer composites desirable for a variety of transportation uses, including lightweight and energy-efficient vehicle structures, self-healing and self-sensing

Table 5. Properties of light responsive polymers.

Polymer	Property altered by light exposure
Spiropyrans	Refractive index, optical absorption
Azobenzene polymers	Refractive index, optical absorption, shape
Polymer dispersed liquid crystals (PDLCs)	Optical transmittance, refractive index
Hydrogels	Shape, swelling, mechanical properties
Liquid crystal polymers (LCPs)	Optical birefringence, mechanical properties

composites for aerospace and marine vessels, and multifunctional materials for advanced transportation systems.

4.2 Aerospace Applications

Smart polymer composites are a type of material made up of a polymer matrix and smart fillers or particles that can react to external stimuli like temperature, light, or pH [36]. These materials could revolutionize the aerospace industry by offering enhanced performance characteristics, such as smart polymer composites for aerospace applications, lightweight and fuel-efficient aircraft structures, repair of minor cracks and damage in aircraft structures, deployment of wing flaps and other aerodynamic devices, and advanced aerospace systems such as self-sensing systems for structural health monitoring [37].

4.3 Construction Applications

Smart polymer composites are a type of material made up of a polymer matrix and smart fillers or particles that can react to external stimuli, such as temperature, light, or pH [38]. These materials could revolutionize the construction industry by offering enhanced performance characteristics. Smart polymer composites can be engineered to adjust to fluctuating loads and conditions, offering improved performance in dynamic and extreme circumstances, making them suitable for use in high-performance and disaster-resistant structures [39]. Smart polymer composites can be engineered to possess shape-memory properties, enabling them to revert back to their original form after being exposed to external loads or distortions. Smart polymer composites can be engineered to self-repair in the event of damage, thereby reducing maintenance and repair costs and extending the life of the structure. Smart polymer composites can be engineered to regulate temperature and thermal insulation, thereby reducing energy costs and creating a comfortable living environment. It can be engineered to incorporate multiple functionalities like self-healing, self-lubrication, and self-sensing into a single material [40]. Smart polymer composites have a variety of applications in the construction industry, such as the following. (i) Structures with high performance and that are resistant to disasters; (ii) composites with self-healing and shape-memory capabilities for the repair and upkeep of building structures; (iii) insulation materials that are smart for energy-efficient buildings; and (iv) multifunctional composites for advanced building systems, such as self-sensing systems for structural health monitoring.

5 Challenges and Opportunities

Smart polymer composites face the challenge of being compatible with the polymer matrices. Incongruous fillers can lead to phase separation and deterioration of composite materials, thus diminishing their overall performance [41]. Despite advances in the laboratory, scaling up and commercializing smart polymer composites is still a challenge. This is due to the expensive cost of production and the limited availability of smart fillers, as well as the requirement for dependable and efficient production processes. Smart polymer composites can experience a decline in performance over time, which can be caused by environmental elements like UV light and humidity, as well as the natural aging of the material [42]. Figure 4 illustrates the difficulties associated with smart polymer composites.

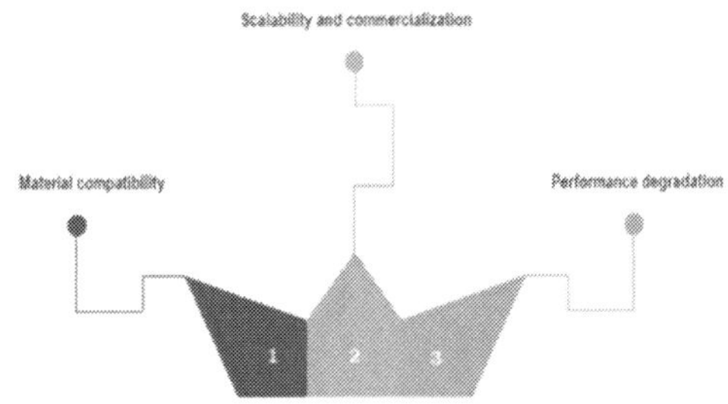

Fig. 4. Challenges for smart polymer composites.

Despite the difficulties, there are a number of opportunities and potential future developments in the area of smart polymer composite materials. The creation of new smart fillers with enhanced performance, stability, and scalability is essential for the progress of this field [43]. Enhancing processing techniques for the manufacture of smart polymer composites, such as 3D printing, is essential for their commercialization and scalability. It will be essential for the advancement of this field to create new applications for smart polymer composites, such as in energy storage, biomedicine, and wearable technologies. Ongoing progress and enhancement of smart polymer composites necessitates collaborative interdisciplinary research that involves materials science, engineering, physics, chemistry, and biology [44]. Figure 5 illustrates the potential of smart polymer composites for future growth.

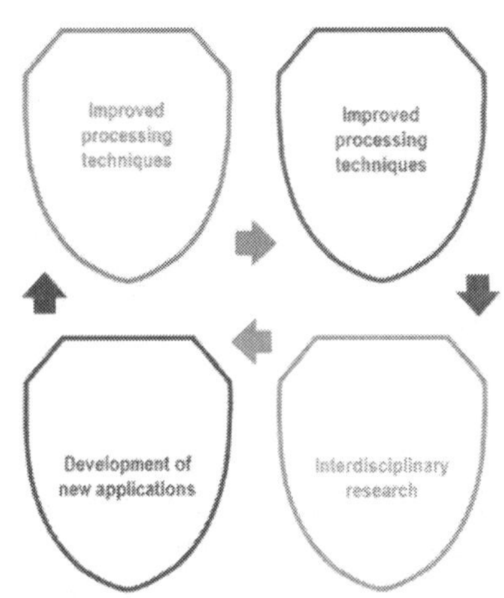

Fig. 5. Opportunities for smart polymer composites.

6 Conclusion

Smart polymer composites are a rapidly expanding area of research, with numerous potential applications that are exciting to explore. Smart polymer composites, made up of a polymer matrix and responsive fillers or particles that can react to environmental factors like temperature, light, and pH, have the potential to revolutionize industries like construction, aerospace, and transportation due to their ability to provide adjustable properties that can satisfy the rigorous demands of these fields. Despite this, there are still many challenges in this field, including material compatibility, scalability, and performance deterioration. Despite the difficulties, there are numerous possibilities and future directions in the field, including the creation of new intelligent fillers, enhanced processing methods, and novel applications. Interdisciplinary research is essential for the ongoing expansion and advancement of this area. In conclusion, the field of smart polymer composites has the potential to revolutionize the world, but further research and development is needed to unlock its full potential.

Availability of data and materials
All the data were included within the article.

Competing interest
The authors do not have any conflicts of interest regarding the publication of this paper in this journal.

Funding
The authors have not claimed any funding for this study. All data are interpreted in this paper and have not been discussed in any of the existing journals.

Acknowledgements

The authors thank KIT-Kalaignarkarunanidhi Institute of Technology, Coimbatore for providing the facility support to complete this research work.

References

1. J. Zhang, G. Lin, U.Vaidya, H.Wang, Past present and future prospective of global carbon fibre composite developments and applications, Composites Part B: Engineering, (2022): 110463
2. M.E. Hoque, A.M. Rayhan, S.I. Shaily, Natural fiber-based green composites: processing properties and biomedical applications, Applied Science and Engineering Progress, **14**, 4 (2021): 689-718
3. V. Chauhan, T. Kärki, J. Varis, Review of natural fiber-reinforced engineering plastic composites their applications in the transportation sector and processing techniques, Journal of Thermoplastic Composite Materials, **35**, 8 (2022): 1169-1209
4. C.I. Idumah, Recent advancements in self-healing polymers polymer blends and nanocomposites, Polymers and Polymer Composites, **29**, 4 (2021): 246-258
5. P. Jagadeesh, M. Puttegowda, S.M. Rangappa, S. Siengchin, Role of polymer composites in railway sector: an overview, Applied Science And Engineering Progress, **15**, 2 (2022): 5745-5745
6. R.C. Verpaalen, T. Engels, A.P. Schenning, M.G. Debije, Stimuli-responsive shape changing commodity polymer composites and bilayers, ACS Applied Materials and Interfaces, **12**, 35 (2020): 38829-38844
7. X. Bi, R. Huang, 3d printing of natural fiber and composites: a state-of-the-art review, Materials and Design, (2020): 111065
8. G. Ehrmann, A. Ehrmann, 3d printing of shape memory polymers, Journal of Applied Polymer Science, **138**, 34 (2021): 50847
9. I.O. Oladele, T.F. Omotosho, A.A. Adediran, Polymer - based composites: an indispensable material for present and future applications, International Journal of Polymer Science, (2020): 1-12
10. M.C. De Souza, I. Moroz, I. Cesarino, A.L. Leão, M. Jawaid, O.A.T. Dias, A review of natural fibers reinforced composites for railroad applications, Applied Science and Engineering Progress, **15**, 2 (2022): 5800-5800
11. Z. Wang, H. Jiang, G. Wu, Y. Li, T. Zhang, Y. Zhang, X. Wang, Shape-programmable three-dimensional microfluidic structures, ACS Applied Materials and Interfaces, **14**, 13 (2022): 15599-15607
12. N. Zheng, Y. Xu, Q. Zhao, T. Xie, Dynamic covalent polymer networks: a molecular platform for designing functions beyond chemical recycling and self-healing, Chemical Reviews, **121**, 3 (2021): 1716-1745
13. N. Maity, A. Dawn, Conducting polymer grafting: recent and key developments, Polymers, **12**, 3 (2020): 709
14. V. Dogra, C. Kishore, A. Verma, A.K. Rana, A. Gaur, Fabrication and experimental testing of hybrid composite material having biodegradable bagasse fiber in a modified epoxy resin: evaluation of mechanical and morphological behavior, Applied Science and Engineering Progress, **14**, 4 (2021): 661-667
15. A.M. Youssef, M.S. Hasanin, M.E. Abd El-Aziz, G.M. Turky, Conducting chitosan / hydroxylethyl cellulose polyaniline bionanocomposites hydrogel based on graphene oxide doped with Ag-Nps, International Journal of Biological Macromolecules, **167** (2021): 1435-1444
16. X.X. Wang, G.F. Yu, J. Zhang, M. Yu, S. Ramakrishna, Y.Z. Long, Conductive polymer ultrafine fibers via electrospinning: preparation, Physical Properties and Applications, Progress In Materials Science, **115** (2021): 100704

17. P.S. Tan, A.A. Somashekar, P. Casari, D. Bhattacharyya, Healing efficiency characterization of self-repairing polymer composites based on damage continuum mechanics, Composite Structures, **208** (2019): 367-376
18. J. Xu, X. Wang, X. Zhang, Y. Zhang, Z. Yang, S. Li, T. Wang, Room-temperature self-healing supramolecular polyurethanes based on the synergistic strengthening of biomimetic hierarchical hydrogen-bonding interactions and coordination bonds, Chemical Engineering Journal, **451** (2023):138673
19. A.N. Santos, D.J.D. Santos, D.J. Carastan, Microencapsulation of reactive isocyanates for application in self-healing materials: a review, Journal of Microencapsulation, **38**, 5 (2021): 338-356
20. Z. Li, R. Yu, B. Guo, Shape-memory and self-healing polymers based on dynamic covalent bonds and dynamic noncovalent interactions: synthesis mechanism and application, ACS Applied Bio Materials, **4**, 8 (2021): 5926-5943
21. S.M. Rangappa, S. Siengchin, Natural fibers as perspective materials, Applied Science and Engineering Progress, **11**, 4 (2018)
22. J. He, D. Lin, Y. Chen, L. Zhang, J. Tan, One - step preparation of thermos - responsive poly (N - Isopropylacrylamide) - based block copolymer nanoparticles by aqueous photoinitiated polymerization - induced self - assembly, Macromolecular Rapid Communications, **42**, 18 (2021): 2100201
23. A. Okudan, A. Altay, Investigation of the effects of different hydrophilic and hydrophobic comonomers on the volume phase transition temperatures and thermal properties of N-Isopropylacrylamide-based hydrogels, International Journal of Polymer Science, (2019): 1-12
24. I. Łukaszewska, A. Bukowczan, E. Hebda, K.N. Raftopoulos, K. Pielichowski, Calorimetric study of hydrated poloxamer - based polyurethanes - thermoresponsive transition and peculiar antiplasticization.
25. H. Chi, Z. Xu, T. Zhang, X. Li, Z. Wu, Y. Zhao, Randomly heterogeneous oleophobic/ph-responsive polymer coatings with reversible wettability transition for multifunctional fabrics and controllable oil – water separation, Journal of Colloid and Interface Science, **594** (2021): 122-130
26. N. Deirram, C. Zhang, S.S. Kermaniyan, A.P. Johnston, G.K. Such, pH - responsive polymer nanoparticles for drug delivery, Macromolecular Rapid Communications, **40**, 10 (2019): 1800917
27. S.C. Ko, S.H. Lee, Protocatechuic aldehyde inhibits α – msh - induced melanogenesis in b16f10 melanoma cells via pka / creb-associated mitf downregulation, International Journal of Molecular Sciences, **22**, 8 (2021): 3861.
28. A. Romano, I. Roppolo, E. Rossegger, S. Schlögl, M. Sangermano, Recent trends in applying ortho - nitrobenzyl esters for the design of photo - responsive polymer networks, Materials, **13**, 12 (2020): 2777
29. E. Pantuso, G. De Filpo, F.P. Nicoletta, Light-Responsive Polymer Membranes, Advanced Optical Materials, **7**, 16 (2019): 1900252
30. P. Talianov, L.I. Fatkhutdinova, A.S. Timin, V.A. Milichko, M.V. Zyuzin, Adaptive nanoparticle-polymer complexes as optical elements: design and application in nanophotonics and nanomedicine, Laser and Photonics Reviews, **15**, 9 (2021): 2000421
31. B. Sana, A. Finne – Wistrand, D. Pappalardo, Recent development in near infrared light - responsive polymeric materials for smart drug - delivery systems, Materials Today Chemistry, **25** (2022): 100963
32. K. Umar, A.A. Yaqoob, M.N.M. Ibrahim, T. Parveen, M.T.U. Safian, Environmental applications of smart polymer composites in smart polymer nanocomposites, Woodhead Publishing, (20221): 295 - 312
33. D.M. Correia, L.C. Fernandes, P.M. Martins, C. García - Astrain, C.M. Costa, J. Reguera, S. Lanceros - Méndez, Ionic liquid – polymer composites: a new platform for multifunctional applications, Advanced Functional Materials, **30**, 24 (2020): 1909736.
34. C. Zhao, X. Jia, K. Shu, C. Yu, G.G. Wallace, C. Wang, Conducting polymer composites for unconventional solid - state supercapacitors, Journal of Materials Chemistry A, **8**, 9 (2020): 4677-4699
35. H. Moustafa, A.M. Youssef, N.A. Darwish, A.I. Abou - Kandil, Eco - friendly polymer composites for green packaging: future vision and challenges, Composites Part B: Engineering, **172** (2019): 16-25
36. F. Li, Y. Liu and J. Leng, Progress of shape memory polymers and their composites in aerospace applications, Smart Materials and Structures, **28**, 10 (2019): 103003
37. W.S. Chow, Z.A. Mohd Ishak, Smart polymer nanocomposites: a review, Express Polymer Letters, **14**, 5 (2020)
38. M.Y. Khalid, Z.U. Arif, R. Noroozi, A. Zolfagharian, M. Bodaghi, 4d printing of shape memory polymer composites: a review on fabrication techniques, applications and future perspectives, Journal of Manufacturing Processes, **81** (2022): 759-797
39. A. Mirabedini, A. Ang, M. Nikzad, B. Fox, K.T. Lau, N. Hameed, Evolving strategies for producing multiscale graphene - enhanced fiber - reinforced polymer composites for smart structural applications, Advanced Science, **7**, 11 (2020): 1903501
40. H.N. Kim, S. Yang, Responsive smart windows from nanoparticle – polymer composites, Advanced Functional Materials, **30**, 2 (2020): 1902597

41. S.M. Rangappa, S. Siengchin, S. Fischer, Sustainable natural fibers for environmental - friendly materials, Applied Science and Engineering Progress, **15**, 4 (2022): 5802-5802
42. H. Moustafa, A.M. Youssef, N.A. Darwish, A.I. Abou - Kandil, Eco - friendly polymer composites for green packaging: future vision and challenges, Composites Part B: Engineering, **172** (2019): 16-25
43. S. Malekmohammadi, N. Sedghi Aminabad, A. Sabzi, A. Zarebkohan, M. Razavi, M. Vosough, H. Maleki, smart and biomimetic 3d and 4d printed composite hydrogels: opportunities for different biomedical applications, Biomedicines, **9**, 11 (2011): 1537
44. M.Y. Khalid, Z.U. Arif, R. Noroozi, A. Zolfagharian, M. Bodaghi, 4d printing of shape memory polymer composites: a review on fabrication techniques applications and future perspectives, Journal of Manufacturing Processes, **81** (2022): 759-797

Understanding the Environmental Distribution and Potential Health Risks of Pollutants from Deodorant Products: A Review

Meenakshi Kakara[1], *Srideep* Dasari[2], *Marttin Paulraj* Gundupalli[3], *Tawiwan* Kangsadan[4], and *Keerthi* Katam[1,*]

[1] Department of Civil Engineering, École Centrale School of Engineering, Mahindra University, Telangana, 500043, India
[2] Department of Chemistry, Indian Institute of Technology Hyderabad, Kandi, Telangana, 502285, India
[3] Department of Food and Nutrition Science, Faculty of Agricultural, Life and Environmental Science, University of Alberta, Canada
[4] Chemical and Process Engineering, The Sirindhorn International Thai-German Graduate School of Engineering, King Mongkut's University of Technology North Bangkok, Bangkok, 10800, Thailand

Abstract. Deodorants are frequently used personal care products; however, questions have been raised concerning their possible toxicity to cause air and water pollution, and their potential impact on human health. The degree to which deodorant ingredients, such as fragrance chemicals, antibacterial compounds, aluminium compounds, and preservatives, are toxic depends on their chemical composition. Many of these chemicals have been connected to adverse health effects, such as skin rashes, allergic reactions, endocrine disruption, and respiratory problems. Understanding these chemicals' toxicity is crucial for determining any potential risks to human health. Spray formulations have the potential to release volatile organic compounds into the air, such as propellants and fragrance chemicals, which can be harmful to human respiratory health and lead to indoor and outdoor air pollution. Improper disposal and wastewater treatment can lead to the contamination of water bodies, potentially impacting aquatic ecosystems and human water supplies. This review provides an overview of the toxicity of deodorant ingredients in various formulations, including sprays, roll-ons, and sticks. The partition coefficients Log K_{aw} (air-water partition coefficient), Log K_{oa} (air-organic carbon partition coefficient), and Log K_{ow} (octanol-water partition coefficient), values of deodorant ingredients were summarized for assessing their potential for long-range transport, persistence in the environment, and bioaccumulation in organisms.

Keyword. air pollution, breast cancer, environmental impact, partition coefficients, phthalates

1 Introduction

Aromatherapy has been used in India for ages, with the rise of technology and increased consumption, India's traditional fragrance sector has seen significant shifts. India is among the top countries in terms of fragrance production, consumption, and market size. The Indian perfume market is anticipated to increase by USD 1328.31 million between 2022 and 2027 [1]. The three type-based categories of fragrance goods are comprised of perfumes, deodorants, and other fragrance products. In terms of revenue in 2019, deodorants occupied the highest percentage (60.65%), followed by perfumes (32.14%) [2]. Deodorant is the most often used scented product in the country because of its affordable price. Recently, roll-ons and sticks are also becoming popular among Indian consumers.

The toxic nature of the propellant and its contaminants is taken into account throughout the formulation of aerosol items. For instance, the propellant isobutane, which is used in aerosol sprays, may include the cancer-causing compound butadiene. Aerosol sprays produce incredibly tiny particles, that are harmful and may amplify their damaging effects if inhaled more deeply [3,4]. Aerosols frequently include very dangerous and harmful substances such as formaldehyde, xylene, neurotoxins, and carcinogens. The Environmental Protection Agency has classified these as hazardous. These components are utilized for a variety of purposes, yet despite this, they pose a serious danger to the environment and cause a great deal of pollution.

The ingredients that go into fragrance formulae remain trade secrets and are not listed on labels for the fragrance section of the product. More and more people are citing fragrance as a cause of illnesses including asthma, allergies, and migraines [5,6]. Additionally, it has been shown that certain scent components build up in adipose tissue and are identified in the mother's milk. There is speculation that other substances disrupt hormones. The consequences are not completely understood since systemic impacts have not received much attention. Fragrances are volatile molecules, which contribute to both indoor and outdoor air pollution [7-9]. Synthetic musk components pollute streams and aquatic life and are persistent in the environment [10].

In addition to fragrance, deodorants also include aluminium and zinc salts to block sweat ducts and prevent perspiration from reaching the skin's surface. The majority of traditional antiperspirants use aluminium compounds such as Aluminium trichlorohydrex glycine.

* Corresponding author: Keerthi.katam@mahindrauniversity.edu.in

https://doi.org/10.1051/e3sconf/202342802015

There is some evidence to support the claims that certain aluminium compounds are neurotoxic, irritate the skin, and interact with estrogen, which raises the risk of breast cancer [11,12]. Deodorants also include heavy metals, which can contribute to pollution, in addition to organic compounds. For example, the Nivea Silver Protect deodorant had 0.3 ppm of silver [13]. Some deodorant sprays and roll-ons included chloride ions (Cl), chromium ions (Cr), cobalt ions (Co), fluoride ions (F), molybdenum ions (Mo), and antimony ions (Sb) [14].
This review aims to examine the environmental and human health effects associated with typical ingredients found in three common types of deodorants: sticks, roll-ons, and sprays. The partition coefficients Log K_{aw} (air-water partition coefficient), Log K_{oa} (air-organic carbon partition coefficient), Log K_{ow} (octanol-water partition coefficient), and Log K_{oc} (organic carbon-water partition coefficient) values of deodorant ingredients were summarized for assessing their potential for long-range transport, persistence in the environment, and bioaccumulation in organisms.

2 Composition and usage of deodorants

Deodorants can be applied as a stick, a liquid roller, or an aerosol can. Deodorant sticks are solid formulations typically packaged in plastic containers. Roll-ons consist of liquid solutions applied through a ball applicator, while sprays are aerosol-based products. The primary components of deodorants include antimicrobial agents (such as ethanol, and triclosan), odor-masking compounds (natural essential oils and/or perfume fragrances), odor absorbers, antiperspirant agents (several aluminum-containing substances), anti-oxidants, preservatives (such as parabens), and others. A small percentage of deodorant sprays contain antiperspirants and antibacterial chemicals which are used to control the growth of microorganisms on the skin that cause body odor. Essential oils (perfume) are used in some formulations as an antibacterial agent. Some of the deodorant ingredients function as a moisturizing agent for the skin since ethanol decreases natural oils in the epidermis.

The specific data regarding the percentage and concentration of ingredients in different types of deodorants can vary depending on the brand, formulation, and region. The details of the general composition and commonly found ingredients in different types of deodorants are given in Table 1 [15]. Typically, aerosol deodorants contain active ingredients like aluminum chlorohydrate, aluminum zirconium tetrachlorohydrex glycine, or triclosan. The concentration of these ingredients can range from 10% to 25%. Aerosol deodorants often contain propellants such as butane, isobutane, or propane, which help release the product from the container. The concentration of propellants can range from 10% to 30%. Fragrance compounds are added to provide a pleasant scent. The concentration of fragrance can vary, typically ranging from 0.5% to 5%. Roll-on deodorants commonly contain antiperspirant active ingredients ranging from 10% to 25%. They often contain water as a base ingredient, which can make up a significant percentage of the formulation, ranging from 50% to 70%. Ingredients like glycerin, propylene glycol, and cyclomethicone may be included to provide moisturization and help the product adhere to the skin. The concentration of these ingredients can range from 5% to 15%. Stick deodorants often incorporate waxes (e.g., beeswax, candelilla wax) and oils (e.g., coconut oil, mineral oil) to provide a solid consistency. The concentration of these ingredients can range from 10% to 60%.

The majority of deodorants contained four specific phthalates: Dibutyl phthalate (DBP), Diethyl phthalate (DEP), Di (2-ethylhexyl) phthalate (DEHP), and Dimethyl phthalate (DMP). Only two deodorants contained all four phthalates together. The concentration ranges of these phthalates were estimated as follows: DEP (23-924 ug/ml), DEHP (255-1402 ug/ml), DBP (7-2119 ug/ml), and DMP (16-84 ug/ml). Among these phthalates, DBP had the highest concentration, followed by DEHP and DEP. DMP was only detected in four samples, and its concentration was lower compared to the other phthalates [16]. Among the many fragrance compounds found in perfumes and deodorants, Benzyl salicylate (3346 μg/g), Lilial (11477 μg/g), Citronellol (2200 μg/g), Hexylcinnamic aldehyde (4664 μg/g), Limonene (1748 μg/g), Linalool (1557 μg/g), and Isomethyl ionone (1822 μg/g) exhibited the highest concentrations [17].

3 Distribution in environmental compartments

The toxicity of deodorant ingredients is primarily influenced by their chemical composition, as well as the specific type of deodorant products that dominate the market. Partition coefficients Log K_{aw}, Log K_{oa}, and Log K_{ow} play a crucial role in understanding the fate and behavior of deodorants in the environment. The transfer of the chemical compounds in the environmental compartments based on the partition coefficients is given in Figure 1 [18]. These partition coefficients along with the physio-chemical properties of the compounds provide insights into their potential transport and accumulation in air, organic carbon, and water compartments. The physical properties and partition coefficients of the typical organic compounds (about 40) used in the deodorants are given in Table 2. The data of vapor pressure, water solubility, Log K_{aw}, Log K_{oa}, Log K_{ow}, and Log K_{oc} of the selected organic compounds were collected from PubChem and EPI Suite software.

The air-water partition coefficient (K_{aw}) represents the distribution of a compound between air and water. It is a critical parameter for understanding the volatility and potential for atmospheric transport of deodorant ingredients. High K_{aw} values indicate a greater tendency for partitioning into the gas phase, potentially leading to long-range transport and subsequent deposition in water bodies. Commonly, Log K_{aw} values can range from approximately -5 to +10 or more, depending on the compound's properties and environmental conditions.

Table 1. Typical composition of deodorants: sticks, roller, and spray [15,19].

Ingredient	Compounds	Stick	Roller	Spray	Purpose
Anti-bacterial agents	Triclosan, Chlorhexidine, Alcohol, Polyhexamethylene Biguanide, Propylene Glycol, Quaternary Ammonium Compounds, Octoxyglycerin, 2-Ethylhexylglycerin, and Ethyllauryl Arginate Hydroxychloride	0.5%	1-3%		Kill bacteria
Antiperspirant (Aluminium and Zirconium compounds)	Aluminium Chlorohydrate (In Roll-Ons), Aluminium Zirconium Tetrachlorohydrex Glycine (In Stick), Aluminium Hydroxybromid, Aluminium Sesquichlorohydrate, Aluminium Bromide, Aluminium Lactate	10%	10%	10 - 30%	To clog pores, blocking body's ability to perspire
Emollient and Emulsifying	Cyclopentasiloxane, Stearyl Alcohol, Alkyl Benzoate, Hydrogenated Castor Oil, Dimethicone, Helianthus Annuus Seed Oil, Cetyl Alcohol	60%			Improves products consistency
Moisturizing and Skin conditioning agents	Glycerin, Citric Acid, Oils	5%	5-15%		Soothe and soften skin
Perfume	Citronellol, Limonene, Linalool, Phthalates, Eugenol, Geraniol, Hexylcinnamaldehyde	1.5%	0.3%	1%	Odour masking agents, usually labelled as "fragrance"
Odour absorbers	Sodium Acid Carbonate, Zinc Carbonate, And Talc				
Humectants	Polyols, Propylene Glycol		5%		Prevent the product from drying out
Propellant (in the case of aerosol formulation)	Butane, Isobutane, Propane			10 - 30%	Carry the product to the skin
Water and Solvent	Alcohols (Ethanol), Cyclomethicone, Decamethylcyclopentasiloxane	10%	60 - 80% (water)	37 - 47%	Carry active ingredients
Additives	Silica, EDTA, Sodium Benzoate, Parabens, Triethanolamine, Diethanolamine	8%	2-5%	2.5%	pH control, colorants, filler, preservatives, and chelating agents

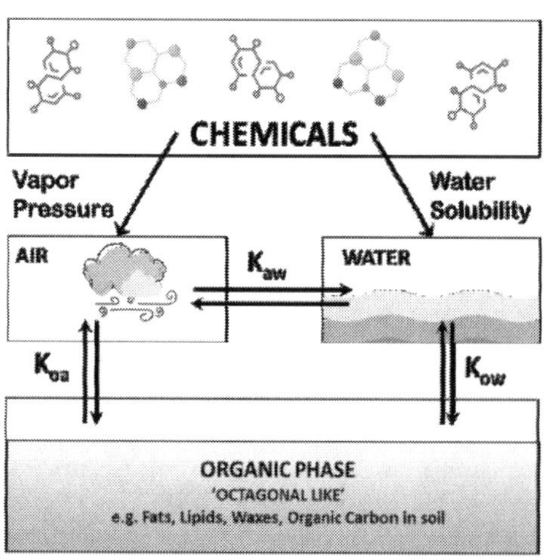

Fig. 1. The transfer of organic compounds between different environmental compartments based on partition coefficients.

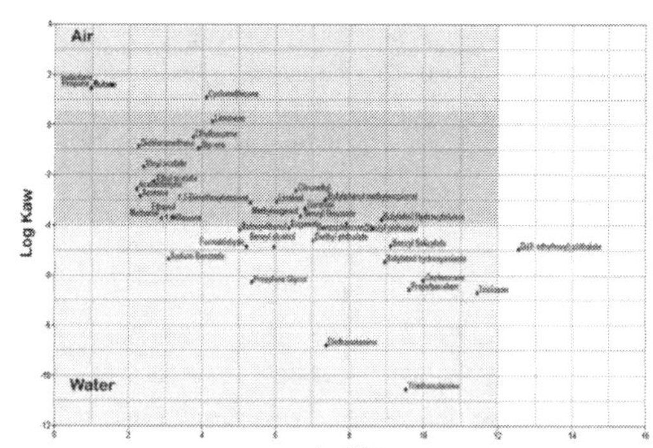

Fig. 2. Distribution of compounds present in the deodorants, based on Log Koa and Log Kaw.

Table 2. The physical properties and partition coefficients at 25°C of the typical organic compounds used in the deodorants.

Name	Formula	Vapor pressure (mm Hg)	Solubility in water (g/L)	Henry's law constant (atm-m³/mol)	Log K_{ow}	Log K_{aw}	Log K_{oa}	Log K_{oc}
1,3-Dimethoxybenzene	$C_8H_{10}O_2$	0.195	1.105	2.45×10^{-5}	2.21	-3.112	5.322	2.259
1,4-Dioxane	$C_4H_8O_2$	38.1	>800	4.80×10^{-6}	-0.27	-3.707	3.18	1.23
Acetaldehyde	C_2H_4O	902	256.8	6.67×10^{-5}	-0.34	-2.564	2.224	0.613
Acetone	C_3H_6O	231	1000	3.97×10^{-5}	-0.24	-2.844	2.310	0.73
Benzophenone	$C_{13}H_{10}O$	1.93×10^{-3}	0.14	1.94×10^{-6}	3.18	-4.101	7.281	2.634
Benzyl alcohol	C_7H_8O	0.094	42.9	3.37×10^{-7}	1.1	-4.861	5.961	1.1
Benzyl Benzoate	$C_{14}H_{12}O_2$	2.24×10^{-4}	0.015	2.34×10^{-7}	3.97	-3.941	7.911	3.8
Benzyl Salicylate	$C_{14}H_{12}O_3$	7.8×10^{-5}	0.025	2.7×10^{-6}	4.31	-4.824	9.134	3.41
Butane	C_4H_{10}	1820	0.0612	0.95	2.89	1.589	1.530	2.508
Butoxyethanol	$C_6H_{14}O_2$	0.88	64.47	1.6×10^{-6}	0.83	-4.184	5.014	0.882
Butylated hydroxyanisole	$C_{11}H_{16}O_2$	2.48×10^{-3}	0.2128	2.6×10^{-6}	3.06	-5.456	8.956	3.084
Butylated Hydroxytoluene	$C_{15}H_{24}O$	0.01	0.0006	3.38×10^{-6}	5.1	-3.774	8.874	3.913
Butylphenyl methylpropional	$C_{14}H_{20}O$	3.58×10^{-3}	0.008	8.48×10^{-6}	4.36	-2.992	7.352	3.107
Citronellol	$C_{10}H_{20}O$	0.02	0.3	2.1×10^{-5}	3.91	-2.634	6.544	2.676
Cyclomethicone	$C_{10}H_{30}O_5Si_5$	0.3	1.7×10^{-5}	33	8.06	1.097	4.103	4.513
Di(2- ethylhexyl) phthalate	$C_{24}H_{38}O_4$	1.42×10^{-7}	0.0003	2.7×10^{-7}	7.6	-4.957	12.5557	4.94
Dibutyl phthalate	$C_{16}H_{22}O_4$	2.01×10^{-5}	0.0112	1.81×10^{-6}	4.50	-4.131	8.631	3.14
Dichloromethane	CH_2Cl_2	435	13.2	3.25×10^{-3}	1.25	-0.877	2.27	1.44
Diethanolamine	$C_4H_{11}NO_2$	2.8×10^{-4}	1000	3.87×10^{-11}	-1.43	-8.801	7.371	-0.732
Diethyl phthalate	$C_{12}H_{14}O_4$	2.1×10^{-3}	1.08	6.10×10^{-7}	2.47	-4.603	7.023	1.84
Ethanol	C_2H_6O	59.3	1000	5×10^{-6}	-0.31	-3.689	3.25	0.2
Ethyl acetate	$C_4H_8O_2$	93.2	64	1.34×10^{-4}	0.73	-2.261	2.7	1.263
Ethylbenzene	C_8H_{10}	9.6	0.17	7.88×10^{-3}	3.15	-0.492	3.74	2.23
Eugenol	$C_{10}H_{12}O_2$	0.0221	2.46	1.92×10^{-6}	2.49	-4.09	6.36	2.403
Formaldehyde	CH_2O	3890	57	3.37×10^{-7}	0.35	-4.861	5.211	0.889
Geraniol	$C_{10}H_{18}O$	0.03	0.1	1.15×10^{-5}	3.56	-3.328	6.798	2.433
Isobutane	C_4H_{10}	2610	0.05	1.19	2.76	1.687	1.073	2.395
Limonene	$C_{10}H_{16}$	1.55	0.008	0.032	4.57	0.115	4.265	3.801
Linalool	$C_{10}H_{18}O$	0.176	1.59	2.15×10^{-5}	2.97	-3.056	6.026	2.156
Methanol	CH_3OH	127	1000	4.55×10^{-6}	-0.77	-3.730	2.88	0.44
Methyleugenol	$C_{11}H_{14}O_2$	0.012	0.5	5.6×10^{-6}	3.03	-3.64	6.670	2.713
Oxybenzone	$C_{14}H_{12}O_3$	6.62×10^{-6}	0.0037	1.5×10^{-8}	3.79	-6.212	10	3.440
Propane	C_3H_8	7150	0.0624	0.707	2.36	1.461	0.970	2.048
Propylene Glycol	$C_3H_8O_2$	0.13	811.1	1.3×10^{-8}	-0.92	-6.278	5.358	0.36
Propylparaben	$C_{10}H_{12}O_3$	3.07×10^{-4}	0.5	4.25×10^{-9}	3.04	-6.584	9.624	2.708
Sodium Benzoate	$C_7H_5NaO_2$	2.9×10^{-12}	556	7×10^{-16}	-2.27	-5.351	3.081	-1.1
Styrene	C_8H_8	6.4	0.31	2.75×10^{-3}	2.95	-0.949	3.899	2.96
Triclosan	$C_{12}H_7Cl_3O_2$	4.65×10^{-6}	0.005	2.1×10^{-8}	4.76	-6.69	11.45	3.925
Triethanolamine	$C_6H_{15}NO_3$	3.59×10^{-6}	1000	7.05×10^{-13}	-1.00	-10.54	9.54	-0.516
Vinyl acetate	$C_4H_6O_2$	115	30.25	5.11×10^{-4}	0.73	-1.68	2.41	1.23

The octanol-water partition coefficient (K_{ow}) describes the distribution of a compound between octanol (representing a lipophilic environment) and water. It is an indicator of the hydrophobicity or lipophilicity of a deodorant ingredient. High K_{ow} values suggest a greater affinity for partitioning into lipids or organic matter in water, which can lead to bioaccumulation in aquatic organisms. The typical range for Log K_{ow} values is from -3 (indicating high water solubility) to +10 (indicating strong water repellence) [20]. The air-octanol partition coefficient (K_{oa}) is a measure of the relative distribution of deodorant compounds between the air and octanol phases. It represents the ratio of the concentration of a compound in the air to its concentration in octanol at equilibrium. A higher K_{oa} value indicates a greater affinity for octanol, suggesting that the deodorant compound has a propensity to accumulate in lipid-rich environments. Log K_{oa} values may range from -10 to 10 or even beyond, depending on the volatility and affinity of the compound for organic carbon [21,22]. The K_{oa} parameter is essential for understanding the potential for bioaccumulation and assessing the environmental fate of deodorant compounds in relation to air pollution and their potential impacts on ecosystems and human health. Log K_{oc} represents the ratio of the concentration of a substance in organic carbon to its concentration in water at equilibrium. It helps assess the potential for adsorption onto organic matter, providing insights into the fate and transport of deodorant ingredients in soils and sediments. The typical values for the high water solubility range can vary, but it is generally considered to be above 1 g/L or even higher. Compounds with high water solubility are readily dissolved in water and can disperse easily. About 19 compounds namely, Diethyl phthalate, 1,3-Dimethoxybenzene, 1,4-Dioxane, Linalool, Eugenol, Dichloromethane, Vinyl acetate, Benzyl alcohol, Formaldehyde, Methanol, Ethyl acetate, Butoxyethanol, Acetaldehyde, Sodium Benzoate, Propylene Glycol, Diethanolamine, Triethanolamine, Ethanol, and Acetone had water solubility greater than 1 g/L and low Log K_{ow} values indicating their distribution mainly in water. According to Wanna (2016), compounds with log K_{aw} values below -2 and log K_{oa} values below 12 are referred to as "swimmers" because their low log K_{aw} values indicate a tendency to remain in water. On the other hand, compounds with log K_{aw} values above 0.5 and log K_{oa} values below 6 are categorized as "fliers" due to their high log K_{aw} values. Compounds with log K_{oa} values above 12 are defined as "hoppers," while an intermediate group called "multiple hoppers" typically have log K_{aw} values above -4 and log K_{oa} values below 12 [23,24]. Based on the above values the compounds that transfer to air and water is shown in Figure 2. Most of the compounds are in multiple hopper groups exhibiting substantial capability for transportation from sources, both directly and through association with particles (for compounds with extremely high Log K_{oa}). The compounds Butylated Hydroxytoluene, Di(2-ethylhexyl) phthalate, and Cyclomethicone exhibited high Log K_{ow} values (>4), as well as low vapor pressure and water solubility. This suggests that these compounds have a strong affinity for sediment or bioaccumulation. The compounds with Log K_{ow} greater than 8.5 are very hydrophobic and exhibit greater affinity to be present in the terrestrial food chain [25,26]. Most of the compounds in deodorants have Log Kow values less than 8.5 (Table 2). Chemicals falling within the range of Log K_{ow} = 2 to 5 and log $K_{oa} \geq 5$ represented a category of substances that have the potential for bioaccumulation, especially within food chains that involve air-breathing organisms [27,28]. About 50% of the compounds fall in this category and can accumulate in the air-breathing food chain. However, it is important to note that the partition coefficients of deodorants can also be influenced by environmental conditions, such as pH, temperature, and the presence of other chemicals. Additionally, the presence of organic matter in the environment can significantly affect the partitioning behavior of deodorant compounds.

1,4-Dioxane exhibits persistence in water and shows limited biodegradability. It has a high solubility in water, allowing for its easy migration into groundwater, where it maintains its resistance to biodegradation [29,30]. Benzyl Benzoate is considered moderately persistent in the environment. The low water solubility indicates that Benzyl Benzoate has a limited ability to dissolve in water, reducing its potential for distribution in aqueous environments such as surface water or groundwater. The higher log Koa suggests that Benzyl Benzoate has a little higher affinity for partitioning into the octonal phase, making it more likely to penetrate the skin and contribute to airborne concentrations. This indicates that skin contact, such as through the use of topical products containing Benzyl Benzoate, can result in its release into the surrounding air [31]. While some portion of Benzyl Benzoate may be washed off during activities like bathing or swimming, the majority is expected to remain on the skin, potentially leading to prolonged exposure and absorption through dermal contact. Benzyl Salicylate is known to be persistent and bioaccumulative. Benzyl Salicylate and Cyclomethicone, with their low water solubility and high log Koa and log Koc, are expected to persist and remain predominantly in the air and soil compartments without significant degradation. Cyclomethicone compounds have a relatively high vapor pressure, which means they readily volatilize into the air. Once in the atmosphere, they can undergo atmospheric degradation through various mechanisms, such as reaction with hydroxyl radicals (OH·) and photolysis by sunlight. These degradation processes can contribute to the removal of cyclomethicones from the air [32].

Butylated Hydroxyanisole does not persist in air, water, or soil, and it is not likely to accumulate significantly in organisms. It is also not considered to be highly toxic to aquatic organisms [33]. Butylated Hydroxytoluene is persistent in water and soil. DEHP is persistent in the environment and has the ability to accumulate in sediments and organisms as it had high Log K_{oa} (12.6) and Log K_{ow} values. This means that it does not readily degrade and can persist for a long time, posing a potential risk to the environment and organisms. Similar to DEHP, DBP is also persistent in the environment and can accumulate in organisms as it also had a high Log K_{oa} value. It does not easily break down and has the potential to pose environmental and biological risks. Diethyl phthalate is biodegradable in the environment. It has a much lower tendency to adhere to aquatic sediments compared to other phthalates. Approximately 70% to 90% diethyl phthalate is found in the water column instead of adhering to sediments. Furthermore, biomagnification, the process by which a substance increases its concentration up the food chain, is not expected to occur in the case of diethyl phthalate [34]. Styrene has the potential to be released into the air and is regarded as a volatile organic chemical. It can engage in photochemical interactions with other contaminants in the environment, contributing to the formation of smog. Styrene does not stay in the air for a long period because of its short atmospheric lifetime [35]. Styrene is poorly soluble in water and tends to partition into sediments as opposed to staying in the water column. Triclosan may accumulate in organisms and is persistent in the environment. The fact that triclosan is hydrophobic and has a high log Koa suggests that it has a greater affinity to lipids and organic materials. Due to this property, it can partition into lipid-rich tissues of organisms as opposed to staying in the water [36].

4 Potential health threats

These substances can provide a variety of health concerns, depending on the concentration, length of exposure, personal sensitivity, and overall product design. Table 3 lists the probable health impacts of the typical deodorant ingredients. More than 50% of the compounds can irritate eyes, skin, and lungs. Antiperspirant deodorants frequently contain aluminium compounds, such as aluminium chlorohydrate and aluminium zirconium tetrachlorohydrex gly, to decrease sweating and regulate body odor. However, concerns have been raised about the potential health dangers associated with the usage of these substances.

Table 3. Potential health hazards posed by common deodorant ingredients

Health effects	Compounds
Skin irritation	1,3-Dimethoxybenzene, Benzyl alcohol, Benzyl Benzoate, Benzyl Salicylate, Butylphenyl methylpropional, Citronellol, Diethanolamine, Eugenol, Geraniol, Limonene, Linalool, Methyleugenol, Propylene Glycol, Styrene, Triethanolamine
Respiratory irritation	1,4-Dioxane, Acetaldehyde, Acetone, Benzophenone, Benzyl alcohol, Benzyl Benzoate, Butane, Butoxyethanol, Butylated hydroxyanisole, Butylated Hydroxytoluene, Butylphenyl methylpropional, Citronellol, Cyclomethicone, Di(2-ethylhexyl) phthalate, Dibutyl phthalate, Diethanolamine, Diethyl phthalate, Ethanol, Ethyl acetate, Ethylbenzene, Eugenol, Formaldehyde, Geraniol, Isobutane, Limonene, Linalool, Methanol, Methyleugenol, Oxybenzone, Propane, Propylene Glycol, Styrene, Triclosan, Triethanolamine, Vinyl acetate
Carcinogenic	1,4-Dioxane, Acetaldehyde, Benzophenone, Dichloromethane, Formaldehyde, Methyleugenol, Styrene
Endocrine disruption	Benzophenone, Di(2-ethylhexyl) phthalate, Dibutyl phthalate, Diethyl phthalate, Oxybenzone, Propylparaben, Triclosan
Dizziness, Drowsiness, Headache, Nausea, and flammability	Butane, Isobutane, Propane
Eye irritation	Butoxyethanol, Ethyl acetate
Allergic reactions	Benzyl Salicylate
Developmental Toxicity	Di(2-ethylhexyl) phthalate, Dibutyl phthalate, Diethyl phthalate
Liver and Kidney Damage	Dichloromethane
Central nervous system (CNS) depression	Ethanol

Numerous studies have looked at the potential connection between aluminium exposure and health problems, such as Alzheimer's disease and breast cancer [37,38]. Aluminium compounds may also interfere with endocrine and hormonal functions. Although further research is needed to determine the degree of these effects and their implications for human health, they have the potential to mimic estrogen in the body and interfere with hormonal signaling. It is significant to highlight that the body has systems to remove aluminium and that only a little amount of aluminium may be absorbed via the skin. However, those with kidney problems could be less capable to eliminate aluminium, which might possibly raise their risk of aluminium buildup. To protect consumers, regulatory agencies like the European Chemicals Agency (ECHA) and the U.S. Food and Drug Administration (FDA) have set restrictions on the amount of aluminium in cosmetic items like deodorants [39].

Liver, lung, and kidney cancers have been linked to prolonged exposure to high amounts of 1,4-dioxane, benzophenone, dichloromethane, and styrene [40-44]. Styrene vapors can irritate the respiratory system, the eyes, and the central nervous system, resulting in symptoms including headache, weariness, and dizziness. Prolonged or repeated exposure to styrene has been associated with potential neurological and hematological effects. Triclosan exhibits an impact on the body by reducing serum thyroid hormone concentrations, as observed due to its structural similarity to thyroid hormones [45]. It acts as a disruptor by interfering with the estrogen, androgen, and thyroid systems of the body. Its ability to disrupt these hormone systems classifies it as an endocrine disruptor. Additionally, studies conducted on mice suggest that triclosan may have an allergic effect. When exposed to the skin, simulating the application of a lotion or deodorant, the mice displayed heightened reactions to allergens introduced into their lungs [46].

At high concentrations, Chlorhexidine can be harmful, and there have been reports of anaphylactic reactions [47]. Additionally, the by-products of chlorhexidine decomposition are considered more harmful to the environment than chlorhexidine itself. The substance can accumulate in aquatic organisms, leading to long-term harmful effects [47]. Prolonged or high-dose use of propylene glycol can result in toxicity, with reported adverse effects on the central nervous system, hyperosmolarity, hemolysis, cardiac arrhythmia, seizures, agitation, and lactic acidosis [48]. Phthalates, including DEP, are known as endocrine disruptors and have been associated with adverse effects on reproduction and development in animals and humans. Phthalates have been linked to abnormalities, nervous system sensitivity, reduced development and birth weight, and maternal mortality in mice. They may also irritate mucous membranes and the skin. Studies on people have connected phthalate exposure to issues with reproduction, diabetes, obesity, allergies, and asthma [49,50]. Parabens have been found in a number of human tissues and body fluids. In addition to being endocrine disruptors, paraben chemicals have also been linked to changes in hormone action, immunological function, lipid homeostasis, blood sugar levels, thyroid function, and tumors, notably breast tumors and male infertility [51]. Deodorant silica is known to irritate the skin, and it may contain crystalline quartz, which has been linked to respiratory conditions and the development of cancer cells [52].

Sustainable practices and alternatives must be considered to minimize the potential negative effects. One way to accomplish this is to choose deodorant products that are free of or contain less dangerous ingredients, opt for environmentally friendly packaging, promote recycling and proper disposal methods, and develop greener and more environmentally friendly formulas. Exploring bacterial-derived, plant-derived, and essential oil-derived compounds as substitute deodorant components has received a lot of attention recently [19]. While chemicals originating from plants offer a variety of useful qualities including odor control and skin-soothing benefits, compounds generated from bacteria have special antibacterial capabilities. Along with attractive fragrances, essential oils also have antibacterial and antioxidant qualities. Consumers often perceive nature-derived compounds as safer and more environmentally friendly alternatives to synthetic compounds. The emphasis on these all-natural options should be a part of a larger trend that aims to use natural components to make more powerful, environmentally responsible, and healthy deodorants.

5 Conclusion

In summary, this review article provides an overview of the presence and potential health hazards of contaminants used in deodorant products. Gaining knowledge about how these pollutants behave in the environment (air, water, and soil) and their potential effects on ecological systems and human well-being is vital in developing sustainable and safe deodorant formulations. Common substances like benzyl alcohol, diethyl phthalate, and ethanol may cause skin irritation, allergic responses, respiratory irritation, and, in certain circumstances, impacts on reproductive hormones. Furthermore, these substances are not confined to a specific environmental compartment. When applied, they can enter the atmosphere and then travel through several different channels to get to water and soil. While some substances naturally degrade, others linger in the environment for extended periods, which can cause bioaccumulation and subsequent human exposure via the food chain. It is essential for effective risk management and the creation of safer substitutes to have a thorough understanding of the environmental fate and potential health concerns related to deodorant pollutants. More research is needed to investigate the long-term effects of exposure, particularly among vulnerable populations. Given the potential health risks associated with certain deodorant compounds, manufacturers, regulators, and consumers must prioritize the use of safer ingredients and encourage the development and adoption of environmentally friendly formulations.

References

1. Perfume Market size in India, https://www.prnewswire.com (2022)
2. nsights Into India's Fragrance Products Market, 2020: Pocket Perfumes Have Rose to Popularity, https://www.businesswire.com
3. V.T. Seller, C.D. Brilliant, C. Morgan, S.P. Lewis, J. Duckers, F.A. Boy, P.D. Lewis, Anti-perspirant deodorant particulate matter temporal concentrations during home usage, Building and Environment, **195** (2021): 107738
4. M. Ago, K. Ago, M. Ogata, A fatal case of n-butane poisoning after inhaling anti-perspiration aerosol deodorant, Legal Medicine, **4**,2 (2002): 113-118
5. A. Steinemann, Fragranced consumer products: effects on asthmatics, Air Quality, Atmosphere and Health, **11**,1 (2018): 3-9
6. A. Steinemann, International prevalence of fragrance sensitivity, Air Quality, Atmosphere and Health, **12**,8 (2019): 891-897
7. J.H. Kim, T. Kim, H. Yoon, A. Jo, D. Lee, P. Kim, J. Seo, Health risk assessment of dermal and inhalation exposure to deodorants in Korea, Science of The Total Environment, **625**, (2018): 1369-1379
8. B. Bridges, Fragrance: Emerging health and environmental concerns, Flavour and Fragrance Journal, **17**,5 (2002): 361-371
9. W. Wei, J.C. Little, O. Ramalho, C. Mandin, Predicting chemical emissions from household cleaning and personal care products: A review, Building and Environment, **207** (2022): 108483
10. T. Wang, H. Zou, D. Li, J. Gao, Q. Bu, Z. Wang, Global distribution and ecological risk assessment of synthetic musks in the environment, Environmental Pollution, **331** (2023): 121893
11. M.C. Martini, Déodorants et antitranspirants, Annales de Dermatologie et de Vénéréologie, **147**,5 (2020): 387-395
12. Z. Kazemi, E. Aboutaleb, A. Shahsavani, M. Kermani, Z. Kazemi, Evaluation of pollutants in perfumes, colognes and health effects on the consumer: a systematic review, Journal of Environmental Health Science and Engineering, **20**,1 (2022): 589-598
13. L.L.M. Modika, L. Matsheketsheke, J.R. Gumbo, Assessment of silver metal released into wastewater after using a silver deodorant, WIT Transactions on Ecology and the Environment, **228** (2018): 121-129
14. G. Tjandraatmadja, C. Pollard, C. Sheedy, Y. Gozukara, Sources of contaminants in domestic wastewater : nutrients and additional elements from household products, Water for a Healthy Country Flagship Report: CSIRO, Canberra (2010)
15. D. Missia, T. Kopanidis, J. Bartzis, G.V. Silva, E.D.O. Fernandes, P. Carrer, P. Wolkoff, M. Stranger, E. Goelen, Literature review on, product composition, emitted compounds and emissions rates and health end points from consumer products, (2010)
16. M. Atiq, V.R.C. Sekar, Identification and estimation of phthalate esters in the commonly used deodorants

in UAE by using HPTLC method, Gulf Medical University: Proceedings, **6**,5-6 (2014): 114-119
17. C.H. Lu, M.C. Fang, Y.Z. Chen, S.C. Huang, D.Y. Wang, Quantitative analysis of fragrance allergens in various matrixes of cosmetics by liquideliquid extraction and GCeMS, Journal of Food and Drug Analysis, **29**,4 (2021): 700
18. Interest Group Environmental Chemistry, Emerging organic contaminants & antimicrobial resistance, CIBR, www.envchemgroup.com, Access on February 2018
19. P. Teerasumran, E. Velliou, S. Bai, Q. Cai, Deodorants and antiperspirants: New trends in their active agents and testing methods, International Journal of Cosmetic Science, (2023): 1-18
20. H. Cumming, C. Rücker, Octanol-Water Partition Coefficient Measurement by a Simple 1H NMR Method, ACS Omega, **2**,9 (2017): 6244-6249
21. M. Odabasi, E. Cetin, A. Sofuoglu, Determination of octanol-air partition coefficients and supercooled liquid vapor pressures of PAHs as a function of temperature: Application to gas-particle partitioning in an urban atmosphere, Atmospheric Environment, **40**,34 (2006): 6615-6625
22. M. Odabasi, B. Cetin, Determination of octanol-air partition coefficients of organochlorine pesticides (OCPs) as a function of temperature: Application to air-soil exchange, Journal of Environmental Management, **113** (2012): 432-439
23. F. Wania, Potential of degradable organic chemicals for absolute and relative enrichment in the Arctic, Environmental Science and Technology, **40**,2 (2006): 569-577
24. D. Muir, P.H. Howard, W. Meylan, Identification of new, possible PB&T substances important in the Great Lakes region by screening of chemicals in commerce, www. epa. gov, Access on May 2012
25. G. Hodges, C. Eadsforth, B. Bossuyt, A. Bouvy, M.H. Enrici, M. Geurts, M. Kotthoff, E. Michie, D. Miller, J. Müller, G. Oetter, J. Roberts, D. Schowanek, P. Sun, J. Venzmer, A comparison of log K ow (n-octanol-water partition coefficient) values for non-ionic, anionic, cationic and amphoteric surfactants determined using predictions and experimental methods, Environmental Sciences Europe, **31**,1 (2019): 1-18
26. J. De Bruijn, F. Busser, W. Seinen, J. Hermens, Determination of octanol/water partition coefficients for hydrophobic organic chemicals with the "slow-stirring" method, Environmental Toxicology and Chemistry, **8**,6 (1989): 499-512
27. B.C. Kelly, M.G. Ikonomou, J.D. Blair, A.E. Morin, F.A.P.C. Gobas, Food web-specific biomagnification of persistent organic pollutants, Science, **317**,5835 (2007): 236-239
28. F.A.P.C. Gobas, B.C. Kelly, J.A. Arnot, Quantitative Structure Activity Relationships for Predicting the Bioaccumulation of POPs in Terrestrial Food-Webs, QSAR & Combinatorial Science, **22**,3 (2003): 329-336
29. Q. Wang, R. He, J. Xu, F. Jin, Removal of 1,4-dioxane from wastewater by copper oxide catalyzed WAO with mild condition, in: E3S Web Conf., EDP Sciences, (2021): 01131
30. F.J.B. Rodriguez, Evaluation of 1, 4-dioxane biodegradation under aerobic and anaerobic conditions, Doctoral dissertation, Clemson University, (2016)
31. M.A. Pearson, G.W. Miller, Benzyl Benzoate, (2014): 433-434
32. J. Kim, S. Xu, Quantitative structure-reactivity relationships of hydroxyl radical rate constants for linear and cyclic volatile methylsiloxanes, Environmental Toxicology and Chemistry, **36**,12 (2017): 3240-3245
33. G. Rychen, G. Aquilina, G. Azimonti, V. Bampidis, M. de L. Bastos, G. Bories, A. Chesson, P.S. Cocconcelli, G. Flachowsky, B. Kolar, M. Kouba, M. López-Alonso, S.L. Puente, A. Mantovani, B. Mayo, F. Ramos, M. Saarela, R.E. Villa, R.J. Wallace, P. Wester, A.K. Lundebye, C. Nebbia, D. Renshaw, M.L. Innocenti, J. Gropp, Safety and efficacy of butylated hydroxyanisole (BHA) as a feed additive for all animal species, EFSA Journal, **16**,3 (2018): 5215
34. M. Bährle-Rapp, Diethyl Phthalate, Springer Lexikon Kosmetik und Körperpflege, (2007): 155-155
35. Department of Climate Change, Energy, the Environment and Water, Styrene (ethenylbenzene), www.dcceew.gov.au, Access on 6 October 2021
36. O.I. Dar, R. Aslam, D. Pan, S. Sharma, M. Andotra, A. Kaur, A.Q. Jia, C. Faggio, Source, bioaccumulation, degradability and toxicity of triclosan in aquatic environments: A review, Environmental Technology & Innovation, **25** (2022): 102122
37. K. Klotz, W. Weistenhöfer, F. Neff, A. Hartwig, C. Van Thriel, H. Drexler, The Health Effects of Aluminum Exposure, Deutsches Ärzteblatt International, **114**,39 (2017): 653
38. A. Pineau, B. Fauconneau, A.P. Sappino, R. Deloncle, O. Guillard, If exposure to aluminium in antiperspirants presents health risks, its content should be reduced, Journal of Trace Elements in Medicine and Biology, **28**,2 (2014): 147-150
39. U. Bernauer, L. Bodin, Q. Chaudhry, P.J. Coenraads, M. Dusinska, J. Ezendam, E. Gaffet C.L. Galli, B. Granum, E. Panteri, V. Rogiers, OPINION ON the safety of Aluminium in cosmetic products-Submission II, (2021): 0-136
40. Centers for Disease Control and Prevention, 1,4-Dioxane, www.cdc.gov, Access on 21 June 2019
41. Environmental Public Health, Oregon Health Authority : High Priority Chemicals of Concern for

Children's Health : Toxic Substances : State of Oregon, www.oregon.gov
42. J. Huff, P.F. Infante, Styrene exposure and risk of cancer, Mutagenesis, **26**,5 (2011): 583
43. P.M. Schlosser, A.S. Bale, C.F. Gibbons, A. Wilkins, G.S. Cooper, Human Health Effects of Dichloromethane: Key Findings and Scientific Issues, Environmental Health Perspectives, **123**,2 (2015): 114
44. P.P. Phiboonchaiyanan, K. Busaranon, C. Ninsontia, P. Chanvorachote, Benzophenone-3 increases metastasis potential in lung cancer cells via epithelial to mesenchymal transition, Cell Biology and Toxicology, **33**,3 (2017): 251-261
45. J.K. Aronson, Antiseptic drugs and disinfectants, Side Effects of Drugs Annual, **35** (2014): 435-445
46. O. Health, A. Program, E.H. Section, Triclosan Technical Fact Sheet, http://www.ct.gov/dph, Access on January 2014
47. C. Disinfectant, R. Card, Disinfectant #14 : Chlorhexidine : Safe for humans, but at what risk to the environment ?, www.viroxanimalhealth.com
48. T.Y. Lim, R.L. Poole, N.M. Pageler, Propylene Glycol Toxicity in Children, The Journal of Pediatric Pharmacology and Therapeutics : JPPT, **19**,4 (2014): 277
49. J.L. Lyche, A.C. Gutleb, Å. Bergman, G.S. Eriksen, A.J. Murk, E. Ropstad, M. Saunders, J.U. Skaare, Reproductive and developmental toxicity of phthalates, Journal of Toxicology and Environmental Health. Part B, Critical Reviews, **12**,4 (2009): 225-249
50. J.K. Hyun, M.L. Byung, Estimated exposure to phthalates in cosmetics and risk assessment, Journal of Toxicology and Environmental Health. Part A, **67**,23-24 (2004): 1901-1914
51. J. Lincho, R.C. Martins, J. Gomes, Paraben Compounds-Part I: An Overview of Their Characteristics, Detection, and Impacts, Applied Sciences, **11**,5 (2021): 2307
52. A. Wilson, The Mystery of Deodorant: What's Really In There?, www.greenamerica.org (2022)

Pharmaceuticals and Agro-Chemicals in Groundwater of Hyderabad, India

Kalyani Subbalakshmi Golakoti[1], *Sneha* Maloth[1], *Madhu Kumar* Kumara[2], *Murali Krishna* Sabavath[1], *Sukanya* Areeya[3], *Debraj* Bhattacharyya[2], and *Keerthi* Katam[1,*]

[1] Department of Civil Engineering, École Centrale School of Engineering, Mahindra University, Telangana, 500043, India
[2] Department of Civil Engineering, Indian Institute of Technology Hyderabad, Kandi, Telangana, 502285, India
[3] Biorefinery and Process Automation Engineering Center, Chemical and Process Engineering, The Sirindhorn International Thai-German Graduate School of Engineering, King Mongkut's University of Technology North Bangkok, Bangkok, 10800, Thailand

Abstract. Organic micropollutants continue to worsen groundwater pollution, especially in many areas of the world where water resources are becoming scarce. India uses groundwater more than any other nation. The main objective of this study is to evaluate the groundwater quality of Hyderabad, India by comprehensively analyzing organic micropollutants. Samples were collected from groundwater borewells in eight different sites (Begumpet, Bharatnagar, Dundigal, Jubilee Hills, Kukatpally, Sanath nagar, Tarnaka, and Tirumalagiri). The non-targeted screening analysis was performed using liquid chromatography-quadrupole time-of-flight (LC-QTOF). About 250 different compounds were detected in total from all the samples. This includes pharmaceuticals, herbicides, fungicides, pesticides, hormones, steroids, cosmetics, plasticizers, cyanotoxins, and metabolites. In all samples, pharmaceuticals accounted for approximately 50% of the detected compounds. The Sanath nagar groundwater sample had been detected with more than 130 compounds and the least number of compounds were detected in Taranaka, Jubilee Hills, and Kukatpally areas. Apramycin (veterinary drug) and Bis(2-ethylhexyl) phthalate (plasticizer) had been found in all eight samples. The high abundance values were observed for 17αβ - Dihydroequilin, Avobenzone, Butachlor, Clarithromycin-N-oxide, Dibutyl phthalate, Doxepin, Estriol, Napropamide, and Nefazodone. Estriol and 17αβ - Dihydroequilin are the largest endocrine disruptors. The presence of various pharmaceuticals and agrochemicals in groundwater reveals pollution either directly or indirectly, by the discharge of domestic and industrial wastewater.

Keyword. Cyanatoxin, EDC, Non-target screening, LC-QTOF, PCA, PFAS

1 Introduction

The Telangana region has few surface water sources due to its hard-rocky terrain, and as rains become shorter, more intense, and irregular, groundwater serves as the main source of surface water for the local population. As a result, groundwater usage is rising, particularly in urbanizing cities. Unfortunately, human activity in urban areas is the primary driver of pollution that impacts adjacent cities and watershed aquifers. Among the many different kinds of micropollutants, people frequently use hormones, insecticides, personal care products (PPCPs), and pharmaceuticals. These hazardous compounds may endanger aquatic life after being released into the environment, mostly through sewage discharge [1]. According to several research investigations, micropollutants and their metabolites are extensively distributed in urban aquatic habitats, which has raised global concerns [2-6]. Humans as well as livestock are often treated with pharmaceuticals and hormones; nevertheless, these drugs have the potential to contaminate groundwater. Even at low concentrations, these bioactive compounds may have negative effects on human health such as endocrine disruption and propagate antibiotic resistance genes within the human microbiome [7].

Agrochemicals are any substances that are used to prevent, decrease, control, or repel pests from crops. In modern agriculture, pesticides are frequently employed to increase crop productivity to meet the food demand of the increased population. There are several different types of pesticides, including termiticides, algaecides, fungicides, germicides, herbicides, insecticides, miticides, molluskicides, and rodenticides. They are substances used by human civilization to ward off or subdue pests including germs, nematodes, insects, mites, birds, rodents, and other organisms that are harmful to human health or food production. They could be chemical, biological, or a combination of the two. In India, the most common pesticides used are insecticides (51%), followed by herbicides (16%) and fungicides + bactericides (33%) [8]. An average of only 0.1 percent of pesticides are known to reach the intended species; the remainder infiltrates different parts of the ecosystem.

* Corresponding author: keerthi.katam@mahindrauniversity.edu.in

The level of contamination risk depends on the relative rates of infiltration and degradation within the soil profile. Several factors, including climate, soil properties, chemical composition, application rate, depth of the aquifer, and agricultural practices, influence these processes.

India is one of the largest manufacturers of medicines in the global market. Hyderabad is the country's primary pharmaceutical manufacturing hub. There are over 800 biotech and pharmaceutical companies in the Hyderabad area. The groundwater sample from Patancheru, Hyderabad, consisted of a total of 12 pharmaceuticals, with cetirizine, ciprofloxacin, enoxacin, and metoprolol being the most prevalent [9]. Sewage in the Patancheru-Bollaram industrial region had high levels of voriconazole, fluconazole, and moxifloxacin [10]. In many parts of Hyderabad, groundwater concentrations of dichlorodiphenyltrichloroethane, endosulfan, and lindane exceeded their corresponding acceptable daily intake values established for human consumption [11]. This study aims to detect micropollutants and evaluate the magnitude of groundwater pollution resulting from human activities in different areas of Hyderabad.

2 Materials and methodology

2.1. Sample collection

Samples were collected from groundwater borewells in eight different sites (Begumpet, Bharatnagar, Dundigal, Jubilee Hills, Kukatpally, Sanath nagar, Tarnaka, and Tirumalagiri) which are densely populated urban areas in Hyderabad, Telangana. The map with sampling sites is given in Figure 1.

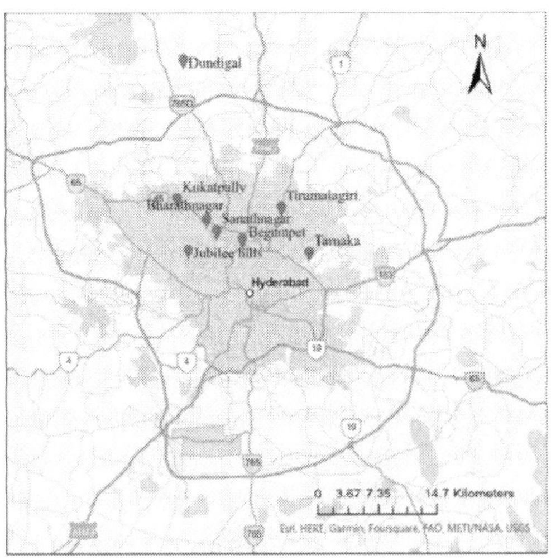

Fig. 1. Selected sampling sites.

Samples were collected in March and April of 2023. Collected samples were passed through a 0.22 µm filter and filtered samples were stored at 4 °C until analysis.

2.2 Analysis of Micropollutants

The filtered samples were transferred to 2 mL amber LC vials and injected into the instrument via an auto-sampler for the identification of micropollutants. Screening of the samples was conducted using an Agilent 6545 Liquid Chromatography-Quadrapole Time of Flight (LC-QTOF) system. The system was equipped with a 1260 Infinity II pump, and a 10 µL portion of the sample was injected for screening. Gradient flow was employed for the separation and identification of target compounds. For this study, a mobile phase consisting of an aqueous solution of 5 mM ammonium acetate and 0.1% acetic acid (mobile phase A), and 0.1% acetic acid in MeOH (mobile phase B) was used. All chemicals and solvents used were of MS grade.

The mobile phase A was initially set at 95% for 0.5 minutes and then gradually increased to 100% B over the next 10.5 minutes. The system maintained 100% B for 2 minutes, followed by a ramp back to 95% A over 5 minutes. Subsequently, 95% A was held for 2 minutes. The total run time for each sample was 20 minutes. A 1-minute post-run was performed after each sample to eliminate any residual interference from the previous sample before the next injection. A Zorbax Eclipse plus C18 (Narrow Bore RR) column with dimensions of 2.1 x 100 mm and a diameter of 3.5 microns was used, maintaining a mobile phase flow rate of 0.22 mL/min. The maximum allowable column pressure was set at 450, and the column temperature was held steady at 40±0.4 °C.

Mass spectrometry was conducted using an Agilent Jet Stream Electrospray Ionization source operating in both positive and negative modes. The mass range was set from m/z 100 to 1200 with a data acquisition rate of 3 spectra/s. Specific parameters were maintained during the measurement, including a gas temperature of 150 °C, drying gas (N2) flow rate of 10 L/min, nebulizer gas pressure of 35 psi, sheath gas temperature of 375 °C, sheath gas flow of 11 L/min, 3500 V capillary voltage, and 125 V fragmentor voltage. Additionally, a reference compound solution with m/z values of 121.0509, 922.0098 (positive ionization mode), and m/z 112.9856, 966.0007 (negative ionization mode) was injected for mass drift correction.

The spectra files were processed using Agilent MassHunter Qualitative Workflows B.08.00 software for target/suspect screening. Data files were screened using the Agilent MassHunter Personal Compound Database and Library (PCDL)-water library to identify compounds, along with their respective abundance and Q-Score.

2.3 Statistical analysis

The principal component analysis (PCA) for each compound's abundance values detected at different sampling sites was carried out using the Microsoft Excel XLSTAT statistical program. PCA is a multivariate statistical technique for data visualization and dimensionality reduction. The popular statistics software XLSTAT has a PCA analysis tool. The PCA analysis equations in XLSTAT involve several mathematical operations. Each variable is standardized by subtracting the mean from each variable and dividing by the standard deviation, to have a mean of zero and a standard deviation of one. The covariance matrix is derived from the standardized data. The eigenvalues and eigenvectors of the covariance matrix are calculated. The eigenvectors are used to represent the principal components, which are orthogonal (uncorrelated) linear combinations of the starting variables. The eigenvalues are variances of each basic component. For calculating the main component scores, the eigenvector matrix is multiplied by the standardized data matrix. The data points for the new main component space are based on these findings. The variance that each major component contributes was determined by simply dividing each eigenvalue by the sum of all eigenvalues. This demonstrates the proportion of the total variability of the data that each basic component was able to record. The two main components and the relationship between each original variable and the loading scores are presented. These findings show which variables have the most effects on each key parameter. PCA assists in better understanding the underlying structure and patterns in the data by using these equations.

2.4 Geospatial analysis

The spatial mapping of the compounds that are identified in at least seven sampling sites was shown using the "inverse distance weighted (IDW)" interpolation method in the ArcGIS pro application. ArcGIS Pro is a well-known geographic information system application that has reliable capabilities for creating interpolation maps. It provides an extensive range of interpolation methods suitable for various data types and geographic patterns one sort of interpolation that is regularly used is IDW. This method makes use of weights that are based on the distance between nearby sample sites in order to estimate values in unsampled areas. To project values at locations that weren't sampled, ArcGIS's IDW interpolation technique employs the equation below:

$$Z(x) = \frac{\sum_{i=1}^{n}\left(\frac{Z_i}{d(x,x_i)^p}\right)}{\sum_{i=1}^{n}\left(\frac{1}{d(x,x_i)^p}\right)} \quad (1)$$

In this equation, $z(x)$ represents the estimated value at the desired location x, Z_i is the measured value at the sampling location i, $d(x,x_i)$ designates the distance between the target location x and the sampling location i, p is the power parameter that calculates each sample point's effect based on its location. The weighted average of the observed values at the sample sites is calculated using the IDW interpolation method, where the weight given to each point is inversely proportional to the distance raised to the power p. IDW interpolation uses a power value of two by default, which is also a typical number.

3 Results and discussion

The number of compounds detected in the groundwater samples is given in Figure 2. The Sanath nagar groundwater sample had been detected with more than 130 compounds and the least number of compounds were detected in Taranaka, Jubilee Hills, and Kukatpally areas.

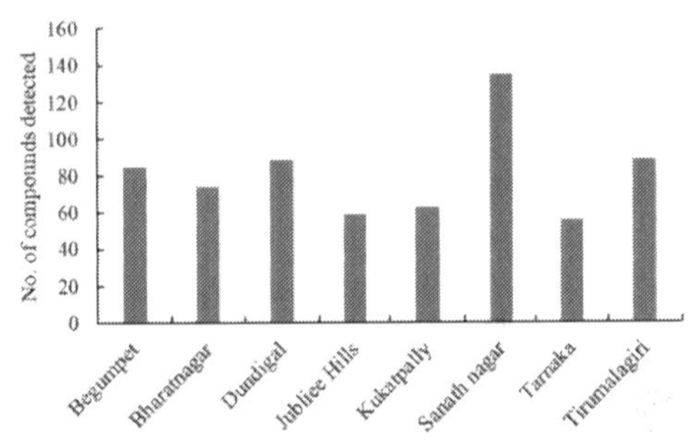

Fig. 2. Total number of compounds detected in the sampling sites.

These detected compounds were categorized as pharmaceuticals, metabolites, herbicides, fungicides, insecticides, pesticides, hormones and steroids, plasticizers, cyanotoxins, cosmetics (primarily UV filters), and miscellaneous. The average composition of the detected compounds at all locations is represented as a pie chart in Figure 3. In all the samples the pharmaceuticals accounted for more than 50% of the detected compounds. Agrochemical compounds (insecticides, herbicides, fungicides, and other pesticides) varied between 10 - 20% of the total detected compounds. Overall, more than 70% of the detected compounds belong to pharmaceuticals and agrochemicals. The Sanath nagar sample had 63% of pharmaceutical compounds and 20% of agrochemical compounds in the total detected compounds. Tarnaka and Jubilee Hills samples had the least number of pharmaceuticals (30% of the total) and 12% of agrochemicals.

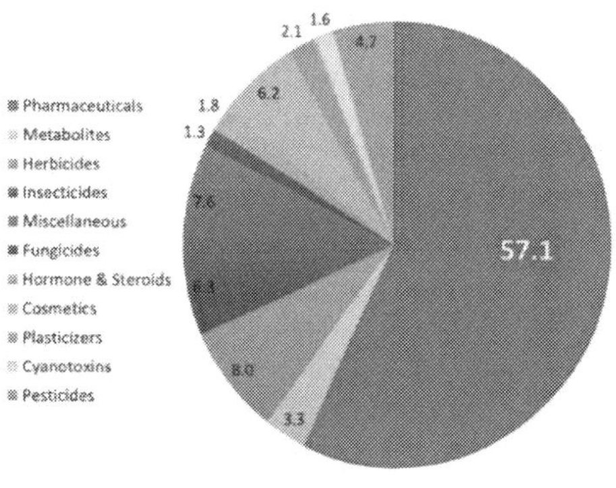

Fig. 3. Composition of the detected compounds.

The principal component analysis (PCA) results of all the identified compounds across all samples and sampling sites is shown in Figure 4. The eigenvalues are depicted as red segments, which represent sampling sites that have the greatest influence on each principal component. Results of the PCA showed a separation of the parameters related to herbicides, hormones, personal care products, pharmaceuticals, and plasticizers on the two independent axes. The first component (PC1), accounts for 51.1% of the variance and the second component (PC2), explains 22.7% variance. PC2 effectively separated the selected sampling sites into two sets. The sampling sites Sanath Nagar, Dundigal, Begumpet, and Tirumalgiri were situated in the positive direction of PC2. Within this cluster of groundwater samples, over 85 compounds were detected. The sampling sites with fewer than 85 detected compounds formed the second cluster of sample sites. The second set of sampling sites, including Tarnaka, Jubilee Hills, Kukatpally, and Bharat Nagar, were distributed in the negative direction of PC2. The micropollutant cluster with positive loading in both PC1 and high PC2 values consists of six pollutants, namely Avobenzene, Estriol, 17α-Dihydroequilin, Butachlor, Sibutramine and Bis(2-ethylhexyl) phthalate. These pollutants were detected in high abundance in the sampling sites of Sanath Nagar, Dundigal, Begumpet, and Tirumalgiri. On the other hand, the other cluster consists of five compounds, namely Clarithromycin-N-oxide, Dibutyl phthalate, Doxepin, Nefazodone, and Napropamide, which were abundantly detected in Tarnaka, Jubilee Hills, Kukatpally, and Bharat Nagar. The remaining compounds (~225) were mainly located on PC1 component axis with low PC2 values (both negative and positive). The compounds Nefazadone, Napropamide, Microcystin-LR, N-Methylpyrrolidone, and Apramycin had been detected in at least seven sample sites. Apramycin and Bis(2-ethylhexyl) phthalate had been found in all eight samples. The compounds Dextilidine, Erythromycin, and Narasin are majorly detected in Begumpet, Dundigal, Sanath nagar, and Tirumalagiri groundwater samples. The remaining (~200) compounds were identified in at least one sampling site. The compounds like Simetryn, Methadone-d3, N-Methylacetanilide, Naftidrofuryl, Pindolol, Nuarimol, Reserpine, and Codeine-d6 which are primarily on PC2 are mainly detected in Sanath nagar samples.

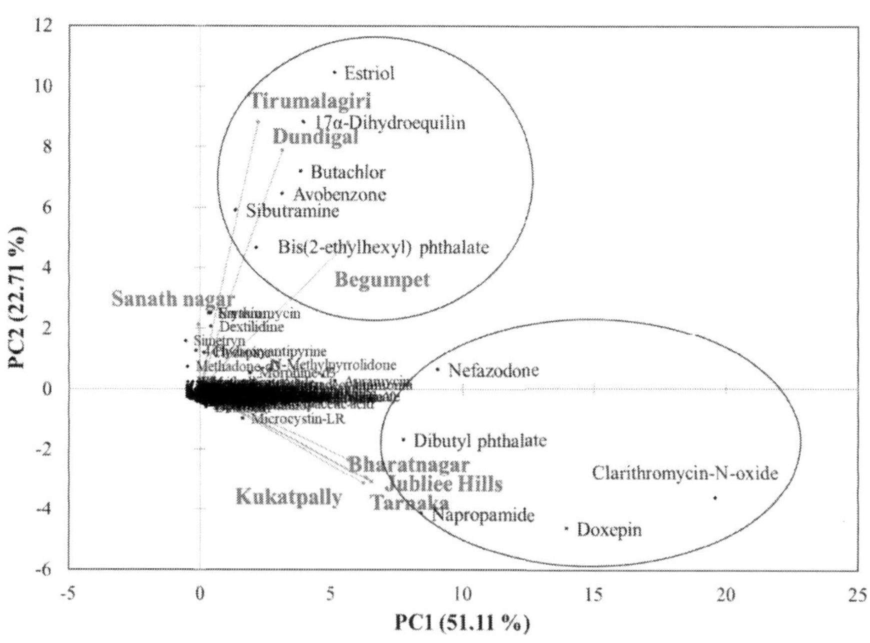

Fig. 4. Principal component analysis of all compounds detected in all the samples at all sampling sites.

Clozapine is an antipsychotic drug used to treat symptoms of schizophrenia: hallucinations and delusions was also detected in five sampling sites in low abundance (<30,000). The groundwater samples contained perfluorooctanoic acid (PFOA), perfluorohexanoic acid (PFHxA), perfluoropentanoic acid (PFPeA), and perfluorotetradecanoic acid (PFTDA). These chemicals belong to the class of poly- and perfluoroalkyl substances (PFASs), which are highly stable fluorinated aliphatic compounds. PFASs are commonly utilized in various applications such as cosmetics, firefighting foams, nonstick cookware, water- and oil-resistant garments, and carpets. PFOA had been detected mainly in the Bharat nagar groundwater sample. PFHxA was detected in Jubilee Hills. Exposure to PFAS can lead to health effects such as kidney cancer, increased liver weight, elevated cholesterol, decreased fertility, obesity, thyroid issues, and immunosuppression [12,13].

The compounds that are detected at high abundance greater than 30,000 were given in Table 1. Thirty compounds showed high abundance values greater than 30,000 among them 16 belong to pharmaceuticals and 5 compounds are agrochemicals. Clarithromycin N-oxide is a urinary metabolite of Clarithromycin, an antibiotic that was detected in almost all the samples indicating the pollution of groundwater with domestic wastewater. The pharmaceutical compounds Apramycin, Doxepin, and Nefazodone were detected in almost all the samples. Apramycin is an aminoglycoside veterinary antibiotic used to treat infections in animals. Doxepin and Nefazodone are medications belonging to the antidepressant class of drugs used to treat major depressive disorder, anxiety disorders, chronic hives, and insomnia. These are detected in seven groundwater samples. Sibutramine an anti-obesity drug was found in high abundance in Dundigal and Tirumalgiri groundwater samples. 4-Hydroxyantipyrine is a major human metabolite of antipyrine which is used for ear infections. Codeine is commonly prescribed as a pain reliever that is converted to its metabolite, morphine, in the liver by an enzyme known as cytochrome P450 isoenzyme 2D6 (CYP2D6). Morphine has been detected as a urinary metabolite of codeine [14] and excessive levels of morphine in the breast milk of codeine-prescribed mothers have been associated with infant mortality [15]. Codeine had been detected in only two sampling locations (Bharat nagar and Sanath nagar) whereas Morphine had been identified in seven groundwater samples indicating the discharge of domestic wastewater. Erythromycin an antibiotic had been detected in five locations with high abundance in the Tirumalgiri sample. Exposure to Erythromycin at 0.1 μg/L concentration in aquatic environments delayed hatching and decreased the survival rate of zebrafish [16,17]. Pindolol a beta blocker used to treat high blood pressure is detected in Sanath nagar groundwater. Fish exposed to these substances may experience cardiovascular dysfunction, which might decrease their growth rate [18].

Butachlor is a common herbicide, used for stopping weeds from developing new plant tissues, highest abundance values were detected in Begumpet and Dundigal groundwater samples. The majority of butachlor enters the environment through various agricultural, horticultural, and forestry practices, which include improper water management, rainfall, and runoff from agricultural areas to watersheds and aquatic habitats [19]. Butachlor ingestion is not highly toxic. However, there have been some rare instances of serious neurological and cardiovascular effects, particularly after oral consumption [20]. Butachlor is not permitted in Hokkaido, Japan, during the rice-planting season due to the herbicide's potential to contaminate aquatic environments. Butachlor-containing formulations for "Machete" also include inert ingredients such as xylenes and N-butyl alcohol. Either of these chemicals has the potential to affect the liver and kidneys. Memory, attention, and hearing issues can develop in the brain as a result of prolonged exposure to xylenes. Other consequences include decreased bone marrow production and low blood cell count. Napropamide is a herbicide that is widely utilized. Although it exhibits low toxicity to mammals, it can cause irritation to the skin and eyes. It possesses moderate solubility in water and displays persistence in soil systems. Available data suggests that, under specific conditions, it may also persist in water. Significant quantities of Napropamide were found in Jubilee Hills, Kukatpally, and Tarnaka. On the other hand, the insecticide Picaridin, commonly used as an insect repellent, was detected in samples from Bharat Nagar and Sanath Nagar. The most commonly reported side effects following exposure to insect repellents were nausea, vomiting, red eyes/conjunctivitis, and mouth irritation.

Dibutyl phthalate is a synthetic compound that is incorporated into plastics and various other chemicals. In the context of plastics, it serves as a plasticizer, contributing to their softness. It is also utilized in elastomers, lacquers, explosives, printing inks, solvents for resin and perfume oils, paper coatings, adhesives, and nail polish. The highest abundance values were observed in Begumpet, Bharat nager, and Jubilee Hills samples. Prolonged exposure to butyl phthalate may be harmful to the liver, kidneys, developing fetus, and male testes. Bis(2-ethylhexyl) phthalate (DEHP) is detected in all the samples with high abundance in Dundigal groundwater. The U.S. Environmental Protection Agency has determined that DEHP is a probable human carcinogen that can cause cancer, birth defects, development of the fetus, and male reproductive damage [21].

The compound Avobenzone is a UVA blocker used as an active ingredient in sunscreens. The highest concentration of Avobenzone is detected in Tirumalgiri and Begumpet groundwater samples. In early pregnancy, avobenzone can trigger mitochondrial dysfunction-mediated apoptosis, which results in abnormal placentation [22]. Estriol and 17αβ - Dihydroequilin had high abundance values in Begumpet, Dundigal, and Tirumalgiri. These compounds are estrogens which are classified as the greatest endocrine disruptors among many micropollutants. The concentration of these hormones, which play a role in the development of feminine features in a variety of living creatures, has increased recently in aquatic environments [23]. Humans as well as animals regularly produce the natural estrogens estriol and 17-Dihydroequilin [24]. Microcystin-LR a cyanotoxin that is generated by cyanobacteria during eutrophication, was also identified at seven sample locations with the highest abundance in the Kukatpally sample indicating the contamination of water with high nutrients or algae.

Table 1. Micropollutants identified in different groundwater samples of Hyderabad.

	Names	Begumpet	Bharat nagar	Dundigal	Jubliee Hills	Kukatpally	Sanath nagar	Tarnaka	Tirumalagiri
Cosmetic	Avobenzone	**163403**	4158	25187	N.D.	N.D.	21113	N.D.	**169373**
Cyanotoxins	Microcystin-LR	2237	N.D.	7555	2286	**105749**	671	3375	3966
Fungicide	Nuarimol	N.D.	415	N.D.	N.D.	N.D.	**39050**	N.D.	N.D.
Insecticide	Picaridin	N.D.	**48966**	N.D.	N.D.	N.D.	1913	N.D.	N.D.
Herbicide	Butachlor	**163403**	N.D.	**216699**	N.D.	N.D.	19692	N.D.	26746
	Napropamide	7938	16300	7604	**124720**	**149439**	2113	**122073**	N.D.
	Simetryn	N.D.	N.D.	N.D.	N.D.	N.D.	**223937**	N.D.	N.D.
Hormones and Steroids	17α-Dihydroequilin	**146019**	11487	**100076**	N.D.	N.D.	6193	N.D.	**217578**
	Estriol	**175638**	27280	**169976**	N.D.	N.D.	15518	N.D.	**208464**
Metabolite	Clarithromycin-N-oxide	**219218**	**204354**	62738	**200859**	**236678**	N.D.	**182870**	11689
Miscellaneous	N-Methylpyrrolidone	44707	51350	44699	38276	**59370**	N.D.	48541	42282
	N-Methylacetanilide	869	N.D.	N.D.	N.D.	N.D.	**52625**	N.D.	1608
	4-Nonylpenoxyacetic acid	N.D.	38727	N.D.	N.D.	N.D.	853	N.D.	N.D.
Pharmaceuticals	4-Hydroxyantipyrine	N.D.	N.D.	18057	N.D.	N.D.	**42877**	N.D.	31784
	Apramycin	28237	**73373**	47297	50564	57976	2523	50579	51914
	Codeine-d6	N.D.	572	N.D.	N.D.	N.D.	37347	N.D.	N.D.
	Dextilidine	26272	N.D.	18939	N.D.	N.D.	721	N.D.	**66004**
	Doxepin	**112908**	**255076**	4776	**129622**	**174821**	N.D.	**117224**	1629
	Erythromycin	5360	838	53874	N.D.	N.D.	1564	N.D.	**63655**
	Lovastatin	1245	30989	625	N.D.	N.D.	2484	N.D.	N.D.
	Methadone-d3	N.D.	822	N.D.	603	607	**123497**	564	N.D.
	Morphine-d3	26408	25221	33572	25274	N.D.	20335	31313	15143
	Naftidrofuryl	N.D.	N.D.	N.D.	N.D.	N.D.	43395	N.D.	N.D.
	Narasin	1922	N.D.	51583	N.D.	N.D.	14217	N.D.	**62789**
	Nefazodone	**103249**	N.D.	88061	**102249**	**126016**	3778	**101246**	46716
	Pindolol	1196	N.D.	N.D.	N.D.	N.D.	**39216**	N.D.	N.D.
	Reserpine	N.D.	N.D.	983	N.D.	N.D.	**38177**	N.D.	957
	Sibutramine	2385	N.D.	**103655**	N.D.	N.D.	N.D.	N.D.	**164261**
Plasticizer	Bis(2-ethylhexyl) phthalate	9982	20789	**210045**	8258	4903	29380	3365	14598
	Dibutyl phthalate	**109689**	**223355**	5684	**129622**	12070	N.D.	6469	1507

N.D. = not detected.

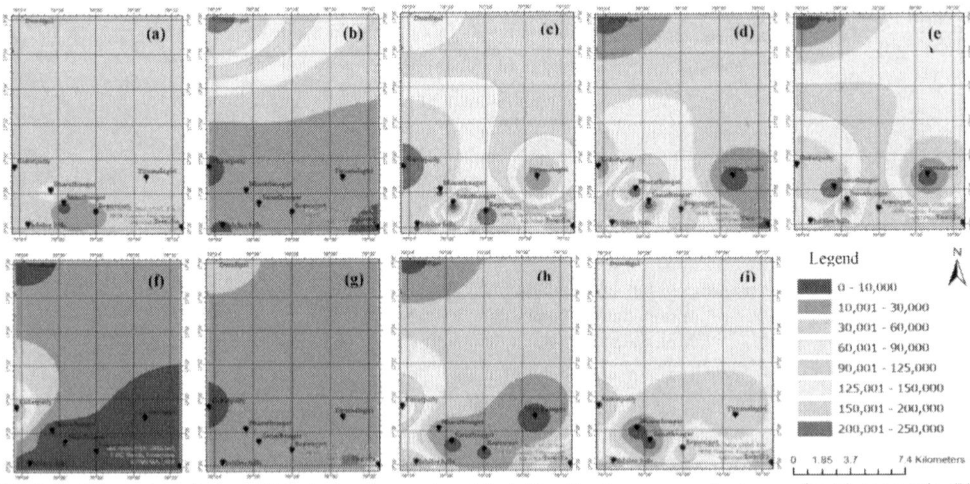

Fig. 5. Spatial mapping of micropollutants abundance values detected in at least seven groundwater samples (a) Apramycin, (b) Bis(2-ethylhexyl) phthalate, (c) Clarithromycin-N-oxide, (d) Dibutyl phthalate, (e) Doxepin, (f) Microcystin-LR, (g) Morphine-d3, (h) Napropamide, (i) Nefazodone

The Spatial mapping of micropollutants (Apramycin, Bis(2-ethylhexyl) phthalate, Clarithromycin-N-oxide, Dibutyl phthalate, Doxepin, Microcystin-LR, Morphine-d3, Napropamide, Nefazodone) detected in at least seven groundwater samples is shown in Figure 5. The spatial mapping of the Apramycin shows that the most prevalent abundance value range between 30,000 to 60,000. The highest abundance value of the compound is detected in Bharat nagar. The veterinary hospitals and poultry farms are majorly located in Begumpet, Kukatpally, Tarnaka, Sanath nagar, Jubilee hills, and Tirumalgiri areas. The spatial distribution of DEHP shows that most of the contamination of plasticizer is in Dundigal areas (Figure 5(b)). The spatial mapping of Clarithromycin-N-oxide metabolite indicates the groundwater contamination with domestic wastewater near Kukatpally, Begumpet, Bharat nagar, Jubilee hills, and Tirumalgiri areas. The spatial distribution of Dibutyl phthalate suggests that the higher abundance is near Bharat nagar areas. The presence of Dibutyl phthalate could be due to domestic wastewater discharge as it is also used in perfumes and nail polish. The mapping of Doxepin shows that regions near Kukatpally and Bharat nagar have a higher abundance of antidepressant. The prevalent abundance values of Microcystin-LR and Morphine-d3 ranged between 0 to 30,000. The highest abundance values of Napropamide and Nefazodone were detected mainly in Kukatpally, Jubilee Hills, and Tirumalgiri areas. The spatial mapping indicated that the Kukatpally, Bharat nagar, and Jubilee hills had high abundance value of the detected compounds even though the number of compounds detected are less than 80 indicating the intensity of pollution.

Based on the internet search about 200 pharmaceutical companies were located in the premises of the sample collected areas. The approximate number of pharmaceutical companies in Begumpet, Bharat nagar, Dundigal, Jubilee Hills, Kukatpally, Sanath nagar, Tarnaka, and Tirumalagiri were 14, 4, 5, 4, 12, 10, 6, and 14 respectively. Approximately 40 pharma companies are located near the premises of Sanath nagar and Begumpet areas. Although the number of companies in the region was less, the discharge from these surrounding companies could be one of the reasons for the high number of pharmaceutical compounds detected in groundwater samples from Sanath nagar and Begumpet. The next highest number of pharmaceuticals were detected in Dundigal area which had around 14 pharma companies nearby. Among the top 30 compounds, 13 pharmaceuticals were detected in Sanath nagar, 11 in Dundigal, and 10 in Begumpet and Tirumalgiri areas. The number of agrotech companies were also densely located near Jubilee Hills, Sanath nagar, and Begumpet areas where there is a possibility of discharge of the compounds through these industries. The urinary metabolites detected in the groundwater indicate the discharge of domestic wastewater or sewage mostly into the soil which would have contaminated the groundwater. Most of Hyderabad's residential communities have decentralized wastewater treatment plants where part of the treatment takes place and the treated water is recycled for daily needs such as gardening and toilet flushing. In most cases, the partially treated wastewater is sent to a centralized wastewater treatment facility. The inefficiencies of these treatment plants, leakage of wastewater during transportation, or infiltration of solid waste leachate could be the reasons for contamination. Almost all the sampling sites have at least one dumping yard.

The absence of monitoring micropollutants in these plants can be attributed to the lack of strict regulations and guidelines addressing these pollutants. Historically, the focus of wastewater treatment plants has been on conventional pollutants (like chemical oxygen demand, biological oxygen demand, and nutrients) than micropollutants. Furthermore, it is difficult for many treatment facilities to maintain the sophisticated equipment needed for micropollutant analysis in order to monitor micropollutants. To address these concerns, it is crucial to establish stricter regulations and guidelines specifically addressing micropollutants in wastewater treatment. Efforts should also be made to improve treatment plant efficiency, minimize wastewater leakage, and prevent solid waste leachate infiltration. Proper waste management practices and the implementation of monitoring systems can help identify and mitigate potential sources of contamination. Additionally, public awareness should be increased regarding the risks associated with micropollutants, and advanced treatment processes should be promoted in wastewater treatment plants. Regulatory agencies should work towards establishing guidelines and regulations for monitoring and controlling micropollutants, ensuring the protection of water resources and public health.

Source control measures should be implemented to prevent the introduction of micropollutants into groundwater. This can include stricter regulations and best management practices for industrial, agricultural, and residential activities. By reducing the use of harmful substances or implementing proper containment and disposal methods, the potential for micropollutant contamination can be minimized. Upgrading wastewater treatment plants, implementing constructed wetlands, managing aquifer recharge, and monitoring groundwater quality are among the recommended measures. Advanced treatment technologies such as activated carbon adsorption, ozonation, UV irradiation, and membrane filtration have shown promise in removing a wide range of micropollutants. Education and awareness campaigns are also important in promoting the responsible use and disposal of chemicals and fostering sustainable behaviors and practices. It is essential to customize the approach to each specific situation and micropollutant, as effectiveness may vary based on local conditions and characteristics. A comprehensive and site-specific strategy is necessary to effectively address emerging micropollutants in groundwater.

4 Conclusion

The groundwater samples of Hyderabad had been contaminated with many different classes of micropollutants with the majority belonging to pharmaceuticals and agrochemicals. The detected pharmaceuticals consist of veterinary medications, narcotic pharmaceuticals, pain killers, anti-psychotic, anti-depressant, and anti-obesity drugs. Sanath nagar and Begumpet areas which are surrounded by more pharmaceutical and agrochemical companies had shown more pharma and pesticide compounds in groundwater indicating the discharge of the industrial wastewater. The presence of urinary metabolites Clarithromycin N-oxide, 4-Hydroxyantipyrine, and Morphine indicates the discharge of domestic wastewater into the aquifers. The majority of the compounds identified have concerning effects on human health. The presence of micropollutants in groundwater, despite the short duration of this investigation, suggests that appropriate wastewater and solid waste treatment procedures should be implemented. Since a lot of new pollutants are consistently entering the market, continuous tracking measures and emission controls must be executed.

References

1. J. Rogowska, M. Cieszynska-Semenowicz, W. Ratajczyk, L. Wolska, Micropollutants in treated wastewater, Ambio, (2019): 1-17
2. C.L. Spindola Vilela, T.L. Damasceno, T. Thomas, R.S. Peixoto, Global qualitative and quantitative distribution of micropollutants in the deep sea, Environmental Pollution, **307** (2022): 119414
3. W. Busch, S. Schmidt, R. Kühne, T. Schulze, M. Krauss, R. Altenburger, Micropollutants in European rivers: A mode of action survey to support the development of effect-based tools for water monitoring, Environmental Toxicology and Chemistry, **35**,8 (2016): 1887-1899
4. K.O. K'oreje, F.J. Kandie, L. Vergeynst, M.A. Abira, H. Van Langenhove, M. Okoth, K. Demeestere, Occurrence, fate and removal of pharmaceuticals, personal care products and pesticides in wastewater stabilization ponds and receiving rivers in the Nzoia Basin, Kenya, Science of The Total Environment, **637** (2018): 336-348
5. H. Ou, E.Y. Zeng, Occurrence and fate of microplastics in wastewater treatment plants, in: Microplastic Contam. Aquat. Environ. An Emerg. Matter Environ. Urgency, Elsevier, (2018): 317-338
6. M.K. Kim, K.D. Zoh, Occurrence and removals of micropollutants in water environment, Environmental Engineering Research, **21**,4 (2016): 319-332
7. Y. Ben, C. Fu, M. Hu, L. Liu, M.H. Wong, C. Zheng, Human health risk assessment of antibiotic resistance associated with antibiotic residues in the environment: A review, Environmental Research, **169** (2019): 483-493
8. P. Nayak, H. Solanki, Pesticdes and indian agriculture A review, International Journal of Research Granthaalayah, **9**,5 (2021): 250-263
9. J. Fick, H. Söderström, R.H. Lindberg, C. Phan, M. Tysklind, D.G.J. Larsson, Contamination of surface, ground, and drinking water from pharmaceutical production, Environmental Toxicology and Chemistry, **28**,12 (2009): 2522-2527
10. C. Lübbert, C. Baars, A. Dayakar, N. Lippmann, A.C. Rodloff, M. Kinzig, F. Sörgel, Environmental pollution with antimicrobial agents from bulk drug manufacturing industries in Hyderabad, South India, is associated with dissemination of extended-spectrum beta-lactamase and carbapenemase-producing pathogens, Infection, **45**,4 (2017): 479-491

11. G. Shukla, A. Kumar, M. Bhanti, P.E. Joseph, A. Taneja, Organochlorine pesticide contamination of ground water in the city of Hyderabad, Environment International, **32**,2 (2006): 244-247
12. K.Y. Kim, O.D. Ekpe, H.J. Lee, J.E. Oh, Perfluoroalkyl substances and pharmaceuticals removal in full-scale drinking water treatment plants, Journal of Hazardous Materials, **400** (2020): 123235
13. X. Dauchy, Per- and polyfluoroalkyl substances (PFASs) in drinking water: Current state of the science, Current Opinion in Environmental Science & Health, **7** (2019): 8-12
14. D.A. Yee, R.S. Atayee, B.M. Best, J.D. Ma, Observations on the urine metabolic profile of codeine in pain patients, Journal of Analytical Toxicology, **38**,2 (2014): 86-91
15. G. Koren, J. Cairns, D. Chitayat, A. Gaedigk, S.J. Leeder, Pharmacogenetics of morphine poisoning in a breastfed neonate of a codeine-prescribed mother, Lancet, **368**,9536 (2006): 704
16. M. Yang, H. Fu, W.X. Wang, Responses of zebrafish (Danio rerio) cells to antibiotic erythromycin stress at the subcellular levels, Science of The Total Environment, **853** (2022): 158727
17. V.T. Minski, C. Garbinato, N. Thiel, A.M. Siebel, Erythromycin in the aquatic environment: deleterious effects on the initial development of zebrafish, Journal of Toxicology and Environmental Health. Part A, **84**,2 (2021): 56-66
18. S.F. Owen, E. Giltrow, D.B. Huggett, T.H. Hutchinson, J.A. Saye, M.J. Winter, J.P. Sumpter, Comparative physiology, pharmacology and toxicology of β-blockers: Mammals versus fish, Aquatic Toxicology, **82**,3 (2007): 145-162
19. J. Ok, N.H. Doan, H. Watanabe, D.Q. Thuyet, J. Boulange, Behavior of butachlor and pyrazosulfuron-ethyl in paddy water using micro paddy lysimeters under different temperature conditions in spring and summer, Bulletin of Environmental Contamination and Toxicology, **89**,2 (2012): 306-311
20. Y.C. Lo, C.C. Yang, J.F. Deng, Acute alachlor and butachlor herbicide poisoning, Clinical Toxicology, **46**,8 (2008): 716-721
21. S.S.S. Rowdhwal, J. Chen, Toxic effects of Di-2-ethylhexyl phthalate: an overview, BioMed Research International, (2018)
22. C. Yang, W. Lim, F.W. Bazer, G. Song, Avobenzone suppresses proliferative activity of human trophoblast cells and induces apoptosis mediated by mitochondrial disruption, Reproductive Toxicology, **81** (2018): 50-57
23. B. Karami Matin, E. Shakiba, M. Moradi, E. Zereshki, A. Karami, Y. Vasseghian, E.N. Dragoi, A.M. Khaneghah, The concentration of estrogen in water resources: a systematic review and meta-analysis, International Journal of Environmental Analytical Chemistry, **101**,15 (2021): 2937-2946
24. F.H. Pusceddu, L.E. Sugauara, M.R. de Marchi, R.B. Choueri, Í.B. Castro, Estrogen levels in surface sediments from a multi-impacted Brazilian estuarine system, Marine Pollution Bulletin, **142**, (2019): 576-580

A Comparison of Fiber Types in Community for Mist Collection

Thana Ananacha [1], and *Onvalee* Amornleetrakul [1,*]

[1]Faculty of Architecture and Design, King Monkut's University of Technology, Bangkok, Thailand

Abstract. The production of clean water from evaporated water in fog has been very attractive in recent decades. Massive fog accumulation combined with simple concepts and technologies with respect to water production has resulted in sustainable environmental impact in producing clean, low-cost water for arid areas around the world. Mist collection systems work best in locations with repetitive fog conditions where fog is driven by wind especially coastal areas. However, the technology can also be used in mountainous areas where there is water in the Stratocumulus clouds at elevations of about 2,000-6,500 feets. The purpose of this research was to compare the fiber types that collect mist water by testing with atmospheric conditions in Khao Yai Thiang, Nakhon Ratchasima Province, which is 800 meters above sea level to produce water for the community and suitable for Thailand. The test was carried out by stretching 12 different fibers to a wooden frame measuring 0.50 x 0.50 m^2 and installing it horizontally. Field tests found that three types of horizontal water droplet materials, which were the best mist water collector, are synthetic fibers: nylon net, plastic net, and polyethylene net. All three materials behave very differently. Especially, the temperature profile of the plastic net has the highest temperature in the afternoon and the lowest temperature in the night. Nylon net has a temperature close to the air temperature throughout the day but slightly lower. These materials will be used in the design of the moisture trap tower in the next experiment. In the first experiment, there was not much water and water droplets clinging to the fibers as blotted dots with tissue paper because the fog period is not long enough.

Keyword. Fiber, Fog, Mist water, Water tower, Water trap

1 Introduction

Nowadays, there are many building designs that take advantage of the natural environment and improve the quality of life for people to live more comfortably, such as concrete block wall (CBW) blocks that reduced the internal temperature to 1.9 - 2.9 °C lower than ordinary glass [1], Thai Modem Façade (TMF) and Thai Modem Façade Wall with Fin (TMF-WF) wall that reduced heat flux flowing into room [2], vapor recovery tower (VRT) roof that include flow rate and reduce average room temperature about 1.41 °C compared with ordinary concrete tiles [3] or even the technology of big tree stilts that make the environment better [4].

Misty water is a freshwater source that is available at low cost. It can be a source of drinking water for communities in foggy conditions. There are studies on the accumulation of mist water in more than 20 countries around the world on all continents, especially, in areas where the phenomenon of high fog occurred. Additionally, collecting mist water is beneficial when rivers or lakes are far away or dehydrated and suitable for countries with a semi-arid climate in the tropics or subtropics [5].

Mist is the presence of water droplets that fall on the ground level as part of the water cycle. Mist form overnight, with diameter range of 1 - 50 μm [6]. This is because the cold ground causes water vapor to condense in the air above [7]. Many studies found that a steady decrease in fog was observed in many areas with dense fog, including large coastal cities like California in the United States and many areas of Europe [8-10]. However, China and India were found to have increased fog [11,12]. Global warming is a theory that reduces the phenomenon of fog in some areas. It affects local atmospheric and wind circulation patterns, as well as inversion patterns [10]. The method of harvesting fog water is quite simple, using a net stretched to the frame. When the mist hits the net, it condenses into water droplets and flows to gather in the prepared water reserve container. However, the difficulty is prediction of the amount of fog.

Due to the lack of standards for measurement and reporting of data [13], only the mean or maximum value was considered in many studies. In 1994, Schemenauer and Cereceda designed a Standard Fog Collector (SFC) [14], which consisted of a 1.00 x 1.00 m^2 frame stretched by a net, attached to the 2 side posts with a height of 2.00 meters, with a distance of 0.10 meters from the posts. Under the net frame, the water chute dimension L x W x D is 1.04 x 0.15 x 0.10 m^3, whose details are shown in Figure 1. Mist collection rates range from 1 - 10 l/m^2.day, but can reach 40 l/m^2.day in some regions [14].

* Corresponding author: onvalee.a@archd.kmutnb.ac.th

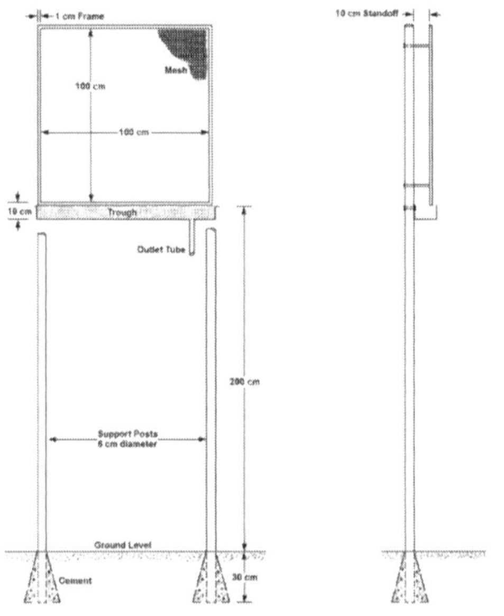

Fig. 1. Standard Fog Collector: SFC [14]

2 Materials and methods

The main objective of this research is to provide an alternative water resource from fog water for people in areas with difficult access to water such as mountainous areas by choosing technology that is easy for the community. In this experiment, it is a preliminary experiment to test the quality of fibers available in the market to collect mist water and to extend the design of the fog trap tower in the next experiment. To achieve these objectives, we, therefore, selected the investigated area based on the published research data.

From the study of air humidification towers in many countries around the world, such as Chile, Namibia, Spain, Greece and others. The optimum climate is on mountainous terrain 400 - 1,200 meters above sea level. Most of them are near water sources because the terrain is hot during the day and cool at night. In case of high humidity from being near a water source, it can create a mist texture easily. Nakhon Ratchasima Province is a province in the northeastern region and has a plateau and mountains. Therefore, it is suitable in many areas around the world. Khao Yai Thiang has a height of 650 meters above sea level witch close to Lam Ta Khong Dam making the environment suitable complete the components of the fog. Field test location has taken into account various factors, the location that is expected to cause a lot of humidity power supply and the safety of experimental equipment. The inner cliff area was the good choice, which is next to the viewpoint, safe for experimental equipment and near the waterway that drains from the reservoir above. With these reasons, it is expected to help generate a lot of humidity. The location of the field test is at approximate coordinates 14°48'11.21"North and 101°33'11.13"East as seen in Figure 2.

Fig. 2. Field test area at Lam Ta Khong Dam, Nakhon Ratchasima

Field testing is a test of the properties of commercially available fibers, both natural and synthetic fibers to find the best fiber for water retention. In this experiment, a small frame was made, consisting of two main parts: the frame for holding the fibers and the stand structure. The fiber was tested horizontally because of the small-sized fibers and in a location covered by trees, which the vertical panel cannot be set to a high height and there is no misty wind in this area.

The frame for fixing fibers is made from structural timber, size 1x 1.5 inches, with a total size of 0.50 x 0.50 m^2, 12 pieces, used for fixing fibers in the test as shown in Figure 3. The stand structure is made up of structural timber measuring 1.5 x 1.5 inches in total size of 2.00 x 0.50 x 0.50 m^3, 3 sets. The frame used to hold the fibers can be removed and placed on the stand structure as shown in Figure 4.

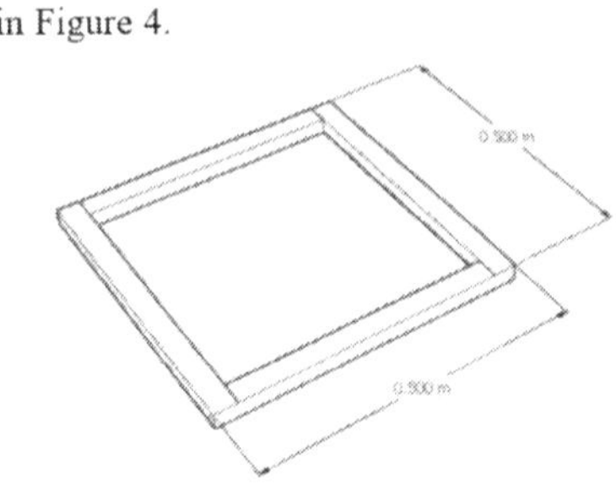

Fig. 3. Frame for fixing fibers

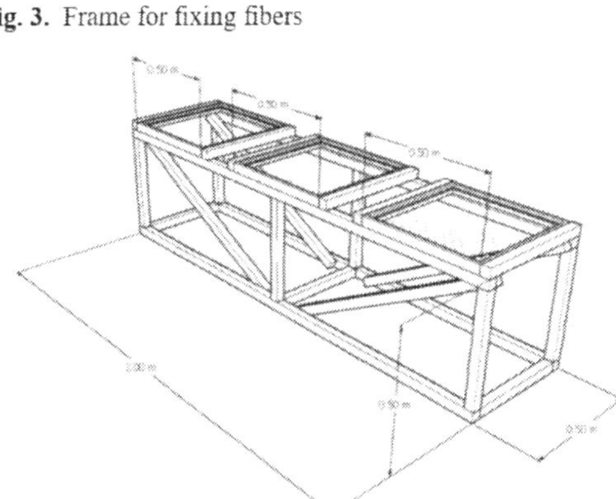

Fig. 4. Stand structure and frame placed on stand structure (1 stand set)

Twelve different fibers were stretched to a wooden frame measuring 0.50 x 0.50 m^2 and mounted horizontally. There are two types of fiber types: natural fibers and synthetic fibers. Natural fibers are hemp fiber, pineapple fiber, woven bamboo and cotton yarn (holy thread). Synthetic fibers are nylon mosquito net, plastic netting, small nylon net, plastic netting (onion bag), hexagonal eye PVC grille, nylon rope, big nylon net and polyethylene mesh (Figure 5). The temperature sensors were attached to the skin in the middle of the fiber sheets to investigate the thermal behavior as arranged in Figure 5. The field test was conducted during April 10-17, 2020, and the following weather data was collected.

- Dry Bulb Temperature: (T,°C)
- Dew Point Temperature: (Td, °C)
- Relative humidity (Relative Humidity: RH, %)
- Wind speed (Wind Velocity: V, m/s)

3 Results and Discussion

The overall climate is shown in a continuous graph in Figure 6. The graph shows results between 0.00 a.m. on April 11, 2020 to 7.00 a.m. on April 17, 2020. It can be observed that in different positions circled as follows:

- **1** - On April 12th, rain occurred between 2.10 - 3.50 p.m., causing the temperature to drop sharply from 31.8oC to 22.7°C or a decrease of 9.1°C.
- **2** - And thus the relative humidity increased from 52.1% to 84.4% during the period.
- **3** - When combined with the decrease in temperature in the evening and moisture accumulation, the humidity increased to reach 100% between 1.35 a.m. and 2.05 a.m. and the humidity exceeds 100% (more than the devices can collect data) between 6.20 a.m. to 8.00 a.m. on April 13, 2020.
- **4** - The same temperature between T and Td between 6:20 a.m. and 8:00 a.m. was observed on April 13, 2020, which was the timing for fog to form and fall on the fibers as water droplets and can absorb moisture.

Fig. 5. Fiber installation in the test area

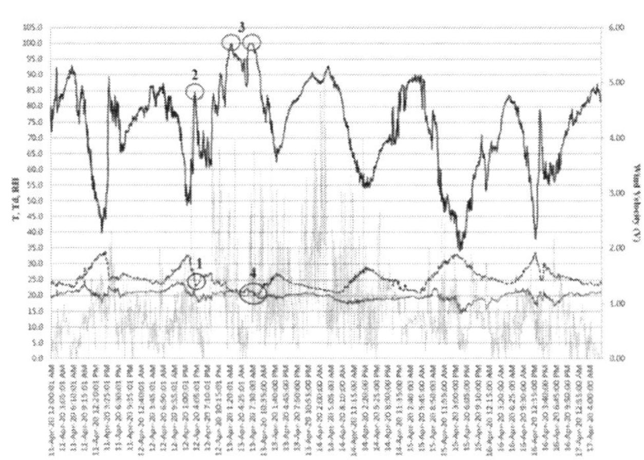

Fig. 6. Climate conditions in the experimental area during 11 - 17 April 2020

Figure 7 shows a graph of climate phenomena on April 12 - 13, 2020 (fog day), which is clearly visible to overlapping curves of apparent dry bulb temperature: T, dew point temperature: Td and relative humidity: RH reaching 100% as far as the instrument can be measured. During 1.35 a.m. - 2.05 a.m., the average wind speed was 0.85 m/s, the maximum wind speed was 1.38 m/s, and during 6.20 - 8.00 a.m., the average wind speed was 1.61 m/s and maximum measurement up to 3.80 m/s.

Temperature results of various materials can be seen in Figures 8 and 9. Figure 8 shows the continuous temperatures of 12 materials for 6 days from 11 April 2020 at 0:00 a.m. to date April 17, 2020 at 7:00 a.m. can be seen that, during the night until early morning, all materials have a temperature drop below the dry bulb temperature. If the temperature profile is divided into 2 time periods, which are:

- Low temperature period, 4:00 p.m. - 9:00 a.m.
- High temperature period, 9.00 a.m. - 4.00 p.m.

The results show that at the low temperature range, the materials with the lowest temperature are nylon mosquito nets. At the high temperature range, the highest temperature material is plastic net.

Figure 9 shows a graph comparing the temperature of various materials and the dry bulb temperature on April 13, 2020 (fog day) from 0.00 a.m. - 23.55 p.m. to see more clearly the temperature of each material. In order to see more clearly the temperature of each material, a comparison chart of skin temperature separation between natural fibers and synthetic fibers are shown in Figures 10 and 11, respectively.

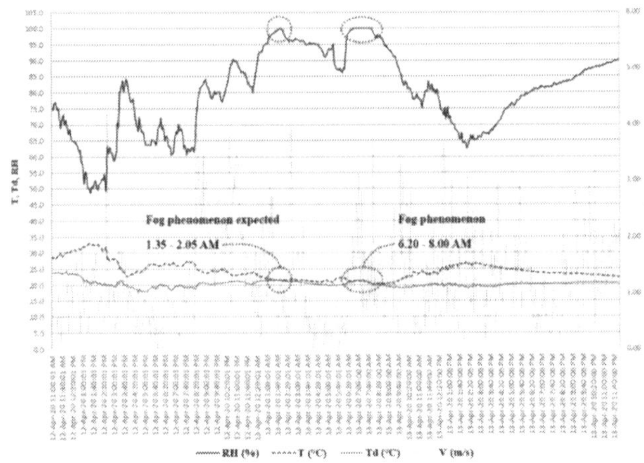

Fig. 7. Climate conditions in the test area during 12 - 13 April 2020.

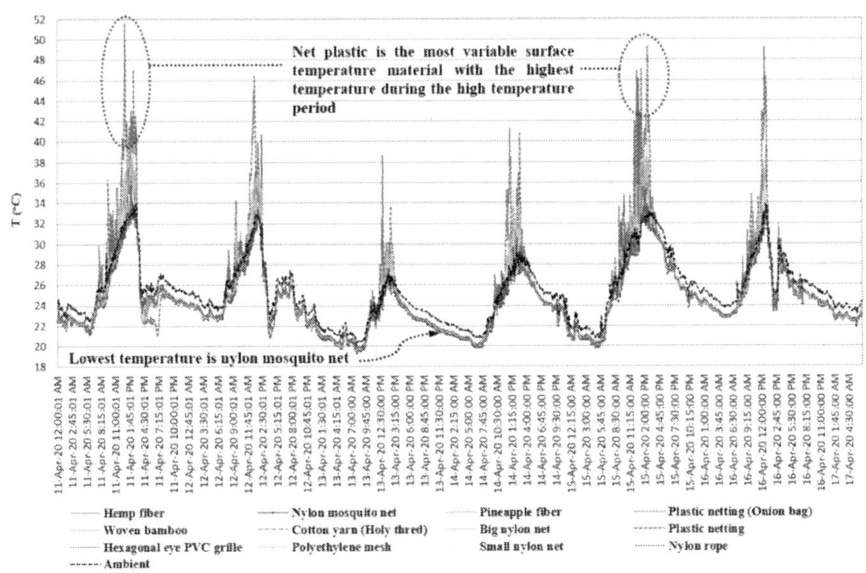

Fig. 8. Comparison graph of the surface temperature of 12 material fibers for 6 days during 11 - 17 April 2020

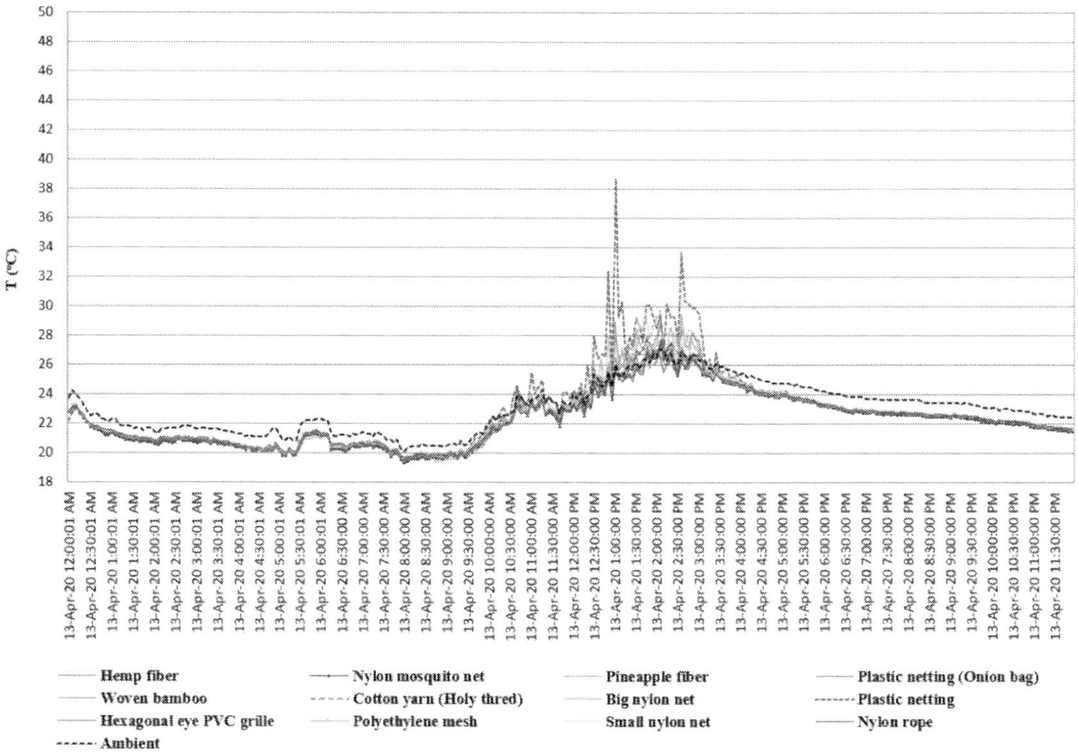

Fig. 9. Comparison graph of the surface temperature of material fibers on April 13, 2020

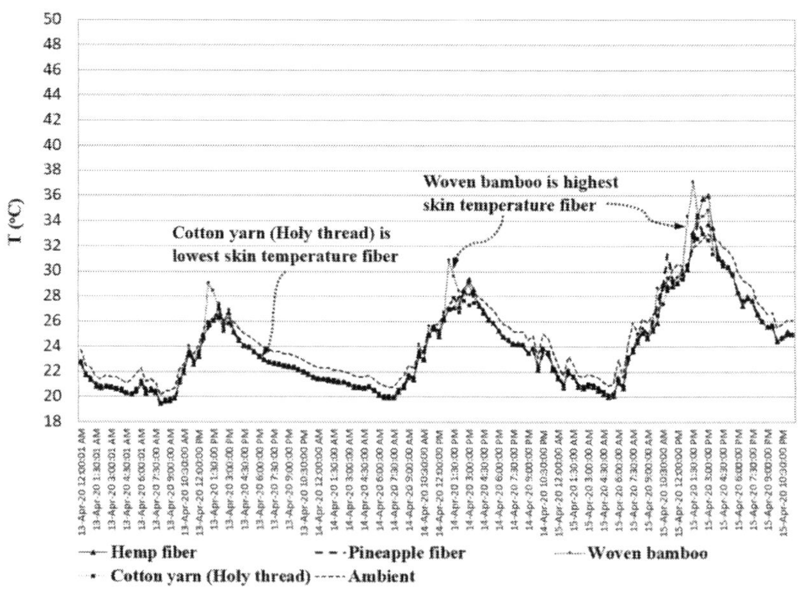

Fig. 10. Natural fiber surface temperature comparison during 13 - 15 April 2020

 https://doi.org/10.1051/e3sconf/202342802017

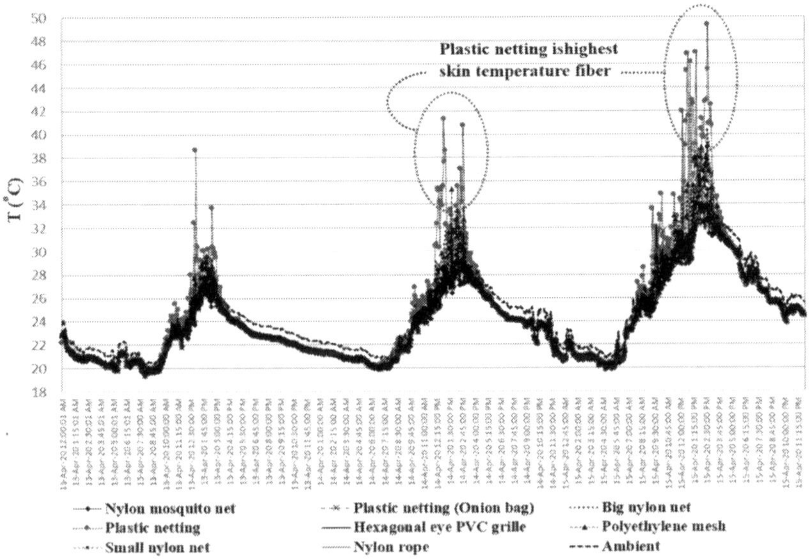

Fig. 11. Synthetic fiber surface temperature comparison during 13 - 15 April 2020

In Figures 10 and 11, fibers can be divided into 2 groups:

- High-temperature fibers sorted in order: woven bamboo, pineapple fiber, plastic net, small nylon net, plastic net (onion bag), big nylon net and polyethylene mesh.
- Low-temperature fibers sorted in order: hemp fiber, cotton yarn (holy thread), nylon net (blue), hexagonal eye PVC grille and nylon rope.

From the 6-day observation, it was found that the material with the highest temperature during 12.00 p.m. - 3.00 p.m. was plastic net and the lowest temperature material in the low temperature range (4.00 p.m. - 9.00 p.m.), they include nylon net, plastic net and pineapple fiber with maximum, minimum and average temperatures as shown in Table 1.

For fiber mist water collection effect in this experiment, we tested the water that was absorbed with toilet paper on the fiber sheet on April 13, 2020, which has a fog period of approximately 1 h and 40 min (6.20 a.m. - 8.00 a.m.). During approximately 7.00 a.m.- 7.30 a.m. and found that among three types of fibers that had the most water droplet adhesion were nylon net, plastic net and polyethylene mesh. Other materials absorbed very little or no water at all, therefore showing only three types that could absorbed water as in Figure 12.

a) Nylon mosquito net b) Plastic Net c) Polyethylyne mesh

Fig. 12. Three materials with the best retained water from mist.

Figure 13 showed a comparison graph of three materials that absorbed water the best, namely nylon mosquito net, plastic net and polyethylene mesh, respectively. Environmental condition data of 6 consecutive days, during 11 - 17 April 2020, showed the behavior of different materials. Nylon mosquito net had a surface temperature value similar to air temperature. It was slightly lower in both high and low temperature ranges and had the lowest average surface temperature on foggy days, 21.67°C and the lowest average temperature for several days.

The plastic net had the greatest fluctuations in surface temperature. When the air temperature was higher, the surface temperature was significantly higher than that of other materials. Especially, on a hot day in April 11, 2020, the maximum surface temperature had increased to 51.64°C, while the low temperature range value of the plastic net was relatively low. It also had a minimum temperature of 22.05°C, which was lower than the nylon net. Therefore, plastic net is the material with the widest temperature range.

Polyethylene mesh was the most woven fiber that had the highest surface temperature after the plastic net, with the highest surface temperature reaching 39.42°C and the lowest temperature was even higher than that of nylon net and plastic net.

Fog water collection in the first experiment was quite difficult to explain which of these 3 fibers collected the most fog. Due to the difference in water droplets characteristics, nylon mosquito net water droplets are distributed in small pellets. Plastic net produced large droplets, but are far apart and polyethylene mesh produced droplets of both small and large water droplets. However, the problem with polyethylene mesh is the complexity of the fibers. This makes water droplets trap inside and harder to extract water out.

Table 1. The max., min., and avg. temperatures of 12 material fibers and dry bulb temperatures.

List	Values	11 Apr.	12 Apr.	13 Apr.	14 Apr.	15 Apr.	16 Apr.
1. Hemp fiber	Max.	36.34	35.98	27.27	30.59	36.01	34.39
	Min.	21.32	22.54	19.45	19.95	19.92	22.85
	Avg. (12.00-15.00)	33.30	31.11	25.34	27.25	32.48	28.77
	Avg. (16.00-9.00)	24.17	22.10	21.69	22.92	25.29	24.23
2. Nylon mosquito net	Max.	34.59	34.82	26.98	30.16	34.08	33.47
	Min.	21.33	22.51	19.33	19.89	19.83	22.82
	Avg. (12.00-15.00)	32.10	30.49	25.53	26.88	31.67	28.52
	Avg. (16.00-9.00)	24.20	22.10	21.67	22.94	25.30	24.24
3. Pineapple fiber	Max.	34.53	34.66	26.87	29.38	34.99	33.65
	Min.	21.38	22.57	19.27	19.95	20.09	22.79
	Avg. (12.00-15.00)	31.95	30.56	25.34	27.24	31.94	28.82
	Avg(16.00-9.00)	24.07	22.06	21.70	22.96	25.21	24.21
4. Plastic Net (onion bag)	Max.	37.98	38.08	28.84	32.46	37.19	34.02
	Min.	21.34	22.53	19.40	19.90	19.92	22.81
	Avg (12.00-15.00)	34.57	32.19	26.05	28.49	33.68	29.14
	Avg. (16.00-9.00)	24.01	22.09	21.71	22.96	25.29	24.22
5. Woven bamboo	Max.	37.48	36.82	28.42	31.42	37.12	37.76
	Min.	21.48	22.61	19.44	19.96	20.10	22.78
	Avg.(12.00-15.00)	33.87	31.95	25.98	28.48	33.56	29.66
	Avg.(16.00-9.00)	24.04	22.08	21.74	23.01	25.22	24.22
6. Cotton yarn (Holy thread)	Max.	33.84	33.21	26.56	29.94	34.56	33.85
	Min.	21.40	22.61	19.46	19.98	20.09	22.83
	Avg. (12.00-15.00)	32.05	30.57	25.18	27.09	31.55	28.71
	Avg. (16.00-9.00)	24.14	22.13	21.75	22.98	25.27	24.25
7. Big nylon net	Max.	38.16	37.87	29.57	33.87	40.45	39.50
	Min.	21.50	22.62	19.39	20.06	20.08	22.88
	Avg. (12.00-15.00)	35.05	32.54	26.52	29.54	34.52	29.86
	Avg. (16.00-9.00)	24.12	22.18	21.80	23.07	25.38	24.32
8. Plastic net	Max.	51.64	46.36	38.68	41.31	49.32	49.22
	Min.	21.50	22.60	19.57	20.07	20.20	22.76
	Avg. (12.00-15.00)	39.56	35.73	28.39	33.03	39.74	32.61
	Avg. (16.00-9.00)	23.77	22.05	21.84	23.20	25.35	24.47
9. Hexagonal eye PVC grille	Max.	34.47	33.29	27.41	31.52	34.18	35.60
	Min.	21.47	22.66	19.56	20.07	20.16	22.86
	Avg. (12.00-15.00)	32.56	30.89	25.54	27.85	32.19	29.08
	Avg. (16.00-9.00)	24.14	22.18	21.82	23.08	25.32	24.34
10. Polyethylyne mesh	Max.	39.42	36.69	29.58	35.24	38.78	37.12
	Min.	21.54	22.66	19.63	20.06	20.14	22.90
	Avg. (12.00-15.00)	35.74	32.72	26.66	29.60	34.47	29.59
	Avg. (16.00-9.00)	24.18	22.22	21.84	23.08	25.38	24.35
11. Small nylon net	Max.	35.50	34.06	27.48	31.03	34.74	35.64
	Min.	21.51	22.69	19.68	20.10	20.16	22.91
	Avg. (12.00-15.00)	33.30	31.30	25.77	28.28	32.38	29.50
	Avg. (16.00-9.00)	24.24	22.24	21.86	23.08	25.36	24.34
12. Nylon Rope	Max.	34.71	33.41	27.44	30.62	35.23	33.05
	Min.	21.51	22.71	16.67	20.04	20.08	22.94
	Avg. (12.00-15.00)	32.11	30.53	25.32	27.43	31.51	28.75
	Avg. (16.00-9.00)	24.24	22.22	21.85	23.07	25.34	24.34
13. Ambient temperature	Max.	34.00	33.00	27.10	29.20	33.10	33.90
	Min.	22.40	23.60	20.10	20.80	20.80	23.80
	Avg. (12.00-15.00)	32.40	31.10	25.70	27.50	31.50	29.50
	Avg. (16.00-9.00)	24.85	25.25	23.13	22.61	23.93	26.37

4 Conclusions

The field test found three types of materials that collected water droplets horizontally, all of which are synthetic fibers: nylon mosquito net, plastic net and polyethylene mesh. They had very different behavior, especially, the plastic net with both the highest and lowest temperatures. Nylon nets had a temperature close to the air temperature throughout the day but slightly lower.

We have noticed that on foggy days, there was often strong wind. This may be caused by high temperatures during the day that caused a temperature difference within the mountain, resulting in strong winds, and strong winds caused a sharp drop in temperature at night, condensation and drop of water. It is also possible that the wind carries fog or steam from elsewhere.

For fibers, we found that materials with low surface temperatures during the night is synthetic materials and they could collect mist water better than natural fibers. The texture of the material and the grid spacing of the fibers have a great effect. Natural materials absorb too much water, causing no water droplets to form on the surface.

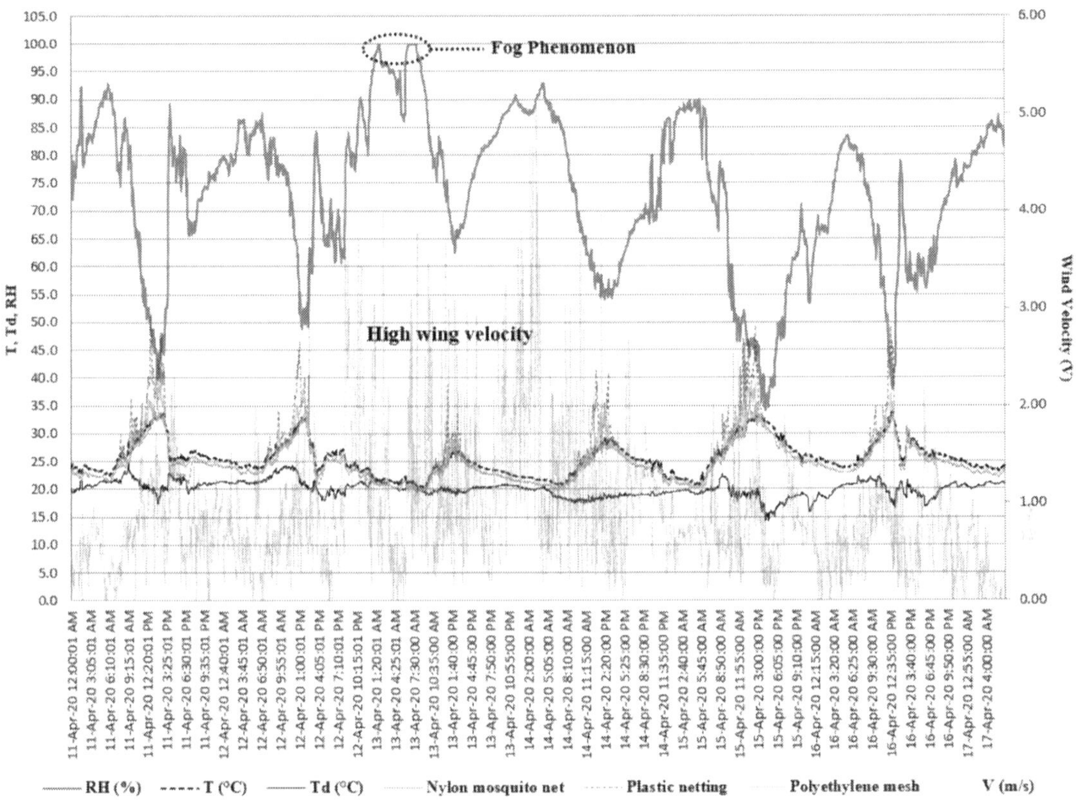

Fig. 13. Comparison graph of surface temperature of three materials and weather conditions for 6 consecutive days during 11 - 17 April 2020

However, on April 13, 2020, when there was fog, the working group surveyed at the cliff area and found that the cliff area had misty wind (like a drop of water) and had more dense mist than the observed area and the wind blown horizontally. The working group therefore agreed that it was appropriate to conduct a second field test by doing it vertically on the cliff and using the above three types of fibers with larger areas to see results more clearly. From the aforementioned experiments, it reveals the possibility of collecting mist water. This is a preliminary experiment to select fibers for further experimentation in a larger scale.

Acknowledgement

The working group would like to thank Electricity Generating Authority of Thailand (EGAT), Thailand for providing financial support for research work.

References

1. T. Ananacha, Thermal Performance of the Clear Block Wall for Ventilation, GEOMATE Journal, **23**,96 (2022): 25-31
2. T. Ananacha, W. Puangsombut, J. Hirunlab, Experimental Performance and Numerical Simulation of a Thai Modern Facade Wall, International Journal of Ventilation, **14**,3 (2015): 255-263
3. O. Amornleetrakul, W. Puangsombut, J. Hirunlab, Field investigation of the small house with the Ventilated Roof Tiles, Advanced Materials Research, **931** (2014): 1233-1237
4. N. Lattikapong, O. Amornleetrakul, S. Kambung, Analysis of Crutches System to Select and Guide the Design of Crutches Suitable for Different Sizes of Siege Timber and Development of Tree Crutches, Mathematical Statistician and Engineering Applications, **71**,4 (2022): 6436-6448
5. S.A. Abdul-Wahab, V. Lea, Reviewing fog water collection worldwide and in Oman, International Journal of Environmental Studies, **65**,3 (2008): 487-500
6. A. Ritter, C.M. Regalado, G. Aschan, Fog water collection in a subtropical elfin laurel forest of the Garajonay National Park (Canary Islands): a combined approach using artificial fog catchers and a physically based impaction model Journal of Hydrometeorology, **9**,5 (2008): 920-935
7. D.J. Straub, J.W. Hutchings, P. Herckes, Measurements of fog composition at a rural site, Atmospheric environment, **47** (2012): 195-205

8. J.A. Johnstone, T.E. Dawson, Climatic context and ecological implications of summer fog decline in the coast redwood region, Proceedings of the National Academy of Sciences, **107**,10 (2010): 4533-4538
9. G.J. van Oldenborgh, P. Yiou, R. Vautard, On the roles of circulation and aerosols in the decline of mist and dense fog in Europe over the last 30 years, Atmospheric Chemistry and Physics, **10**,10 (2010): 4597-4609
10. S. LaDochy, M. Witiw, The continued reduction in dense fog in the Southern California region: possible causes, Pure and Applied Geophysics, **169** (2012): 1157-1163
11. F. Niu, Z. Li, C. Li, K. Lee, M. Wang, Increase of wintertime fog in China: potential impacts of weakening of the Eastern Asian monsoon circulation and increasing aerosol loading, Journal of Geophysical Research: Atmospheres, **115**,D7 (2010)
12. F.S. Syed, H. Ko¨rnich, M. Tjernstro¨m, On the fog variability over south Asia, Climate dynamics, **39** (2012): 2993-3005
13. O. Klemm, R.S. Schemenauer, A. Lummerich, P. Cereceda, V. Marzol, D. Corell, J. Van Heerden, D. Reinhard, T. Gherezghiher, J. Olivier, P. Osses, Fog as a fresh-water resource: overview and perspectives, Ambio, **41** (2012): 221-234
14. R.S. Schemenauer, P. Cereceda, A proposed standard fog collector for use in high-elevation regions, Journal of Applied Meteorology and Climatology, **33**,11 (1994): 1313-1322

AUTHOR INDEX

AUTHOR INDEX

EDP Sciences – Web of Conferences
17, Avenue du Hoggar
Parc d'Activité de Courtabouf
BP 112
F-91944 Les Ulis Cedex A
France

ISBN 978-1-7138-8427-9

CURRAN ASSOCIATES INC.
proceedings.com

Computing in Science and Technology (CST 2018)

ITM Web of Conferences Volume 21 (2018)

Rzeszow-Muczne, Poland
11 – 14 June 2018

edp sciences